*A Guide to Implementing*

# Oracle Siebel CRM 8.x

*A Guide to Implementing*

# Oracle Siebel CRM 8.x


**Vivek Kale**

*Cupertino, CA and Mumbai, India*



**Tata McGraw Hill Education Private Limited**

**NEW DELHI**

*McGraw-Hill Offices*

**New Delhi** New York St Louis San Francisco Auckland Bogotá Caracas
Kuala Lumpur Lisbon London Madrid Mexico City Milan Montreal
San Juan Santiago Singapore Sydney Tokyo Toronto

**Tata McGraw Hill**

Published by Tata McGraw Hill Education Private Limited,
7 West Patel Nagar, New Delhi 110 008.



ISBN-13: 978-0-07-068007-4
ISBN-10: 0-07-068007-8

Managing Director: *Ajay Shukla*
Head—Professional and Healthcare: *Roystan La'Porte*
Executive Publisher—Professional: *R Chandra Sekhar*
Asst. Sponsoring Editor—Computing: *Ritesh Ranjan*
Manager—Production: *Sohan Gaur*
Manager—Sales & Marketing: *S Girish*
Sr. Product Manager—Science, Technology & Computing: *Rekha Dhyani*
General Manager—Production: *Rajender P Ghansela*
Asst. General Manager—Production: *B L Dogra*



Typeset at Text-o-Graphics, B1/56 Arawali Apartment, Sector 34, Noida 201 301

Cover Design: Kapil Gupta, New Delhi

RZAYCRAFDZALB

*The* **McGraw·Hill** *Companies*

*To*

*My professional mentors and dear friends*

*Dr. Dhananjay G. Mahajan*

*for his unfailing encouragement and support*

*and*

*Dr. Frank W. Davis*

*for being such a genius and a great inspiration*

*by showing the way in Customer Responsiveness*

# Advance Praises

In his new book, *A Guide to Implementing Oracle Siebel CRM 8.x*, Vivek Kale successfully bridges the gap between technology and business by exhibiting a remarkable conceptual grasp of both. His book is not merely about implementing a computer application but shows how Siebel software can be used to enable any degree of customer responsiveness a firm desires. Kale describes how the software can be used to manage relationships with customers in traditional product-oriented firms. He includes a variety of implementation strategies which can be used depending upon the business's resources, the size of the supply chain network, and the customer base. He does not give just a list of rules-of-thumb but explains the principles underlying each of the options. After reading this book, the reader should have a clearer understanding of the business and technology options available in Siebel software to achieve business goals within the available budget.

Who should read this book? Managers who seek to understand the maze of computer concepts and how technology can be used to enable their businesses to be what they envision; technologists who want to become more familiar with business strategy and better understand what technology needs to accomplish; entrepreneurs who want to develop more competitive business organizations and learn about strategies to make their vision a reality—all can benefit from this book. Most importantly, the astute reader will realize that many computer concepts such as networking, modularity, integration of components, and network economics are also applicable in developing new business strategies. The same concepts used in organizing computer applications can be used in organizing supply chains. For this reason, academics should view this book as a blueprint for future business practices. Kale has accomplished the task of making technology and business strategies seem simple and logical. The book is a must read!

*Dr. Frank W. Davis, Jr.*
Professor
Department of Marketing, Logistics and Transportation
The University of Tennessee
Knoxville, TN

*A Guide to Implementing Oracle Siebel CRM 8.x* is a well-written guide to a rich, complex, and ever-evolving domain. It's a one-stop reference for Siebel practitioners and, moreover, a comprehensive overview of any CRM project. A must for the CRM practitioner's library!

*Jill Dyche*
Partner, Baseline Consulting, CA
Author of *The CRM Handbook* (Addison Wesley, 2002)

*A Guide to Implementing Oracle Siebel CRM 8.x* is lot more than about implementing Siebel!

It is a rich treatise on Customer Relationship Management that blends business and technology concepts. Of great interest are Kale's own ideas such as 'information is relationship', 'management by collaboration', and 'survival and success of enterprises based on the theory of natural selection from Biosciences'.

*Dr. Jagdish N. Sheth*
Charles Kellstadt Professor of Marketing
Emory University
Atlanta, GA

An important insight Vivek Kale offers in this book is that organizations mistakenly identify CRM as a technology project confined to certain aspects and areas of the enterprise's operation. His corrective to this perception is to emphasize that CRM implementation can significantly benefit the organization only if the company first transforms itself into a customer-centric and customer-responsive organization. This unique and pragmatic insight underlies *A Guide to Implementing Oracle Siebel CRM 8.x* and makes it a 'must read and consult' book for all managers who are about to or have set sail in the journey of enterprise-wide CRM deployment.

*Jerry Rao*
Founder MphasiS
Former Chairman, Nasscom and current Chairman, Nasscom Foundation, New Delhi

In the complexity of today's media world...with their ever-increasing options, along with their ever increasing costs...sometimes we lose track of how to most effectively and efficiently get across our message to a specific customer, who resides at the core of our business proposition and to whom we want to reach out again and again. Sharply targeted Customer Relationship Management approaches significantly reduce the cost of customer acquisition and retention. In this book Vivek has vividly brought forth the proposition as to how technology and effective data management can be as good a tool as breathtakingly creative advertising executions to meet our end objectives of shareholder value addition...

*Aniruddha Deshmukh*
President—Retail and FMCG, Raymond Ltd.
Mumbai

This book is unique in introducing all aspects of Customer Relationship Management as well as its application catering to a wide reader base ranging from students to all stake holders of any modern customer-centric enterprise. It uses Siebel CRM application to explain all implementation and operational aspects of CRM, as Siebel CRM is one of the most mature CRM applications available in the marketplace today. I recommend this wonderful book to all educational institutes which train students in managing customer-centric enterprises as well as information technology. I also recommend this book as "must to have" to libraries of all medium and big enterprises for reading, training and inducting their employees.

*Vishwas Kulkarni*
Founder Director, Penta Computing Pvt. Ltd.
Pune

Vivek Kale's book is a significant step in deepening the theoretical knowledge of CRM and simultaneously creating a clear path for its practical and profitable application in industry. In his work, he combines his vast knowledge of Siebel and CRM systems with his technological and managerial experience. He has provided not only an instruction manual for Siebel CRM deployment but, equally importantly, created a companion knowledge tool kit in the practice of management. This book is a compulsory asset for those undertaking the CRM deployment.

*Rajesh Pant*
Director & Founder of Kandor Solutions, Mumbai
Former COO Sony Entertainment Television

Customer Relationship Management has become an important component of any industry and, especially in retail, has a very specific customer-centric use. The level of knowledge and first-hand approach in guiding and implementing quick-value propositions described in this book will be the key to deriving business benefits from implementing Siebel CRM.

This book will give insights, learning, and check lists on Siebel CRM to each and every one of us on our path to build businesses which will excel and thrive in the new era of constant changes and uncertainties.

*Meheriar Patel*
GM & Head IT, HR & Admin., Globus Stores Pvt. Ltd.
Mumbai

Vivek's book clearly brings forth the basic idea, for the first time ever, that CRMs are able to treat enterprise-level customer information not merely as 'records of information' but as meaningful 'customer relationships'.

*Gibson G. Vedamani*
Executive Director, Kirtilal Kalidas Jewellers Pvt. Ltd.
Director, Governing Board, Retailers' Association of India, Mumbai

# Preface

As customer-facing applications, CRM systems are expected to be implemented by companies as a top-most priority. However, the reality is quite different. CRM implementations usually follow in the wake of ERP implementation. Not all companies go as far as implementing an enterprise-wide CRM strategy and application(s). Of the several reasons for this apparent lack of enthusiasm for implementing the most critical customer-oriented application for a company, a major one is the non-availability of a single-point resource on all aspects of implementing a CRM system like Siebel. This book attempts to fill that gap.

Oracle Corp.'s Siebel Business Applications is one of the best CRM systems in the market. Its advanced architecture and design provide for comprehensive and flexible adoption and also permit the development and release of functional upgrades of individual modules without disrupting the already functioning systems at various customer installations in a major way.

Adopting CRM not only means a new way of looking at a business's operational processes, but also requires a nearly complete overhaul of Information Technology systems. This book helps technologists and managers come to grips with the vision, concept and technology of CRM, particularly Siebel software. This provides a framework for making optimal decisions necessary for the successful implementation of Oracle Corp.'s Siebel CRM 7.x, 8.x in organizations. The book begins with laying down the groundwork for understanding CRM by explaining the concept and context of CRM, and tangible business benefits of CRM adoption. Then it demonstrates the professional approach to evaluation and selection of Siebel as the best CRM suit of applications, its technology, architecture, functionality, project cycle, plan and methodology of implementation, development and customization, project management, support and administration. Besides, it provides detailed Critical Success Factors (CSF), and patterns and anti-patterns for a successful Siebel implementation.

Further, the book delves deep into the specifics of Siebel CRM 7.x, 8.x:

- Siebel Enterprise including Sales Enterprise, Service Enterprise, Marketing Enterprise, Field Service, Call Center and ERM
- Siebel eBusiness including eSales, eService and eChannel
- Optional functionality including Product Configurator, Email Agent and Expense Reporting
- Vertical market applications including Consumer Goods, Finance and Insurance

- Application environment including Siebel Enterprise Server, eBusiness Application Integration (eAI), EIM and Workflow
- Application development environment including Siebel Tools and Repository

Moreover, it provides summaries and checklists to help managers deal with Siebel in different stages: planning, installation, configuration, administration and support. The last part deals with the Balanced Scorecard (BSC) for companies and concludes with a discussion of other important CRM-related issues like privacy and future trends in ASP-based CRM services.

## What Makes this Book Different?

This book studies the late 90's phenomenon of the emergence of Customer Relationship Management (CRM) software packages from both business and technological perspectives. Then, it moves to demystifying CRM systems like Siebel and their power and potential to transform business enterprises. Unlike customary works on CRM systems which seldom discuss the key differentiator of Siebel from the earlier mission-critical systems, this book brings to fore the fact that with Siebel, *CRMs, for the first time, are able to treat enterprise-level information not merely as a 'records of information' but as 'customer relationships'.* This importance of customer relationships is based on a simple fact: *it can cost four to seven times more to replace a current customer than it does to retain one.* A major step in retaining a customer is to realize that whereas customer relationships are not all about information, all customer-related information is certainly about customer relationships. Thus, this book provides a reference framework for business operations based on customer relationships rather than the traditional four P's (product, positioning, price and promotion).

This is one of the first books to focus on a company's internal operations and business processes to show how greatly they impact external, i.e., customer-facing strategies, services and relationships. Further, it spells out strategies to configure internal business processes and operations in order to improve the customer-facing strategies, services and relationships.

Many companies have been struggling with the implementation of CRM projects primarily because they have mistakenly identified CRM implementations only as technology projects and that too confined to only certain aspects and areas of the enterprise's operations. Nothing can be farther from the truth. CRM implementations can add significant value to a company's bottom-lines only if the company first transforms itself into a customer-centric and customer-responsive enterprise. The book thus begins with an overview of what it means to be a customer-centric and customer-responsive enterprise and then discusses the technology of CRM systems.

Secondly, this book recommends that CRM implementation be undertaken as an *enterprise-wide* effort. In this big-bang approach to CRM implementation adopted in the book, all facets of CRM relevant for the enterprise operations are implemented at the same time. Thus, CRM implementations should entail enterprise-wide communications, participation, planning, resourcing, risk and change management, quality-checking and training.

This book also touches upon certain aspects of Siebel implementation that would be of particular interest to company executives and decision-makers. For instance, the ROI of implementing CRM is covered in Part VI.

Far from developing in isolation from the IT industry, the design and architecture of Siebel have picked on the best developments in IS/ IT in the latter half of the 20th century. Hence, at relevant stages the book highlights Siebel's connections with the parallel developments in software development technologies and methodologies to make the context of several outstanding features of Siebel more meaningful.

The book has used many concepts for the first time in the context of CRM systems, such as Collaborative Enterprise, Extended Collaborative Enterprise (ECE), Critical Value Determinants (CVDs), Management by Collaboration (MBC), Customer Triggered Company, etc. But, some new terms and concepts have also been introduced, such as the Private ASP, the vision of 'Decisions on Desktops' or 'Relationships on Demand' (Chapter 17) and the concept of *Infosphere* (Chapter 7).

Other novel features of the work are: an overview of the Oracle Fusion Architecture which is the basis for Oracle's next generation Fusion Applications combining the best ideas and processes of the Oracle E-business Suite, PeopleSoft, JD Edwards and Siebel applications (Appendix E); and an alternate view on the success and survival of companies based on market selection and inspired by Darwin's theory of evolution by natural selection (Appendix F).

## How is this Book Organized?

### Part I: Setting the Stage

Chapters in first part of this book describe the context and significance of CRMs in general and Siebel in particular for increasing competitiveness of organizations. Chapters 1 and 2 introduce the key idea of CRM: *information is relationship.* Chapters 3 and 4 present a framework for evaluation and selection of CRMs. Chapter 5 demonstrates Siebel as the best CRM system in the market. Chapter 6 presents an overview of a Siebel implementation project. Chapter 7 touches upon Enterprise Business Process Management (BPM), an important aspect of any CRM implementation project.

### Part II: Siebel Business Applications

This part has three chapters which cover three main components of Siebel. Chapters 8 and 9 are on the heart of the Siebel system—various application modules catering to the functional requirements of different areas of the enterprise. Chapter 10 deals with Siebel's operating environment and related products. Chapter 11 is on Siebel tools which form the complete development environment within Siebel.

### Part III: The Pre-implementation Stage

This part presents various activities which are pre-requisites for starting a Siebel project. Chapter 12 discusses various activities and tasks necessary for Siebel implementation. Chapter 13 provides a brief on the Siebel installation and its administrative aspects.

### Part IV: The Implementation Stage

This part presents in detail Siebel's eRoadmap implementation methodology through all its phases. Chapter 14 introduces the concept and context of eRoadmap and details the eight stages of eRoadmap viz., Project Plan, Definition, Discover, Design, Configure, Validation, Deployment and Sustain.

### Part V: The Post-implementation Stage

In this part, Chapter 15 gives a brief overview of the post-implementation issues associated with the support of a Siebel system in production.

### Part VI: Siebel Implementation and Beyond

Chapter 16 presents various aspects related to valuing the ROI of a Siebel implementation using the method of Balance Scorecard (BSC). Chapter 17 visits several aspects of the intelligent customer-centric enterprise and shows how Siebel is geared up for enabling relationship-based enterprises to address the emerging challenges in the $21^{st}$ Century.

## Who Should Read this Book?

All readers who are involved with any aspect of a Siebel project—Sales, Marketing, Service and Support personnel, Siebel CRM implementation project and IS/IT personnel—will profit by using this book as a roadmap to make a more meaningful contribution to the success of their Siebel implementation project.

This complete and comprehensive guide to CRM Siebel has been so designed that it can be selectively read with a view to understand specific components of the system relevant to a reader's purpose.

Following are the sets of chapters that can be recommended for reading to different categories of stakeholders:

- Chapters 1, 2, 4, 7, 16 and 17 for executives and business managers.
- Chapters 1, 2, 4 through 9, 16 and 17 for operational managers.
- Chapters 1, 2, 3, 4, 5, 16, and 17 for CRM evaluation and selection team members.
- Chapters 1, 2, 5-10, and 12-15 for project managers and module leaders.
- Chapters 1-9, and 12-17 for functional members of the Siebel team.
- Chapters 1-6, 9-15 and 17 for technical managers.
- Chapters 1, 2, 3, 5, 6, and 8-15 for technical members of the Siebel team.
- Chapters 1, 2, 5-9, 12, and 14-17 for professionals interested in Siebel.
- Chapters 1 through 17 for students of computer courses.
- Chapters 1-9, 12 and 14-17 for students of management courses.
- Chapters 1, 2, 5-9, 12, 16 and 17 for general readers interested in CRM and Siebel.

I believe that companies can greatly benefit from implementing end-to-end CRM strategic solutions in their organizations. Even if this book inclines executives and their companies toward seriously considering the task of undertaking such enterprise-wide CRM initiatives, it would have achieved its objectives. Any thoughts, suggestions or feedback can be sent to SiebelCRM@vkale.com.

# Acknowledgements

I would like to thank all those who have helped me with their clarifications, criticism and valuable information during the writing of this book, were patient enough to read the entire or parts of the manuscript and made many valuable suggestions. They include Jayant Kulkarni of Siebel, Nilesh Acharya of Oracle, Pawan Gupta, Mukesh Dhebar, B. Sreenivas and Kedar Purohit. I thank my professional mentors Dr. D. G. Mahajan and Dr. Frank W. Davis, Jr. for their constant encouragement and support over the years, as also for this book. I was also fortunate to get advice and feedback on several chapters of this book from Dr. Frank W. Davis, Jr. of University of Tennessee and Dr. Jagdish Sheth of Emory University.

This book would not have seen the light of the day without help from many people including Daniel Cooperman, Christopher Andrews, Sheila Cepero and Todd Adler of Oracle Corp. and Chris Van Buren.

And, of course, the book would not have ever been finished without the invaluable assistance of R. Chandra Sekhar, Vishwanath Ghanekar, Ritesh Ranjan and the entire publishing team at Tata McGraw Hill Education who directly or indirectly contributed to the production of this book.

I thank my beloved daughters Tanaya and Atmaja for their understanding and support, and, for not persistently asking when the book would really get published. Finally, I owe my greatest thanks to my wife, Girija without whose continuing love, support and sacrifice this book would not have been possible. For this and much more, I am deeply and forever thankful to her.

**Vivek Kale**

Cupertino, CA and Mumbai, India

# Contents

# PART I: SETTING THE STAGE

This part sets the background and context of undertaking *Customer Relationship Management* (CRM) implementation project within a company.

The phenomenon of CRMs like Siebel that is being witnessed in the last few years is fascinating. Technically, there have always been several application software systems to cater to all aspects of organizational interaction with its customers. Thus one may be intrigued by the question of what's so special about CRMs in the 00's? I feel the answer is that CRMs, for the first time, are able to treat customer-related information not merely as 'records' of customer interactions, expectations and transactions, but also as relationships. This enables CRMs to leverage the totality of this information, across all channels and customer touch points, to manage customer relationships more effectively and optimize the realized customer value throughout the life cycle of the customer. The importance of customer relationships is based on a simple fact—*it can cost four to seven times more to replace a current customer than it does to retain one*. A major step in this direction is to realize that while customer relationships are not all about information, all customer-related information is certainly about customer relationships.

Chapters in the first part of this book provide the context and significance of CRMs and Siebel CRM in particular for increasing competitiveness of organizations. Chapter 1 introduces a reference framework based on customer relationships rather than traditional approach based on products (positioning/price/promotion). Chapters 1 and 2 introduce the key idea that *information is relationship.* These also unravels the mystery of CRMs like Siebel and their power and potential to transform enterprise relationships.

Chapters 3 and 4 present a framework for evaluation and selection of CRMs. Chapter 5 presents the supporting logic behind the claim that Siebel is the best CRM system among the other systems operating in the market. Chapter 6 presents an overview of a Siebel implementation project, which would help in understanding how all other pieces, discussed in the following chapters, fit into the overall scheme. Chapter 7 discusses enterprise Business Process Management (BPM), which is an important aspect of any CRM implementation project.



**Companies have a wealth of knowledge in the files and records that customer-facing employees have on customer and customer interactions. The best way to leverage this knowledge is to free it from the shackles of experience, institutionalize it and transfer it in real-time to all employees, so that they are empowered to build relationships with customers.**

Chapter 1

# The Relationship-based Enterprise

Customer Relationship Management (CRM) is a holistic approach to identifying, attracting and retaining customers. CRM deals with creating a customer-centric enterprise. This involves two major aspects, customer centricity and customer responsiveness. All activities must eventually add value to the customer reflected in their willingness to pay for the products and/or services. Non-value adding elements should be excised swiftly in Internet time because customers have numerous other choices. This entails focusing all strategies, plans and actions on the customer rather than the traditional focus on the products and/or services. As pointed out by Fred Reichheld, it is a question of transitioning from zero defects to zero defections. Additionally, enterprises must ensure seamless and real-time integration between:

- Customer-facing demand generation
- Back-end demand fulfilling intra- or inter-enterprise supply chain processes.

An effective CRM strategy aims at achieving the following:

- Continuously attract new customers
- Gain customer insight and manage intimacy
- Retain profitable customers and phase-out non-profitable customers
- Establish long-term relationships with current customers
- Increase the customer spend and profits by cross-selling and up-selling

This book takes a stance that customers are not the exclusive preserve of the marketing function, but are the key to an enterprise's enduring and compounding competitiveness and success.

## 1.1 ORACLE: THE COMPANY AND ITS SIEBEL CRM PRODUCT

Siebel Systems, Inc., which was taken over by Oracle Corporation in 2005, was founded in 1993 to address the growing need of organizations of all sizes to acquire, retain and better serve their customers. Today, Oracle's Siebel CRM division with sales revenues of $1.79 billion is the world's leading provider of e-business applications software, with over 8,000 employees who operate in more than 34 countries. More than 4,700 organizations in 107 countries run on Siebel e-business applications. By any standards, these are impressive numbers coming from a company that has a great vision and is destined to play a significant role even in the internet-driven markets of this century. Since, Siebel is now a part of Oracle Corporation, which is primarily a database company we will continue to refer to Oracle's Siebel division as Siebel Systems to avoid confusion and maintain focus on the Siebel CRM. Readers should keep in mind that whenever we refer to Siebel Systems and Siebel CRM, we are referring to Oracle's Siebel division and Oracle's Siebel CRM product only.

Throughout this book, we will refer to Oracle's Siebel division as a company and its products by the term 'Siebel'. This should not lead to any confusion because we believe that, at any point, the context would make it clear as to which meaning is intended.

The phenomenal success of Siebel comes from the fact that Siebel systems are comprehensive but at the same time configurable to the specific needs of any company. Companies prefer off-the-shelf packages like Siebel because they are flexible and can be configured to satisfy most requirements of any company in any industry. Siebel can be deployed on various hardware platforms providing the same comprehensive and integrated functionality and flexibility for addressing the requirements of individual companies. Siebel implements a process-oriented view of the extended enterprise.

> There is a substantial difference between the concept of customer relationship management (CRM) and Customer Relationship Management systems (CRM systems).
>
> CRM is a concept with a much broader scope than the CRM systems that implement a sub-set of the tenets of CRM. In the next section, we will take an overview of the concept of CRM, while in Chapter 2 on "Customer Management Relationship (CRM) System" we will look at the basic characteristics of a CRM system of which Siebel is a prime example. Notwithstanding all this, in the next few chapters we will first familiarize ourselves with the background and significance of CRM before we introduce Siebel in Chapter 5. Figure 1.1 presents the underlying customer relationship framework for the whole book.

## 1.2 THE CONCEPT OF CUSTOMER RELATIONSHIP MANAGEMENT (CRM)

**Customer relationship management (CRM) is a customer-centric business strategy that encompasses all business models, processes, methodologies and techniques for closing the gap between an organization's current and potential performance in acquisition, growth and retention of valuable customers for mutual benefit.**

In an era where advantages based only on product features and add-on services are shortened to a 'click of a customer' (see Chapter 2, Section 2.5 "The Customer-triggered Company"), the key to success is to forge long-term, profitable relationships with valuable customers. This involves two major aspects namely, customer centricity and customer responsiveness. CRM aims to identify the customers that are most profitable to the company and optimizes relationships with them.

Whereas, this view may lead to increased services and incentives for customers that provide the greatest returns to the company, it may also result in reduced services or even strong disincentives for non-profitable customers. If a company or organization were to put more of its efforts into its existing customers, it would make sense to do this with customers that had the greatest potential. This means that at some point, it has to start to lose those customers that do not offer long-term future value either because of transaction spend, the value of a customer, or the cost of transacting or dealing with that customer or customer group. This requires costing information at the customer level (see Chapters 7, sub-section "Activity-Based Costing (ABC) for BPM"). All customers are not created equal! Consequently, the traditional customer-centric slogan should be transformed to: *Valuable (i.e., Profitable) customers are always right.* Thus, even customers compete for bestowing their custom!

Customer retention is extremely important for companies because it is more efficient and effective to retain a current customer than to gain a new one. Companies can generate additional revenue and profits without incurring the costs for acquiring new customers. In light of this, management is really concerned with having the right product in the right place, at the right price, at the right time, in the right condition, for the right customer.

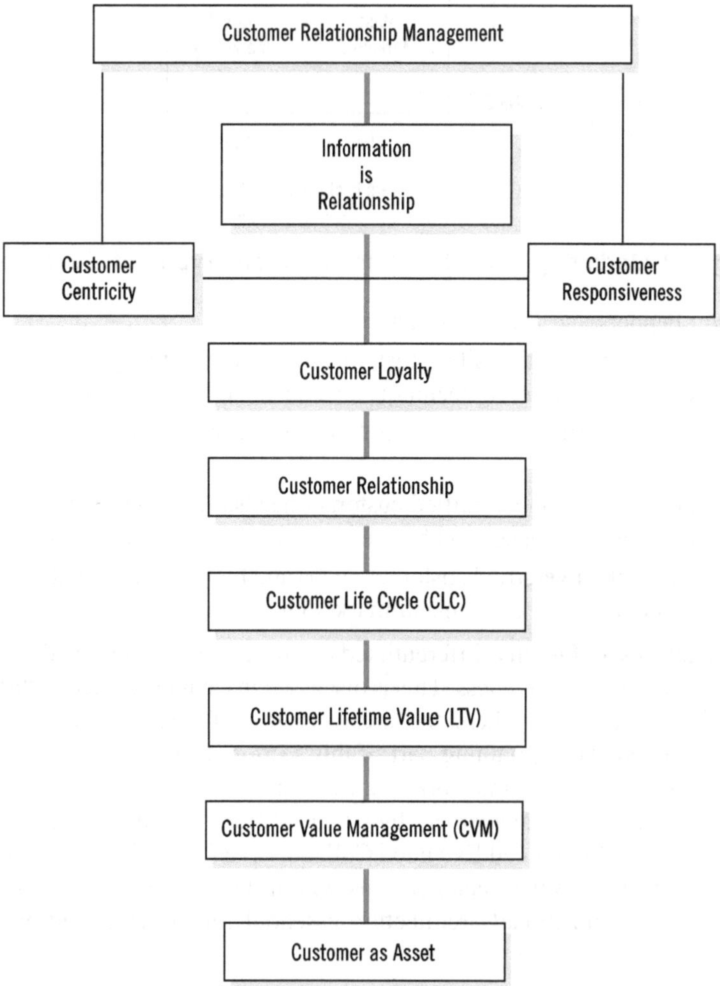


**Fig. 1.1 The Customer Relationship Framework**

Don Peppers and Martha Rogers pioneered the concept of one-to-one marketing made possible by the advent of computer-assisted database marketing. Figure 1.2 represents the entire spectrum of customers and the corresponding marketing techniques. The horizontal axis measures the diversity of 'customer needs' and the vertical axis measures the differentiation in 'customer valuations'. The representative businesses for each of the quadrants are as follows—gas station, bookstore, airlines, and a computer systems company.

**Fig. 1.2 Marketing Techniques for Different Types of Customers**

According to Don Peppers and Martha Rogers:

1. Businesses with relatively undiversified customer needs and relatively uniform customer valuations will do best with mass marketing techniques (refer to sub-section on "Customer Value" )
2. Businesses with diversified customer needs but uniform valuations can benefit from target marketing
3. Businesses with relatively undiversified customer needs but with highly differentiated customer valuations will benefit immensely with a key accounts management approach
4. Businesses with highly diversified customer needs and highly differentiated customer valuations will benefit from one-to-one customized marketing

How does one handle a set of highly differentiated customers having a large diversity of needs? The answer is, through customer responsiveness. This is discussed in Chapter 2, section "Electronic Customer Relationship Management (eCRM)" where, the latest variation of the traditional CRM geared to handle such customers is described. The remaining part of this section deals with the various facets of CRM. There is also a need for a unifying framework that ties together the various aspects of a CRM system implementation. The section on "Management by Collaboration" introduces a unifying framework for the various aspects of the CRM-enabled Extended Collaborative Enterprise (ECE), and sets the tone for the rest of the book as well. The next chapter ends with a discussion of how CRM systems such as Siebel provide the new organizational architecture essential for the extended enterprise of the 21$^{st}$ century.

The enterprises' business model governs both its business strategy and its use of IT. Figure 1.3 shows the product-process change matrix that illustrates the four distinct business models based on:

- The dimensions of change (product or process change)
- The fundamental nature of change (dynamic or stable)

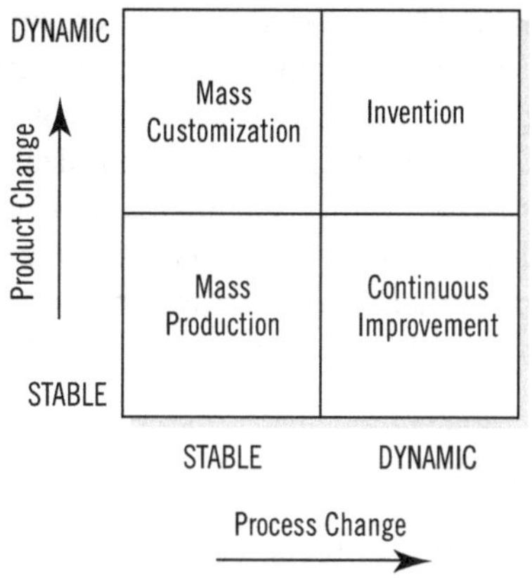


**Fig. 1.3 Business Models**

On the vertical axis, product change reflects changes in the demand for goods or services because of competitor moves, shifting customer preferences, or entering new geographical or national markets. On the horizontal axis, process change means altering the procedures or technologies used to generate, produce or deliver the corresponding products or services. Taken together these factors result in four distinct business models.

1. Mass production—In these enterprises the primary use of technology is to automate tasks.
2. Invention—In these enterprises, technology must support collaborative efforts amongst teams or a set of individuals.
3. Continuous improvement—In these enterprises, technology must augment tasks by enhancing people's deep process knowledge and skills. It can also link people and processes across functions to provide customer-focused, horizontal, informational flows enabling them to continuously improve the processes they execute
4. Mass customization—In these enterprises, technology must not only automate tasks, and augment knowledge and skills, but most significantly must also automate relationships between processes and people.

The advent of the Total Quality Management (TQM) movement in the USA led to the emergence of customer satisfaction measures, and efforts aimed at improving and sustaining them led to greater emphasis on customer centricity. The total quality management focused attention on customer needs and forced a rethinking of traditional management methods.

One of the keys to mass customization is the use of dynamic business networks within and amongst enterprises. These are formed out of a set of loosely coupled autonomous business process capabilities with a linkage system that allows them to be reconfigured instantly for any particular customer order. By engineering the flexibility of the processing units and coordinating the flow of resources (materials or services) between these units, the mass customizer can produce an almost infinite variety of base products or services, at a cost that is competitive when compared even with a mass producer. Whereas labor in the mass production design is organized to perform repetitive tasks according to a singular command and control system, the mass customizer organizes labor to routinely respond to an ever-changing set of rules and commands. The mass customizer organizes labor to work effectively in a dynamic network of relationships and to respond to work requirements defined by the dynamically changing customer needs. Although there is apparently a great degree of centralization in both of these models, there is a fundamental difference in the nature of centralization. In case of mass production, all decision-making is centralized, whereas in the case of mass customizer only the coordination and control are centralized. The mass customizing organizations centralizes the allocation of work to different processing units to produce the customer's product or service order. [see sub-section "The Agile Enterprise" at the end of this chapter and Chapter 7, sub-section "Business Webs (B-webs)".]

## 1.2.1 Customer Centricity

CRM is a different approach to business that involves relationship marketing, customer retention and cross-selling leading to customer extension (see sub-section "Customer Life Cycle (CLC)" below). CRM represents a culmination of a long-evolutionary shift in the traditional thinking of business. Until the last few decades, the business of the global economy was essentially, manufacturing. The focus on goods rather than on services led to a product-focused, mass market marketing strategy resulting in a high cost of acquiring new customers, and a low cost for customers switching to other brands.

***The Logics of Business***

The fundamental logics of business that have been identified are as follows.

1. Product-centric business—These types of business believe that customers primarily choose products with the best quality, performance, design or features. These are characteristically highly innovative and entrepreneurial firms usually driven by the founders' vision but with marked descent on market research or hearing the 'voice of the customer'. Their managements usually make assumptions regarding what the customers want, resulting in over-specified or over-engineered products that are normally costly for the majority of the customers. They actually target a relatively small segment of price-insensitive customers called, innovators.
2. Production-centric business—These types of business believe that customers primarily choose low-price products. Consequently, they strive to keep operating costs low.
3. Sales-centric business—These types of business believe that if they invest enough in advertising, selling, public relations (PR) and sales promotion, customers will be persuaded to buy their products or services.
4. Customer-centric business—These types of business believe in the primacy of the customers and their specific wants at a particular moment. Based on customer and competitive information, they develop better value propositions that are attractive for the customers. Customer-centric businesses are learning organizations that constantly adapt to customer requirements and competitive conditions.

CRM and CRM systems like Siebel enable customer-centric business, though they also support the other logics of business that may become essential at a certain stage of the market development, products or services.

Table 1.1 compares the traditional mass marketing approach with that of the relationship-oriented customized marketing.

**Table 1.1 Traditional Mass Marketing versus Customized Relationship Marketing**

| | | Traditional Mass Marketing | Customized Relationship Marketing |
|---|---|---|---|
| 1. | Objective | Mass marketing | Customer as an individual |
| 2. | Focus | Customer acquisition cycle | Throughout customer life |
| 3. | Time table | Transaction term | Medium to long-term |
| 4. | Performance indicators | Market share, product profitability | Wallet share of the valuable (i.e. profitable) customers |
| 5. | Customer knowledge | Segment-based habits, Behavior modeling, Occasional market research | Individual-based habits, Behavior modeling and Prediction |
| 6. | Product | Standalone product | Product and service |
| 7. | Price | General price reductions | Customer loyalty based differential pricing |
| 8. | Channels | Traditional channels | New technology channels |
| 9. | Sales | Salesman as the 'lone hunter' | Team sales<br>Sales automation |
| 10. | Communication | One-way<br>brand-oriented | Two-way, interactive<br>personalized |

There has always been a focus on customer needs, but with the advent of computers, there has been a shift away from producing goods or providing services, towards discovering and meeting the needs of the individual customer. The challenge to the company's future is not necessarily from competitors, but from its own complacency towards its customers. Product differentiation is eroding. The change is driven by intensified compensation, deregulation, globalization, and saturation of market segments. Internal business processes are being re-engineered as never before, but process changes are initiated, designed, implemented, and evaluated in terms of meeting the needs of the customer (see Chapter 7 "Siebel and Business Process Management"). These businesses are organized for customer centricity and responsiveness, not for the routine performance of standardized pre-defined tasks.

The customer needs and values can itself be defined in terms of the following.

- The need for relationship—Customers with a high need for relationship place a high value on the supplier's ability to understand their needs, their organization, strategy and challenges; and their future plans.

- The need for information—Customers with a high need for information place a high value on the supplier's ability to provide all relevant information about the company, its products and services enabling them to make an informed decision regarding using the company's products and services.

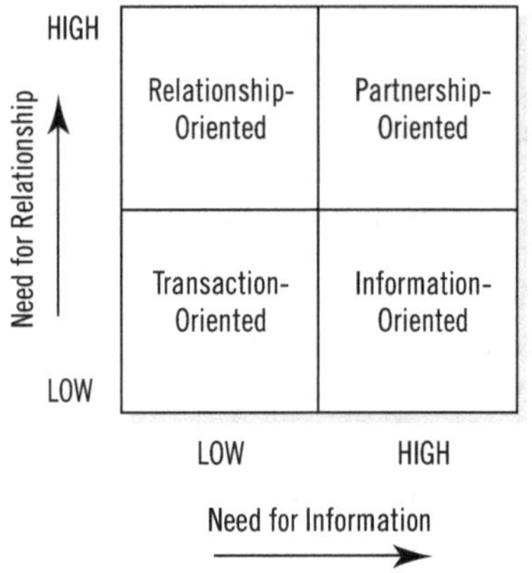


**Fig. 1.4 Type of Customer Relationship**

Accordingly, Figure 1.4 presents a map that classifies customers depending on what customers value most:

- Transaction-oriented
- Relationship-oriented
- Information-oriented
- Partnership-oriented

For a successful CRM program that can produce bottom-line financial results, the customer-centricity needs to pervade the whole of the demand and supply chain. A process view, as embodied in Siebel, assists in achieving this by integrating the downstream customer-facing processes with upstream supply chain processes. As emphasized throughout this book, the process view cuts through the impeding organizational boundaries to focus on business results for the satisfaction of the end-customer.

### 1.2.1.1 From Products to Services to Experiences

By the middle of the last century, products, goods and property came to increasingly mean an individual's exclusive right to possess, use, and most importantly, dispose as he/ she wished in the market. By the 1980s, the production of goods had been eclipsed by the performance of services. These are economic activities that are not products or construction, but are transitory, are consumed at the time that they are produced (and thus cannot be inventoried), and primarily provide intangible value. In a service economy, it is time that is being commodified, not prices, or places, or things. This also leads to a transition from P&L to market cap as the base metric of success (see Chapter 16, sub-section "Time Value of Customers and Shareholder Value"); what the customer is really purchasing is the *access for use* rather than *ownership* of a material good. Since the 1990s, goods are becoming more information-intensive, interactive and are continually upgraded, and are essentially evolving into services. Products are rapidly being equated as cost of doing business rather than as sales items; they are becoming more in the nature of containers or platforms for all sorts of upgrades and value-added services (see Chapter 7, sub-section "Customer Service Management"). Giving away products is increasingly being used as a marketing strategy to capture the attention of potential customers. But with the advent of electronic commerce, feedback and workflow mechanisms, services are being further transformed into multifaceted relationships between the service providers and customers, and technology is becoming more of a medium of relationships. In the *servicized* economy, defined by shortened product life cycles and an ever-expanding flow of competitive goods and services, it is customer attention rather than resources that is becoming scarce.

> The true significance of a customer's attention can be understood the moment one realizes that time is often used as a proxy for attention. Like time, attention is limited and cannot be inventoried or re-used. In the current economy, attention is the real currency of business and to be successful, enterprises must be adept in getting significant and sustained mindshare or attention of their prospects or customers. As with any other scarce and valuable resource, markets for attention exist both within and outside the enterprise. For extracting optimum value, the real-time and intelligent enterprises must impart optimal attention to the wealth of operational and management information available within the enterprise. This fact alone should automatically put a bar on overzealous re-engineering and downsizing efforts (although re-engineering and other cost-cutting tactics are necessary, it is essential to ascertain if undertaking such tactics will contribute to the delivery of superior or at least 'on par' value to the customers). This is the fundamental vision underlying the emergence of outsourcing strategies (see section "The Virtual Enterprise" and Chapter 17, sections "Application Outsourcing" and "Application Functionality as Web Services").

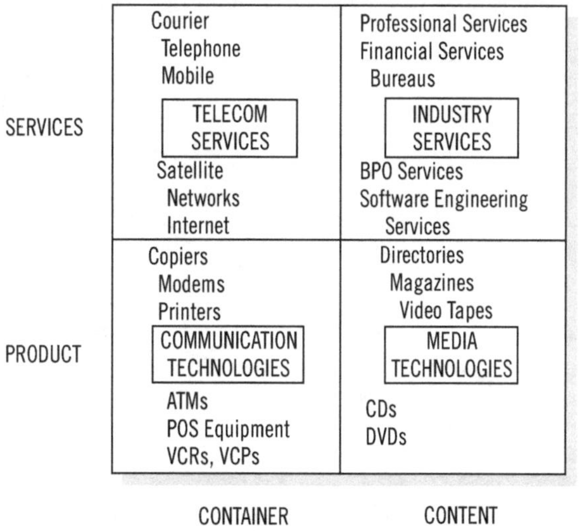


**Fig. 1.5 Spectrum of Offerings vs. Medium (Container)/Message (Content)**

One major result of this trend towards the importance of experience has been the blurring of lines between the content (the message) and container (the medium) in the market. This is described in the next section (see Figure 1.5).

### 1.2.1.2 Convergence: From Marketplaces to Market Spaces

Traditional capitalism considered market share as the prime determinant of profits. Market share was a classic example of the zero sum game, where increase of market share by one company was typically at the expense of corresponding loss by other(s). Market share, which is a lagging indicator, does not distinguish in favor of valuable, satisfied or repeat customers. On the other hand, market spaces are defined with reference to a customer's perception of the delivered value and the resulting market size may be essentially limitless. Market spaces typically emerge because of the convergence across disparate or differing industries. For instance, the convergence of computers, data communication and telecommunications, and media industries has resulted in the emergence of one of the biggest market spaces with possibly the largest growth opportunities in recent times.

Convergence describes the phenomenon in which two or more existing technologies, markets, producers, boundaries, or value chains combine to create a new force that is more powerful and more efficient than the sum of its constituting technologies. The value chain migration alludes to the development of real-term systems that integrate supply chain systems and customer-facing systems, resulting in a single and unified integrated process.

This convergence occurs primarily because of three factors:

- The digitization of information to enable the preparation, processing, storage and transmission of information regardless of its form (data, graphics, sound and video or any combination of these)
- The rapidly declining cost of computing that has enabled computing to become ubiquitous and available with sufficient power (see Chapter 7, note on "Moore's Law")

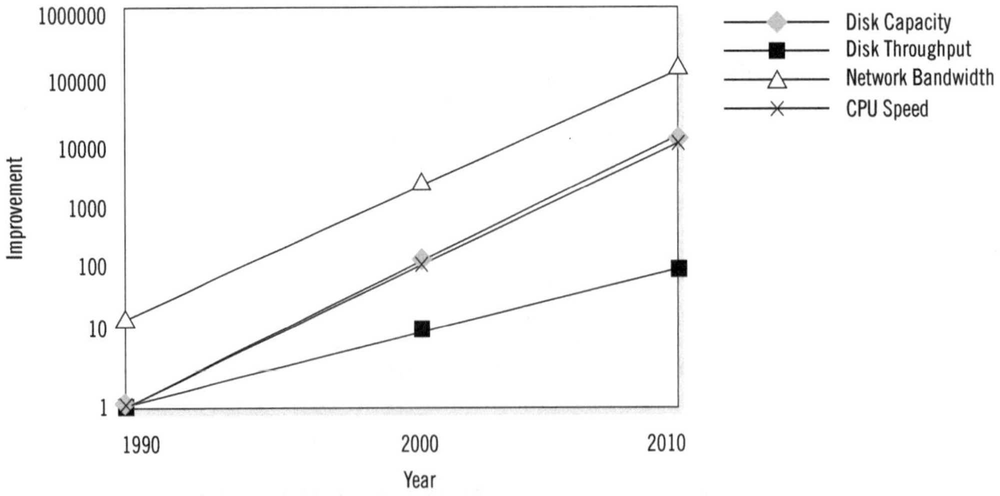


**Fig. 1.6 Hardware Trends in the 90's and the Current Decade**

- The availability of broadband communications is critical to convergence because multimedia is both storage-intensive and time-sensitive

Figure 1.6 presents the hardware trends in the 90's and the current decade.

Table 1.2 gives a comparison of communications technologies in terms of the approx. time required to send file with a size of 1 MB.

**Table 1.2 Comparison of Communications Technologies**

| Communications Technology | Bandwidth | Time for Sending 1 MB file |
|---|---|---|
| Modem using analog signal over phone line | 28.8 KB/sec | 1 min |
| ISDN using digital signal over phone line | 128 KB/sec | 30 sec |
| T1 using digital signal over private phone line | 1.5 MB/sec | 16 sec |
| Cable using modem digital signal over Ethernet | 10 MB/sec | 0.80 sec |
| T3 using digital signal over private phone line | 45 MB/sec | 0.53 sec |
| ATM using digital signal over ATM switched network | 155 MB/sec | 0.05 sec |
| ATM using digital signal over ATM switched network | 1 GB/sec | 0.008 sec |

The merging of previously disparate technologies, products and information to give rise to compelling new products and services also underscores the concept of the merging of the container and content that we referred to earlier. Convergence increasingly means that products in the experience economy (see earlier sub-section "From Products to Services to Experiences") combine the attributes of both content and container in novel ways to create new value chains.

### 1.2.1.3 Customer Relationship as a Strategy

Customer relationship strategy is emerging as one of the most important components of corporate strategy. A well-executed customer relationship strategy can result in a number of quantitative benefits including greater ability to up-sell and cross-sell, improved customer retention, and reduced cost of service and support.

Customer relationship management has emerged as a corporate strategy driven by the following factors:

- Implosion of product life cycles—This has robbed companies from enjoying the sustained financial benefits of being product innovators for sustained periods. Competitors introduce alternative, substitute and even improved products much more rapidly.
- Explosion of new technologies—They are enabling even nascent players to compete effectively with established players not only in terms of superior technology but in terms of flexibility, reliability, maintainability, costs and so on.
- Explosion of new distribution channels—Companies need to effectively integrate interactions through newer technology-driven channels like internet, wireless, telephone, mobile sales, kiosks, ATMs, etc.

- Explosion of competitors—The convergence of industries like computers, networking and data communications, TV and print media, publishing and so on, have radically re-defined the traditional boundaries between industries resulting in an explosion in the number and kinds of competitors (see earlier sub-section "Convergence: From Marketplaces to Market Spaces").

Ongoing changes rule the marketplace. The only permanent factor is the customer, and abiding relationships with the customer alone can buffer the impact of change. Thus, only those organizations that nurture customer relationships can survive product obsolescence, overcome the onslaught of superior competitors and still manage to maintain profitability.

Traditionally, competitive advantage came from strategies based on the following value determinants:

| | |
|---|---|
| Cost | Ownership, use, training support, maintenance, and so on |
| Time | Cycle time, lead time, and so on |
| Response time | Lead time, number of hand-offs, number of queues, and so on |
| Flexibility | Customization, options, composition, and so on |
| Quality | Rework, rejects, yield, and so on |
| Innovation | New needs, interfaces, add-ons, and so on |

Most enterprises have squeezed (and continue to do so) as much as they can from these value determinants in the last few decades. Now, one of the sources of substantial value for competitive advantage that remains to be exploited in a major way is from the enterprise relationships especially customer relationships, which are truly the real source of revenue.

For instance, in a B2B environment, a leading supplier of aggregates and industrial materials harnessed its CRM systems to help build loyalty and retain customers. However, the company faced the challenge of rapid growth through acquisition of synergetic businesses. The company grew from $140 million in revenues and seven locations in 1997 to $360 million in revenues and 21 locations in 2000. Now it was distributing throughout the United States. With the addition of many new products to its products portfolio (through the acquisitions) the company wanted to be sure that it was maximizing its cross-selling opportunities and that the salesmen had as much information about the different products and each of the customers as possible. This was because the company could no longer depend on the sales representatives "*knowing it all*" at any point of time.

### *1.2.1.3.1 Information is Relationship*

Companies cannot have relationships with the customers unless they 'know' them, i.e., unless they have detailed information on them. Companies have a wealth of knowledge in the files and records that customer-facing employees have on customer interactions. The best way to leverage this knowledge is to free it from the shackles of experience, institutionalize it and transfer it in real-time to all employees, so that they are empowered to strengthen relationships with customers.

As stated earlier, companies are finding it more difficult to differentiate on factors that prevailed in the 1980s namely, product quality, operations, logistics, and business processes. Across the last decade, the quality of products has improved, many companies have undertaken business process re-engineering (BPR) with reference to the enterprise processes, and many businesses have also streamlined their supply and distribution channels. In this environment it has become essential for companies to identify new ways to attract new customers, to maximize the value from each existing customer, and to retain the most profitable ones. Studies show that maintaining loyalty can increase customer profitability between 25% and 85%. Knowing who your customers are and what they are buying is a major step toward ensuring their loyalty without necessarily increasing the costs.

The approximate value of a customer can also be estimated easily based on the information on the defection rate and the profitability of customers by year. Since,

$$\text{Average life of a customer} = \frac{1}{\text{Attrition rate}}$$

It is evident that profits are determined not by sales but by the retention rate.

A major step in this direction would be to realize that whereas customer relationships are not all about information, all customer-related information is certainly about customer relationships. And everything else being the same, there is a huge potential in leveraging on the totality of information that is gathered from all the interactions that the company has with each customer. This is achievable by:

(a) Knowing the customer better than the competition does
(b) Employing that knowledge to create better and more personalized interactions in the future
(c) Incorporating or embedding the costs of switching to competing solutions into the current customer relationships

It is interesting to realize that as much as 80% of the sales process maybe controlled by specific knowledge of a customer's business. Information as relationships can help in enhancing the effectiveness of the various functions within the company.

- In sales, it helps companies to make the offers that are most likely to be accepted, and to focus sales efforts on the highest lifetime value customers.
- In after-market service, it reduces customer hassles, lowers costs, and streamlines repair and return processes.
- In marketing, it is the key to planning, executing, and evaluating campaigns.
- In manufacturing and distribution, it helps to forecast optimally delivered solutions.
- In design, it guides in the development of product features and style.
- In finance, it helps to manage credit risks and opportunities.

Customer information bases within CRM systems like Siebel consist mainly of two components namely, a customer database and an enterprise-level statistical database. A customer database typically contains:

- Descriptive data such as the customers' name, address, and phone number
- The customer's status data, such as outstanding balance, line of credit, and pre-existing conditions
- The customer's lifestyle preference data, such as meals, clothes, cars, housing, and allergies
- The customer's history, such as search history, purchase history, returns, failed deliveries, complaints, recommendations, and any other data that could affect the customer's relationship with the firm

#### 1.2.1.4 Customer Capital—Customer Knowledge as the New Capital

Adam Smith helped start the industrial revolution by identifying labor and capital as the economic determinants of the wealth of a nation. In this century however, the size of the land, mass of labor, and materials that you may possess might be worthless if you do not control the related know-how including customer know-how.

> The information about an asset is more important than the asset itself. This stance also opens up possibilities ranging from co-ownership, options on ownership, etc., to ownership for access/use or even ownership by consumption.

In the 21st century, know-how will reside and flourish in people's minds; what might matter more are how many enterprising and innovative people you have and the freedom that they have in realizing their dreams. It will be the century of information economics, and in particular, customer economics. Traditional capitalism made companies more efficient by the classical means of cutting costs of producing and distributing volumes of offerings rather than giving customers the value they were looking for. This is why more than two-thirds of the companies identified in the search for excellence in 1982 fell from grace within five years. Similarly, this is also why so many companies in the Fortune 1000 improved their margins between the mid-80s and '90s, but fewer than 40 companies actually increased their total shareholder value by more than 25 percent (see also Chapter 16, sub-section "From 'Built to Last' to 'Built to Perform' Organizations"). In contrast to traditional capitalism where it was the scarce offerings (and thus, resources) that produced wealth, in customer capitalism it is the intangible customer relationships that are driving growth and prosperity in the networked economy (see Chapter 7, sub-section "Network of Resources").

CRM systems like Siebel also act as transformers of the knowledge which resides in the heads of the operational and subject experts into a more explicit and accessible form. This corresponds exactly to the *tacit knowledge* talked about by I. Nonaka and H. Takeuchi in their book titled *The Knowledge Creating Company*. These could be learning experiences, ideas, insights, rules of thumb, business cases, and so on. They exhort companies to convert the illusive, un-systematized, un-codified and 'can-be-lost' knowledge of the corporation and its customers into *explicit knowledge* that can be codified, collated, and managed like any other capital investment. This could be in the form of documents, case studies, analysis reports, evaluations, concept papers, internal proposals, and so on. Most importantly, it is available for scrutiny and can be improved on an ongoing basis. Siebel performs the invaluable service of transforming the implicit customer related knowledge into the explicit form (see Chapter 7, sub-section, "Best Practice Guideline Management").

Customer capital has gained importance because of the following trends:

- Information-based targeted marketing is becoming more efficient and effective than unfocused mass marketing because of factors like affordable information technology, sophisticated statistical modeling, low-cost communications and flexible fulfillment.
- Enterprises are no longer dependent solely on the vertical channel systems to control customers' buying behaviors.
- Enterprises utilizing all the data on customer purchase behavior are not only acquiring new customers, retaining existing ones and cross-selling more effectively, but are also linking this data with the corresponding cost data much more efficiently.

- Customers have access to comprehensive comparative data on competing solutions, resulting in barriers to switch to competing solutions dropping dramatically.
- Competitors' targeted acquisition efforts to wean away more attractive customers are undermining the mass marketing strategies of enterprises, entailing more profitable customers subsidizing less profitable ones to achieve targeted profits.

### *Information as the New Resource*

All computerized systems and solutions in the past, used past-facing information merely for the purpose of referring and reporting only. As pointed out in an earlier book "Implementing SAP R/3", for the first time in the history of computerized systems, ERP began treating information as a resource for the operational requirements of the enterprise. Furthermore, unlike the traditional resources, information resources as made available by ERPs can be re-used and shared multiply without dissipation or degradation. Among all resources, this is one, which in practical terms almost defies the universal law of increase of Entropy as understood in the physical sciences. The impressive productivity gains resulting from the ERPs, truthfully arises out of this unique characteristic of ERPs to use information as an inexhaustible resource.

It was emphasized there that the importance of packages such as Siebel and SAP are not due to the total integration of various modules, single-point data entry, data integrity, ad hoc reporting, instant access to information, end-user computing, and so on. The importance of ERP and CRM packages arises primarily from the fact that information is by now the fifth resource (the first four being manpower, materials, money, and time) and unlike other resources, is inexhaustible. It can be shared infinitely without any reduction. Thus, if we can use information as a substitute for other resources (as seen in the following discussion), we can use it many times over without any appreciable additional cost.

For instance, just-in-time (JIT) inventory permits us to order just the right kind of material, at the right time and place. Therefore, it reduces inputs of manpower in ordering, handling and storing, and so on. It also results in reduced materials inventory and hence, cost of storage mechanisms, cost of locked capital, and so on. The availability of detailed and up-to-the-minute information on (for example) production runs can result in up-to-the-minute information on:

- Production plans for the next run
- Material requirements for the next run
- Issue of materials from the main stores for the next run
- Stock-on-hand in the stores for the next run
- Material to be ordered for the next run
- Etc.

It is not difficult to see that this ultimately results in drastically increased throughputs and reduced business cycle times, which is equivalent to improved production or technological processes through the use of improved resources. Traditionally, appreciably higher throughputs and lower production/ business cycles were possible only through innovation in technology, or production methods or processes. How information provided by CRM systems and ERPs is a resource of an organization can be seen from the analogy with fuel which drives automobiles—

information made available by Siebel and SAP R/ 3 greatly increases the velocity of business processes within the organization. These gains are a class apart from what is achievable with the manual or even fragmented legacy computerized systems. Enterprise-wide JIT (just-in-time), and not just the one confined primarily to the production department, is impossible without integrated computerized systems like CRM/ ERP packages for correct, current, consistent, and complete information.

It should be specially noted that only a CRM/ ERP implemented within an enterprise enables the optimal utilization and efficient conversion of such a seemingly intangible resource as information into a tangible commercial resource, which is also a highly perishable resource!

Enterprises that use customer capital as the defining component of the marketing system benefit because of the following:

- They address the customer as a whole who uses myriad services and products
- They utilize customer interactions to reinforce relationships and attain customer extensions
- They adjust marketing investment levels as customer relationships move through their dynamic life cycles
- They organize processes and structures around acquisition, retention and add-on selling to maximize the profitability of each over the customer life cycle.

### 1.2.1.5 Increasing Returns and Customer Capitalism

Traditional capitalism encourages managers to focus on short-term rewards that eventually lead to diminishing returns. In contrast, customer capitalism focuses on becoming the customer's preferred choice to ensure an enduring and compounding competitive advantage and sustainable growth, eventually leading to increasing returns, that is, positive, disproportionate gains over time. With customer capitalism, customers 'lock in' to a corporation and such customers become the most effective barrier to competitive entry. However, this 'lock in' is very different from the product 'lock in' envisaged in the traditional offering-based mass marketing approach. The latter is primarily based more on the product architectures and standards, which once established give the customer little or no option, and give the corporation quasi-monopolistic powers for as long as that particular technology wave lasts.

Increasing returns are the consequence of a combination of network effects (see Chapter 7, note on "Metcalfe's Law and Network Effects") and minimal marginal costs. This situation typically occurs when enterprises have very large start-up costs but very low marginal costs; this effect becomes pronounced with incidences of network effects. Network effects is manifested as a change in the benefit or surplus that a customer derives from goods when the number of other customers using similar kind of goods changes. The classic example of this case is the use of fax machines, whose value rises rapidly dependent on the number of other people using similar machines.

Please note that while the positive loops of increasing returns reinforce successes, in reverse, they will also aggravate losses. If an enterprise falters in delivering value to its customers, the 'value gap' will get amplified rapidly to pull the enterprise down a descending spiral of ever-decreasing customer values and number of customers.

## 1.2.2 Customer Responsiveness

It comes as a revelation that customers are neither necessarily looking for more products and services, nor are they looking for a wider range of choices. Customers simply want solutions to their individual needs—when, where and how they want it. The goal of a responsive enterprise is the cost-effective delivery of an interactively defined need of a customer.

In the traditional mass marketing, the primary focus is on the offering and the goal is the sales transaction. It is the offering (whether tangible or intangible), that must be defined, produced and distributed. All measures of activity namely, cost, revenue and profits are based on the offering. Mass marketing organizations emphasize deterministic planning for example, the best offering, the best way to produce and deliver the offering, and the best way to inform potential customers about the offering and so on. The 'best' method is typically based on the anticipated need of a prototypical customer who represents the needs of the target market, and success depends on how many customers buy the offering. In customized marketing, the focus is on flexibility—the flexibility to obtain the capability and capacity needed to respond quickly to a wide variety of individual customer requests. Customer responsive activities are used to find the best way to solve the individual customer needs. In customized relationship marketing (or in short, customized marketing) the emphasis is on delivered solution effectiveness (i.e., how well the individual problems are communicated, diagnosed and solved) and delivered solution efficiency (how few resources are required to solve the problems).

While mass marketing enterprises try to sell a single product to as many customers as possible, customized marketing enterprises try to sell as many products across several different product-lines over as long a period of time as possible, to a single customer. CRM systems like Siebel give enterprises the ability to interact one-to-one with individual customers and the ability to produce goods in response to individual customer requests.

The mass marketing and customized marketing approaches are organized very differently. The mass marketing approach anticipates customer needs and defines solutions before interacting with the customers, while the customized marketing approach involves developing a process that allows interaction with each individual customer one-to-one to define his or her need and then customize the delivered solution in response to that need. Each type of marketing requires a different type of organization.

When the inflexibilities are due to natural causes beyond the control of the enterprise, competitors will not be able to gain a responsive edge and hence, competitive advantage. However, to the degree that inflexibilities are institutionally caused by organizational structure, processes or strategies, the inflexibility is self-inflicted and the enterprise should definitely be liberated from such inflexibilities to make it customer responsive. True, customer-centricity is reflected in the enterprise transitioning from providing customers a range of choice offerings to providing solutions to the specific needs of the customers; but until the organization becomes customer-centric the emphasis will be on the offering and not on the responsiveness. In the offering-based approach, when the range of offerings is small and demand is relatively stable, enterprises can focus on producing and mass marketing more new offerings and rely on the customer attending to the best of these offerings. As against this, in the customer responsiveness based or customized marketing approach, rather than merely increasing the number of offerings, enterprises focus on meeting the individual needs of the customers. These issues are discussed in Chapter 7, section "Customer Responsive Management."

***Enterprise Networks***

It must be emphasized that contrary to the common perception, customer-centricity and responsiveness as an alternative logic of business (or management) has applications not only for services but also for production activities. The achievement of CRM objectives like customer acquisition, retention and value delivery requires enterprises to develop and manage a business network comprising suppliers, partners, distributors, investors and employees. An enterprise network is a coalition of enterprises that works collectively, and collaboratively to create value for the customers of a focal enterprise. Sometimes the coalition is loosely connected; at other times it is tightly defined, as in the relationship between Dell and its component suppliers. An enterprise network consists of a wide range of companies—suppliers, joint venture (JV) partners, contractors, distributors, franchisees, licensees and so on—that contribute to the focal enterprise's creation and delivery of value to its customers. Each of these enterprises in turn will have their own enterprise networks focused around themselves. Thus, relationships between enterprises in the network both enable and constrain focal companies in the achievement of their goals. Therefore, liberating the potential value in customer relationships hinges on enterprises effectively managing their non-customer network relationships.

CRM performance is more assured when the resources of the network are aligned and coordinated to contribute to the responsive creation and delivery of value to the focal company's customers. Consequently, CRM now includes applications for the extended enterprise encompassing relationships with the partners, suppliers, investors, employees and of course, the ERP systems (see Chapter 2, sub-section "Extended Collaborative Enterprise").

Whereas, offering-based enterprises are characterized by "top-down management", customer responsive organizations are "bottom-up management" oriented. As the response is guided by prior organizational experience that is embodied in the best practice guidelines that are readily available to all the frontline workers, the delivery is necessarily effective and efficient. Customer responsive enterprises are knowledge-based rather than plan-based. This knowledge base consists of knowing how to divide the envisaged work into tasks, identifying individual delivery units capable of performing it, assigning the work/tasks, and monitoring activities to ensure that the tasks are completed as per agreed requirements. Unless the knowledge is captured, it will only be available to those who have experienced it or learned about it. Because it is modifiable, rather than a fixed plan, the captured knowledge becomes a list of best practices to guide responses to requests in the future. Conditional best practice guidelines specify the processes required for diagnosing needs and developing customized delivery plans. Development of best practices is discussed in Chapter 7, section "Best Practice Guideline Management".

### 1.2.2.1 Advantages of Customer Responsiveness

The various advantages of customer responsiveness are:

- Improves the fit between the customer's need and what the enterprise delivers
- Increases profits through customer retention
- Increases profits by reducing costs
- Makes the enterprise capable of more change

Responsiveness reduces costs for the providers by reducing capital costs, making planning activities more efficient and effective and increasing capacity utilization. Chapter 7, section "Economics of Customer Responsiveness" looks at the different aspects of costs associated with customer responsiveness.

#### 1.2.2.2 Responsiveness Reduces Costs

Can an enterprise be more responsive at a reduced cost? Yes! In a career spanning about four decades, Taiichi Ohno spent years fine tuning the principles for controlling costs that became the foundations of the world famous Toyota Production System. He surprisingly discovered that not only the best way for increasing revene but also the best way to reduce cost of automobile production was to make the system more flexible and responsive! This is akin to the situation in the '60s and '70s when manufacturing quality and costs were mistakenly believed to be in opposition to each other. However, by the early '90s it was clearly established that not only can an enterprise achieve excellent quality at reduced costs but this was also imperative for its success.

Ohno discovered that the best way to reduce cost was also the best way to make the enterprise more responsive—customer responsive management was the most cost-effective way to solve customer needs. Toyota found that in order to control costs, they had to separate capacity scheduling (capacity management) from work dispatching (task assignments) as the responsiveness was not necessarily limited because of the constraints, inflexibilities or limitations of the infrastructure, but primarily because of the inflexible way in which deliveries are scheduled and assigned (i.e., coordinated, monitored and if delayed, expedited).

#### 1.2.2.3 Customer Responsiveness is Activity Based

Customer responsiveness is activity-based, where every activity is constituted of four parts.

- The first is an event (whether internal, external, regular or dramatic) that triggers the response.
- The second defines the actions or tasks (guided by existing or customized best practice guidelines) that need to be taken in response to the event.
- Third, is the assignment (i.e., JIT coordination) of the identified actions to resources with appropriate capability and capacity, in response to the event. Assignment minimizes lead time and thus contributes towards enhancing the flexibility.
- Lastly, the desired benefits are delivered to the customer.

### 1.2.3 Compelling Customer Experiences

For an enterprise to get the positive reinforcing loops that produce the increasing returns of customer capitalism depends on its ability to link benefits and deliver a totally integrated experience to its customers over a period of time. The pervasiveness and convergence of information technology is transforming the traditional feature–benefit oriented marketing to experiential marketing. As recognized by B. Joseph Pine II and James Gilmore, experiences have emerged as the latest step in the *progression of economic value*. However, the experience economy envisaged by them is only another manifestation of the overarching customer economy whereby customers are now demanding not only the quality of the enterprise solutions and services, but also the quality of the experience of *using* these solutions and services. While solutions and services are external to the customer, experiences are inherently individualistic, involving and engaging the customer's attention directly. In the future, the competitive edge will lie in staging engaging, compelling and memorable experiences. Thus the same product delivered with the same portfolio of surround services may still be perceived to generate varying levels of value depending on the final rendering or performance for individual customers.

Customer responsive enterprises recognize that customers may not be aware of what they really need unless they experience it and hence, realize the importance of anticipating rather than reacting to expressed need after it is too late.

### 1.2.3.1 Personalization

Relationships evolve and grow through trust, responsiveness and the mutually beneficial exchange of value. Personalization is a combination of technology and prior information to tailor customer interactions with the enterprise. Using information previously obtained or provided in real-time about these and other customers, the conversation between the parties can be altered dynamically to fit the customers' interests, preferences and needs so that the interaction/transaction locates the best suited product or service with minimal expenditure of time and cost. Deliveries are personalized to suit the evolving, unique and multiple needs of individuals, as opposed to only providing the standard offering in that range that the company makes or has in stock at that moment of time. This strengthens the bonding that enables the corporation to be proactive, and the deliveries to be more customized—this is what gets customers to 'lock in' (see earlier sub-section on "Increasing Returns and Customer Capitalism").

Delivering content, products or services, and pricing specific to a customer's interests and needs is based on collection of information about individual customer preferences, interests and buying behavior by employing the following techniques:

- Customer profiling aggregates data from allied websites based on the identification (ID) made available when the customer arrives on an event venue or a website.
- Collective filtering involves utilizing the prior experiences of a customer or similar customers to devise responses to individual customers.

The advantages of personalization are as follows:

- Higher degrees of customer service to the customer by anticipating their needs delivering content, products, services or pricing information that meets their needs
- Improving the efficiency of the interaction and thus, enhancing the likelihood of a purchase being made during the current visit
- Increasing the level of knowledge about customers and understanding why and how they prefer to do business with your organization
- Establishing a relationship that encourages customer relationship and enhanced customer bonding
- Improving the performance with the customer site by using tracking to provide insight into factors that have a salutary effect on the performance of the application

## 1.2.4 Customer Loyalty

Traditionally, companies have focused on winning customers rather than retaining them. The conventional wisdom was that a dominating market share typically translated into production economies of scale and the ability to become a low-cost producer. The goal was to continually add customers to replace those that defected to competitors and also to increase the market share.

However, lately, financial analysis of the cost of customer acquisition versus the cost of retention has shown that, for most organizations where the cost of acquisition is high, keeping customers can be a more profitable strategy. It is estimated that it can cost four to 7 times more to replace a current customer than it does to retain one. On the average, US companies lose half of their customers every five years. It is easier to get existing customers to try new capabilities than to engage and acquire new ones. The cost of contacting existing customers, researching their needs, and getting them to begin using new services is minimal compared with acquiring new customers. It is easy to see how effective this approach of 'customer loyalty' can be if we recognize that the revenue accruing from customers follows the Pareto's Law, that is, 20% of the customer base accounts for 80% of the revenues and more than 110% of the profits generated by a company. A study published in *Harvard Business Review* by Reichheld and Sasser concluded that some companies could boost profits by almost 100% by retaining just 5% more of their customers (however, for a different view, see Timothy Keiningham et al). Mass unfocused marketing is a thing of the past. As stated earlier, as much as 80% of the sales process may be controlled by specific knowledge of a customer's business. As the marketing spend needs to show a higher return on investment, a longer-term relationship becomes essential.

The relative costs for acquiring, retaining and winning back a lost customer is as follows:

| | |
|---|---|
| Cost of retaining a current customer | $1x$ |
| Cost of acquiring a new customer | $5x$ to $10x$ |
| Cost of winning back a lost customer | $3x$ to $8x$ |

Customized relationship marketing recommends that companies identify their Most Valuable Customers (MVC) and then have a close relationship with them. Companies may use an ABC analysis (for example, identify top 20% customers who account for 80% of sales) to identify their MVCs. However, this may be a misguided effort because, being a lag measure, it would lead to concentration of efforts on customers who, although they are currently contributing to the profitability of the company may not necessarily have a long-term profit potential. The best way of assessing the long-term profit potential of customers is through their Lifetime Value (LTV), which we will discuss in the section on "Customer Lifetime Value (LTV)" later.

While most companies measure some form of customer satisfaction, that measure does not determine customer loyalty as reasonably satisfied customers often defect to the competition. Customer loyalty is different from customer satisfaction per se. For instance, higher levels of customer satisfaction do not necessarily translate into repeat purchases and therefore, increased sales and profits. A related problem is that even enterprises such as departmental stores that are critically dependent on access to data on loyalty schemes, may possibly be using only about 2 percent of the data to which they have access. One of the primary reasons for this is the sheer volume of data that is being captured within these organizations. For instance, a regular shopper may buy 50 to 100 items during a monthly visit. Many of these stores have 10 to 20 check-out points operating at any given time. These can process on an average about 12 customers an hour for 10 hours a day. So, each day they are open, they gather between 60,000 and 240,000 data points per store. Even for a mid-sized supermarket chain with about 200 stores working 7 days a week, this would result in something like 65 million to 340 million data points per working week!

Table 1.3 compares the traditional customer satisfaction-oriented approach with that of the value orientation of relationship marketing.

**Table 1.3 Customer Satisfaction-orientation of Traditional Mass Marketing versus Value Orientation of Customized Relationship Marketing**

| | Traditional Mass Marketing<br>Customer Satisfaction-Orientation | Customized Relationship Marketing<br>Customer Value Orientation |
|---|---|---|
| 1. | Focuses on the product, emphasizes the firm's offering or tactical solution needs of customer | Focuses on the customer/product interaction, emphasizes fundamental |
| 2. | Emphasizes product attributes and features | Considers all aspects of the customer/ product interaction viz. attributes, values, consequences, etc. |
| 3. | This is inherently more short-term and unstable, leads to incremental or marginal product/service change and improvement, and results in historical orientation | Is inherently more long-term and stable, leads to innovation and radical improvements and has a future orientation |
| 4. | Typically fails to measure trade-offs that determine customer value | Measures the trade-offs that determine customer value |
| 5. | Often difficult to assess in absence of consequence-level information | Helpful to assess because of available interaction-level information and is actionable |

Customer loyalty is characterized by repeat purchases and a willingness to continue the relationship. Loyal customers:

- Stay longer
- Cost less to service
- Buy more
- Provide higher margins
- Purchase across product lines
- Demonstrate immunity to the lure of competition
- Demonstrate less price sensitivity

There are various ways to represent progress up the ladder of customer loyalty. Customer pyramid is one such approach that assists in planning for enhanced relationship with the company's prospects and customers, and is also helpful in visualizing the progress towards higher value relationships.

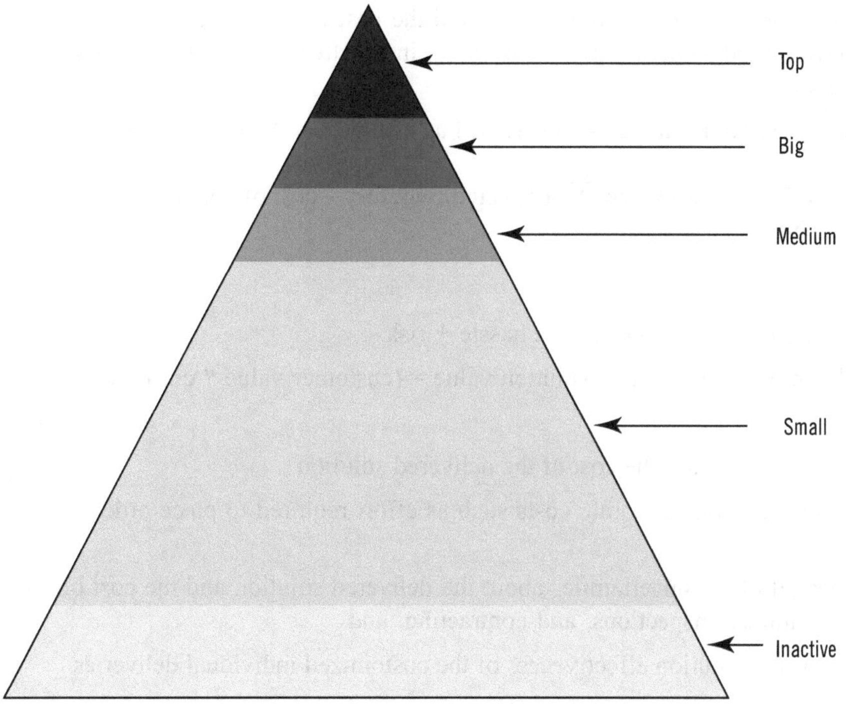


**Fig. 1.7 Customer Pyramid**

Figure 1.7 presents the Customer pyramid consisting of the following:

(a) 'Top'—the top 1% revenue customers
(b) 'Big'—the next 4% revenue customers
(c) 'Medium'—the next 15% revenue customers
(d) 'Small'—the next 70% revenue customers
(e) 'inactive'—the remaining 10% revenue customers

The objective of enhanced customer loyalty then translates into the movement of customers within, up and out of this pyramid. It helps in getting new customers into the pyramid, getting a larger share of the business of the existing customers, and prevents losing those who are most profitable. A 2% upward migration in the customer pyramid can mean 10% more revenues and 50% more profit. This is why CRM initiatives that are targeted at getting, growing and keeping valuable customers result in revenue and profit increases that represent very high returns on the company's CRM investments.

## 1.2.5 Customer Relationships

In today's world of decreasing margins, increasing competition and ever-changing business environment, corporate success depends on an enterprise's ability to build and maintain loyal and valued customer relationships.

In a market where loyalty has plummeted and the cost of acquiring new customers is prohibitive, companies have turned to their current customers in an attempt to retain and maximize the business potential from them.

The value of a relationship can be expressed as a sum over $M$ offerings as follows:

$$\text{Value of a relationship} = \text{future value} \sum_{l=1}^{M} (\text{Expected Benefits}_l - \text{cost of obtaining the benefits}_l)$$

where,

Expected benefits = economic cost + hassle + risk

Cost of obtaining the benefits = solution value = (customer value * customer fit)

and,

*economic cost* is typically the cost of the delivered solution

*hassle* includes all non-economic costs such as effort required to place orders and locate potential providers

*risk* includes all of the uncertainties about the delivered solution and the cost of protecting against risk such as insurance, inspections, and contracting, and

*fit* is the delivered solution effectiveness of the customized individual deliveries

The customer responsive enterprise adds value for the customer even by eliminating the hassle required to research the product and to learn how to use it. When relationships exist uninterruptedly for extended periods of time, they improve need diagnosis and delivered solution effectiveness as well as establish procedures that minimize the hassle of communicating needs and responses.

### 1.2.5.1 Why Cultivate Customer Relationship?

The relationship-oriented organization sees the customer not as a single sale but as a long-term relationship in which the value of future solutions will always be greater than the value of any existing transactions. Relationships not only define and determine expectations but also minimize transaction costs. Good relationships obtain substantial outcomes with a minimum of effort (i.e., cost and hassle). When relationships are positive, solutions are more effective, and the effort expended for making these solutions also gets reduced (e.g., the hassles, risks or transactions).

Such a relationship results in several benefits because:

- The parties understand and trust each other
  - have shared values
  - have confidence in each other
  - rely on each other
  - communicate clearly
  - work easier
- The parties are more committed and responsive. They
  - are willing to pay a premium for mutual commitment

  - are mutually persuasive rather than coercive
  - resolve delivered solution errors or other differences amicably
- The parties are predictable to each other
- It not only reduces the time to diagnose needs of the customer but also reduces diagnosis errors
- The parties develop the solutions jointly
- The parties integrate schedules mutually

Relationships based purely on contracts may not be long-lasting because no contract can be comprehensive enough to cover all possible future eventualities. The purpose of a contract is primarily to eliminate uncertainties regarding delivered solution commitments in terms of scope, functionality, schedule, costs, etc. Consequently, especially in these times of market change and turbulence, contracts tend to restrict responsiveness of the relationships and hence, eventually the responsiveness of the respective organizations.

Customer relationships are important because they establish customer expectations. When expectations are realistically high, customers call to seek solutions for their needs. Once the customer does call, the provider needs to respond and reassure the customer. Customers empower the people and organizations they trust. Each time their needs are met, the customers' trust is increased. Even if the delivered solution is below expectations, trust levels get restored if the provider accepts responsibility for the problems and makes a good recovery. Few managers realize that more than 80% of customers return if their complaints are resolved quickly.

### 1.2.5.2 Customer Interaction Channels

Companies draw on and integrate information from a wide range of resources to strengthen customer relationships and develop insights into customer wants, needs and values. These sources may include direct contacts, customer information systems, sales reports, call center data, market surveys, focus groups, billing data, demographic studies and so on. This may also include prior records and analysis of interactions of the customer with the enterprise. The customer may interact with different units of the business through different channels but the enterprise must have a coordinated, consistent and complete picture of the customer available throughout the enterprise. All these impart a greater degree of stability, continuity and predictability to the customer base, which eases the planning and operations all along the supply chain.

Customers are demanding more access and interaction points with their suppliers. In addition to getting more information from the companies with which they do business, customers are demanding more ways of interacting with those companies, including phone, fax, e-mail, Web, mail, on-site and so on. Most companies practicing CRM set up call centers, which are able to provide customized services to individual customers. This further enhances the enterprise's organizational memory about the customers' interactions with the company. While these interactions are momentary and could be across many interaction channels, the organizational memory about these interactions (and therefore, the customer) can be made persistent by incorporating them within the growing customer knowledge base.

Accessibility creates responsiveness. In terms of sales, responsiveness depends upon how easy it is for the prospect or the customer to reach the company through multiple modes of communication and how fast the enterprise can respond. On the other hand, responsiveness in service also depends upon the speed of reply and action (which in turn is dependent upon the speed of executing the corresponding business processes). More than the product itself, it is often the degree of responsive support and service received by a customer that decides between a loyal customer and a lost customer.

#### *1.2.5.2.1 Internet—The Web of Relationships*

The Web is a key factor in the emergence of CRM as an important technology. The emergence of the Web, like printing and telegraph earlier, has caused a fundamental change in the ease with which people communicate with each other. It has enhanced by a quantum measure, the ability of many more people to produce information, disseminate it to a much larger audience and that too at much lesser costs, and more easily. In some cases, the Web simply offers a new and better way to perform existing services such as, checking an account balance. But other Web applications offer novel products and services that are possible only through Web technology. Customer self-service is the best example of the Web's enablement of customer relationships. It is estimated that a typical banking transaction at a local branch costs about 50% by telephone, 30% at an ATM, and only 1% on the Web! (see Chapter 9, note on "The Significance of Internet").

#### *1.2.5.2.2 Customer Channel Integration*

Once we have a proliferation of channels, the objective is to make the sales and marketing as efficient and effective as possible whilst also delivering rapid growth, reduced sales expenses and seamless services.

### 1.2.5.3 A 360-degree View of the Customer

In the customer centric approach, the goal is to provide personal service—recreating the individual attention, flexibility and understanding that the best neighborhood stores have always provided to their most valued customers—on a mass scale. Meeting this goal involves solving the 'many-to-many' problem, that is, many people within different departments of the enterprise interacting with many different customers. None of the information on interactions is shared across these different departments, leaving all employees involved with only partial information. Each employee has at the most only a fragmentary view of the customer resulting in possibly below par service, inappropriate product offering and pricing, and ineffective branding. To address this effectively and efficiently, each of the company's representatives who interacts with the customer needs to have a clear and complete picture of that customer's activity. This holistic picture is termed, the '360-degree view'.

Achieving a 360-degree view of the customer is critical in order to:

- Interact with a customer in a fully informed way
- Assess the customer's potential value correctly
- Determine the programs that could realize this potential value from each customer

The key is to integrate in a single environment the related data that comes from all points of interaction with the customer. This can be achieved effectively by a CRM system like Siebel (see Chapter 2, "Customer Relationship Management (CRM) Systems"), which gives each employee at each customer touch point, a 360-degree view of the customer. Siebel eBusiness Application Integration (eAI) that is a critical enabler of enterprise-wide integration of diverse applications across various products and divisions, affords the enterprise a 360-degree view of its customer relationships across multiple channels of interaction. It enables every customer to perceive the enterprise as a whole and also to expect to be recognized and valued by the enterprise as a whole. By tracking and managing interactions with individual customers and making the customer history available across the enterprise, such a system provides companies with the data they need to improve relationships across the board.

### 1.2.5.4 One-to-One Marketing

In the traditional mass marketing approach, companies use demographic segments—segments based on standard demographic measures like age, income, geography, gender and marital status—to divide up their customer base and define the marketing program. While this is a step towards recognizing the fact that not all customers are the same, it does not address the problem adequately. The problem is that demographic segments tend to be very large or coarsely grained because of which major differences among individual members of such segments and the corresponding marketing opportunities, are overlooked. This is also the primary reason that standard response rates for direct marketing, such as direct mail, are only about 2 percent.

Don Peppers and Martha Rogers introduced the notion of one-to-one marketing in their popular book, *The One to One Future*. This advocates the move towards more fine-grained segments, with the ultimate goal of reaching the segment of one. One-to-one marketing treats each customer as an individual, based on a holistic view with consistent actions across all touch points, and thinks in terms of wallet share of each customer rather than market share.

### 1.2.5.5 Permission Marketing

It is estimated that by 2004, eBusiness marketers took advantage of the e-mail channel by sending more than 200 billion e-mails to reach customers, increase their brand visibility and jump-start sales. This is primarily because e-mail marketing has been assessed to achieve purchase rates as high as four times those achievable using the traditional direct mail methods. But with the increasing use of internet and other digital channels as vehicles for marketing or selling, the need to manage customer data more effectively in line with government rulings has become very important (see Chapter 17, section on "Privacy and Security").

The Distance Selling Directive implemented from 4 June 2000 requires:

- The consumer to be provided with information in a clear and comprehensible manner and in good time before concluding any distance contract
- The consumer has the right to cancel a distance contract within a specified 'cooling off' period
- The consumer cannot be targeted for unsolicited e-mails, faxes and automatic calling systems for distance selling purposes, unless he has consented to be contacted by the vendor enterprise in that way.

Permission marketing is an approach to selling goods and services in which a prospect explicitly agrees in advance to receive marketing information. Conceived by Seth Godin, Yahoo!'s internet marketing pioneer, permission-based marketing seeks to build trust and involve the customers by putting them in control of asking the enterprise to keep them informed on information and offers that are of specific interest to them. The objective is to gain permission from customers to keep them informed about things that are of interest to them, by e-mail, SMS, WAP or through official channels, on a regular basis.

## 1.2.6 Customer Life Cycle (CLC)

Customer relationships, along with their needs and expectations from the companies at various stages, evolve over a period of time. The concept of a customer life cycle provides a framework for understanding and managing these differences at various stages of relationship with the company. Support for the existence of CLC comes from various studies and research undertaken on new product acceptance, and Recency, Frequency and Monetary (RFM) analyses.

The different types of customers are as follows.

- Prospects—This is the pre-customer stage where the prospects are not customers yet, but they represent potential value for the enterprise. In fact, managing prospects is much more difficult than managing even disgruntled customers at a later stage. This is because all customers have pre-defined thresholds of cost, quality and price for making the 'buy' decision. If the company's offerings are not perceived to exceed such thresholds, it may not result in a purchase. On the other hand, exceeding them overly may also prove to be counter-productive, as very high expectations are likely to be unmet resulting in difficulty in retaining such customers later.
- First-time buyers—A company's customer capital is heavily dependent upon the potential value of the first-time buyers. Customers achieve this stage upon making their first purchase. At this stage, the customer is highly vulnerable to defections due to even minor disappointments or lure of the competitor's offerings.
- Core customers—Customers advance to this stage when they begin to make repeat purchases regularly. At this stage, the relationship has stabilized, the expectations too have stabilized and finally, there are no major changes in the customer's needs or product specifications. An occasional product failure does not trigger defection or even a re-evaluation of the firm's offerings. Core customers have the highest and most stable retention rates and also account for the highest sales per customer.
- Defectors—Customers may reach this stage either because of a massive, though rarely occurring, failure on the part of the company or a compelling alternative offering from a competitor, or in a few cases, frequently recurring failure that goes un-addressed by the company for an extended period of time despite repeated reporting by the customer.

Figure 1.9 shows the various stages during the Customer Life Cycle (CLC). The focus of activities during the various phases is as follows:

### *(a) Customer engagement*

To contact a new customer through marketing, advertisement, telemarketing, personal selling, direct mail, promotions and publicity.

### *(b) Customer acquisition*

To increase customer involvement through collection of as much information about him as possible, understand the buying context, purchase conditions and associated costs, offer post-purchase reassurance, promote the price–value relationship and finally, develop the foundation for a long-term relationship.

### *(c) Customer retention*

To create long-term, committed and loyal customers, develop a service philosophy, identify and close service gaps, manage your retention-related costs, increase responsiveness to customers, measure customer satisfaction and reward positive customer behavior.

### *(d) Customer extension*

To extend your customer's loyalty through first defining loyalty parameters and discover customer lifetime, determine customer lifetime value, learn customer needs and extended needs (e.g., up-sell), search and communicate solutions (e.g., cross-sell), counter defection rates and patterns, bond closely with your customers, manage your loyalty costs and reward loyal behavior. Initially, Amazon only sold books, then it added CDs, and now it also sells DVDs, toys, electronics, computer peripherals and much more. The customer capital model leads to greater customer value once the firm understands how to apply it as a business model.

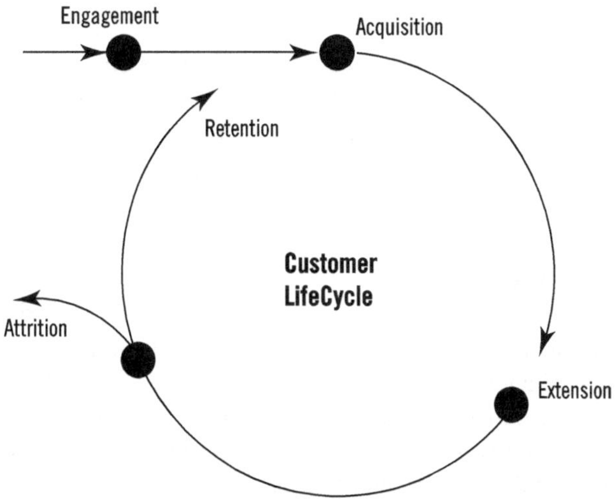


**Fig. 1.8 Customer Life Cycle (CLC)**

### *(e) Customer attrition*

To reduce defection rates and patterns through identification of defection parameters (both controllable and uncontrollable), focus on 'at risk' customers, arrange loyalty schemes, programs and events, felicitate and reward loyal customers, improve customer satisfaction ratings, extend customer lifetime, discover customer 'wish lists' to propose effective customized solutions and improve customer spend. Despite questionable on-time reliability and poor customer service, the airline industry has been able to foster high loyalty by instituting barriers to the customer's exit including increasing customer's cost of switching to the competitors. For instance, frequent-flyer programs pitch the customer's status in the next year dependent upon the mileage clocked in the current year.

To grow, an enterprise needs to acquire customers at a rate greater than their defection or attrition rate. Unlike customer satisfaction, the attrition rate being unambiguous is an excellent predictor of long-term (non-)profitability. To increase its profits, an enterprise must place as much emphasis on reducing customer defections as it does on new customer acquisitions.

#### 1.2.6.1 Customer Value

Customer Value (CV) is the long-term financial value that a customer delivers to a business and is therefore, a result of the following factors:

- All income streams, right from the initial purchase through all the subsequent purchases
- All direct variable costs associated with managing the customer
- The envisaged length of the customer's relationship with the enterprise
- The customer's propensity to recommend the company to other prospective customers
- The resulting final value discounted at an appropriate rate, to calculate the net present value

Customer value could be of different kinds:

(a) Historic value—What has been the total CV till date

(b) Current value—Assuming the current customer behavior to remain the same, what will be the CV in the future

(c) Potential value—What could the customer be worth if we cost-effectively cross-sell, increase their useful life with the company and encourage them to recommend us to others

(d) Influence value—What is the value of the sales that the customer indirectly influences through reference, referrals, and the like (see Chapter 7, note on "Power Law and Small Worlds Networks (SWN)").

**Co-creation of Customer Value**

Co-creation or co-production of customer value occurs when enterprise delivers the value desired by the customer with the active participation of the customer. This is such a significant concept that it would need another book in itself to explore it to its full potential and depth. In co-creation of value, the customer contributes time, effort or resources essential for the selection, production, packaging and delivery of the offering or services. Because of co-participation of customer in production and delivery of the offering and services, inherently, there is an assured minimum level of customer satisfaction. ATM systems, Self-service Restaurants etc. are typical examples of value co-creating systems, but the best exemplars of the value co-creating systems are the Internet-based applications (also see earlier section 'Customer Relationships', and Chapter 16, sub-section 'Aspects of Enterprise Value').

#### 1.2.6.2 Customer Lifetime Value

As mentioned earlier, the Customer Lifetime Value (LTV) is measured typically on an individual customer basis by tracking all transaction and expense details. This information is used to project the net present value of the future revenue streams from this customer throughout his envisaged lifetime. The focus on net margins rather than gross margins is because of the necessity to include cost-to-serve considerations in computing customer profitability. Enterprises that do not have the costing processes in place to trace costs to the customers, do not have the net margin data and therefore, must work either with gross margin or sales revenue data.

The kinds of data that are essential for calculating LTV include:

(a) Customer transaction history
- What was the revenue generated from the purchase
- What was purchased
- How much was purchased
- When was it purchased
- Where was it purchased
- What were the special offers/promotions
- What was returned/cancelled

(b) Revenue history
- Initial revenue
- Incremental revenue
- Service and support revenue

(c) Promotion history

(d) Costs
- Acquisition costs
- Product costs
- Incremental sales costs
- Incremental product costs
- Ongoing service and support costs

A general formula for LTV can be defined as follows:

Customer LTV = Value (Initial Revenue – Costs)
+ Net Present Value (Loyalty * (Future Revenue – Costs))
+ Net Present Value (Loyalty * Influence Value)

The LTV for various customers may also be helpful in identifying several groups of customers who have similar patterns of behavior, which in turn could be helpful in tailoring value propositions to such identified groups of customers

The Customer Lifetime Value (LTV) is easier to predict if it incorporates recurring numbers of the corresponding product's use cycle(s). For instance, if the average use cycle of a vehicle costing $20,000 is five years, the CV for a single vehicle owning customer with the relevant customer lifetime of about 40 years, may range between $140,000 and $200,000. The LTV of this customer will be much larger because of additional values representing warranty, maintenance, repair and other services during the use cycle of a vehicle.

This is based on the powerful idea of the business cycles or the constituent product use cycles. A database of the ownership and use history of product(s) can be used to perform sales projections at any moment of time, for a specific period for a named prospective customer. It is possible to predict the requirements of a company with a reasonable accuracy based on:

- The average use life cycle of a product
- The average innovation cycle of the underlying technology
- The business cycle of the particular company as well as the concerned industry
- The purchase history of the company for the relevant product

This kind of information on enterprises used strategically for sales and marketing could help too improve:

- Efficiency of the sales by reducing the time-to-sell
- Effectiveness of the sales by entering the natural procurement cycle at an appropriate time as predicted by this analysis.

## 1.2.7 Customer Value Management (CVM)

In the process of re-orienting the business around the customer, companies are increasingly realizing that not all customers are equal. Different customers provide different revenues to the companies, they choose its products and services for different reasons and they also defect for different reasons. This range of customer behavior results in widely differing values across the customer base, in terms of customers' future revenue to the business. To maximize profitability, it is important for companies to determine the future value of prospects and customers, so that they can differentiate their marketing activity and business processes to optimize future revenues and return on investment.

Customer Value Management (CVM) is the management of processes and communications designed to maximize Customer Lifetime Value (LTV) by closing the gap between the current and potential Customer Value (CV). CVM provides a way of measuring and improving the value delivered by the customer to the business and using this as the basis for decision-making. It identifies those customers that really count; identifying what it is that they want as individuals (or as groups) and determining how to deliver it profitably.

CVM improves profitability and delivers greater Return on Investments (ROI) by assisting in the following:

- Targeting acquisition efforts and activities at those prospects with the greatest CV
- Developing stronger and more profitable relationships with existing customers
- Observing shifts in CV that reflect changes in customer behavior
- Identify the gap between the current value and potential value, that is, the value gap to drive targeted cross-sell/up-sell campaigns as well as measure improvements in CV
- Ensuring that the scarce financial and staff resources are allocated to interactions with those customers with the largest proven CV or potential CV.

Any business initiative can be assessed in terms of the how much it contributes to increasing the CV versus the costs involved. But CVM is more than just a new method for calculating the value of customer relationships or a new way that a business allocates marketing resources and efforts. It is a total marketing system that entails the need to build organizations, processes and performance measures that work together to maximize the value of the customer capital. In contrast to the traditional brand management approaches that focus primarily on the brand equity, CVM treats customer capital as the primary marketing asset. Figure 1.9 compares the features of these two approaches. Whereas, the traditional mass marketing and tactics revolve around segmentation, targeting and positioning; CVM is driven by acquisition, retention and an add-on selling model. In the case of CVM, the marketing mix is determined by the stage of the customer life cycle.

| | Customer Capital Approach | Brand Equity Approach |
|---|---|---|
| Production and service quality | Create strong customer preference | Create high customer retention |
| Advertising | Create brand image and position | Create customer affinity |
| Promotions | Deplete brand equity | Generate repeat buying and enhance customer lifetime value |
| Product development | Use brand extensions to sell related products | Use relationships to sell other products |
| Segmentation | Based on customer characteristics and benefits | Based on observed customer buying behavior |
| Channels of distribution | Multi-stage distribution system | Direct distribution to customer |
| Customer service | Enhance brand image | Enhance customer affinity |

**Fig. 1.9 Comparative Features of the Customer Capital and Brand Equity Approaches**

Mass customization of products and services enables companies to market off-the-shelf products and services as tailored to the individual customers. This reduces the need for standard offerings and their associated carrying costs. However, this is possible only if the vendor has an accurate profile of the individual customer; a good CRM program will generate and maintain this kind of information. Building such a profile also facilitates cross-selling of products and services through the different delivery channels available, adding incremental revenues. It can also reduce time to market new products as potential latent demand can be quickly identified and addressed.

## 1.2.8 Customers as Lifelong Investments

Relationship-based enterprises view customers as lifelong investments (see Sunil Gupta and Donald Lehman) and therefore, their primary objective is to maximize the sum total of the time value of current and envisaged future customers. Relationship-based enterprises focus on accomplishing the intricate and long-term goal of 'owning' the customer.

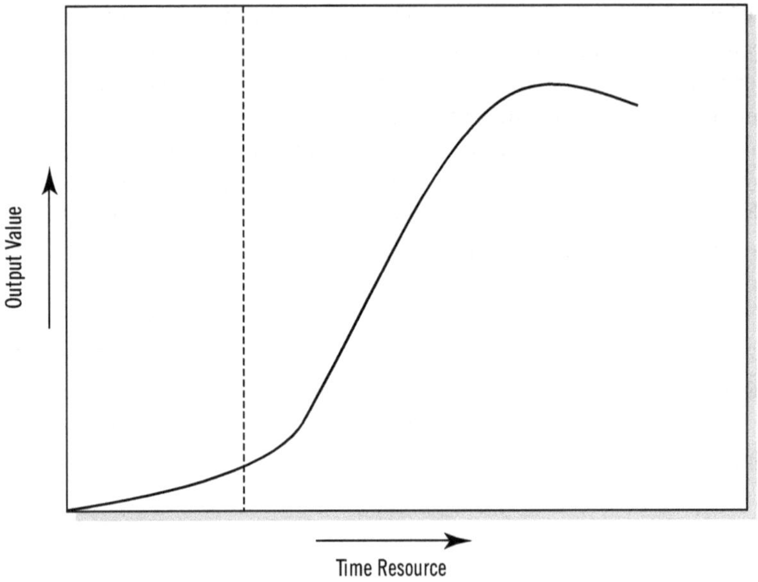


Fig. 1.10 Value Curve for Offering-based Enterprises

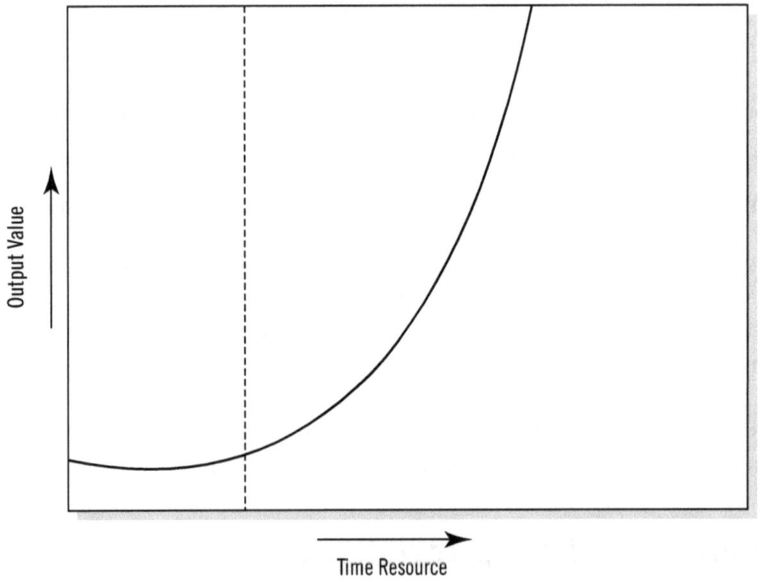


Fig. 1.11 Value Curve for Relationship-based Enterprises

**Table 1.4 Marketing Mix for Customer Equity and Brand Equity Approaches**

| Element of the Marketing Mix | Customer Equity Approach | Brand Equity Approach |
|---|---|---|
| Segmentation | Behavioral segmentation based on the customer base | Customer characteristics and benefit segmentation |
| Product and Service Quality | Creates high customer retention rate | Create strong customer preference |
| Product Development | Acquire products to sell to the installed customer base | Use brand name to create line extensions into new areas |
| Advertising | Create customer bonding and affinity | Create brand image and position |
| Promotions | Create repeat buying and enhance customer lifetime value | Momentarily enhance perceived value for money; but this depletes brand equity |
| Customer Service | Enhance customer bonding and affinity | Enhance brand image |
| Channels of Distribution | Direct distribution to customer | Multistage distribution system |

Traditional offering-based organizations are focused on maximizing the ROI on customers as early on in the relationship as possible because once the competition sets in, the margins and pay-off would invariably go down leading to the regime of rapidly diminishing returns. Figure 1.10 shows the classic product lifecycle or the 'S' curve for offering-based enterprises. On the other hand, customer responsive organizations are more focused on maximizing the sum of the area under the curve, that is, the sum total of time value of the current and envisaged future customers. Figure 1.11 shows the characteristic exponential curve for the relationship-based enterprise. Initially the returns are minimal or even reducing; thereafter with increasing inputs of resources the returns increase exponentially.

Enterprises that take a customer asset approach differ significantly from those that treat brand equity as the primary marketing asset. Brand approach focuses on activities that maximize a brand's total revenues and the greatest possible returns on the brand investment. Rather than confining attention to singular brands, the customer asset approach focuses on the sum total of the net income stream across all brands and services. Table 1.4 compares the characteristic features of the marketing mix for the customer equity and brand equity approaches.

Chapter 16, section on "Time Value of Customers and Shareholder Value" elaborates on the concept that a company's market valuation/capitalization is truly dependent on the sum total of the envisaged lifetime value of its current and future customers. The market valuation in turn, determines the company's share price on the stock markets. Patricia Seybold was the first to point out that the success in the customer economy will depend on companies managing their enterprises by and for customer value—they will have to use Customer Lifetime Value (LTV) as a strategic management tool. The source of investor value for companies will increasingly be based on the value of their customer franchise and the customer lifetime value of their present and future customers (see Chapter 9, sub-section on "Basic eBusiness Strategy Patterns").

## 1.3 MANAGEMENT BY COLLABORATION (MBC)

The business environment has witnessed tremendous and rapid changes in the '90s. There has been an increasing emphasis on being customer-focused and on leveraging and strengthening the company's core competencies. This has forced enterprises to learn and develop abilities to change and respond rapidly to the competitive dynamics of the global market.

Companies have learned to effectively re-engineer themselves into flatter organizations with closer integration across the traditional functional boundaries of the organization. There is increasing focus on employee empowerment and cross-functional teams. In this book, we are proposing that what we are witnessing is a fundamental transformation from the manner in which businesses have been operating for the last century.

This change, which is primarily driven by the information revolution of the past few decades, is characterized by the dominant tendency to integrate across transaction boundaries, both internally and externally. The dominant theme of this new system of management with significant implications on organizational development is *collaboration*. We will refer to this emerging and maturing constellation of concepts and practices as Management by Collaboration (MBC). CRM packages such as Siebel are major instruments for realizing MBC-driven organizations.

MBC is an approach to management primarily focused on relationships; relationships by their very nature are not static and are constantly in evolution. With organizations and environmental conditions becoming more complex, global and therefore more competitive, MBC provides a framework for dealing effectively with the issues of performance improvement, capability development, and adaptation to the changing environment. MBC, as embodied by CRM packages such as Siebel, has had a major impact on the strategy, structure and culture of the customer centric organization.

The beauty and essence of MBC is that it incorporates in its very fabric the basic urge of humans for a purpose in life, for mutually beneficial relationships, for mutual commitment and for being helpful to other beings that is, for collaborating. These relationships could be at the level of the individual, a division, an enterprise, or even between enterprises. Every relationship has a purpose and manifests itself through various processes as embodied mainly in the form of teams; thus, the relationships are geared towards attainment of these purposes through the concerned processes optimally.

Because of the enhanced role played by the individual members of an enterprise in any relationship or process, MBC promotes not only their motivation and competence, but also develops the competitiveness and capability of the organizations as a whole. MBC emphasizes the roles of both the top management and the individual member. Thus, the MBC approach covers the whole organization through the means of basic binding concepts such as relationships, processes and teams. MBC addresses readily all issues of management, including organization development. The issues range from organizational design and structure, role definition and job design, output quality and productivity, interaction and communication channels, and company culture to employee issues such as attitudes, perception, values and motivation.

The basic idea of collaboration has gained tremendous ground with the increasing importance of business processes and dynamically constituted teams in the operations of companies. The traditional bureaucratic structures, which are highly formalized, centralized and functionally specialized, have proven too slow, too expensive and too unresponsive to be competitive. These structures are based on the simple assumption that all the individual activities and task elements in a job are independent and separable. Organizations were structured hierarchically in a 'command and control' structure, and it was taken as an accepted fact that the output of the organization as a whole could be maximized by maximizing the output of each constituent organizational unit.

On the other hand, by their very nature, teams are flexible, adaptable, dynamic and collaborative. They encourage flexibility, innovation, entrepreneurship and responsiveness. For the last few decades, even in traditionally bureaucratic manufacturing companies, teams have manifested themselves and flourished successfully in various forms as super-teams, Self-directed Work Teams (SDWT), quality circles and so on. The dynamic changes in the market and global competition that companies are now facing, necessarily lead to flatter and more flexible organizations with a dominance of more dynamic structures like teams.

People in teams, representing different functional units, are motivated to work within constraints of time and resources to achieve a defined goal. The goals may range from incremental improvements in responsiveness, efficiency, quality and productivity to quantum leaps in new product development. Even in traditional businesses, the number and variety of teams instituted for various functions, projects, tasks and activities has been on the increase.

Increasingly, companies are populated with worker teams that have special skills, operate semi-autonomously and are answerable directly to peers and to the end-customers. Members must not only have higher level of skills than before, but must also be more flexible and capable of doing more jobs. The empowered workforce with considerably enhanced managerial responsibilities (pertaining to information, resources, authority and accountability) has resulted in an increase in worker commitment and flexibility. Whereas workers have witnessed gains in the quality of their work life, corporations have obtained returns in terms of increased interactivity, responsiveness, quality, productivity and cost improvements.

Consequently, in the past few years a new type of non-hierarchical network organization with distributed intelligence and decentralized decision-making powers has been evolving. This entails a demand for constant and frequent communication and feedback among the various teams or functional groups. A CRM package such as Siebel essentially provides such an enabling environment through its modules like Siebel Office, Siebel Workflow, EIS, etc.

## 1.3.1 The Relationship-based Enterprise (RBE)

A Relationship-Based Enterprise (RBE) builds customer relationships to sustain business growth and to increase the profitability of the business. A relationship is a series of dialogues each consisting of numerous instantaneous interactions with the customer. The relationship-based enterprise has the ability to recognize and interact with different types of customers. The enterprise uses these dynamic interactions to discover its customers through customer-related and customer needs-related information and creates value by organizing itself to serve these customers. Customers and their corresponding needs are changing constantly depending on the market environment and therefore, it is only because of these dynamic interactions that it can continue to discover the current needs of its customers.

## 1.3.2 The Information-driven Enterprise

The combined impact on companies of increasing product complexity and increased variety has been to create a massive problem of information management and coordination. Information-driven activities now constitute a major fraction of all activities within an enterprise. Information-driven organizations alone can survive in the dynamically changing global competitive market. Only integrated, computer-based information systems such as Siebel are (and can be) enablers for this kind of enterprise-level collaboration.

The information-based organization as proposed by management theorist Peter Drucker is a reality today; correspondingly, companies are compelled to install both end-user and work group oriented enterprise-level integrated computing environments. Only information-driven extended organizations can possibly store, retrieve, analyze and present colossal amounts of information at the enterprise-level that is also up-to-date, timely, accurate, collated, processed and packaged dynamically for both external and internal customers. It should be noted that the title of this sub-section uses the phrase 'information-driven' rather than 'information-based'. The primary reason for this is that technology in the 90's permits us to use information as a resource that is a legitimate substitute for conventional resources.

## 1.3.3 The Process-oriented Enterprise

CRM packages like Siebel enable an organization to truly function as an integrated organization; integration across all functions or segments of the traditional value chain—sales order, production, inventory, purchasing, finance and accounting, personnel and administration, and so on. They do this by modeling primarily the business processes as the basic business entities of the enterprise rather than by modeling data handled by the enterprise (as done by the traditional IT systems). However, every CRM might not be completely successful in doing this. In a break with the legacy enterprise-wide solutions, Siebel CRM treats business processes as more fundamental than data items.

Collaborations or relationships manifest themselves through the various organizational and inter-organizational processes. A process may be generally defined as the set of resources and activities necessary and sufficient to convert some form of input into some form of output. Processes are internal, external or a combination of both; they have cross-functional boundaries, they have starting and ending points and they exist at all levels within the organization.

The significance of a process to the success of the enterprise's business is dependent on the value, with reference to the customer, of the collaboration that it addresses and represents. In other words, the nature and extent of the value addition by a process to a product or services delivered to a customer is the best index of the contribution of that process to the company's overall customer satisfaction or customer collaboration. Customer knowledge by itself is not adequate; it is only when the organization has effective processes for sharing this information and integrating the activities of frontline workers and has the ability to coordinate the assignment and tracking of work, that organizations can become effective.

Thus, MBC not only recognizes inherently the significance of various process-related techniques and methodologies such as Process Innovation (PI), Business Process Improvement (BPI), Business

Process Redesign (BPRD), Business Process Re-engineering (BPR), Business Process Management (BPM) and so on, but also treats them as fundamental, continuous and integral functions of the management of a company itself. A collaborative enterprise enabled by the implementation of a CRM is inherently amenable to business process improvement, which is also the essence of any Total Quality Management (TQM) oriented effort undertaken within an enterprise. We will deal with such process improvement related issues in Chapter 7, "Siebel and Business Process Management".

## 1.3.4 The Value-add Driven Enterprise

Business processes can be seen as the very basis of the value addition within an organization that was traditionally attributed to various functions or divisions in an organization. As organizational and environmental conditions become more complex, global and competitive, processes provide a framework for dealing effectively with the issues of performance improvement, capability development and adaptation to the changing environment.

Along a value stream (i.e., a business process), analysis of the absence or creation of added value or (worse) destruction of value critically determines the necessity and effectiveness of a process step. The understanding of value-adding and non-value-adding processes (or process steps) is a significant factor in the analysis, design, benchmarking and optimization of business processes leading to BPM in the companies. As will be discussed in Chapter 7, "Siebel and the Business Process Management," Siebel provides an environment for analyzing and optimizing business processes.

Values are characterized by both value determinants such as time (cycle time and so on), flexibility (options, customization, composition and so on), responsiveness (lead time, number of hand-offs and so on), quality (rework, rejects, yield and so on), and price (discounts, rebates, coupons, incentives and so on). We must hasten to add that we are not disregarding cost (materials, labor, overhead and so forth) as a value determinant. However, the effect of cost is truly a result of a host of value determinants such as time, flexibility, responsiveness, etc.

Consequently, in this formulation one can understand completely the company's competitive gap in the market in terms of such process-based, customer-expected value and the value delivered by the enterprise's processes for the concerned product or service. We will refer to such customer-defined characteristics of value as Critical Value Determinants (CVDs). Therefore, we can perform market segmentation for a particular (group of) products or services in terms of the most significant of the customer values and the corresponding CVDs.

## 1.3.5 Enterprise Change Management

Strategic planning exercises can be understood readily in terms of devising strategies for improving on these process-oriented CVDs based on the competitive benchmarking of these values. The strategies resulting from analysis, design and optimization of especially the customer-facing processes would in turn result in a focus on the redesign of all relevant business processes at all levels. This could result in the modification or deletion of the concerned processes or even the creation of new process.

Today, initiating change and confronting change are the two most important issues that enterprises face. The ability to change business processes contributes directly to the 'innovation' bottom line. The traditional concept of change management is usually understood as a one-time event. But if an organization is looking for the capability not only to handle change management, but also management of changes on a continual basis, then CRM like Siebel, is a must!

Siebel enables the essential changing of customer-facing processes that are so critical to the success of the enterprise. Business processes that reside or are internalized within an organization's employees are difficult to change simply because human beings naturally find it more difficult to change. However, processes that reside within any computerized systems are much easier to change. The consequences of using information technology/information systems (IT/IS) can itself be managed by using more IT! The abstraction and electronic manipulation that has increased the speed of change can itself be used to manage (transparently to the end-users) these changes. It is reported that in the mid-1980s, managers at the Australian bank Westpac concluded that the bank's adaptability to change could be enhanced by first modularizing and then codifying core functions, policies and knowledge in a computerized system. By linking this separate system to the regular operational systems, the bank was able to reduce their time to market with new products; thus it was able to enhance its ability to meet changed market conditions in weeks or months instead of in months or years.

## 1.3.6 The Learning Enterprise

RBE builds customer relationships based on customer-related information. Evidently, all this information is necessarily finite in nature and also keeps on changing with changes in the customer environment. RBE recognizes that perfect information at any instance and especially on an ongoing basis is impossible and therefore, incorporates them incrementally. Customer responsive management enables enterprises to be more adaptable to changing conditions and responsive to smaller markets. It recognizes that forecasting and planning become more difficult as the marketplace and environment become more turbulent. It gives frontline workers more responsibility and authority so that they can innovate. The delivered solution may be expensive, but it is probably less expensive than the traditional deterministic planning and approval process. The solution may not be optimal, but the customer gets served (called 'single loop' learning) and the first delivered solution occurrence serves as a learning process for new guidelines that will need to be developed (called 'second loop' learning). Thus, the detailed planning of work is done at the frontline. Customer responsive management develops numerous best practice guidelines to guide frontline workers as they interact with customers to plan solutions, and also enables them to modify these if necessary, to improve the customer fit. After the problem has been identified and resolved, it is added dynamically to the best practice guidelines. Thus, CRM would not only assist in the immediate problem-solving efforts in the present, but would also define the problem in a new way. The essential difference between the two types of learning is between being adaptive and having adaptability. CRM provides and increases the adaptability of the enterprise. It is the dynamic development of best practice guidelines that keeps the organization flexible in responding to new needs and in making continual improvements to the process as new techniques and technologies develop. CRM also automatically transforms the tacit knowledge within the enterprise to its explicit form for every one to know it, feel it, analyze it, and, if possible, improve it further.

MBC also underlies the contemporary notion of the learning organization. To compete in an ever-changing environment, an organization must learn and adapt. Because organizations cannot think and learn themselves, it is truly the individuals constituting the organization who have to do this learning.

The amount of information in an organization is colossal. A single individual, however intelligent and motivated, cannot learn and apply all the knowledge required for operating a company. Moreover, even this colossal amount of information does not remain constant, but keeps changing and growing.

The only effective solution is collaborative learning or, sharing this learning experience among a team of people. This not only caters to differences in the aptitudes and backgrounds of people but also enables them to do this learning simultaneously, thus drastically shortening the turnaround time on the learning process itself. If organizational learning is seen in terms of the creation and management of knowledge, it is very easy for us to see the essential need to share the learning experience among the various member teams at the enterprise level and, within each team, among the members of the teams. Thus, we see another reason for collaboration among and within teams for contributing effectively to the learning process of the organization as a whole.

> What distinguishes learning from mere training is the transformation that results from the former. This again, can be implemented successfully only by collaborations between various teams as becomes apparent when such collaborations are embodied in the form of a CRM package such as Siebel.

## 1.3.7 The Virtual Enterprise

Along with the general economic growth and globalization of markets, personal disposable incomes have increased and so, the demand for product variety and customization has increased appreciably. Additionally, technological progress driven by the search for superior performance is already increasing the complexity of both the products and especially customer-facing processes. Because volume, complexity and variety are mutually exclusive, this has invariably led to collaborative endeavors for achieving this with greater flexibility in terms of enhancing of capabilities, minimization of risks, lower costs of investments, shortened product life cycles, and so on.

These collaborative endeavors, which have been known variously as partnering, value-added partnering, partnership sourcing, outsourcing, alliances, virtual corporations, and so on (see Chapter 2, sub-section "The Collaborative Enterprise"). These collaborative endeavors recognize the fact that optimization of the system as a whole is not achievable by maximization of the output at the constituting sub-system levels alone. Only CRMs with mature partner relationship management (PRM) packages such as Siebel can provide a backbone for holding together the virtual value chain across all these collaborative relationships. In Part VI, Chapter 17, section "Application Outsourcing (AO)" we look at such issues that are beyond the borders of the conventional enterprise.

Outsourcing will become a dominant trend in the millennium enterprise, whereby the enterprise concentrates only on being competitive in its core business activities and out sources the responsibility of competitiveness in non-core products and functions to third parties for mutual benefit. The development and maintenance of its core competencies are critical to the success of its main business; an enterprise cannot outsource these because it is these core functions that give it an identity. On the other hand, competitiveness in non-core functions, which is also essential for overall efficiencies, is outsourced to enterprises that are themselves in the business of providing these very products or services; the outsourced products and services offerings are *their* core competencies.

Most of the major manufacturers the world over have become to a large extent 'systems integrators', providing only some of the specialized parts and final assembly of sub-systems from a network of suppliers (see Chapter 7, sub-section "Network of Resources"). Their economic role has transformed mainly into basic planning, coordination, design, marketing and service, but not complete production per se. For the existence and growth of such virtual organizations, it is important that the company is able to manage the complexities of handling such relationships on a day-to-day basis. A PRM system provides all the functionality and processes for managing and accounting for such outsourced jobs. But more significantly, only a PRM can make it possible for such a collaborative enterprise to exist and grow to scales unimaginable with traditional organizational architectures.

## 1.3.8 The Agile Enterprise

Agile companies produce the right product, at the right place, at the right time, at the right price for the right customer. In an agile enterprise products will be built quickly and at a lower cost for a customer because of the detailed data received at the point of sale.

The organizational requirements of an agile enterprise include:

- A flat, fast, flexible organization with continuous interaction, support and communications among various functions
- Highly decentralized management that recognizes its knowledge base and manages it effectively
- A multi-skilled, flexible workforce that is proactive and responsible
- Extremely flexible strategies and relationships with suppliers
- Complete control of lean production and concurrent engineering
- Flexible tooling and automation
- Deep understanding of the customer based on operating integration and real-time market data collection and analysis

Though they appear similar, there are fundamental differences between the 'agile' and 'lean' approaches for running a business. Lean production is at heart simply an enhancement of mass production methods, whereas agility implies breaking out of the mass production mold and into mass customization. Agility focuses on economies of scope rather than economies of scale, ideally serving ever-smaller niche markets—even quantities of one—without the high cost traditionally associated with customization. A key element of agility is an enterprise-wide view, whereas lean production is usually associated with the efficient use of resources on the operations floor.

As pointed out by Jagdish Sheth in these times of market change and turbulence, the 'half life', (i.e., the time within which it loses currency by 50%) of customer knowledge is getting shorter and shorter. The difficult challenges facing businesses today require organizations to transition into flexible, agile structures that can respond to new market opportunities quickly with a minimum of new investment and risk. As enterprises have experienced the need to be simultaneously efficient, flexible, responsive and adaptive, they have turned increasingly to the network form of organization with the following characteristics.

- Networks rely more on market mechanisms rather than on administrative processes to manage resource flows. These mechanisms are not simple 'arm's length' relationships usually associated with independently owned economic entities. Instead, to maintain the position within the network, members recognize their interdependence and are willing to share information, cooperate with each other and customize their product or service.

- While a network of subcontractors have been common for many years, recently formed networks expect members to play a much more proactive role in improving the final product or service.
- Instead of holding all assets required to produce a given product or service in-house, networks use the collective assets of several firms located along the value chain.

The agile organization is composed of small, autonomous teams or subcontractors who work concurrently and reconfigure quickly to thrive in an unpredictable and rapidly changing customer environment. Each constituent has the full resources of the company or the value chain at its disposal and has a seamless information exchange between the lead organization and the virtual partners. Chapter 7, "Siebel and Business Process Management" discusses aspects of the customer centric and responsive enterprises.

## 1.4 SUMMARY

Customer relationship strategy is emerging as one of the most important components of corporate strategy for competitive differentiation and shareholder value. The concept of CRM aims at identifying the customers that are more profitable to the company and helps in optimizing relationships with those customers. In today's world of decreasing margins, increasing competition and ever-changing business environment, corporate success depends on an enterprise's ability to build and maintain loyal and valued customer relationships. The key to forging long-term, profitable relationships with valuable customers involves two major aspects: customer centricity and customer responsiveness. The importance of customer relationships is based on a simple fact: *it can cost four to seven times more to replace a current customer than it does to retain one*. A major step in this direction is to realize that whereas customer relationships are not all about information, all customer related information is certainly about customer relationships.

This chapter looked at the concept of Customer Relationship Management (CRM). We presented a definition CRM and the importance of customer centricity and customer responsiveness. Following this, we positioned customer relationship as the core strategy to achieve the objective of delivering value to customers at a profit. After explaining the concept of 'information is relationship' as the underlying theme of CRM, we discussed related topics such as customer capital, customer responsiveness, customer loyalty and measures to cultivate it. With a view to judging the profitability of customers, we then looked at the concept of customer value and customer lifetime value. Finally, we introduced the concept of Management by Collaboration (MBC) as a unifying framework in the context of the Customer centric enterprise.

> It must be highlighted that this chapter discussed major concepts, factors and issues in the CRM space without major references to the Internet, the defining characteristics fo which are natural manifestations of many of these very concepts.

# Chapter 2 Customer Relationship Management (CRM) System

What is a Customer Relationship Management (CRM) system? Not only is there little agreement on what it really stands for, but there is even less agreement on what constitutes an CRM system, how it should be used, the potential of profitability gain, the impact on customer loyalty, the costs involved, the personnel needed, and the training they require. The characteristics of a CRM system are not limited to the CRM products and tools that are currently available in the market, and CRM is certainly not a technique or methodology. There is every reason to believe that the boundaries described for CRM in this book will be constantly enlarging in the coming years (see Chapter 3, section "The Anatomy of a CRM System").

## 2.1 INTRODUCTION TO CUSTOMER RELATIONSHIP MANAGEMENT (CRM) SYSTEMS

Notwithstanding all these caveats, a CRM system could be defined reasonably as follows:

**A Customer Relationship Management (CRM) system is a suite of pre-engineered, ready-to-implement, integrated application modules that focus on automating and improving all customer-centric functions—sales, marketing, service and support—of an enterprise and possessing the flexibility for configuring, customizing and personalizing dynamically the delivered functionality of the package, through any channel of interaction, to suit even the specific requirements of an individual customer. CRM enables an enterprise to operate as a relationship-based, information-driven, integrated, enterprise-wide, process-oriented, real-time, intelligent customer-centric enterprise.**

CRM system applications provide the framework for executing the best practices in customer-facing activities; it provides a common platform for customer communication and interaction. The use of CRM system applications helps in improving the customer responsiveness and also provides a comprehensive view of the entire customer life cycle. With reference to Figure 1.2, one can state that CRM systems, like CRM, are useful to companies that have customers with large variability both in their needs and their value to the company's business.

A CRM system like Siebel can provide this comprehensiveness and flexibility because at the heart of the system resides a CASE-like repository that stores all details of these pre-developed applications.

These details include every single data object, business objects and user interface (UI) programs that are used by the complete system. It also has additional support sub-systems that help it to manage, secure and maintain the operations of this package on a day-to-day basis.

Off-the-shelf packages and especially enterprise-wide solutions such as CRM systems were considered as the best approach for confronting the software crisis of the '80s. This was because CRM systems

(i) Ensure better validation of user requirements directly by the user
(ii) Ensure consistent quality of delivered functionality
(iii) Provide cohesive and integrated information system architecture
(iv) Ensure a fair degree of standardization
(v) Provide a consistent and accurate documentation of the system
(vi) Provide outstanding quality and productivity in the development and maintenance of the system

One and half a decade later, as companies report their experiences in implementing a CRM system, a base of experience seems to support the fact that companies that plan and manage the use of a CRM system are usually successful. Today, the recognized management decision is not *whether* to use a CRM system, but rather *when* to use it, and *which* CRM system to use. As we go through the book, it will become evident that Siebel is the best-of-breed product in this genre.

The success of CRM systems is based on the principle of re-usability. The origin of re-usability goes back almost to the beginning of the computer era, when it was recognized that far too much program code was being written and rewritten repeatedly, and uneconomically. Very soon most of the programming languages provided for routines or packets of logic that could be re-used multiple times within individual programs or even by a group of programs. Databases enabled the re-use of data, resulting in a tremendous surge in programmer productivity. Similarly, networks permitted re-use of the same programs on different terminals or workstations at different locations.

CRM systems, like ERPs earlier, extended the concept of re-usability to the functionality provided by a system. For instance, Siebel was based on the essential commonality observed in the functioning of companies within an industry. Siebel built a re-usable library of normally required processes in a particular industry and all that implementing Siebel customers had to do was select the processes that were required by their company from this library. From the project effort and cost that were essential for the development and implementation using the traditional Software Development Life Cycle (SDLC), CRM reduced the project effort and cost to that associated only with the implementation phase of the SDLC. Even though the cost of 'implementing' a CRM system like Siebel might seem higher than that of a traditional system, the CRM system gets implemented sooner and therefore, starts delivering all of its benefits much earlier than the traditional systems.

Although there have not yet been any published results, it has become an accepted fact that enterprises that implemented CRM systems for only a part of their organizations or for only a few select functions within their organizations, did not benefit greatly. CRM systems, like ERPs earlier, recognize the fact that business processes of an organization were much more fundamental than data characterizing various aspects of the organization. Most importantly, CRM systems elevated IS from a mere enabler of the business strategy of an organization to a significant part of the business strategy itself.

Thus, CRM systems brought to an end the subsidiary and support role that IT had played throughout the last few decades. But in turn, the very nature of IS has also undergone a complete transformation. Implementing a CRM system within an enterprise is no longer a problem of technology; it is a business problem. CRM systems have been the harbingers of a paradigm shift in the role of the IS/IT function within an enterprise. This book was motivated by the need to address these fundamental changes in the very nature of IS/IT activity within an enterprise.

The distinguishing characteristics of a CRM system are as follows:

- It transforms an enterprise into an information-driven enterprise
- It fundamentally perceives an enterprise as a global enterprise
- It reflects and mimics the integrated nature of an enterprise
- It fundamentally models a process-oriented enterprise
- It enables the real-time enterprise
- It enables the intelligent enterprise
- It elevates IT strategy as a part of the business strategy
- It represents an advance on the approaches to manufacturing performance improvement
- It represents the new department store model of implementing computerized systems
- It is a mass-user oriented application environment

> We have differentiated between the concept of Customer Relationship Management (CRM) and customer relationship management systems (CRM systems) that implement possibly a part of this holistic concept. This book mainly relates to Siebel as a system to realize the CRM programs of a company. Hereafter, for the sake of convenience, CRM will usually refer to aspects of a comprehensive CRM program that are embodied into a CRM system like Siebel and implemented within the enterprise.

## 2.1.1 CRM Transforms an Enterprise into an Information-driven Enterprise

In the past, all computerized systems and solutions used past-facing information merely for the purpose of referrals and reporting only. For the first time in the history of computerized systems, ERP began treating information as a resource for the operational requirements of the enterprise. But unlike the traditional resources, information resource as made available by CRMs (and ERPs) can be re-used and shared multiply without dissipation or degradation. The impressive productivity gains resulting from the CRMs truthfully arise from the unique characteristic of CRMs (and earlier ERPs) to use information as an inexhaustible resource.

Customer interactions, which are the mainstay of CRMs, create real-time organizational knowledge providing insights into customer behavior. CRMs enable an organization to use the real-time knowledge and information gained at any touch point to manage and synchronize the communications and marketing messages it delivers to its customers in all its touch point applications.

> This is also the root cause of one of the major problems leading to failures of Siebel implementations. Sales persons, sales consultants and sales managers are extremely possessive of their customers and related interaction information. Such withholding of critical customer information prevents the information stored in CRMs to be treated fully as customer relationships and to be leveraged for maximum benefit.

### 2.1.2 CRM Perceives an Enterprise as a Global Enterprise

In these times of divestitures, mergers and acquisitions, this is an important requirement. Unlike some of the earlier enterprise-wide solutions available on mainframes, CRM packages like Siebel cater to corporation-wide requirements even if an organization is involved in disparate businesses such as discrete industries (manufacturing, engineering and so on), process industries (chemicals, paints, etc.), and service industries (banking, media, etc.). CRM packages enable the management to plan, operate and manage such conglomerates without the impediment of mismatching systems for different divisions.

Although it might seem a minor point, CRM packages also permit the important functionality of enabling seamless integration of distributed or multi-location operations. This aspect is considered in the next sub-section.

### 2.1.3 CRM Reflects and Mimics the Integrated Nature of an Enterprise

By promoting cross-functional processes and work teams CRMs like Siebel, provide a powerful medium for supporting, reconciling and optimizing the conflicting goals of different functions within an organizations. For instance, marketing may want production of more customized products to cater to the requirements in the market whereas production function will want to standardize products for reducing set-up times and related costs. The tussle between these two functions may result in releasing products that incur (say) five times the normal failure rates, the brunt of which is borne by the service function. Thus, marketing and to a large extent manufacturing, obtain their short-term sales forecasts at the expense of the service function. The longer-term adverse effect on customer retention and loyalty may not even become evident until after many months have elapsed.

Companies interact with their customers across a variety of channels—offline channels such as branch stores and direct mail, as well as online channels like call centers, e-mail and the Internet. In any CVM strategy, all of these interactions are part of an integrated communications strategy to realize the full value-creation potential of these interactions. In fact, as customers continue to use more channels to interact with the enterprise, the company must ensure that it has the infrastructure to provide consistent and optimal marketing messages across each of its touch point applications.

CRM provides an integrated view of an enterprise's customers to everyone in the organization so that the customer can be serviced effectively throughout the customer life cycle. For instance, if marketing runs an outbound campaign, all the information about the customers and the program should be retained for:

- The sales people to follow up
- The customer service people to answer any queries
- Technical support to provide any field support.

Similarly, CRM enables even the customer to experience that they are dealing with the different functions of the same enterprise rather than independent departments that force them to run from pillar to post when trying to meet their demands.

## 2.1.4 CRM Fundamentally Models a Process-oriented Enterprise

As organizational and environmental conditions become more complex, global and competitive, processes provide a framework for dealing effectively with the issues of performance improvement, capability development and adaptation to the changing environment. Process modeling permits capturing of the true nature of the characteristic structure and dynamics of the business.

Conventional systems primarily store only snapshots of customer interactions in terms of discrete groups of data at pre-defined or configured instants of time, along a business process within an organization. *This predominating data-oriented view of the enterprise as implemented by traditional IT systems is a most unnatural and alien way of looking at any area of human activity.* The stability of the data models as canonized in the conventional IT paradigm may have been advantageous for the systems personnel, but for the same reason it would have been unusable (and unacceptable) to the business stakeholders within the organizations. Traditional systems could never really resolve this simple dichotomy of the fact that systems based on leveraging the unchanging data models, although easy to maintain, can never describe the essentially dynamic nature of businesses. This is the post-modern version of C.P. Snow's 'two cultures', which he had initially mooted to talk meaningfully about the worlds of humanities and sciences in the middle of the last century. Business processes are the most important parts of the reality that had been ignored by the traditional information systems. The traditional IT process modeling techniques, methodologies and environments are a misnomer for they truly model only the procedures for operating on the data associated at various points of the business sub-processes, which themselves are never mirrored within the system.

CRM packages recognized the fundamental error that was perpetuated all these past decades. Although many CRM packages still carry the legacy of the data-oriented view, the parallel view of business process and business rules is fast gaining prominence. This is the reason for the rapidly maturing groupware and workflow sub-systems within the core architecture of current CRM systems.

## 2.1.5 CRM Enables the Real-time Enterprise

The real-time responsiveness of the enterprise coupled with the earlier mentioned enterprise-wide integration also enable enterprises with the powerful capability of *concurrent processing* which would be impossible without systems like Siebel. Enterprises can obtain tremendous efficiencies and throughputs because of this ability to administer in parallel, many processes that are related but independent of each other. In non-ERP enterprises, such closely related processes are typically done sequentially because they are usually handled by the same set of personnel who may be obviously constrained to address them only in a sequence.

Customer responsiveness is an outcome of real-time sharing of current, complete and consistent information on interactions with individual customers. Furthermore, it implies instantaneous, transparent connectivity and visibility between customer-facing processes with the corresponding order fulfilling processes. This visibility not only permits the salesman to give accurate Available-To-Promise (ATP) information to the customer but also enables him to assess for himself the latest Capable-To-Promise (CTP) status for a particular order prior to making any commitments. In turn, the various members of the supply chain also have a better visibility and understanding of the customer requirements and commitments made to the customer, thus ensuring On-Time Delivery (OTD). The tight integration with the fulfillment processes enable coordination, monitoring and managing of goods across the ECE. It also provides instant notifications and alerts on exceptions and problem that may delay the on-time-delivery of the order.

Furthermore, this integration also helps to match the growing trend of customers postponing the buying decision closer to the purchasing decision, with the corresponding ability of the enterprise to postpone the point of product differentiation as close as possible to the point of demand by the customer. Every action of the customer needs to be met by a highly automated and tightly integrated response across the supply chain to fulfill the need of the customer. More succinctly, one can say that 'sell one, make one' has become the manufacturing watchword and corresponds closely to the current marketing watchword of 'the market of one'.

### 2.1.6 CRM enables the Intelligent Enterprise

The ability to access, collect and analyze information in real-term is an essential prerequisite of a customer responsive enterprise. In order to remain competitive, provide good customer service and optimize eBusiness operations, enterprises have to enable a Zero Latency Enterprise (ZLE) that supports real-term decision processing providing rapid access to information and analyses from any place at any time, for making real-term business decisions. Such decision processing systems are also required to integrate with the corresponding business processes to attain a closed-loop system whereby the output of the decision processing applications is delivered as inputs to influence favorably the business operations of the enterprise.

A real-term decision processing system typically consists of the following:

- An event-driven hub that (via messaging and EAI) captures, transforms and loads operational data into a data warehouse
- An analysis engine that generates business analyses from any place at any time
- A rule-driven decision engine that generates recommendations or eBusiness action messages in the real-term

Business Intelligence (BI) applications are decision support tools that enable real-time, interactive access, analysis and manipulation of mission-critical corporate information to provide users with valuable insight into key indicators to identify business problems and opportunities. BI enables users to access and leverage vast amounts of information to analyze relationships and trends to support real-term business decisions. BI systems enable enterprises to become proactive and information agile (see Chapter 1, sub-section "The Agile Enterprise" and Chapter 7, sub-section "Enterprise Agility") by delivering information to:

- Empower enterprise users in the assessment, enhancement and optimization of organizational operations and performance
- Deliver real-term business information to users about customers and partners
- The BI components of Siebel include Siebel Data Warehouse and Siebel Analytics (see Chapter 10, sub-section "Siebel Data Warehouse").

## 2.1.7 CRM Elevates IT Strategy as a Part of the Business Strategy

The coming of CRM heralded an enhanced role for IT systems. They are no longer the support functions of the earlier years. Anyone under that illusion will pay a very high price. Today, the real focus of IS/IT systems is no longer its alignment with the business strategy of the enterprise but with that of the customer.

## 2.1.8 CRM Advances on the Earlier Approaches to Performance Improvement

CRM is the latest in the succession of approaches that have been adopted throughout the history of enterprises for improvement of enterprise-level performances. CRMs have realized the failed dream of improvements that were expected from the MRP-II based manufacturing resources planning systems of the 70's. They have enabled combining the 'hard' approach of Quality Function Deployment (QFD) with the much broader scoped 'soft' approaches to customer satisfaction, like support and services that were widely adopted during the 80's in the last century.

Figure 2.1 gives a list of major enterprise performance improvement movements during the last century. CRMs like Siebel provide the basic platform for devising techniques and tools for better implementation of the earlier approaches.

## 2.1.9 CRM represents the New Department Store Model of Implementing Computerized Systems

The coming of packaged solutions such as CRM (like ERP before them) has been the death knell of the development model of IS systems. Along with it went the concept of requirements capture, modeling languages, development of software programs, testing, and so on that have usually been associated with the conventional developmental model. In its place, for the first time, is the end-user friendly model of what one could call the department store model of computerized systems—you pick and choose the functionality you require from the array of functional goodies on display!

Today, an organization solves critical information management needs by purchasing the best-of-class application software package available in the relevant domain. This package is then configured, customized and integrated to its specific requirements. The benefits of such an approach over the traditional full custom development project include the following.

- Immediate access to the best technologies and industry practices. A typical package represents the synthesis of many years of business analysis and software engineering.

| | | |
|---|---|---|
| 1690 | Division of Labour | Adam Smith |
| 1890 | Scientific Measurement | Frederick Taylor |
| 1900 | Mass Production | Henry Ford |
| 1920 | Industrial Engineering | F. Gilbreth and Frederick Taylor |
| 1930 | Human Relations Movement | Elton Mayo |
| 1950 | Japanese Quality Revolution | J.M. Juran and W. E. Dimming |
| 1960 | Materials Requirement Planning | William Orlicky |
| 1970 | Manufacturing Resources Planning | Oliver Wright |
| 1970 | Focused Factory | Wickham Skinner |
| 1980 | Total Quality Management | Philip Crosby |
| 1980 | Just-In-Time | Taiicho Ohno |
| 1980 | Computer Integrated Manufacturing. | |
| 1980 | Optimised Production Technology | Eliyahu Goldratt |
| 1980 | ISO 9000 | NASI |
| 1980 | World Class Manufacturing | Richard Schonberger |
| 1990 | Mass Customisation | Stan Davis and B. Joseph Pine II |
| 1990 | Lean Manufacturing | Jones & Roos |
| 1990 | Business Process Re-engineering | Michael Hammer |
| 1990 | Enterprise Resources Planning | |
| 1990 | Customer Relationship Management | Frederick Reichheld |

**Fig. 2.1 Timeline of Performance Improvement Movements in the 20$^{th}$ Century**

- Quick Return on Investment (ROI) because the organization can begin to implement and deploy a packaged application immediately.
- Lower software application life cycle costs in every aspect—business and technical expertise, initial configuration and customization, maintenance, and future enhancements.
- Mitigation of financial and delivery risks.
- Much higher probability of overall success due to the use of a proven solution.

A comprehensive CRM like Siebel is the analogue of the great department store of functionalities or processes required within an organization. CRM makes the transition from the world of carefully engineered and running systems to the world of consumers, in which the value of the delivered functionality is based not on its pedigree but only on what, how, where and when it can be used gainfully.

This is the final commoditization of the IS/ IT products and services!

Traditional Software Development versus Commercial Off-The-Shelf (COTS) Applications

In the past few decades, all of us have witnessed a procession of different methodologies, tools and techniques emanating from the software industry that have had a tremendous impact on the very nature and operations of business enterprises. But in the midst of all this turmoil, one fact has remained constant and that has been the lack of productivity improvements, irrespective of the extent and nature of computerization.

But right from the start there was an even more basic problem in terms of the number of software applications that were actually completed and implemented successfully. Much has been written on the software crisis that engulfed information service groups in the '80s. The reasons were multifold:

- With the advent of PC-like functionalities, users were becoming more aware and demanding
- Consequently, applications were becoming bigger and more complex.
- Correspondingly, productivity was reducing rather than increasing.
- Software development times were increasing and cost and time overruns were fairly routine.
- Quality, trained professionals were always in short supply, resulting in increased costs for programmers; hence, systems development costs were ever-increasing.
- Mortality of systems was very high.

On average, out of the total number of IT systems under development more than half used to be cancelled; of the remaining half only about two-thirds were delivered. Half the delivered systems never got implemented, while another quarter were abandoned midway through the implementation. Of the residual quarter of the delivered systems, half failed to deliver the functionality required by the management and were therefore scrapped. Only the remaining half of the systems was used after great modifications, which entailed further delays and costs in an almost never-ending process.

One of the root causes identified for these problems was the inherent weakness of the phase in which requirements were captured and analyzed. This phase never seemed to get the correct and complete requirements. As a result, completed projects never seemed to deliver on the promised functionality and had to be recycled for more analysis and development. Maintenance and enhancements were called for indefinitely and became harder to undertake as time went by. Because individuals often changed midway, both on the development and user sides, system requirements changed frequently and the whole process continued indefinitely. This is primarily because there is a fundamental disconnect between the business and the IT/IS people. Notwithstanding how much both the parties try to bridge the gap, there is a fundamental chasm between the perception of a business user and what is understood by the systems staff; both classes of people speak different languages. Even if the systems personnel tried to increase precision by using methodologies and specification tools, they were never able to ratify the documented requirements completely because users were unfamiliar with these tools.

Typically, surveys found that 50 to 80 percent of the IT/ IS resources were dedicated to application maintenance. The return on investments in IT was abysmally low by any standard of measurement and expectation. With IT/IS budgets stretching beyond the capabilities of most organizations, there was a compelling need for a radically new approach that could result in actual usable functionality that was professionally developed, under control, and on time.

The traditional software implementation involving the development of applications was characterized by:

- Requirement-driven functional decomposition
- Late risk resolution
- Late error detection
- Use of different language or artifacts at different phases of the project
- Large proportion of scrap and rework
- Adversarial stakeholder relationship with non-IT users
- Priority of techniques over tools
- Priority of quality of developed software rather than functionality per se
- Greater emphasis on current, correct, complete and consistent documentation
- Greater emphasis on testing and reviews
- Major effort on change control and management
- Large and diverse resource requirements
- Schedules always under pressure
- Greater effort on projected or estimated target performance
- Inherent limitations on scalability
- Protracted integration between systems

Many alternate strategies were devised like CASE and prototyping; however, none were able to cross this basic hurdle. CASE provided more rigorous environment for requirements analysis and design, and automated to a large extent the subsequent development of code, testing and documentation efforts. The increased time spent on requirements definition with the users was envisaged to lead to systems that were closer to the user's actual requirements. On the other hand, prototyping was designed to address the requirements capture issue by making the users directly participate in the process of defining the requirements. This was mainly focused on the screen and reports design because these were the elements that could be visualized directly by the user. However, none of these strategies really resolved the problem. Packages like ERP and CRM adopted a totally different approach by providing the most comprehensive functionality within the package. Company personnel were only expected to pick and choose whatever was required by the company actually using the package. Thus, ERP/CRM packages effectively short-circuited the whole issue of capturing requirements. The traditional project life cycle consisting of analysis, design, development, testing and implementation was transformed to the ERP/ CRM implementation life cycle consisting merely of requirements mapping, gap analysis, configuring and customizing, testing and implementation (see Chapter 14, 'Siebel eRoadmap Methodology').

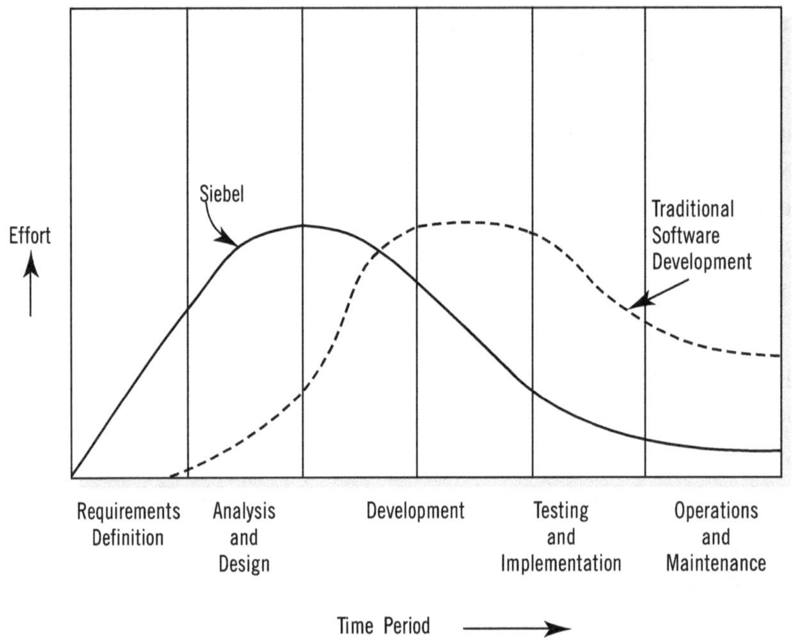


**Fig. 2.2 Comparison of Effort Expended during ERP and the Traditional Software Development Life Cycle**

Figure 2.2 shows a comparison of effort expended during ERP/CRM and the traditional software Development life cycle.

This ultimately led to the ERP revolution that we are witnessing today.

Unlike the traditional systems, the CRM software implementations involving the implementations of pre-engineered ready-to-implement application modules are characterized by:

- Primacy of the architecture; process-oriented configurability
- Primacy and direct participation of the business user
- Early risk resolution
- Early error and gap detection
- Iterative life cycle process; negligible proportion of scrap and rework
- Changeable and configurable functionality
- Participatory and cohesive stakeholder relationship with non-IT users
- Priority of functionality over tools followed by techniques
- Quality of the functional variability and flexibility of the available functionality
- Greater emphasis on current, correct, complete and consistent documentation of customizations
- Greater emphasis on integration testing

- Actual demonstration of functionality at all phases of the project
- Twin categories of resource requirements—functional and technical
- Schedules devoid of long-term cascading impact
- Demonstrated performance
- Larger span of scalability
- Efficient integration between systems

### 2.1.10 CRM is an End-User Oriented Application Environment

Compared to the degree of involvement of functional managers and end-users in traditional software project implementations, their participation as recommended here in Siebel implementations might seem unusual. CRM brings computerization and decisions to the desktops and in this sense is an end-user oriented environment in the true sense of the word (see Table 2.1). Unlike traditional systems in which users accessed the system directly only in well-defined pockets within the enterprise, in CRM, end-users are the personnel actually involved with the operations of the business. Because of the intense involvement of a sizable portion of the workforce of the company with the CRM implementation from the beginning, the probability of users embracing the system (and not struggling against it) is much higher. Users also act as the advocates and facilitators during and after the implementation phase.

## 2.2 TYPES OF CRM SYSTEMS

The CRM ecosystem comprised three categories of applications.
**(a) Operational CRM**—These applications help the sales people to become more productive and effective. These include automation software for sales, marketing and services. These systems hold transactional level data on individual products, customers and transactions. They provide support for customer-facing processes done by direct mail, phone, the Internet, third party agents and field sales. These applications are also referred to as the front office applications. Operational CRM is focused on the automation of the customer-facing parts of the businesses like:

- Marketing automation
  - Market segmentation
  - Campaign management
  - Event-based marketing
- Sales force automation
  - Opportunity management, including lead management
  - Contact management
  - Proposal generation
  - Product configuration
- Service automation
  - Contact and call center operations
  - Web-based service

- Field service

Marketing Automation (MA) applies technology to marketing process and includes market segmentation, campaign management and event-based marketing. Marketing automation enables companies to develop, budget and execute communications campaigns. For instance, a print-based communication campaign will involve a number of people such as a marketing manager, market analyst, copywriters, artists, printers, sales staff and media buyers. MA automates the multi-person workflow and coordinates their contributions to deliver the output. It can also audit and analyze campaign performance and direct leads from advertising campaigns to the most appropriate sales channel. Event-based marketing refers to sales or service actions that are initiated in response to some action by the customer.

Sales Force Automation (SFA) refers to application of technology to the company's selling activities, which are the core of CRM. The selling process is composed of stages such as lead generation, lead qualification, needs identification, development of specifications, proposal generation, proposal presentation, handling objections and closing the sale. SFA applications are constituted of capabilities like opportunity management, contact management, proposal generation and product configuration. The success of SFA is primarily based on its ability to provide the right customer information to the right sales person and/ or customer at the right time.

Service Automation (SA) allows companies to automate their service operations whether delivered through a retail outlet, a call center, a contact center, the Web, or face-to-face in the field. It enables companies to manage and coordinate their service related in-bound and out-bound communications across all channels.

**(b) Analytical CRM**—These applications are concerned with employing customer data to enhance both the customer and the company value. It is based on customer information, including sales data (purchase history), financial data (payment history, credit score), market data (campaign response, loyalty scheme data) and service data. Analytical CRM offers the prospects of more powerful cross-selling and up-selling programs and more effective customer retention and customer acquisition programs. These applications support the one-to-one customized marketing programs. They hold aggregated data where a unit of analysis is the campaign, market segment, key account, market, or product group. These applications provide support for the strategic planning processes.

**(c) Collaboration CRM**—These applications help in smoothing the dialogues with the customers. They constitute the traditional and new groupware/Web technologies to facilitate customer, staff and business partner communications, coordination and collaborations.

Figure 2.3 shows the relationships between the three categories of applications.

Strategic CRM is a combination of these three characteristic applications and is focused on the development of a customer-centric business culture. This culture is dedicated to winning and keeping customers by creating and delivering better value than their competitors.

### 2.2.1 Closed-loop CRM

Closed-loop CRM systems not only enable execution of customized marketing campaigns but also measure their effectiveness, which in turn is used to improve their performance even further (the next time around).

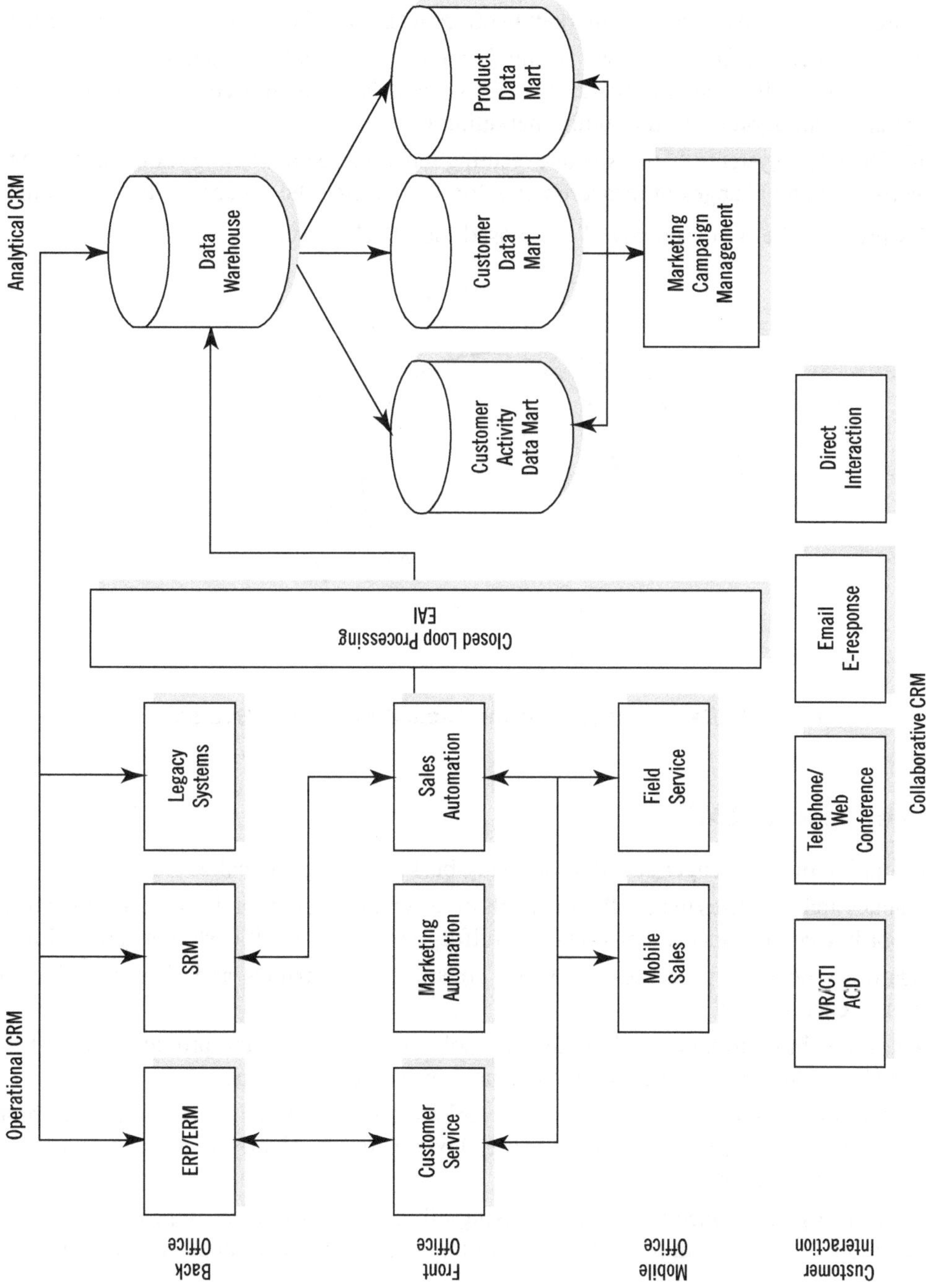


**Fig. 2.3 Types of CRM Systems**

Closed-loop marketing consists of three basic steps that lead to an ever-improving marketing performance.

(a) Measure—the effectiveness of the marketing effort in terms of the resulting customer profitability.

(b) Predict—Analyze the available data for modeling consumer behavior and predicting consumer behavior close to the actual observations. These models are then used to focus and refine the design and configuration of the future marketing campaigns.

(c) Act—The CRM systems then assist in executing the modified marketing campaigns along with the corresponding changes in measurements for ascertaining the success of the new campaign.

Figure 2.4 presents the basic schema of the closed-loop CRM system.

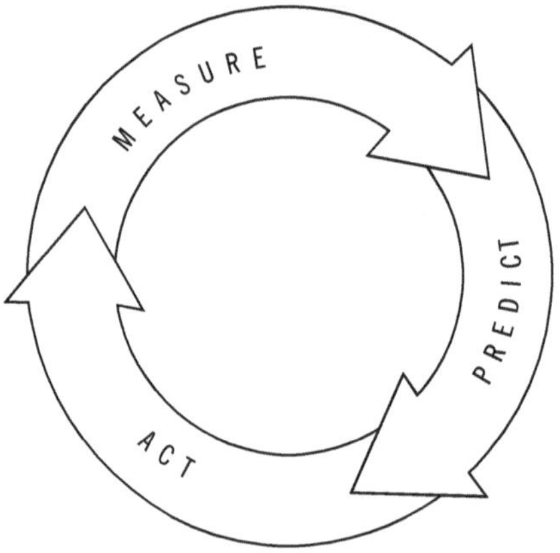


**Fig. 2.4 Basic Schema of the Closed-loop CRM System**

## 2.2.2 Why Use CRM?

The implementation of CRM engenders the following business and technical advantages.

- Reconciles and optimizes the conflicting goals of different divisions or departments for consistent and coordinated customer interactions and fulfills experience at all customer touch points.
- Standardizes business processes across all constituent companies and sites, thus increasing their efficiencies.
- Provides the ability to know and implement global best practices and provides the best means for benchmarking the organization's customer-centric competitiveness.
- Alters the function-oriented organization toward a more team-based, cross-functional, process-oriented organization, thus leading to more flexible, flatter, tightly integrated and customer responsive organization.
- Provides a responsive medium for undertaking all variants of process improvement programs and methodologies, including process innovation, process improvement, interaction channels, and so on.

- Provides a responsive medium for quality improvement and standardization efforts including QC, QA, TQM and QFD.
- Is process-oriented and therefore is fertile ground for implementing activity-based management (ABM) efforts be they for budgeting, costing, efficiency or quality.
- Provides the best conduit for measuring the benefits accruing to an organization by monitoring the Return On Investment (ROI) of not only money, but also manpower, materials, time and information. This could be in terms of various parameters like cost, quality, responsiveness, cycle time and so on. Thus, CRM could assist in the implementation of for instance, the balanced scorecard within the enterprise.
- Enables an enterprise to scale up its level of operations drastically or even enter into different businesses altogether without any disruption or performance degradation.
- Enables real-time creation of data directly during the actual physical transaction of processes by the persons who are responsible for it.
- Pushes latest data and status to the actual operational-level persons for better and faster decisions at least on routine issues; empowers and gives ownership to the customer-facing operational personnel at the customer touch points (this automatically does away with problems associated with collection of voluminous data, preparation, entry, corrections of inaccuracies, backups and so on).
- Integrates data of the organization into a single comprehensive database.
- Provides online availability of correct, current, consistent, complete, clear and authentic operational data across multiple channels and touch points that could be populated into the enterprise data warehouse for analysis and mining.
- Greatly reduces the cost of maintaining systems.

As mentioned in the introduction to this chapter, all these characteristics of CRM implemented organizations arise primarily from the fact that what they handle is not merely organizational data, but relationships that are of strategic importance to the customer-centric enterprise.

In the next section, we turn to this aspect of the relationship-based organizations.

### 2.2.3 ERP versus CRM

The two primary chains within an enterprise are:

- The supply chain—covering the back-of-office to external suppliers and distributors. This includes functions and processes associated with finance, accounting, inventory, human resources, manufacturing, shipping and logistics.
- The demand chain—covering the front-of-office to external customers and the channel. This includes functions and processes associated with sales, marketing, service and support.

The ERP and CRM approaches differ in their focus and tactical objectives. The ERP orientation for example, views business as a set of rigid back office processes and customers are modeled as 'resources' that fall under the control of internally focused, command-and-control systems. Because domain expertise in ERP and other back office applications focuses on algorithmic optimization of structured and deterministic processes, the ERP perspective does not accommodate the random, unstructured and highly dynamic nature of customer behavior.

Table 2.1 compares the traditional back office automation technology like ERPs with relationship building technology such as CRM.

**Table 2.1 Back Office Automation Technology versus Relationship Building Technology**

| | | Traditional Back Office Automation Technology | Relationship Building Technology |
|---|---|---|---|
| 1. | Strategic focus | Internal: Operational efficiency | External: Customer relationship |
| 2. | Key business benefit | Control cost | Drive corporate performance |
| 3. | Expertise required to develop applications | Algorithmic optimization | Business knowledge (e.g. sales, marketing, customer service) |
| 4. | Industry focus | Manufacturing | Services |
| 5. | Nature of process flows | Structured, deterministic | Unstructured, spontaneous |
| 6. | Process focus | Transactional | Relationship building |
| 7. | Number of internal users | 10's to 100's | 1000's to million's |
| 8. | Number of external users | 10's to 100's | Million's |

ERP vendors have been acquiring or building new modules for Sales Force Automation (SFA) and CRM to front-end traditional sales order, billing and Accounts Receivable (AR) application modules. This streamlines the information flow from initiating the sales forecasting activity to servicing an established customer. While this extends the business functions and activities supported by information processing, it also extends the reach of the traditional back-of-office ERP products. However, this does not necessarily deliver functionality of a true CRM. Extended ERP is seldom more than a vendor's best-of-breed and piecemeal application add-on functionality, intended simply to extend the market share of their ERP product. Front-of-office applications grafted on an ERP may not be as functionally rich as Siebel, but may have a certain advantage in terms of the in-built provisions for integration with back-of-office modules. A judicious balance needs to be struck between these aspects to evaluate and select the most appropriate vehicle for delivery of CRM functionality for the enterprise. These issues are the focus of Chapter 3, "CRM Evaluation" and Chapter 4, "CRM Selection".

## 2.3 CRMs AS KEEPERS OF CUSTOMER KNOWLEDGE ASSETS

CRM implementations must ultimately be business driven and not dictated or driven by technology issues. The survival and success of an enterprise depends on how it differentiates itself and its products and services from those of its competitors. In this era of mass customization, what organizations need is not more standardization and generic processes, but the ability to be more dynamic, more flexible, more proprietary and more customized. Because the CRM strategy basically embodies the 'theory of business' of a company (Peter Drucker), it must also mirror these differences in strategies and processes. To leverage their competencies, distinct advantages, edges or competitive advantages, companies cannot abandon the corresponding differentiating processes and will have to incorporate such fundamental variants in their CRM implementations or interface with such systems. Siebel's Industry Specific (IS) solutions are primarily efforts driven by recognition of this fundamental need of its customer organizations.

All of these unique value propositions and differentiating factors are information assets of an organization, and are captured and configured into the CRM system. These information assets include the business rules and procedures or methods of operations, customer analytics, parameters of analysis, ranges for defining credit limits, credit periods, discounting structures, ratings and so on. Like any other assets CRM packages like Siebel register, maintain, monitor and report on these informational assets. This helps in keeping these assets current and useful.

## 2.3.1 The Collaborative Enterprise

CRM provides the design and architecture for the collaborative enterprise as has been discussed in this chapter. It provides the basic platform for enabling the enterprise-wide, integrated, information-based, process-driven, real-time intelligent enterprise. This has a direct impact on many aspects that traditionally have been more relevant to issues of organizational development.

- Vision—CRM enables the realization of an organization that has a customer-centric vision to be competitive by raising the level of skills and competencies of its personnel so that they can respond better, faster and at the optimal cost to the changing customer expectations every day.
- Strategic Goals—CRM enables access to customer-sensitive data for all customer-related personnel to enable them to keep track of the organization's overall performance with reference to the company's customer-centric goals as well as their own contribution to the same on a daily basis. This engenders a sense of involvement and transparency that was not achievable earlier.
- Culture—CRM truly makes it possible to operate a collaborative, value addition driven and customer-centric organization in real-time mode. CRM permits learning taking place in any part of the enterprise to be incorporated into the system, even on a daily basis.
- Structure—CRM system provides visibility to the responsibility-oriented organization structure rather than the designation-oriented structure of earlier times. It provides instant communication and interaction with all customer-facing members irrespective of their reporting department or designation.
- Systems—CRM provides for adequate control without encumbering the work that directly contributes to the value addition delivered to the external or internal customers.
- Processes—CRM enables the process-oriented enterprise that might not always be feasible to realize physically; for instance, by locating all concerned members of a team in one place. It makes it possible for members to participate in multiple customer interactions efficiently and effectively.

## 2.3.2 Extended Collaborative Enterprise

The future of CRM is closely related with the efforts to re-engineer such inter-enterprise interfaces and foster closer collaborations across multiple enterprises, that is, the Extended Collaborative Enterprise (ECE). This is in contrast to the traditional adversarial relationships that have been known to exist among the suppliers, manufacturers, distributors and retailers. True economies of production can only be gained by the economies of cooperation. The virtual organization that we referred to in Chapter 1 spans all such members of the traditional supply and demand chain.

In the '90s, the enterprise resource plans focused attention on enhancing performance within the enterprise. Yet, more than 50 percent of the variable costs that affect the performance of an organization are mainly driven by decisions outside the boundaries of the organization. After benefiting from streamlining and re-engineering the internal processes, enterprises will address the potential for major gains obtainable from these cross-company processes. But why is this extended value chain considered important for the next quantum leap in organization performances? Enormous opportunities exist for enhanced efficiencies at the interfaces between contributing value chain partners, as also the potential for a greater level of customer satisfaction.

Like the non-value adding hand-offs within an organization, many of the interfaces and hand-offs between partners are non-value adding, efficiency-depleting, and time-consuming. The customer ends up paying for all these inefficiencies regardless of how far removed or hidden he or she may be from the source. Similar to the inefficiencies associated with typical internal processes (before the implementation of enterprise-wide solutions like Siebel), value chain inefficiencies can easily account for up to 25 percent of the company's operating costs.

Thus, an ECE differs from a traditional supply chain in the extent to which a company can integrate with its partners.

## 2.3.3 Extended Relationship Management

ERM provides a unique global view that consolidates all information about stakeholders, their interactions and activities into a centralized repository for both real-time and analytical use. The objective of Extended Relationship Management (ERM) is to build and maintain profitable business relationships with all key stakeholders of the company, namely, customers, suppliers, partners and employees. Relationships that continually engage, satisfy, sustain and enhance these relationships across all channels and touch points result in greater loyalty, revenues and profitability. ERM enables an integrated business experience that spans service, marketing and commerce, and extends outside the enterprise to incorporate customers, partners and suppliers in collaborative business processes. By integrating and sharing information and processes across various constituents, the enterprise enables precisely targeted marketing campaigns, increase up-sell and cross-sell opportunities, and ensures consistent and personalized treatment of every customer throughout this extended value chain. Such an extended dialog between its stakeholders creates collaborative relationships that yield greater customer loyalty.

Unlike the problems that confronted the traditional supply chain, the issues extend beyond the conventional static and predefined individual supply chains. This is because of the dynamic reconfigurations that are possible by the Internet. The Internet enables the formation and dissolution of momentary supply chains even for individual customer transactions depending on the optimal combination of collaborations to deliver a product and/or service triggered by the customer. More than supply chains, these will be a network of suppliers and partners. The extended collaborative enterprise will be more like a community of enterprises guided by the major value adding players within the communities. Instead of the competitive advantage of individual enterprises, the competition today will exist among different communities of enterprises, that is, ECEs. The success of an enterprise will depend on the 'collaborative advantage' of the corresponding supply chain or more correctly, the supply network to which it belongs. Since the threat of substitution is available not only to the end-customers but also to the other constituents of the ECE, it may be vital to become a valued member of a successful supply chain.

## 2.4 ELECTRONIC CUSTOMER RELATIONSHIP MANAGEMENT (eCRM)

The Internet has altered forever the ways in which enterprises interact and work with their customers, suppliers and even their own members. The Internet has enabled a dramatic reduction in the cost of transactions and interactions between the enterprise and its customers. Online customers expect shorter sales cycles, personalized information, quicker resolution of issues and added value at each stage of the transaction. Internet supported customer relationship management (eCRM) is rapidly emerging as the 'killer app' of the Web of the 00's.

eCRM provides a standard-based Web architecture for information, process and application integration so that the enterprise can integrate information and processes across marketing, commerce and service. The enterprise can integrate existing databases, legacy applications and systems to create a virtual centralized information repository so that the company can market, sell and service its offerings more effectively. And, the Web architecture's scalability and flexibility enables it to be more responsive leading to rapid growth.

### 2.4.1 Data Warehouse and Customer Analytics

Many enterprises find it necessary to complement their CRM systems as well as their ERP systems with Business Intelligence (BI) tools that support decision-making. BI includes a range of tools such as query and reporting, business graphics, Online Analytical Processing (OLAP), statistical analysis, forecasting and data mining. Data warehousing, OLAP and data mining are the 'killer app' for CRM. CRM tries to capture information from each customer touch point and store it in a single repository so that all customer-facing personnel have a complete understanding of the company's relationship with each customer.

More than merely gathering information, it is the accurate analysis of the information that gives businesses the opportunity to improve their customer relationship and maximize their bottom lines. OLAP software helps an enterprise to maximize the profits from its customer base by focusing on:

(a) What is done, when and how (processes, activities and communications)
(b) To whom (i.e. to which specific segment of the customer base)
(c) Its effect on the behavior, loyalty and value of the targeted customers

Being able to monitor the effect that various actions have on the customer base will allow a company to make sure that they retain the 'best' customers and that the candidates with the best growth potential are identified and appropriately targeted

### 2.4.2 Data Mining

Data mining is of great interest because it is imperative for enterprises to realize the competitive value of the information residing within their data repositories. The goal of data mining is to provide the capability to convert high volume data into high value information. This involves discovering patterns of information within large repositories of enterprise data. Enterprises that are most likely to benefit from data mining:

- Exist in competitive markets
- Have large volumes of data
- Have communities of information consumers who are not trained as statisticians
- Have enterprise data that is complex in nature

More traditional business intelligence (BI) tools enable users to generate ad hoc reports, business graphics and test 'hunches'. This is useful for analyzing profitability, product line performance, and so on. Data mining techniques can be applied when users don't already know what they are looking for. Data mining provides an automatic method for discovering patterns in data (R. Delmater and M. Hancock).

Data mining accomplishes two different things:

(i) It gleans enterprise information from historical data.

(ii) It combines historic enterprise information with current conditions and goals to reduce uncertainty about enterprise outcomes.

Customer-centric data mining techniques can be used to build models of past business experience that can be applied to predict customer behavior and achieve benefits in the future. Data mining provides insights that can be used to:

- Learn patterns that allow rapid, proper routing of customer enquiries
- Learn customer buying habits to suggest likely products of interest
- Categorizing customers for focused attention (e.g., churn prediction, prevention)
- Providing predictive models to reduce cost and allow more competitive pricing (e.g., fraud/ waste control)
- Assist purchasers in the selection of inventory of customer-preferred products

## 2.5 THE CUSTOMER TRIGGERED COMPANY

The Internet has engendered a dramatic shift in the business environment from a production-centric model to a customer-centric one. It has led to a tidal wave that has swept the market beyond the model of a customer-driven company to the more recently witnessed phenomenon of what we can term as the customer-triggered company. The outstanding potential for the survival and success of customer-triggered companies is amply demonstrated by the ubiquity of customer-centric e-commerce services companies.

Currently, more than computers and computing it is the customer that is all-pervasive. The pervasive customer wants the following:

(a) Personalized attention
(b) To buy in smaller quantities
(c) Customized products
(d) To postpone the buying decision closer to the purchasing decision
(e) To enjoy the buying experience at any convenient time or place with any convenient mode of payment
(f) Easy access to the status of the order
(g) Instant gratification
(h) Increased excellent service and support at a lower cost

In the Internet-based economy, success hinges on establishing a 'pull'. In this century, instead of the four P's of marketing (product, price, place and promotion), the four C's (content, cost, convenience and communications) all centered on the individual customer, rather than the products as earlier, will reign. Figure 2.5 shows the old and the new marketing mix. The content includes information on the products and services as well as the direct context of the presentation.

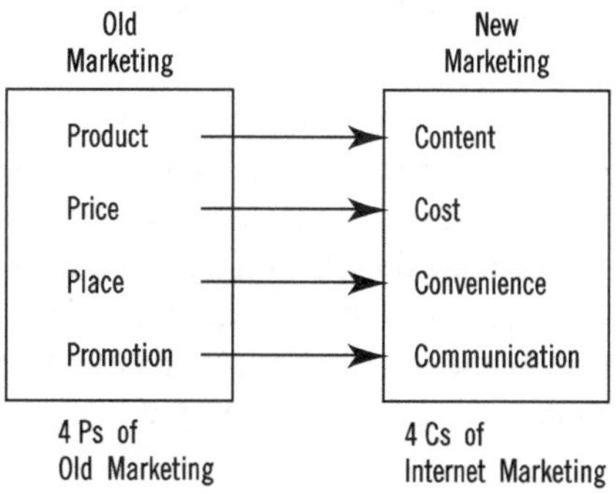


**Fig. 2.5 Internet Marketing Mix**

Never before has it been so easy for a customer to find a desired product or service along with contextual data necessary to make an informed purchase decision. Companies need to truly focus on sensing, feeling, thinking, relating and acting to each individual customer. This is the best example of a 'high tech and high touch' organization. Customers are no more than a click away from a world of comparative information about products, prices and alternatives that are resulting in heightened competition among the suppliers. Companies need to respond rapidly and profitably to this generation of net-savvy and opportunistic customers who are perpetually on the verge of switching or clicking to alternate suppliers.

The power of the customer will continue to grow to unprecedented levels with the ever-increasing ability to shop and buy anything from anyone, at any price, at any time, anywhere.

### 2.5.1 Event-driven Business Systems

Unlike the make-to-stock strategy that has dominated since the '80s, the millennium enterprises must adopt the strategy of make-to-order, or even beyond to a 'sense and respond' to the customized requirements of individual customers. In fact, the JIT philosophy for increasing the efficiencies and effective responsiveness of the supply chains would have to surpass itself to become synchronized with the actual event of an order being placed by the customer, which will truly become the universal point of purchase (POP). It is in this sense that the market is moving rapidly towards the event-driven enterprise where all actions are actually triggered by the customer simply clicking on the personalized Web user-interfaces (WUIs) of enterprises.

All actions of procurement, production, dispatch and collection will result from the subsequent cascade of events triggered within the enterprise and the extended enterprise. The lines among the CRM, eCRM, ERM and back-of-office systems like ERP and SCM are blurring. This will lead organizations to shed the monolithic, vertically integrated infrastructures of the past and embrace loosely coupled, independent and Internet agile organizations that engage collectively to address a momentary customer transaction.

## 2.6 SUMMARY

In this chapter we presented a definition of a Customer Relationship Management (CRM) system, after which we described in detail the characteristics of such a system. Following this, we presented various types of CRM systems, namely, operational, analytical and collaboration.

The real power of the CRM concept can be seen when we go beyond the boundaries of an enterprise. In the last few sections of this chapter, we looked beyond the physical confines of an enterprise to include its partners like vendors and customers into an extension of the enterprise and to the next higher level of what we term as the Extended Collaborative Enterprise (ECE). We also introduced the powerful notion of the *Customer Triggered Company* as an event-driven enterprise where all actions are triggered by a 'click of the customer' on the personalized Web User-Interfaces (WUIs) of the enterprises. Siebel has adopted a symbiotic strategy to go beyond simple integration to collaboration between the customer-centric enterprises.

Chapter 3

# CRM Evaluation

This chapter outlines the concepts and criteria for evaluating the CRM package most suitable to the requirements of a company. Managers must initially make a careful decision on the functional requirements that are desired, and the characteristic features and facilities expected of the CRM system as a whole. Managers can then make an objective selection of the best CRM to deploy considering the various factors described in this chapter.

## 3.1 THE ANATOMY OF A CRM SYSTEM

A comprehensive CRM system is immensely complex. As mentioned in the section "Introduction to Customer Relationship Management (CRM) Systems", CRM essentially treats an application development environment as an application *in itself.* The integrated application repository holds a full set of correlated information regarding the application as well as the data that will reside in the system when it is in production, which also greatly facilitates documentation, testing and maintenance. In this section, we will briefly give an overview of the various systems that constitute a comprehensive CRM like Siebel. Figure 3.1 presents an overview of a customer relationship management (CRM) system. Every system described below has two simultaneous aspects—managing the application data and also the metadata related to the very nature and configuration of the implemented CRM itself.

The exhaustive list provided later will illustrate the complexities of modern off-the-shelf packages. It can also act as a reference list when we look at the issues related to the evaluation and selection of CRM packages in later sections of this chapter.

### 3.1.1 Application Maintenance-related Systems

***(a) Application Repository System***

The application repository system forms the core of the CRM system. It provides the essential information on the structure and design of the whole application to all other modules or systems. It records the information regarding the information model of the system in terms of the entities, attributes, relations, processes, views, user scenarios and so on. It also promotes a methodology that is native to the development and maintenance of the CRM system. It contains information on every single program, file and data item in the system. This includes information on the various components and elements such as identity, purpose, type and nature, defining attributes, 'where used' list, tables accessed, processing cycles and times, sizing, and so on.

This module provides facilities to check the consistencies and integrity of definitions for all system components and elements within the CRM.

The application repository needs analysis and design modeling sub-systems. It also needs a graphics environment to represent the processing requirements of the company operations. The graphic module provides a diagram representation of the processes that enable rapid changes whenever necessary. Detailed requirements can be defined and stored in a related database that can be analyzed for dependencies, consistencies, impact analysis, and so on. This is usually called the *data dictionary* and provides support for the database and data tables or file design (including forming data tables, normalization, indices, referential integrity, and so on).

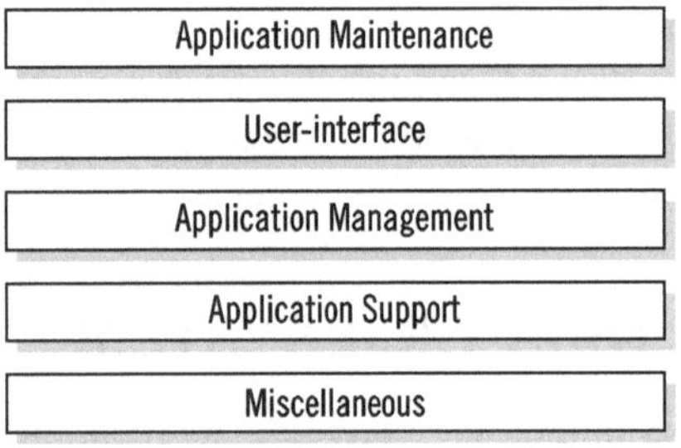


**Fig. 3.1 Overview of a Customer Relationship Management (CRM) System**

### *(b) Fourth Generation Language Development Environment*

This environment provides facilities to customize or extend the CRM system's functionality to meet the specific requirements of an enterprise. This has the standard tools set for the development, testing, debugging and documentation of the programs, especially data entry programs.

### *(c) Query Management System*

This system provides extensive querying facilities on the system details stored in the application repository (and data dictionary). These details include process information, entities, data tables, programs, and also the data stored in the tables of the application database. This query management system enables the painting of query screens; the specification of tables to be accessed, fields to be displayed and their sequences; the selection of a set of records to be displayed, and so on.

### *(d) Report Management System*

This report management system is similar to the query management system except that it permits the queried information to be printed for reference. It defines customized reports for specific requirements of the company related to pre-printed documents like purchase orders, invoices, and so on. It provides advanced features for rapidly programming break totals, page breaks, line details, and so on within a report.

### *(e) Configuration Management System*

This permits the CRM to be configured to the specific organizational structure of a company. This may include the physical locations, operational divisions, profit/loss (P/L) entities and accounts, the fiscal period, the taxation and discount structures, the categories of customers, suppliers, and products, and so on. All subsequent reporting and analyses are based on the details of configuration defined at the time of inception. This system also customizes the CRM system to embody the various functions and processes specific to an enterprise.

### *(f) Change Management System*

This system provides the facility to register, release and control all changes introduced into the system. This permits control over system components being changed or tested and those that are released in the production environment for access and use by all. It also enables gathering and monitoring details on dates, persons and the duration required for affecting changes. This helps both in the security as well as the productivity of the CRM operations.

### *(g) Version Management System*

This system provides facilities to keep track of the current versions of the various systems constituting the CRM. This enables prompt diagnosis of any malfunction that may arise because of incompatible systems, wrong interfaces, non-compliant systems, and so on.

### *(h) Application Programming Interface (API) System*

This system provides facilities for a standardized interface of the CRM to upload or download data from legacy systems; specific application systems like Supply Chain Management (SCM), Customer Relationship Management (CRM), Electronic Data Interchange (EDI), and so on; high end project management systems; or scientific and industrial application systems. These interfaces could be in batch or asynchronous modes or, for ongoing operations, in synchronous mode. Even multiple installation of the same CRM at different sites for the organization will need such interfaces. These may also be needed as basic enablers for such sophisticated facilities like data replication, database mirroring, and so on.

## 3.1.2 User-Interface-Related Systems

### *(a) Graphical User Interface (GUI) Management System*

This module provides the standard facilities of any presentation manager in terms of layouts, navigation among and within screens, help features, error recoveries, and so on. The Graphical User Interface (GUI) management system controls the design and functioning of the dialog flow on the screen, validations and table look-ups, default values, lists of values, and so on. This system will usually be one of the standard Relational Database Management Systems (RDBMS) like Oracle, DB2, and so on.

### *(b) Menu Management System*

This system presents the various choices that are available in various areas of functionality. It also lets you dynamically define the choices that are available to a particular user, depending on his level of access and authorization in different areas within the CRM.

### *(c) Help Management System*

This system provides the specific or contextual help at every field or processing step within the system. At any moment, it provides information on programs, screens or particular fields of interest. This system also incorporates the architecture to report on errors and warnings, as well as give more specific diagnosis or suggestions on resolving problems encountered during the usage of the system.

## 3.1.3 Application Management-related Systems

### *(a) Database Management System*

This module is responsible for the storage of information required or supplied by all other modules of the CRM product. This will usually be one of the standard RDBMSs like Oracle, DB2, and so on.

### *(b) Application Administration and Management System*

This provides facilities to guide and assist in installation, upgrades, system maintenance, printer/spool management, and so on. This application administration and management system interfaces with other related systems for managing software distribution, configuration and change releases, versions, security and authorization, disaster recovery, archival, and so on. It also provides facilities for operational requirements of performance monitoring, back-ups, background processing, creating and managing jobs, and so on.

### *(c) Software Distribution Management System*

This system enables the facility to upgrade the client-based software automatically from a centralized place. The system can enforce the access and authorization profiles at the various users' PCs.

### *(d) Security and Authorization Management System*

In an integrated environment of CRM, this system provides the architecture for the security and hence the access and usage available to the system. This enables maintaining the profiles of authorized access, assigning such profiles to specific user accounts, authenticating the users in the production environment, logging user access and usage, tracking attempts to breach the system security, changing access profiles and passwords, and so on.

### *(e) Audit Management System*

This system provides monitoring for user access and usage, system processing and updates, system and data change management, error logs, and so on.

### *(f) Disaster Recovery Management System*

This provides the facility to define the alternate disaster recovery servers and systems, triggering or initial response procedures, databases recoveries, activating back-up resources, full recovery procedures, and so on.

### *(g) Archival Management System*

This provides the facility to archive system and application data that has been identified as essential for future reference. This defines details on data, the data sources, duration, frequency, the target archival system, and so on.

### *(h) Communications Management System*

This provides the communication layer for the CRM system. It provides features like distributed processing, distributed databases, security, and so on.

## 3.1.4 Application Support-related systems

### *(a) Online Documentation System*

This provides the ability to make system documentation available on the system while one uses it and more importantly, in the context of the particular functionality being used at any moment. This system provides links to related issues as well as the facility to pursue individual topics in full detail.

### *(b) Print Documentation System*

This provides facilities for printing the full technical details and the application design of the system for offline reference. Moreover, it enables updates to this documentation depending on upgrades, enhancements and new releases of functionality in any of the above systems.

### *(c) Online Tutorial, Training and Demonstration Management System*

This system provides an online tutorial carefully designed to highlight the comprehensiveness of the application and also advanced features that are available within the system. This training and demonstration system provides a path to be followed during the learning phase on the CRM. The system also provides the ability to measure and assess the progress made by the trainees during such exercises.

### *(d) Implementation Project Management System*

This system provides integrated capabilities for monitoring and managing the progress during implementation of the CRM. It provides the capability to define the work steps, dependencies, schedules, estimates on duration and effort, work in progress, work completed, work under testing, and so on.

### 3.1.5 Miscellaneous

#### *(a) Office Automation System*

This system provides the functionalities provided by word processors, document formatters, spreadsheets, and so on. This office automation system is used for recording annotations on the system or for project management, defining preformatted letters generated by the systems, and so on.

#### *(b) Groupware and Workflow System*

This system provides extensive communication between users of the CRM system. More significantly, it provides direct interfaces between itself and the mail system in order to inform and alert concerned personnel about pre-defined events occurring during processing, like released purchase orders, dunning notices, alarms on exceeding credit limits, and so on.

This system also provides for broadcasting mail to multiple persons, routing mail in the operating sequence, triggering reminders at various stages along the workflow, soliciting approvals or authorizations, and so on.

#### *(c) Data Warehouse and Data Analysis System*

This system provides for mapping and populating operational data from the CRM tables into the multidimensional tables of the data warehouse for manipulation and analysis. It provides advanced tools for detecting data patterns, trends, co-relations, and so on within the available data and prospecting for any significant relationship between data across the organization.

## 3.2 PREPARING A BUSINESS CASE FOR CRM

Before proceeding with the evaluation, selection and implementation of a CRM, it is essential to prove that its introduction will have demonstrable benefits for the organization. Each application has a different purpose, nature, certainty and risks. This is achieved by preparing a business case for the implementation of a CRM. The basic premise of a business case is that an investment will have an impact and payback that spans a timeline spreading across a few months or years. However, to be relevant it is essential that the input costs and the resulting outcomes must be directly related to the specific investment decision. This is difficult because of the following reasons:

- There is no baseline data available prior to the implementation of the CRM, making before and after comparisons impossible
- There are too many independent variables to be accounted for
- Many of the resulting benefits are soft (or intangible) and hard to quantify

There are several approaches for assessing the payback potential and period of any investment. Some of these approaches are as follows.

### 3.2.1 Financial Approach

The financial approaches use techniques like Return On Investments (ROI) based on the calculations of the Net Present Value (NPV) or the Internal Rate of Return (IRR). But, one of the simplest methods is to compute the breakeven/payback period, when the cumulative flow of income or benefits exceeds the cumulative flow of the costs. Clearly, the shorter the payback the better is the opportunity. However, this is not very reliable beyond a period of a couple of years, as it does not take into account the time value of money.

Financial benefits from the implementation of CRM can be assessed in terms of the increased revenues. This increase could result either from the generation of new revenue or because of more efficient production of erstwhile revenue.

Revenue growth envisaged from the implementation of CRM systems could result from:

***(a) Increased sales through***

- Gaining new customers
- Retaining customers for longer
- Realizing higher price for existing products or from new sales (up-sell and cross-sell)
- Drastic reduction in the costs of closing the first sale through reduced number of calls, accelerated search and evaluation

***(b) Better sales mix or customer mix through***

- Increasing sales of higher margin products or platform products (see details under sub-section "Strategic Approach")
- Bonding strongly with higher value customers and at the same time motivating other customers to exit from the company's customer base

***(c) Enhanced customer benefits resulting in improved retention through***

- Improved response time to customer requests
- Easy access to current order status
- Reduced costs of searching, evaluating and buying the product/solution or service
- Reduced costs of using and supporting the product/solution or service
- Delivered product/solution or service meeting or exceeding customer expectations
- Greater range of products/solutions or services addressing varying needs of the customer

### 3.2.2 Cost Reduction Approach

This is one of the most direct ways of justifying an investment for the introduction of information systems. Assuming that the benefits from the new systems are equal to or greater than the existing system, one simply compares the costs of the proposed system with the existing system. A variation on this approach is the value add analysis of the related business processes within the organization. In this approach, which is the essence of the BPM approach presented in Chapter 7, the organization essentially identifies the non-value add tasks and either eliminates them or substitutes them for more efficient processes via automated systems like CRM.

### *(a) Sales Support*

Major factors that contribute to reducing sales costs are:

- Automation of proposals, configuration and quotations
- Referencing and reviewing notes and files before calls
- Managing samples, demo stock, sales literature, etc.
- Preparing sales forecasts and customer call reports
- Providing better quality leads in usable format
- Reducing the number of customer calls necessary to close a sale by enabling capture of critical information at the point-of-sale, better customer information, on-the-spot reports on different configuration and costs
- Finding and providing product or technical information to the customers
- Information and learning about new product/solutions and services, best practice templates, domain knowledge guides, etc.

### *(b) Direct Marketing*

Cost savings can result from better targeting, personalization and elimination of duplicates and blank calls. In fact, better targeting and validated data should enable the volume of direct mail to be reduced while simultaneously increasing the response rates.

### *(c) Call Centers/Customer Contact Centers*

Staff is the most expensive element in setting up and running a contact center. By automating as many processes as possible—number of calls, call routing and assisted call answering—companies can save up to 70 percent on staff costs.

### *(d) More Accurate Sales Forecasts*

For some organizations, better sales forecasting will enable

- Reductions in inventory resulting in savings on stockholding costs
- More efficient production schedules resulting in reduced per unit costs

### *(e) Staff Motivation and Loyalty*

Like customer loyalty, employee loyalty also has a positive effect on profitability. High sales staff turnover has an adverse effect on the sales relationship and the potential of subsequent up-sell and cross-sell opportunities.

### 3.2.3 Strategic Approach

Unlike the earlier approaches the strategic approach takes a view of the future. CRM systems provide support for organizational change as also for rapid delivery of strategic changes to product, pricing and customer information. For a better payback it is important that the CRM strategies should be linked to the company's business and marketing strategies.

> While CRM strategies are based on the fundamental premise of enhancing customer relationships this does not necessarily imply that CRM systems require a single view of the customer across all channels and customer touch points. As noted in Chapter 1, section "The concept of Customer Relationship Management (CRM)", all customers are not equal and may prefer certain specific channels or touch points over others.

Thus, it is critical to identify and develop models for managing different types of profitable customer relationships. Each of these models may need a different business and market strategy and therefore, a different approach to implementing the CRM systems. Some of these profitability models relevant to CRM systems projects are as follows.

***(a) Solutions Profit***

This strategy demands up-front investment commitment to understand customers' economics and identify ways to make them more favorable. This demands working closely with customers to discover how they search, evaluate, test, buy and use their products and then finding ways to help them to improve the difficult, time-consuming or expensive areas of their functions and processes. This strategy is characterized by

- Early negative cash flow
- Customized products that are finely integrated with customer's operations
- Mid to long-term payback horizon
- High customer retention

For this model, the CRM systems have to provide a unified view of key customers across all channels and touch points.

***(b) Time Profit***

This strategy enables exploitation of the early mover advantages for innovative solutions; being first allows innovators to generate excess returns but only until imitators begin to erode margins. Price premiums exist but the opportunity window is only for a short period of time. This strategy is characterized by

- Sporadic but large investments
- Constant innovation as value migrates away from the current innovation
- Ability to bring new products and services to market quickly
- High prices and abundant profits but for short periods of time
- Immediate to short-term payback horizon

- High customer satisfaction resulting from acquiring unique products or solutions

For this model, the CRM systems require rapid development and quick deployment.

### *(c) Multiplier Profit*

This strategy churns out gains from the same product, character, trademark, capability or service, over and over again. Technologically, this corresponds to the economics of 'increasing returns' that is a characteristic of the network-effect phenomenon as witnessed in media, software and related industries (see Chapter 1, sub-section "Customer Capitalism and Increasing Returns"). Business-wise, this is closely allied to brand-building strategy. This strategy is characterized by

- Large and even huge investments in building brands
- A unified brand across a broad array of products
- Risk of brand erosion or dissipation if extended to unrelated areas
- Payback horizon highly dependent on the rapidity of build-up of the installed base
- Brands are valuable but intangible assets like customer relationships

For this model the CRM systems must support international brand management as also localization for identifying and developing opportunities in specific markets.

### *(d) Platform Profit*

This strategy demands maintenance and management of a user base of high value customers focused around its product platform. Such a group of committed customers can then be promoted through up-selling and cross-selling to higher margin add-on solutions and services. The more proprietary is the base product platform, the more powerful is this strategy as a profit generating mechanism. This strategy is characterized by

- Comprehensive platform architecture and design standards
- Establish conformance programs for qualifying third-party co-products
- Comprehensive interface design, preferably proprietary standards
- A product/service portfolio that meets the needs throughout the Customer Life Cycle (CLC)
- Efforts to establish the industry-wide standard and achieve ubiquity

For this model, the CRM systems must cater to the company's standardized architecture and interfaces for integrating best-of-breed solutions.

### *(e) Innovation Profit*

This strategy demands that companies remain in direct contact with the customers to dynamically solicit feedback and also remain lean and agile to quickly re-configure their business operations and processes more suitably to the altered requirements or expectations. Successful companies tend to become more risk-averse, more formalized, more bureaucratic, more insulated from the customers and, finally, more lethargic in their responses to demanding circumstances. However, the most damaging factor is the widening gap from the actual customers where direct feedback from customers is reduced, filtered and often ignored. The twin forces of direct customer contact and agile operations create potential for enormous profits. This strategy is characterized by

- Organizational design that emphasizes direct customer contact and agile responsiveness
- Smaller autonomous and agile Strategic Business Units (SBUs)
- Early positive cash flow, but volatile P/L scenarios
- Unalloyed direct feedback from the customers
- High performance-based rewards and compensation resulting in highly responsive sales operations

For this model, the CRM systems have to focus on becoming highly responsive to the top 20 percent of the customers including customized requirements, rapid implementations and deployments.

***(f) Exchange Profit***

This strategy brings multiple sellers and buyers together and enables them to place and match offers, and execute the deals. The exchange reduces the costs for both the buyers and sellers coupled with assured throughputs, security and integrity of the system. This strategy is characterized by

- Increasing profits with increasing transaction or business volumes
- Easy access to accredited customers
- Control of the information flow through the exchange
- Myriad value added services for payments, settlements, account maintenance, and so on

For this model, the CRM systems must enable robust and high performing systems.

## 3.3 CRM ACQUISITION DECISION PROCESS

The evaluation and selection of the CRM packages for implementation within organizations is a major exercise. Specific effort needs to be taken for the evaluation of highly complex CRM packages like Siebel, in terms of their functionality and technology. The package needs to be selected by judiciously balancing both, the dimensions of functionality and technology, and the mutually contradictory requirements for complexity and flexibility of the CRM packages. Companies have processes ranging from make-to-order to continuous flow. For certain shortcomings in functionality they may also have to decide to build, rather than buy some of the applications.

In the following section we discuss the various aspects to be considered when evaluating the CRM packages suitable for an organization. The actual process of selecting a CRM is the topic of the next chapter.

### 3.3.1 General Considerations of CRM Evaluation

The general characteristics of CRM packages to be reviewed include the following:

- Comprehensive functionality
- Ease of use
- Capability for customizing
- Controls and reliability
- Ease of installation

- Efficiency of operation
- Ease of user management
- Open system architecture
- Open system interfaces; legacy system and third-legacy products
- Data synchronization
- Internationalization and euro currency
- Online documentation and contextual help
- Future upgrades and enhancements
- Skill transfer and training programs
- User group activity

### 3.3.2 Checklists for CRM Evaluation

The exercise of evaluating CRMs becomes easier if detailed checklists of major points of interest are prepared beforehand. These checklists can be used to gather relevant information that can be analyzed and used as the basis for the selection process.

Tables 3.1 through 3.8 are included for reference:

(i) CRM vendor issues are illustrated in Table 3.1
(ii) CRM product issues are illustrated in Table 3.2
(iii) CRM technical issues are illustrated in Table 3.3
(iv) CRM installation and operation issues are illustrated in Table 3.4
(v) CRM integration and interface issues are illustrated in Table 3.5
(vi) CRM modification and maintenance issues are illustrated in Table 3.6
(vii) CRM audit and control issues are illustrated in Table 3.7
(viii) CRM standards and documentation issues are illustrated in Table 3.8

The meaning of the column headings is as given below:

**Available**: Indicates that the functionality is currently available as standard functionality in the CRM system.

**Configured**: Indicates that the functionality is not available as the standard functionality, but the CRM system can be configured easily to deliver the required functionality.

**Upgraded**: Indicates the functionality is planned and would become available in future named upgrades or release versions of the CRM system.

**Third-party**: Indicates that the functionality is not available but is available with third-party packages that have been specifically qualified for the CRM system.

**Absent**: Not available at the time of the evaluation.

**Table 3.1 CRM Evaluation: Vendor Issues**

| Item | Description | Available | Configured | Upgraded | Third-Party | Absent |
|---|---|---|---|---|---|---|
| (a) | **Sales Channel Management** | | | | | |
| 1 | How long has the CRM under consideration been sold by the vendor in the market? | | | | | |
| 2 | Has it been developed in-house or acquired? Is the core development team still with them? | | | | | |
| 3 | What is the gross annual turnover and profit of the company? What is the ratio of sales to support revenue? | | | | | |
| 4 | How long has the vendor been in the packaged solution market? | | | | | |
| 5 | What is the installed base of this CRM? | | | | | |
| 6 | What are the hardware and operating systems that it is currently available on? | | | | | |
| 7 | How are they distributed? Industry-wise or location-wise? | | | | | |
| 8 | What is the geographical spread of the vendor/s development, sales, and support offices? | | | | | |
| 9 | How many employees does the company have in technical and support functions? | | | | | |
| 10 | What are vendor/s support and service policies? | | | | | |
| 11 | Does the vendor provide online modem-based support? | | | | | |
| 12 | What are vendor's training programs and facilities? | | | | | |
| 13 | How many employees does the company have in development, technical support, training, and commercial areas? | | | | | |
| 14 | Does the company's products have user groups? How are they organized? | | | | | |
| 15 | Who are the technical and business partners of the vendor? | | | | | |
| 16 | What is the company's strategy for industry-specific solutions? | | | | | |
| 17 | Is the vendor itself ready to implement the CRM package within the company? | | | | | |

**Table 3.2 CRM Evaluation: Product Issues**

| Item | Description | Available | Configured | Upgraded | Third-Party | Absent | |
|---|---|---|---|---|---|---|---|
| 1 | How many actual package users are there? | | | | | | |
| 2 | How many years have they been using the package? In how many locations has the package Been operational? | | | | | | |
| 3 | Have the users been satisfied with the package? | | | | | | |
| 4 | Can the vendor provide references of companies where the CRM under consideration is in operation? | | | | | | |
| 5 | Can the vendor provide details of installations at these customer sites? | | | | | | |
| 6 | Can the vendor provide professional references who can be contacted in these companies? | | | | | | |
| 7 | Can the vendor arrange a visit to one or two sites where the package has been operational? Can this visit include detailed demonstrations and a review of experiences, operations, and problems? | | | | | | |
| 8 | Is the package user-friendly? | | | | | | |
| 9 | What is the product map? Is it comprehensive? | | | | | | |
| 10 | Does it cover all functions of a CRM? | | | | | | |
| 11 | How scalable is the CRM in terms of the number of users that can be supported as well as its ability to be deployed as a company-wide solution? | | | | | | |
| 12 | Does it follow the principle of one-point data entry? | | | | | | |
| 13 | Does it have a centralized database for enterprise data? | | | | | | |
| 14 | Are the transactions updates done in batch or online mode? | | | | | | |
| 15 | Can it be integrated? Can its modules work in a standalone mode? | | | | | | |
| 16 | How easy is it to integrate with third-party systems and solutions? | | | | | | |
| 17 | Does it have an open architecture with adherence to worldwide standards? | | | | | | |
| 18 | Is it based on nonproprietary technology? Can it work on standard hardware and operating system platforms? | | | | | | |

**Table 3.2 CRM Evaluation: Product Issues (*Continued*)**

| Item | Description | Available | Configured | Upgraded | Third-Party | Absent |
|---|---|---|---|---|---|---|
| 19 | Does it follow standard protocols and interfaces? Can it interface with legacy and other systems like ERP, SCM, CRM, EDI, CTI, and so on? | | | | | |
| 20 | Is the source code made available along with the system? | | | | | |
| 21 | Is it accessible for making modifications? How will modifications and corrections be made? | | | | | |
| 22 | Will modifications of the CRM be necessary to obtain efficient and effective operations? | | | | | |
| 23 | Will the CRM markedly affect other users services? | | | | | |
| 24 | How easy is it to configure the CRM to the specific requirements of a company quickly and simply? | | | | | |
| 25 | Does the system enable the uploading of data from the legacy systems used by the enterprise? | | | | | |
| 26 | Does the system have utilities for doing the data conversion? What is the cost of such utilities? | | | | | |
| 27 | What is the development status of the product? Is it slated to go through a major revamping or major additions? | | | | | |
| 28 | Does the package contain current technological features? | | | | | |
| 29 | What is the enhancement and upgrade strategy of the product? | | | | | |
| 30 | How many releases or upgrades have been introduced in the last two years? | | | | | |
| 31 | How often are the new releases introduced? | | | | | |
| 32 | Did the releases meet the customers' schedule? | | | | | |
| 33 | What is the design strategy for addressing Euro currency and international languages? | | | | | |
| 34 | What is the product strategy to make it Web-enabled? | | | | | |
| 35 | Does the system have e-commerce functionality or does it have third-party e-commerce solutions? | | | | | |

**Table 3.2 CRM Evaluation: Product Issues (*Continued*)**

| Item | Description | Available | Configured | Upgraded | Third-Party | Absent |
|---|---|---|---|---|---|---|
| 36 | What is the product strategy to introduce and enhance country-specific functionality | | | | | |
| 37 | What is the product strategy to introduce industry-specific functionality? | | | | | |
| 38 | What is the market view of the product? Has it been analyzed, compared, and benchmarked? | | | | | |
| 39 | Does the package rate well in surveys? | | | | | |
| 40 | What is the cost of the package? | | | | | |
| 41 | Is the cost based on the envisaged number of users? | | | | | |
| 42 | What are the licensing policies of the product? | | | | | |
| 43 | What is the cost of additional features and modules required by the enterprise? | | | | | |
| 44 | What is the cost of periodically purchasing updated versions? | | | | | |
| 45 | What is the cost of installation? | | | | | |
| 46 | What is the cost of training? | | | | | |
| 47 | What is the cost of system documentation? | | | | | |
| 48 | What is the cost of vendor support and services? | | | | | |

**Table 3.3 CRM Evaluation: Technical Issues**

| Item | Description | Available | Configured | Upgraded | Third-Party | Absent |
|---|---|---|---|---|---|---|
| 1 | Does the CRM run on the target platform identified by the enterprise including Windows NT/2000, UNIX (AIX, HP-UX, Solaris), OS/390? | | | | | |
| 2 | Does the CRM support a variety of architectures like three-tier, multi-tier, and n-tier? | | | | | |
| 3 | What is the minimum configuration required for the target computer for installing the CRM including the application Serve, Database Server, Connected Client, Thin Client, and Mobile/Handheld Client? | | | | | |
| 4 | Does the package support the following main servers: MS Exchange, MS Outlook, MS Mail, cc:Mail, and Lotus Notes? | | | | | |
| 5 | Does the package support the Web scripting languages like Hyper Text Markup Language (HTML), Dynamic Hyper Text Markup Language (DHTML), eXtended Markup Language (XML), Java Server Pages (JSP), JavaScript, and Visual Basic VBScript? | | | | | |
| 6 | Does the package need any optional features from the operating system? | | | | | |
| 7 | Does the CRM have an application repository system? | | | | | |
| 8 | Does it have a GUI System? | | | | | |
| 9 | Does the system provide for defining default screen characteristics, function keys, fonts, and so on? | | | | | |
| 10 | Does the menu have pictures or icons? Is the status information displayed on the screen for reference? | | | | | |
| 11 | Does it have a menu management system? | | | | | |
| 12 | Is the system startup satisfactory, including date, time, operator identification, control numbers, security controls, and so on? | | | | | |
| 13 | Are there clear, brief, and well-documented instructions to guide the user through the system? | | | | | |
| 14 | Are error messages well-formatted, clear, and well-documented? | | | | | |
| 15 | Are single-key action commands used to speed the interaction of the user? | | | | | |
| 16 | Does it have a help management system? Is contextual help available on a field or a program? | | | | | |

**Table 3.3 CRM Evaluation: Technical Issues (*Continued*)**

| Item | Description | Available | Configured | Upgraded | Third-Party | Absent |
|---|---|---|---|---|---|---|
| 17 | Does it have a database management system or utilize a variety of standard RDBMSs like Oracle 8. IBM Db2, MS SQl Server, Sybase, Informix, and so on? | | | | | |
| 18 | Does the package provide ability to record emails, voice files, multimedia files (including compression mechanisms), and so on? | | | | | |
| 19 | Does it have facility for database reorganization? | | | | | |
| 20 | Does the system provide direct access to the data within the database outside of the system? | | | | | |
| 21 | Are the record sizes, key structures, and other elements relatively independent of the target environment? | | | | | |
| 22 | Are the detailed layouts available for all data tables? | | | | | |
| 23 | Do the data tables contain sufficient audit trails including date changed, by whom, and the type of change? | | | | | |
| 24 | Does the system test for the existence of numbers such as account numbers, document numbers, and code numbers? | | | | | |
| 25 | Does the package have adequate input and output edits and controls? | | | | | |
| 26 | Does the package have adequate controls for maintaining the integrity of tables and data? | | | | | |
| 27 | Does it have a 4GL development system? | | | | | |
| 28 | Does it have a query management system? | | | | | |
| 29 | Does it have a report management system? | | | | | |
| 30 | Can the user select documents, formats, and fields and control the output to the screen or to the printer? | | | | | |
| 31 | Can the user select documents, formats, and fields and control the output to the administration system? | | | | | |
| 32 | Does the system provide mirroring or data replication? | | | | | |
| 33 | Does it have the facility for data replication and synchronization? | | | | | |

**Table 3.3 CRM Evaluation: Technical Issues (*Continued*)**

| Item | Description | Available | Configured | Upgraded | Third-Party | Absent |
|---|---|---|---|---|---|---|
| 34 | Can the system tolerate errors and difficulties at the terminals and continue operating? | | | | | |
| 35 | Does the system save the data needed for recovery in case of power failure, entry of improper data, and so on? | | | | | |
| 36 | Are terminal users prevented from stopping, disrupting, or destroying the operation of the system? | | | | | |
| 37 | Are there simple nondestructive methods for EXIT, GO BACK, OR PREVIOUS SCREEN? | | | | | |
| 38 | Does it have a software distribution system? | | | | | |
| 39 | Does the system provide for defining an access profile at specific terminals? | | | | | |
| 40 | Does it have a configuration management system? | | | | | |
| 41 | Does the system help in guiding the user through the configuration system? | | | | | |
| 42 | Does it have a change management system? | | | | | |
| 43 | Does the system have facilities to control the release of new or changed programs into production? | | | | | |
| 44 | Does it have a version management system? | | | | | |
| 45 | Does it have a security and administration system? | | | | | |
| 46 | Does the system provide for defining and maintaining access profiles and passwords? | | | | | |
| 47 | Does it have an audit management system? | | | | | |
| 48 | Does it have a disaster recovery system? | | | | | |
| 49 | Does the system provide automatic recovery procedures? | | | | | |
| 50 | Does it have an archival management system? | | | | | |
| 51 | Does it have a communications management system? | | | | | |

**Table 3.3 CRM Evaluation: Technical Issues (*Continued*)**

| Item | Description | Available | Configured | Upgraded | Third-Party | Absent | |
|---|---|---|---|---|---|---|---|
| 52 | Does the package support the following communications channel: telephone, Web, fax, email, dial-up modem, Interactive Voice Response (IVR), wireless/PDA, and so on? | | | | | | |
| 53 | Does the package have the capability to handle and route inbound and outbound faxes to selected destinations/groups/users? | | | | | | |
| 54 | Does the system have a Computer Telephony Integration (CTI) architecture based on a Telephony Application Programming Interface (TAPI), Java Technology Application Programming Interface (JTAPI), or CallPath Services and Telephony Architecture (CSTA)? | | | | | | |
| 55 | Does the package support intelligent responses to callers by identifying them via Automatic Number Identification (ANI), Dialed Number Identification Services (DNIS), Calling Line ID (CLID), or caller information given via IVR? | | | | | | |
| 56 | Does the system provide facilities for Automatic Call Distribution (ACD) depending on the type of routing to be employed based on skill, predefined rules, or customer information? | | | | | | |
| 57 | Does the system provide facilities or real-time monitoring of ACD queues and outbound call activity? | | | | | | |
| 58 | Does the CRM provide facilities for recording phone conversations? | | | | | | |
| 59 | Does the system provide softphone support for functions such as dial, answer, transfer, conference, hold, and speed dial? | | | | | | |
| 60 | Does the system support call scripting? | | | | | | |
| 61 | Does the system support Web callback facility? | | | | | | |
| 62 | Does it have an API system? | | | | | | |
| 63 | Does it have an online documentation system? | | | | | | |
| 64 | Does it have a powerful search facility as well as suggestions on related topics? | | | | | | |
| 65 | Does it have a print documentation system? | | | | | | |

**Table 3.3 CRM Evaluation: Technical Issues (*Continued*)**

| Item | Description | Available | Configured | Upgraded | Third-Party | Absent |
|---|---|---|---|---|---|---|
| 66 | Does it have an online tutorial, training, and demonstration system? | | | | | |
| 67 | Does it have an office-automation system? | | | | | |
| 68 | Does it have a Groupware and Workflow system? | | | | | |
| 69 | Does the system have a built-in system for the following: workflow/routing capabilities, escalation, and flexible query system? | | | | | |
| 70 | Does the workflow system interface with the email system? | | | | | |
| 71 | Does it have a data warehouse and data analysis system? | | | | | |
| 72 | Does the CRM have an integrated knowledge engine and built-in knowledge bases (especially for industry specific functionality) and/or support third-party knowledge engines and knowledge bases? | | | | | |
| 73 | Does the system have the ability to support and access multiple knowledge engines and knowledge bases concurrently? | | | | | |
| 74 | Does the system provide capability for a group to build and populate knowledge bases as needed (including any attached files such as text, binary, and multimedia files)? | | | | | |
| 75 | Does the knowledge engine support capabilities like boolean logic processing, rule-based representation, explanatory facility, pattern matching, rule performance/efficiency algorithms, case-based matching algorithms, and so on? | | | | | |
| 76 | Does the system enable the knowledge engine and knowledge bases to support databases, Internet. Hyperling/hypertext, Web pages, reporting software, batch import/export of data, customization/ upgrades/ updates/new releases of knowledge engine and knowledge source databases, APIs (for IVR, ACD, and MS Exchange/Lotus Notes), and testing and validation of the knowledge engine and knowledge base? | | | | | |
| 77 | Does it have an implementation project management system? | | | | | |
| 78 | Does the system report on missed milestones, schedules, and so on? | | | | | |

**Table 3.4 CRM Evaluation: Installation and Operation Issues**

| Item | Description | Available | Configured | Upgraded | Third-Party | Absent | |
|---|---|---|---|---|---|---|---|
| 1 | Are the vendor's and purchaser's installation responsibilities clearly defined? | | | | | | |
| 2 | Are installation specifications defined clearly? | | | | | | |
| 3 | Does the vendor have a manual or computer-assisted installation procedure? | | | | | | |
| 4 | Does the configuration of the installation depend on the specifies of the enterprise and is there enough assistance available via documentation or vendor personnel? | | | | | | |
| 5 | Are the acceptance criteria clearly defined? | | | | | | |
| 6 | Does the operation of the system need extensive training for computer operators and system programmers? | | | | | | |
| 7 | Does the vendor provide sample operating standards and procedures that can be adapted and used? | | | | | | |
| 8 | Does the system documentation conform to the installation's documentation standards? | | | | | | |
| 9 | Can the system be installed in the operating system environment, database, Local Area Network (LAN), and so on without major modifications? | | | | | | |
| 10 | Are the system's performance criteria for acceptance clearly stated? | | | | | | |
| 11 | Does the system have guidelines for maximization of performance of the software for the following: network bandwidth requirements, database sizing threshold, number of concurrent users, and synchronization of remote clients? | | | | | | |
| 12 | Does the system provide for audit trails for the following activities: backups, failures in the system, and recovery in case of failure? | | | | | | |
| 13 | Does the vendor promise full support until the system is installed satisfactorily? | | | | | | |
| 14 | Will the vendor be available for the data conversion effort? | | | | | | |

**Table 3.5 CRM Evaluation: Integration and Interface Issues**

| Item | Description | Available | Configured | Upgraded | Third-Party | Absent | |
|---|---|---|---|---|---|---|---|
| 1 | Does the CRM support APIs for interfacing to customized modules or third-party applications? | | | | | | |
| 2 | Does the package have APIs developed in any of the common standards like Component Object Model (COM) ro Distributed Component Object Model (DCOM), Common Object Request Broker Application (CORBAS), and Enterprise JavaBeans (EJB)? | | | | | | |
| 3 | Does the package provide facilities to access these APIs through 4GL environments like Microsoft VB, Visual C++, PowerBuilder (PB), Java, and so on? | | | | | | |
| 4 | Does the package support APIs or specific connectors to other packages like ERPs, CRMs, SCMs, and so on? | | | | | | |
| 5 | Does the CRM system provide an interface to its database? | | | | | | |
| 6 | Does the CRM system provide an interface to other databases and systems? | | | | | | |
| 7 | Does the CRM system conform to known communications protocols and standards? | | | | | | |
| 8 | Does it conform to known standards of encryption? | | | | | | |
| 9 | Does the system provide online or batch interfaces? | | | | | | |
| 10 | Does the system provide for controlling the upload of data into the system? | | | | | | |
| 11 | Does it provide facilities for quickly mapping the external data into the system tables and vice versa? | | | | | | |
| 12 | Does the system provide for defining and scheduling the upload or download of data in an online mode? | | | | | | |
| 13 | Does the system provide a report or audit trail on the transfer of data? | | | | | | |
| 14 | Does the package provide email integration through various interfaces such as Simple Mail Transfer Protocol (SMTP) or Microsoft Windows Messaging Application Programming Interface (MAPI)? | | | | | | |
| 15 | Does the system provide an interface with the workflow system? | | | | | | |
| 16 | Does the system provide an automatic interface for loading data into a data warehouse system? | | | | | | |

**Table 3.6 CRM Evaluation: Modification and Maintenance Issues**

| Item | Description | Available | Configured | Upgraded | Third-Party | Absent | |
|---|---|---|---|---|---|---|---|
| 1 | Can the system function on an as-is basis without modification? | | | | | | |
| 2 | Can the users change the administrative procedures to suit their requirements? | | | | | | |
| 3 | Are all the system requirements defined through parameters and tables, making modifications easy to accomplish? | | | | | | |
| 4 | Does the vendor inform others about customers that have made similar modifications that may be available rapidly? | | | | | | |
| 5 | Are customers advised of outstanding problems that other users have discovered? | | | | | | |
| 6 | Are new releases available regularly and automatically to all the purchasers? | | | | | | |
| 7 | Can a system dump be sent to the vendor for review? | | | | | | |
| 8 | Does the vendor provide onsite support and maintenance? | | | | | | |
| 9 | Will the vendor support an installation that has the package modified by a customer? | | | | | | |
| 10 | Does the system provide for controlling the upload of data into the system? | | | | | | |

**Table 3.7 CRM Evaluation: Security, Audit, and Control Issues**

| Item | Description | Available | Configured | Upgraded | Third-Party | Absent | |
|---|---|---|---|---|---|---|---|
| 1 | Does the system have adequate backup if the operational version of the system is destroyed? Are all transactions properly recorded at the point of origin? | | | | | | |
| 2 | Does the system have controls to ensure that all data recorded enter the computer for processing? | | | | | | |
| 3 | Does the system provide for determining the proper authorization of transaction? | | | | | | |
| 4 | Does the system provide facilities to ensure that all data received by the system are accurate and complete? | | | | | | |
| 5 | Can the system ensure the complete and accurate processing of data through the system? | | | | | | |
| 6 | Does the system provide controls to detect the loss of data or non-processing of data? | | | | | | |
| 7 | Does the system ensure that all transactions are recorded in the proper accounting period and also posted to the proper records? | | | | | | |
| 8 | Can the system ensure that the organization's procedures and processing rules have been followed? | | | | | | |
| 9 | Can the system ensure that the data in the tables are accurate and complete? | | | | | | |
| 10 | Does the system have information on when the file was created, when it was modified, by whom, and for what purpose? | | | | | | |
| 11 | Does the system provide audit trails for varied activities such as security breaches, user logins, profile logins, group logins, report format modifications, and generations? | | | | | | |

**Table 3.7 CRM Evaluation: Security, Audit, and Control Issues (*Continued*)**

| Item | Description | Available | Configured | Upgraded | Third-Party | Absent | |
|---|---|---|---|---|---|---|---|
| 12 | Does the system provide capabilities to maintain audit trails for varied activities like database structure modification, data fields modifications, database entry, query generation, and so on? | | | | | | |
| 13 | Does the system provide safeguards such as passwords or authorized terminals to protect the tables from unauthorized access? | | | | | | |
| 14 | Does the system provide for varied access rights for activities related to system configuration, systems administration, systems development, Management Information System (MIS) activities, data field modifications, files/database viewing, files/database editing, report format modifications, report generation, printing, viewing screens, and so on? | | | | | | |
| 15 | Does the system ensure that the processed data do not include unauthorized alterations? | | | | | | |
| 16 | Does the system have controls to ensure that all errors detected by the system get corrected? | | | | | | |
| 17 | Do the transmitted messages include sufficient identification including the message number, terminal, date, transaction type, and so on? | | | | | | |
| 18 | Does the system maintain logs to ensure that lost or garbled messages can be recreated? | | | | | | |
| 19 | Does the system retain information to permit the reconstruction of transactions to prove the accuracy completeness of the processing? | | | | | | |

**Table 3.8 CRM Evaluation: Standards and Documentation**

| Item | Description | Available | Configured | Upgraded | Third-Party | Absent |
|---|---|---|---|---|---|---|
| 1 | Does the package have standard documentation that is available online and in printed form? | | | | | |
| 2 | Does the package provide documentation on the system's functionality, technical design, and operating environment? | | | | | |
| 3 | Is the documentation easily referenced? | | | | | |
| 4 | Does the system provide extensive cross-referencing facilities? | | | | | |
| 5 | Does the system provide the capability to automatically change the relevant documentation when making modifications in the system, such as to tables, fields, screen formats, and report layouts? | | | | | |
| 6 | Does the user documentation have clear representations of menus, screens, and so on? | | | | | |
| 7 | Does the system provide the ability to prepare relevant training material on the modified system? | | | | | |
| 8 | Does the system describe the programming standards and procedures in sufficient detail to establish conformity and make documentation easy? | | | | | |
| 9 | Does the system enable easy maintenance of the modifications in the system as well as the corresponding documentation? | | | | | |

### 3.3.3 Checklists for CRM Functional Requirements

When evaluating the suitability of a CRM package the detailed functional requirements of an enterprise need to be analyzed and enlisted for detailed scrutiny later. This also acts as the baseline for the comparative evaluation of the various CRM packages.

CRM applications are sub-divided into three segments—marketing automation software, sales automation software, and customer support and call center software. Sales software is designed to manage functions, from high-end processes like account/ contact management and list management, to low-end processes like simple content management. Marketing software assists with such things as campaign management and execution, and list management and telemarketing. Customer support and call center applications are designed to enhance management of the relationship with existing customers.

In the CRM space, Sales Force Automation (SFA) represents the oldest set of functionality that has been addressed by IT solutions in the past, but is also the more difficult because of the inherent relationship-orientation of the processes involved. SFA applications focus on functionalities like lead distribution and tracking, pipeline management, contact centralization and management, and group collaboration. The advent of the Internet has also altered the fundamental premise of SFA by attempting to make the sales process devoid of the salesman by providing RFP/ RFI type of capabilities through an automated interface.

Applications that offer marketing automation primarily provide two major functions, namely, campaign management and demographics analysis. A campaign revolves around marketing budget management, advertisement management and placement, targeting campaigns, response management, and the like. While these activities have always involved a degree of statistical analysis, the variety and colossal amount of data that is captured on the websites has led to a quantum jump in the level of such analysis.

In the past, typical customer service automation and management consisted of setting up a contact center with access to a customer database. With the advent of Internet the norm is a totally integrated contact center where customer agents respond to e-mails, phone calls and chat requests using a fully integrated customer database connected to various sub-systems like the ERPs, sales and procurement portals, and supply chain applications.

A detailed checklist of functional requirements needs to be compiled for the various functional areas within the company, as follows.

(a) Sales function

Field/ mobile, indirect (resellers, brokers and distributors) and retail sales

Opportunity management and pipeline analysis

Forecasting

Sales cycle analysis

Sales metrics

Activity reporting and management

Mapping tools and territory alignment

Time and expense reporting

Quotas and incentive design, and compensation management

Sales training

A sample checklist of sales requirements is shown in Table 3.9.

(b) Contact and account management function

Contact profile

Activity management and history

Organization chart

Correspondence

Business relationships

Order entry, history and tracking

Presentations, proposal and sales contract generation

Internet account maintenance

email system and CTI integration and process

Wireless

Sales calendar

Multi-platform data synchronization

(c) Telemarketing/ telesales function

Call planning

Call lists assembly

Dynamic branch scripting

Call history and statistics

Auto-dialing

Productivity and performance analysis

Literature fulfillment

(d) Lead management function

Internet lead generation

Lead enhancement

Routing to partners

(e) Marketing function

Campaign planning and budgeting

Marketing event management

Marketing encyclopedia

Content management and literature material

Database marketing

Campaign ROI analysis

Customer retention

Word processor integration

(f) Services function

Service call management

Incident analysis
Incident assignment and escalation
Incident tracking
Multiple issues per incident
Self-service
Warranty and contract management
Order tracking
Solutions repository
Service calendar
Quality management
Customer feedback system and satisfaction survey
Cross-sell and up-sell

(g) eCommerce
Order catalog
Interactive advisor
Auction management
Order configurator
Shopping cart
Online ordering
emailed order confirmation

(h) Business intelligence
Reporting—standard and ad hoc
List management
Dashboard
Alerts and alarms scheduling
Real-time productivity monitoring

**Table 3.9 CRM Functional Requirements: Sales**

| Item | Description | Available | Configured | Upgraded | Third-Party | Absent | |
|---|---|---|---|---|---|---|---|
| (a) | **Sales Channel Management** | | | | | | |
| 1 | Does the CRM Support territory management? | | | | | | |
| 2 | Does the system provide support for territory realignment or reassignment? | | | | | | |
| 3 | Does the CRM provide the ability to identify channel partners? | | | | | | |
| 4 | Does the system support/help in developing a profile of the desired channel? | | | | | | |
| 5 | Does it help in identifying channel requirements by matching desired with existing channel coverages? | | | | | | |
| 6 | Does it help in identifying channels resource requirements (by matching desired with existing channel resources) and the enablers to bridge thee gaps? | | | | | | |
| 7 | Does the system provide fcr a Geographical Information System (GIS) for mapping out the existing channels? | | | | | | |
| 8 | Does the CRM provide facilities for management of a distribution policy, strategic partnering guidelines, channel partner review policy, and other information generated by internal sources? | | | | | | |
| 9 | Does it provide a facility to create joint agreements/programs in conformance with the predefined agreement standards, methods, and procedures and furnish the requisite information for the same? | | | | | | |
| 10 | Does it provide the capability to (or interface with another application to) set up contracts, manage a contract against objectives, monitor/manage contract consumption, set up payment schedules, and manage terms? | | | | | | |
| 11 | Does it provide support for project planning and administration to ensure timely fulfillment of these requirements? | | | | | | |

**Table 3.9 CRM Functional Requirements: Sales (*Continued*)**

| Item | Description | Available | Configured | Upgraded | Third-Party | Absent |
|---|---|---|---|---|---|---|
| 12 | Does the CRM enable evaluating performances of individual channels on selected measurement criteria? | | | | | |
| 13 | Does it provide maintaining a repository for performance objectives against these channel partner agreements and provide performance analysis? | | | | | |
| 14 | Does the CRM provide for ready read-only access to a channel partner and write access to the enterprise product catalogs and related information? | | | | | |
| 15 | Does the system provide for management of external information from external sources such as governmental regulations, service bulletins, documents, and spreadsheets? | | | | | |
| 16 | Does it provide for electronic distribution of collateral materials (including product and pricing information) through fax on demand or automated voice response? | | | | | |
| 17 | Does the system make online product-related information accessible to employees and channel partners in the form of their choice (viz/ audio, video, or multimedia)? | | | | | |
| 18 | Does the CRM support forecasting of sales by product, customer segment, and promotional campaign and track the actual sales results against the forecast by sales region, sales manager, sales person, or any other user-defined criteria? | | | | | |
| 19 | Does it trend actuals, campaign management, advertising and sales events, and identify potential future shortfalls? | | | | | |
| 20 | Does it track variance on sales discounts, margins, and so on as well as identify any correlation between compatible and/or mutually exclusive products and services? | | | | | |
| 21 | Does the system predict the most effective sales method for a particular market, product, and/or promotion? | | | | | |
| 22 | Does it provide the capability to evaluate, on a continuous basis, the relative success of the sales channel by tracking the conversion leads/prospects into customers and the associated sales events? | | | | | |

**Table 3.9 CRM Functional Requirements: Sales (*Continued*)**

| Item | Description | Available | Configured | Upgraded | Third-Party | Absent |
|---|---|---|---|---|---|---|
| 23 | Does the CRM provide the capability to assign and track sales quotas and sales performance by region, by sales person, channel, or product/service? | | | | | |
| 24 | Does the system provide for numerous details on rebates, such as special price agreement costs, rebate amounts, and volume discounts? | | | | | |
| 25 | Does it provide support for suppliers sponsored bonus/special supplier incentives to a singular or multiple recipients? | | | | | |
| 26 | Does the system provide for calculating commissions, gross margins, and related rebates at sales, person, region, or enterprise level? | | | | | |
| 27 | Does it support payment and reporting on commissions period over a predetermined period (weekly, monthly, and quarterly) to sales people or distribution channels/agents? | | | | | |
| 28 | Does the system support in-depth reporting on amount and timeliness of bills collected in respect to actual and estimated sales? | | | | | |
| 29 | Does it track receivables versus sales performance measurement by commission with number of sales, revenue per customer, margin per customer, customer service, and so on? | | | | | |
| 30 | Does the system provide sales performance measurement by commission with number of sales, revenue per customer, margin per customer, customer service, and so on? | | | | | |
| 31 | Does the CRM analyze channel data for fraud detection and reduce commissions for bad debt, returns, and so on? | | | | | |
| 32 | Does it track and store historical data to help in devising a future commissions plan for different market segments, products, and services? | | | | | |
| 33 | Does it produce an accounts payable (A/P) transaction file with data on commissions, bonus/special supplier incentives, rebates, and so on, for interfacing with the accounting system. | | | | | |
| **(b)** | **Sales Campaigns Management** | | | | | |
| 1 | Does the CRM support the collection and analysis of standard and segment-specific information to assist in the selection and evaluation of marketing materials and of media selection and placement? | | | | | |

**Table 3.9 CRM Functional Requirements: Sales (*Continued*)**

| Item | Description | Available | Configured | Upgraded | Third-Party | Absent | |
|---|---|---|---|---|---|---|---|
| 2 | Does the system help in identifying campaigns by matching desired objectives with results of earlier campaign? | | | | | | |
| 3 | Does it assist in planning, monitoring, assessing, and analyzing the effectiveness of a campaign? | | | | | | |
| 4 | Does it provide facilities to define the type of campaign plan, the eligibility rules, campaign conditions, and the campaign components for both the customer and the sales person or agent? | | | | | | |
| 5 | Does it analyze competitive pricing options in support of the objectives of a campaign plan by utilizing internal and external data? | | | | | | |
| 6 | Does the system provide facilities for automatic selection of the channel to be used (face-to-face, phone, IVR, fax, or Internet)? | | | | | | |
| 7 | Does the CRM provide for detection of customers ineligible for specific campaigns and discounts (depending on prior discounts being availed by the customer), and determine alternative options? | | | | | | |
| 8 | Does the CRM provide the ability to track total revenue from customers over monthly, yearly, and customer lifetime periods, awards, and bonus point programs? | | | | | | |
| 9 | Does the system have facilities to identify "at risk" customers through "early warning" signs such as returns, customer service enquiries, and/or significant decreases in purchasing? | | | | | | |
| 10 | Does it provide facilities to access the desirability of maintaining an "at risk" customer based on the corresponding payment history, profitability, and projected LTV of the customer? | | | | | | |
| 11 | Does the system identify customers who have stopped purchasing products and services for "win back" considerations? | | | | | | |
| 12 | Does it generate a retention call and/or survey distribution to valuable but "at risk" customers to gauge the degree and reasons for dissatisfaction. | | | | | | |
| 13 | Does the system provide for undertaking win-back programs and special campaigns for selected valuable customers? | | | | | | |

**Table 3.9 CRM Functional Requirements: Sales (*Continued*)**

| Item | Description | Available | Configured | Upgraded | Third-Party | Absent |
|---|---|---|---|---|---|---|
| (c) | **Opportunity Management** | | | | | |
| 1 | Does the CRM provide for capturing all sales leads and all associated criteria? | | | | | |
| 2 | Does the CRM provide facilities for opportunity management using a variety of methods including logging in a lead, generating a lead from customer history, or validating the lead from third-party sources? | | | | | |
| 3 | Does the system provide for qualifying, profiling, categorizing, and prioritizing of leads for effective and efficient opportunity management? | | | | | |
| 4 | Does the CRM support the selection and evaluation of direct marketing material as well as the corresponding target customers? | | | | | |
| 5 | Does the system provide automated generation and distribution of product information to target customer segments? | | | | | |
| 6 | Does it provide support for numerous methods of selling to customers including Direct Sales, Telemarketing, Internet, and IVR? | | | | | |
| 7 | Does it provide facilities for integrated team selling including Head Office Sales Managers, Area Office Sales Officers, and Channel Partner Sales Managers? | | | | | |
| 8 | Does it support territory assignment to various members of the sales team including Area Manager, Territory Manager, Channel Partner Sales Person, and so on? | | | | | |
| 9 | Does the CRM provide the ability to search for customers within proximity of a channel partner of the enterprise? | | | | | |

**Table 3.9 CRM Functional Requirements: Sales (*Continued*)**

| Item | Description | Available | Configured | Upgraded | Third-Party | Absent |
|---|---|---|---|---|---|---|
| 10 | Does the system predict potential customers for an existing product/new product or service? | | | | | |
| 11 | Does the system provide facilities for automatically assigning leads to appropriate sales persons based on geographical location, type of customer, vendor, and so on? | | | | | |
| 12 | Does the system support contact profiles (public addresses, phone numbers, information sent or received, calls, sales visits) for all contacts including leads, prospects, existing customers, and previous customers? | | | | | |
| 13 | Does the CRM provide the facility to capture opportunity profiles (including status), summarize opportunity status, and view pipelines across the territory? | | | | | |
| 14 | Does the system provide the ability to prioritize opportunities? | | | | | |
| 15 | Does it provide the ability to track and display a customer's contact history across all channels? | | | | | |
| 16 | Does the CRM have the ability to generate a "to do" list from the contact history and also have the activities assigned automatically or manually? | | | | | |
| 17 | Does it provide the ability to automatically notify the sales persons of expected future activity? | | | | | |

**Table 3.9 CRM Functional Requirements: Sales (*Continued*)**

| Item | Description | Available | Configured | Upgraded | Third-Party | Absent |
|---|---|---|---|---|---|---|
| (d) | **Sales Management** | | | | | |
| 1 | Does the CRM assist in identifying the offering (products and services) to fit the customer's needs on the basis of captured information? | | | | | |
| 2 | Does the system provide an "offering configurator" to fit the customer's need based on captured information? | | | | | |
| 3 | Does it provide for the development of requirements for selling compatible products and services (i.e., Up-sell/cross-sell offerings)? | | | | | |
| 4 | Does the system provide templates for proposals/quotes, opportunity/call allocation report, call report for sales person, route plan report for sales person, expense report for sales person, and so on? | | | | | |
| 5 | Does it provide for customizations of these templates? | | | | | |
| 6 | Does the system provide for the generation of proposal/quotation incorporating the relevant customer, product, pricing, commercial, and statutory information? | | | | | |
| 7 | Does it provide for automatic transposition of the proposal information to the order (in case of receiving a confirmation on the proposal)? | | | | | |
| 8 | Does the system provide facilities for generation of performa invoice or invoice incorporating the relevant customer, product, pricing, commercial, and statutory information? | | | | | |
| 9 | Does the CRM provide for tracking order completion and provide automated notifications of orders that are not completed within a specified due date or within a predefined period? | | | | | |
| 10 | Does it provide ability for notifying a customer of the order status? | | | | | |
| 11 | Does the system provide prompts/alerts for campaign management, opportunity management, proposal/quote generation, product configuration, performa invoice/invoice generation, expected future activities for sales personnel, development of offerings, and so on? | | | | | |

# 3.4 SIGNIFICANT ISSUES TO BE CONSIDERED WHILE EVALUATING CRM

In this section we describe a set of issues that need to be considered while evaluating a CRM.

## 3.4.1 CRM Product Functionality and Features

Just as for a vendor company, a similar exercise would have to be taken for the company's suite of CRM products. Product evaluation criteria would involve queries as illustrated in Table 3.2.

Unlike the traditional computerized systems, which take a data-oriented view of the operations of the company, the enterprise-wide systems primarily emphasize the process-oriented view of the organization. Hence, special attention needs to be paid to ascertain whether the CRM package can configure, support and maintain the business process of the organization.

### *(a) Support for Standard Processes and Best Practices*

Companies that are multi-divisional and multi-located develop differently at different sites and acquire a character of their own at each site that may not fit into a uniform mold across the organization. A CRM package must have the ability to provide a comprehensive functionality to implement such deeply ingrained, differing ways of operations at different locations. It should be able to provide ready-to-use, best practice processes that incorporate such varying ways of executing any business transaction or process.

A standardization of processes usually leads to tremendous gains in terms of maintenance, future upgrades, documentation, training and even routine operations and the administration of the CRM applications system.

### *(b) Support for Customizing the Processes*

This custom support is counter to the general emphasis on standardizing the processes and implementing generic ones. It is a business truism that the survival and success of a company depends on how it differentiates itself and its products or services from those of its competitors. To leverage on their competencies or advantages, companies cannot abandon the corresponding differentiating processes and will have to incorporate such fundamental variants in their CRM implementations.

Therefore, in addition to the best-of-class processes a CRM package must provide a basic framework and philosophy for the customization of processes for a company or even for a different division of the company. As is suggested in Chapter 6, "The Siebel Implementation Project Cycle", a company should rationalize, standardize, and as far as possible use the process configurations that have been made available in Siebel.

Customization requirements could arise because of:

- Country-specific rules and regulations
- State-specific differences, if any
- Country-specific business requirements

- Company-specific business strategy and tactics
- Division and location-specific business and operational requirements

#### *(c) Support for Cinderella Process*

These processes are also known as *exception* processes or *strange* processes. Process scenarios that may result from particular or peculiar circumstances at any moment of time can occur in an organization. Such exceptions can either be treated as erroneous scenarios or be handled as specifically identified exception processes. For instance, occasionally every organization makes or is required to make an exception in the procedures for selection of suppliers, proposals submitted to prospective customers, delivering supplies to defaulting but otherwise loyal customers, releasing of delayed payments, partial payments against unverified invoices, and so on.

Exception processes are major targets for customizations. However, as discussed in relation with customizations earlier, decisions on customizations need to be taken after assessing the resulting complexity in terms of use, training and maintenance of these, and dependent processes.

#### *(d) Support for Application Users*

A CRM package must be able to support and enable access to different kinds of users of the corporate database:

- Connected users—Telesales or call center agents connected via LAN and WAN
- Mobile users—Field sales executives with a local database on their laptops who synchronize with the central database
- Thin client users—Channel partners/dealers who log on to the corporate database via Internet
- Handheld device users—Typically field service engineers with a palm device to manage their field activities
- WAP users—Customers accessing critical information by logging on to the corporate database via mobiles or WAP-enabled devices

## 3.4.2 Vendor Credibility

An organization may select a CRM primarily on the basis of the product credibility to be discussed in the next section. However, the credibility of the vendor company to upgrade and continuously improve its suite of offerings is important because of the rapid changes in the technology and market requirements. The relevant issues are listed in Table 3.1 for reference.

## 3.4.3 CRM Architecture and Technology

The CRM system should been implemented using the latest technology, architecture and methodology. As technology continues to undergo rapid change, the product architecture becomes very important because this enables relevant portions of monolithic packages like Siebel to be upgraded modularly without disrupting the function of the full package.

### *(a) Graphical User Interface (GUI)*

It may seem strange that we are talking about the importance of GUIs, but what are generally accepted standards of GUI functionality today were not available even a few years ago. This was more so for CRM-like solutions where the emphasis tended to be on comprehensive functionality and flexibility to make changes. Basically, the GUIs enable the systems to become more user-friendly by providing and controlling features like:

- Structuring and nesting of menus
- Facilitating cursor movement on the screen
- Navigating between different screens
- Providing context-sensitive help
- Flashing of error messages
- Etc.

With the advent of the Internet the importance of a separable GUI has become even more pronounced.

### *(b) Open System Interfaces and APIs*

Information Technology (IT) developments in the past decade have amply demonstrated the importance of open systems, that is, the need for non-proprietary systems, protocols and interfaces. CRM systems are conceptually easy to understand but very difficult to deliver. Developing such monolithic products at one instance is simply inconceivable. Therefore, CRM architecture and interfaces must permit the evolutionary development of the various components of the CRM system without disrupting its integrated functionality.

CRM systems should permit easy interfacing with legacy systems and other specialized systems like SCM, CRM, Product Development Management (PDM), Automatic Data Recording (ADR), data capturing like bar codes, EDI, computerized telephony, and so on. It is impossible for any vendor to develop a suite of products to address all these functionalities provided by all these systems with the same panache as its core product.

### *(c) Web-based Functionality*

With the growing importance of the Web as a primary medium of interaction and executing transactions, CRMs have to be flexible by design to enable not only business-to-business commerce but also enable personalized interactions with end-customers. The architecture of CRM should permit easy conversions to Web-enabled functionality. In this regard, a CRM like Siebel with a user interface layer, which is separate from the underlying business logic, just like the corresponding database layer, is ready for its functionality to be seen on an Internet browser.

## 3.4.4 CRM Implementation and Use

In CRMs, which are end-user-oriented systems, there is a major emphasis on the ease of implementation and use. This refers especially to the ease of operations and management of the end-users.

### *(a) Ease of Installation*

Although the installation of packages like CRMs are not envisaged to be simple, a systematic and menu-driven facility for installation of the various components of the system is in vogue. But more importantly, the installation application component should make the installation process independent of (say) the operating system.

### *(b) Ease of Configuration*

After the installation, facilities for configuring the system for the existing or envisaged IT infrastructure of the company is very important. The system should have an easily understandable path and method for gathering the company-specific details of the IT infrastructure. Using present empirical models or theoretical models and the information furnished at the various stages, the system should be able to suggest various default values that would define the configuration of the installation for a particular company.

### *(c) Ease of Operations*

The CRM system should provide sample procedures and documentation for routine operations of the system. The system should also provide for automated backup and recovery procedures.

### *(d) Ease of User Management*

CRM being an enterprise-wide and end-user-oriented system must enforce complete control on the access and authorization profiles of its users. Unlike the traditional computerized systems, the number and categories of people who operate the CRM system on a routine basis have undergone a change. It is now operated directly by the end-user operational persons. They create all the business transactions and functions directly on the system or with the help of the CRM system.

The CRM system must provide a judicious mixture of role-oriented and individual-oriented access profiles. This is necessary to cater to the needs of personnel working in rotation on different production shifts during a month.

## 3.4.5 Investments and Budgets

The ratio of the implementation expenses is broadly as follows:

| | | |
|---|---|---|
| (i) | Hardware infrastructure | $x$ |
| (ii) | Siebel license and other software infrastructure | $x$ |
| (iii) | Siebel implementation project | 2 to 3 $x$ |

The breakup of the Siebel implementation project cost could be as follows:

| | |
|---|---|
| External consultants | 35% |
| In-house consultants | 25% |
| Travel and local expenses | 15% |
| Training | 7% |
| Miscellaneous | 13% |
| Contingency | 5% |

For capital equipment, the operating costs that are not directly related to the implementation effort are as follows:

| | |
|---|---|
| Annual maintenance contracts | 10% |
| Depreciation | 20% |

A full CRM package from a vendor like Siebel, Vantive or Nortel's Clarify can cost upwards of $1 million and as much as $3 million; the necessary integration and consulting work can then double that amount.

## 3.4.6 The CRM Infrastructure

An important element that must be considered while evaluating the CRM for an organization is the type and size of the envisaged hardware infrastructure essential for the enterprise-wide operations.

### *(a) Hardware*

This is the central horsepower that is required to drive the functioning of the CRM throughout the enterprise. The nature of CRM will dictate whether this will be a monolithic server or a cluster of servers, each focusing on a part of the envisaged load. The number of computers within the cluster can be based on either the particular functional areas or the sub-locations that are to be served by the cluster as a whole. The sizes of the individual computers may depend upon

- The envisaged processing load of the system
- The number of terminals through which the system will be accessed

### *(b) System Software*

Usually, deciding on the system software is coupled with the selection of the hardware boxes. The operating system environment should have the capability to provide fault-tolerant operations with facilities for automatic backup, mirroring and replication across sites, and automatic failure recovery features.

### *(c) Networking*

Since CRMs are end-user-oriented systems, the usage and load expected on the terminals will be substantial. The network should be able to provide enough throughputs so as not to impair the performance of access at these terminals.

## 3.4.7 The CRM Implementation Time

The time required for implementing a whole suite of CRM applications within an organization, is important. As will be discussed later, this book recommends that for real payoffs from a CRM implementation, an organization should adopt the big-bang strategy of implementing all the Siebel modules that cater to the company's sales and marketing operations. This includes basic modules like sales, contact and account management, telesales/ call centers, marketing, campaign management, service, support, and so on.

The CRM project duration is dependent upon the characteristics of the company such as its cultural, organizational and technical readiness, as well as on the innate complexity of the CRM product. The cultural readiness of an organization is dependent upon its vision for the future as well as its willingness to embrace change towards that end. The organizational readiness has to do with the management's commitment, empowerment of the employees, streamlined systems and procedures, standardized processes, and so on. Technical readiness deals with the maturity of the infrastructure for hardware and communications, training, help desks, office automation, groupware, and so on.

The complexity of CRM products arises because of the multiple demands for comprehensiveness as well as flexibility of customization. When implementing CRM it becomes critical to have prior familiarity with the functionality provided by the CRM system. In an integrated system, any wrongly configured process may have adverse and unforeseen effects on processing in some other related function. And this may not be detected until a rigorous integration-testing phase of the implementation or worse, when the system is in actual production! Consequently, the effort to identify the all-functional gaps between the required and available functionality, coupled with the effort required to configure the resulting processes in an integrated CRM package, leads to comparatively longer implementation times.

## 3.5 SUMMARY

This chapter introduced the concept and criteria for evaluating a CRM package that is suitable for the requirements of a company. The chapter discussed the anatomy of a CRM system by sub-dividing it into five major parts, namely, application maintenance, user-interface related, application management related, applications support related and miscellaneous. After considering the basic characteristics of a full-featured CRM system, the chapter discussed aspects related to preparation of a business case for the implementation of a CRM system like Siebel. We then considered in detail various checklists for ascertaining several issues related to vendor, product, technology, installation and operations, integration and interface, modification and maintenance, audit and control, and standards and documentation. Following this we dwelt on the functional requirements expected of the envisaged CRM system. In the last part of this chapter we discussed other significant dimensions of a CRM system that are essential for any enterprise-wide customer-centric solution.

Chapter 4

# CRM Selection

## 4.1 SIEBEL FOR THE MID-MARKET ENTERPRISES (MME)

The majority of companies that will be implementing enterprise resource planning (CRM) systems in the millennium will be the Mid-Market Enterprises (MMEs). MMEs are usually defined as companies that have revenues ranging from $250 million to $1 billion. These companies have modest IT/ IS resources and budgets and are expected to benefit the most from implementing off-the-shelf application products like CRMs. This is because they do not have the depth of experience and a constant availability of adequate expertise to be able to handle the in-house development of an enterprise-wide system.

Like the large enterprises within their markets, MMEs are impacted by the rapidly changing market-place and their own ability to respond to these changes. CRMs provide MMEs with a platform to address the competitive demands of the marketplace and be successful in terms of

- Improved customer responses and experience
  - Increase customer satisfaction
  - Improve communications
- Improved customer relations and management
  - Consolidate critical information about each customer
  - Target the most profitable customers and develop programs to increase their loyalty to your company
  - Virtually eliminate the possibility of prospects or customers 'falling through the cracks' of an obsolete or overloaded system
  - Yield faster and more accurate follow-up on sales leads, referrals and customer inquires
  - Personalize the service and product offerings to each customer
  - Boost the revenue per salesperson and territory performance, while reducing both cost per lead and cost of closed business expenses
  - Give top managers a detailed and accurate picture of all sales and marketing activities
- Improved quality sales

  - Improve sales effectiveness
  - Improve sales management
  - Support team selling
- Improved margins and reduced buying and using costs
  - Reduce sales costs
  - Improve forecasts
  - Increase revenues
  - Effective channel management
- Reduced product development time
- Reduced manpower for routine operations

CRM implementations in MME enterprises also need a completely different type of skills set as compared to the implementation of the same system in a Fortune 500 company. We will touch upon this aspect again in Appendix A.

## 4.2 THE CRM SELECTION PROCESS

The objective of a systematic selection of CRM is to optimize the benefits for the organization. Careful selection to acquire the most acceptable enterprise-wide system is important as it has a salutary effect on the overall acceptability, usefulness, cross-functionality and collaboration within the customer-centric enterprise.

An enterprise must select the most suitable CRM system based on the pre-defined, predetermined and pre-agreed criteria of evaluation. The process should follow the organizational policies and procedures in reaching the final decision.

The use of checklists for such purposes has proved especially valuable. We discussed a handful of checklists in Chapter 3, "The CRM Evaluation", to evaluate the different characteristics of the CRM systems. These checklists should be supplemented or altered depending on the requirements of the organizations. It is important however, to use such checklists because it helps in focusing discussions on issues that matter objectively. Later in this chapter we will discuss using metrics to compare CRMs.

The process of selecting a CRM system for a customer-centric enterprise involves the following steps.

(i) Establish the CRM selection team (discussed later in section "The Selection Team").

(ii) Establish the functional requirements of the envisaged customer-centric enterprise-wide system (discussed in detail in Chapter 3, sub-section "Checklists for CRM Functional Requirements").

(iii) Search and screen for prospective CRM systems.

(iv) Prepare detailed checklists of different class characteristics in order of priority, such as necessary, desirable, good-to-have and great-to-have. This can be cued from the list of features available from the CRM vendors (see Table 4.1).

**Table 4.1 Sample List of Features for Architecture (from Oracle Siebel)**

| | Description Characteristics |
|---|---|
| 1. General Architecture Characteristics | Extensible<br>Multi-tiered<br>Object-oriented<br>Component architecture<br>Multiple language support<br>Rapid application development<br>Internet-enabled<br>Multiple deployment technologies<br>Global enterprise support<br>Compliance with important standards<br>Graphical configuration<br>Open application programming interfaces<br>Enterprise-class scalability and performance |
| 2. Global Enterprise Support | Multiple language support<br>Externalized message strings<br>Bi-directional character display support<br>Euro currency support<br>Multi-lingual list of values |
| 3. Standards Compliance | Microsoft COM<br>CORBA<br>Microsoft IE4<br>Netscape 4<br>Crypto-2 security |
| 4. Rapid Application Customization | Powerful, extensible object classes<br>Graphical development tool<br>Base-of-class functionality provided in repository<br>Metadata repository<br>Integrated scripting language<br>Multi-developer tools<br>Object versioning and modification control |
| 5. Component Architecture | In-process objects<br>Lightweight, server or client-based<br>Support re-usability<br>Published application program interfaces<br>Accessible from Web page editors |
| 6. Open Application Programming Interfaces | COM compliant<br>CORBA compliant<br>Intuitive methods<br>Common events exposed |
| 7. Automatic Object Up grader | Automatic repository upgrade<br>Three-way object definition evaluation |

| | |
|---|---|
| | Retains user customizations<br>Business rules used to define upgrade behavior<br>Upgrade behavior can be overridden |
| 8. Web-based n-tiered Architecture | Well-defined layers<br>Applet layer for user interface control<br>Applets re-usable in multiple views<br>Applet manager support multiple applet technologies simultaneously<br>Support Java, ActiveX, HTML, Netscape plug-in<br>Configurable business object support<br>Data manager abstraction from physical database<br>Ability to deploy without persistent software |

(v) Screen the available CRM products that most nearly meet the agreed criteria against the necessary requirements that have been established. The company can also partner with the vendor companies at this stage by issuing an RFP based on the finalized checklists.

(vi) Evaluate the resulting shortlist of CRM products against the detailed desirable requirements like those presented in Chapter 3, "CRM Evaluation".

(vii) Select the few remaining CRM systems for demonstrations, site visits and hands-on trials.

(viii) Direct and help the vendors to conduct script tests and stress tests and report on the results of these tests using the same test data provided by the company to all of the CRM vendors.

(ix) Conduct a comparison and rating of the various CRMs using metrics by compiling, collating and analyzing the submitted information.

(x) Compile the findings of the product ratings and test reports with special emphasis on the cost of installing and operating the CRM, the timeframe for implementing the package, the experience and strength of the vendor, and the risks associated with each of the alternative CRMs.

(xi) Prepare the recommendations report to the management.

A systematic and metrics-based approach would not render the decision process as foolproof, but it would help to make the decision clearer. The recommendation report will give clear descriptions of how the CRM systems were rated, for what reasons and how the selection decision was reached. At a later stage, others can know the principal points that were considered and why certain CRM systems were rejected while others were considered more suitable. This approach leaves a clear "audit trail" of the route taken in the decision-making process used for the final selection of the CRM for the organization.

## 4.3 THE SELECTION TEAM

Implementation of enterprise-wide systems like Siebel can be successful only when all stakeholders are willing participants in such an effort. To ensure the future interest and involvement of all concerned it is essential that all stakeholders and their views should be properly represented and incorporated during the planning, organizing, executing and managing the implementation of the CRM system. In the MME enterprise, the mistakes committed while implementing computerized systems in the last century should be avoided. In the remaining part of this section we will discuss the important constituents of the selection team.

### *(a) Functional Team*

This team is the major constituent of the selection team. Its members should consist of senior officers who are knowledgeable about the company's business operations, manufacturing technology, competencies and the competitive gaps. Since the CRM implementation projects are user-driven, involving the functional team members in the evaluation and selection phase is the best prescription for ownership during the implementation of the selected package. They should preferably be members who have participated in similar customer-centric enterprise-wide performance improvement efforts like TQM, BPR, BPM, and so on.

### *(b) Technical Team*

The members of this team should have extensive experience at least in the traditional application development and implementation projects. They should be familiar with conventional development environments and the traditional methodologies employed during the Software Development Life Cycle (SDLC). They should be perceptive of the rationale for deploying CRM solutions in the organization and the reasons for the implementation project to be driven and led by the functional users.

### *(c) Technology Team*

The members of this team should be conversant with the latest hardware, networking issues and solutions. They should be familiar with issues of portability, scalability and interoperability. They need to be aware of the latest standards and protocols to make an informed judgment on the infrastructure issues for the CRM implementation within the organization. They must be comfortable with issues of compatibility, upgrade paths, network traffic on LANs and WANs, and estimating systems loads and system responses.

Technology team members should also be familiar with solutions for backup, archival and disaster recovery systems. The members of this team need to be conversant with site preparation, cabling, installation, maintenance and support requirements for the CRM system installation.

### *(d) Commercial Team*

The members of this team need to be conversant with the issues of negotiating with vendors, signing commercial contracts, defining deliverables and milestones, laying out acceptance criteria and approval procedures, performance guarantees, payment terms, legal liabilities, licensing procedures, upgrades and releases, regulatory issues and taxes, and so on.

## 4.4 CRM CORE SELECTION METHODOLOGY

As CRM fundamentally implements a process-driven customer-centric enterprise, the selection of processes for implementation is of primary significance. The selection team will make its choice depending on how easily the CRM can implement the process considered critical for the company operations. It will depend upon the flexibility with which the system implements the business processes of interest to the organization.

### *(a) Process Selection*

This involves systematically compiling all processes and variants that are prevalent within the organization. These could be processes at every level within the organization, irrespective of whether it has been computerized or not. Compared with the financial systems (generally defined by FASB) and manufacturing systems (generally defined by MRP II) the processes used in sales, marketing, customer service and other parts of the customer life cycle are not very well-established.

### *(b) Enterprise Process Mapping*

This involves painstakingly mapping a selection of processes that are considered critical for the business operations of the company. It entails detailing each process in terms of its name, purpose, responsible owner, process description (including inputs and outputs), quality and efficiency, sub-processes, interfaces with other functions and systems, exceptional conditions, areas for improvement, impact analysis of suggested scenarios, and so on. This compilation of process mapping is helpful in preparing the script tests. The topic of process mapping is discussed in detail in Chapter 7, "Siebel and the Business Process Management".

### *(c) Script Tests*

Script tests are process scenarios that have to be demonstrated by the vendor in the product licenses. These tests are a handful of process scenarios that are considered especially critical for the business operations and are not easily configurable within the standard functionality provided by the CRM systems.

The approach recommended for handling these specifically identified processes indicates the robustness, depth and inherent flexibility of the CRM systems. CRM systems may have the following approaches for mapping a process within the package:

- Provide it as a basic or standard functionality
- Suggest a workaround for achieving the same functionality and configure it accordingly
- Indicate if this functionality is to be introduced in the next scheduled release of the system
- Suggest third-party add-ons or plug-ins that provide the desired functionality and have been qualified for compatibility with the concerned CRM
- Program the required functionality in the CRM system by developing the same in the 3GL/ 4GL native to the CRM system

CRMs that can accommodate such processes, even if these are achieved only by resorting to workarounds, are preferable to others where the only options are to either wait for these functionalities to be addressed, possibly in the next released version of the system, or for the company to customize the package itself by programming such functionality directly into the system.

### *(d) Stress Test*

This is similar to the stress test administered for traditional systems. This involves estimating the load anticipated in the production environment and simulating the same in the test environment to ascertain whether the suggested configuration can handle the expected load. This test can involve predictable volumes of data in the database, transaction throughputs on the LAN/ WAN, or interactive sessions on the terminals serviced by the central servers. Industry-level benchmarks for the relevant areas should be used for reporting on the observed performances. This could be a full-scale test conducted on the company site or at the technology demonstration centers of the concerned vendor.

## 4.5 CRM VENDORS AND PRODUCTS

CRM is a customer-focused business strategy designed to optimize profitability, revenue and customer satisfaction. To improve business processes associated with selling, servicing and marketing, enterprises across a number of industries are launching CRM initiatives. To realize CRM enterprises must implement collaborative processes and technologies that support customer interactions throughout all channels. The problem is that many of those software vendors provide only single-function-focused or single-channel-focused offerings and are often not strong in each of the three domains relevant to CRM.

Most CRM packages are targeted at three types of companies:

- Enterprise, with more than 500 employees
- Mid-market, with between 100 to 500 employees, and
- Small businesses with less than 100 employees

By about 1994, CRM had clearly been identified as the emerging market with a great potential. Siebel and Pivotal emphasized sales management aspects while Vantive, Clarify, Onyx and Remedy developed customer service applications. Newer entrants such as BroadVision and Silknet concentrated on e-commerce. Since then all of the leading vendors have undergone significant consolidation by moving towards a model of an all-encompassing system that covers all functional areas and all customer interaction channels and touch points.

The major players like Siebel, Vantive, Clarify, Oracle and SAP have been targeting the enterprise and are moving slowly into the mid-market area by reason of its great growth potential. Other vendors such as Onyx, Pivotal, Remedy and Applix, who are typically associated with the mid-market, are trying to capture some of the enterprise market. Finally, vendors such as Goldmine and SalesLogix target the small enterprises by providing a one-stop shop for a spectrum of functionalities.

### 4.5.1 Application Suites or Best-in-class

### *(a) Suite of Applications*

An integrated application suite is a set of applications that employs a common architecture, referencing a common logical database with a single schema. Some suites are more of an interfaced application bundle, that is, a set of interfaced applications from a single vendor containing more than one technical architecture, or more than one logical database, frequently assembled by the vendor through the process of acquisition or partnership. This approach attempts to standardize on a single vendor's application suite and compromise on functionality that is good enough for minimum requirements but engenders the disadvantageous of vendor lock-in.

Adherents of the single vendor suite approach are primarily motivated by cost and risk avoidance, believing that delivered integration and the requirement of a single set of IT skills outweigh tradeoffs in the timing, breadth and depth of the business process functionality. But application suites turn out to be quite difficult and expensive to implement or upgrade. The engineered complexities of suites can lessen the benefits of delivered integration in many cases. In a few extreme cases when implementation and upgrades are not planned properly or when companies lack adequately trained resources in vendor-specific IT skills, such projects can potentially de-stabilize a company.

Finally, suite vendors are even more challenged while addressing the requirements of inter or cross-customer-centric enterprise collaborative activities that are becoming pervasive with the advent of Internet. Getting a customer-centric enterprise to standardize on a single vendor's application suite is fairly difficult, but to get an entire value chain to adopt and standardize on a proprietary set of applications and interfaces is highly impossible.

### *(b) Integrated Best-in-class Applications*

An alternative approach to suites is an interfaced best-in-class or best-of-breed solution—an approach whereby an enterprise selects from multiple vendors a set of applications that must be interfaced to work together, either by the enterprise, one of the selected vendors or a third-party integrator. Customer-centric enterprises select the applications because they best meet the particular needs. Such process-specific applications generally lead in the areas of time-to-market, and the breadth and depth of functionality, especially for industry-specific processes. The benefits of this approach are:

- Streamlining operating cycles on high volume business processes
- Reducing processing and inventory costs
- Improving compliance with contracts
- Enhancing collaboration whilst strengthening long-term relationships with strategic trading partners

The downside of this approach is the higher effort and cost of integration. The challenge with this approach is that in some cases, the enterprise fails to complete the necessary interfaces to get the individual applications working together; consequently, the applications remain stovepipes.

Thus, this approach attempts to deploy state-of-the-art application functionality from multiple vendors at a markedly increased cost of integration. A variation on this theme, called 'the best-of-cluster' is similar to best-of-class except that instead of individual applications, suites or bundles are interfaced.

## 4.5.1.1 Component-based Architectures

A component-based architecture can eliminate the customary tradeoff between best practice functionality and large integration, and ongoing support costs. A standards-based architecture provides a unified framework on which componentized applications from multiple vendors can be easily and cost-effectively:

- deployed and distributed across servers on heterogeneous networks
- integrated directly with the logic layer of other component-based applications

- extended to support customer-specific business processes
- upgraded individually

Because the business components share and open common programming standards, they can communicate with other similar components by exchanging messages, whether located on the same memory space or distributed across a network. Each component is self-identifying and self-contained, and is wrapped with communications, event handling, relationship management and data validation services. Functions, objects or data located within one component can be accessed and re-used by another. This also enables it to be better positioned to take advantage of the shift to Web services (see next sub-section).

Component-based solutions rely on application servers to deliver robust scalability and apportion the functionality into several self-contained units of business process. Encapsulating business logic in components and delivering it through an open interface allows companies to deploy and integrate functionality very systematically. Such rolling deployments speed up time to payback and minimize upgrade expenses by shortening both the planning cycles and extended implementations that are usually associated with traditional upgrades. Componentization also enhances the company's ability to extend or modify a particular business functionality without disrupting the other applications' data structures and process flows. By eliminating direct exposure to or interaction with data elements of a component, component-based solutions like Siebel make it easier for companies to link not only with their other internal processes but also with those of their partners. Such flexibility facilitates easy access to market-leading functionality and process and can make the entire value chain more responsive to the market conditions. Moreover, such flexibility can better position a company to meet the challenges of rapidly changing business requirements resulting from rapid growth, process re-engineering and M&As (mergers and acquisitions).

#### 4.5.1.2 Applications as Web Services

Web services are new standards for creating and delivering cooperative applications over the Internet. Web services allow applications to communicate irrespective of the platform or the operating system. By using Web services developers can eliminate major porting and quality testing efforts, potentially saving millions of dollars. They will radically change the way that applications are built and deployed in the future.

Please refer to Chapter 17, sub-section "Application Functionality as Web Services".

### 4.5.2 Large Enterprieses

This cateegory comprises vendor solutions primarily targeted toward organizations with revenues of more than $1 billion per year and/ or more than 1000 employees. CRM vendors focused on the enterprise-class organizations typically offer a full range of functionalities, can scale to serve large user populations, and offer support for multiple languages and countries. They offer their products primarily through the traditional on-premise license model. However, hosted and SaaS (software-as-a-service) deployment options are now offered by several of the leading players. Oracle offers Siebel On Demand and SAP Business By Design. The typical cost paid by large enterprises for products from such vendors as Oracle's Siebel and PeopleSoft CRM, and SAP CRM is about $2500 and higher per user.

Oracle's CRM product lines, specifically its Siebel CRM are market leading solutions in almost every aspect of the CRM technology. Oracle strategically positions Siebel CRM as the most fully-featured solution with a breadth and depth of functionality for many industry verticals. SAP CRM strategy is closely linked to the success of its enterprise applications portfolio; SAP CRM customers benefit from the enormous depth of industry expertise accumulated in the past in its products and the group as a whole. Similarly, Oracle's eBusiness Suite (EBS) CRM and PeopleSoft CRM are also good options for the respective ERP customers. Oracle EBS or PeopleSoft CRM customers benefit from the ease of integration into the rest of the Oracle EBS or PeopleSoft suites. Both products offer strong capabilities across most of the CRM functionalities including marketing, sales, service, field service and partner channel management. However, both SAP CRM and Oracle Siebel CRM implementations are characterized by comparatively lengthy time-to-value, relative inflexibility for changing business processes and higher costs.

#### 4.5.2.1 Oracle Siebel CRM

Siebel remains the key market shareholder in technology-enabled selling and is a leader in large enterprise customer service and support, making it the only front office suite vendor with a dominant position in two of the three front office domains. Siebel also provides solutions tailored to the following verticals—automotive, public sector, communications, consumer goods, apparel and footwear, energy, finance, insurance, healthcare, pharma and retail.

**Table 4.2 Industry-specific CRM Requirements**

| Industry | Applications/Functionality |
|---|---|
| Commercial Banking | Contact center, profitability analysis, integrated target marketing, data mining |
| High Technology | Full field sales, e-sales, reseller extranets, contract management, blended sales and service contact center, integrated field service, sales commission management, bottom up/ top down forecasting |
| Insurance | Blended sales and service contact center with Web integration, consumer credit checking and lease underwriting process |
| Telecom | Blended sales and service contact center, competitive pricing analysis, integration with billing system, churn management |
| Utilities | Integrated customer service and support call center and field service, integration with billing system |
| Consumer Goods | Category management, trade promotions, demand planning, interactive selling |
| Manufacturing | Bottom up/ top down forecasting, available and capable to promise sales data, supply chain integration |
| Pharmaceuticals | Contract management, portable marketing analysis, regulatory compliance |
| Retail | E-tailing, space planning, merchandizing, integration with point-of-sale systems |

In addition to Oracle Siebel CRM for enterprise customers, the product family also includes Oracle's Siebel On Demand and Oracle's Siebel Professional Edition for the mid-market. The Siebel product for enterprise-class customers has achieved best-of-breed status for most CRM functionalities, with the exception of customer service and e-commerce. It also boasts good industry vertical adaptations. However, it faces the challenges arising out of application complexity, high cost and lengthy implementation. The product is best suited for buyers who value advanced functionality tailored for specific industries, customer insight through strong analytics and customer data management, and the ability to support global organizations. For instance, Siebel CRM's superior analytics enable closed-loop analysis delivering marketing management metrics that can optimize the customer's marketing strategy.

> Oracle also plans to integrate its CRM product lines through Applications Unlimited, Application Integration Architecture and Fusion Strategies (see Appendix E "Oracle Fusion Architecture").

### 4.5.2.2 SAP CRM

SAP has steadily built up comprehensive functionality in the SAP CRM product. Most recently, the company has focused on improving usability and deepening support for strategic business processes as part of the SAP Business Suite. SAP CRM is particularly strong in sales, marketing, partner channel management and analytics but offers less support for customer data management requirements. The product can scale to support global deployments and offers many industry-specific process solutions. The SAP CRM SaaS offering provides more deployment flexibility, while cost, complexity, and lengthy implementations schedules remain drawbacks of the on-premise product. SAP CRM is best suited for global buyers committed to SAP and its ERP platform who need to support end-to-end industry processes.

The SAP customer relationship management (SAP CRM) application provides best-in-class functionality for marketing, sales and service. By supporting customer-facing business processes across multiple interaction channels, SAP CRM enables organizations to focus on strategies for customer-driven growth and to differentiate themselves in the market by providing a superior customer experience.

With its latest release in December 2007, SAP has evolved CRM beyond traditional task automation to a flexible, user-driven, end-to-end business process execution platform. SAP CRM is architected to help companies achieve a complete 360-degree view of customers, which is one of the most critical factors in enabling successful CRM strategy.

### 4.5.2.3 Oracle PeopleSoft CRM

Oracle's PeopleSoft CRM product line has a significant base of loyal customers who value the integration benefits and usability of PeopleSoft's HR and ERP suite. Oracle's Applications Unlimited announcement gives those customers much-needed assurance of continued ongoing support. Oracle's PeopleSoft CRM solution offers a broad range of functionality across all the major components of CRM with particular strengths in sales, customer service and analytics. PeopleSoft's background in human capital management renders PeopleSoft CRM particularly suitable for HR and IT help desk applications. The product has good industry specialization in sectors including higher education, public services and telecommunications and financial services. It is well suited for existing PeopleSoft customers who need a broad-based CRM platform to build upon.

#### 4.5.2.4 Oracle EBS CRM

Oracle's EBS CRM, a comprehensive enterprise application suite, includes a broad range of CRM capabilities. Oracle is also investing heavily in a next generation product strategy, fusion applications, to fully modernize its technology architecture. The EBS CRM solution provides capabilities across all major customer-facing functionalities. It is strong in sales, field service and partner channel management, and has the ability to scale for global deployments. The product is particularly suitable for field-oriented customer services due to excellent field service and depot repair features, and seamless integration with the rest of the Oracle EBS enterprise application suite. EBS CRM is a leading solution in situations where ERP integration is judged as more important than marketing support and customer analytics. EBS CRM is best suited for buyers committed to Oracle infrastructure platform and applications.

#### 4.5.2.5 Salesforce.com

This company is growing quickly by making CRM solutions available through the SaaS deployment model. As with other SaaS vendors the value proposition has found success in the SMB market, which values quick time-to-value, usability and lower upfront costs compared with traditional on-premise solutions. Enterprise-class customers seeking these benefits are increasingly turning to salesforce.com to understand whether SaaS deployment can meet their more complex CRM requirements. As indicated by its name, it is very strong in supporting SFA requirements and recently moved to expand its partner channel management offerings. But other CRM functional capabilities are still relatively underdeveloped. The company's strategy is to fill out its product line using an 'ecosystem' of allies who work through its AppExchange to develop solutions on the salesforce.com platform.

### 4.5.3 Small and Mid-market Enterprises

Mid-size enterprises are defined as those with annual revenues between $200 million and $1 billion, and an overall staff strength of fewer than 1000. CRM vendors in this group also offer a breadth of CRM functionalities but these often have more limited capabilities in specific areas and are simpler to use than solutions built for the enterprise market. These vendors are less suitable for large-scale global deployments. Vendors in this group also offer a variety of deployment options, including on-premise license, hosted and SaaS. Some vendors in this category have upgraded their solutions to be more suitable to enterprise-class buyers and are gaining acceptance in that segment as well. The typical cost of a front office application from a vendor targeting the mid-size enterprise is $600 to $1700 per user.

#### 4.5.3.1 Onyx CRM (now Consona)

Onyx is a leader in mid-market customer service and support solutions. Onyx was one of the first vendors to determine portals as the focus of the various components of their CRM offerings. The portals act as the information aggregators and toolboxes to maximize the efficiency of their target groups, which include internal users, external customers and external partners. All portals employ a common engine that serves to provide data, workflow and integration capabilities.

The Onyx CRM solution was one of the first enterprise CRM solutions to adopt a flexible, three-tier architecture, with tight alignment to Microsoft technologies. The company was acquired by M2M

Holdings in August 2006, which also subsequently acquired Knova to consolidate its product lines under the brand name of Consona. The product's strongest functional areas are in sales and customer service. But it lacks deep functionality in many areas including marketing, field service, customer data management, e-commerce and partner channel management. Onyx is best suited for customers who want a flexible CRM solution incorporating a BPM capability that also leverages Microsoft infrastructure technologies.

Onyx Front Office manages critical customer, prospect and partner information across your entire enterprise. Information is organized around relationships with individuals and companies, not incidents, events and records. User-specific interfaces make it easy to access, share and leverage valuable information for quantifiable returns.

#### 4.5.3.2 Microsoft Dynamics CRM

Microsoft leverages its desktop applications strength in large enterprises and promotes its now more robust business applications to this sector. Customer interest in Microsoft Dynamics 4.0 solutions is high in the SMB market and is growing in the enterprise segment. Enterprise customers that have made a commitment to a Microsoft infrastructure to lower their TCO (Total Cost of Ownership) are attracted to Microsoft Dynamics CRM. Customers also like Microsoft Dynamics CRM usability and its quick time-to-value compared with traditional CRM applications. The product provides basic capabilities in sales, customer service and field service adequately but is weaker in marketing and customer data management. On the other hand, sales force automation, integration and interoperability across the whole suite of products are very strong. But partner channel management and e-commerce capabilities are not very strong, and there are no industry-specific solution sets.

#### 4.5.3.3 RightNow

This company is gaining success by offering a CRM suite solution available through the SaaS deployment model. To date, its value proposition has found success with the SMB market, which values quick time-to-value, strong usability and lower upfront costs compared with traditional on-premise solutions. While the RightNow 8 excels in customer service features, it is perceived as weak in marketing, sales force automation and process automation, and customer analytics. Unlike the other 'on demand' vendors that rely on mass adoption primarily in the mid-market segment, RightNow positions its 'on demand' offerings higher up the market. RightNow's value proposition is also beginning to attract the attention of enterprise-class customers interested in these benefits.

### 4.5.4 CRM Products Comparison

Table 4.3 presents a comparison of CRM systems, namely, Siebel, PeopleSoft, Oracle EBS and Onyx (now Consona).

**Table 4.3 Comparison of Systems**

| Description | Siebel Systems | PeopleSoft | SAP | Oracle | Onyx Software |
|---|---|---|---|---|---|
| **General** | | | | | |
| URL | www.siebel.com | www.peoplesoft.com | www.sap.com | www.oracle.com | www.onyx.com |
| Product Name | Siebel eBusiness Applications 7.5 | PeopleSoft & CRM | MySAP.com | Oracle eBusiness Suite | Onyx Enterprise 2001 |
| Total Sales for 2002 | $205 billion | $207 billion | $6.43 billion | $10.52 billion | — |
| Percentage Growth | 15.0% | 23.9% | — | -.80% | — |
| **Functions/Features** | | | | | |
| Sales campaign management | X | X | X | X | X |
| Opportunity managemet | X | X | X | X | X |
| Sales lead management | X | X | X | X | X |
| Account management | X | X | X | X | X |
| Contact management | X | X | X | X | X |
| Activity tracking | X | X | X | X | X |
| Content management | X | X | X | X | — |
| Status tracking | X | X | X | X | X |
| Marketing campaign management | X | X | X | X | X |
| Loyalty programs | X | X | X | X | — |
| Customer profiling | X | X | X | X | X |

**Table 4.3 Comparison of Systems (*Continued*)**

| Description | Siebel Systems | PeopleSoft | SAP | Oracle | Onyx Software |
|---|---|---|---|---|---|
| Segmentation | X | X | X | X | X |
| Personalization | X | X | X | X | X |
| Analytical capabilities (including mining) | X | X | X | X | X |
| Reporting tools | X | X | X | X | X |
| Workflow automation | X | X | X | X | X |
| Call scripting | X | X | X | X | X |
| Dynamic scripting | X | X | X | X | — |
| field service/dispatch | X | X | X | X | |
| Incentive compensation | X | — | X | X | — |
| Partnership relation Management | X | X | X | X | |
| **Vertical Market Functionality** | | | | | |
| Retail | X | X | X | X | — |
| Distribution | — | X | X | X | — |
| Manufacturing | X | X | X | X | X |
| Financial Services | X | X | X | X | X |
| Hotel/restaurants | — | X | — | — | — |
| Entertainment/gaming | — | = | X | — | — |
| Telecommunications/ utilities | X | X | X | X | |

**Table 4.3 Comparison of Systems (*Continued*)**

| Description | Siebel Systems | PeopleSoft | SAP | Oracle | Onyx Software |
|---|---|---|---|---|---|
| Cable TV/Internet service providers | X | X | X | X | X |
| Other | Automotive, Public sector, Pharma, Insurance, Clinical, Consumer goods | Education and Government | Insurance, consumer products, Public sector, Higher education, Healthcare | | Professional Sports, Software Mfg., Hardware Mfg. |
| **Operating Systems** | | | | | |
| Window 2000 | X | — | X | — | X |
| Window NT | X | X | X | X | X |
| Window XP | — | — | — | — | — |
| Sun Solaris | X | X | X | X | — |
| IBM AIX | X | X | X | — | |
| HP UX | X | X | X | X | — |
| Linux | X | X | X | — | — |
| **Database Offerings** | | | | | |
| Oracle | X | X | X | X | — |
| DB2 | X | X | X | — | — |
| Sybase | X | X | — | — | — |
| Microsoft SQL server | X | X | X | — | X |

**Table 4.3 Comparison of Systems (*Continued*)**

| Description | Siebel Systems | PeopleSoft | SAP | Oracle | Onyx Software |
|---|---|---|---|---|---|
| **Hardware Platform** | | | | | |
| Mainframe | X | X | — | — | — |
| Windows/Intel (Wintel) Industry Standard Architecture | — | X | X | — | X |
| IBM Series | X | X | X | X | — |
| Sun Sparcserver | X | X | X | X | — |
| Hewlett-Packard | X | X | X | X | — |
| **Connectors to ERPs** | | | | | |
| Siebel | X | X | X | X | X |
| SAP | X | X | X | X | X |
| Oracle | X | X | X | X | X |
| PeopleSoft | X | X | X | — | X |
| J.D.Edwards | X | X | X | — | X |
| Other | X | Deliver standard open framework for third-party solutions | SAP's open interface allows it to link to other non-SAP systems | | Great Plan etc. |
| **Wireless Access** | | | | | |
| Links to pagers | X | X | X | — | X |
| Cell phones | — | X | X | X | X |
| Handheld computer | — | X | X | X | X |
| Integration with | | X | X | X | X |
| Fax | X | X | X | X | X |

**Table 4.3 Comparison of Systems (*Continued*)**

| Description | Siebel Systems | PeopleSoft | SAP | Oracle | Onyx Software |
|---|---|---|---|---|---|
| Email | — | X | X | X | X |
| Instant messaging | — | — | X | X | X |
| Web sites | — | X | X | X | X |
| **Middleware** | Yes | Yes | Yes | Yes | Yes |
| **Integration with Marketing data Warehouse** | Yes | Yes | Yes | Yes | Yes |
| **Deliverable through Web-Based ASP** | Yes | Yes | Yes | Yes | Yes |
| **Security** | | | | | |
| Firewalls | X | X | X | X | X |
| Encryption | X | X | X | X | X |
| Password access | X | X | X | X | X |

## 4.6 CRM SELECTION REPORT

When reporting on a selection of systems like CRM, which are large, complex and integrated, functionalities are not very easy to compare. Moreover, the participation of members from different functional areas into the selection team also brings forth widely differing views on every aspect of the envisaged customer-centric enterprise-wide system.

As noted in section "The CRM Selection Process", it is best to state the variables involved as objectively as possible and to apply some sort of measuring scale for each of these variables. A metrics approach is the best way to assign values and resolve disputes. Although the assigned numbers are only comparisons on a relative scale and not actual costs, they help in focusing the discussions more on the specific numbers assigned to definable points. The relative scale or the weighty factors assigned to various aspects can always be reworked until most participants are satisfied with the scale. The resulting conclusions will arise from all such smaller agreements made along the way.

In the next sub-section, we will discuss a metrics approach for comparison of the CRM systems.

### 4.6.1 CRM Systems Comparative Chart

Table 4.4 presents a form that can be used for comparison of CRM systems.

The steps to be used by the selection team for using this form are as follows.

1. Using the information gathered in response to the various criteria for evaluation as suggested in Chapter 3, prepare a list of characteristics that are mutually acceptable as important for the envisaged customer-centric enterprise-wide systems.
2. Place these characteristics in the order of importance as agreed by all the members of the selection team.
3. Decide on which of these characteristics are necessary.
4. Decide on which of these characteristics are desirable.
5. Assign factors on a scale of 1 to 10 for each of the characteristics; the higher the factor is, the more important the characteristic for the envisaged CRM. Characteristics that are considered necessary should definitely be assigned a factor closer to 10, using a scale like the following:

   Vital = 10

   Critical = 9

   Essential = 8

   Significant = 7

   Important = 6

   Mandatory = 5

   Required = 4

   Useful = 3

   Desirable = 2

   Optional = 1

   The actual weights should be decided by consensus.

6. Next, rate the various CRM systems for each of these characteristics on a scale of 1 to 5. Five indicates excellent, while 1 denotes poor or unacceptable A good rule of thumb is to agree on the best package for a particular characteristic and give only that package a rating of 5.

   Excellent/Best = 5

   Remarkable = 4

   Moderate = 3

   Acceptable = 2

   Poor/Worst = 1

   Then agree on ratings for other packages by consensus.
7. Compute the score for each CRM system by each characteristic by multiplying the weighting factor by the corresponding rating as follows:

   Score = Weighting Factor × Rating
8. Total all the scores for each CRM system.

**Table 4.4 Evaluative Comparison of CRM Systems**

| CRM System Characteristics | Weighting Factor | Oracle | Siebel CRM | SAP CRM |
|---|---|---|---|---|
| | | | Rating Score | Rating Score |
| **Technical** | | | | |
| Comprehensive functionality | | | | |
| Ease of use | | | | |
| Extendibility, flexibility and configurability | | | | |
| Ability of customization and modification | | | | |
| Open systems architecture and interfaces | | | | |
| One-point data entry | | | | |
| Data synchronization | | | | |
| Centralized database | | | | |
| Interfacing of other devices, barcodes, EDI, CTI, and so on | | | | |
| Integration with legacy and ERP, SCM, DW and other third-party products | | | | |
| Internationalization and euro compliance | | | | |
| Online documentation and contextual help | | | | |
| Future upgrades and enhancements | | | | |
| Skill transfer and training programs | | | | |
| User's group activity | | | | |
| **Total Score** | | | | |
| **Operational** | | | | |
| Controls and reliability | | | | |
| Ease of installation | | | | |

| |
|---|
| Efficiency of operations |
| Ease of performance tuning |
| Ease of user management |
| Security and authorization |
| Backup and disaster recovery |
| Availability |
| Resource requirements |
| **Total Score** |
| **Financial** |
| System costs |
| Hardware, system software and networking |
| Base license |
| Enhancements |
| Third-party solutions |
| Site preparation |
| Installation |
| Services |
| Staffing |
| Training |
| Implementation consultancy |
| Documentation |
| Travel |
| Communications |
| Maintenance |
| Spread of investment |
| **Total Score** |
| **GRAND TOTAL** |

## 4.6.2 Script and Stress Test Reports

The results of the script test and stress test reports could also be included as one of the characteristics for comparing the CRM systems. This should be considered if the test results vary widely among the various CRM systems.

## 4.6.3 Recommendations Report

The report on the recommendations for the CRM submitted to the company's management should include the following:

- The advantages and disadvantages of the selected CRM system. This would be based on the information collected on evaluation criteria presented in the earlier chapter.

- A detailed profile of Siebel is presented in the next chapter. By the end of the chapter it will be clear as to why Siebel is a clear winner amongst all other CRM systems available on the market today.
- The CRM systems comparative chart.
- The estimate of cost and benefits for the implementation of the CRM. This would be based on the information collected in Table 4.4 for costs of the requisite hardware, system software, CRM software, networking software, installation, training, yearly maintenance, implementation consultancy services, travel, communications, and so on.
- The implementation project schedule with dates of key milestones. An overview of a Siebel implementation project is discussed in Chapter 6, "The Siebel Implementation Project Cycle".
- A recommendation for the approval by the management.

## 4.7 SUMMARY

In this chapter we presented the methodology for selecting the CRM package most suitable for the requirements of a company. We looked at a selection of actual CRM vendors and their products that targeted mainly the large enterprises and SMEs. In the latter part of the chapter we discussed the preparation of the CRM systems comparative chart and the final recommendation report. In the following chapters, we will talk about Siebel and its enterprise and e-business applications products. We will talk in sufficient detail about the architecture, structure and design of Siebel to understand the comprehensiveness and complexity of this system. Chapters 5 through 11 will amply demonstrate why Siebel has been the leading CRM product on the market in the last decade. It will also substantiate to a great extent our claim that Oracle's Siebel CRM will be the CRM system of choice for any customer-centric enterprise in the 21$^{st}$ century.

Chapter 5

# The Oracle Siebel CRM Solution

In this chapter and in the remaining part of the book, we talk in detail about Oracle Corporation's CRM product Siebel. We present the architecture and salient features of the system in sufficient detail to highlight its overwhelming superiority. It will become evident from this and the following chapters that Siebel is indeed the best CRM system on the market today. With its n-tiered distributed architecture, excellent repository-driven development environment and comprehensive componentized business functionality covering all customer-facing functions across several industries, Siebel represents perhaps one of the best software development efforts in recent times.

## 5.1 ORACLE'S SIEBEL DIVISION

Siebel Systems Inc. was taken over by Oracle Corporation in 2005. Siebel Systems, Inc. was founded in 1993 to address the growing need of organizations of all sizes to acquire, retain and better serve their customers. Today, Oracle's Siebel division with sales revenues of $1.79 billion is the world's leading provider of eBusiness applications software, with more than 8000 employees who operate in more than 34 countries. More than 4700 organizations in 107 countries run on Siebel eBusiness applications. By any standards, these are impressive numbers coming from a company that has a great vision and is destined to play a significant role in the Internet-driven markets of this century as well.

Siebel Systems is the world leader in Web-based front office solutions for sales, marketing and customer service. The phenomenal success of Siebel comes from the fact that its systems are comprehensive but at the same time configurable to the specific needs of any company. Companies prefer off-the-shelf packages like Siebel because they are flexible and can be configured to satisfy most requirements of any company in any industry. Siebel can be deployed on various hardware platforms providing the same comprehensive and integrated functionality, flexibility for addressing individual company-specific requirements as well as ensuring independence from specific technologies deployed in the company. Siebel implements a process-oriented view of the extended enterprise.

Siebel ensures success in a number of ways. The closed-loop sales, marketing and customer service solution available from Siebel is one of the most functionally complete solutions in the market. The company also aligns with world class partners that provide certified systems integration, hardware and software solutions. Siebel solutions are designed to enable rapid implementation and customization to unique business requirements; provide for fast application upgrades; provide upwardly compatible enterprise application interfaces; allow for automatic software distribution to mobile, handheld, connected and thin client users; and are easy to administer and support. Siebel also provides a systematic and responsive service and support infrastructure that contributes to the success of each of the Siebel implementation projects.

This chapter understandably banks heavily on the Oracle Siebel's product messages and documentation. At this level, it is not very easy to make objective assessments of Siebel's architecture, strategies and products vis-à-vis other CRM products on the market. Therefore, hereafter this book assumes that Siebel is the pre-eminent CRM solution on the market, which it is! Scores of Siebel features and characteristics are par excellence and need to be applauded. These include Siebel Architecture, Siebel Tools, Siebel Application Customization and Upgrades, Synchronization and Replication, Siebel's lowest Total Cost of Ownership (TCO) and many others.

## 5.2 THE SIGNIFICANCE OF ORACLE SIEBEL CRM

The remaining part of this chapter will provide an overview of the salient features and advantages of Siebel as a CRM system. Although not patterned on our discussions in Chapter 3 "CRM Evaluation" and Chapter 4 "CRM Selection" for the evaluation and selection of a CRM system, it will become evident that Siebel excels in all of these dimensions compared to any other competing product on the market today. This chapter covers the most significant characteristics of the Siebel product and the related services provided by Siebel. More details on aspects like query facilities, reporting facilities, online help, documentation, training, and so on will be covered later in the book.

Siebel 8.x is a fully integrated suite of applications for Customer Relationship Management (CRM) and related applications for Partnership Relationship Management (PRM) and Employee Relationship Management (ERM), all based on a common Web architecture. Siebel helps organizations by providing three key technologies that together enable organizations to fully align their partners, employees and customer touch points, processes and channels around the goal of maximizing the value of customer relationships. These three key technologies are as follows.

### *(a) Customer Relationship Management (CRM)*

Siebel enables organizations to more effectively identify, select, acquire and retain customers. By providing a centralized repository of customer data captured from all customer interactions across all channels and touch points, Siebel enables organizations to maintain an ongoing and seamless dialog with its customers regardless of when, where or how the interactions occur. Companies are able to understand, anticipate and respond to customer needs and are able to do so more effectively and efficiently over time. Siebel gives managers better visibility into market dynamics and customer demand by providing real-time views of customer activity.

### *(b) Employee Relationship Management (ERM)*

Organizations also face the problems of their employees not being fully aligned with the organization's focus on customers. Siebel ERM helps organizations to rapidly communicate the corporate policies and decisions to the entire workforce, mobilize employees to execute those decisions and monitor workforce performance in real-time. As employees are able to perform their job more effectively, organizations benefit from increased employee satisfaction and hence, increased customer satisfaction (as happier and better informed employees provide better customer service).

### *(c) Partner Relationship Management (PRM)*

Siebel eBusiness Applications for PRM allow organizations to manage their business partner's ecosystem as a virtual extension of their sales, marketing and service organizations. Organizations can maximize their partners' efficiency and productivity by ensuring that their partners' incentives, resources and objectives are fully aligned with those of the organization.

By providing organizations with real-time analytical ability to track and understand both customer behavior and key performance indicators of corporate performance, Siebel enables them to be 'digitally wired' to their customers, partners and employees. The result is a total solution enabling organizations to fully focus the resources of their entire company on maximizing the value of their customer relationships. Siebel enables organizations to overcome the five major obstacles that typically thwart its way towards becoming a customer-centric organization. These are as follows.

- Information silos—Organizations have a tendency to get fragmented into silos based on product or line of businesses. This results in the customer data being scattered throughout the organization in a disjointed fashion, which gives a highly fragmented and incomplete view of their customers
- Disconnected channels—The organization lacks the ability to maintain a unified and coordinated interface with the customer across different interactions through different channels. This lack of synchronization invariably leads to a disjointed customer experience.
- Business processes that do not reflect best practices—The organizational processes may not be aligned with the customer-centric focus of the organization; for instance, instead of being customer-focused, business processes are often optimized with reference to the back office functions of the organizations. Though this may not be without some advantages in terms of back office efficiencies, this may deny the organization the opportunity to achieve increased revenues while reducing the costs.
- Poorly coordinated business partners—Organizational partners are not aligned with the organizational objectives of delivering value to its customers. Thus, though organizations increasingly rely on partners to deliver value to its customers they may not be able to monitor and manage the performance of its partners.
- Unaligned employees—Organizations lack systems to keep their employees informed and the resources to enable them to do their jobs effectively; managers do not have a means to optimize workforce performance.

In addition to enhanced customer loyalty and retention, Siebel's customer-focused eBusiness technology also delivers other measurable benefits that directly enhance an organization's effectiveness, productivity and revenue. All these collectively have a positive impact on the company's performance in terms of:

(i) eBusiness Applications improve the organization's effectiveness in sales, marketing and customer service, resulting in increased revenue because of factors such as more selling time for salesman, higher order sizes and improved close rates for new leads.

**Table 5.1 Benefits Achieved from Siebel eBusiness Technology**

| Area of Activity | Benefits Achieved |
|---|---|
| Sales | Increased selling time per sales representative |
| | Increased revenue per sales |
| | Shorter sales cycle |
| | Improved prospect targeting |
| | Increased close rate |
| | Increased prospect-to-customer conversion rate |
| | Increased order size |
| | Increased revenue per customer ('wallet share') |
| | Incremental revenue gains from new channel capabilities |
| | Reduced training costs |
| | Reduced sales overhead |
| | Improved team selling effectiveness |
| | Reduced costs for collateral distribution |
| | Increased order accuracy |
| | Decreased cost to manage partner/channel interactions |
| | Increased partner/reseller satisfaction |
| | Increased salesperson satisfaction |
| | More accurate sales forecasting |
| | More accurate and complete information to support sales managers |
| | Improved visibility into sales pipeline |
| Marketing | Reduced marketing campaign overheads |
| | Increased marketing campaign response rate |
| | Decreased cost to generate new leads |
| | Decreased cost to acquire new customers |
| | Decreased cost to identify potential customers |
| | Better, more detailed information on lifetime value of customers |
| | Faster cycle time to create, execute and analyze marketing campaigns |
| | Faster lead generation |
| | Improved ability to test campaigns (offers, lists, etc.) |
| Service | Increased customer retention |
| | Decreased cost to retain existing customers |
| | Reduced customer service costs |
| | Faster response times to service requests |
| | Shorter wait times for callers requiring customer service |
| | Decreased time to resolve service requests |
| | Higher rate of service issues resolved on first call |
| | Increased productivity of customer service representatives |
| | Higher rate of service issues resolved on first field service visit |
| | Decreased rate of service issue escalation |
| | Extended customer service through 24x7 self-service options |
| | Increased customer service representative satisfaction |
| | More accurate information concerning customer service operations |

(ii) eBusiness applications increase the productivity of the organization's sales, marketing and service operations; thus effectively reducing the costs of the revenue producing resources and increasing the availability of productive resources substantially.

## 5.2.1 n-tier Principle

n-tier computing is a style of computing where the computer processing load is distributed across several synchronously or asynchronously cooperating computer programs running on a single computer or on a group of computers. During the last decade of development this has become one of the architectures of choice for computerized systems because of the tremendous flexibility permitted by this approach. Applications can be installed, configured and run on a central computer or distributed across several numbers, depending on the type and load of the applications. Moreover, as the processing requirements and loads change, the corresponding systems can be upgraded selectively. This approach provides a path for the companies to achieve greatly enhanced performance at only incremental costs, while preserving the investments made in the earlier hardware.

In Siebel, n-tier computing forms the basis of cooperative processing of disparate software components that could reside either on a centralized or distributed configuration on many servers that are networked to each other. The communication between the servers could be based on:

- Synchronous program-to-program communication
- Asynchronous message exchange
- Remote SQL

These disparate software components could be meant for graphical presentation, for processing applications or even for the storage of data. Special application servers can also be installed for individual work areas. Allocating separate servers not only helps to balance loads, but also enables allocation of individual server configurations that are appropriate for the concerned tasks. This not only helps to improve the throughput and response times, but also optimizes costs.

The n-tier approach with its distribution of presentation, applications and database functions on separate computers, truly provides a viable foundation for extended enterprise client/server solutions. For integrated systems like Siebel however, the real achievement is to implement the multi-layer client/server concept without losing the integration of data and the processes across the entire system.

## 5.2.2 Comprehensive World Class Functionality

Siebel provides a suite of pre-packaged, best-in-class applications to manage customer, partner and employee relationships on a global basis, delivering the broadest and deepest set of features in the marketplace. The pre-built features and business processes are designed to satisfy the majority of an organization's business requirements out of the box. Siebel covers most of the significant business processes within several industries and businesses. Organizations can utilize divisional operations that are discrete or continuous in nature, or both. Similarly, a company can also have operations in service industries like banking, financial services, and so on. Such organizations, and many such enterprises exist now, need a uniform enterprise-wide system that can span customer-related functions across all such disparate business activities and help in controlling and managing them on a day-to-day basis. It is understandable that organizations that have interests in heterogeneous business activities across different regions of the world can be handicapped when managing day-to-day operations if different, incompatible and non-integrated systems are functioning at all these locations.

### *(a) Application Components*

Siebel's standard application components address functionality that is commonly used across a broad spectrum of industries. They are mainly divided into three major groups—Sales, Marketing and Service. Siebel Sales consists of standard components like Opportunity Management and Pipeline Management, Account Management, Contact Management, Activity Management, Quotas and Incentives, and so forth. Siebel Marketing consists of major components like Marketing Analysis, Customer Management, Marketing Communications, Content Management and Literature Material, Database Marketing, and so forth. Siebel Services consists of components like Service Request Management, Self-service, Account Management, Activity Tracking, Service Calendar, Customer feedback system and satisfaction survey. The Siebel product map is shown in Figure 5.1.

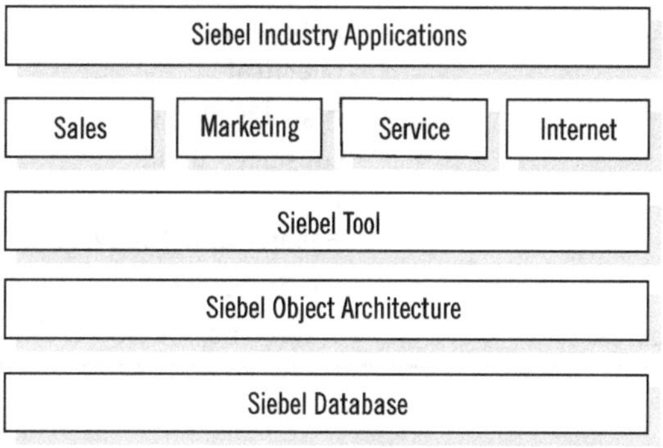


**Fig. 5.1 The Siebel Product Map**

We will discuss these modules in greater detail in Chapter 8, "Siebel Enterprise Applications".

### *(b) Industry-specific Applications (IA)*

Almost every industry has characteristic requirements that are specific to the companies operating in that industry. Each industry has different needs—different competitive challenges, customer requirements, business processes, and so on. Siebel provides a wide array of industry-specific vertical solutions that address such unique requirements through Industry Applications (IA) that are complementary to the base solution. Siebel Systems has invested extensively in developing these industry-specific applications with deep out-of-the-box functionality and embed the industry best practices for customer-facing processes such as sales, marketing and customer service.

**Table 5.2 Siebel Industry Applications**

| Industry | Industry-specific Applications |
|---|---|
| Financial Services | Retail Banking and Brokerage<br>Institutional Finance<br>Insurance<br>Healthcare |
| Communications | Welfare<br>Wireless<br>Media |
| Energy | Energy<br>Oil and Gas |
| Life Sciences | Pharmaceutical<br>Clinical<br>Medical Products |
| Industrial | Automotive<br>Chemicals<br>High Technology |
| Consumer Sector | Consumer Goods<br>Retail<br>Apparel and Footwear |
| Public Sector | Public Sector |
| Travel and Transportation | Travel and Transportation |

## 5.2.3 Lowest Total Cost of Ownership (TCO)

Siebel enables rapid implementation and customization to unique business requirements, provides fast application upgrades, provides upwardly compatible enterprise application interfaces, allows for automatic software distribution to mobile, handheld, connected and thin client users, and is easy to administer and support.

Siebel is built on a scalable Web architecture that pre-packages several important core technologies critical to eBusiness deployments. These include a fully-featured rules-based personalization engine, a content management platform and a business rules or workflow engine, among others. The n-tier architecture increases portability and allows business objects and logic to be built in a modular fashion. This allows for business logic to be shared among multiple applications and multiple client devices, including connected and offline browser clients, Personal Digital Assistant (PDAs), phones that are enabled with Web Application Protocol (WAP), and voice.

Siebel allows organizations to leverage industry best practices embedded in the software, while enabling them to easily make modifications and provide a business edge. The pre-built features and business processes are designed to satisfy the majority of an organization's business requirements out of a box. These features are upgradable from one version to the next, which allows customers to leverage a steady stream of new features and enhancements.

### 5.2.4 Customization and Upgrades

Organizations increasingly rely upon the strategic value of their customer, partner and employee relationships to achieve higher revenues, greater loyalty and increased competitive advantage. Cultivating those relationships requires sound business processes that are dynamic and require frequent modifications. For example, businesses frequently change marketing campaigns, realign territory assignments and alter escalation procedures in a call center to deal with changing market conditions or because of constraints on internal resources. Consequently, eBusiness applications need to provide industry-specific functionality that can be easily modified to fit the needs of an ever-changing business. Siebel provides the tools for a company to tailor Siebel to its specific requirements by configuring the parameters at the time of implementation. This custom support is counter to the general emphasis on standardizing the processes and implementing generic ones. It is a business truism that the survival and success of a company depends on how it differentiates itself and its products or services from those of its competitors. To leverage on their competencies or advantages, companies cannot abandon the corresponding differentiating processes and will have to incorporate such fundamental variants in their CRM implementations.

Traditional client/server applications, typically developed using 4GL tools, used to be customized by changing the source code of the application to customize the screens, business logic, triggers or even the database schema of the application. This approach led to problems in the ability to upgrade and support the applications, thereby dramatically inflating the full life cycle costs of application maintenance.

Because of the way Siebel applications are designed, they are highly configurable and easy to upgrade. Siebel eBusiness applications are *declaratively configured,* that is, they are defined as metadata in the Siebel Repository. The customizations are implemented by configuring or setting properties of business objects using the graphical toolset of Siebel Tools rather than traditional programming (see sub-section "Siebel Tools"). Furthermore, because the customizations are defined in terms of metadata, configurations and integrations can be upgraded to the next release of software without additional effort. Not only does this obviate the need for expending additional time and effort; it also provides a smooth upgrade path that accelerates the deployment of the new version of applications. Overall, this strategy helps to preserve the organization's investment in custom configurations and integrations.

Competing solutions do not allow for a high level of configurability to tailor the application to unique requirements of businesses. Generally, such applications are developed using a Fourth Generation Language (4GL) against a relational database management system (DBMS). The customer's ability to tailor the application revolves around changing the source code of the application by changing the business logic using the 4GL or the database schemas. Such changes not only render supporting and upgrading such customized applications extremely difficult, if not impossible, but they also make them costlier. Compared to Siebel, competing solutions have much higher TCO's. Some packaged applications permit a certain degree of configuration, like being able to turn on or off various switches or being able to set parameters that effect the behavior of programs constituting the application. However, when this is inadequate to meet the needs of the business, the customer is forced to change its business to suit the needs of the application—this is not BPM! (see Chapter 7, "Siebel and Enterprise Business Process Management").

## 5.2.5 Highly Interactive Browser Interface

Siebel Enterprise Applications provide a familiar, intuitive Web browser user interface. Based on the Web browser and Microsoft Windows interface standards, the Siebel user interface employs common icons and a graphical representation of user controls. Siebel provides support for personalized fonts, colors, layouts, toolbars and most other attributes of the appearance of the application. Users also have the ability to personalize the appearance of the application to suit their preferences through the Options dialog. For instance, end-users can tailor the application to start-up with their favorite view, default to their most commonly used price list, and route correspondence using their default delivery method, fulfillment center, and timeframe. Users with varying skill levels benefit from the efficient navigation mechanisms such as hyperlinks for drill down, forward and back buttons, history pull down lists and drag-and-drop support.

Siebel's Smart Web Architecture combines a zero-footprint browser-based client with levels of interactivity that normally is only associated with Windows applications. Consequently, the browser does not have to be refreshed every time the user makes a field-level change. This not only contributes to improved network performance but also makes the user's experience highly interactive. This results in a higher level of user productivity, satisfaction and acceptance for both employees and customers.

In designing the Siebel Smart Architecture, Siebel Systems leveraged extensive domain expertise in CRM to develop best practices for both information presentation and business process flows. For instance, stepping off a record automatically triggers a request for saving the validated changes made by the user; the user does not have to explicitly request for saving the changes by clicking a 'Save' button. Siebel supports easy system navigation, promotes intuitive context management and provides comprehensive user assistance through standard context-sensitive help, field-level help and tool tips.

## 5.2.6 Internationalization and Localization

To operate effectively in multiple countries, applications must be able to operate in multiple languages and be localized to the unique business requirements of each locale. Global organizations can implement Siebel applications in multiple languages, while maintaining a single, unified repository of customer data across the different languages. The applications are packaged for global deployments in more than 20 languages—pre-translated and pre-configured with regional settings. This includes the ability to support single as well as double byte European and Asian character sets. Advanced localization techniques such as bi-directional character display allows the system to render text processing from right to left, for languages such as Hebrew and Chinese. The availability of local language releases of an application enables sales, marketing and service professionals to access customer information using screens, reports, online help text and data in their language of choice. Siebel provides multilingual, multi-currency support as well as support for multiple time zones. Features such as multilingual list of values enable users of different languages to work within the same system while using their native language.

Siebel supports multiple currencies and provides full support for automatic currency conversions across the system with exchange rate interfaces to online services such as Reuters. Full support for multiple currencies (including the euro) enables sales, marketing and service professionals to track sales opportunities, quotations, price lists, forecasts, service requests and service agreements in the currency that is appropriate for the customer. On the other hand, this also enables organizations, for example, to consolidate sales forecasting information across different global regions and analyze data regardless of the language of the underlying customer interactions.

## 5.2.7 Siebel Bus Object Repository

As mentioned in Chapter 3, section "The Anatomy of an CRM System", the repository is the central collection area for access or information on every kind of development object in the Siebel system.

Metadata, that is, data that defines the structure and the behavior of the business objects, is an important aspect of Siebel's application architecture. Siebel's metadata repository contains properties and attribute-value pairs that determine the behavior of Siebel business objects. The use of metadata enables Siebel to customize rapidly without changing the source code of the application as well as the Siebel automatic upgrade capability. This is primarily because structured metadata allows for automated analysis and manipulation.

Well-defined metadata repositories like Siebel's reduce the cost and time required to train new developers to customize an application easily with the aid of graphical development tools like Siebel Tools that obviates the need to learn a new procedural language.

### 5.2.7.1 Object-orientation

Before delving into the object-oriented aspects of Siebel, we need to elaborate briefly on what object-orientation means. The object-oriented paradigm is based on a new way of looking at the old dichotomy of data and computational procedures.

#### *(a) The Object-oriented Paradigm*

A *paradigm* is the totality of techniques, tools, attributes and patterns of thinking or exemplars that constitute a world view. The '60s were characterized by the 'algorithmic view', wherein the primary concern was to design and implement correct and efficient algorithms, which were related mostly to the performance issues of the numeric computations within the hardware constraints of main memory and offline storage memory. Subsequently, attendant problems of programming such as writing, debugging, modifying, and so on led to the progressive crystallization of the 'procedural view'. In the procedural view, algorithms were packaged into sub-programs or procedures and handled independently of the programs using them. This gradually led further to the 'structural view' of the functional paradigm. In the functional paradigm, the focus is on the various functions and sub-functions that a system has to perform and the manner in which those functions have to be performed. The object-oriented view extends and couples this trend of abstractions not only to operations (such as sub-programs and procedures), but also to the data.

There are four principal building blocks of the object-oriented paradigm:

- Object
- Class
- Message
- Method

These broadly correspond to the record, record type, procedure and procedure call in traditional language systems. An interface is a particular set of methods.

An *object* is a thing that exists and has identity (that is, it occupies memory and is addressable). An object consists of data that is tightly coupled with all the operations that can act against it. The operations are referred to as *methods*, and the communication to the object triggering some method is the *message*. A collection of such messages defines the public interface of the object and an object may be inspected or altered only through this pre-defined protocol of messages.

Because there is a considerable amount of commonality between the methods of several objects, objects with the same internal structure and methods are grouped into classes called the Class Defining Object (CDO) and are themselves called instances of this class. A class may have multiple instance classes; however, each instance has only one CDO and keeps reference to its CDO. Thus, a computation is performed by sending a message to an object, which inherits or invokes a method of its CDO. This method in turn might invoke other objects by addressing them, and so on. This chain might terminate when a primitive object is invoked that either changes the instance variable or affects external entities such as the printer, hard disk, and so on. For instance, gasoline and diesel cars can be seen as the instance (sub) classes of the four-wheeled vehicle object, which itself is an instance (sub) class of the automobile class.

### *(b) Inheritance and Encapsulation*

A class is also a template from which newer objects can be quickly generated and used. This logically leads to many important characteristics of object-oriented environments, such as *inheritance* and *encapsulation*. We will illustrate these with reference to Figure 5.2, which shows the various sub-classes and instance classes of the Class Defining Object (CDO) called 'automobile'.

In the automobile illustration, inheritance can be understood in terms of certain standard characteristics and components, such as the fuel, fuel tank, wheels, gears, axle, engine, and so on that can be presumed to be constituents of gasoline and diesel cars. These are properties inherited from the four-wheeler class, which in turn is inherited from the automobile class. It is not difficult to imagine that this phenomenon of objectification can be carried out in either direction, from locomotion objects down to the combustion engine parts, through the Bills of Materials (BOM). In fact, the BOM itself is an example of a legitimate object! This results in a hierarchy or ladder at each level or step of classes and objects, not unlike the classification hierarchies of species in biology.

The second important characteristic of encapsulation refers to the transparency of any object within such a hierarchy of objects. Thus, each object (for instance, X) merely performs a service and questions on how that service is accomplished, or on the constituting objects of X, are immaterial. If one Persists in getting answers to these queries, one might have to ascend or descend the ladder of inheriting objects for an appropriate answer.

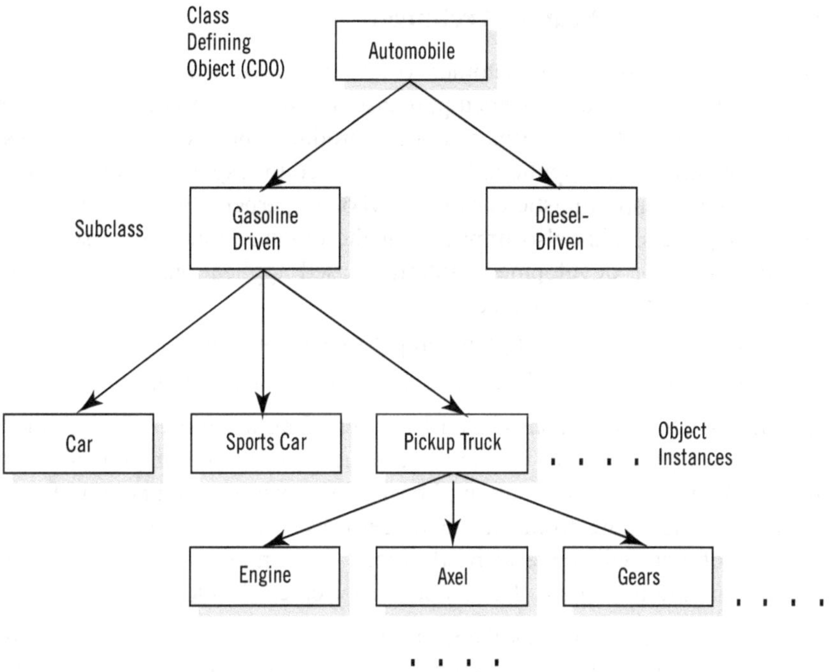


**Fig. 5.2 Sub-classes ad Instance Classes of the Class Defining Object (CDO) 'Automobile'**

### *(c) Advantages of Object Orientation*

Object orientation has gradually matured, and now it also subsumes activities of planning, analysis and design not only of information systems, but also of enterprise modeling and engineering. Uses of the object model produces systems that are built upon stable intermediate forms, and thus, are more resilient to change. Object-oriented methodologies, when fully developed, can also provide a smooth and seamless transition across the various stages in the SDLC, such as the requirement definition, detailed specification, detailed design and code generation stages. This also implies that such a system can be allowed to evolve over time, rather than being abandoned or completely redesigned when the first major change in requirements comes along.

Thus, the basic advantages of the object-oriented paradigm are drastically increased opportunities for re-use of software components, the development methodology of rapid prototyping and incremental redesigning, and increased maintainability and environmental portability of finished applications. One is tempted to refer to the object-oriented approach as the re-engineered version of the traditional software engineering process!

This completes the introductory framework necessary for us to tackle an object-orientated environment like Siebel. Although there are a host of other related complex issues, such as composite objects, multiple inheritance, polymorphism, threads, concurrency, persistence, and so on, this is sufficient for us to appreciate the object orientation of the Siebel environment as a whole.

### 5.2.7.2 Componentized Application Architecture

Never before has it been so easy for a customer to find a desired product or service along with the contextual data necessary to make an informed purchase decision. Customers are no more than a click away from a world of comparative information about products, prices and alternatives that result in heightened competition among the suppliers. Companies need to respond rapidly and profitably to this generation of net-savvy and opportunistic customers who are perpetually on the verge of switching or clicking to alternate suppliers. This also implies that the organization's processes and infrastructure must support rapid application development. Internet-based applications will need to operate in an environment of constant change, precipitated by:

- External pressures to compete and gain competitive advantage
- Internal pressures to increase efficiency and accountability, and cut costs

Flexible applications need to be constructed by assembling a variety of components (functional modules) to create newer products and services. Although the initial components would have to be developed from scratch, with the accumulation of basic components over a period of time, applications will be assembled more and more from increasing re-use of the existing components. However, to accomplish this, the software will have to be designed as component-based applications and there needs to be an infrastructure to support the component-oriented development of applications.

An organizational structure that enables change is based on reusable elements that are re-configurable in a scalable framework. In the componentized architecture, a system is considered as a group of components sharing a common interaction framework and serving a common purpose. A framework is a set of standards constraining and enabling the interactions of compatible system components; where the component itself is an autonomous system sub-unit with a self-contained identity, purpose and capability, and is capable of interacting with other components.

A component-based architecture can eliminate the customary tradeoff between best practice functionality and large integration, and ongoing support costs. A standards-based architecture provides a unified framework on which componentized applications from multiple vendors can be easily and cost-effectively:

- Deployed and distributed across servers on heterogeneous networks
- Integrated directly with the logic layer of other component-based applications
- Extended to support customer-specific business processes
- Upgraded individually

Figure 5.3 presents Siebel's Componentized Application Architecture. Siebel's enterprise component architecture and the corresponding development and maintenance environment have been discussed in more details in Chapter 11, "Siebel Tools".

> However, the focus of the componentized application architecture is at a too fine level of granularity. The recent trend and developments towards Web Services and Service Oriented Architecture (SOA) corrects this bias towards enterprise-level services.

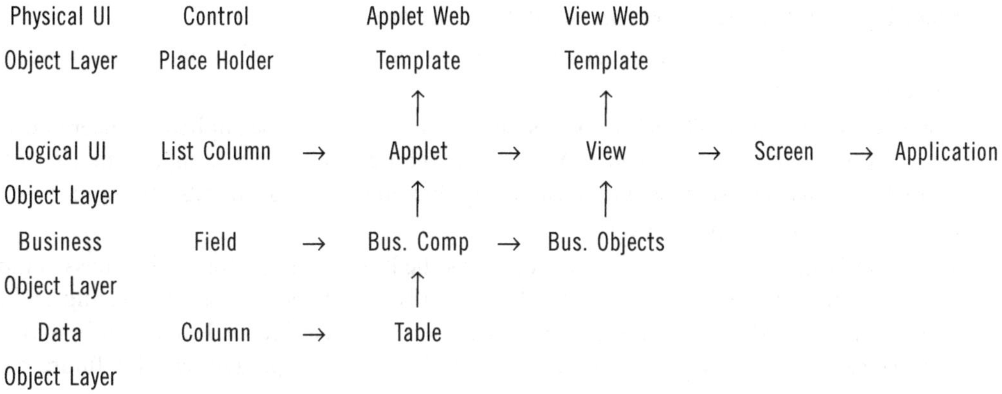


**Fig. 5.3 Siebel's Componentized Application Architecture**

## 5.2.8 Siebel Architecture

Siebel Enterprise Architecture is based on an n-tiered (that is, multi-tiered) and object-oriented architecture that is entirely Web-based. The salient features of Siebel's Web-based architecture are:

- It is the result of a powerful, component-based, object-oriented kernel that has enabled Siebel to produce an advanced yet highly modular system quickly.
- It provides customers with a platform for rapid application customization while maintaining a clear and consistent upgrade path to future releases of Siebel enterprise applications.
- It provides the foundation for moving to the next level of sophistication that are inevitable due to the relentless growth of Internet-based functionality.

The critical elements of Siebel's comprehensive and competitive application architecture include:

- Familiar Web browser user interface
- Global enterprise support
- Standards compliance
- Complete development tools
- Automated application upgrades
- Open application integration
- Enterprise class scalability and performance

### *(a) Web-based Software Architecture*

Siebel is built on a scalable Web architecture that pre-packages several important core technologies critical to eBusiness deployments. These include a fully-featured rules-based personalization engine, a content management platform, a business rules or workflow engine, and an assignment or routing engine, among others. The n-tier architecture increases portability and allows business objects and logic to be built in a modular fashion. This also allows for business logic to be shared among multiple applications and multiple client devices, including connected and offline browser clients, Personal Digital Assistants (PDAs), phones that are enabled with Web Application Protocol (WAP) and voice.

The major layers of the Siebel Web-based architecture are:

- Applet Layer—This layer manages the user interaction for Siebel and customer-developed applications and components.
- Applet Manager Layer—This layer is responsible for rendering the application user interface and managing user interactions. Applet Manager combines and displays applets in views that are accessible to users as screens within Siebel applications. It also extends programs by exposing the interfaces to its applet objects.
- BusObject Manager Layer—This layer contains the business logic for the business components as well as behavior-determining methods for various entities in sales, marketing and service entities. Siebel BusObjects are designed to be configured via Siebel Tools rapidly to meet their business requirements while ensuring a clear and consistent upgrade path for future releases.
- Data Manager Layer—This layer maintains an object-oriented abstraction of the native data stored in the databases; this abstraction frees developers from knowing and working with the particulars of a specific database. It creates the SQL objects that automatically generate the most effective and efficient SQL code for the access, manipulation and updation of the required data for the underlying database.
- Universal Data Exchange Layer

Figure 5.4 shows Siebel's Web-based n-tier software architecture framework.

### *(b) Siebel Enterprise Server Architecture*

The Siebel Enterprise Server architecture fully exploits the 'configure once, deploy everywhere' capabilities of Siebel's n-tiered software architecture. Siebel Enterprise Applications are built on an

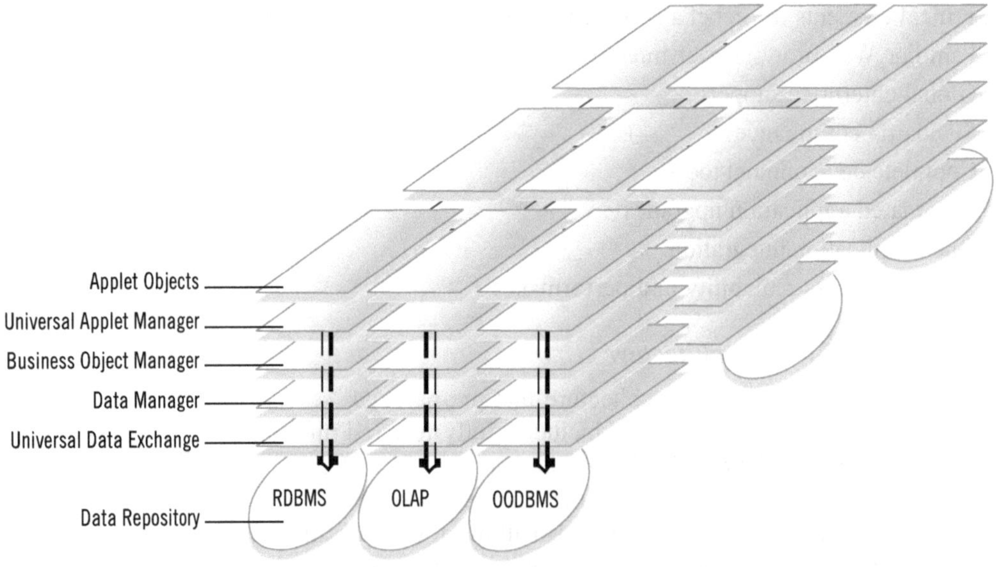


**Fig. 5.4 Siebel's Web-based n-tier Software Architecture Framework**

advanced, Web-based enterprise server architecture that provides a wide variety of features for deploying and supporting heterogeneous Siebel users enterprise-wide. Figure 5.5 shows the major components that make up the Siebel Server architecture. It corresponds broadly to the common 3-tier architecture with the following layers.

- The presentation-tier clients including the HTML and thin clients, mobile clients and connected clients.
- The middle-tier enterprise server which deploys BusObjects and includes the Siebel Server, Gateway Server (providing Name Server and connection brokering services), and Server Manager components.
- The database-tier for storing data in the Siebel Database Server and Siebel File System.

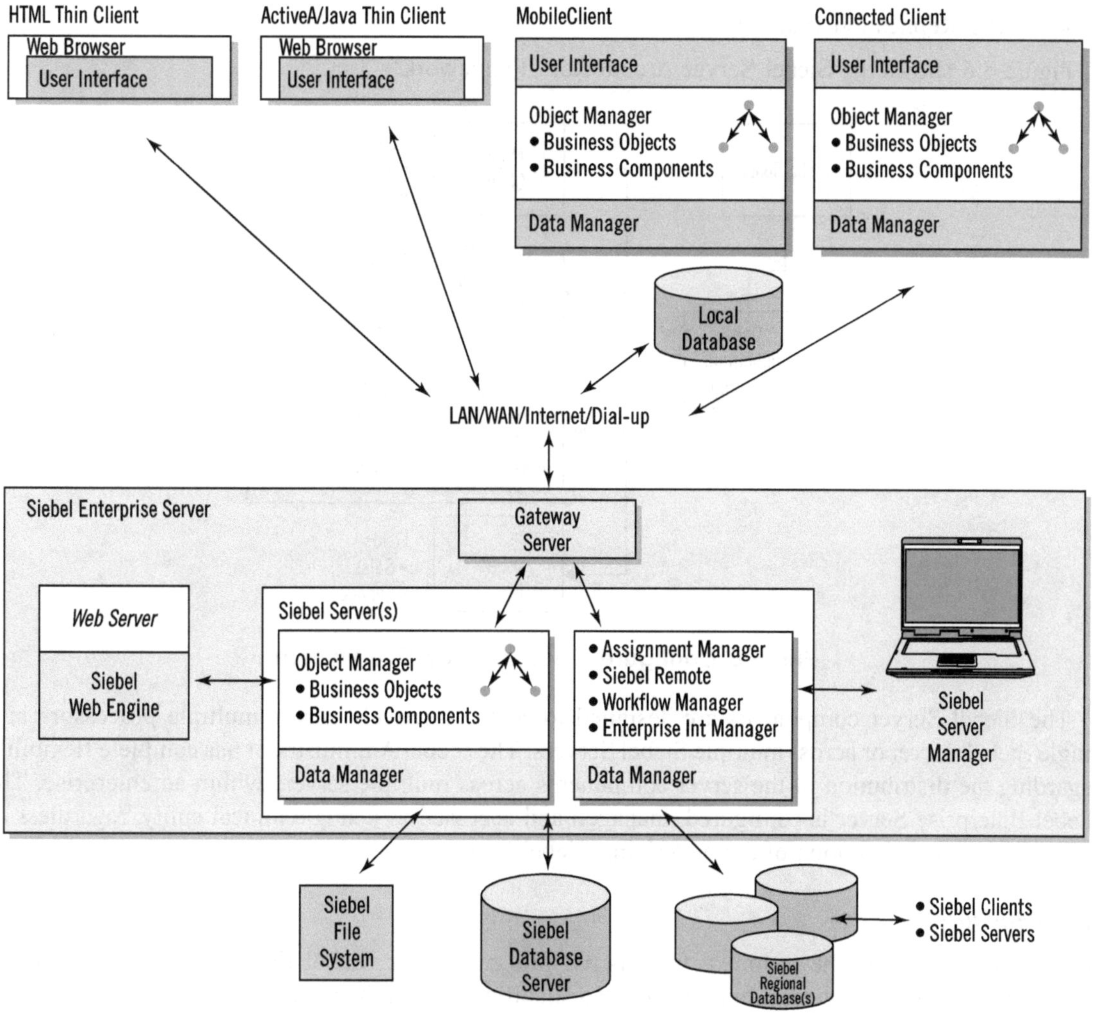


**Fig. 5.5 Siebel Server Architecture**

The Siebel Server is the application server platform within the Siebel Enterprise Server. Applications that execute on the Siebel Server are implemented on components that share common control, administration and monitoring functionality regardless of the different processes they execute. Some components interact directly with the Siebel Clients; others are batch-oriented and interact only with the Siebel Database Server. The Siebel Server supports a wide variety of components, executing in both multi-process and multi-threaded models, as follows.

- Siebel Workflow
- Siebel Assignment Manager
- Siebel Enterprise Integration Manager
- Siebel Object Manager
- Siebel Remote
- Siebel Replication Manager

Figure 5.6 shows the Siebel Server Architecture Framework.

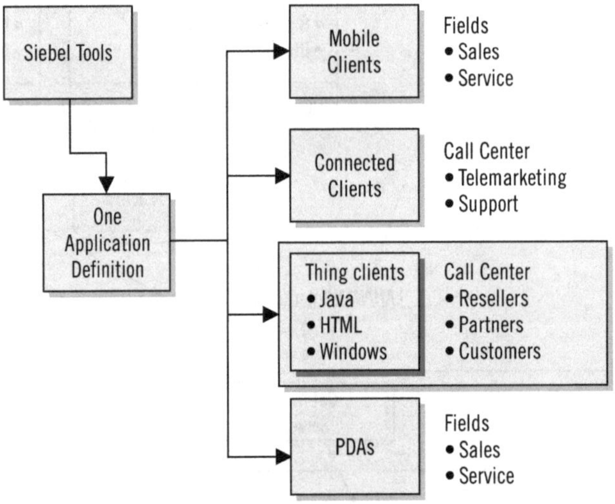


**Fig. 5.6 Configure Once, Deploy Everywhere**

The Siebel Server components are designed to scale effectively across multiple processors in a single Siebel Server or across multiple Siebel Servers. The Siebel Administrator has complete flexibility regarding the distribution of the server components across multiple servers within an enterprise. The Siebel Enterprise Server is configured, managed and accessed as a single logical entity, regardless of the number or configuration of the underlying Siebel Servers.

### *(c) Scalability*

Siebel's scalability on the technical front is easy to grasp. The Siebel Enterprise Server's parallel processing approach provides a high degree of scalability to meet the processing requirements of even the largest deployments. Each server component is implemented as a multi-threaded application that can process multiple tasks. The multi-layer client/server architecture enables Siebel to easily scale the operations from a configuration for few hundred to a few thousand users. On particular sites, this scaling might also be dictated by the implementation of additional modules or third-party specialized applications that are interfaced with Siebel.

The use of the Enterprise Server components also ensures a high degree of Siebel Database Server scalability. For instance, during synchronization sessions mobile users and replication agents do not need to open synchronous connections with the central database server, ensuring a low load on the Siebel Database Server and eliminating surges in usage that could throttle other use during peak synchronization periods. The Siebel Enterprise Server components also use sophisticated memory and file-based caches to reduce the database load as well as enhance the performance of each component. The component operations can be executed against data held in local memory much faster than that required for executing them against a remote relational database. Moreover, the data is also shared across multiple processing steps rather than being continually retrieved from the database server.

Siebel however, also provides scalability on the business front, where an MME may commence using only a sub-set of the functionality provided by the Siebel system. As a result of business successes an organization may witness rapid growth and expansion in terms of volume, type and the complexities of business activities. Siebel can keep pace with such positive developments in the nature and structure of a company's business by customizing its delivered functionality on an ongoing basis (suitable to the increased scale and complexity of its business). This is the genesis of Siebel's configure-to-order strategy for MMEs.

### *(d) Performance*

Siebel applications are the most scalable enterprise front office products available on the market providing the following.

- Fast user response times ensuring quick end-user response regardless of client type, database location or network connectivity including LAN, WAN, Internet and dial-up.
- Support for large numbers of concurrent heterogeneous users including a mix of field-based mobile sales and service professionals, call center sales and service representatives and thin client users.
- Fast data synchronization ensuring minimal user impact and reducing data latency for mobile and regional database users between disparate user communities.
- High performance, throughput and scalability ensuring fast, reliable performance and scalability for all server side components including volume data interfaces, batch-oriented automation services and middle tier clients.
- Reasonable server, client, network and other resource requirements ensuring optimal scalability and also controlling deployment cost.
- Support for large databases that allow effective operation against the data volumes of businesses with tens of millions of global customers.
- Scalable enterprise interfaces that provide well documented, upwardly compatible enterprise interfaces, which allow full two-way information exchange between the customer information system and leading manufacturing, accounting and human resource information solutions.

Enterprise interfaces are useful for both the initial data loads and for ongoing bi-directional exchange of transactions between the various enterprise systems.

Poor application performance and scalability can be addressed to a certain extent by upgrading the basic infrastructure resources at additional costs. However, the basic performance and scalability characteristics of an application are really determined by the application architecture. The Siebel applications are carefully designed to meet all demanding performance and scalability requirements, in all deployment scenarios, at all layers of the Siebel Enterprise Architecture (that correspond broadly to the conventional 3-tier architecture).

- Siebel Database Server—This uses the relational database purely as a data store; the business logic is not implemented in the database in the form of triggers or stored procedures (the database-centric model), but rather on the scalable, middle tier Siebel Enterprise Server and on the Siebel Client. The data-centric model is not only difficult to scale, customize, maintain and upgrade, but it can be scaled only by augmenting the single database server.
- Siebel Enterprise Server—The components of the Siebel Enterprise Server are designed to scale across multiple Siebel Servers in the Enterprise Server, providing a high degree of scalability in the middle tier of Siebel applications.
- Siebel Client—The Object Manager executes Siebel Business Objects and Components on the native Siebel Client and on the middle tier Object Manager that supports the Siebel Thin Client. The Object Manager supports configurable data caching at the business component level, eliminating the need to re-query data from the database server with each use of the business component. Data caching typically is applied to the business components that support PickLists.

### *(d) Application Integration*

IT heterogeneity is a reality that all businesses have to take into account while planning future IT strategies. Siebel's n-tier architecture offers open interfaces for application integration at each one of the constituting layers namely; user interface, application server and database server layer (see Figure 5.4). Integration at each of these layers involves different tradeoffs with regards to:

- Implementation complexity and solution robustness
- Performance as measured by overall throughput and transactional response time
- Real-time versus deferred business event processing
- Business logic independence across access channels
- Extent of data replication
- Mobile user support

As an approach to integration, Siebel has adopted the newer paradigm of 'application networks'. Based on a bus architecture, an application network acts as the backbone for inter and intra-enterprise data synchronization and business processes execution. A key benefit of an application network is that it provides a vendor independent architecture for inter-application integration; any compliant application can be easily plugged into or removed from the application network.

Siebel applications attach themselves to the application network using open, standards-based models, namely:

- Tight-coupling using programmatic interfaces such as COM, CORBA, or Java libraries
- Loose-coupling using XML over HTTP, IBM MQSeries and MS MQ

Siebel Object interfaces are the technology foundation for such online real-time integration with legacy desktop, Web-based, server-based and mainframe-based legacy applications. They are well-defined, open, customizable and up gradable online interfaces to the Siebel Objects both at the client and application server levels. Object interfaces are also defined through the Siebel Repository and can be customized by changing attributes in the repository and scripting with Siebel VB to adopt them to the existing external models (see Chapter 10, sub-section, "eBusiness Application Integration (eAI)").

On the other hand, Siebel Enterprise Integration Manger (EIM) provides *batch* interface for highly efficient data integration with external applications. EIM supports bi-directional exchange of large volumes of transaction and event data through pre-built and extensible interfaces.

Siebel Pre-built Interfaces provide for out-of-box enterprise scalability of the Siebel applications with major ERP vendors like SAP and PeopleSoft. Siebel also provides pre-built adapters for use by organization standardizing on middleware platforms such as Microsoft BizTalk, webMethods, SeeBeyond, Vitria and TIBCO.

### 5.2.8.1 Siebel on Unix

Siebel Systems can be used on a variety of systems. In fact, its platform independence permits different hardware/O/S platforms like Unix, Linux, etc. for presentation, application and database servers with tremendous consequential advantages in terms of performance and costs. This also enables any installations to avail of the latest developments in infrastructure technologies (hardware, O/S, networking, DBMS, etc.) without disrupting the Siebel system in production.

Because of the open architecture, Siebel can work flexibly with multiple solutions options at all levels:

(a) Graphical interface level
(b) Desktop level
(c) Application level
(d) Database level
(e) External Interfaces level
(f) Communication protocol level
(g) Hardware and O/S level

### 5.2.8.2 Siebel Applets

Siebel Smart Web Architecture's zero-footprint browser-based client is based on Applets. The very first computing model was the large mainframe computer serving multiple users to share the same applications, which in turn shared the same mainframe CPU. With the advent of personal computers (PCs) (each storing individual copies of software applications) connected by networks, emerged the client/server computing model. This model allowed PC users to query, view and manipulate a centralized database on the server. While users shared the server CPU running the server processes, but to the extent that data processing was performed locally at the individual PC clients, the burden on the central

CPU hosting the server process was reduced drastically. Thus, PC's connected by networks were able to replicate the multi-user data access capability of the mainframes without the crippling load on the central CPU. However, the client/server model and the following 3-tier and the more generalized n-tier architectures (see section "n-tier Client/Server Principle" earlier) embodying the distributed processing computing model, were much more difficult to administer with regards to installation, upgrades, etc., than the centralized mainframe systems.

Applets represent a more evolved computing model that addresses the difficulties involved in the system administration of distributed processing systems and entails:

- Automatic delivery of applets from the server across networks to computers that run the applets.
- User being relieved of the burden of installation, keeping track of versions, version management, upgrades, etc., on the individual client computers; only the server needs to be updated for the user to access the latest applets during the next invocation.
- Delivery of data along with the corresponding software code (that processes and displays this data).

> ***Network is the Computer***
>
> *Once the network begins to move software as well as data, it begins to appear and behave more and more like a computer in its own right—this is the basic rationale behind Sun's vision of 'Network is the Computer'!*
>
> (see Chapter 7, note "Network is the Resource Provider").

Devoid and transparent of the versions, the indistinguishable combination of data and software (content) manifests more in terms of self-evolving 'content services'.

### 5.2.9 Siebel Tools—A Comprehensive Application Development Environment

Siebel Tools is the integrated and fully-featured development environment for custom development or enhancement of Siebel standard functionality. It is not a programming language but a declarative software development tool. It is a powerful object-oriented, client/server application development environment designed to meet the customization needs of Siebel deployments. Built on the latest industry-standard development platform from Microsoft, Siebel Tools enables unprecedented levels of application customization and ease of use for Siebel customers seeking to extend Siebel Enterprise Applications.

Siebel customers can use Siebel Tools to rapidly configure the various aspects of Siebel applications like the look and feel, behavior and workflow; without modifying the application source code or SQL. The advanced repository management capabilities of Siebel Tools allow developers to work efficiently on configuring Siebel Enterprise Applications. The Siebel Application Upgrader provides an automated process for upgrading customizations to future product releases, thereby protecting customization investments. Overall, the ease, comprehensiveness, scalability and upgradability of the customization process helps reduce the total life cycle cost (i.e. TCO) of customizing Siebel Enterprise Applications.

The primary components of Siebel Tools are as follows:

(a) Siebel Business Object (BusObject) Designer

The BusObject Designer gives developers the ability to customize Siebel products quickly and easily. It includes:

- Siebel BusObject Explorer used to modify and manage object definitions.
- Siebel Object Visualization Views, which provides graphical representations of the relationships between the various object definitions in the Siebel BusObject Repository that in turn helps in configuration process for developers.
- Siebel Applet Designer, which is an intuitive drag-and-drop visual programming interface that is used to modify and extend applets like list, form, dialog and chart.
- Siebel View Designer, which enables developers to visually modify existing views and construct new ones by simply dragging-and-dropping the desired applets on the view canvas.
- Siebel Menu Designer, which is a visual programming tool for customizing and extending Siebel menu structures.
- New Object Wizards, which assists developers to create new objects in the Siebel Repository only by clicking on the type of new object that needs to be created; this Wizard guides through the entry of properties essential for that type of object.
- BusObject Repository Manager, which is an efficient multi-user development environment that also provides check-in/check-out functionality and version control.
- Siebel BusObject Compiler, which enables full or incremental compilation of the repository to generate a repository file that is used to run the Siebel Application.

(b) Siebel VB

This is a complete Visual Basic (VB) complaint environment for integrating Siebel Enterprise Applications with thrid-party cooperative applications and extending the base functionality of the Siebel application screens and business components.

(c) Siebel Object Interfaces

These are used to access Siebel data from third-party applications, to provide integration with legacy systems and automate Siebel applications from external applications. These interfaces expose selected Siebel objects and are available as COM, ActiveX and CORBA components.

(d) Siebel Database Extension Designer

This provides a point-and-click interface for extending Siebel application tables when developers need extension even beyond the built-in database extensions. New columns are reflected automatically in the Siebel BusObject Repository and named appropriately to ensure easy migration to future releases of the Enterprise Applications.

(e) Siebel Application Upgrader

This radically reduces the time, effort and hence, cost of version upgrades by enabling customers to better determine and compare the changes available in a new release with the customizations from an earlier release. It notifies system administrators about any such conflicts and after merging differences between object definitions, it allows administrators to manually override and apply any of the changes. By obviating the need to manually migrate changes from one release to the next, this tool reduces the total life cycle cost of ownership (TCO) of Siebel Applications tremendously.

Siebel Tools enables developers to become productive quickly by enabling them to work top down or bottom up. Top down development, often favored by business-oriented professionals, starts with the development of the user interface, then proceeds to business component definition and then data structure design. Bottom up development, often favored by technical professionals, enables developers to start with the database design and then work their way up to the user interface. This flexibility of Siebel Tools enables developers, for instance, to accommodate businesses where visual prototyping is required in the early stages of the project in order to validate the approach with the users. More details on "Siebel Tools" are described later in Chapter 11.

## 5.2.10 Comprehensive Data Model

Siebel has built a rich set of structures that includes the data elements required for a broad range of enterprises; a comprehensive and complete database schema minimizes the need for database extensions or modifications. Many Siebel customers discover that Siebel Data Model and the corresponding database schema deliver all the required data structures right out-of-the-box.

Siebel Data Model is characterized by the following:

- A rich information model to support cross-industry requirements—Siebel has the most comprehensive customer information data model which takes into account the requirements of a broad range of industries and is also continuously updated on an ongoing basis.
- A leading-edge strategy for integration with other systems within the enterprise—Siebel supports multiple integration methodologies including APIs that support business functions not only across components of Siebel Enterprise Applications but also across other applications like ERP, SCM, HRMS, KM/BI, and so on.
- A flexible architecture with full support for database extensions—Siebel supports full configurations and adaptations to support specific requirements of the enterprise.
- A future-proof strategy to protect customer investments in customization—Siebel Enterprise Applications architecture allows users to make customizations to the data model while preserving the ability to seamlessly upgrade to future product releases.
- A comprehensive and seamless support for internationalization—Siebel Data Model has built-in support for multiple languages as well as currencies.
- A high-performance database design—Siebel Enterprise Applications have been benchmarked to perform excellently against very large databases with a large number of users.

Siebel database configuration tools are integrated with the Siebel applications data dictionary called Siebel Repository and delivered as a part of Siebel Tools resulting in a level of configurability and adaptability that far exceeds traditional modeling techniques. The Siebel configurable business object technology provides Siebel Systems customers with a high level of configurability while maintaining a clear and simple upgrade path.

#### 5.2.10.1 Siebel Data Model Extensibility

For enterprises that determine a need for additional data elements or structures, Siebel Systems provide several built-in mechanisms to achieve this objective easily. Siebel applications provide complete flexibility to modify and extend the Siebel Data Model to accommodate the specific and unique needs of enterprises. Siebel Data Model supports three levels of configurability:

- Adding additional columns to existing tables
- Configuring and using pre-defined extension tables and columns
- Adding additional extension tables to store additional entities

Siebel applications provide more than 1000 additional database columns as a part of the base Siebel Data Model that, though available, are not used by the default Siebel applications. These fields can be used by customers to capture information specific to their business. The pre-defined extension columns on both base and extension tables can be used simply by adding fields to Siebel application screens, reports and business components that reference the extension columns. Because the Siebel SQL objects dynamically generate the appropriate SQL to retrieve and manipulate data based on the particular applet and business component, the Siebel extension tables are referenced only when actually needed. Customers who do use extension tables do not experience significant performance degradation because the built-in database tables are joined to the base table with a single field.

Siebel applications also provide additional database tables as part of the base Siebel Data Model that are not used by the default Siebel applications. Customers whose needs exceed the pre-defined extension tables and columns can use the Database Extension Designer option of Siebel Tools to further extend the data model by adding extension tables and columns to contain additional entities and attributes.

### 5.2.11 Siebel Worldwide Services

Siebel provides companies with a comprehensive set of services during the implementation and support phases of their implementations. As part of this program, Siebel provides services designed to work directly with customers as well as to complement its system integration partners. The comprehensive set of services includes the following.

***(a) Technical Account Management (TAM)***

TAM plays the role of the lead Siebel technical advisor and also the customer's advocate within the Siebel organization. TAM assists and supports the customer project teams in areas of project planning and reporting, implementation issues, requirement mapping issues, product knowledge, customer liaison and customer satisfaction. TAM also recommends the specific expert services that may be required for the implementation.

***(b) Consulting Services***

These services can be used either as a complete package for total implementation or as select services for staff augmentation. These services include areas of project management, business analysis, design, interfaces, operations and support. Through the use of the Siebel RAD (Rapid Application Development) methodology Siebel Consulting Services is able to ensure that customers achieve benefits through a rapid process of prototyping, testing, and deployment.

(c) ***Expert Services***

Expert Services provide valuable assistance with the most critical implementation points and ensure that a project is on track and follows best practice recommendations. Expert Services entail specific review checkpoints and targeted services for:

- System architecture—design, hardware capacity planning, implementation benchmarks and system testing, data mapping and extensions design, and Enterprise Integration Manager (EIM) processing design
- Design reviews—data mappings, database extensions, and configuration designs
- Configuration consultation and configuration reviews
- Visual Basic (VB) design reviews—Siebel VB and OLE design reviews

(d) ***Technical Support***

As Siebel expects its products to be mission-critical tools for its customer's sales, marketing, and services activities, Siebel Technical Support ensures that customers enjoy seamless use of Siebel products by providing 24 × 7 technical support options and an online solutions database.

Siebel offers a variety of support packages specifically designed to meet any need of an organization:

- Standard Support package offers technical support during business hours, software updates and two designated contacts for communication with Siebel's technical support organization
- Gold Support package adds a corporate sponsor, 24-hour support for severity-one and -two issues, an option for onsite technical support, four designated contacts, etc.
- Platinum Support package adds a personal support representative assigned to the account, additional designated contacts, etc.

Siebel maintains an updated support Web site support@siebel.com, where customers have access to Siebel's extensive technical support knowledge base. Siebel provides around-the-clock access to information and answers through two areas, namely, self-help Support Search and Service Requests mailed or telephoned to Technical Support. Support Search enables a customer to find FAQs, technical notes (on updated information), and Siebel alerts (on new product information) within Siebel's extensive knowledge repository.

(e) ***Operations Services***

SiebelNet is a set of application outsourcing services designed to help customers to quickly deploy and manage their Siebel systems. SiebelNet services include the underlying database software, operating systems, server hardware, data storage, support staff and network connectivity required for a successful implementation. SiebelNet offers network or Internet-based access to customers' configured Siebel applications.

Siebel HelpDesk provides customers with 24 × 7 end-user technical support. It is designed to increase an end-user's overall productivity without the customers being required to staff an internal help desk for application support. Siebel works closely with the customer to design, develop and carry out efficient, cost-effective help desk support. Siebel HelpDesk improves the quality of end-user support, reduces deployment risk and scales with the need of the client's organization.

(f) ***Customer Education***

Siebel offers a broad spectrum of training courses covering all stakeholders of a Siebel project. These courses cover a range of topics from a general overview to in-depth coverage of individual topics.

Siebel University technical courses provide comprehensive training for the entire implementation team. Siebel's courses are designed to get a team up to speed quickly and efficiently; some of which are:

- Core courses
- Migration courses
- Application workflow courses
- Advanced technical courses

(g) ***End-user Education***

Siebel end-user education provides training to the end-users to ensure the quality of end-user deployment. This is achieved through a customized training process to maximize the benefits of the software as it applies to the company's business, and integrates a variety of delivery methods including:

- Instructor-led training
- Online training
- Distance learning
- Custom documentation

### 5.2.12 Partnering for Growth

Partnering has been one of the driving forces in the growth of Siebel. Siebel has adopted partnering as a growth strategy not only with its business and technology partners, but also with its customers. It partners with more than 750 technology providers thereby enabling organizations to implement the best solution possible from an array of best-in-class products.

The partnership with customers has led to the success of its Industry Applications (IAs). Siebel combines the horizontal functionality of its base solution with focused, vertical functionality provided by IAs that are developed along with specific, best-in-class Siebel customers in each industry.

## 5.3 OTHER SIGNIFICANT ASPECTS OF SIEBEL

In this section, we will mention briefly some aspects of Siebel system operations that may not get highlighted in Siebel literature yet are nonetheless, in my opinion, of great value in terms of their potential for leading to major gains in productivity. They are also indicative of the exactness of the research done by Siebel in the usability engineering of their system.

### 5.3.1 Configure Once, Deploy Everywhere

Siebel enables developers to configure once and deploy everywhere, thus enabling them to re-use customization and deploy them to any of the clients.

- Mobile clients
- Handheld clients
- Connected clients
- Browser-based thin clients
  - Siebel Thin Client for Windows
  - Siebel Java Thin Client
  - Siebel HTML Thin Client

The Siebel Applet Manager enables Siebel Enterprise Applications to be used on a wide variety of platforms because it uses a single applet definition stored in the Siebel Repository. Using the Applet Manager delivered with the Siebel Thin Client, the same applet can be deployed in either the Windows (ActiveX-based) Thin Client or also in the Siebel Java Thin Client. If appropriate, the very same applet can also be similarly rendered on a Personal Digital Assistant (PDA) by using the Siebel Handheld Client without any additional programming. This architecture enables Siebel applications user interface objects, including Views and Applets, to be configured once in the Siebel Repository and deployed in any environment.

This approach to application customization dramatically reduces the full life support costs of the applications and enables customers to benefit quickly from the clear and consistent path from one release to another.

## 5.3.2 Synchronization

Siebel Remote and Siebel Replication Manager are the only proven, enterprise class synchronization solutions that meet all the needs of mobile and distributed deployments, and are configured completely out-of-the-box for quick and easy deployment. They provide complete capabilities for both mobile user and server-to-server synchronization. They are also fully integrated with Siebel Anywhere to support rapid application deployment, low maintenance costs and seamless upgrades to thousands of distributed users.

All Siebel databases are tracked as synchronization transactions. Following a standard store-and-forward model, these transactions are written into files that are used to transport them between databases. Both, the transactions and the files that contain them are tracked by several control mechanisms that include sequential numbering and CRC verification to ensure that each database receives and successfully applies all transactions in the exact order in which they were applied in the originating database. This maintains transactions-level integrity and allows the process to be stopped and re-started from the next transaction at any time. Even if a synchronization session does not run to completion, Siebel Remote is not only efficient but also resilient enough to ensure data integrity. Dial-in lines are notorious for dropping unexpectedly, but unlike the case of snapshot-based 'all-or-nothing' solutions that abort the entire session when this occurs, Siebel Remote applies all transactions retrieved during a synchronization session and resumes from the point of failure in the next session.

Siebel Remote and Siebel Replication Manager provide transparent, fast and robust data sharing across the enterprise, supporting truly enterprise-wide relationship management. They provide users with a single, unified, consistent view of all customers' information regardless of where users are located geographically or how they operate.

Competing solutions that use snapshot mechanisms do not offer the requisite level of synchronization robustness. These competing solutions 'sweep' the server database during the synchronization session and create a record-level snapshot of all changes. No integrity controls are applied when retrieving data from multiple tables, so the snapshots can contain inconsistencies like incomplete parent-child relationships that are replicated to the client. The snapshot is typically written into a single, potentially very large file that must be re-transmitted at any point of interruption in transmission. Finally, the client database itself maybe left in an inconsistent state if the entire snapshot is not applied successfully.

### 5.3.3 Authentication and Access

Siebel Remote and Siebel Replication Manager provide totally transparent, user-controlled data sharing across all members of enterprise-wide virtual customer teams, supporting truly enterprise-wide customer relationship management. For example, a given account may have a local sales representative and sales consultant, a key or national account manager, several support engineers and an executive sponsor assigned to the team. Routing rules based on memberships of such teams for key entities are used to determine the appropriate data that is visible to each user and the information is synchronized according to the corresponding databases. All team members have the same visibility and comprehensive picture of the account. The key entities include accounts, contacts, opportunities and service requests.

Teams are defined for each record in these key entities; each record level team can comprise any user from across the enterprise, providing complete flexibility in determining which users have access to the data for a given record. Users are provided differing levels of visibility to the same entity, depending on their team membership. For instance, the members of an account team can be provided with full visibility to that account and all related records including opportunities, contacts and products. On the other hand, a user may be added to the team for a specific opportunity, which will allow him to see only the summary level information about the related account, but not other opportunities related to that account. Once a team member has been added to an account team, all data related to that account including contacts, products, opportunities, service requests and related entities, including file attachments stored on the Siebel File System, are synchronized automatically. Similarly, the removal of a team member also results in the deletion of all related data from their laptop or regional database at the next point of synchronization.

The Siebel Assignment Manager server component is used to automate these team assignments and maintenance using the corresponding assignment rules. Collectively, these capabilities provide complete support for territory realignments and other organizational changes as well as enable the results to be disseminated enterprise-wide, seamlessly.

## 5.4 SIEBEL STRATEGIC INITIATIVES

In the past few years, Siebel has taken the initiative to address the concerns reported by their customers. These initiatives have also been based on the experiences gained from thousands of Siebel implementation projects that have been undertaken by Siebel and its partners over the last few years. The thrust of all these initiatives has been to increase the efficiency of project efforts, decrease project completion times and make Siebel easy to use and operate.

*(a)* ***Customer Satisfaction Surveys***

Customers have the opportunity to provide Siebel with valuable feedback on their interactions with Siebel products, services and employees. Results are distributed to the executive staff and are used to develop quarterly action plans. The collected data is used as a major input by Siebel Systems for defining and fine-tuning its consulting services and support services, as well as to drive priorities for new features in Siebel Enterprise Applications.

The data is also used as the basis for determining employee compensation.

*(b)* ***Customer-driven Initiatives***

To ensure success of Siebel implementations, Siebel has established the following programs.

- Sales commissions and compensation—All Siebel employees are compensated based on the satisfaction of Siebel's customers. Sales representatives receive a large portion of their sales commissions based on their customer's satisfaction ratings. Even non-sales personnel receive an incentive compensation based on the company's independently audited customer satisfaction levels.
- Weekly status reports—Customer issues have executive visibility and all customer account information is tracked in detailed weekly reports to Siebel management.
- Customer communication—Siebel sponsors several events and programs focused on direct dialog with customers. These programs include Siebel user week, Siebel magazine and weekly audio conference call.

*(c)* ***eRoadmap Implementation Methodology***

The eRoadmap implementation methodology devised by Siebel is a comprehensive solution for achieving successful Siebel implementations with optimal resources, costs, and time periods. It is based on the experiences obtained from hundreds of Siebel implementations in the past few years. It includes technical guides for expediting all stages of the eRoadmap methodology, especially the business blueprint and realization phases. It contains sample project plans that guide you through project management in order to optimize time, ensure quality and make efficient use of resources throughout the duration of a project.

*(d)* ***Siebel SupportWeb***

Siebel Technical Support maintains Siebel SupportWeb to provide users with a comprehensive resource for product information and solutions, including issues previously encountered by other companies. Designated support contacts are provided with full access accounts. Through Siebel SupportWeb, Siebel Technical Support provides around-the-lock access to product information and answers to common support issues raised by Siebel customers. Siebel SupportWeb is the primary means for designated contacts to log Service Requests (SRs) to Siebel Technical Support.

*(e)* ***SiebelNet Managed Services***

SiebelNet managed services provide customers with a remote management solution for in-house Siebel eBusiness developments. It is designed specifically for enterprises that have implemented Siebel but do not have the IT resources to manage and optimize their Siebel implementations.

Siebel managed services include:

- Remote DBA services
- Network and system administration
- Performance planning and tuning
- Application upgrade support
- Report creation
- Complete second level help desk support

## 5.5 SUMMARY

In this chapter, we looked at several aspects of Siebel to substantiate the fact that Siebel is the best CRM solution that there is on the market. Even though it is not directly patterned on various evaluation criteria discussed in Chapter 3, "Siebel Evaluation", this chapter clearly demonstrates the overwhelming superiority of Siebel in relation to all these criteria. We presented the significance of Siebel by highlighting aspects of its world class functionality, lowest TCO, ease of customization and upgrades, user-friendly GUIs, provision for internationalization and localization, Siebel Repository, Siebel architecture and the powerful Siebel Tools development environment, and comprehensive data model, and rounded this off with a description of the comprehensive program of Siebel Services.

The intelligent use of Internet technology for business operations has already become a critical success factor for many enterprises. The sudden explosion in eBusiness implies that intra-enterprise issues such as Employee Relationship Management (ERM) and beyond-the-enterprise issues such as Partner Relationship Management (PRM) have already become crucial for the competitiveness of many companies. Siebel has moved rapidly to provide excellent offerings in both these areas. Siebel has always worked with tremendous foresight and vision that have powered its growth to its present position as one of the pre-eminent business applications software company.

# Chapter 6 The Siebel CRM Implementation Project Cycle

In this chapter, we will take an overview of a Siebel implementation project life cycle. First, we will consider the context of launching such a project, which includes the objectives of the project, implementation strategies and resource requirements of a company. We will also provide an overview of the pre-implementation, implementation and post-implementation phases of the project. The chapter will conclude by identifying some of the aspects involved with the deployment of Siebel at remaining sites, as well as the issues of supporting a Siebel production environment.

It is assumed that after the evaluation and selection of the CRM system for the company, it would have decided to implement Siebel as the core solution throughout the organization. All other systems, whether they are legacy or likely to be implemented in the future, have to interface with the Siebel backbone that will be implemented within the company. We will also assume that the company has evaluated, selected and contracted for the hardware and networking infrastructure and the Siebel implementation partners, as well as any other vendors for training, testing, system and network management support and services, and so forth.

It must be noted that the approach being presented here is based on the author's experience and perception of Siebel projects. The situations in particular projects might certainly be different, and the measures presented here might not be applicable. Siebel projects should still be considered recent phenomena and no one is in a position to take a definitive stance on various aspects of such projects. We urge readers to modify the prescriptive message, particularly of this and subsequent chapters, to suit the particular circumstances of individual companies. This might also be true by reason of the fact that Siebel implementations for MME enterprises might differ qualitatively from implementations for the earlier Fortune 500 enterprises.

## 6.1 MISSION AND OBJECTIVES OF THE SIEBEL PROJECT

The mission of the Siebel project should dovetail into the mission and objectives set forth by the company for the following 3 to 5 years.

The Siebel implementation project itself could have a mission similar to the following:

**To prepare, implement and support Siebel throughout the organization in the planned period of 2 years, with the full participation of all stakeholders of the company and to their satisfaction.**

Project objectives set for the Siebel effort are quantifiable items such as:

- Increasing by 3% the percentage of customers that deliver 80% of revenues (in total, by product category, by specific product, etc.)
- Increasing by 5% the percentage of customers that deliver more than 100% of the profits
- Increasing the marketing spend on existing customers by 15%
- Increasing customer retention by 5%
- Increasing process throughputs by 30%
- Reducing transaction turnaround times by 50%; these could be related to collecting or making payments, responding to internal requisitions or external queries, and so forth

The success of the CRM strategy, which is directly related to engaging, acquiring, retaining and growing customers, can be assessed using various CRM metrics like:

- Customer Value Metrics
- Customer Behavior Metrics
- Customer Loyalty Metrics

### 6.1.1 Examples of Cited Reasons for Implementing Siebel

At present there are more than 4700 Siebel installations throughout the world. The reasons cited for undertaking Siebel vary markedly from company to company. Some of these are:

- Limitations in expanding on the existing applications
- Application's ability to function on heterogeneous hardware and infrastructure
- Applications' ability to provide company-wide uniform user-interface across incompatible front-end hardware
- Application's ability to enable all business events online
- Application's ability to provide access to real-time information
- Application's ability to provide support for cross-functional processes
- Application's ability to enable flexible adjustment of business processes to market demands
- Application's ability to enable integration of customer-facing systems with back office systems
- Application's ability to ensure that business processes are not be hampered by system or national boundaries
- Application's ability to provide support country-specific functionality
- Application's ability to provide reduction in lead time

## 6.2 GUIDING PRINCIPLES FOR CRM BEST PRACTICES

CRM is the sum of the people, processes and technologies working together to:

- Attract target customers

- Increase the value of the existing customers
- Retain profitable customers for as long as possible

The guiding principles to create CRM best practices are as follows.

(a) Define the customer relationship strategies required to:
   - Acquire new customers by creating awareness of your differentiated product and service offering
   - Retain your best customers by better responding to their needs
   - Increase the value of the relationship with your customers

(b) Design and implement the CRM processes and programs which will allow you to:
   - Create a closed-loop relationship with the customer
   - Manage the customer throughout their relationship and life cycle with the company and its employees
   - Respond and respond in real-time to customer needs, inquiries, problems and opportunities across all channels and touch points
   - Anticipate customer needs and expectations in order to differentiate the experience you deliver to the customer

(c) Select, develop and integrate the applications, tools and technology infrastructure needed to:
   - Capture all relevant transactions and relationship information about the customer's behavior, requirements, attitudes and expectations
   - Analyze the information and data in order to create a meaningful relationship experience regardless of the marketing, sales, service or communication objective
   - Plan the programs, initiatives and tactics for interacting with the customer based on anticipated customer needs and corporate objectives
   - Execute the process, programs and initiatives in real-time, providing the necessary decision-making support for people within the company who are called upon to flawlessly execute the specific customer interactions

## 6.3 PROJECT INITIATION AND PLANNING

For business-driven projects such as Siebel it is vital that the top management should not only be involved, but should also drive the project at every stage. Therefore, the project initiation would start with the appointment of an executive sponsor for the project. Usually the executive sponsor should be the CEO of the company. That appointment should be followed by the formation of a project executive committee and a steering committee. These should be followed by the appointment of a Chief Project Officer (CPO) and also the finalization of the scope of the project.

The CPO, under the guidance of the executive and steering committees should assemble the implementation team, including the identification of module and site managers. The project management policies and guidelines should be finalized. The central project office should be established, including the critical support staff such as the training manager, the resources manager and the project administrative staff. This team will have to prepare a plan and schedule for the implementation project, including the various activities, the manpower required, the duration and the schedule for completing each of these activities.

The CPO will have to form another team to look after the procurement, installation and productive operation of the basic infrastructure, including the hardware servers and clients, networking hardware and software, operating systems, databases, office automation software, and so forth.

## 6.4 CRITICAL SUCCESS FACTORS

Various factors are considered critical for the success of the Siebel projects. We will look at each of them in this section.

### 6.4.1 Direct Involvement of the Top Management

Siebel implementation is not an IT project but a business strategy project. As with any other business strategy project for new product development, new marketing strategy, BPM project, and so on, a Siebel project should get the direct attention and involvement of the senior management. If this involvement is confined only to the initial stages of the project, the project is certain to falter later.

One of the issues in which top management is required to demonstrate and encourage full commitment to the Siebel project is the deputation of key managers from different departments. Particularly in consumer goods industries, participating in IT-oriented projects might be considered a non-value adding activity in terms of its ability to further managers' career goals. This perception must be corrected because Siebel implementation is not an IT-driven effort. Furthermore, the full participation in the project of all the employees who will use Siebel for their routine operations is very critical. This can be ensured only by deputing the key managers of the company for this effort.

### 6.4.2 Clear Project Scope

It is very important for a project to have a well-defined scope. Any ambiguities lead only to diffusion of focus and dissipation of effort. There are always adherents especially for increased scope, and a series of such increments in scope would render any project unsuccessful. This is also referred to as 'scope creep'. Hence, the CPO must be vigilant on any creep in the scope of the project.

### 6.4.3 Covering as Many Functions as Possible Within the Scope of the Siebel Implementation

Companies that are multi-divisional and multi-located develop differently at different sites and acquire a character of their own at each site that may not fit into a uniform mould across the organization. A CRM package must have an ability to provide a comprehensive functionality to implement such deeply ingrained, differing ways of operations at different locations. It should be able to provide ready-to-use, best practice processes that incorporate such varying ways of executing any business transaction or process. We have mentioned that more the functions that are integrated and performed in real-time, the more competitive the organization will be. For this, it is essential that as many functions as possible should go productive together on Siebel. This 'big bang' strategy will have to be adopted at a beginning stage of the projects, such as the discovery and design stage. Hence, it is critical that at least all the basic components of Siebel like eBusiness Applications, Sales, Services and Marketing, should be implemented at the pilot site.

### 6.4.4 Standardizing Business Process

Every office or customer service center of a company develops its own character and culture, which is the result of the company's recommended corporate environment blending with the local situations. Such local practices have strong adherents and generate fierce loyalty and pride. These factors often hinder the progress of a system implementation across the organization at all of its sites and offices, even if it is a computerized system such as Siebel. As a prerequisite, it is important to streamline and standardize a business process.

### 6.4.5 Proper Visibility and Communication on the Siebel Project at All Stages

It is important to give proper visibility to the Siebel project. This might entail communicating about the strategic direction of the company, the relevance of Siebel, the Siebel implementation project and team, and the implementation plan and schedule. Either there could be a bulletin exclusively focused on the Siebel project or the company's in-house newsletter must have regular features and articles on Siebel project related issues and milestones.

### 6.4.6 Allocation of Appropriate Budget and Resources

After the company has made the strategic decision to undertake the Siebel implementation effort, it must also prepare and approve the budget plan and estimates for the complete Siebel project. Because the project schedules are dependent non-linearly on the prerequisite at all stages, any changes or deferment of release of funds and therefore resources, will always have an adverse effect on the successful commencement of the project.

Many times the controllers or decision-makers will withhold sanction for the resources at a particular stage at a pilot site or for other sites in order to optimize costs. It must be noted that when any business project is launched, and Siebel implementation is no exception, any deferment of such strategic programs only *increases the opportunity cost* for the period that the project is delayed. Moreover, for an integrated project such as Siebel, that opportunity cost is not confined only to the local activity or site that contributes to the delay, but applies to the whole company. Thus, a company with a turnover of $500 million would effectively incur an opportunity cost of $25–50 million for every delayed month in the schedule after launch of the Siebel project.

### 6.4.7 Full-time Deputation of Key Managers from All the Departments

In traditional IS/IT projects the personnel normally allocated to such efforts are either members who are young and newly recruited, or are older members who could be spared from their respective departments. In either case, this will not help greatly to lead the projects to success. Siebel being a strategic project, should get allocation of the key personnel of different departments because only if the inputs are accurate and functionally correct will the Siebel system truly deliver when it goes into production. Unlike the large enterprises, MME enterprises whose staff strength is small, must allocate their best people with the conviction that after Siebel is in production correctly, it will give better returns not only in terms of money but also in other dimensions like relationships, satisfaction surveys, improved brand, and so on.

### 6.4.8 Completing Infrastructural Activities in Time and with High Availability

Consistent with the approach being taken in this book, the infrastructure for a Siebel project, whether it is the computers and networking infrastructure or human infrastructure in terms of skills acquisition and training, must not be treated as an IS/IT infrastructure. It must be monitored like any other non-IS/IT infrastructure. Any mismatch between the readiness of the infrastructure and the overlaying Siebel system will only lead to delays in the project and hence, incur opportunity costs.

### 6.4.9 Instituting a Company-wide Change Management Plan

Like any other strategy implementation plan Siebel implementation is a prime case of an organizational change. It should be recognized and planned as such. In parallel with the Siebel implementation effort, it makes sense to undertake a change management program to address the disorientation and lost sense of direction that might be experienced by a large number of members. If not managed properly, this could jeopardize the success of the whole project.

Top management should note that unlike traditional IS/IT projects, most Siebel implementations do not have *parallel runs* in which incumbent systems are run along with the older ones for a predetermined time period until the new systems are declared operational and the company switches over to the new regime. This happens because after Siebel goes productive, the transactions and the actual operational tasks are done on the Siebel System itself; any major error could turn fatal for the company. The situation might seem alarming based on the past experiences of the traditional IT systems going productive; however, that is the exact point we are trying to make in this book. Siebel is not like a traditional IT/IS project; it represents a totally different model of computerization (see Chapter 2, sub-section "CRM Represents the New Departmental Store Model of Implementing Computerized Systems").

### 6.4.10 Training of Siebel Team Members

The training needs for all the members of the team should be identified and corporate training programs should be arranged, either on-site or at external training programs. For the MME enterprise where project schedules are shorter and the manpower base in the organization is smaller, it is essential that training is initiated and completed before the scheduled start of the program. Members should be encouraged to take certification tests in their concerned area of activity.

### 6.4.11 Training of User Members

Awareness as well as familiarity training for all users who are likely to use the Siebel productive system is important. Training plans should provide not only for training programs but also budget for refresher courses for all members. Sometimes, when the Siebel project is reaching critical mass, the user community as a whole may be disadvantaged because of a time lag between the actual training and the commencement of Siebel going into production. In such cases, refresher courses may have to be undertaken either very close to the actual commencement of implementation or, if all sites and offices go live on Siebel, on a staggered schedule. Again, top management should allocate a good contingency training budget in view of the fact that when Siebel goes into production there is no fallback arrangement; once launched, it has to reach 'critical mass'.

### 6.4.12 Scheduling and Managing Interface of Siebel with Other Systems

There are many legacy systems, non-Siebel systems, external systems and even manual functions that may be considered out of the scope of the Siebel project. Siebel does not address all the functional requirements of a company. This may be involved with solutions for security and access, e-mail, CTI, digitizing system, and so on. Siebel has a complete program of interfacing with and qualifying third-party products to leverage on companies with special expertise and products (see Chapter 5, sub-section "Partnering for Growth"). Interfacing these systems should be scheduled in such a way that the interfaces are operational when Siebel goes into production.

In cases where a peripheral or support system could be replaced by some functionality provided by Siebel, the steering committee must judge the schedule of that functionality's implementation in Siebel. Considering the onerous agenda of the Siebel project itself, the committee could decide to continue using the earlier system and transit to the functionality in Siebel at a more appropriate time.

### 6.4.13 Transition Plan for Cut-over to Siebel

The company must have a subsidiary project plan for transitioning from the earlier systems to the Siebel system, whether they are computerized or manual. This may entail uploading data in a timely fashion into the Siebel system. The timeliness of the data may be dictated by whether it is master unchangeable data or transaction data; or it may be like opening balances for General Ledger (GL) accounts and party ledger accounts. It could also be processing jobs that are done on a periodic basis, which may have to be transferred to the Siebel production system. Because everything cannot just be transferred automatically to Siebel, a phased approach starting with uploading of data, to transactions, to posting statuses and subsequent processing steps may have to be designed and executed.

## 6.5 IMPLEMENTATION STRATEGY

In this section, we consider what should be adopted by a MME enterprise for its Siebel implementation projects.

*(a)* ***Big Bang Implementation of Siebel Components***

The organization should consider a 'big bang' implementation of Siebel, wherein all the base components of Siebel (relevant to the enterprise's area of business) are implemented and put in production together. The company should not hope to reap more significant benefits than those accruing from the traditional systems if it implements only certain components of the system. If Siebel is not to be used as a past-facing system merely for recording and reporting purposes but more as a future-facing handler of strategic information and relationships, implementation of all the *basic components* corresponding to the businesses of the company is essential. The Siebel system is componentized and thus, allows component-wise implementations. However, this is one feature that we recommend should be ignored unless it is unavoidable because of extreme circumstances. A piecemeal approach of progressive implementation should be abandoned because delaying the implementations of all basic components together only delays the benefits of a fully-functional Siebel and therefore, incurs opportunity costs.

*(b)* ***Base Components Implemented First***

This strategy clearly dictates that the base components should be implemented with the highest priority, though the definition of base component may vary from industry to industry. But, in contrast other components or interfaces to other systems could be handled more appropriately after the base components as a whole have stabilized.

*(c)* ***Implementation of Siebel Standard Functionality***

A standardization of processes usually leads to tremendous gains in terms of maintenance, future upgrades, documentation, training and even routine operations, and the administration of the CRM applications. Custom support is counter to the general emphasis on standardizing the processes and implementing generic ones. It is a business truism that the survival and success of a company depends on how it differentiates itself and its products or services from those of its competitors. To leverage on their competencies or advantages companies cannot abandon the corresponding differentiating processes and will have to incorporate such fundamental variants in their CRM implementations. But, as far as possible, avoid the bugbear of customization by altering and additional programming in Siebel Tools. Additional programming should be evaluated and adopted only as a last resort. Siebel keeps upgrading its suite of products and if custom software is built for a particular version, it will have to be upgraded every time Siebel releases new upgrades. Like any other product, Siebel goes through oscillating cycles between major functional upgrades followed by technical upgrades and vice versa.

The best solution is to:

- Use Siebel standard functionality
- Accommodate the variation of the business process by using Siebel's flexibility for configuring variant processes
- Adopt a workaround that indirectly takes care of the required functionality; for example, in the absence of the HR module some accounts interfacing HR functions can be managed by treating employees as customers
- Use third-party products that are properly certified and qualified by Siebel

***(d) Pilot Site Deployment Followed by Rollouts at Other Sites***

This strategy entails deploying as comprehensive a functionality as possible at the pilot site and preparing the base reference Siebel configuration at the first site. This configuration is merely rolled out rapidly with minimal changes at other sites. These changes may have to do, for instance, with loading separate master data for a different portfolio of products or services or marketing programs that may be sold or promoted at different sites. Thus, subsequent to the implementation at the pilot site, the project effort at the other sites will mainly involve:

(i) Installing Siebel
(ii) Functional training of super users and end-users
(iii) Training technical personnel in Siebel system administration and management functions
(iv) Uploading corresponding data
(v) Integration testing

***(e) Utilize External Consultants to Primarily Train In-house Functional and Technical Consultants***

No external consultant can match the know-how of the functional and operational requirements of the company better than its own members who have the requisite expertise and experience working in various capacities and on different functions in the company. External consultants should be used as facilitators for getting their own key members familiarized with the functionality and navigation of the Siebel system (see Appendix A, "Selecting Siebel Implementation Partners").

Considering the tight schedules, external consultants would have to shoulder the main effort and deliverables during the business design and configure stages of the eRoadmap methodology. But the focus of their participation should be in transferring the Siebel product know-how to the key members of the implementation team. The key members of the implementation team will have the key responsibility of not only rolling out Siebel to other sites, but also of providing the necessary support for the Siebel effort in the future. As maybe noted, it is not as simple as it may sound because after gaining expertise on Siebel product know-how such key members have a marked tendency to quit their jobs and join the growing number of independent Siebel consultants or join one of the Siebel consultancy firms.

Because of their backgrounds, the IS/IT professionals have a critical role in acting as facilitators for non IS/IT-savvy functional members to clarify, define and decide on their business requirements, and in assisting the functional members in configuring the system to obtain the desired functionality.

***(f) Centralized or Decentralized Siebel Configuration***

Siebel installations have had centralized database servers. The enterprises of the millennium with distributed database servers may need to use the decentralized configuration. As we have noted in Chapter 5, "The Siebel Solution", Siebel distributed architecture enables the integration of data and processes across the entire system.

***(g) User-driven Functionality***

In marked contrast to traditional IS/IT projects, Siebel projects are user-driven. The key members on the implementation team from the functional and business departments play the critical role of documenting and mapping the 'AS IS' (or existing) processes and deciding on the 'TO BE' processes. The mapping and configuration of the desired functionality proceeds by an approach, closer to the Joint Application Development and prototyping methodology of the '80s.

## 6.6 SIEBEL IMPLEMENTATION PROJECT BILL OF RESOURCES (BOR)

Taking a cue from the Bill of Materials (BOM) employed in Production Planning and Control (PPC) functions, we can define a generalized version of the same for the Siebel implementation project called the Bill of Resources (BOR). It enables one to define the hierarchy of the inputs, resources and costs in the same structure. In this section, we provide an overview of what resources are needed for a Siebel implementation project.

Siebel recommends the eRoadmap methodology as the primary implementation methodology for MME enterprises (discussed in detail in Part IV, "The Implementation Stage").

### 6.6.1 Money

Although it is obviously dangerous to make any kind of generalization, an average Siebel project for MMEs may range from $3 million to $5 million.

In a typical CRM implementation, 28 percent of the total cost goes towards buying software, while 38 percent goes towards services such as software customizations, application integration and training. Hardware makes up 23 percent of the cost, while telecommunication expenses make up the remaining 11 percent.

> Companies may spend about $10,000 per user per year on hardware, software, customization, support and training.

### 6.6.2 Materials

The material inputs needed are:

(a) Hardware—Servers (database, application, data warehouse, communications, network, e-mail, and so on) and client PCs

(b) Networking—Hardware and software

(c) Software—CRM, front-end GUI software, data warehouse, DBMS, operating system, office automation systems, and so on

(d) Project office and Siebel Center infrastructure

### 6.6.3 Manpower

The manpower resources essential are:

(a) Executive management

(b) Senior officers
(c) Technical personnel
(d) System administrative and support personnel
(e) Office administrative and support personnel
(f) Super Power or Key users
(g) End-users

### 6.6.4 Time Period

The duration of a Siebel project for MMEs may range from 4 to 9 months.

### 6.6.5 Information

The significant input is the documentation of business process for the whole of the enterprise. This includes documentation on each process, including inputs, outputs, duration, labor, frequency, processing, purpose, interfaces, initiator, supervisor, and so on.

## 6.7 IMPLEMENTATION ENVIRONMENT

The implementation environment consists of several components, discussed in the following sub-sections.

(a) Siebel Enterprise Server Architecture—Siebel Enterprise Applications are built on an advanced, Web-based enterprise server architecture that provides a wide variety of features for deploying and supporting heterogeneous Siebel users enterprise-wide. It corresponds broadly to the common 3-tier architecture with the following layers:
   - The presentation tier clients including the HTML and thin clients, mobile clients and connected clients
   - The middle tier enterprise server which deploys BusObjects and includes the Siebel Server, Gateway Server (providing Name Server and connection brokering services), and Server Manager components
   - The database tier for storing data in the Siebel Database Server and Siebel File System

(b) Siebel Server is the application server platform within the Siebel Enterprise Server. The Siebel Server supports a wide variety of components, executing in both multi-process and multi-threaded models, as follows:
   - Siebel Workflow
   - Siebel Assignment Manager
   - Siebel Enterprise Integration Manager
   - Siebel Object Manager
   - Siebel Remote
   - Siebel Replication Manager

(c) Siebel Tools is the integrated and full-featured development environment for custom development or enhancement of Siebel standard functionality. Built on the latest industry-standard development platform from Microsoft, Siebel Tools enables unprecedented levels of application customization and ease of use for Siebel customers seeking to extend Siebel Enterprise Applications. It is composed of:

- Siebel Business Object (BusObject) Designer gives developers the ability to customize Siebel products quickly and easily. It includes:
    - Siebel BusObject Explorer
    - Siebel Object Visualization Views
    - Siebel Applet Designer
    - Siebel View Designer
    - Siebel Menu Designer
    - New Object Wizards
    - BusObject Repository Manager
    - Siebel BusObject Compiler
- Siebel VB is a complete Visual Basic (VB)-complaint environment for integrating Siebel Enterprise Applications with third-party cooperative applications and extending the base functionality of the Siebel application screens and Business Components.
- Siebel Object Interfaces are the technology foundation for such *online* real-time integration with legacy desktop, Web-based, server-based and mainframe-based legacy applications. Object interfaces are also defined through the Siebel Repository and can be customized by changing attributes in the repository and scripting with Siebel VB to adopt them to the existing external models.
- Siebel Database Extension Designer provides a point-and-click interface for extending Siebel application tables when developers need extension even beyond the built-in database extensions.
- Siebel Application Up grader radically reduces the time, effort and hence, cost of version upgrades by enabling customers to better determine and compare the changes available in a new release with the customizations from an earlier release.

(d) Siebel Enterprise Integration Manager (EIM) provides for *batch* interface for highly efficient data integration with external applications. EIM supports bi-directional exchange of large volumes of transaction and event data through pre-built and extensible interfaces.

(e) Siebel Remote and Siebel Replication Manager are the only proven, enterprise-class synchronization solutions that meet all the needs of mobile and distributed deployments; they provide complete capabilities for both mobile users and server-to-server synchronization.

## 6.8 IMPLEMENTATION METHODOLOGY

Under ideal conditions, projects can be completed in the most efficient manner in time and on budget. However, what is essential is to have a standardized approach of systems and procedures that could guide a company, which is new to Siebel, to implement Siebel successfully without any major risk of failure. Such an approach is called a *methodology*. A methodological approach may not be the *most*

efficient one but it ensures success under *optimal conditions*. Companies survive and grow not by planning for the most ideal or adverse conditions but by planning for optimal conditions. In the case of a Siebel implementation project, the implementation methodology must ensure success given the usual complexity of businesses, resources, organizational structures, time schedules, and so on.
An enterprise implementation methodology broadly covers the following:

(a) Modeling business processes—where the company defines the envisaged or to-be business processes
(b) Mapping business processes onto the processes supported by Siebel—where the company discovers the Siebel standard processes and functionality that address the requirements of the modeled process
(c) Performing the gap analysis—where the company assesses the difference or gap between the Siebel standard and functionality, and the requirements of the modeled processes
(d) Finalizing the scope of the Siebel implementation project—where the company decides on the scope of the Siebel implementation in terms of the processes that would be implemented in the Siebel system
(e) Configuring the Siebel system—where the company configures the basic parameters in the Siebel system
(f) Validating the customized Siebel system—where the configured system is tested for delivered functionality with actual data

The identified gaps in functionality can be rectified by any of these measures:

- Devise a workaround for achieving the same functionality and configure it accordingly
- Program the required functionality in CRM system via user exits
- Suggest third-party Siebel add-ons or plug-ins that provide the desired functionality and that have been certified for compatibility through Siebel's Complementary Software Program (CSP)
- Defer its implementation to the next wave of implementation or defer it until the Siebel release update (that will introduce this functionality) becomes available
- Change the business process radically so that it is suitable to the functionality available in Siebel to achieve the same objectives
- Modify Siebel software directly, although modified software may lead to incompatibility with future releases of Siebel

## 6.8.1 eRoadmap Methodology

The Siebel eRoadmap is a phased project implementation method designed to ensure the success of a Siebel Business Applications implementation. Siebel consultants use the method to identify and address key strategic and tactical issues and to develop a blueprint for the progress of the project.

The Siebel eRoadmap prescribes eight iterative stages of activities. These are as follows:

- **Plan stage**—The team develops comprehensive strategies that serve as the baseline for the various subsequent stages of the implementation. This ensures that measurable objectives have been established, alignment of the enterprise has occurred and a vision has been articulated.

- **Define stage**—Siebel consultants work with client personnel to organize the project team, set the project approach and scope, and establish project management controls. The project sponsor then officially launches the project by presenting its objectives and timetable to the extended project team.
- **Discover stage**—The project team refines and documents the functional and technical requirements of the company's business goals. This consists of creation of detailed business process flows, documentation of detailed system requirements and completion of a gap analysis of stated requirements against Siebel functionality.
- **Design stage**—The project team designs the solution using application screen flows and design layouts to map the requirements developed in the discover stage.
- **Configure stage**—The project team configures the application, creates any required extensions and integrates any external interfaces needed to support the system.
- **Validation stage**—The project team completes this in two parts. First, the project team conducts a full-function system test of the application with production data. Key users then perform an acceptance test to validate user requirements. The test environment will evaluate functionality, usability, scalability, reliability and performance.
- **Deploy stage**—The team conducts a production pilot that provides all the system's features to users in a segment of the organization's business environment, such as a region or district. Feedback from the production pilot guides the full rollout. Activities in this stage include final configuration revisions, production environment tuning, user training and data conversion.
- **Sustain stage**—The team measures the results, including user adoption and customer satisfaction. These are used as the inputs for the next cycle of the implementation.

We will discuss eRoadmap methodology in detail in Part IV of this book.

## 6.9 PROJECT MANAGEMENT

The purpose of project management is to help define the tasks that are necessary to complete a project, control the progress of the activities and account for the resources expended through the project.

### 6.9.1 Project Organization

Project organization consists of constitution of the various teams that are assigned to different tasks of the project. It entails nominating the various members of all teams, appointing team leaders and reporting structures for compiling the progress reports of each team, which are consolidated progressively into higher level progress reports. Usually, the team will consist of the technical team, the Siebel Tools programming team, and many teams corresponding to major components within Siebel. Each of these will later contain sub-teams for performing analysis and design as well as undertaking documentation and testing of the various components.

### 6.9.2 Project Control

It is essential that the work of all teams and groups of teams in different areas be controlled for gauging the progress, or lack of it, in the corresponding tasks. For this, the effort and time expended will have to be recorded and monitored on a daily basis. This would be helpful in detecting delays and slippage, reconstituting the teams and reinforcing any team with additional resources wherever necessary.

(a) Time Recording

Time recording involves recording the time expended under various categories of activities by every member of the team. This is essential not only for the external consultants but for company members as well. An analysis of the time spent in various activities could be helpful in identifying the effort and cost expended in identifying gaps, resolving gap issues, talking with end users, configuration, documentation, functional and technical testing, debugging functional and technical errors, and so forth.

(b) Meetings

Project meetings could be for all project-related issues such as:

- Scope of the project
- Project strategy
- Constitution of teams
- Project schedule and milestones
- Requirements and business processes
- Gap issues and their resolution
- Issues that have not been resolved
- Decisions on standardizing processes
- Preparation of test plans and data
- Test reports
- Debugging and candidate solutions
- Documentation and updates
- Software upgrades
- Scheduling training programs
- Nominating team members for training
- Resource availability and utilization
- Conflicts and resolutions
- User accounts, access and authorizations
- Performance and availability
- Hardware and networking vendors
- Providers of implementation services and consultancy
- Bill payments
- Leave and resignations

(c) Project Monitoring

The actual effort and time expended need to be compared to the planned effort and schedule on a frequent basis. Any observed deviations or pattern of deviations, are corrected immediately. Any rescheduling of the project plan is addressed only in the project reviews.

(d) Project Reviews

The main objective of project reviews is to ascertain the progress made with reference to the planned schedule. Progress on the action points of the last review is reassessed. Any shortfalls in achieving milestones or delays are diagnosed for the reasons, and corrective measures taken are endorsed or changed. Any suggestions for changing strategies are considered during the reviews. Any unforeseen problems cropping up during the project are analyzed here.

## 6.10 SIEBEL IMPLEMENTATION

Unlike the traditional software development project, this involves three main phases—pre-implementation, implementation and post-implementation. The pre-implementation issues have been discussed in Chapters 12 and 13. Implementation by using the eRoadmap methodology is presented in Chapter 14. The post-implementation phase is discussed in Chapter 15.

### 6.10.1 Pre-implementation

Pre-implementation involves the formation of the project and steering committees, the constitution of the implementation project team, and the installation of hardware and Siebel software. The latter involves readying the hardware and infrastructure, installing the operating systems, database software, client software and Siebel software. The Siebel administration function entails systems administration, applications administration, ISS transaction server administration, communications server administration, network administration, database administration, printer administration, client administration, user's authentication and access security administration, and so forth. Another major activity during this phase is training for the implementation team and other users, which is very critical to the success of the project.

(a) Training

Considering the short timeframes of the Siebel implementation projects, Siebel has identified training as an important determinant in the success of any project. Siebel offers a broad spectrum of training courses covering all stakeholders of a Siebel project. These courses cover a range of topics from a general overview to in-depth coverage of individual topics.

Siebel University technical courses provide comprehensive training for the entire implementation team. Siebel's courses are designed to get a team up to speed quickly and efficiently. Some of these are:

- Using Siebel 7x
- Siebel Server Administration
- Siebel Tools
- Migrating Siebel
- Siebel Sales Enterprise

- Siebel Service Enterprise
- Siebel Field Service
- Siebel Finance
- etc.

Similarly, Siebel End User Education provides training to the end-users to ensure the quality of end-user deployment. This is achieved through a customized training process to maximize the benefits of the software as it applies to the company's business and integrates a variety of delivery methods including instructor-led training, CBT, self-directed study, Internet-based training, distance learning, etc.

(b) Siebel Installation

This basically involves installing the base license and designing the system landscape including the ISS Transaction Server, Enterprise Integration Manager (EIM), Communications Server, eBizConn, Anywhere, and so on.

(c) Implementation

For the MMEs, Siebel recommends the eRoadmap methodology (mentioned earlier). It consists of the following eight stages:

(i) Plan
(ii) Define
(iii) Discover
(iv) Design
(v) Configure
(vi) Validate
(vii) Deploy
(viii) Sustain

### 6.10.2 Post-implementation

The post-implementation phase involves instituting support and services such as the Siebel Call Center, Employee Relationship Management (ERM), Siebel Anywhere and so on. Following the implementation of the base components, other components such as Siebel Data Warehouse, Siebel Workflow, and so on can be implemented.

For effective Siebel operations, training of implementation team and user personnel is essential. This could also be achieved through implementation of Siebel eTrain which is Siebel's solution for Web-based training.

## 6.11 SIEBEL SUPPORT

Support includes various measures or activities that are undertaken to ensure availability in terms of the application functionality or continued functioning of the system.

It deals with design, organization and operation of a help desk or a call center for the Siebel users within the company. Users can register their complaints and queries, and get specific responses that can be implemented by the end-users with the help of the super users in their respective departments.

Hardware availability is ensured by various measures, such as disaster recovery systems and archiving of data.

## 6.12 SIEBEL DEPLOYMENT

After Siebel goes into production at the pilot site, it is important to have scheduled the focus to immediately shift to the other sites. In fact, at those other sites certain activities including training of super users and preparation of data for uploading into the Siebel system should be undertaken in parallel with the last stages of implementation at the pilot site. It is advised to immediately commence implementation at other sites because doing so enables the company to leverage the momentum generated by the implementation at the pilot site. Moreover, any breaks between the implementations may cause members of the core team to look for other challenging opportunities.

If training super users and data loading are done in parallel with the finishing stages of the deployment at the pilot site(s), what remains during the actual Siebel project at the sites is:

(i) Deploying the base configuration prepared at the pilot site
(ii) Conducting the integration test
(iii) Conducting the training of the end-users at the concerned site
(iv) Going live

## 6.13 WHY SOME SIEBEL PROJECTS FAIL

There are various reasons why Siebel projects may be less than successful. CRM is a complex endeavor requiring significant change management expertise, business process experience and domain knowledge. Failure in CRM projects may be because of the following reasons:

- Top management involvement and interest falters or is perceived as faltering
- Lack of clear project scope and strategies; project is too narrowly focused
- Implementation of non-optimized processes in Siebel
- Decisions regarding changes in processes and procedures may not be effected; they may be ignored or subverted
- Lack of proper visibility and communication on the Siebel project at all stages
- Lack of adequate budget and resources such as, for training of large groups of envisaged end-users
- Not deputing the key managers on the implementation team
- Support infrastructure and systems are delayed inordinately
- Disputes and conflicts in the team are not resolved quickly
- Company members of the team may not get along with the external consultants
- External consultants may have differences with end-users or user managers

- Core team members may have differences with user departments
- A company-wide change management plan is not implemented
- Too much time between the implementation at the deployment/pilot site and rollout sites
- Members of the company do not participate actively because
    - Sales persons, sales consultants and sales managers are extremely possessive of their customers and related interaction information; such withholding of critical customer information prevents the information stored in CRMs to be treated fully as customer relationships and to be leveraged for maximum benefit of the enterprise as a whole
    - Members feel the system has been implemented in haste and that it does not address their requirements; they feel they have not been taken into confidence
    - Members feel they have not been given adequate training
    - Members of the company are apprehensive of their future roles
    - Members of the company are afraid that they may not be able to learn the new system and perform satisfactorily
    - Members of the company feel unsettled by the lack of hierarchy in the system
    - Members feel they have been reduced to data entry operators
- Members of the core implementation team may resign and leave the company
- Members of the core team may be averse to moving on projects at rollout sites
- Inexperienced consulting resources
- Slow decision-making process
- Scope creep

The solutions for tackling these problems will vary from company to company. The approach to be adopted will depend upon the industry, culture and history of the company. An approach to handling these kind of issues is referred to in an earlier section "Critical Success Factors" and is discussed further in the next section.

## 6.14 THE PEOPLE FACTOR

Siebel implementation has a fundamental and far-reaching effect on the organizational and human resources aspects of the company. Customer relationships are enabled, controlled and managed by people and not by the CRM systems. When planning the CRM strategy, the users' reaction to change, their learning curve and their commitment to adoption of the new system needs to be incorporated into the whole strategy.

CRM often provokes large and disruptive change within the work environment. Whether the change is positive or negative, resistance is inevitable. The best way to handle this change is to put in place a change management plan that employs systematic methods to ensure that the organizational change necessitated by a CRM initiative is guided in a cost-effective and efficient manner. With careful planning and consideration of the human element of change, a CRM initiative can avoid some of the pitfalls that stymie many CRM projects.

The organizational change management task deals with a series of change processes that facilitates diagnosing and managing change issues in order to optimize the benefits accruing from the implementation of a CRM solution like Siebel. Siebel recommends an array of processes like impact analysis, assessment of baseline risks, the sponsorship strategy, user-adoption strategy, training and skills development, know-how transfer process, and so on.

### 6.14.1 Business Impact Map

This is the starting point of the change management process and its aim is to determine the potential impact of the envisaged Siebel implementation. The business impact map helps greatly in assessing the scope, degree and priority of the anticipated changes.

The business impact map is prepared based on the following inputs:

(a) Divisions and units expected to be impacted by the envisaged Siebel implementation and hence, the planned change management process

(b) Perception of the senior personnel in each of these units of the expected changes both within their own and other units

(c) Assessment of the timing, magnitude and relative importance of the various changes

Based on these inputs, the change team compiles a matrix of business units' verses the degree of anticipated change. An effective and comprehensive change management strategy can be devised based on the critical areas highlighted by the resulting business impact map. This enables the change team to develop the organizational change management plan that is in tune with the overall Siebel implementation plan and at the same time is aligned with the perceptions and concerns of the individual departments.

### 6.14.2 Baseline Risk Assessment

This assesses the degree to which the company's environment facilitates or inhibits the rapid implementation of Siebel. The results of the assessments provide the critical inputs to the change management process. This task gauges the initial support for the Siebel implementation project. Furthermore, the assessment also reveals the factors that may adversely affect the control and management of the project. Siebel has provided risk assessment guidelines, which should be referred to when developing a strategy suitable to a particular company. The results of this exercise enable the change team to identify the risks associated with the envisaged changes, the potential implications of these risks and possible remedial actions.

The objectives of the risk management are to minimize the impact of unplanned incidents on the project by:

- Identifying the nature, probability and likely impact of potential risks before they occur
- Identifying and implementing preventive measures where possible
- Implementing contingency actions to deal with the risks when they occur

A well-defined risk management strategy focuses on:

(a) Risk management planning

(b) Risk identification

(c) Risk analysis

(d) Risk response planning
(e) Risk monitoring
(f) Implementing risk response plans

The assessment of the risks is also used to shape the communications and sponsorship programs and other change processes. The risk assessment process also identifies the key messages that should be disseminated throughout the organization and that are also suitably tailored to the conditions of the individual organizational units.

## 6.14.3 Sponsorship Strategy

The project leadership is the most critical element of a comprehensive change program. There is a need to assess the facilitation or inhibiting factors inherent in the leadership itself that will directly accelerate or undermine the momentum of the implementation project. The baseline leadership risk assessment is the essential input to the sponsorship process. The sponsor point is a senior executive champion of change who by his/her actions and communications helps in maintaining project credibility, momentum as well as committed support throughout the company.

The leadership risk assessment tool enables the change team to:

- Get a measure of the risks associated with the envisaged Siebel implementation
- Uncover the potential implication of these risks on the Siebel project
- Identify the actions for mitigating these risks to acceptable levels

The change management team needs to work closely with the project and site sponsors as well as the communication point person to consistently address the key negatives and reinforce the potential benefits of implementing Siebel. Periodic administration of the risk assessment process described earlier helps in ascertaining the effectiveness of the sponsorship process. Any perceived deviation towards increasing risks should be countered immediately by specifically targeted communications and credible actions.

A consistent message on the organization's demonstrative commitment and focus to see the CRM system implementation through to a successful end is a powerful enabler for sustaining the right context for achieving the successful completion of the project.

## 6.14.4 Communications Strategy: Aligning the Organization

A key component of a change management plan is the communication plan. This handles the design of the framework for sharing project-related information and status throughout the organization. While doing so, it incorporates the results of the latest risk assessment processes to address the member's genuine concerns and apprehensions about the Siebel implementation and its perceived impact at the organizational level as well as at the individual level. This could be direct communication through formal channels like project and site sponsors or indirectly through the active involvement and participation of a cross-section of the members of the company during project-related events, risk assessment processes, focus group sessions, feedback schemes, etc.

This involves identifying the communication point person who works closely with the change management team as well as the key site sponsors to fine-tune the message and the medium of communication depending on the audience and criticality of the stage, and status of the Siebel project effort. It is important to ensure that the messages are also customized to the differing ground realities at different sites to discuss how Siebel would change jobs, skills, roles, responsibilities, and standards and measurement of performance. Tailoring communications on an organizational unit level also provides the opportunity to enlist the support of the unit level management or even the line management.

This task also includes ascertaining the effectiveness of the communications strategy through:

(a) Informal feedback from focus groups and 'influencers' or 'opinion leaders' or 'thought leaders'

(b) Formal feedback through the periodic risk assessment processes wherein specific questions regarding the project communications process can be presented

## 6.14.5 User-adoption Strategy

Enterprises reap the full business benefits of implementing the Siebel applications only if they adopt a user-focused approach to the Siebel implementation.

A comprehensive user adoption strategy focuses on the following key elements:

- Business alignment
- Communication
- Measurement
- Training and support
- Reinforcement

The associated best practices are as follows:

- Identify and communicate performance expectations
- Assess and grade user adoption
- Identify support structures and develop expert users
- Plan for training

Some of these practices are discussed below.

### 6.14.5.1 Training and Skills Development Process

This task is concerned with forming the skills development team, identifying the important constituencies of the Siebel project effort, compiling the skills inventory, analyzing the gaps in skills, assessing the training needs, and arranging for the content and logistics of the skills development training program. The various constituencies are all members of the Siebel core and the extended team, including senior executives, project and site level sponsors, project team members, Siebel consultants, site level executives, managers, supervisors, and workers.

The type of training required for the various constituencies is as follows:

- Siebel implementation project impact training
- Business process-related training

- Technical and functional training in Siebel
- Siebel skills training

The skills development team would decide on the following:

(a) Content, such as the prototype, tutorial, workshop, case study, testing, or Quality Assurance (QA).

(b) The delivery mechanism for the different kinds of skills training, such as instructor-led or Computer Based Training (CBT) programs.

(c) The delivery system for imparting this training, like Siebel training partners

The skills development team must also set the procedures for assessing the effectiveness of the training given to members covering their identified roles in the Siebel project.

### 6.14.5.2 Know-how Transfer Process

We have spoken about the tacit (or implicit) and explicit knowledge in Chapter 1, "Customer Capital Customer Knowledge as the New Capital" and seen how Siebel acts as a medium for converting the tacit knowledge of a company into a valuable resource. Further, in Chapter 1, note on "Information as the New Resource", we discussed how information acts as a tangible resource that drives the operational processes faster without expending more conventional resources. eRoadmap does for the Siebel implementation process exactly what productive Siebel does for the company as a whole; it uses all of this relevant information to drive the very process of Siebel implementation itself faster!

Implementing the know-how transfer process is related to the achievement of the following objectives.

(a) Converting and codifying the tacit knowledge scattered across the organization into a coherent and integrated body of knowledge for driving the accelerated implementation of Siebel within the organization.

(b) Preventing history from repeating itself in the case of problems occurring during a Siebel implementation by codifying and disseminating the knowledge generated during a Siebel implementation to all the concerned stakeholders. It can also be useful for other organizations to benefit from the experience and expertise gained from past implementations.

The valuable experience and insights gained by all members of the Siebel team should not be lost to other members in the company. All this know-how is an asset and the organization needs to capitalize on it. The eRoadmap know-how transfer process taps the information and experience found both outside and inside the organization. It builds and leverages on the knowledge base that accelerates the Siebel implementation by helping the Siebel project team and the extended team to make correct decisions and enact them quickly.

eRoadmap defines the know-how transfer process to consist of the following aspects:

- Knowledge drivers, which relates to the research, collection, authentication, rationalization, standardization and benchmarking of the information, know-how, and technology
- Knowledge delivery process, which relates to the storing, presentation, sharing and application of the project knowledge

The know-how transfer process is administered and managed by the change team.

## 6.15 SUMMARY

This chapter gave an overview of a complete implementation cycle of a typical Siebel project. Starting with the setting of the mission and objective of a Siebel project, we discussed various aspects related to project planning, implementation strategy, environment, implementation methodology, project management and the phases of implementation, deployment and support of a Siebel CRM system. The chapter also presented Critical Success Factors (CSF) as well as reasons for failures of some of the Siebel projects. With this as a reference, we have highlighted several people-related issues that are critical to the success of Siebel implementation projects like risk management, communications and user adoption strategies including training and skills development programs. Later in the book, Chapters 12 and 13 discuss the prerequisites for undertaking a Siebel implementation project. In Part IV, Chapter 14 discusses the various phases of the eRoadmap methodology for implementing Siebel. Chapter 15, "Supporting Siebel" deals with the post-implementation issues of a Siebel CRM project.

# Chapter 7 Siebel CRM and Business Process Management

This chapter clarifies the role played by Siebel in re-engineering an enterprise while implementing Siebel in the organization. After introducing the concept of Business Process Management (BPM), we look at the full cycle of an enterprise BPM methodology. The relevance and role that Siebel can play at every stage in the re-engineering effort within an enterprise are considered in the section "BPM and Siebel Implementation".

Siebel implementation can result in BPM (or top down dramatic improvements through re-designed, re-engineered or completely new processes); however, it all depends on the approach taken by the enterprise. Some companies implement Siebel trying to duplicate their existing business practices. Although implementing Siebel will result in some improvements in such a case, BPM will not result. For achieving BPM, top down management focus on BPM during the implementation of Siebel is required; the timeframe and project plan must also reflect the goal of BPM.

## 7.1 BACKGROUND OF BUSINESS PROCESS MANAGEMENT (BPM)

Business Process Management (BPM) addresses the following two important issues for an enterprise:

- The strategic long-term ***positioning*** of the business with respect to the current and envisaged customers, which will ensure that the enterprise would be competitively and financially successful, locally and globally
- The enterprise's **capability/capacity** that is the totality of all the internal processes that dynamically realize this positioning of the business

Traditionally, positioning has been considered as an independent set of functional tasks split within the marketing, finance and strategic planning functions. Similarly, capability/ capacity has usually been considered the preserve of the individual operational departments that may have mutually conflicting priorities and measures of performances (see Chapter 2, sub-section "CRM System Reflects and Mimics the Integrated Nature of an Enterprise").

The problem for many enterprises lies in the fact that there is a fundamental flaw in the organizational structure—organizational structures are *hierarchical*, while the transactions and workflows that deliver the solutions (i.e., products and services) to the customers are *horizontal*. Quite simply, the *structure* determines who the customer really is. The traditional management structures condition managers to put functional needs above those of the multi-functional processes to which their functions contribute. This results in:

- Various departments competing for resources
- Collective failure in meeting or exceeding the customers' expectations
- Inability to coordinate and collaborate on multi-functional customer-centric processes that would truly provide the competitive differentiation in future markets

The traditional mass marketing type of organization works well for researching market opportunities, planning the offering, and scheduling all of the steps required to produce and distribute the offering to the marketplace (where it is selected or rejected by the customer). It takes a very different kind of organization, namely, the customized marketing type organization to build long-term relationships with customers so that they call such organizations first when they have a need because they trust that such enterprises will be able to respond with an effective solution. This is customer responsive management, which we will discuss in the section that follows.

- BPM is the process that manages and optimizes the inextricable linkage between the positioning and the capability/capacity of an enterprise.

## 7.1.1 Value-add View of Business Processes

Business processes can very easily be seen as the basis of the value addition within an enterprise that has been traditionally attributed to various functions or divisions. As organizational and environmental conditions become more complex, global and therefore competitive, processes provide a framework for dealing effectively with the issues of performance improvement, capability development and adaptation to the changing environment. Along a value stream (that is, a business process), the analysis of the absence, creation, addition of value, or (worse) destruction of value critically determines the necessity and effectiveness of a process step. The understanding of value adding and non-value adding processes (or process steps) is a significant factor in the analysis, design, benchmarking and optimization of business processes in the companies leading to BPM.

Values are characterized by value determinants like time (such as the cycle time), flexibility (options, customization and composition), responsiveness (lead time, number of hand-offs and duration), quality (rework, rejects and yield), and price (discounts, rebates, coupons and incentives). We must note that we are not disregarding cost (such as materials, labor and overheads) as a value determinant, but the effect of cost is truly a result of other value determinants like time, flexibility, responsiveness, and so on.

The nature and extent of a value addition to a product or service is the best measure of that addition's contribution to the company's overall goal for competitiveness. Such value expectations are dependent upon:

- The customer's experience of similar product(s) and/or service(s)
- The value delivered by the competitors
- The capabilities and limitations of locking into the base technological platform (see Chapter 1, sub-section "Increasing Returns and Customer Capitalism").

However, value as originally defined by Michael Porter in the context of introducing the concept of the value chain, is meant more in the nature of the cost at various stages. Rather than a value chain it is more of a cost chain! Porter's value chain is also a structure-oriented and hence a static concept. Here we mean value as the satisfaction of not only external but also internal customers' requirements, as defined and continuously redefined, as the least total cost of acquisition, ownership and use.

Consequently, in this formulation one can understand the company's competitive gap in the market in terms of such process-based, customer-expected levels of value and the value delivered by the company's process for the concerned products or services. Customer responsiveness focuses on costs in terms of the yield (see section "Activity-Based Costing for BPM" that follows). Therefore, we can perform market segmentation for a particular product or services in terms of the most significant customer values and the corresponding value determinants, or what we term as Critical Value Determinants (CVD). We will look at CVDs in detail in the next section.

Strategic planning exercises can then be understood readily in terms of devising strategies for improving on these process-based CVDs, based on the competitive benchmarking of these 'collaborative' values and processes between the enterprise and customers. These strategies and the tactics resulting from analysis, design and optimization of the process will in turn focus on the re-strategizing of all relevant business process at all levels. This can result in the modification or deletion of the process or creation of a new one.

## 7.1.2 Business Process Re-engineering (BPR)

Although, BPR has its roots in Information Technology (IT) management, it is basically a business initiative that has a major impact on the satisfaction of both the internal and external customer. Michael Hammer, who triggered the BPR revolution in 1990, considers BPR as a 'radical change' for which IT is the key enabler. BPR can be broadly termed as ***the rethinking and change of business processes to achieve dramatic improvements in the measures of performances such as cost, quality, service and speed.***

Some of the principals advocated by Hammer are as follows:

- Organize around outputs, not tasks
- Put the decisions and control, and hence all relevant information, into the hands of the performer
- Have those who use the outputs of a process to perform the process, including the creation and processing of the relevant information
- The location of user, data and process information should be immaterial; it should function as if all were in a centralized place

When perusing the above points it will become evident that the implementation of Siebel possesses most of the characteristics mentioned.

The most important outcome of BPR has been viewing business activities as more than a collection of individual or even functional tasks; it has engendered the process-oriented view of business. However, BPR is different from quality management efforts like TQM, ISO 9000, and so on, that refer to programs and initiatives that emphasize bottom up incremental improvements in existing work processes and outputs on a continuous basis. In contrast, BPR usually refers to top down dramatic improvements through redesigned or completely new processes on a discrete basis. In the continuum of methodologies ranging from ISO 9000, TQM, ABM, and so on, at one end and BPR on the other, Siebel implementation definitely lies on the BPR side of the spectrum when it comes to corporate change management efforts.

### 7.1.3 Business Process Management (BPM)

As stated earlier, BPM is based on the principle that there is an inextricable link between positioning *and* capability/capacity. A company cannot position the organization to meet a customer need that it cannot fulfill without an unprofitable level of resources, nor can it allocate enhanced resources to provide a cost-effective service that no customer wants!

***Theory of Constraints (TOC)***

One factor that drives down customer loyalty is the primary focus on cost and the waves of downsizing, with the resulting adverse impact on the customers. Dr. Eliyahu M. Goldratt's conceived the Theory of Constraints (TOC) by focusing on the concept of throughput as a panacea for the disastrous decisions resulting from misguided overhead cost allocations to different products, services, facilities and other entities. With unfailing regularity, companies end up treating these wrongful allocations as the actual costs that lead to disastrous results like termination of 'apparently' un-profitable product lines, manpower layoffs and plummeting employee morale, and customer confidence.

Dr. Goldratt first introduced TOC in the 1980s, with its application to manufacturing planning and scheduling. He later expanded the theory to systematically and holistically address the problems of complex organizations with many interrelationships and dependencies.

Within TOC,

Throughput (T) = (Sales – Direct variable costs)

Where,

Direct variable costs are usually raw materials

In terms of TOC, enterprises can be considered either to be focused on cost or throughput. The enterprise's focus is directly related to:

- *Measurements focused either on reducing cost or building throughput*
- *Policies that dictate the enterprise's responsive behavior*
- *Training that dictates improvement in the efficiency and effectiveness in executing identified job responsibilities*

A primary focus on throughput includes dealing with issues of customer loyalty and value, and increasing throughput through employee initiative and productivity. In contrast, a primary focus on cost only deals with decreasing the operating expenses (plant labor, administrative costs, utilities, corporate overheads, depreciation, sales and marketing expenses, and so on) and investments (assets like buildings, equipment, fixtures as well as cost of the inventory). Figure 7.1 contrasts the characteristics of a throughput-oriented versus a cost-oriented enterprise. Cost-focused enterprises via cost cutting efforts initially experience quick and dramatic improvements that are eventually followed by stagnation, financial losses and loss of competitiveness. In contrast, the throughput-focused enterprises show a slower start to improvement that reflect time expended on analysis, understanding and confirming customer needs, researching offerings, gaining buy-in from employees and partners for the proposed offering, devising the offering, launching and testing the offering, and finally, installing, servicing and supporting the offering. But this is usually followed by a phase of exponential improvement.

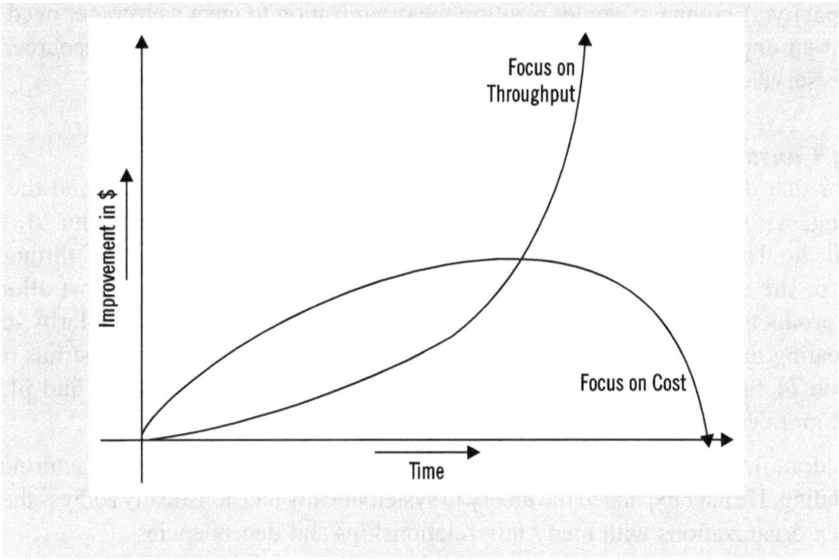


**Fig. 7.1 Throughput-oriented Versus Cost-oriented Enterprise**

Costs cannot be ignored and cost cutting may seem to work in the short-term, but this cannot create the kind of Return of Investment (ROI) that keeps shareholders around for the long-term.

Positioning leads to higher levels of revenue through increasing the size of the market, retaining the first-time customers, increasing the size of the wallet share and so on. Positioning has to do with factors such as:

- Understanding customer needs
- Understanding competitor initiatives
- Determining the businesses' financial needs
- Conforming with legal and regulatory requirements
- Conforming with environmental constraints
- etc.

The capability/capacity has to be aligned with the positioning or else it has to be changed to deliver the positioning. Capability/capacity has to do with internal factors such as:

- Key business processes

- Procedures and systems
- Competencies, skills, training and education
- etc.

The key is to have a perceived differentiation of being better than the competition in whatever terms the customers choose to evaluate or measure, and to deliver this at the lowest unit cost.

In practice, BPM has developed a focus on changing capability/capacity in the short-term to address current issues. This short-term change in capability/capacity is usually driven by the need to:

- Reduce the cycle time to process customer orders
- Improve quotation times
- Lower variable overhead costs
- Increase product range to meet an immediate competitor threat
- Re-balance resources to meet current market needs
- Reduce work-in-progress stocks
- Meet changed legislation requirements
- Introduce short-term measures to increase market share (e.g., increased credit limit from customers hit by recessionary trends)
- etc.

In contrast, BPM focuses on first determining the future positioning of the enterprise and then changing the processes in order to attain this identified capability/capacity.

### 7.1.3.1 Salient Aspects of Customer Relationship Management

A major part of the following sections has been inspired by the insightful book titled, *Customer Responsive Management: The Flexible Advantage* by Frank W. Davis and Karl B. Manrodt. The literature on enterprise responsiveness is rather limited, but this book is an exception and had a lasting impression on the author in that it ignited an abiding interest into the nature of responsiveness and characteristics of responsive enterprises.

Salient aspects involved with customer relationship management are as follows:

#### *7.1.3.1.1 Needs Diagnosis Management*

This involves activities related to identifying, discovering or understanding the needs of prospects or newer needs of existing customers. Traditional offering-based or mass marketing organizations typically achieve this through product catalogues, demonstrations or even product data-sheets. However, responsive organizations achieve this through dialog with the customer regarding their operational or design issues problems, inefficiencies, and so on.

#### *7.1.3.1.2 Best Practice Guideline Management*

Best practice guidelines management is to response-based enterprises what strategic and tactical planning is to the offering-based or mass marketing enterprises. It is the management of the enterprise's knowledge base by collecting newer needs encountered, solutions proposed and delivered by the frontline workers, and disseminating to the entire frontline workforce on a continual basis. It involves activities like development of new guidelines when new resources become available; dynamic modification of existing guidelines when new situations are encountered, and the periodic review of existing guidelines for continuous improvement.

There are two major categories of best practice guidelines:

- Needs diagnosis
- Defining work, identifying resources/capacity, assigning work and coordinating deliveries

The guideline should identify each task required, the skill needed to perform that task, the timing of the task, the conditions under which the task needs to be performed, and the capacity required to perform the task.

Processes are under continual review to verify the result and assess the delivered solution effectiveness and efficiency of adopting the best practice guidelines.

#### *7.1.3.1.3 Responsive Task Management*

Responsive task management is not unlike project management except that:

- Customer requirements are often more similar than different, but never completely identical
- Instead of a single big project, it is a series of smaller projects or tasks
- Lead time is typically shorter

It deals with the prioritized assignment list that is used to determine, plan, assign and coordinate the work steps composing the deliveries to the individual customers. It also deals with the best practice guidelines that must be developed to oversee the assigning, tracking and delivery process.

#### *7.1.3.1.4 Responsive Capacity Management*

Responsive capacity management is the process of maximizing capacity utilization to deliver benefits to customers. It is the process of minimizing unutilized capacity because while delivered capacity generates revenue, unutilized capacity creates only additional cost as this wasted capacity cannot be inventoried. As will be discussed, capacity is scheduled in the short-term but sold only in the real-term.

The various methods utilized to maintain high utilization are as follows:

- Forecasting needs so that excess capacity is not scheduled in the short-term—the ideal situation being the matching of capacity scheduling to the capacity utilization.
- Cross training of employees so that the same capacity can be used for a wider variety of tasks; this is counter to the tendency of specialization in mass production or offering-based enterprises.
- Developing cooperative networks for real-term flexibility. The main driver for this method is the fact that cost of transactions coupled with the cost of interfacing, collaboration, coordination and communication between enterprises may be lower than the cost of those transactions being undertaken by a vertically integrated enterprise. Mass production or offering-based enterprises are more amenable to 'cooperative partnerships' that are oriented towards long-term, steady-state and continuous relationships. Typically, a customer will have a limited number of cooperative partnerships because while it ensures the customer a consistent and reliable supply of

know-how and offerings, it also ensures a steady business for the provider. However, customer responsive enterprises rather then limiting the number of partners lay more emphasis on developing a large network of providers (each having their own special core competency) to increase the range of capabilities that they can access to meet their customer's needs. Instead of emphasizing steady-state relationships, customer responsive enterprises focus more on obtaining a greater diversity of capabilities by enabling ready access to a broader network of solution delivering units (i.e., resources) that are available for assigning on as-need basis at any instant, at a lower cost, seamlessly and with minimal friction.

Please also see the sub-section "Economics of Customer Responsiveness" that follows later.

### *7.1.3.1.5 Resource Interface Management*

Interface management is not unlike channel management where the prime objective is to minimize the number of interfaces and to continuously optimize the performance of the existing interfaces in line with the business objectives and strategies of the enterprise. The more diverse the final customer needs are, the broader is the network necessary to provide access to more core competencies (i.e., capabilities), the greater is the variation in capacity needs and the greater is the depth of the network required to ensure the capacity needed for each core competency. For enterprises to be flexible they need access and the ability to integrate, assign and coordinate the delivered solution at a very low cost. Whereas, efficient network interface management enables network members to actually become additional solution delivering units for the response-based enterprise just as in-house delivery units do, inefficient interface management forces the enterprises to integrate vertically thus, limiting its options for access solely to the capabilities (i.e., core competencies) of its in-house delivery units.

With successful interface management an enterprise has advantages like:

- Virtually all enterprises can become part of the delivery network
- Thus, the enterprise has virtually unlimited capability and capacity at its disposal to serve the needs of its customers
- The enterprise can thus, focus on meeting the needs of the customer unfettered by the need to find a revenue-generating use for the existing unused in-house capacity

### *7.1.3.1.6 Customer Service Management*

As discussed in Chapter 1, sub-section "From Products to Services to Experiences", products are rapidly being equated as cost of doing business rather than as sales items; they are becoming more in the nature of 'containers' or 'platforms' for all sorts of upgrades and value added services. This allows the enterprise to initiate and maintain a long-term relationship with the customer. For this reason platforms are often sold at cost or even given away free, with the expectation of selling even more lucrative services to the customer over the lifetime of the product, or rather more correctly, the lifetime of the customer!

In these times of rapid product obsolescence and continual onslaught of superior competitors a sustainable competitive advantage can only be obtained through services such as:

- Tailor-made designs
- Just-in-time logistics

- Installation of the equipment
- Customer training
- Documentation of goods
- Maintenance and spare part service
- Service recovery and complaints management
- Handling of enquiries
- Customer-oriented invoicing
- Pricing below the market standard, and so on

In the *servicized* economy defined by shortening product life cycles and ever-expanding flow of competitive goods and services, it is customer attention rather than the resources that is becoming scarce. Giving away products is increasingly being used as a marketing strategy to capture the attention of potential customers. A growing number of enterprises are giving away their products *for free* to attract customers and then charging them for managing, upgrading and servicing for uninterrupted availability and usage of the products. Microsoft, after initially missing the Internet wave, invested massively to come up with a reasonably competitive Internet Explorer (IE) Web browser but decided to give away this Web browser free to its customers.

Especially in the case of software companies, the cost of producing and delivering individual product orders is almost zero; hence if a sufficient number of customers 'hook' on to the company's product and if the enterprise can set its product as an industry standard, it can sell upgrades and services at significant margins. The more the number of customers that are linked together through an enterprise's program (see note on "Metcalfe's Law and Network Effects" later), the more are the benefits to each of the participating customers and consequently, more valuable are:

- The services provided by the enterprise (at much lower cost, because the costs are spread across a much larger installed base of customers)
- The attendant long-term relationships with the customer

## 7.1.4 Leveraging the Customer Capital

Each piece of information in the enterprise including that residing in the company's information systems has a value. This value is primarily associated with the manner in which this piece of information is utilized by the enterprise for remaining competitive, providing good customer service and optimizing eBusiness operations. If Siebel is not to be used as a past-facing system merely for recording and reporting purposes but more as a future-facing handler of strategic information and relationships, implementation of all the basic components corresponding to the businesses of the enterprise is essential. As recommended in the last chapter the organization should consider a 'big bang' implementation of Siebel wherein all the base components of Siebel (relevant to the enterprise's area of business) are implemented and put in production together. By implementing only certain components of the system, the company cannot hope to reap more significant benefits than those accruing from the traditional systems. A piecemeal approach of progressive implementation should be abandoned because delaying the implementations of all basic components together only delays the benefits of a fully-functional Siebel and therefore, incurs opportunity costs.

In analogy with the Metcalfe's Law for networks (see note on "Metcalfe's Law and Network Effects" later), the value of customer information can be assessed to be proportional to:

$$n^m \times d$$

where,

$n$ is the average number of active users

$m$ is the average number of employees involved in any business process from different departments

$d$ is the number of interacting departments involved in the primary business processes of the enterprise.

Some of the major users of CRM are database marketers whose objective is to automate the process of interacting with the customers in order to:

- Identify the customers or prospects with high profit potential using mountains of data about prospective customers and their buying behavior
- Build and execute campaigns that impact this behavior favorably to the benefit of the enterprise's business

Data mining applications automate the process of searching these mountains of data to find patterns that are good predictors of purchasing behaviors based on analyses of past activity. Data mining uses well-established statistical and machine learning techniques to build models that predict customer behavior.

Table 7.1 lists the various mechanisms that an enterprise can employ to retain, leverage and enhance its customer capital.

## 7.1.5 Customer Responsive Management

The traditional philosophy of management focused on mass production was developed during the 20th century. The foundation of mass production is based on:

- Eli Whitney's concept of interchangeable parts
- Ford's development of the production line
- Frederick W. Taylor's scientific management
- GM and Dupont's cost accounting methods

Mass production management is focused on large-scale production and mass marketing of standardized, low-cost products produced for homogenous markets. Customers' are researched so that the right product is offered to the marketplace. This approach results in centralized product planning, process planning, production scheduling and market planning that is separated from the daily operations. When the change is gradual and incremental, the traditional make-and-sell enterprises focus on optimizing the efficiency of execution in terms of the following:

- Predicting or forecasting or projecting the market demand
- Minimizing the cost of making and selling the corresponding offering

In contrast, when the customer-driven change becomes rapid and essentially unpredictable, adaptability takes precedence over efficiency; the enterprises need to sense early the need of the customer and respond in real-term, individual customer by individual customer. The sense-and-respond enterprise becomes a pool of modular capabilities that can be dynamically configured and re-configured to respond

**Table 7.1 Loyalty Models**

| Name | Description |
|---|---|
| Personal profile/data | Customers are averse to furnishing or confirming the same information again. This model involves maintaining and sharing existing customer databases to obviate the need to demand the same information again across related functions or corresponding call centers, service centers, Web sites, etc. |
| Lethargy | Customers are averse to negotiating the interaction or dialog mechanisms with the enterprise again and prefer to stick to the familiar experiences including searching, assessing, evaluating, configuring, ordering, paying, etc. Loyalty through lethargy is a very powerful mechanism for loyalty. |
| Customized service | Customers vote for an identified and customized service that creates a personalized experience of excellence attributable to the enterprise. The customized service can get configured over time through either user-selected options or a customer profile that is maintained current. |
| Making it easier to do business with the enterprise | Customers appreciate informed and non-intrusive assistance while doing business with the enterprise. The information and assistance gets calibrated to dynamically suit the available customer profile and the current flow of the interaction or dialog. |
| Personal involvement | In later stages of customer bonding, customers have a great desire to be involved and identify with the specific product design, development and production support activities or with the brand or even the enterprise as a whole. User groups, vendor sponsored development communities, sponsored case studies, etc., are manifestations of the customers wanting to share a sense of ownership with the enterprise. |
| Free services, discounts and promotional incentives | All customers get reassured with occasional rewards for continued relationship with the enterprise, even if in real-terms these only have a notional value. |
| Payments | Customers are gratified if they are rewarded even with small monies or points, for specific actions or activities, be that satisfaction surveys, suggestions on promotional slogans, etc. |
| Sole supplier | This is akin to attaining the Everest of loyalty whereby customers return again and again despite of numerous other hardships. |

to the customer's latest requirements. Therefore, in make-and-sell enterprises the plan comes first, while in the sense-and-respond enterprises the customer comes first; make-and-sell enterprises primarily focus on what is common among many customers rather than what is different about individual ones (see Chapter 1, sub-section "One-to-One Marketing"). The customer commitment rather than the command-and-control structure defines the dynamic interactions between the modular capabilities.

Customer Responsive Management (CRM) enables enterprises to be more adaptable to changing conditions and responsive to smaller markets. The responsiveness could be in terms of:

(a) Timeliness (e.g., a schedule)

(b) Time window (i.e., by a specified time range)

(c) Priority (e.g., a dynamic dispatch list).

It recognizes that forecasting and planning become more difficult as the marketplace and environment become more turbulent. The detailed planning of work is done at the frontline. The purpose of flexible planning is not to plan all the details of the work but to plan the infrastructure that is necessary to enable and facilitate individual level changes. CRM emphasizes taking steps that minimize the time and cost required to recognize and respond to changes. Whereas mass production was based on defining a product and designing the most efficient means of producing large quantities of a product, CRM designs flexible processes that can make it easier to respond to changing conditions.

Thus, CRM consists of two major relationships—one with the customers to identify and diagnose needs, and the second with the network of suppliers who make the delivery. For offering-based enterprises, the former corresponds to the marketing function (e.g., market research, product planning, advertising, sales and customer service) and the later corresponds to the operations function (e.g., purchasing, production, supply chain logistics and human resources). For traditional offering-based enterprises, logistics is generally understood as the process of managing the efficient flow and storage of raw materials, in-process inventory, finished goods and information for conformance with the customer requirements. But within the CRM framework, this logistics concept transforms to the coordination of deliveries that are responsive to individual customer requests using a network of resources and integrated by flexible processes and communications.

As emphasized brilliantly by Frank Davis (Frank W. Davis and Karl B. Mandrot), for achieving responsiveness, the separation of assignment and delivery is critical. It is the frontline worker that interacts with the individual customer to determine individual needs. These individual needs are then used in conjunction with the conditional best practice guidelines to develop the individual delivery plan. The individual delivery plan, which itemizes each task, schedule and the responsible person, becomes the prioritized assignment list or Kanban. This list is used to assign each task dynamically to the resource network as also for recording the results.

The offering-based deterministic enterprises use highly structured systems or channels to develop a plan that not only includes the product design but also the channels that will be used to deliver the product to the customer. When enterprises do not have the flexibility to respond to a wide variety of needs, a different system must be established to meet each type of need. This makes it very expensive to respond to new markets. In contrast, the customer responsive enterprise tends to build and use networks of resources that it can call upon to respond to a wide range of needs. The customer responsive enterprise is able to put together a large combination of resources to respond according to initial conditions determined, best practice guidelines to a wide range of needs.

The role of the responsive enterprise is to develop an infrastructure that facilitates the integration of the provider network into the solution process, and the assigning and monitoring of each delivery. When the infrastructure works the relationship is effective and hassle-free; otherwise it is frustrating and unresponsive. Similarly, when the infrastructure works the delivery is efficient and coordination cost is low; otherwise the delivery is late and ineffective and special recovery mechanisms such as expediting, inspection, signoffs and approvals must be implemented to work around these shortcomings of the infrastructure. These recovery mechanisms unduly increase expense, slow delivery and make the enterprise inflexible and unresponsive.

Thus, to be able to respond, the enterprise must create an organizational infrastructure that includes:

- Best practice guideline development to maintain a repertoire of delivery practices
- Resource network development that identifies resources, interfaces and builds relationships to ensure that the resources are available when needed
- Information infrastructure development that integrates and coordinates individual deliveries

We touch upon these topics briefly in the sections that follow.

Surely, Internet is the classic illustration of a 'neural network' on a large-scale that displays a top down oversight combined with a bottom up cooperative delivery of digital content.

It displays characteristic features of:

- *Network Effects*
- *Small Worlds Networks (SWN)*
- *Cooperative Patterns*

etc.

#### 7.1.5.1 Network of Resources

The customer responsive enterprise is not aware of the exact needs of the customer until the customer calls it. Therefore, the enterprise cannot ever be more responsive to its customers than its delivery units are to it. The enterprise's ability to respond is determined by the capability and capacity available for assignment. Consequently, customer responsive enterprises constantly seek to expand the core competencies, that is, capabilities and capacity for assignment to serve customers. The more capability and capacity that is available, the more customers can be served.

Because responsive enterprises typically deliver benefits to customers in the form of products, information or even money, an enterprise utilizes a wide range of resources. Resources typically provide functions (or services) such as transport, storage, security or processing. The range of resources includes:

- Transportation networks resources like satellites (for communication movement), datacom (for data movement), truck lines (for products movement), airlines (for people movement)
- Storage resources like computer hard disk storage banks (for eData or eContent), voice mails (for messages), emails (for information messages), warehouses (for products), hotels (for people)
- Security resources like PINs and e-passports (for computer authentication), vaults or refrigeration units (for products), escort services or smart cards or identity cards (for people)
- Processing resources like data processing centers (for data and information), fulfillment centers (for products), janitorial services (for facilities), healthcare providers (for people)

Each of these resources would have a core competency. An enterprise cannot be more responsive than their resources enable them to be. To make responsive deliveries the enterprise must be able to build a network of resources, develop guidelines that allow the integration of the resources into the delivery task and create information systems that allow the coordination and assigning of work to these resources. The resource units may either be owned by the responsive enterprise or may have a relationship with the responsive enterprise. Notwithstanding the legal nature of these collaborative relationships, which could either be a collaborative exclusive partnership or intermittently used network, these resources have to be 'always-on', that is, available when needed, and have the capability and capacity needed to respond to the responsive enterprise's dynamic assigning and monitoring requirements.

Infrastructure development is not a one-time effort but must evolve continually to allow the organization to stay ahead of competition and keep pace with technology and environmental changes. For instance:

- As new customer needs evolve the infrastructure must enable these needs to be satisfied.
- As new resources become available the infrastructure must integrate the new resource into the delivery process readily.
- When new technology becomes available the infrastructure must allow newer options for communicating, coordinating deliveries and relating with customers.
- As new measurement techniques become available the infrastructure must incorporate them to enhance delivery coordination and monitoring.

The network of resources achieves two apparently contradictory goals—a greater ability to respond to customer needs and a reduction in the cost of the response.

***Network is the Resource Provider***

In-fact, in analogy with Sun's vision of "Network is Computer" one can say that "Network is the Resource Provider"! (see Chapter 5, sub-section "Siebel Applets"; Chapter 1, sub-section "CRM Application Services Provider (ASPs)", "Infosphere" later in this chapter and Chapter 5, note "Network is the Computer").

### *7.1.5.1.1 Business Webs (B-Webs)*

Don Tapscott introduced the concept of a Business Web (B-Web) as a cluster of businesses coming together particularly over the Internet. B-Webs are the mechanisms for accumulation of digital capital consisting of three parts:

(1) Human capital—is the sum of the capabilities of individuals in the enterprise including skills, knowledge, intellect, creativity and know-how

(2) Customer capital—is the wealth contained in an enterprise's relationships with its customers

(3) Structural capital—is the knowledge embodied in enterprise procedures and processes

The rise in affiliate marketing and the existence of Internet-based Extranets or Exchanges are examples of the rise of B-Webs.

***Moore's Law***

Gordon Moore, one of the Intel founders, observed that computer processor performance for transport, storage and processing of data doubled roughly every 18 months at constant cost. This law has held true for the last few decades and has potential to hold valid in future as well. The true significance of this law is its indication of the rapidly shrinking footprint of the computing devices. Moore's law continues to be valid, not for the number of transistors but for the number of CPUs.

***Metcalfe's Law and Network Effects***

Robert Metcalfe, the inventor of the Ethernet and founder of 3Com, evaluated that the value of a network increases as the square of the number of users; consequently additional users are attracted to connect to the network resulting in a virtuous cycle of positive feedback. Considering that the original observation was inspired by telephonic systems that are typically bilateral, the value associated with computer networks that admit multi-lateralism are many fold. Thus, for computer networks with $n$ number of nodes allowing conversations of m users simultaneously, the value of the computer network may increase as $n^m$! This phenomenon has important implications for corporations competing in network markets. While in the traditional economy value is derived from scarcity, in the network economy critical mass supercedes scarcity as a source of value. Positive feedback works to the advantage of big networks and to the detriment of smaller networks. Consequently, the bigger networks continue to grow bigger while the smaller networks are sucked into a vortex of negative feedback and shrink to insignificance. The classic examples of this phenomenon is Microsoft's Windows rapid ascendancy to market domination against other alternatives like Apple or UNIX operating systems or the VHS vs. Betamax standards battle.

***Gilder's Law***

The technologist George Gilder conjectured that the communication capacity triples every 12 months at constant cost (see Figure 1.6).

***Power Law and Small Worlds Networks (SWN)***

The phenomenon of networks is pervasive and they deeply affect all aspects of human life and relationships. Networks matter because local actions have global consequences, and the relationship between local and global dynamics depends on the network structure. The idea of small worlds is applicable to diverse problems—community of prospects or customers, organizations, national markets, global economy, flying routes, postal services, food chains, electrical power grids, disease propagation, ecosystems, language or firing of neurons. In 1998, Cornell mathematician Duncan Watts with his advisor, Steve Strogatz, recognized the structural similarity between graph problems describing any collection of dots connected by lines and:

- *The coordinated lightning of fireflies*
- *The 1967 idea of sociologist Stanley Milgram that the world's six billion people are all connected by six degrees of separation, that is, the average number of steps needed to get from one selected person to another is six.*

They showed that when networks of connected dots have a degree of order to their clustering, the degree of separation is correspondingly high, but adding random links shrinks the degree of separation rapidly. Real world networks are far from being a bunch of nodes randomly linked to each other; instead, a few well-connected hubs keep most of the networks together. They showed that networks operate on the Power Law, the notion that 'a few large interactions carry the most action' or 'the rich get richer'! This explains why the Internet is dominated by a few highly connected nodes or large hubs such as Yahoo! or Amazon.com as also the dominance of

Microsoft Windows on desktops. Similarly, in a separate context, a few individuals with extraordinary ability to make friendships keep the society together.

Thus, networks combine order and randomness to reveal two defining characteristics of the 'small worlds' networks—local robustness and global accessibility. Local robustness results from the fact that excepting the hubs, malfunctioning at other smaller nodes does not disrupt or paralyze the network; it continues to function normally. However, paradoxically, the elegance and efficiency of these structures also make them vulnerable to infiltration, failures, sabotage and, in case of the Internet, virus attacks.

***Infosphere***

The implications of Moore's Law and Metcalfe's Law lead us to conceive of the concept of Infosphere along with other factors like:

- Pervasiveness and convergence of information technology (see Chapter 1, sub-section "Convergence: from Marketplaces to Market spaces").
- Ubiquity of the Internet (see Chapter 9, note "The Significance of Internet").
- Application Service Providers (ASPs) (see Chapter 17, sub-section "Application Outsourcing").
- Future developments in Web Services (see Chapter 17, sub-section "Application Functionality as Web Services").

Infosphere is a highly dense network of apparently invisible intelligent computing nodes permeating across the world that could be tapped into dynamically for supplementing existing computing capabilities with additional resources for processing power, Random Access Memory (RAM), data storage, peripherals, etc.

### 7.1.5.2 Economics of Customer Responsiveness

Unlike the case of a mass production enterprise that defines average cost per unit in terms of the constituent fixed and variable costs, a customer responsive enterprise classifies costs into three components, namely:

- Fixed capacity costs that are incurred to acquire or develop facilities, tools and skills
- Scheduled capacity costs that are incurred when the acquired facilities, tools and skills are scheduled so that they become available to serve customers
- Service delivery costs that are the costs incurred when the benefits are actually delivered to the individual customer

Consequently,

(i) The total capacity costs are the combination of both fixed capacity and scheduled capacity costs

(ii) Total service delivery costs are the sum of total capacity costs and service delivery costs.

While fixed capacity costs remain unchanged even in the long-term; scheduled capacity costs are variable costs in the short-term, and the service delivery costs are variable costs even in the real-term.

For the responsive enterprises revenues are determined in real-time when the organization interacts with the customer. Therefore, for responsive activities capacity acquisitions, modifications or abdications are decided on a long-term basis, capacity is scheduled on a short-term basis and capacity is committed on a real-term (or real-time or immediate-term) basis. While the capacity acquisition costs are based on the long-term trends analysis, the capacity is usually scheduled on a periodic basis like accounting periods because of the availability of the relevant information on sales, production, costs, revenue and inventory on which the schedule is based. As against this, the capacity is committed on the basis of a real-term operational data available in CRM systems like Siebel.

Moreover, the role of inventory changes radically in the process of the enterprise becoming more customer responsive. In the mass production (i.e., mass marketing) approach, inventory greatly simplifies the task of managing an offering-based enterprise because it allows the enterprise to manufacture products and ship finished goods to the marketplace in anticipation of market demand. It is the key for enabling various functions like purchasing, production, distribution and sales to function independently and also seek optimal performance independently. There is no major emphasis on extensive coordination, planning and scheduling, as inventory is used to buffer purchasing, planning and scheduling. In times of market uncertainty and turbulence inventory:

- Desensitizes decision-making
- Enables longer lead times
- Reduces flexibility
- Reduces complexity of coordination

Thus, in offering-based enterprises the local functional efficiencies and strategies are truly at the cost of increased inventory and inventory carrying costs at the enterprise level. However, in the mass customization (i.e., customized marketing) approach, enterprises seek minimization of inventory because this not only reduces the costs but also enhances the organization's flexibility, that is, ability to respond to changing conditions. But increase in flexibility also increases the complexity of coordination; the enterprise has to shift from the deterministic planning and scheduling management approach to the protocol and assignment method of coordination.

> However, inventory could change from a large user of capital (because inventory turns slower than payment terms) to a source of capital for financing retail outlets by dramatically increasing the normal inventory turns to much more rapid inventory churns. An inventory churning 24 times per year generates cash flow fast enough to provide its value in working capital to help finance the building of a new store.

> One can conceive the concept of 'Chart of Inventory' in analogy with 'Chart of Accounts' which involves the use of a hierarchy of actual and virtual stores to segregate and aggregate inventory of various types like nature (aging, damaged, returns, rejects, in-transit etc.), usage (moving or non-moving), and so on. This has many advantages like independent valuation, stock taking, effective inventory control, stock analysis and so on. Normal transactions can be performed at either of these storage locations—actual or virtual.

As pointed out by Frank Davis, a customer responsive enterprise does not have the luxury of inventory to buffer real-term variations and reduce management complexity. Although capacity has to be scheduled in anticipation of customer requests, the use of capacity can only be scheduled after receiving such a customer request. If the provider has scheduled too much capacity, the excess capacity gets wasted because capacity cannot be preserved in an inventory. On the other hand, if inadequate capacity is scheduled some customers or users are likely to go un-served. As the service delivery costs are typically less then 10 percent of the total delivery costs explained earlier, the profitability of the enterprise depends on reducing the fixed and scheduled capacity costs and maximizing the percent utilization.

To minimize wasted capacity, responsive enterprises have to enable more flexible scheduling in the short-term and higher utilization in the real-term. This can be achieved through the following:

- Economies of scope—an approach that allows the provider to increase capacity utilization (e.g., percentage billable hours, load factors, occupancy rates, etc.) through cross-training of the workforce.
- Economies of use—an approach that seeks to utilize every unit of scheduled capacity to generate revenue to minimize the amount of non-revenue generating and wasted capacity.
- Economies of modularity—an approach that seeks greater flexibility to schedule capacity by developing modules so that less capacity can be scheduled when the demand is expected to be low. The more modular the organizational structure, the more efficiently the enterprise can respond to variations in expected capacity utilization. One way of increasing modularity is through networking.
- Economies of networking—an approach that seeks to allow enterprises the flexibility to focus on the changing customer needs rather than be burdened with finding a revenue-generating use for the inflexible resources. Resources can either be acquired or networked. A responsive enterprise will typically acquire resources where expected demand is continual and stable; whereas, if there is a greater variation in the expected capability and capacity needs, it will network with resources on as-needed basis. Acquired resources become fixed capacity costs, whereas networked resources become variable service delivery costs because they are paid on a per use basis. It maybe more efficient to have the resource in-house on a per hour basis, but it is more efficient to network for the resources on a per use basis. Thus, the network approach not only enhances the flexibility to respond to customer needs but it also makes this possible at a much lower cost!

> The purpose of a network is to provide the enterprise with the range of capabilities and capacities it needs to serve its customers' diverse needs while at the same time maintaining the cost of the resource as a service delivery cost (which is a variable cost in the real-term) rather than as a capacity cost (which is a fixed cost in the real-term).

## 7.1.6 Activity-based Customer Responsiveness

The customer responsiveness of an enterprise is really dependent on the corresponding business processes or activities. As explained in Chapter 1, in CRM the focus is on flexibility—the flexibility to obtain the capability and capacity needed to respond to a wide variety of individual customer requests. Customer responsive activities are used to find the best way to solve the individual customer needs. In customer responsive activities, the emphasis is on delivered solution effectiveness (i.e., how well the individual problems are communicated, diagnosed and solved) and delivered solution efficiency (how few resources are required to solve the problems).

Enterprises that deploy customer responsive activities have the following objectives:

- Build relationships so that customers become 'conditioned' to contact the enterprise first whenever they have a need
- Establish the enterprise to provide effective diagnoses and responses whenever customers make such a contact with the enterprise
- Create the capability and processes to enable customer-facing members to cultivate deep and long-term relationships with the customers, and cost effectively coordinate each individual delivery of benefits.

The traditional mass marketing or mass production approach considers a process to be a way to produce a product; it focuses on limitations (e.g., setup time, resource availability, capability of the existing workforce) and develops the most efficient process that can function within the constraints. The focus is on coping with internal limitations (often self-inflicted) instead of on becoming more responsive to customers and the changing business climate. The emphasis is on control rather than performance. As against this, mass customization obtains its flexibility by viewing the process as a way of converting resources into products so that a single process can be used to produce many different products. The balance of control and power has shifted from producers to the customers. Mass customization develops processes to minimize or eliminate limitations (e.g., reduce setup time, locate alternative resources, expand capabilities of current workforce and develop a network of resources). Customer responsiveness management develops numerous best practice guidelines to guide frontline workers as they interact with customers to plan deliveries and enable them to modify them if necessary, to improve the customer fit.

Therefore, for an enterprise to be totally flexible in responding to individual customers it must develop three things:

- Process(es) for interacting with individual customers and defining their individual needs
- Conditional best practice guidelines for defining how the organization will respond to various types of customer requests
- A dynamic assigning system that allows JIT (Just-in-Time) assignment of work for delivery to resources with appropriate capability and capacity

### 7.1.6.1 Activity-Based Costing (ABC) for BPM

CRM's success depends on an understanding of the profitability of customers that in turn requires costing information at the individual customer level. Traditional product-centric standard costing systems are not detailed enough to permit costs to be analyzed by the channel and the customer. The traditional systems typically used only three cost categories namely, labor, materials and overhead. While the enterprises could trace the labor and materials used by individual products, their cost systems allocated the indirect and support costs—the overheads—with measures already being recorded, such as direct labor hours and costs expended. With decreasing labor costs driven by industrial automation and improved efficiencies but with the increasing focus on customer-centricity to offer expanded variety and new options, features and services, overhead costs have been increasing progressively by leaps and bounds (see Chapter 1, section "Customer Centricity").

Activity-based costing resolved the inaccurate allocation of the overhead costs derived from the standard costing systems by tracing these indirect and support costs first to the activities performed by the enterprises' shared resources, and then mapping the activity costs down to the relevant orders, products and customers, on the basis of the quantum of each organizational activity consumed by them, respectively. Managers employed the more accurate ABC and profitability information to better decisions regarding business process improvements, order acceptance and rejection, pricing, customer relationships, and so on. The decisions led to near-term and sustainable improvements in offerings and customer profitability.

ABC is essential to achieve a suitably accurate assessment of customer profitability as many customer-related costs are activity-based (like sales effort and service calls). ABC effectively converts indirect costs (like marketing expenses and sales time) to direct costs by tracing them back to channels or customers. ABC splits costs into two major groups—volume-related costs and order-related costs. Volume-related costs are variable only against the size of the order, but are fixed per unit for any order or customer. On the other hand, order-related costs vary according to the product and process requirements of each order or customer.

ABC is a way of linking an enterprise's market positioning to its internal cost structure, that is, capability. The basic premise is that activities that are realized via the business processes consume resources and convert them into products and services that are usable by customers. Thus, costs are the consequence of resource decisions and income is the consequence of the business processes that deliver value to the customers. In other words, the requirement is to improve resourcing decisions as a means of managing costs, and improve business processes as the means of improving business effectiveness leading to improved customer loyalty and therefore, revenue.

The ABC data is useful as a source to support:

- Profitability management such as costing and profitability analysis, customer and product mix decisions, and support for marketing decisions
- Revenue and performance management such as resource to volume and service level changes, activity budgeting and cost driver analysis

The principle of ABC is based on knowledge of activities, the reason for their existence and the factors that drive them. The BPM effort helps in identifying a list of cost drivers that are allocated to the various activities. These could include:

- Volume of materials used, labor hours consumed, parts produced
- Number of new parts, new suppliers, new prototypes
- Number of customers, orders raised, invoices sent
- Number of design modifications, customer warranty claims, and so on

The database of activities can then be aggregated into 'pools' of activities that have common cost drivers. By assigning such pools of activities to 'objects' (such as products, distribution channels, customer groups, etc.), a proper allocation of product and customer costs can be derived.

To build up activity-based product costs, the total for any one product (or a group) summed over M activities would be:

$$\sum_{l=1}^{M}\{\text{Activity-based product costs}\}_l = \sum_{l=1}^{M} \begin{array}{l}\{\text{Direct material and labour} + \\ \text{volume dependent overhead} + \\ \text{variable cost driver dependent overheads}\}_l\end{array}$$

Similarly, to build up activity based customer costs, the total for a customer (or a group) summed over $M$ activities would be:

$$\sum_{l=1}^{M}\{\text{Activity-based customer costs}\}_l = \sum_{l=1}^{M}\left\{\begin{array}{l}\text{Activity based product costs +}\\ \text{volume dependent customer costs (e.g.}\\ \text{packaging materials or cost of delivery) +}\\ \text{variable cost driver dependent overheads}\end{array}\right\}_l$$

ABC provides the basis to understand product and customer profitability and allows the management to make decisions both on positioning and capability—the twin pillars of BPM. The understanding of product and customer costs that comes from using ABC provides its real value when the revenue resulting from the total activity within a business area is related to the costs of achieving that revenue.

It is usually possible to trace revenue to customers only if the enterprise operates a billing system requiring customer details or if there is in place a membership scheme like a store card or loyalty program. Costs vary from customer to customer on account of:

- Customer acquisition costs—sales calls and visits, free samples, engineering advice and so on
- Terms of trade or transaction—price discounts, advertising and promotion support, extended invoice due-dates, and so on
- Customer service costs—handling queries, claims and complaints, demands on sales person and contact center, and so on
- Working capital costs—cost of carrying inventory for the customer, cost of credit, and so on.

If an enterprise wants to assess which of its customers are profitable, it has to be able to trace costs as well as revenues to the customers (see Chapter 16, section "Customer-centric Activity-Based Revenue Accounting (ABRA)"). In Chapter 16, section "Economic Value Add (EVA)", we look at the EVA concept for assessing performance of responsive enterprises.

### 7.1.6.2 Time-Driven Activity-Based Costing (TDABC)

The conventional ABC systems had many drawbacks in that they were expensive to build, complex to sustain and difficult to modify. Their reliability was highly suspect as the cost assignments were based on individuals' subjective estimates of the percentage of time spent on various activities. It also made unrealistic assumptions like:

- Identified activities (e.g., processing customers orders or enquiries) take about the same amount of time without any variations for particular circumstances
- Resources work at full capacity without discounting for idle or unused time

Moreover, implementing an ABC system for realistic enterprise scenarios (a few hundred activities, few hundred thousand cost objects and time duration of a couple of years) quickly ended-up confronting computational challenges of gargantuan proportions requiring huge computational resources that were beyond the capabilities of normal enterprises. Because of the subjectivity, time-consuming surveying and data-processing costs of ABC systems, many enterprises either abandoned ABC entirely or localized it in isolated units or ceased updating their systems, which left them with out-of-date and highly inaccurate estimates of the business process, product and customer costs.

Time-Driven Activity-Based Costing (TDABC) gives enterprises an elegant and practical option for determining the cost and capacity utilization of their processes and the profitability of orders, products and customers. Based on this accurate and timely information, enterprises can prioritize for business process improvements, rationalize their offering variety and mix, price customer orders and manage customer relationships.

TDABC avoids the costly, time-consuming, error-prone and subjective activity surveying task of the conventional ABC by skipping the activity definition stage and therefore, the very need to estimate allocations of the departments' costs to the multiple activities performed by the department (Robert Kaplan and Steven Anderson).

TDABC defines activity costs with only two parameters:

(a) Capacity cost rate for the department executing the activity or transaction
(b) Capacity usage time by each activity or transaction processed in the department

Thus,

$$\text{Activity-based cost} = \text{Capacity cost rate} * \text{Capacity usage time}$$

where,

$$\text{Capacity cost rate} = \frac{\text{Cost of capacity supplied}}{\text{Practical capacity of resources supplied}}$$

And,

Cost of capacity supplied is the total cost of the department executing the activity or transaction.

Practical capacity of resources supplied is the actual time employees, machines and equipments perform productive work.

Capacity usage time is observed or estimated time for performing the activity or transaction.

Both of these parameters can be estimated and validated easily and objectively. These estimates are not required to be precise; a rough accuracy is adequate. Cost of capacity includes cost of all the resources like personnel, supervision, equipment, maintenance and technology, and so on, that are supplied to this department or business process. However, the practical capacity of resources supplied is usually lower as compared to the rated capacity because it excludes the cost of unused resources on account of scheduled breaks, training, meetings, setting time, maintenance, and so on.

Table 7.2 compares the conventional Activity-Based Costing (ABC) and Time-Driven Activity-Based Costing (TDABC).

TDABC does not require the simplifying assumption, unlike that for the conventional ABC, that all customer orders or transactions are the same and require the same amount of time for the processing. TDABC is not only more accurate but also granular enough to capture the variety and complexity of actual operations. For example, it allows time estimates to vary on the basis of particular requirements of individual customers, or orders such as manual or automated orders, orders for fragile or hazardous goods, expedited orders, international orders or orders from a new customer without an existing credit record. It achieves this through the simple mechanism of altering the unit time estimates or adding extra terms to the departmental time equation on the basis of the order's activity characteristics. Thus, TDABC can readily incorporate many more variations and complexities (in business process efficiencies,

**Table 7.2 Conventional ABC Versus Time-driven ABC**

| Conventional Activity-Based Costing | Time-driven Activity-Based Costing |
|---|---|
| Tedious, costly and time-consuming to build a that is error-prone, difficult to validate, and enterprise-wide model and localized model | Easier, inexpensive and faster to build an accurate model |
| Drives cost first to the activities performed by a department and then assigns the activity costs down to orders, products and customers on the basis of subjective estimates (based on interviewing and surveying process) of the quantity of departmental resources consumed by various activities | Drives costs directly to the transactions or orders using specific characteristics of particular business processes, products and customers |
| Complexity and variations are incorporated by adding more activities to the model increasing its complexity and subjectivity, resulting in lower accuracy; creates an exploding demand for estimates data, storage and processing capabilities | Incorporates complexity and variations that add accuracy at little additional cost and effort without creating and exploding demand for estimates data, storage and processing capabilities |
| Calculates cost driver rates by taking into account the full rated capacity of resources without discounting for idle or unused resources | Calculates cost driver rates by taking into account only the practical capacity of resources supplied by discounting for idle or unused resources, rather than the full rated capacity of the resources |
| As most of the data are estimates furnished by employees in respective areas, it has to be fed separately into systems for further processing; data being localized, this model cannot provide integrated view of enterprise-wide profitability opportunities | Integrates well with order and transaction-specific data already available from ERP/CRMs like Siebel thus providing integrated view of enterprise-wide profitability opportunities |
| Cannot be easily updated to accommodate changing or anticipated circumstances | Can be easily updated by simply estimating the unit times required or by adding additional terms in the time equation for each changed or anticipated activity |
| Being based primarily on users insights and conjectures, cannot provide visibility into process efficiencies; since it ignores idle or unused capacity, capacity utilization is at 100% by definition | Provides transparent visibility to process efficiencies and capacity utilization |
| Being already based primarily on users insight and conjectures cannot guide user with identifying the root cause of problems | Furnishes granular information to assist users with identifying the root cause of problems |
| Not an universal model; cannot be applied to other companies even within the same industries | Can easily be applied to other companies in same or even industries with similar business processes; hence, useful in M&A |
| Being based primarily on users insights and conjectures cannot act as a correct or consistent basis for initiatives like business process re-engineering, benchmarking, lean management, enterprise performance management, etc. | Potentially usable in initiatives like business process re-engineering, benchmarking, lean management, enterprise performance management, balance scorecard, supply chain management, and so on. |

product volume and mix, customer order patterns and channel mix), which adds accuracy at little additional cost and effort, and with fewer number of equations compared (i.e., without creating an exploding demand for estimates data, storage or processing capabilities), than the conventional ABC. TDABC models expand only linearly with variation and complexity by merely adding terms in the time equation; but a department is still modeled as one process with one time equation.

Consequently, the expressions for the total costs presented in the previous section get modified to:

$$\sum_{l=1}^{M} \{\text{Activity-based product costs}\}_l = \{(\text{capacity cost rate}) * (\sum_{l=1}^{M} \{\text{ capacity usage time})_l\}$$

and

$$\sum_{l=1}^{M} \text{Activity-based customer costs}_l = \{(\text{capacity cost rate}) * (\sum_{l=1}^{M} \text{capacity usage time})_l\}$$

***Significance of Time-Driven Activity-Based Costing (TDABC)***

TDABC plays an increasingly significant role in strategy and operations of an enterprise because of reasons like:

(i) Time is a decisive factor in all efforts for process improvements, Business Process Re-engineering (BPR), Enterprise Performance Management (EPM), Balance Scorecard (BSC) and so on, because of the criticality of wait times, lead times, cycle times, handover processes across department boundaries, etc. By contributing through increased accuracy at dramatically reduced complexity, efforts, resources, costs, etc., TDABC plays a determining role in enabling all such exercises.

(ii) Along the critical path of departmental business processes, any drastic imbalances in the capacity usage times of the various process or sub-processes will highlight the potential for dramatic improvements in terms of complexity, efforts, resources, materials, technology, costs and so on, and will become obvious candidates for detailed scrutiny. This will usually result either in a BPR initiative or even in restructuring or re-configuration of the department(s).

(iii) Based on the analysis of capacity cost rate, TDABC plays a crucial role in deciding the boundaries of an enterprise i.e., in bifurcation of core activities (that get executed in-house) from non-core activities (that can get outsourced). TDABC is critical for addressing the issues of dramatically reduced response times, turnaround times, high throughputs, increased accuracy, etc. Hence, the reason that all customer-facing processes like call centers or contact centers, customer service or customer response desks, help desks, etc., are usually outsourced.

The TDABC model simulates the actual business processes deployed across the enterprise. In addition to addressing the improvement of inefficient processes and transforming non-profitable products and customers, an enterprise can also use TDABC to tackle the issue of excess capacity revealed by the application of this model. An enterprise can use the TDABC model as the core of its budgeting process to link its strategic plan, and sales and production forecasts to the specific demands for capacity required to implement the plan and realize the forecast. Thus, TDABC can assist in deciding on the capacity the company needs to supply in the future.

### 7.1.6.3 Responsive Activity Pricing

For the sake of completeness, we will touch briefly on the issues related to the pricing of responsive activities for BPM.

Some of the relevant characteristics of customer-responsive activities are as follows:

- There is no standardized product for which there is a market price. As the delivered solution is customized to each individual customer's need, the value of the delivered solution is determined by how well the solution solves the customer's need and must be priced separately.
- There are no products that are tradable as delivery services are not tradable. Therefore, there is no market price for the delivery service.
- There are no products to inventory; only capacity, which continuously perishes if it is not utilized to deliver benefits.
- Commitments to the customers are made on the real-time basis.

Thus, the emphasis must be on pricing in the immediate run to maximize the yield that can be obtained from the capacity scheduled in the short run that is, minimizing wasted capacity (or maximize capacity utilization) and maximizing the customer value of capacity. The objective must be to not only collectively cover the fixed capacity costs but also to profit through contributions from customers; or in other words, the objective is to maximize contribution to fixed capacity and to profit from each sale. The price will range between the customer value at the upper limit and either the cost of delivery or the competitor's price, whichever is larger, at the lower limit.

However, the final price is determined by the customer's perception of a reasonable price in light of the corresponding hassles (to identify the right solution) and the risks (see Chapter 1, sub-section "Customer Relationships"). Evidently, the customer will pay a premium for response commitments like guaranteed response, time-of-day, lead time, response level, and so on.

The frontline worker can make the pricing decision based on information like customer value, cost of delivery, competitor's charges and alternative use of capacity.

## 7.1.7 Enterprise Agility

The difficult challenges facing businesses today require organizations to be transitioned into flexible, agile structures that can respond to new market opportunities quickly with a minimum of new investment and risk. As enterprises have experienced the need to be simultaneously efficient, flexible, responsive and adaptive, they have transitioned themselves into agile enterprises with small, autonomous teams that work concurrently and re-configure quickly, and adopt highly decentralized management that recognizes its knowledge base and manages it effectively.

Enterprise agility is the ability to be:

1. Responsive—Adaptability is enabled by the concept of loosely coupled interacting components re-configurable within a unified framework. This is essential for ensuring opportunity management to sustain viability.

   The ability to be responsive involves the following aspects:

   - An organizational structure that enables change is based on re-usable elements that are re-configurable in a scalable framework. Re-usability and re-configurability are generic concepts that are applicable to work procedures, manufacturing cells, production teams or information automation systems
   - An organizational culture that facilitates change and focuses on change proficiency

2. Intelligence intensive or ability to manage and apply knowledge effectively whether it is knowledge of a customer, a market opportunity, a competitor's threat, a production process, a business practice, a product technology or an individual's competency. This is essential for ensuring innovation management to sustain leadership.

The ability to be intelligence intensive involves the following aspects:

- Enterprise knowledge management
- Enterprise collaborative learning

> When confronted with a competitive opportunity a smaller company is able to act more quickly, whereas a larger company has access to more comprehensive knowledge, options, resources etc and can decide to act sooner and more thoroughly.

### 7.1.7.1 Patterns of Enterprise Agility

Christopher Alexander introduced the concept of patterns in the late 70's in the field of architecture. A pattern describes a commonly occurring solution that generates decidedly successful outcomes.

A list of success patterns for agile enterprises (and systems) in terms of their constituting elements or functions or components are as follows.

(a) Re-usable

**Agility Pattern 1**: The components of agile enterprises are autonomous units cooperating toward a shared goal.

**Agility Pattern 2**: The components of agile enterprises are re-usable and multiply replicable, that is, depending on requirements multiple instances of the same component can be invoked concurrently.

**Agility Pattern 3**: The components of agile enterprises share well-defined interaction and interface standards, and can be inserted, removed and replaced easily and non-invasively.

(b) Re-configurable

**Agility Pattern 4**: The components of agile enterprises communicate, coordinate and cooperate with other components concurrently and in real-term sharing of current, complete and consistent information on interactions with individual customers.

**Agility Pattern 5**: The components of agile enterprises establish relationships with other components in the real-term to enable deferment of customer commitment to as late a stage as possible within the sales cycle, coupled with the corresponding ability to postpone the point of product differentiation as close as possible to the point of purchase by the customer.

**Agility Pattern 6**: The components of agile enterprises are defined declaratively rather than procedurally; the network of components display the defining characteristics of any 'small worlds' network, namely, local robustness and global accessibility.

**Agility Pattern 7:** The components of agile enterprises are self-aware and they interact with other components via on-the-fly integration, adjustment or negotiation.

(c) Scalable

**Agility Pattern 8**: The components of agile enterprises operate within pre-defined frameworks that standardize inter-component communication and interaction, determine component compatibility, and evolve to accommodate old, current and new components.

**Agility Pattern 9**: The components of agile enterprises replicate components to provide the desired capacity, load-balancing and performance, fault-tolerance as well as variations on the basic component functionality and behavior.

**Agility Pattern 10**: The components of agile enterprises enable dynamic utilization of additional or a reduced number of resources depending on the requirements.

Chapter 10, section "Component Enterprise Architecture" presents the current approaches to enterprise agility and architecture that is embodied in post-Internet packaged applications like Siebel.

## 7.2 A BPR METHODOLOGY

In this section, we look at the full life cycle of an enterprise's BPR methodology. We will indicate opportunities where Siebel can be of assistance in an ongoing BPM effort within the enterprise.

> Outsourcing is distancing the company from non-core but critical functions; as against this re-engineering, that is associated with BPM, is exclusively about the core.

We present an overview of the seven steps in a BPR methodology. These steps are as follows.

(1) Develop the context for undertaking the BPR and in particular re-engineer the enterprise's business processes. Then identify the reason behind redesigning the process to represent the value perceived by the customer.

(2) Select the business processes for the re-engineering effort.

(3) Map the selected processes.

(4) Analyze the process maps to discover opportunities for re-engineering.

(5) Redesign the selected processes for increased performance.

(6) Implement the re-engineered processes.

(7) Measure the implementation of the re-engineered processes.

The eight steps of the enterprise BPR methodology are shown in Figure 7.2.

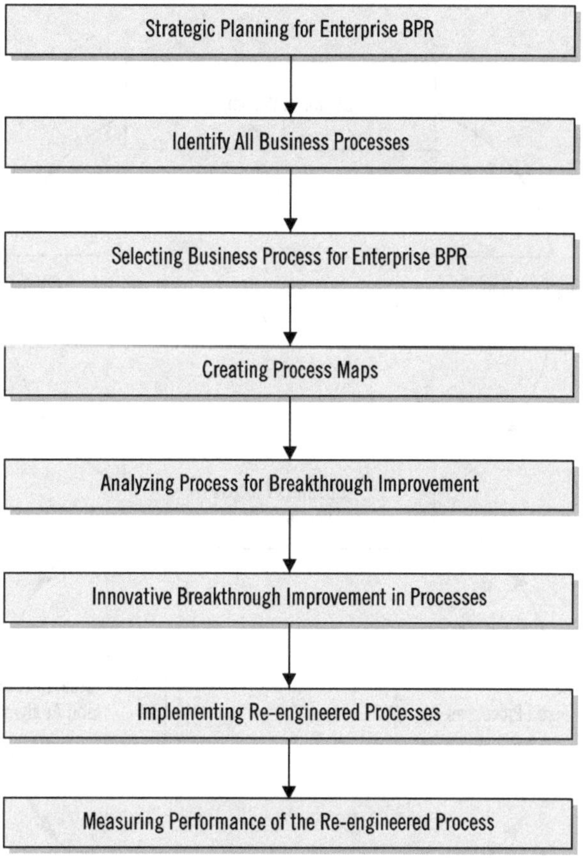


**Fig. 7.2 A Cycle of Enterprise BPR Methodology**

The BPM effort within an enterprise is not a one-time exercise but an ongoing one. One could also have multiple BPR projects in operation simultaneously in different areas within the enterprise. The BPM effort involves business visioning, identifying the value gaps and hence, selection of the corresponding business processes for the BPR effort. The re-engineering of the business processes might open newer opportunities and challenges, which in turn triggers another cycle of business visioning followed by BPR of the concerned business processes. Figure 7.3 shows the iteration across the alternating activities without end.

## 7.2.1 Strategic Planning for Enterprise BPR

All markets are fluid to some degree and these dynamic forces and shifting customer values necessitate changes in a company's strategic plans. The significance of a process to the success of a company's business is dependent on the nature and extent of the value addition to a product or service. Consequently, as stated earlier, one can understand the competitive value gap in terms of the customer expected level of value and the value delivered by the enterprise for the concerned product or service.

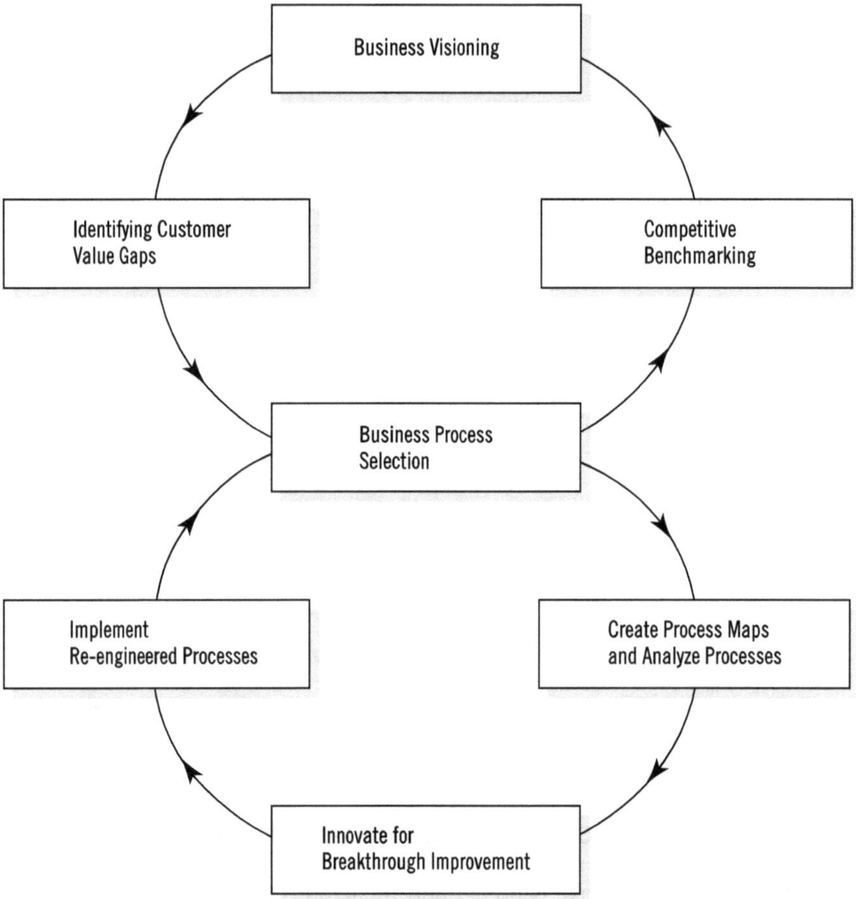


**Fig. 7.3 The Alternating Activities of Business Visioning and BPR**

The competitive gap can be defined as the gap between the customer's Minimum Acceptance Value (MAV) and the customer value delivered by the enterprise. Companies that consistently surpass MAVs are destined to thrive, those that only meet the MAVs will survive, and those that fall short of the MAVs may fail.

CVDs are those business imperatives that must happen if the enterprise wants to close the competitive gap and are similar to the Critical Success Factors (CSF) at the enterprise level. CVDs relate to factors like

- Time (lead time, cycle time, and so on)
- Flexibility (customization, options, composition, resource network interfaces, and so on)

- Responsiveness (lead time, duration, number of handoffs, priorities, number of queues, and so on)
- Quality of work (rework, rejects, yield, and so on)

Market segmentation is performed based on the customer value and the corresponding CVDs. Such market segmentation helps in suggesting corrective strategic and tactical actions that may be required, such as in devising a process-oriented strategic business plan. The strategic plan can in turn help identify the major processes that support these critical value determinants that must be innovatively improved and re-engineered.

### 7.2.1.1 Identifying the Business Processes in the Company

All business processes in an enterprise are identified and recorded. A process can be defined as a set of resources and activities necessary and sufficient to convert some form of input into some form of output. Processes can be internal or external, or a combination of both. They cross functional boundaries, have starting and ending points, and exist at all levels within the organization, including the section, department, division, and enterprise levels. In fact, processes exist across enterprise boundaries as well. Processes evolve and degrade in terms of their efficiency and effectiveness.

A process itself can consist of various sub-steps. These could be:

- Value added steps
- Non-value added steps
- Legal and regulatory steps (which are treated as value added steps)

## 7.2.2 Selecting Business Processes for BPR

Selecting the right processes for an innovative process re-engineering effort is critical. The processes should be selected for their high visibility, relative ease of accomplishing goals, and at the same time their potential for great impact on the value determinants.

Customers will take their business to the company that can deliver the most value for their money. Hence, the MAVs have to be charted in detail. MAV is dependent upon several factors, such as

- The customer's prior general and particular experience base with an industry, product, and/or service.
- What competition is doing in the concerned industry, product or service.
- What effect technological limitations have on setting the upper limit.

As mentioned earlier, MAVs can be characterized in terms of the CVDs; only four to six value determinants may be necessary to profile a market segment. CVDs can be defined by obtaining data through:

(i) The customer value survey
(ii) Leaders in non-competing areas
(iii) The best-in-class performance levels
(iv) Internal customers

A detailed customer value analysis analyzes the value gaps and helps in further refining the goals of the process re-engineering exercise. The value gaps are as follows:

- Gaps that result from different value perceptions in different customer groups
- Gaps between what the company provides and what the customer has established as the minimum performance level
- Gaps between what the company provides and what the competition provides
- Gaps between what the organization perceives as the MAV for the identified customer groups and what the customer says are the corresponding MAVs

It must be noted that analyzing the value gaps is not a one-time exercise; neither is it confined to the duration of a cycle of the breakthrough improvement exercise. Like the BPM exercise itself, it is an activity that must be done on an ongoing basis.

As a goal for the improvement effort, a clear, competitive advantage can be gained if best-in-class performance levels can be achieved in some key customer value areas and at least some MAVs can be achieved in all others.

## 7.2.3 Creating Process Maps

A process map documents the flow of one unit of work (the unit may be one item, one batch or a particular service that is the smallest unit possible to follow separately) or what actually happens to the work going through the process. A process map is developed at several process levels, starting at the highest level of the enterprise. It documents both value added and non-value added steps. A process map could either be sequential or concurrent in nature.

A process could be mapped in two forms:

- Workflow chart form
- Work breakdown structure form

Process workflows fall into three categories—continuous workflows, balanced workflows and synchronized workflows.

A workflow becomes non-synchronized because of:

(a) Steps or tasks produced at different rates, that is, an imbalanced workflow

(b) Physical separation of operations causing work to move in batches, that is, a non-continuous workflow

(c) Working in batches causing intermittent flow

(d) Long setup or change-over times resulting in batched work along with its problems

(e) Variations in process inputs in terms of quality and availability on time

All these add time and costs to the process and reduce flexibility and responsiveness.

Using the value added workflow analysis of the process map, we can:

(i) Identify and measure significant re-engineering opportunities

(ii) Establish a baseline of performance against which to measure improvement

(iii) Determine which tools may be most useful in the re-engineering effort

Evidently, the major goal in re-engineering the process is to eliminate non-value added steps and wait-times within processes. A good rule of thumb is to remove 60 to 80 percent of the non-value added steps, resulting in the total number of remaining steps to be no more than one to three times the number of value-added steps. Even this would be a credible goal for the first iteration of the BPR effort.

## 7.2.4 Analyzing Processes for Breakthrough Improvements

An enterprise's competitive strength lies in eliminating as many costly non-value added steps and wait times as possible. The key to eliminating any non-value added steps is to understand what causes them and then eliminate the cause.

For breakthrough improvements the process maps are analyzed for

- Organization complexity—commonly organizational issues are a major deterrent to efficiency of the processes.
- Number of handoffs—especially other than those associated with resource network interfaces.
- Work movement—workflow charts are utilized to highlight move distances, that is, work movements.
- Process problems—several factors may have a severe affect on the continuity, balance or synchronicity of the workflow. Examples are loops of non-value added steps designed to address rework, errors, scraps, and so on. These may be on account of
  - (i) Long change-over times
  - (ii) Process input/output imbalances
  - (iii) Process variability
  - (iv) Process yields

These problems need to be identified, measured, analyzed and resolved through an innovative problem-solving methodology.

## 7.2.5 Innovative Breakthrough Improvement in Processes

The steps involved in innovative problem-solving methods are as follows:

(a) Define a problem
(b) Find alternate solutions
(c) Evaluate the solutions
(d) Implement the best solution
(e) Measure and monitor the success

The responsive process consists of the following components:

- Diagnosing customer need
- Developing customized solutions specific to organizational interfaces
- Dynamically assigning work to the appropriate delivery unit
- Tracking performance as each task is completed

Business problems fall into three basic categories:

- System problems (methods, procedures, and so on)
- Technical problems (engineering, operational, and so on)
- People problems (skills, training, hiring, and so on): these problems arise because 'if you change what a person does, you change what he or she is'.

### 7.2.6 Implementing Re-engineered Processes

This involves the following:

- Re-engineered vision and policies
- Re-engineered strategies and tactics
- Re-engineered systems and procedures
- Re-engineered communication environment
- Re-engineered organization architecture
- Re-engineered training environment

### 7.2.7 Measuring the Performance of Re-engineered Processes

Measuring the performance of any process is very important because lack of measurement would make it impossible to distinguish such a breakthrough effort from an incremental improvement effort of a Total Quality Management (TQM) program.

Measurements are essential because they are:

- Useful as baselines or benchmarks
- A motivation for further breakthrough improvements, which are important for future competitiveness

The measures for innovative process re-engineering should be:

- Visible
- Meaningful
- Small in number
- Applied consistently and regularly
- Quantitative
- Involve personnel closest to the process

Table 7.3 enlists tools and techniques for continuous improvement and Table 7.4 lists some of the advanced techniques.

## 7.3 BPM AND SIEBEL IMPLEMENTATION

While perusing the various steps of a BPM methodology presented above, it becomes evident that Siebel can play a critical role in enabling and assisting any BPM effort in an enterprise in a major way.

**Table 7.3 Benefits, Tools and Techniques for Continuous Improvement**

| Tools or Techniques | Use |
|---|---|
| External customer survey | To understand the needs of the external customers |
| Internal customer survey | To understand the perceptions of internal services |
| Staff survey | To obtain employees feedback on work environment |
| Brainstorming | To generate ideas for improvements |
| Cause and effect diagrams | To prompt ideas during brainstorming |
| Benchmarking | To compare similar processes to find the best practice |
| Service performance | To quantify the importance/performance of services |
| Activity data | To understand the allocation of time in processes |
| Activity categories | To obtain the level of core/support/diversionary activities |
| Activity drivers | To relate volumes of activity to causes |
| High-low diagram | To group objects using two variables |
| Force-field analysis | To show the forces acting for/against a variable |
| Histogram | To show frequency of a variable in a range |
| Scatter diagram | To view the correlation between two variables |
| Affinity analysis | To measure the strength of functional relationships |
| Bar chart | To plot the frequency of an event |
| Run chart | To show how a variable changes over time |
| Pie chart | To show frequency of a variable in a range |

**Table 7.4 Advanced Techniques for Continuous Improvement**

| Tools or Technique | Use |
|---|---|
| Statistical Process Control (SPC) | SPC is a means to understand if a process is producing and is likely to produce an output that meets the specifications within limits |
| Failure Mode and Effects Analysis (FMEA) | FMEA is a means to understand the nature of the potential failure of components and the effect this will have on the complete system |
| Quality Function Deployment (QFD) | QFD is a structured process to build customer requirements in all functions at all stages of production |
| Taguchi methods | The design of experiments to create robust processes/products where final quality is subject to many variables |

### (a) Siebel Reference CRM Processes

There are different degrees of process automation:

- Time-out processing on external interactions is the ability to time-out and take action upon non-completion of an asynchronous interaction

- Internal activity is automatically triggered upon successful completion of an asynchronous interaction with an external application
- Workflow automation across applications; multiple automated activities distributed across applications are coordinated through the exchange of events and monitored for exception conditions.

A world class application like Siebel includes the tools to achieve process integration and integrate with third-party middleware, as appropriate. The Siebel architecture includes several mechanisms for supporting automation across a wide range of business processes:

- An assignment manager for apportioning and sharing critical information such as leads, customers and service requests across members of an enterprise
- Rules-based data synchronization for the coordination of a mobile force
- A workflow manager for workforce collaboration in reacting to business events
- An assignment engine to automate the assigning of resources to a set of planned activities
- Call scripting to support call center agents in their interactions with customers

The Siebel strategy is to integrate all business operations in an overall system for planning, controlling, optimizing and monitoring all customer-related activities of a given business. Siebel has included hundreds of best business practices or scenarios that can help an enterprise to restructure its processes. These scenarios provide logical models for the optimization of the specific business processes and can be modeled around primary and support business activities. Siebel guides an enterprise to automatically integrate all primary and support functions of logistics like customer orders, production, procurement, packaging, delivery, service, accounting, and so on. Companies can simply print out the relevant data models and analyze the most critical processes quickly and efficiently. The customizing features of Siebel can then help in implementing the required changes.

**(b) Real-time Siebel Operations Make Processes Transparent**

Transparent Siebel transactions are immediately updated in the concerned functional areas, be they inventory, party ledgers, accounting, and so on. Siebel re-engineers the business immediately to eliminate all wait times and minimize the time period required for communication between various functions. All of these postings are done simultaneously so that a consistent view is always available for any transactions; there is no lag between the material, management or financial accounting of any transaction. All this adds up to tremendous transparency in the functioning of the Siebel system and hence, the enterprise.

With traditional systems, which were not integrated and had batch-oriented processing cycles, a consistent picture was available only for a short period of time near the close of a month or a year. It also permitted different functions a certain amount of latitude in exercising a manner of ownership and degree of authority, even to the detriment of the overall functioning of the company's operations.

By making all transactions in real-time, Siebel enables an enterprise to minimize reaction times to changing situations in the market and take immediate corrective action. This also makes the enterprise more efficient, which is discussed in the following sub-section.

**(c) Integrated Siebel Operations Eliminate Handoffs**

The integration of an organization's functions and processes through Siebel eliminates various kinds of handoffs between departments, wherein tasks and copies of related documents are handed over to the next department for further processing. At every stage, this generates the need for in-warding, reconciliation, negotiations and follow-up with upstream and downstream activities along the process path, and so forth. All this merely adds more overheads, elapsed time, manpower effort, information overload and therefore, costs. The inherent integration provided by Siebel eliminates all such overheads and non-valued added activities. Reduced time cycles encourage various operational decision-makers not to inflate plans, projections, estimates, requisitions, material and purchase orders, production orders, and so on, in order to accommodate contingencies. Overall, implementing Siebel helps companies become more lean and efficient. However, one cannot discount the possibility that an enterprise under some misguided zeal for accountability may enforce highly restrictive authorization and access profiles that may essentially negate the advantages of the basic transparency, real-time interfaces and integration provided by Siebel.

## 7.4 SIEBEL AND CHANGE MANAGEMENT

In the last chapter, which gave an overview of a Siebel implementation project, we identified the fact that a Siebel implementation project is like any other business performance improvement program. Because of the enterprise-wide character of these projects, the issues arising out of Siebel project necessitate that a formal change management program be undertaken within the enterprise.

### 7.4.1 Change Champions—Core Team

The key members from the various functional departments of the Siebel team are the ideal 'change champions' for the Siebel project. They can best communicate to the end-users of their department with whom the key members already have a good standing. After mapping and configuring the processes in Siebel suitable for their requirements, the key members are also in the best position to talk to the other members of their respective departments and quickly address their particular common requirements and apprehensions. The change process is furthered by the core team members being directly involved in training the super users from their respective departments.

### 7.4.2 Change Facilitators—Super Users

Super users are the key to a full-scale implementation and subsequently the productive operation of Siebel. Super users are trained by the key members of their respective departments. Their training consists of an overview of their module (and related modules) and all the critical processes of interest within their departments.

Under the guidance of the key users, the super users participate in the full-scale validation and integration testing with other departments. This helps them to see the power and potential of Siebel through actual experience with the system. It also helps them to understand the practical implications of the tight integration, immediate updates and transparency available in the Siebel system. The super users can then convey the real power of the system as experienced by them, especially during the integration testing phase, to the end-users in their respective departments. The super users would be the messengers who would not only advocate changes in the processes, but also demonstrate its actual functioning and benefits.

## 7.4.3 Change Agents—End Users

The super users train the end-users in their respective departments, covering an overview of the processes in their area of operation, the details of the process and programs of direct relevance to their daily operations.

The transparent and instant access to relevant information that Siebel provides from other departments is always a great motivator, but the implications of instantaneous updates and integration also make all members conscious of the enhanced responsibility and discipline that the system demands from all the concerned participants. Although new systems are always viewed with suspicion, the sense of involvement and ownership inherited from contacts and interaction far outweighs all misgivings about using a Siebel system in production.

## 7.5 SUMMARY

In this chapter we introduced the concept of Business Process Management (BPM) especially for customer responsive enterprises, including aspects like need diagnosis, best practices, task and capacity, resource interface and customer service management. We then focused on exploring the fundamental economic and financial characteristics (like costing and pricing) of customer responsive networks of resources. This chapter introduced Activity-Based Costing (ABC) as the basis of ascertaining customer profitability and then described the significance of its latest innovation, the Time-Driven Activity-Based Costing (TDABC). With this detailed insight into customer responsiveness behind us, we summarized it by presenting the patterns of enterprise agility.

In the latter part of the chapter, we detailed the full cycle of an enterprise BPR methodology. We also presented the relevance and role that Siebel can play at various stages in the re-engineering effort within an organization. We looked into the change management aspects enabled by implementation of Siebel within an organization. The valuation of processes and Measurement of Performances (MOPs) has been tackled in greater detail in Chapter 16.

***Significance of Time***

This chapter touched upon many ideas like separation of assignment and deliveries, coordination of deliveries, minimization of inventories and, especially time, which are significant underpinnings of many enterprise-wide initiatives like JIT, Kanban, Theory of Constraints (TOC) and so on. Thus, this chapter also extended application and relevance of these ideas to areas beyond the normal areas of production, namely, to Marketing and Sales.

The activity-based cost could also be interpreted in terms of cost rate of time thereby implying that the cost of time is an order of magnitude costlier on the production floor than that outside the factory or even at the administrative office (see section "Time-Driven Activity-Based Costing" earlier). This automatically highlights the reason for the importance given to reduction of utilization or consumption of time (lead time, cycle time, wait time, duration, priority etc.) in BPR exercises (see Chapter 1's note "Information as the New Resource", and, Chapter 7's section "An Enterprise BPR Methodology").

# PART II: SIEBEL BUSINESS APPLICATIONS

This part has four chapters covering the three main components of the Siebel. Chapters 8 and 9 discuss the heart of the Siebel system—the various application modules catering to the functional requirements of different areas of the enterprise. Chapter 10 is on Siebel's operating environment and related products. Chapter 11 introduces Siebel Tools which is the complete development environment within Siebel.



**Siebel CRM did not develop in isolation from the IT industry. The design and architecture of Siebel CRM include the best of development in IS/IT in the latter half of the 20$^{th}$ century. At relevant stages, we have taken the opportunity to highlight the connections with parallel development in software development technologies and methodologies to make the context of several outstanding features available in Siebel more meaningful.**

Chapter 8

# Siebel Enterprise Applications

This chapter presents the business functionality available in Siebel. Considering that Siebel caters to all customer-related functions within a company in various industries, it is not surprising that it is a huge and complex system. It is not easy to give an overview of an integrated system such as Siebel. Hence, we have attempted to highlight the functionality that is made available by the major application modules of Siebel.

## 8.1 SIEBEL MARKETING ENTERPRISE

Siebel Marketing Enterprise provides the following functionality to ensure better returns on the marketing spend:

- Integrated customer datamart that enables business analysis of customers, products, sales and service
- Workflow management tools to implement best practice marketing processes
- Point-and-click call script authoring tool
- One-click generation of trapped, multi-level marketing campaign
- Built-in marketing communications that enable fast publication of product information, pricing, configuration models, competitive information and collateral
- Sophisticated marketing analysis tools that enable precise customer segmentation
- Online, dynamically generated trends analysis

### 8.1.1 Salient Features

***(a) Comprehensive Marketing Automation System***—Siebel Marketing Enterprise empowers marketing professionals to thoroughly analyze and segment customer and marketing information, create uniquely tailored campaigns and promotions, and measure and monitor the results that are helpful in refining subsequent campaigns. It enables marketing professionals to develop, implement, manage and refine their strategies across multiple products, product lines, sales territories, demographics and geographies. It provides a comprehensive set of tools and information including:

- Comprehensive pre-built data mart and an Online Analytical Processing (OLAP) server to perform complex, multi-dimensional analyses of markets, customers, products and geographies
- Sophisticated multi-dimensional pre-built and customizable analyses
- Market segmentation, list and campaign management tools
- Call scripting
- Integrated workflow management tools
- Marketing communications tool

***(b) The Industry's First Pre-built Customer Data Mart***—Siebel Marketing Enterprise represents the industry's first pre-built repository of all customers' interaction information. The Siebel Data Mart Builder is a general purpose facility used to populate the Siebel Data Mart based on data generated within all of the Siebel enterprise applications as well as other enterprise or legacy applications and syndicated external data feeds.

## 8.1.2 Core Business Processes

Core business processes of this component are described below.

### 8.1.2.1 Siebel Customer Management

Siebel Customer Management provides access to the sum total of data contained within Siebel Sales Enterprise, Siebel Call Center and Siebel Service Enterprise across all customers in the customer database. They can assess this data either at the aggregate level or drill down to individual customers and associated opportunities. Such high value information is decisive when

- Reviewing highly valuable customers
- Determining the effectiveness of new product offers
- Validating trends by investigating fine-grained data

Siebel Customer Management provides marketing managers enterprise-wide access to Account Management, Contact Management and Activity Management information, which enables them to review current and past opportunities, specific customer purchases and considerations, salespeople's notes, customer decision issues, and the quotes and proposals submitted to the customer.

### 8.1.2.2 Siebel Data Mart

Siebel Marketing Enterprise provides customers with pre-built customer data mart designed to maximize analytical performances and optimize marketing analysis using star schemas and common aggregates. It is a repository of all customer-related data like:

- Customer
- Sales
- Service
- Product
- Market

It can be configured to incorporate specific requirements of the organization as well as externally sourced data via the Siebel Data Mart Builder which automatically extracts, transforms and populates the Siebel Data Mart.

Siebel Data Mart Builder uses pre-configured procedures to extract data at regular intervals from the Operational Data Stores (ODS) and Online Transaction Processing (OLTP) databases maintained by Siebel Sales Enterprise and Service Enterprise.

#### 8.1.2.3 Siebel Marketing Analysis

Siebel Marketing Analysis enables organizations to rapidly convert customer, sales, service, product and market data into effective marketing strategies and actions. Using the Siebel Web user interface, marketing professionals, business analysts and senior executives can easily navigate, drill down and query this underlying data to identify trends and respond better to the changing customer requirements or market trends. Marketing and business analysts can review the trends in average prices, costs and profitability over time by product, customer or customer segment. Armed with information, marketers can tailor their campaign offers to better target their most valuable customers.

Siebel Marketing Analysis provides a variety of pre-built analyses that helps marketing professionals in measuring, monitoring and managing the performance of the sales, service, call center and marketing functions, namely:

- Customer Analysis
- Product Analysis
- Campaign Analysis
- Sales Analysis
- Pipeline Analysis
- Channel Analysis
- Competitor Analysis
- Service Analysis

Siebel Marketing Analysis helps executives, managers and marketing analysts to view, analyze and present data in a variety of ways to empower them to respond to these changes including:

- Dynamic Chart Views
- List Views
- Online Narratives

#### 8.1.2.4 Siebel Database Marketing

Siebel Database Marketing helps marketing professionals to understand the customer base and its future value potential, define marketing strategies and target segments, and automatically develop focused marketing campaigns or promotions that include select contacts and contacts in those market segments. Siebel's One-click Campaign Creation enables marketing professionals to move seamlessly from analyses directly into campaign definition, management and execution. Siebel Database Marketing establishes the best methods to reach customers and prospects, creates supporting marketing messages and collateral, and immediately publishes new campaigns to fulfillment centers, field centers, call centers and direct to the customer using the Web for e-commerce. It enables the corresponding distribution channel, namely, Siebel Sales Enterprise or Siebel Call Center or even customers who use Siebel Thin Client, to act immediately on the generated campaign.

(a) Siebel List Management enables a list to be handled as an object on its own and can be associated with any number of campaigns. Although, marketing campaigns are generally driven off internally generated customer and prospect lists, Siebel enables not only the import of purchased lists of prospects, but also effectively tracks their responses. Siebel also provides for storing of additional campaign demographic information which maybe imported initially but is thereafter augmented for better customer, company and opportunity profiling.

(b) Siebel Campaign Management enables marketing professionals to define and manage sophisticated marketing campaigns across multiple channels of distribution and via all communications medium including direct sales, call centers, regular mail, email, Web, fax and pagers. It enables focusing on select target segments with:

- Well-tailored marketing campaigns
- Developing dynamic call scripts and workflows for each campaigns
- Assigning campaigns to the appropriate call center professionals

(c) Web-based Marketing enables customers to execute highly effective closed-loop marketing by leveraging Siebel's Web-based architecture along with Siebel Campaign Management, Workflow Management and Assignment Management as also seamless integration of Siebel Marketing Enterprise with Siebel Sales Enterprise and Siebel Call Center.

### 8.1.2.5 Siebel Marketing Communications

Siebel Marketing Enterprise provides marketing professionals with a complete set of tools that enable them to develop and distribute key marketing information across the enterprise. Siebel Marketing Communications enables marketing professionals to manage, update and distribute key content that helps marketing and sales professionals to access or generate high quality product collateral, presentations, quotes, proposals and other documents.

## 8.1.3 Feature Details

(a) Campaign Management allows one to:

- Create complex campaigns that break down into individual marketing events
- Track and manage campaign costs and setup activities for each campaign
- Quickly import and re-use external lists across multiple campaigns
- Assign agents or groups to campaigns for better workload balancing
- Monitor campaign media sources to ascertain which media sources are providing the best return on investment
- Review campaign responses to monitor the success of various marketing initiatives or generate orders for new products and services from campaign responses

(b) Siebel Contact Management enables sales professionals to:

- Manage and track rich contact profiles
- View a complete activity history of every interaction for each contact
- Understand contact relationships within enterprises
- Focus on high value prospects

## 8.2 SIEBEL SALES ENTERPRISE

Siebel Sales Enterprise is a market leading Sales Information System (SIS). Many large as well as mid-market companies around the world use Siebel Sales to increase their revenue and profitability. As a world class SIS, Siebel Sales provides the following functionalities:

- Comprehensive opportunity and account management that fully supports team selling
- Group-enabled contact and activity management
- Group calendars that integrate with leading standard calendar packages
- Visual pipeline management
- Automatic sales territory management
- Product and revenue management
- Forecasts and pipeline multi-level rollups for managers
- One-click quote generation
- One-click proposal and sales presentation generation
- One-click expense report management and approvals
- Integrated product configuration
- Complete marketing encyclopedia including product information, price lists, detailed, comprehensive and decision support information, and online sales tools
- Compiling effective account and competitor briefings that include external content and data
- Automated correspondence and fulfillment
- Campaign and trade promotion management
- Integrated sales assistant that recommends sales activities
- In-built sales methodology support
- Comprehensive reporting and online executive information
- Mobile solutions on laptops and handhelds that support mobile salesman
- Fast one-click synchronization of the mobile database with the server database

### 8.2.1 Salient Features

***(a) Market-leading sales information system***—Siebel Sales Enterprise empowers sales professionals throughout the entire sales cycle with comprehensive tools and information including:

- Opportunity and sales pipeline management
- Profile and account management

- Web-enabled encyclopedia with rich information about products and pricing, competitors, issues, objection handling tools, etc.
- Sales tools including brochures, data sheets, presentations and videos.

***(b) Ensuring customer success***—Siebel Sales enables sales representatives to be authoritative sources of product information and be able to handle objections and construct solutions quickly and accurately, creating possible opportunities for cross-sell and up-sell. With the Siebel solution the entire sales staff is better informed, better equipped to handle customer requests quickly and able to satisfy customers immediately. Because satisfied customers lead to repeat customers Siebel helps to avoid the cost of acquiring new customers and also increasing their lifetime value.

***(c) Full support for team selling***—Siebel empowers a virtual sales team including the appropriate field sales representative, telesales manager, reseller and sales manager by ensuring fast access to new leads by the right members of the organization.

***(d) Mobile and handheld computing support***—Siebel enables mobile users to access the full power Sales Enterprise and supports synchronization between laptops, handheld computers and the corporate server—over LAN, WAN, dial-up connections and the Internet.

## 8.2.2 Core Business Processes

Core business processes of this component are described below.

### 8.2.2.1 Siebel Opportunity and Pipeline Management

Siebel Opportunity Management System (OMS) enables sales professionals to manage all aspects of an opportunity with real-term information from all sales team members about target accounts and partners, key deal participants, product interest and pricing, and historical activity. OMS offers sales representatives and managers immediate access to comprehensive pipeline and sales funnel analysis tools that display pipeline information against sales quotas and objectives. OMS offers one-click access to:

- Siebel's automatic proposal and presentations generators
- Siebel's automatic quoting or product configurator assisted quoting
- All forecasting information related to each deal

### 8.2.2.2 Siebel Account Management

Siebel Account Manager enables sales professionals to build a comprehensive understanding of target accounts, schedule and track account related activities, track products and service delivery, and explore new business opportunities with within existing accounts. It also enhances long-term supplier-oriented sales processes with industry-specific functional requirements (see sub-section "Siebel Industry Applications").

### 8.2.2.3 Siebel Contact Management

Siebel Contact Management enables sales professionals to track and profile contacts, understand their influences on others, and communicate quickly and easily. Siebel Contact Management features tight integration with Siebel Office for effortless correspondence creation and fulfillment.

#### 8.2.2.4 Siebel Activity Management

Siebel Activity Management helps schedule to-do list items, manage complex tasks and delegate actions to others. Sales professionals can exchange activity, contact and calendar information effortlessly with popular personal information managers like Microsoft Outlook, Novell GroupWise, and from there to PDAs including Windows CE-based devices and palm pilots.

#### 8.2.2.5 Siebel Quotas and Incentives Management

Siebel Quotas and Incentives enable sales managers to design compensation plans with the envisaged objectives and incentives needed to support that level of business activity. Sales representatives and managers can compare sales quotas with the respective achievements in either tabular or graphical form.

### 8.2.3 Feature Details

(a) Siebel Opportunity Management System (OMS) enables sales professionals to:

- Quickly find the best deals to work on
- Test deal status throughout the sales cycle
- Handle transactions in any currency
- Perform true ROI-based marketing for actual deal values and lead costs
- Eliminate briefing time
- View automatically generated analyses
- Specify and track additional information to support various types of sales

(b) Siebel Account Management enables sales professionals to:

- Display a comprehensive picture of the status and value of each account
- Capture and track detailed account profiles that are accessible to all members of the sales team
- Prioritize accounts by probability of success
- Specify and track additional information to support various styles of sales

(c) Siebel Contact Management enables sales professionals to:

- Manage and track rich contact profiles
- View a complete activity history of every interaction for each contact
- Understand contact relationships within enterprises
- Focus on high value prospects

(d) Siebel Activity Management enables sales professionals to:

- Manage activities and to-do lists quickly and easily
- Assign and delegate activities to other members of the organization
- Track priorities, due dates and completion dates for key activities
- Automatically assign activities and action items to specific individuals via Siebel Assignment Manager and Siebel Workflow Manager

- Identify expense-related activities enabling automatic expense report creation along with Siebel Expense Reporting

(e) Siebel Quotas and Incentives enables sales:

- Managers to align quotas and incentives with corporate objectives
- Employees to see the exact status of their performance
- Administrators to manage quota plans

## 8.3 SIEBEL SERVICE ENTERPRISE

Siebel Service Enterprise assists customer service professionals throughout the entire customer management life cycle. It is fully integrated into call center, field service, marketing and sales automation systems, and provides comprehensive tools such as service request management, return material authorization and customer correspondence with their internal functions. These include multiple methods of problem resolution, a complete corporate knowledge base, service automatic assignment and workflow and Internet self-service to dramatically increase customer satisfaction and loyalty.

Siebel Service provides the following functionality for ensuring increased customer satisfaction:

- Full-service request management
- Detailed customer and account profiles
- Customer purchase histories
- Automatic entitlement tracking and verification
- Group-enabled contact and activity management
- Complete product information
- Online knowledge base of solution to prior problems
- Multi-method problem resolution capabilities
- Full text search and Case-Based Reasoning (CBR) integration
- Skills-based routings
- Shared service calendars
- Return Material Authorizations
- Comprehensive call management through built-in Computer Telephony Integration (CTI)
- Internet-based self-service
- Robust service center reporting and analysis

### 8.3.1 Salient Features

***(a) Integrated Request Routing and Assignment***—Siebel Service Enterprise ensures that incoming customer requests are immediately assigned to the customer representative with the most appropriate skills, training, expertise and certification levels. It ensures that the employees or partners with the right skills in the appropriate geographic area or channel are assigned to the right customer issues. It also enables the creation of teams to manage more complex issues. Consequently, while customers experience the optimal levels of service and consultation, the organization increases its productivity and profitability.

***(b) Communications***—As stated earlier, Siebel supports global sales and service teams. Any team member can communicate with the customer and other agents via standard methods including telephone, Internet, e-mail, fax and pagers. The system tracks the full history of customer communications, giving service an overview of all interactions associated with a particular customer or case.

***(c) Fast Problem Resolution***—Siebel Service Enterprise enables customer service representatives to resolve customer service issues quickly and efficiently by providing:

- Ready access to comprehensive information within the Siebel Encyclopedia
- Multiple methods of problem resolution

Siebel search methods enable users to quickly isolate answers to FAQs including related case analysis and integrated text retrieval searches across knowledge repositories. Siebel also integrates with Case-Based Reasoning (CBR) engines to provide additional problem-resolution capabilities.

***(d) Scripted Workflow and Process Automation***—Siebel Service Enterprise enables new products, services or policies to be integrated rapidly into the customer relationship activities. It makes possible scripted dialogs that guide the call center agents through the entire customer interactions, dynamically suggesting the right products and services based on the customer's profile, unique circumstances and buying patterns.

***(e) Customer Satisfaction Tracking***—Siebel Service Enterprise enables organizations to assess if they are meeting customer expectations successfully. It enables agents to automatically generate customer satisfaction surveys during or after the service event so that organizations can measure, monitor and track customer satisfaction.

***(f) Comprehensive and Pre-built Computer Telephony Integration (CTI)***—Siebel Services Enterprise provides a comprehensive CTI that provides full support for Dialed Number Identification Service (DNIS), Automated Number Identification (ANI), and Interactive Voice Response (IVR) systems. Siebel also provides off-the-shelf integration with the most popular CTI middleware products in the industry.

## 8.3.2 Core Business Processes

Core business processes of this component are described as follows.

### 8.3.2.1 Siebel Service Request Management

Siebel Service Request Management enables service professionals to create, assign and manage customer service requests. It allows users quick access to the customer's profile, operating circumstances, open issues and related product issues, and service agreement commitments.

### 8.3.2.2 Siebel Activity Tracking

Siebel Service Activity Tracking helps in scheduling not only the sales but also service activities. Sales professionals can exchange activity, contact and calendar information effortlessly with popular personal information managers like Microsoft Outlook, Novell GroupWise, and from there to PDAs including Windows CE-based devices and palm pilots.

### 8.3.3 Feature Details

**(a) Siebel Service Request Management has the following features:**

- It provides customer information, problem description, severity classifications and prioritization, and complete status tracking with open and closed dates and times in one place.
- Service requests are assigned manually or automatically to individuals or groups of individuals with appropriate expertise for problem resolution.
- Case tracking that can be used along with the corresponding Service Level Agreements (SLAs) ensures that all commitments to the customer are met.

**(b) Siebel Account Management enables service professionals to:**

- Display a comprehensive picture of the status and value of each account.
- Maintain detailed information on the customer environment including all related products and services of the enterprise or competitors being utilized by the company.

**(c) Siebel Activity Manager enables:**

- Employees to manage their activities quickly and easily.
- Avoiding overlooking of commitments to the customers.
- Integrating with Siebel Assignment Manager for assigning activities and Siebel Workflow Manager for follow-up and escalation whenever necessary.
- Integrating with Siebel Expenses Reporting for automatic creation of expense reports for submission.

## 8.4 SIEBEL FIELD SERVICE

In today's intensely competitive environment, organizations have turned their focus to customer service in an effort to attract new customers and maintain established customer bases. Siebel Field Service gives companies the tools to execute field service activities with unmatched efficiency, precision and profitability. Siebel Field Service provides the following functionality for ensuring higher level of service:

- Field engineer activity management
- Integrated spare parts and replacement management
- Service management
- Sales order and Return Material Authorization management
- Field engineer route scheduling
- Dispatch integrated with call center applications
- Mobile solutions that support mobile field engineers using laptops and handheld computers
- Fast one-click synchronization of the mobile database with the server database

### 8.4.1 Salient Features

***(a) Increased Customer Satisfaction and Loyalty***—Siebel Field Service contributes substantially to fostering total customer satisfaction that in turn, results in dramatic increases in customer loyalty and new selling opportunities with existing customers. With the intelligent dispatch capabilities, it ensures that the most qualified field engineer gets assigned for a job as well as the right level of resources is employed for completing the same.

***(b) Integrated Field Service Solution***—In today's intensely competitive environment, the corporate enterprise must move forward toward functioning as an organic unit rather than as a collection of isolated activities divided amongst the different departments. Siebel Field Service is an enterprise level application designed to support global service organizations across multiple distribution and support channels. Siebel's integrated solution optimizes field service operations enabling realization of new revenue streams while simultaneously lowering inter-departmental costs. Incorporating the enhanced functionality of Siebel Service Enterprise, Siebel Field Service covers every aspect of the customer's interaction with the enterprise. Integrating the solution to other departments such as sales, fulfillment, and customer service, immediately them know if, and when they should get involved in the account.

***(c) Comprehensive Field Service Management***—Siebel Field Service delivers a comprehensive, fully integrated set of tools that collectively assist the service personnel, including the field service engineers, through the entire service cycle. Field service organizations need to respond to customer's requests with precision, speed and efficiency. Siebel Field Service allows organizations to dispatch the right field engineer, with the right parts, at the right time and location, for right problem diagnosis and resolution at the right cost of service, to result in tremendous increase in customer satisfaction and loyalty. It covers

- Service Call Management that allows users to create, assign and manage customer service requests. Field engineers have ready access to the customer's operating environment, profile, existing open issues, service agreement details, and purchase and service history, including all customer interactions, related product issues and attempted solutions.
- Closed-loop Intelligent Dispatch is ensured via Siebel Assignment Manager, which assigns each activity to the most appropriate engineer based on territory, skills, workload and other criteria. Siebel can also be integrated with IET's W-6 Scheduling Engine that can assign and schedule each activity automatically in real-time based on the latest updates from the field engineers.
- Siebel allows automation of the fulfillment, replenishment and cycle counting processes based on factors like preferred inventory locations, fulfillment and replenishment relationships between different locations, and the allocation and substitution rules at different levels. Siebel Logistics Manager allows implementation of a set of business rules to automate and optimize the management of service parts based on established practices like:
    - Transaction-based inventory
    - Availability and status tracking
    - In-transit inventory
    - Serialized inventory
    - Inventory on a laptop
    - Cycle counting methods
- Siebel Services Inventory manages service inventory throughout the part's life cycle in real-time at any level of granularity like trunk inventories, field offices, service and repair centers and third-party logistics (TPL) firms or providers.

- Siebel Reports provides powerful reporting, analysis and management functionality around requirements of typical field service organizations. A field service manager can review activities for the region, activities pending for assignment and perform trend analyses to identify business changes early enough to re-purpose appropriate resources and processes

***(d) Ready Access to Key Information***—Siebel provides a wealth of relevant information including parts, Bill of Materials (BOM), substitute parts and so on. Siebel's integrated Field Service component transforms the mass of cross-departmental data into a veritable gold mine of relevant information that empowers each customer-facing worker with a knowledge base to maximize the returns on every customer interaction or even a service call. Siebel Service Encyclopedia is a comprehensive knowledge base of diagnostic instructions, system configuration procedures, system specifications, etc. Various attachments can also be introduced into the product information. Previous solutions are populated into the system to give everyone access to this repository of frequently occurring problems, FAQs and standard solutions. Field engineers can also incorporate successful tips and solutions to enrich the knowledge base for the benefit of all members of the service team. Dissemination of the relevant information is automated through a one-click data synchronization process.

***(e) Siebel Field Service*** fully supports mobile computing enabling the field engineers with full support for handheld computers, rapid one-click bi-directional synchronization of the local datastore, and mobile software upgrades and distribution. At the customer site, field agents have the benefit of a searchable corporate and product database at their fingertips via wireless or dial-up connectivity, ensuring that they have all the information needed to resolve issues or cases quickly.

## 8.4.2 Core Business Processes

Core business processes of this component are as follows.

### 8.4.2.1 Siebel Service Request Manager

Siebel Field Service allows users to create, assign and manage customer service requests. It provides a complete purchase and service history including all prior customer interactions and attempted solutions, short and detailed problem descriptions, problem categorization, prioritization, and complete status tracking with schedules and time expended. The system supports the concept of expertise-based routing of activities within the enterprise.

### 8.4.2.2 Siebel Account Management and Profile

As for sales professionals, this enables service professionals to manage all customer information such as company and contact names, designated service contacts, purchased products or services, type of service level agreement and the corresponding maintenance calendar.

### 8.4.2.3 Siebel Contact Management

Siebel Contact Management allows users to manage service events associated with any given customer efficiently.

#### 8.4.2.4 Siebel Field Engineer Activity Tracking

This helps to schedule daily service activities, manage complex tasks and assign tasks across various departments. With Siebel's open scheduling architecture, users can exchange activity, contact and calendar information seamlessly with popular personal information managers like Microsoft Outlook. Once a service event is reported, it defines the procedural steps required to address the problem, the sequence in which these steps need to be performed and the necessary tools, parts and skills that are essential for completing the assignment successfully. The system automatically provides related information like safety, schematics or technical notes on the products, and so on.

#### 8.4.2.5 Siebel Solutions

This enables customer service professionals to create solutions that can be used to resolve similarly occurring service requests and address product defects. Responsive organizations solve problems and leverage such experiences and knowledge to resolve similarly occurring future problems. Such endorsed solutions can be published both for internal use by employees as well as for customer use on an Internet self-service Web site.

#### 8.4.2.6 Siebel Service Parts Information

Siebel Parts Information provides critical information about the availability of parts and identifies important part attributes such as installation instructions, operational constraints, warranty as well as manufacturing data.

#### 8.4.2.7 Siebel Field Engineer Information

Siebel Field Engineer Information tracks a wide range of field engineer-related information such as skill levels, product expertise, location, organization and critical contact data such as paging and cellular phone numbers.

## 8.5 SIEBEL CALL CENTER

Siebel Call Center is the next generation 'high-tech and high-touch' call center, enabling agents to handle a complete set of service, support and sales interaction across a broad range of communications channels such as phone, Web, fax, email, Interactive Voice Response (IVR) or even Electronic Data Interchange (EDI).

Siebel Call Center has the following functionality:

- Multi-level marketing campaign management
- List management for external lists of customers
- Internet-based lead collection and routing
- Intelligent lead scoring and routing based on customer defined criteria
- Comprehensive call management through in-built Computer Telephony Integration (CTI)
- Dynamic and configurable call scripting with full support for complex script branching

- Integrated up-selling and cross-selling capabilities
- Message broadcasting
- Sales order entry
- Blended sales and service functionality for agents
- Online monitoring of call statistics

## 8.5.1 Salient Features

***(a) Blended Service and Sales***—Siebel Call Center enables blended service assistance and sales support by combining the powerful capabilities of Siebel Service Enterprise with Siebel Sales Enterprise. Siebel Call Center agents can alternate between accepting inbound sales or service calls and initiating outbound calls associated with marketing campaigns and promotions. It enables agents to become complete customer contact managers for providing support over a broad range of products and services by providing ready access to a broad range of information.

Siebel Call Center integrates comprehensive information profiles about customers, accounts, products, past purchases, current opportunities, outstanding quotes, service records and service level agreements with powerful workflow engines, problem-resolution systems, and provides intelligent selling support that integrates customer profile information with campaign management, list management, intelligent call scripting and automated lead routing.

***(b) Scripted Workflow and Process Automation***—Siebel Call Center provides a Web-based user interface, call scripts and integrated workflow management that makes the system very easy to learn and use because

- Siebel SmartScript is an intuitive scripting tool that guides the agents through the entire customer interaction, dynamically suggesting the right products and services based on the customer's profile, customer's environment, current requirements and buying patterns. It helps them to overcome objections, ask the right questions to research and resolve problems in a service situation.
- Siebel Workflow enables escalation or fulfillment's to be routed immediately to all the concerned departments.

These scripts and workflows can also be changed even when the campaign and call centers are in operation for continuous improvement in the Call Center productivity.

***(c) Comprehensive and Pre-built CTI***—Siebel Call Center also includes a complete telesales and telemarketing system, which enables marketing and tele-Business managers to quickly design and execute campaigns with intelligent call scripts, assign campaign teams and also incorporate fulfillment and sales activities. Please also refer to details on CTI above. Because Siebel Call Center is tightly integrated with Siebel's List and Campaign management, call center managers can optimize the performance of each campaign, call center and even individual agents, based on critical performance parameters including:

- Average hold times
- Average speed-to-answer times
- Average handling times

***(d) Case-Based Reasoning***—Siebel has partnered with Inference Corporation to seamlessly integrate Siebel enterprise applications with Inference CasePoint to enable agents to easily search for solutions based on information available in Siebel. The identified or devised solution is stored automatically in Siebel for referencing and possible use in the future.

## 8.5.2 Core Businesses Processes

Core business processes of this component are described as follows.

### 8.5.2.1 Siebel Opportunity and Pipeline Management

Please refer to details earlier.

### 8.5.2.2 Service Request Management

Please refer to details earlier.

### 8.5.2.3 Siebel Account Management and Profile

Please refer to details earlier.

### 8.5.2.4 Siebel Contact Management

Please refer to details earlier.

## 8.5.3 Feature Details

**(a) Siebel Opportunity and Pipeline Management features are:**

- It quickly finds the best deals to work on through integration with the Siebel Sales Assistant's assessments
- Specifies and tracks additional information to support various types of sales styles
- Tracks deal status throughout the sales cycle
- Integrates with Siebel Marketing Enterprise, which enables performing true ROI-based marketing from actual deal values and true lead costs

**(b) Siebel Service Request Management features are:**

- It provides place customer information, problem description, severity classifications and prioritization, and complete status tracking with open and closed dates and times in one place
- Service requests are assigned manually or automatically to individuals or groups of individuals with the appropriate expertise for problem resolution
- Case tracking, which can be used along with the corresponding Service Level Agreements (SLAs) ensure meeting of all commitments to the customer

**(c) Siebel Account Management: enables contact center staff to:**

- Display a comprehensive picture of the status and value of each account

- Maintain detailed information on the customer environment including all related products and services of the enterprise or competitors being utilized by the company

**(d) Siebel Contact Management: enables sales professionals to:**

- Manage and track rich contact profiles
- View a complete activity history of every interaction for each contact
- Understand contact relationships within enterprises
- Focus on high value prospects

**(e) Siebel Activity Management: enables contact professionals to:**

- Manage activities and to-do lists quickly and easily
- Assign and delegate activities to other members of the organizations
- Track priorities, due dates and completion dates for key activities
- Automatically assign activities, action items to specific individuals via Siebel Assignment Manager and Siebel Workflow Manager
- Identify expense-related activities enabling automatic expense report creation along with Siebel Expense Reporting

## 8.6 EMPLOYEE RELATIONSHIP MANAGEMENT (ERM)

Siebel Employee Relationship Management (ERM) provides employees with a single point of entry to a wide variety of information resources that enhance communication and improve productivity. Siebel ERM aggregates business data and displays it in easy-to-use Web pages from multiple sources including:

- Siebel Database
- Internet
- Legacy systems
- Third-party news services

Siebel ERM gives employees access to applications data, news, business information, productivity tools and other resources in secure and personalized Web pages.

### 8.6.1 Salient Features

Siebel ERM aggregates business data in easy-to-use Web pages as described.

***(a) Home Page***—provides employees with information such as new opportunities, service requests, company news and literature from the Siebel Encyclopedia. Users can customize and personalize this content appearing on the home pages. Further, the home page also allows users to search the Web using leading search engines, track expense reports and view personalized news topics.

***(b) Briefing Pages***—provide employees with a summary of critical business information about accounts, competitors and other companies that includes recent news, relevant data from the Siebel database and company profiles provided by Siebel eContent Services.

***(c) Portal Pages***—provide employees with information such as corporate announcements, links to literature, files, links to HTML files and other key resources. Portal pages are flexible, giving administrators the ability to integrate unstructured content on the same page with Siebel data.

Siebel ERM also ships with several pre-configured portal pages such as the human resources (HR) page.

## 8.6.2 Core Businesses Processes

Core business processes of this component are described as follows.

### 8.6.2.1 Siebel Performance Management

Siebel Performance Management helps enterprises to manage the employee performance measurement process across the entire workforce. It provides a common and comprehensive format for tracking and managing employee periodic objectives and reviews, and annual reviews. Employees can view the company objectives along with the objectives of their managers to define their own objectives and rate them by assigning relative weights that are used to calculate their overall performance rating at the end of the review period. To initiate the review process at the end of the period or at the end of the year, employees perform self-assessment and submit them for approval. An overall rating calculation for the annual review can be configured to include several weighted components like:

- Average overall rating from previous periodic reviews
- Ratings on shared objectives
- Ratings on specific competencies

### 8.6.2.2 Siebel News Authoring

This allows news authors to create, manage, approve, and view news and information within the ERM application

### 8.6.2.3 Siebel Unified Help Desk

This renders world class employee self-service by providing:

- Alerts
- Assets information
- Products
- Facilities to submit and track service requests
- Solutions to routine problems by providing access to FAQs (frequently asked questions) and interactive diagnostic tools

### 8.6.2.4 Siebel eContent Services

This provides for the following:

- Setup Content Broker allows integration and display of content from Siebel eContent Services or any external source that is properly configured
- Defining content agents that request for required information
- Connecting to Siebel eContent Services
- Configuring ERM to display external content

Building content agents for company vocabulary based on Dun & Bradstreet DUNS number. This link also enables access to other identifiers such as ticker symbols that are useful when requesting information from external content providers.

### 8.6.3 Feature Details

(a) Siebel Performance Management

- Define review periods for periodic objectives, periodic reviews and annual reviews
- Publish corporate objectives
- Define review components like individual and shared objectives
- Assign weight values to review components
- Define rating scale
- Override review statuses

(b) Create News

- Create News Topics
- Create Account Topics

(c) Single Sign-on (SSO) that enables users to access other applications of the enterprise without the need to provide login credentials each time.

(d) Siebel Teams

- Activity Templates
- Service Details
- Reporting Relationships
- Expense Reporting and Time Sheets
- Incentive Compensation

## 8.7 MID-MARKET APPLICATIONS

Siebel CRM and e-business solution, mid-market edition, is a completely Web-enabled suite of functionality for sales, customer service and call center applications. It allows small and mid-size companies to compete more effectively in today's marketplace. Designed for fast deployment, this application enables organizations to completely integrate their enterprise, employees, business partners, stockists and customers.

The product is available for several users—between 2 and 200—and also gives the customer the flexibility to implement only the required features from the available product bundles.

### 8.7.1 Salient Features

Siebel is available as Enterprise Applications and eBusiness Applications. Siebel also provides necessary tools for customization and enhancement of standard Siebel applications.

***(a) Siebel Enterprise Applications***

- Siebel Sales Enterprise—Base Module

- Siebel Service Enterprise—Base Module
- Siebel Call Center—Base Module

In addition to the base modules, Siebel offers advanced modules, which are available as optional modules.

- Advanced Selling Pack
- Advanced Service Pack
- Tele-business Pack
- Product Configurator
- Server Pack

***(b) Siebel eBusiness Applications***

- Siebel eSales
- Siebel eService
- Siebel eChannel
- Siebel eMarketing

***(c) Customization Tools***

- Siebel Tools
- Siebel Visual Basic

## 8.7.2 Feature Details

***(a) Siebel Sales Enterprise—Base Module***

- Opportunity management and sales pipeline analysis
- Account management and contact management
- Organizational charting and expense reporting
- Calendar and activity management
- Extensive reports and charts
- Outlook synchronization
- eMail and fax integration
- Patented mobile synchronization

***(b) Siebel Service Enterprise—Base Module***

- Service request management
- Solution management
- Asset tracking
- Account management and contact management
- Calendar and activity management
- Extensive reports and charts
- Outlook synchronization

- eMail and fax integration
- Patented mobile synchronization

***(c) Siebel Call Center—Base Modules***

- Opportunity management and sales pipeline analysis
- Service request and solution management
- Asset tracking
- Account management and contact management
- Organizational charting and expense reporting
- Calendar and activity management
- Extensive reports and charts
- Outlook synchronization
- eMail and fax integration
- Patented mobile synchronization

***(d) Advanced Selling Pack***

- Fast forecasting
- Quick quotes
- Order entry
- Competitor information
- Sales library
- Product catalog

***(e) Advanced Service Pack***

- Contract and entitlement management
- Product defect management
- Inbound email management with Siebel email response
- Call scripting with Siebel Script Wizard
- RMAs and service order entry
- Service library
- Product catalog

***(f) Tele-business Pack***

- Campaign administration
- Campaign execution
- List management and list import
- Command-central for agent

***(g) Product Configurator***

- Quote assistant
- Model manager
- Rules designer

- Catalog designer
- Model validation

***(h) Server Pack***

- Territory management
- Automatic lead routing
- Workflow management/automatic escalation
- Integration of bulk data feeds (EIM)
- Remote software distribution (Anywhere)

***(i) eSales***

- eCatalog
- eConfigurator
- eQuotes

***(j) eService***

- Customer self-service
- Solution management
- 24 × 7 customer support

***(k) eChannel***

- Opportunity management
- Account and contact management
- Activity management

***(l) Siebel Tools***

- Cooperative work environment for developers
- Rapid application customization
- Need to modify source code or SQL eliminated
- Seamless upward compatibility to future product releases
- Development and maintenance costs dramatically lowered

***(m) Siebel VB***

- Complete Visual Basic programming platform for developers
- Easy integration with third-party cooperative applications
- Further extends Siebel application functionality
- Includes an editor, debugger and compiler

## 8.8 VERTICAL MARKET APPLICATIONS

The breadth and depth of Siebel's industry-specific front office solutions are unmatched in the software industry. Unlike most vendors who pledge support for vertical industries but simply force-fit generic software into all customer environments, Siebel has staked its future on delivering industry-specific solutions. Siebel has underscored this commitment by building dedicated engineering, product marketing and sales teams to support each industry solution. These teams include executives with years of industry experience who are intimately familiar with the business challenges Siebel's solutions are designed to address. Siebel Industry Applications teams have also forged strategic alliances with leading software, hardware and systems integration partners in each industry in order to bring new functionality to the market more quickly. Siebel's commitment to industry applications is absolute.

Siebel Industry Applications are tailored to meet the unique requirements of each industry, allowing organizations to minimize customization costs, dramatically decrease implementation times and leverage critical industry-specific functionality. Only Siebel provides out-of-the-box industry solutions for world class sales, marketing and customer service.

## 8.8.1 Salient Features

***(a) Unparalleled Front Office Functionality***—A cornerstone of Siebel's verticalization strategy has been to provide customers the ability to customize front office solutions to suit their unique business environments. Siebel has built each vertical application using the same data model and object architecture that it uses for its core products. This approach enables customers to select the specific functionality they require and easily upgrade their systems with new features and modules as their business needs change.

Each vertical base application provides the sales and service functionality required to establish, manage and support client relationships. User screens, tabs and views are pre-configured to reflect industry terminology and process flows. Customers wishing to automate other industry-specific processes (negotiating a consumer home loan or tracking a communication work order) may supplement the base application with additional Siebel vertical product options. Customers wishing to automate other common business functions (configuring complex product offers, designing call scripts or enabling Web-based customer service) may enhance the base application with Siebel general product options. These might include Siebel Product Configurator, Siebel SmartScript, or Siebel Interactive.

***(b) Easy Integration with Back Office Systems***—Siebel's enterprise integration approach is based on the recommendation of customers, leading software providers and industry standards organizations. Competitive applications based on parameter-based architectures and reliant on proprietary Application Program Interface (API) are difficult to integrate with back office systems, and are costly to maintain and upgrade. In contrast, Siebel's n-tiered, object-oriented architecture and robust development environment allows customers to integrate Industry Applications easily with back office systems. Siebel Industry Application driver provides seamless user access to back office data, lower total cost of ownership and an increased Return on Investment (ROI).

Siebel Enterprise Object Interfaces, the technology foundation of each Siebel vertical solution, provide well-defined, open, customizable and upgradeable interfaces at the client, object manager and data manager level. They consist of:

- Siebel BusObject Interfaces for tight, real-time communication between Siebel Industry Applications and other desktop and legacy applications
- Siebel ActiveX Container for embedding other desktop or enterprise applications
- Siebel ActiveX Controls—two ActiveX controls, the Siebel ActiveX Application Control and the

Siebel ActiveX Data Control, for embedding Siebel application components in a legacy environment

- Siebel HTML Tags for embedding Siebel BusObjects into Web pages
- Siebel Enterprise Integration Manager (EIM) for bi-directional exchange of large volumes of data (transactions or events) or for synchronization
- The Siebel Pre-built Enterprise Application Interfaces for out-of-the-box integration with the major Enterprise Resource Planning (ERP) vendors such as PeopleSoft and SAP
- A set of middleware integration tools available through Siebel Alliance Partners for the development of high-end, custom, cross-application process integration
- Best-of-class Siebel Integration Partners fully trained on Siebel technology
- On-demand point expertise through Siebel Professional Services to complement the Siebel Integration Partner or the in-house IS department

## 8.8.2 Siebel Industry Applications

De-regulation, privatization and technological innovation have dramatically altered the global business landscape. In this evolving marketplace, companies are competing to find and manage a sustainable competitive position. The winners will recognize that their only lasting competitive advantage is knowledge about their customers, leveraged throughout the enterprise. Siebel is committed to delivering software solutions that allows its customers to build and exploit this competitive advantage. Siebel provides unrivaled breadth and depth of sales, marketing and customer service functionality. Siebel's Industry Applications provide comprehensive front office functionality, customized to address the business requirements of eight critical industries.

In most industries vast amounts of valuable customer information remain isolated in back office systems, largely inaccessible to potential users. Siebel's vision has been to provide sales, marketing and customer service professionals with immediate access to customer information residing in diverse back office systems and to enable them to leverage this information into increased profitability and customer satisfaction. Siebel's flexible object architecture and standards-based integration tools, which facilitate rapid, seamless integration with the back office, make this vision a reality.

Since its inception, Siebel has worked closely with leading companies and standards organizations to 'future proof' its products. Unlike applications based on proprietary technology, which can be expensive to support and quickly become obsolete, all Siebel Industry Applications comply with the most current industry object design and interface standards. The result is a broad vertical product portfolio that anticipates and proactively addresses user needs.

- Siebel Automotive is designed to allow automotive and heavy vehicle companies to increase revenues and customer loyalty by maximizing the effectiveness of every customer interaction and enabling collaboration among vehicle development and delivery sectors.
- Siebel Communications is designed to help wireline, wireless cable and Internet service providers introduce new services faster, dramatically increase customer profitability and reduce churn by delivering consistently superior customer service.
- Siebel Consumer Goods is designed to help consumer goods companies enhance profitability through the improved planning, execution and analysis of retail trade promotions.

- Siebel Finance is designed to help financial institutions of all kinds serve their customers faster and more efficiently, and provide for cross-sales opportunities that increase share-of-wallet, long-term customer satisfaction and retention.
- Siebel High Technology is designed to help providers of high technology products rapidly increase revenue productivity and customer satisfaction across multiple distribution channels.
- Siebel Insurance is designed to help insurance field agents, brokers and call center professionals sell property, casualty, life and health policies, and process customer claims with increased efficiency and responsiveness.
- Siebel Pharma: Designed to help pharmaceutical account representatives manage relationships with physicians, hospitals and HMOs and strategically influence the sale of pharmaceutical products.
- Siebel Public is designed to help local, state and national government agencies deliver more complete, responsive service to their constituents.
- Siebel Utilities is designed to help enhance the profitability and competitiveness of investor-owned and municipal utilities through increased sales productivity and the consistent delivery of superior customer service.

Siebel Industry Applications are the result of a collaborative effort with customers and integration partners to address specific business challenges using Siebel's state-of-the-art information technology. Each industry solution leverages Siebel's unparalleled front office functionality, pre-configured to reflect industry-specific terminology, required functionality and process flows. In contrast to the generic point solutions offered by competitive software providers that require extensive customization, Siebel Industry Applications deliver comprehensive out-of-the-box functionality tailored to unique industry requirements.

### 8.8.2.1 Siebel Automotive

Siebel Automotive leverages the full scope of information systems and technologies, including desktop clients, mobile handled devices and the Internet, streamlining the process of market research, designing, manufacturing, selling and delivering vehicles to establish long-term customer satisfaction.

***(a) Complete Customer Services***—Siebel Automotive enables manufacturers and dealers to respond to the needs of retail and fleet customers via telephone, in person or over the Web. Siebel Automotive offers an integrated suite of tools to effectively manage accounts, opportunities and relationships. With immediate access to accurate product and customer information, users are better equipped to satisfy the needs of their customers. Siebel's unique approach to channel management ensures manufacturers, dealers and authorized service centre share the responsibility of satisfying customers. For example, Siebel Automotive enables manufacturers and dealers to proactively offer customers financing, leasing, insurance and credit card options as they configure vehicle orders online, at the dealership or with a fleet sales representative. This shared information approach results in increased sales, enhanced customer loyalty and a repository or information on which to drive future growth.

***(b) Effective Program and Supplier Management***—Siebel Automotive utilizes workflow management capabilities to assist automotive professionals better manage product development cycles by integrating tasks associated with product portfolios, quality management, quoting, engineering and marketing.

With easy access to complete and accurate information, automotive professionals can perform tasks on time, on scope and on budget. Siebel Automotive also provides tools to manage all facets of supplier relationships from involvement in product development, quality and cost audits, joint marketing events, warranty and service responsibility, and product sourcing.

### 8.8.2.2 Siebel Communications

Siebel Communications is a comprehensive front office solution designed to meet the needs of wireline, wireless, cable and Internet service providers serving consumer and business customers.

***(a) Comprehensive Front Office Functionality***—Siebel Communications, based on Siebel's industry-leading front office functionality, automates several critical communications industry processes out-of-the-box. Siebel Communications users can acquire new customers, up-sell and cross-sell new services to existing customers, and address billing and service inquiries, all from within the same application. Siebel's comprehensive functionality eliminates the need for carriers to purchase multiple customer management systems and delivers a high return on investment.

***(b) Complete Sales and Service Order Management***—Siebel Communications increases sales efficiency by automating the generation of valid sales quotes, the entry of accurate sales orders, and the decomposition and distribution of work orders to back office provisioning systems. Siebel Communications helps carriers shorten sales cycles, improve order accuracy and increase on-time service delivery.

***(c) Integrated Trouble Management***—Customer Service Agents (CSAs) responding to customer service inquiries can enter, assign and monitor the resolution of trouble tickets within the Siebel Communications application. Through seamless integration with network management systems, Siebel can immediately alert CSAs and service technicians to network troubles and empower them to notify affected customers proactively via phone, fax, email or pager.

***(d) Complete Service and Billing Profiles***—Sales teams and CSAs serving large business accounts must be aware of what services already are installed at each customer location when making new service recommendations, placing new/add/change orders, responding to billing inquiries, and troubleshooting network problems. Siebel Communications enables communication companies to build and maintain complex billing and service profiles that enhance the quality of sales proposals, shorten sales cycles and hasten the resolution of billing inquiries and network troubles.

***(e) Easy Integration with Back Office Systems***—In the communication industry, vast amounts of valuable customer information often remain isolated in back office systems, largely inaccessible to potential users. Siebel Communications' flexible, object architecture and standards-based integration tools give users immediate access to customer information residing in back office systems. Service providers effectively leveraging this information can improve the quality and profitability of each customer relationship.

### 8.8.2.3 Siebel Consumer Goods

***(a) Trade Promotions Planning***—Siebel Consumer Goods empower key account managers to create, distribute, manage, monitor and track simultaneous campaigns and promotions across products, categories, accounts and regions. Account managers assign and manage MDF funds, determine merchandizing tactics and leverage national promotions as they structure their account plans in Siebel Consumer Goods.

***(b) Retail Execution***—Retail account managers use Siebel Consumer Goods to ensure the success of promotions by designing and managing associated point-of-sale programs. Siebel assists in optimizing route plans across territories and creating recommended activities for each promotion. Displays, promotional samples and even retail audits can be managed in Siebel.

***(c) ROI-based Promotional Analysis***—With Siebel Consumer Goods promotions can be analyzed easily for their return on investment. Ensuring that stores execute the plans to which they commit, Siebel measures and reports on retail compliance. Product shipment as compared with consumption can be measured easily in Siebel. Not only do key account and retail managers know how well their products sold compared to their promotional plan, but because of Siebel's powerful integration with third-party syndicated data, they also know how well they benchmark against historical sell-through trends.

#### 8.8.2.4 Siebel Finance

Siebel Finance provides a single, comprehensive view of the entire customer relationship, across multiple product lines, in a unified solution. It delivers out-of-the-box functionality specifically designed for the unique needs of financial organizations to serve customers better and provide for cross-sales opportunities that increase share-of-wallet, long-term customer satisfaction and retention.

***(a) Integrated Consumer, Small Business and Corporate Relationship Management***—Siebel Finance supports consumer, small business and corporate relationships in banking and brokerage. Pre-built support for business processes and workflow management guides your financial services representatives through needs analysis, product recommendations and application processing. This provides the best combination of financial products and services that optimize both your customers' financial portfolios and your organization's overall profitability.

***(b) Consistent Sales and Service Delivery Across All Channels***—Siebel Finance provides consistency for sales and service transactions throughout your entire network of delivery channel including branch, call center, kiosk, field relationship management and the Internet. Siebel Finance support such typical financial activities as consumer and commercial loan profiting, institutional knowledge management and prospecting, campaign and lead management, referral network tracking, fee adjustment, reversal and waiver support, issue tracking and lost or stolen credit card processing.

***(c) Targeted Relationship Management for Commercial and Investment Banking***—Siebel Finance also supports investment banking and commercial banking professionals in managing their relationships with corporate clients. Siebel Finance—Corporate Relationship Management provides comprehensive deal pipeline management, client profiling, loan and deposit portfolio tracking and referral network management to increase deal wins, improve cross-selling and maximize client satisfaction.

#### 8.8.2.5 Siebel High Technology

Siebel High Technology is an integrated closed-loop sales, marketing and customer service solution that allows technology providers to rapidly increase revenue productivity and customer satisfaction across multiple distribution channels.

***(a) Increased Sales Effectiveness***—Siebel High Technology allows field sales, telesales, and telemarketing departments to manage sales opportunities, qualify deals and effortlessly generate quotes, proposals, presentations and sales orders tailored to the customer's requirements. The Siebel solution includes a built-in-product configurator that support mass customization by ensuring that quotations and proposals include accurate and complete configurations of products and services. Siebel Remote provides the industry's most scalable data synchronization technology, supporting fast synchronization for thousands of mobile sales professionals.

***(b) Integrated Call Center and Field Service***—Siebel High Technology provides industry-leading call center functionality, Computer Telephony Integration (CTI), intelligent call handling and routing, call scripting and call center agent productivity tools to increase sales and service effectiveness, Service centers immediately capture service requests over the phone, via email or through the Web to resolve difficult technical issues quickly. Telesales centers can develop tailored marketing campaigns and promotions, and up-sell and cross-sell new products and services at lower costs than field sales.

Siebel Field Service provides service functionally for dispatch, repair, spare parts management and route planning. Siebel Field Service allows field engineers to access full service functionality on their laptop, connect to the network via a modem and quickly synchronize their mobile database with the master server database.

### 8.8.2.6 Siebel Insurance

Siebel Insurance empowers field agents, brokers and call center professionals in direct marketing and claim processing with all the information they need to manage every facet of their customers' needs for property, casualty, life and health insurance. Siebel Insurance enables team selling and service across multiple channels including agents, call centers, brokers and customers.

***(a) Comprehensive Quotes and Policies***—Siebel Policies allow insurance professionals to record the pertinent information about drivers, vehicles and insured properties. Used with industry-standard rating engines Siebel Insurance automatically generates comprehensive insurance quotes. Siebel Insurance is fully integrated with policy processing systems, providing seamless new insurance policy creation and issuance, as well as policy amendments.

***(b) Integrated Claims Processing***—Siebel Claims allows insurance professionals to make decisions regarding key incident claim information. Agents, brokers, call center representatives and mobile claims adjusters capture comprehensive claims information with customer and policy information. Automated claims workflow management routes the claim for settlement. Throughout the entire claims process, agents as well as customers can monitor progress directly.

### 8.8.2.7 Siebel Pharma

***(a) Closed-loop Activity Management***—Siebel Pharma enables account representatives to profile, manage and track activities. With Siebel Pharma, pharmaceutical sales representatives create a comprehensive profile of their target professionals including information about special skills, education, professional affiliations and even drugs historically prescribed based on third-party, syndicated data sources. Sales representatives use Siebel Pharma to qualify doctors for meetings and specialist lectures and recommend which doctors they should provide drug samples and product detailing to. Siebel

Pharma helps plan and manage these meetings, proportionally allocate the costs and tract prescription rates of their product drugs.

***(b) Formulary Management***—Siebel Pharma helps national account and plan managers ensure that all hospitals and Health Maintenance Organizations (HMOs) in their territory include their products on the formulary of authorized prescription drugs. Siebel guides and assists managers to identify key formulary decision-makers, create detailed strategies and activities to influence them, and perform formulary pull through analysis, measuring their promotional effectiveness by account, doctor, geography and product.

### 8.8.2.8 Siebel Public Sector

Siebel Public Sector is a complete call center and customer service solution that enables national and local government agencies to be more responsive to customer needs.

***(a) Comprehensive Customer Services***—Siebel Public Sector details and tracks customer profiles and problems, provides access to knowledge bases and automatically assigns problems to the most qualified agent. Siebel Public Sector includes built-in Computer Telephony Integration (CTI) to ensure maximum call efficiency, along with dynamic call scripting and workflow management to ensure best practices and procedures.

***(b) Web-based Self-service***—Customers can enter new requests for service, update existing requests, track progress and access problem resolution tools using standard Web browsers, or email. Information entered through the Web browser or email is available immediately to the agency's call center users.

### 8.8.2.9 Siebel Utilities

Siebel Utilities is a complete sales and marketing solution designed to help electric and gas utilities increase sales productivity, improve customer loyalty, and maintain profitable and lasting relationships with commercial, industrial and residential customers.

***(a) Comprehensive Front Office Functionality***—Siebel Utilities builds upon Siebel's industry-leading front office functionality including the Siebel Sales Enterprise, Service Enterprise, Marketing Enterprise, Call Center and Product Configurator product families. Siebel Utilities provides utility sales, service and marketing professionals a comprehensive view of each customer, enabling them to exploit opportunities to cross-sell and up-sell new products and deliver superior service.

***(b) Enhanced Selling Efficiency***—Siebel Utilities is equipped to assign and distribute leads to utility account managers automatically and to provide them with a unified platform for managing customer opportunities, contacts and sales activities. The application further enhances sales efficiency by automating the process of generating customized price quotes, sales proposals and presentations.

***(c) Integrated Marketing and Call Center Support***—When integrated with back office billing, metering and rating systems Siebel Utilities can help utilities target profitable customers, design service bundles tailored to their needs and launch successful inbound/outbound marketing campaigns. Siebel's industry-leading call center functionality, intelligent call handling and routing, CTI and call scripting increase agent productivity and enhance sales and service effectiveness.

## 8.9 SIEBEL PROFESSIONAL SERVICES AUTOMATION

Professional Services Automation provides comprehensive support for the entire professional services process. Organizations use Professional Services Automation to manage leads for customer engagements, define project scope and work breakdown structure, create contracts, manage resource assignments, select and track subcontractors, manage time, expenses and materials, expose and resolve risks related to the project, creation of customer invoices and guarantee customer satisfaction. Professional Services helps service delivery teams win more deals, deliver services on time with high quality, and accurately track resource needs, delivery dates and accurate recognition of revenue. Professional Services Automation allows companies to maximize its market potential by closing more business and providing a comprehensive solution for managing projects.

### 8.9.1 Salient Features

Professionals Services Automation helps professionals by providing:

- Opportunity Management
- Automated Proposal Generation
- Contract Management
- Risk Tracking and Management
- Project Management
- Resource Management
- Time and Expense Reporting
- Financial Management

### 8.9.2 Core Business Processes

Core business processes of this component are described as follows.

#### 8.9.2.1 Siebel Opportunity Management

Opportunity Management allows engagement managers to access critical sales and customer data, and assess critical opportunities.

#### 8.9.2.2 Siebel Proposals

This takes the details that have been recorded about an account or opportunity and combines them with a pre-defined template to create a proposal specifically tailored to the requirements of the prospective customer. The template defines the initial formatting and structure of the proposal and includes pre-defined components such as text, tables, diagrams, standard terms and conditions, and includes files from a proposal library such as product descriptions and data sheets.

This generated proposal can be further modified to meet the exact requirements of the customer.

### 8.9.2.3 Siebel Agreements

Automated agreement generation optimizes on the effort expended in preparing agreements including the enterprise's best practices along with industry standards.

### 8.9.2.4 Siebel Project Management

This enables effective project management including tracking of activities, schedule, resource utilization and project budgets.

### 8.9.2.5 Siebel Resource Management

Resource Management is designed to manage the process of staffing resources for project assignments. Practice managers, engagement managers or project managers can identify resources requirements and create resource request(s). Resource managers review these requests, search for the appropriate resources, short-list resources for consideration and assign selected and available resources on the project.

### 8.9.2.6 Microsoft Project Integration

Integration with Microsoft Project allows team leaders to track tasks and activities and to share them with their project team. Team leaders can import activity and requirement status into MS Project to monitor and manage the project's status, requirement completion, planned scheduled and deviation, and costs.

### 8.9.2.7 Siebel Time Sheets

Time Sheets tracks time units of activities performed, allowing management to better understand completion of each activity and adjust resource scheduling to keep the tasks and projects on target.

Time Sheets enable the following:

- Sales managers to measure the cost of sales
- Call center managers to get better insight into resource utilization against various tasks and activities
- Field service agents to track different categories of activities for performance optimizing
- Professional service managers to track actual time spent versus budgeted time on an activity or task

### 8.9.2.8 Siebel Expense Reporting

Expense Reporting allows the enterprise to streamline the expense reimbursement process by eliminating the manual, error-prone and time-consuming tasks of completing manual expense forms. Expense reporting also provides for automatic conversions of currencies of the expense amounts.

#### 8.9.2.9 Siebel Financials

Siebel Professional Services Automation integrates with back office systems to export project, time and expense data to create client invoices and track accounts receivable. In reverse, the invoice and payments received information can be imported back to monitor projects budgets and overruns.

### 8.9.3 Feature Details

***(a) Managing Opportunities***

- Entering information about new opportunities in the database
- Viewing Opportunity information including contacts, activities, products, decision issues, competitors, estimated revenue, stage of sales cycle and probability of closure
- Generating presentations, quotes and proposals based on opportunities
- Tracking the status of an opportunity through the sales cycle from creation to closure
- Updating information about opportunities as they move through the sales cycle

***(b) Automated Proposal Generation***

- Creating a proposal
- Generating a proposal draft
- Printing a proposal draft

***(c) Contract Management***

- Creating standard agreements
- Adding agreement line items
- Adding activities

***(d) Project Management***

- Tracking tasks and sub-tasks
- Creating activities
- Attachments to a project
- Tracking the status and appropriate progress of the project
- Administering risks that may potentially affect the outcome of the project
- Generating project status reports for management purposes
- Tracking and approving time, expense and material resources

***(e) Resource Management***

- Placing a request for resources
- Assessing potential resources that may match the request
- Identifying potential candidates for a resource request
- Assigning resources to resource requests
- Monitoring an open queue of resource requests

***(f) Time Sheets***

- Creating Time Sheets

- Recording Activity Time
- Generating Time Sheet
- Submitting Time Sheet
- Approving Time Sheet
- Adjusting Time Sheet
- Preparing Time Sheet Summary

## 8.10 SPECIAL ENTERPRISE OPTIONS

The various optional modules are as follows.

### 8.10.1 Siebel Product Forecasting

Using Siebel Product Forecasting, sales representatives can estimate and submit forecasts based on unit volume and price estimates over time. Product Forecasting includes opportunity product driven forecasts, forecast revisions, complete forecast histories, forecast rollup capabilities and forecast reports. Managers can review forecast information in summary rollups or view the details and then adjust them as appropriate.

### 8.10.2 Siebel Revenue Forecasting

Siebel Revenue Forecasting enables sales representatives to estimate and submit forecasts based on opportunity revenues over time. Revenue Forecasting includes opportunity driven forecasts, forecast revisions, complete forecast histories, forecast rollup capabilities and forecast reports. Managers can review forecast information in summary rollups or view the details and then adjust them as appropriate.

### 8.10.3 Siebel Territory Management

Siebel Territory Management enables enterprises to establish territory schemes and automatically route leads, accounts and other relevant items to assigned personnel across multiple distribution channels.

Siebel Territory Management:

- Automatically assigns virtually all key sales information to any one or any group of sales professionals
- Supports easy, point-and-click territory definition and assignment of employees to territories
- Performs automatic load leveling across territories and sales professionals
- Supports exclusive and overlapping territories as also major territory realignments
- Supports ongoing responsibility changes

### 8.10.4 Siebel Campaign Management

Marketing professionals can use Siebel Campaigns to develop and target specific markets with well-tailored marketing campaigns. Siebel Campaigns provide automated list management capabilities to develop and load lists from both internal and external sources. Campaigns can be assigned and executed by telemarketing and telesales agents resulting in well qualified responses and new sales opportunities.

### 8.10.5 Siebel Expense Reporting

Siebel Expense Reporting helps sales and service representatives ensure they are reimbursed for all expenses and handles complex currency conversions including euro support. With the Auto Expense capability, all activities that caused expenditures are captured automatically and added to the user's newly created expense report with the push of a single button. Administrative access enables an individual's administrator to prepare an expense report for his or her review, which lets sales and service professionals focus on serving customers.

### 8.10.6 Siebel Sales Assistant

The Siebel Sales Assistant is a sales coaching tool that supports popular sales methodologies and best practices. It ensures that the sales organization presents a consistent face to customers, enabling sales representatives to work quickly and efficiently through the sales process. With Siebel Sales Assistant the sales organization is able to define sets of activities or Activity Plans that move their accounts and opportunities from prospect to close. An Activity Plan can be invoked automatically at specified points in the sales process, or on demand by a sales professional. In addition, the Sales Assistant can suggest that one or more assessments be performed to gather critical information about contacts, accounts or opportunities. This information enables sales professionals to understand what they know and importantly, what they do not yet know about a particular situation.

### 8.10.7 Siebel Encyclopedia

Siebel Encyclopedia provides sales and service professionals with access to a complete repository of all company marketing information including complete product information, competitive information, decision support and online literature. Service professionals can view linked problem categories for suggested diagnostic tips and access related technical information. Siebel Encyclopedia information can be published by marketing and made available to all end-users of the system. The built-in communication functionality enables users to immediately send information to customers via the Internet, email, fax or automated correspondence and fulfillment.

### 8.10.8 Siebel Advanced Search

Siebel Advanced Search enhances the ability of agents to easily locate information from the corporate knowledge base. Using Siebel Advanced Search enhances the base Siebel Search capabilities by locating documents using term proximity, word stemming, advanced thesaurus, term inflection, fuzzy searching and other advanced searching features. Siebel Advanced Search uses the Fulcrum search engine (included with the base Siebel Search in each named license of Siebel Sales Enterprise, Siebel Service Enterprise or Siebel Call Center).

## 8.10.9 Siebel Target Account Selling

Provides built in support for the Target Account Selling (TAS) sales methodology from Target Marketing Systems. Sales professionals can reinforce the TAS training curriculum by using TAS to manage account plans, strategies and competitive positioning.

## 8.10.10 Siebel Briefings

Siebel Briefings are online briefing reports that provide charts, tabular displays and a narrative that explains business trends and drivers. Siebel Briefings are displayed in Microsoft Word to enable managers and business analysts to further customize briefing documents.

## 8.10.11 Siebel Computer Telephony Integration (CTI)

Siebel CTI empowers telesales, telemarketing and teleservice professionals with powerful Computer Telephone Integration (CTI), to decrease call times and improve customer intimacy. Siebel CTI supports off-the-shelf integration with popular CTI middleware vendors to provide integrated call handling, call tracking and automated pop-up window capabilities with a broad variety of Automated Call Distributors (ACDs). Siebel CTI includes Siebel Adaptive CTI, a framework that enables middleware vendors, systems integrators, consultants and customers to integrate additional third-party CTI middleware applications and leverage the features of Siebel CTI. It also includes the Siebel CTI Server, which performs intelligent inbound call routing when integrated with the Genesys Telecommunications Laboratories' T Server or Aspect Prospect CTI middleware.

## 8.10.12 Siebel Product Configurator

Siebel Product Configurator enables sales professionals to interactively configure solutions for quoting, building and ordering. The Siebel Product Configurator includes a quote assistant that takes you through an intelligent quoting process and sophisticated administrative tools that enable product managers to model the business rules about product inter-relationships. Sales organizations can dramatically reduce order entry and configuration error and implement mass customization of solutions configured to customer requirements. Siebel Product Configurator works with Siebel Remote, enabling mobile sales professionals to synchronize and download new model and configuration rules.

Siebel Product Configurator Integration Object enables Siebel customers to pass quote information to third-party product configurator applications and import valid configurations into the Siebel Quotes module. Support for integration with select third-party product configurators is provided. In addition, customers can use this object to develop integration to their own custom in-house product configurator application.

## 8.10.13 Siebel Proposals

Siebel Proposal Generator enables sales professionals to build high quality sales proposals and tailor them to customer requirements based on customer profiles. With the press of a single button, the sales professional can create a draft proposal based on the details of the sales opportunity, including the customer's product interest, the competitive landscape and the relevant decision issues. Sales professionals can then further customize the proposal to precisely meet customer requirements by accessing the latest information published in the Siebel Encyclopedia and Proposal Library.

### 8.10.14 Siebel Presentations

At the press of a single button, Siebel Presentation enables sales professionals to build high quality sales presentations tailored to customer requirements. The sales professional creates a complete Microsoft PowerPoint presentation based on the details of the sale opportunity including the customer's product interest, the competitive landscape and the relevant decision issues. Sales professionals can then further customize the presentation to meet customer requirements by accessing the latest information in the Siebel Encyclopedia and Proposal and Presentation Libraries. Completed presentations can include templates embodying the company's culture, positioning and product information, materials pulled automatically or manually from the Presentation Library, slides dragged and dropped by the user from the Windows Explorer and dynamically generated slides designed by marketing professionals.

### 8.10.15 Siebel Quotes

Siebel Quotes enables field sales and telesales professionals to develop, verify, submit and revise quotes tailored to meet customer requirements. Users can quickly generate quotes based on opportunity specific information, price them from price lists, and include volume discounts and contingent services pricing. Quotes can be communicated easily to customers in print or electronically.

### 8.10.16 Siebel Order Entry

Siebel Order Entry provides enterprises the ability to enter and track Return Material Authorization (RMA) and service orders in addressing customer service issues. Each line item may reference different ship-to-bill and bill-to-address information, and price lists with multiple levels of discounts are supported at the line item level. As the RMA/order is processed via the back office application, order status is retrieved via Siebel's enterprise and object interfaces so that order status may be quickly conveyed to the customer.

### 8.10.17 Siebel Contracts

Siebel Contracts assure sales and service representatives that customers receive the proper level of support based on service level agreements and other contractual obligations. Siebel Contracts enables organizations to track details for both sales contracts and service agreements. Entitlement verification automatically locates all the relevant agreements and calculates the time that an issue must be resolved by based on a customer's service calendar.

## 8.10.18 Siebel Customer Profiles

Siebel Customer Profiles provide communications companies with functionality to better qualify prospects, manage their profiles, and improve their customer acquisition, up-selling, and cross-selling efforts. Through open enterprise interfaces to OSS and databases, service providers are able to analyze customer data and usage patterns, identify profitable service opportunities, and design service bundles tailored to their customers' needs. Call centers fielding inbound calls can quickly profile clients to up-sell and cross-sell services more effectively.

Communications providers can use demographic and usage data to calculate potential customer value, assess customer credit risk, and identify and retain vulnerable customers. Call centers running Customer Profiles in conjunction with Siebel SmartScript have the ability to guide sales agents through a series of questions designed to capture valuable profile information and up-sell new services.

## 8.10.19 Siebel Service Orders

When used with the Siebel Product Configurator, the Service Orders option will automate the process of creating an accurate quote for a bundle of communications services and generating syntactically correct order information for submission to back office billing and provisioning systems. This powerful functionality will enhance sales efficiency dramatically, shorten service delivery cycles and reduce the number of orders rejected due to entry orders.

Agents armed with this powerful software tool will be able to:

- Create an accurate quote for a bundle of communications products or services
- Generate a new order from a quote, a case or from scratch
- Change existing orders, add supplemental orders and move orders
- Classify orders by priority, type, organization, contact or any combination of these terms
- Confirm and allocate available inventories such as telephone numbers or wireless handsets
- Perform a credit check on a customer
- Assign standard interval due dates

## 8.10.20 Siebel Work Orders

Siebel Work Orders provide carriers with the ability to decompose and optimize each sales order into one or more work orders based upon criteria such as service provider, due dates, time or other customer-specified requirements. When combined with the Workflow Integration product option this component provides carriers with full visibility of all work orders, regardless of owner, to ensure that due dates are met.

## 8.10.21 Siebel Service Profiles

Siebel Service Profiles enable carriers to manage and maintain profile information about complex services deployed across multiple customer service addresses. This feature employs an easy to use Microsoft Explorer graphical format to display and manage service profiles including physical addresses or areas, installed/provisioned products and services, and associated contact information.

Sales and service agents using this tool in conjunction with the Siebel Product Configurator are empowered to create syntactically correct standalone orders as well as contextually correct orders, which take into consideration the customer's current service configuration.

## 8.10.22 Siebel Billing Profiles

Siebel Billing Profiles assist users in creating, maintaining and managing complex billing and discounting arrangements common with large corporate accounts. Through open enterprise interfaces to OSS, this component leverages the capabilities of existing billing systems to support complex billing hierarchies that may span multiple service address/areas and service types. Billing Profiles also provide users the ability to create and maintain billing aggregation points, and to support complex discounting methodologies. This feature uses a Microsoft Explorer graphical format to display and manage these profiles. Billing profile information such as address and contact name is maintained at each point in a billing hierarchy. Siebel's drag-and-drop capability enables users to assign billing products and services to a customer's invoicing hierarchy.

## 8.10.23 Siebel Reports including Smart Reports

Siebel Reports provides robust report generation and report viewing capabilities. Siebel reports include a built-in report writer and more than 100 pre-built reports. Users have access to the power of 'query by example' to generate ad hoc reports online or view reports in graphical format. Siebel Smart Reports go far beyond traditional tabular lists of information to provide, at a glance, summary dashboards, graphical analysis tools and all the rich detail necessary to make rapid, informed decisions. The summary dashboards provide an overview of the topic covered in the report and enable sales and service professionals to know immediately where to focus their efforts. Siebel Smart Reports cover key areas of sales, marketing, customer service and call center performance. This base application is required for all customers that use the Siebel Report Designer included with Siebel Tools.

## 8.10.24 Siebel Service Assistant

Siebel Service Assistant ensures that the service organization utilizes standard steps for diagnosing and closing service events. With Siebel Service Assistant, the service organization is able to define sets of activities or Activity Plans for various categories of service requests. Activity Plans can be invoked automatically at specified points in the service process or on demand by a service professional, thereby improving consistency across the service organization.

Siebel Customer Service Integration enables sales and marketing professionals to view customer service requests and associated activities stored in third-party customer service applications. Siebel Customer Service Integration provides interfaces with these customer service applications through Siebel Enterprise Integration Manager. This module is designed for organizations using a third-party customer service application.

## 8.10.25 Siebel Field Service Inventory

Siebel Service Inventory provides comprehensive service parts inventory management. Users can track inventory in real-term from many locations including trunk inventories, and easily access this information from anywhere within the system. The parts locator offers real-term access to inventory, enabling everyone in the service organization to make informal decisions on parts availability with accurate information. Siebel Service Inventory provides the parts locator screen during the RMA/order process or during the dispatch operation.

## 8.10.26 Siebel Shipping and Receiving

Siebel Shipping and Receiving builds on Siebel Service Inventory to optimize the pick/pack/ship processes and receiving processes. Siebel Shipping and Receiving tracks and manages customer orders and internal stock transfer orders throughout the entire process. RMAs and orders are received within Siebel Shipping and Receiving, closing the loop with each customer.

## 8.10.27 Siebel Logistics Manager

Siebel Logistics Manager builds on Siebel Service Inventory by providing powerful and configurable engines that leverage inventory information to automate the field service business.

- The fulfillment engine analyzes orders and allocates parts for each line item. It then automatically generates pick tickets and processes them, optimizing the movement of parts from supply depots to customer site.
- The replenishment engine generates replenishment orders based on stock levels at each location.
- The cycle counting engine generates cycle counts based on cycle counting requirements (ABC or XYZ) specified by a Logistics Manager.

Siebel Logistics Manager reduces overstocking and parts delayed service corrections by determining the critical thresholds on desired parts quantities across various product classifications, and then monitoring stock and issue replenishment orders as required.

## 8.10.28 Sales Analysis

Siebel Sales Analysis is a pre-configured analysis tool focused on sales performance, sales pipeline and competitor information. Analyses include charts, tabular displays and online narratives about key performance information.

## 8.10.29 Siebel Service Analysis

Siebel Service Analysis provides pre-configured analysis tools focused on customer service and customer satisfaction information. Analyses include charts, tabular displays and online narratives about essential service center performance information.

### 8.10.30 Siebel Campaign Analysis

Siebel Campaign Analysis provides pre-configured analysis tools focused on campaign management and call center metric information. Analyses include charts, tabular displays and online narratives about key performance information.

## 8.11 SIEBEL ENTERPRISE APPLICATIONS DATA MODEL ENTITIES

Siebel Data Model includes the structure for a complete deployment of Siebel applications. Siebel delivers all the major entities that are required by a global sales, marketing and service enterprise. Moreover, if required it is fully extensible and customizable as well (see Chapter 11, sub-section "Siebel Database Extension Designer "). Siebel Data Model contains more than 1200 tables and 5500 indexes. The Siebel Data Model is designed to be very flexible and can optimize performance for both online users and server processes. It provides a foundation for easily customizable solutions, rapid application development, optimized performance and lower cost of ownership. This flexibility is by reason of its automated integration with the Siebel Enterprise Applications, which also accounts for its unprecedented level of configurability and adaptability. Table 8.1 lists a sample of the important Siebel Data Model Entities.

**Table 8.1 A Sample of Important Siebel Data Model Entities**

| Entity | Description |
|---|---|
| Account | An organization unit (account) that is external to the internal organization deploying Siebel. An account represents a buying organization, business partner or competitor organization. |
| Account External Products | Customer ownership of a product provided by an external vendor. |
| Account File Attachment | An instance of a physical file attachment—MS Word documents, emails, and so on—associated with an account. |
| Account for a Promotion | Detailed plan for the execution of a promotion at the specified account. |
| Account for Opportunity | An account/external organization that is involved in an opportunity. An organization may be the primary purchasing/buying organization of a product. Other accounts involved in the opportunity may be secondary organizations such as integrators or subcontractors. |

Siebel Data Model is characterized by the following:

- A rich information model to support cross-industry requirements—Siebel has the most comprehensive customer information data model which takes into account the requirements of a broad range of industries and is also continuously updated on an ongoing basis.
- A leading-edge strategy for integration with other systems within the enterprise—Siebel supports multiple integration methodologies including APIs that support business functions not only across components of Siebel Enterprise Applications but also across other applications like ERP, SCM, HRMS, KM/BI and so on.

- A flexible architecture with full support for database extensions—Siebel supports full configurations and adaptations to support specific requirements of the enterprise.
- A future-proof strategy to protect customer investments in customization—Siebel Enterprise Applications architecture allows users to make customizations to the data model while preserving the ability to seamlessly upgrade to future product releases.
- A comprehensive and seamless support for internationalization—Siebel Data Model has built-in support for multiple languages as well as currencies.
- A high-performance database design—Siebel Enterprise Applications have been benchmarked to perform excellently against very large databases with a large number of users.

## 8.12 SUMMARY

In this chapter we familiarized ourselves with the main components of Siebel Enterprise Applications including Marketing Enterprise, Sales Enterprise, Service Enterprise, Field Service, Call Center, Employee Relationship Management (ERM), Mid-market Applications, Vertical Market Applications, Professional Services Automation and a host of special enterprise options. For each of these modules, we highlighted the salient features of the module and described its core business processes followed by a detailed list of its features. Under vertical market applications we discussed industry-specific solutions for automotive, communications, consumer goods, finance, high technology, insurance, pharma, public sector and utilities industries.

In the next chapter we will look at the characteristics of Siebel's eBusiness Applications and the various functionality options available within them.

# Chapter 9

# Siebel eBusiness Applications

eBusiness is the relocation of internal and external business processes to the Internet. Customer-led eBusiness has been highly publicized due to the astronomical market valuations attained by hundreds of dot.com companies as well as the unprecedented amounts of venture capital attracted by them during the period of the Internet boom. Research studies suggest that the business-to-business (B2B) segment will prove to be much more significant in terms of the overall eBusiness impact by an order of magnitude. However, there is no denying the fact that the Internet revolution was launched in the business-to-consumer (B2C) arena. Siebel's eBusiness suite of products called Siebel eBusiness Applications, fully addresses the requirements of the entire market spanning the entire spectrum of B2C, B2B and B2E scenarios. In this chapter we discuss the functionality and features of the Siebel eBusiness Applications.

## 9.1 WHAT IS eBUSINESS?

eBusiness refers to an enterprise that has re-engineered itself to conduct its business via the Internet and Web. Successful enterprises need to re-conceptualize the very nature of their business.

As customers begin to buy via Internet and enterprises rush to use the Internet to create new operational efficiencies, most enterprises seek to update their business strategies. Enterprises survey the changing environment and then modify their company strategies to accommodate these changes. This involves major changes in the way companies do business, including changes in marketing, sales, service, product delivery, and even manufacturing and inventory. Changed strategies will entail changed business processes that in turn, imply changed software systems or better still, software systems that are changeable!

Table 9.1 lists the various business models that an enterprise can employ to retain, leverage and enhance its customer capital. Table 9.2 lists the various pricing mechanisms that an enterprise can employ to retain, leverage and enhance its customer capital.

**Table 9.1 Business Models**

| Name | Description | Benefits to Customer | Benefits to Enterprise | Sources of Value |
|---|---|---|---|---|
| Collaboration Platform | - Collaboration, cooperation and coordination between enterprises | - Collaboration on specific functions, design and engineering<br>- Virtual team of consultants | - Low-cost high value activities | - Membership fee<br>- Fee per use<br>- Charging for specialist tools for design, workflow document management |
| Information Brokers, Trusts and other services | - Adding value to the colossal amount of information on the Net | - Up-to-date, quality information available whenever and wherever it is needed<br>- Information management services for ascertaining authenticity and accuracy | - Selling information search results<br>- Selling customer profiling information<br>- Selling business opportunities<br>- Providing Investment advice<br>- Providing trust certificates | - Subscription fee<br>- Service fee<br>- Software sales<br>- Consultancy fee |
| Virtual communities | - Medium of communication between members | - Communities of common interests<br>- Sharing of issues, solutions, workarounds, future requirements | - Establish Customer loyalty<br>- Receive customer feedback<br>- Join third-party marketplaces | - Membership fee<br>- Advertisement fee |
| eShop | - Seeking orders<br>- Commonly for regular goods, groceries and consumables | - Lower price<br>- Wider choice of products and services<br>- Better comparative information<br>- Easy selection<br>- Buying and delivery<br>- 24 × 7 availability<br>- Personalized and customized | - Low-cost option<br>- Increased sales<br>- Advertisement<br>- Global presence | - Lower cost<br>- Newer sales channel |

*(Contd.)*

| Name | Description | Benefits to Customer | Benefits to Enterprise | Sources of Value |
|---|---|---|---|---|
| eProcurement | - Seeking vendors<br>- Electronic tendering<br>- Electronic procurement of goods and services | - Wider choice of vendors<br>- Reduced cost of procurement<br>- Reduced price<br>- Better quality<br>- Improved delivery<br>- Electronic negotiation and contracting<br>- Collaborative work on specification<br>- Convenience<br>- Faster turnaround | - More tendering opportunities<br>- Global reach/ presence<br>- Lower cost of tendering<br>- Small companies can share/ apportion tender work<br>- Collaborating tendering work | - Reduction of procurement cost<br>- More cost-effective offers<br>- Selling technology solution<br>- Transaction fee<br>- Advertising |
| eAuction | - Electronic bidding | - Multimedia presentation<br>- Integration of bidding with contracting, payment and delivery<br>- Increased efficiency and faster turnaround<br>- Bid on smaller quantities and lower value<br>- Reduced purchasing overhead | - Increased efficiency and faster turnaround<br>- New channel for global presence | - Reduced surplus stock<br>- Better utilization of the production capacity<br>- Lower sales overhead |
| email | - Collection of eShops with common functionalities such as common customer database, common target customer segments, | - Common guaranteed payment method<br>- Add value via establishment of a virtual - community<br>- Convenience of related eShops related eShops | - Opportunities for sale of supporting technologies<br>- Cross-sales of other eShops Advertising space<br>- Brand reinforcement<br>- Ease of setting up Web front ends | |

*(Contd.)*

| Name | Description | Benefits to Customer | Benefits to Enterprise | Sources of Value |
|---|---|---|---|---|
| | combined marketing campaigns, promotions, etc. | | - Provide sophisticated payment methods<br>- Benefits from up-selling of competing brands<br>- Ease of outsourcing Web-based operations | |
| Internet Service Provider (ISP) | - Providers of infrastructure and attendant services for management, operations and support | - Easy access to Internet services | - Advertising space<br>- Collaboration with related companies<br>- Direct access to customers for direct marketing | - Subscription fees<br>- Surround services like telephony |
| Portal | - Integrated collection of services providing a seamless and compelling customer experience | - A one-stop shop<br>- A unified experience bound by a common purpose | - Provision of common services<br>- Portal as a distinct brand | - Membership fee<br>- Advertisement<br>- Transaction fee<br>- Service fee |
| Third-party Marketplace | - Third-party marketing<br>- Uniform transaction support to multiple businesses | - Automatic benefits of branding, ordering, secure transactions, payments, logistics, delivery, etc. | - ISP can offer Web-application building services<br>- Bank can offer transaction services | - Joining fee<br>- Service fee<br>- Transaction fee |
| Value Chain Service Provider | - Specific services spanning across the value chain such as ePayment and logistics | - Indirect benefits via efficiencies gained in the enterprises' cost and processes | - Beneficial especially to the Banks<br>- Management of inventory, stock, production, etc. | - Service fee<br>- Percentage of transaction value |
| Value Chain Integrator | - Integrating across the complete value chain | - Beneficial to customers of third-party marketplaces | - A dynamic marketplace with continually changing constituent partners | - Consultancy fee<br>- Percentage of the transaction value |

**Table 9.2 Pricing Models**

| Name | Description |
|---|---|
| eCommerce | The sale of real and electronic merchandize through the medium of an electronic shop via a browseable catalog |
| Subscription | The customer pays a pre-determined amount of money for use of the service; the ownership of the merchandise is not transferred to the customer |
| Charges on per use basis | The customer pays each time they use the service such as video-on-demand; ownership of the merchandise is not transferred to the customer |
| Charges on usage basis | The customer pays based on the duration of usage as in the case of playing interactive games; ownership of the merchandise is not transferred to the customer |
| Advertisement | The customer indirectly pays via interested vendor companies purchasing advertising space on the Web site to target the visiting customers |
| Sponsorship | This is akin to the advertisement model except that the space is purchased only by the sponsor companies and it advertises only their messages |
| Public Support | The public interest Web sites are typically supported by donations from the general public and social and government institutions |
| Indirect | The customer pays indirectly not for use of the Web site but via the use of telephony, etc. |

***The Significance of Internet***

It is not easy to speculate on the reasons that the Internet is undergoing the revolutionary changes that we have witnessed in the past few years. What gives it the power to drive the massive changes that have been witnessed in the last five years, while similar changes in the past have taken ages to sweep across the globe?

In the earlier book "Implementing SAP R/ 3", I had proposed that the fundamental reason is that the medium is always more powerful than the message. It may be that at certain stages in history messages (and their messengers) have had a determining effect on the course of history, but these passages have been few and far between. The impact of the medium has always been more powerful and longer-lasting than any message. Throughout history, the powerful have always recognized this truth and have concentrated on controlling a medium as the most powerful facet of governance, rather than becoming martyrs as revolutionaries with a new message to give to the world. The print medium has outlasted all ideological and technological revolutions seen in past centuries since the dawn of civilization. In one form or another, this has been a known fact in all fields of human endeavor, but Marshall McLuhan brought this out much more forcefully for the electronic media in the middle of the last century.

Computers were always positioned as both the message and medium for the new era but it is clear that right from the beginning the Internet was the medium. Considering that the Internet is not governed or dictated by any specific authority and is one of the most democratic of institutions, one can be absolutely sure that it is destined to herald the next major cultural revolution in human history.

Additionally, underlying all human endeavor, lies the quest for immortality, the desire to transcend space and time forever. It may seem that this is only the concern of spiritualists and philosophers or mathematicians, relativists and other scientists. Similarly, it may seem that all commercial endeavors are driven by the pursuit of money, but that could be wrong! At the base of all commercial transactions lie the fundamental concerns for transcending space and time!

All major technological advance that had a lasting impact on the future course of human development, be they discoveries or inventions, had to do with one of the following:

- *Sliding space and/ or time in a direction that satisfied the basic urge to transcend space and time in practical terms and in a direction that was convenient.*
- *Altering space and/ or time, that is, expanding or contracting space and /or time to satisfy the basic urge to transcend both, again in practical terms and in a direction that was convenient. Although such effects are not unknown in physical sciences, here we are referring to effects that are psychological and experiential in nature.*

**Technological Advances in the Last Century**

| Description | Space | | | | Time | | | |
|---|---|---|---|---|---|---|---|---|
| | Sending | | Altering | | Sending | | Altering | |
| | +ve | –ve | +ve | –ve | +ve | –ve | +ve | –ve |
| Paper | X | X | X | X | X | X | X | X |
| Vericies | | X | | | | | | X |
| Telephones | X | | X | | X | | | |
| Voice Mall | X | X | X | | X | X | | X |
| Photographs | X | X | X | | | X | | |
| Transmitted Pictures | X | X | X | X | X | X | X | |
| Motion Pictures | | X | X | | | X | X | |
| Audio/Video CDs | X | X | X | | X | | | X |
| Audio/Video CD Players | X | X | | X | | X | | X |
| Deepfreezers | | | | | | X | | |
| Microwaves | | | | | X | | X | |
| Credit Card Payments | X | X | | | X | | | |
| Telephone Charge Cards | X | | | | X | | | |
| Computers | | | X | X | | X | X | X |
| Networks | X | X | | X | X | | | X |
| Internet | X | X | X | X | X | X | X | X |

**Fig. 9.1 Technological Advances in the Last Century**

Figure 9.1 shows a snapshot of the technological advancements witnessed in the last century interpreted in this new light. In the figure, the legend used is as given below:

Sliding Space

+ve Bringing near

–ve Taking afar

Sliding Time

+ve Bringing near

–ve Taking afar

Altering Space

+ve Compressing space

–ve Expanding space

Altering Time

+ve Compressing time

–ve Expanding time

For instance, telephones permit you to converse with a person as if he were close (Sliding space +ve and Altering space +ve) and without waiting for a time in future when you can meet him/her in person (Sliding time +ve). It is a simple grid, but it enables us to understand in a powerful way the essential unity behind the technological advances in the last couple of centuries. It also gives a rationale for the difference in the degree of impact that these technological inventions have had on human life and thought. It is evident that the Internet's power on the consumer's mind comes from its unprecedented facility to slide and alter both space and time to a degree that is unlikely to be surpassed for quite some time in the future, and is matched only by that of printed paper.

Frances Cairncross coined the phrase 'the death of distance' to describe the way in which the Internet helps to eliminate geographical constraints. In a 1995 article on telecommunications, she had predicted that 'the death of distance as a determinant of the cost of communications will probably be the single most important economic force shaping society in the first half of the next century'.

### 9.1.1 Basic eBusiness Strategy Patterns

Patricia Seybold was the first person to point out that the Internet economy was first and foremost a *customer* economy because of the power that it gave to customers in terms of the information on competitive products and real-term pricing that it made available to them via any channel of interaction of their immediate choice.

The customer economy heralded the following:

- Significance of the customer relationships in a way that they had never done before
- Fundamental strategy of making it easy for customers to do business with the enterprise

Success in the customer economy will demand that companies manage their enterprises by and for customer value—they will have to use Customer Lifetime Value (CLV) as a strategic management tool. A company's source of investor value will increasingly be based on the value of their customer franchise, or the lifetime customer value of their present and future customers (discussed in Chapter 16, sub-section "Time Value of Customers and Shareholder Value").

Companies will have to focus on the branded customer experience whenever they interact with the company's products at via any touch point (Web, email, phone or face-to-face) and across any channel (retail, dealer, agent or broker). To win in the customer economy, companies will have to build and sustain an exquisite branded experience and to measure and monitor what matters to customers in the real-term, and which may be tracked not unlike financial information and share price information at present. Just as customer satisfaction indices are by now well-established as good indicators of profitability, in the future investment decisions may be made based on the changing values of the customer metrics and value indexes.

In the customer economy, the employees' performance-linked pay may be based on such customer metrics that assess the achievement of customer satisfaction and customer loyalty goals like:

- Growth in active number of customers
- Customers' commitment to the company's products, strategy and vision
- Customers' propensity to defect
- Customer retention
- Customer referrals
- Customer acquisition costs

The concept of pattern was introduced by Christopher Alexander in the late 70's in the field of architecture. A pattern describes a commonly occurring solution that generates decidedly successful outcomes (see Chapter 7, sub-section "Patterns of Enterprise Agility").

The patterns learned from eBusiness efforts in the past few years are listed below.

### 9.1.1.1 Target the Right Customers

Some of the steps involved with this strategy pattern are:

- Know customers and prospects—This involves identifying the customers and then knowing as much as possible about them
- Identify profitable customers—This involves looking not only at the revenue but also at the costs of servicing particular customers or customer segments
- Decide on which customers to attract—This involves deciding on which existing customers should be prevented from defecting and the new customers that should be attracted and engaged
- Locate customers influencing the key purchases in any home or enterprise—This involves identifying, communicating and engaging them directly, for instance, inviting them into community forums (discussed later)
- Discover which customers generate referrals—This involves identifying their wants, delivering solutions and measuring their levels of satisfaction. Repeat customers that are profitable are the best barometers of 'getting it right'
- Differentiate clearly between customers, partners and stakeholders—This involves focusing and caring about the actual consumers

#### *9.1.1.1.1 Know the Customer*

Some of the steps involved with this strategy pattern are:

- Know the customer's business context
- Know the customer's needs and wants
- Know the customer's preferences
- Know the customer's prior interactions and history

#### *9.1.1.1.2 Care about Customer's Wants*

Some of the steps involved with this strategy pattern are:

- Nurture deep commitment to customers and their outcomes
- Enhance mindshare and market space as against market share
- Create a customer-centric culture
- Move from the earlier product-centric to a customer-centric approach

#### *9.1.1.1.3 Value Customer's Time*

Some of the steps involved with this strategy pattern are:

- Streamline decision-making
- Offer ubiquitous and convenient access
- Design, using customer scenarios

#### *9.1.1.1.4 Measure What Matters to Customers*

Some of the steps involved with this strategy pattern are:

- Determine customer's outcomes
- Understand the customer's context
- Identify key customer scenarios within customer life cycle stages
- Determine what tasks matter the most to customers
- Monitor customer scenarios in real-term and take effective action

### 9.1.1.2 Own the Customer's Total Experience

Some of the steps involved with this strategy pattern are:

- Deliver a consistent, high value and enriching experience—The company's branding should not only include the product or the service but also the actual 'experience' of using them
- Value customer's time and convenience—This involves focusing on the customer's convenience for locating, selecting, evaluating and ordering for the company's offerings, rather than the convenience of the company or its partners for manufacturing, distributing and delivering them
- Partner for delivering consistent quality and service—The customer, especially repeat customers, should be assured of and be able to avail of the same seamless experience whenever or wherever they chose to opt for the company's offerings
- Personalize and celebrate the customer's individuality—This involves leveraging on the information from the customer directly or from the customer's profile to tailor the customers experience to

suit their preferences and expectations. This may be related with the look-and-feel, navigation, types of products, range of prices, special options, and so on

- Give customers control over their experience—This involves enabling customers with the flexibility to customize even the personalization factors dynamically

#### *9.1.1.2.1 Deliver Personalized Service*

Some of the steps involved with this strategy pattern are:

- Enable customers to specify and modify their profiles
- Customize information presentations and offers based on customer's profiles
- Provide appropriate service and information based on customer's needs
- Give access to their transaction histories

#### *9.1.1.2.2 Deliver a Seamless Customer Experience across Channels and Touch Points*

Some of the steps involved with this strategy pattern are:

- Create a multi-touch point strategy
- Deal with channel conflict
- Integrate channel partners
- Share customer information

#### *9.1.1.2.3 Provide a 360-degree View of the Customer Relationship*

Some of the steps involved with this strategy pattern are:

- Provide one-stop shopping for the customer to enable them to access information, perform transactions and request service across all the product lines from your organizations
- Improve the company's 'memory' about the customer's interactions with the company by consolidating all the information about each customer's account and relationship in one single, easily accessible place. The company must support and encourage sharing of information
- Ensure that everyone in the company dealing with the customer has access to the complete profile of the customer
- Put in place the technical infrastructure essential to provide a 360-degree view of the customer

#### *9.1.1.2.4 Streamline Business Processes that Impact the Customer*

Some of the steps involved with this strategy pattern are:

- Identify the actual end customer
- Streamline processes from the end customer's point of view
- Streamline the processes for the other key stakeholders
- Continuously improve the processes based on the customer feedback
- Give everyone involved a clear view of the process

#### *9.1.1.2.5 Establish a Customer Centric eBusiness Architecture*

Some of the steps involved with this strategy pattern are:

- Enable multiple touch points
- Enable multiple channels for interaction
- Integrate or inter-operate multiple applications
- Integrate or interface multiple customer and transaction databases
- Integrate or inter-operate with multiple partners
- Make it easy for customers to do business with you anytime, anywhere and via any device

### 9.1.1.3 Foster Customer Loyalty

Some of the steps involved with this strategy pattern are:

- Increase the customer base
- Increase the tenure within the total customer life cycle with the company
- Measure the retention power
- Measure the customer revenue
- Measure customer costs
- Measure customer profitability
- Evaluate defection and loyalty

#### *9.1.1.3.1 Help Customers Do Their Jobs*

Some of the steps involved with this strategy pattern are:

- Establish an understanding of how the customers do their jobs
- Continuously refine the enterprise business processes to make it easier for the customers to do their jobs
- Give customers the tools to assist in making the purchasing decision
- Prepare the bills as desired by the customer
- Enable customers to satisfy their own customer or target entities

#### *9.1.1.3.2 Let Customers Help Themselves*

Some of the steps involved with this strategy pattern are:

- Let customers help themselves to information and perform transactions online
- Let customers check on the status of orders, pay or adjustment of bills and access related services
- Let customers interact using whatever channel or media of communication they like—telephone, voice response, fax, mail, and so on
- Give customers the ability to customize the company's offerings to their requirements and preferences

#### *9.1.1.3.3 Foster Community*

Some of the steps involved with this strategy pattern are:

- Attract and encourage customers to become valuable members of customer communities focused on specific areas of interest

- Facilitate introduction of the customer to others with common interests
- Reinforce the understanding and commitment on common standards, terminology and values
- Enable members of customers to share the issues, resolutions and experiences of using the company's offerings

### 9.1.2 eBusiness Challenges

The challenges of eBusiness are as follows:

(a) Business fit—Most systems are designed as point solutions for intra-enterprise needs. However, as we have seen in Chapter 7, the processes are not necessarily confined to an enterprise alone but can extend to incorporate the business partners as well as the customers. This fundamental shift from enterprise-focused to primarily customer-focused, multi-enterprise spanning business processes is the most fundamental challenge faced by any eBusiness.

(b) Time-to-market—Because of the rapid changes in the market, it is essential that the eBusiness systems are able to adapt themselves quickly to the changes in the market environment and respond with competitive offerings and solutions.

(c) Cost-effectiveness—This ability to change should be achievable in a cost-effective manner without compromising on the quality of the design, maintainability and upgradeability of the eBusiness solutions.

(d) Quality—Since eBusiness solutions are targeted at thousands of anonymous users, its design, both at the user interface and architecture level, needs to be usable, intuitive, reliable, robust and consistent for enhancing the quality of the customer' experience.

(e) Adaptability—eBusiness solutions must enable business innovation and responding to strategic opportunities, while at the same time being able to interface or integrate readily with the existing systems and databases.

(f) Scalability—eBusiness should be able to address the basic eBusiness paradox of 'the more visitors you have, the more successful you are but, the more successful you are the more venerable you are'! A crashed Web site at a critical juncture and the resulting customer ire can jeopardize the very existence of your business. The success of eBusiness Web sites hinges on their ability to attract customers and prospects. But if the deluge of customers does materialize, woe befalls the Web site that cannot service them.

(g) Integration—eBusiness solutions need to interface or integrate with existing systems both Web applications and back end enterprise systems across heterogeneous architectures and protocols, to enable continual returns on earlier investments.

### 9.1.3 eBusiness Applications for a Customer-centric World

Internet supported customer relationship management is rapidly emerging as the 'killer app' of the Web of the 00's. The Internet has enabled a dramatic reduction in the cost of transactions and interactions between the enterprise and its customers. Online customers expect shorter sales cycles, personalized information, quicker resolution of issues and added value at each stage of the transaction.

eBusiness applications like Siebel provide a standard-based Web architecture for information, process and application integration so that the enterprise can integrate information and processes across marketing, commerce and service. The enterprise can integrate existing databases, legacy applications and systems to create a virtual centralized information repository so that the company can market, sell and service its offerings more effectively. And, the Web architecture's scalability and flexibility enables it to be more responsive leading to rapid growth. eBusiness applications like Siebel, are a fully integrated suite of applications for Customer Relationship Management (CRM) and closely related applications for Partnership Relationship Management (PRM) and Employee Relationship Management (ERM), all based on a common web architecture. They help enterprises by providing these three key functionalities to fully align their partners, employees and customer touch points, processes and channels around the goal of maximizing the value of customer-relationships.

### 9.1.3.1 Business to Customer (B2C) Applications

Historically, it was the B2C applications that launched the Internet revolution by extending the reach of the organization directly to the consumer market. B2C applications were typically referred to as eCommerce applications and involved credit or debit payments. Over time, B2C applications have matured to enable organizations to identify, select, acquire and retain customers more effectively. By providing a centralized repository of customer data captured from all customer interactions across all channels and touch points, B2C applications enable organizations to maintain an ongoing and seamless dialog with its customers regardless of when, where or how the interactions occur. Companies are able to understand, anticipate and respond to customer needs and are able to do so more effectively and efficiently over time. CRM's like Siebel give managers better visibility into market dynamics and customer demand by providing real-time views of the customer activity.

### 9.1.3.2 Business to Business (B2B) Applications

B2B applications employ Internet technologies to link one enterprise with another, many of whom are traditional brick-and-mortar companies that have been doing business together for a time, using direct connection technologies like EDI (Electronic Data Interchange) to trade with each other. B2B or related Partnership Relation Management (PRM) applications allow enterprises to manage their business partner's ecosystem as a virtual extension of their sales, marketing and service organizations. Enterprises can maximize their partners' efficiency and productivity by ensuring that their partners' incentives, resources and objectives are fully aligned with those of the enterprise. We will discuss Siebel eChannel in the next section.

### 9.1.3.3 Business to Employee (B2E) Applications

B2E applications typically involve internal business processes that are moved to the Internet specifically for the benefit of employees who are remotely located. Enterprises face the problems of their employees not being fully aligned with the organization's focus on customers. B2E or the related Enterprise Relationship Management (ERM) applications help organizations to rapidly communicate the corporate policies and decisions to the entire workforce, mobilize employees to execute those decisions and monitor workforce performance in real-time. As employees are able to perform their job more effectively, organizations benefit from increased employee satisfaction and hence, increased customer satisfaction (as happier and better-informed employees provide better customer service). We have described Siebel ERM in Chapter 8, section "Employee Relationship Management (ERM)".

## 9.2 SIEBEL eBUSINESS APPLICATIONS

Siebel eBusiness is a comprehensive suit of Web-based products that allow enterprises to leverage the Web as the basic communications channel to acquire new customers and enhance relationships with the existing ones.

Siebel eBusiness includes the following components:

- Siebel eSales
- Siebel eService
- Siebel eChannel
- Siebel eMarketing

Siebel eBusiness enables enterprises to accrue all the benefits entailed in the usage of packaged applications, including profitability, lower software applications, maintenance costs, ongoing enhancements and technical support. Siebel eBusiness provides comprehensive out-of-the-box functionality, scalable Web-based product architecture, flexible application customization capabilities, and a solution that is built on current and emerging Internet and Web computing standards.

### 9.2.1 Salient Features

Siebel eBusiness Applications is a leading example of comprehensive and world class pre-built applications that are scalable, configurable, integrable, readily customizable and easily upgradeable. With Siebel applications customers, field sales, service professionals, call center agents and channel partners can use a uniform customer management architecture that delivers a consistent, integrated store of business-related information and a compelling interface that meets the needs of all these constituencies.

Siebel eBusiness Applications have the following outstanding characteristics.

- Web-based architecture enables geographically dispersed users to access comprehensive functionality on the client through their Web browser with no software installed on the client.
- Rapid development and deployment enables complete application versioning for maintenance revisions, and automated deployment strategies for rapid and continuous eBusiness site customization.
- Support for all channels enables enterprises to coordinate and deploy sophisticated multi-tiered distribution and support strategies across all channels simultaneously. Siebel eBusiness delivers a suite of applications built on a singular set of objects and a common set of business logic valid across multiple interaction channels. Thus, it provides support across the entire spectrum of front office including Web-based sales, marketing and service; field sales and service; indirect sales; and traditional marketing, call centers and customer service.
- Support for multiple platforms enables users to select the platform of choice amongst Web browser-based thin clients, connected clients, mobile clients and handheld computer clients.

- Comprehensive interfaces enables transactions to be processed in real-term and reliably across systems by supporting functional, high performance and maintainable integration with intra and inter-enterprise applications including those of channel partners and third-party service providers.
- A robust middle tier enables flexible and scalable support for large numbers of concurrent users, workflow and process automation, data visibility and security, data synchronization, application integration and other key server processes.
- Customizable yet automatically upgradeable software enables enterprises to customize the eBusiness applications to conform to their specific business practices, yet benefit from the technological advances and functional enhancements of the corresponding software upgrades
- High performances, scalability and availability of functionality enables support of high volume transactions on eBusiness sites accessed by thousands or even millions of users on a 24 × 7 basis.
- Global support enables satisfying the demanding multi-lingual, multiple currency and localization requirements of particular eBusiness implementations.

## 9.2.2 Core eBusiness Applications

The core business processes constituting Siebel eBusiness Applications are described below.

### 9.2.2.1 Siebel eSales

Siebel eSales is a comprehensive Web-based application to support unassisted business-to-business (B2B) and business-to-consumer (B2C) selling over the Web. Siebel eSales includes a visual product catalog. By integrating Siebel eSales with existing Web sites, Siebel customers can quickly set up shop on the Internet, leverage product data and marketing collateral and configure across multiple selling channels including indirect channels, call centers, the field and the Web.

Siebel eSales allows B2B and B2C selling over the Web and provides:

- Customer profiling and personalization using Siebel Personalization
- Multimedia product catalog
  - Product search tools including full-text search and parametric search based on product attributes
  - User-specified product comparison
  - Distributed catalog administration allowing multiple-vendor catalogs
  - Thread bar for easier catalog navigation, customer profiling and personalization using Siebel Personalization
- Customizable order management processes using Siebel Workflow
- Online shopping cart, quotes and orders
  - Favorites lists of items enabling easy recall and repeat buying by the customers
  - Quote template for expediting the buying process
  - Streamlined checkout processes
  - Integration with third-party taxation solutions such as Taxware and payment processing systems such as CyberSource Internet Commerce Suite (ICS)

- Optional modules
  - Siebel eAdvisor for Web-based needs analysis
  - Siebel eAuction for dynamic pricing, and auction creation and management
  - Siebel eConfigurator for Web-based product configuration
  - Siebel ePricer for one-to-one pricing and promotions using custom price lists

Siebel eSales setup involves several activities including:

- Defining User Access
  - Defining external authentication via LDAP
  - Enabling database access by creating database users for LDAP
  - Defining visibility for
    Views
    Catalogs
    Products
  - Assigning proxy employee
  - Associating users with accounts
- Pre-defined responsibilities for Siebel eSales
  - Web Anonymous User
  - Web Registered User
  - Web Corporate User Especially for B2B
  - Web Purchasing Manager
- Defining Access Groups especially for external B2B customers requiring access to particular catalogs
- Setting up price lists
- Customizing user interface
  - Modifying Web templates
  - Changing colors
  - Modifying the behavior caused by clicking a button
  - Adding or removing applets
  - Changing controls
  - Altering fields in forms required or optional fields
  - Deploying Siebel eSales without using frames
- Defining Products Administration Screen
- Setting up full-text search
- Setting up shipping charge calculation
- Customizing Notifications controlled by workflow processes

Siebel eSales uses Siebel Workflow to control the order management processes. Siebel Workflow provides a graphical interface for designing, implementing and modifying user interactions and business processes including:

- Quotes and templates
  - Order Quote Process
  - Edit Quote Process
  - Re-Price Process
  - Save Cart Process
- Checkout
  - Checkout Process
  - Enter Shipping Details Process
  - Enter Payment Details Process
  - Complete Checkout Process
  - Authorize Order Process
  - Save Credit Card
  - Save Shipping Address
  - Shipping Calculation Process
  - Set Primary Account Address Process
  - Save Order Status
- Notifications
  - Send Order Accepted email
  - Send Order Awaiting Approval email
  - Send Order Failed email
  - Send Order Rejected email
  - Send Order Shipped email
- Purchase approval
  - Approve Order Process
  - Modify Order Process
- Order modification
  - Cancel Order Process
  - Modify Order Process
  - Re-order Process
- Error messages and views
  - Display Error Process
  - Login View
  - Order Confirmation View
  - Shopping Cart View
- Auctions

Siebel eCatalog provides a mechanism for users to find products that satisfy their requirements and is also available in conjunction with Siebel eChannel, Siebel Sales and Siebel Call Center. Using Siebel eCatalog customers can browse through categories arranged in a hierarchy to locate products of interest by searching via full-text search or parametric search.

Siebel eCatalog can be deployed in two different ways:

Server-based catalog created and managed via Catalog Administration

Browser-based catalog for feature-based product selection created via Siebel Interactive Designer, and page-sets generated automatically by Siebel Catalog Wizard using existing product definitions contained in the Siebel database. Siebel Catalog Wizard consists of four modules, namely, Data Builder, Module Builder, File Builder and Manager.

> Siebel Interactive Selling Suite (ISS) is a comprehensive suite of products that enables enterprises to acquire, engage and retain customers through the Web as well as their existing field, call center and indirect sales channel. Siebel ISS applications enable an enterprise to leverage the Web as a powerful selling channel to deliver need analysis, interactive advice, multimedia catalog and configuration assistance to maximize the value of every customer interaction across all communication channels by presenting solutions in the context of customer-identified needs. Siebel ISS enables enterprises to provide customers with personalized but consistent service not only on the Web but also across all customer channels by presenting product features and capabilities, compatibility, pricing, and product recommendations.

### 9.2.2.2 Siebel eService

Siebel eService enables enterprises to provide world class customer service and support through the Internet. Service centers can increase customer satisfaction and reduce costs for providing a high quality 24x7 service dramatically, by implementing Siebel eService. Siebel eService can also verify a user's authorization upon login and provide a personalized view of service activity customized for the particular user.

Siebel eService delivers Web-based customer service automation to manage the entire service process including:

- Comprehensive customer self-service, which reduces the load for customer service call center agents
- Multiple channels of communication for customers to choose from, including universal queuing of voice, email, fax, Interactive Voice Response (IVR), or Web interactions that can be achieved through use of Siebel eService in conjunction with Siebel Service Enterprise or Siebel Call Center
- Routing and dispatch of field service engineers via internal service teams or channel service partners

Siebel eService provides enterprises with a Web and email interface to manage service requests, customer billing inquiries and trouble tickets. Customers and partners can create new service requests, enter service details, place billing inquiries or enter trouble tickets, as well as query and track progress of open service requests, existing inquiries and view solutions. Using Siebel eService, customers and partners can interact and collaborate in real-term with CSRs using Siebel Communications. Siebel eService notifies customers of important events via email, both acknowledging receipt of the service request and informing the customer of updates or resolution.

Siebel eService provides a portal page where customers can quickly access service and knowledge information from the same page constituted of:

- User login for anonymous and registered Web users
- Salutation
- Recommended products based on records of earlier purchases or captured preferences
- Contact Us quickly, using a variety of communication channels like telephone, email, online, chat, voice over IP, postal mail and face-to-face communications
- My Account, maintains person and enterprise-specific information including service requests, orders and registered products that have been purchased by the customer. This enables customers to check regularly on outstanding order status (including returns, repairs, etc.) as well as receive timely product news, alerts, track warranty agreements, recommendations on scheduled services, and register and track service requests related to purchased products
- Self-service including an integrated and searchable knowledge base that provides wide range of information, 'how to' instructions, as well as a wide variety of support and service tools
- Ask a Question, enables the customer to perform natural language searches on the knowledge base using Siebel Smart Answer technology.

Siebel eService setup involves several activities including:

- Setting up the security framework including
  - User Authentication
  - Access Control
  - User Administration
  - Web Delegated Administration
  - Data Privacy
- Setting up Siebel Personalization
- Setting up email notification for (say) change of status of an open service request
- Setting up knowledge base
- Setting up of FAQs
- Setting up Siebel eSmartScripts, Siebel Smart Answer and Siebel eSearch
- Setting up of Contact Us
- Setting up of Branch Locator
- Setting up of Siebel eCollaboration
- Setting up of Siebel Communications Server
- Setting up email, Fax, Mail and Phone Accounts
- Setting up of eService Customer Satisfaction Survey

#### *9.2.2.2.1 Siebel eMail Agent*

Through Siebel email Agent, Siebel eService addresses the importance of email as an important channel for interaction between the customers and prospects with the enterprise. Siebel email Agent which is a component of Siebel eService includes:

- email parsing, which enables configuration of a default field for storing the entire content of the email without the keywords being specified by the user
- Flexibility to support multiple business objects

Siebel email Agent provides the flexibility to:

- Monitor an email box
- Parse inbound emails to extract the sender and the purpose of the message
- Store email contents into the fields of the database
- Automatically reply to the sender with email confirmation information
- Querying the database for customer information via email
- Updating existing database records

email has an edge over interactions with the customers or prospects compared to those via the Web. The foremost among them is the fact that whereas the Web requires the user to request information proactively, email can be sent to the customer or prospect directly. Also, Siebel email Agent automatically tracks each of these email interactions to provide a complete email history for each customer interaction.

### 9.2.2.3 Siebel eChannel

Ensuring the success and effectiveness of channel partners is critical to the success of the enterprise because channel partners are critical components of the extended enterprise. A majority of the world's largest enterprises sell to and service their customers through indirect channels as diverse as resellers, distributors, service providers, retailers, system integrators and complementary solution providers.

Siebel eChannel allows enterprises to route leads, sales opportunities and service requests to the appropriate channel using configurable business rules and also tracks their performances on an ongoing basis. Siebel eChannel enables channel partners to browse product and pricing information, generate quotes and place orders online. During all these interactions, advanced security rules ensure that partners and vendors are able to maintain the confidentiality of the relevant information. Siebel eChannel not only enables enterprises to turn channel partners into an extended virtual sales and service enterprise but also automates the entire partner and vendor relationship.

Siebel eChannel enables channel partners to

- Manage opportunities: with the latest information about accounts, contacts, notes and activities. Channel partners view assigned opportunities, create new opportunities and update the status of opportunities ensuring better visibility into the pipeline.
- Manage accounts by viewing assigned accounts, creating new accounts and tracking the latest information about opportunities, contacts and activities.
- Manage contacts by creating a list of contacts, viewing all contacts related to a specific account or opportunity and recording all contact activity.

- Manage service requests by creating and assigning it automatically to proceed with its immediate resolution.
- Manage activities by entering, viewing and tracking all phone calls, meetings and marketing events related to specific opportunities, accounts, contacts or personal activities.
- Create quotes and orders on behalf of the customers.
- View a multimedia product catalog for the latest products and details.
- Access Marketing Encyclopedia including datasheets, product backgrounder, competitive positioning and other marketing and promotional material, point-of-sale items and copies of advertisements, and so on.
- Receive Siebel ActiveBriefings summarizing updates on opportunities, accounts, contacts and current action items coupled with latest news on target accounts and territories.

Siebel eChannel also provides comprehensive functionality for channel managers in vendor enterprises with features such as:

- Automated lead routing, which entails routing the opportunities, accounts and contacts to the channel partner best qualified to handle a particular lead; this can be achieved by the enterprise's channel managers by defining the assignment criteria through the Siebel Assignment Manager
- Automated service request routing, which entails routing the service requests, accounts and contacts to the channel partner best qualified to service a particular service issue
- Activity tracking, which entails tracking of lead status, service requests and activities that have been assigned to channel partners
- Automated notification, which entails sending email, pager and fax notifications to the channel partners whenever new leads and service requests are assigned, activities are overdue or immediate action is required
- Channel forecasting, which enables enterprises to track effectively, revenues on opportunities in the channel's sales pipeline
- Channel program analysis, which enables comparative analysis of the channel partner's performance

### 9.2.2.4 Siebel eMarketing

Customers use Siebel eMarketing to create, execute and assess Web-based marketing campaigns. Siebel eMarketing drives targeted consumers and channel partners to your Web site through URLs embedded in the email campaigns. Once there, they can purchase products and services effortlessly using Siebel eSales.

With Siebel eMarketing, enterprises can:

- Segment the customer and prospect bases
- Target them with a personalized, automatically generated Web or email based communication or promotion
- View OLAP-based graphical reports that assess the effectiveness and Return on Investment (ROI) of each campaign

The information across all channels captured in the Siebel database can be mined in the Siebel Datamart to enable marketing professionals to determine the effectiveness of Web-based marketing campaigns by way of slicing and dicing by performance indicators like channel performance and account profitability. Siebel Marketing Enterprise includes a broad range of pre-built, out-of-the-box performance analyses as well as capabilities to generate briefings and compelling reports that synthesize and summarize the business insights behind the customer data.

## 9.3 SPECIAL eBUSINESS OPTIONS

The various optional modules are now discussed.

### 9.3.1 Siebel InterActive

Siebel InterActive integrates the wealth of data stored in Siebel Enterprise Applications with content from corporate intranets, the Internet and third-party information providers. This critical information is gathered, filtered and formatted by software agents and delivered to users through a standard Web browser in personalized, elegant, online documents known as ActiveBriefings. Siebel InterActive ensures that sales, marketing and service professionals have immediate access to relevant, business-critical information about customers, prospects, markets and competitors. From each active briefing users can follow hyperlinks to the details of news stories and financial information and can also jump directly into other Siebel applications to find out more about the relevant opportunities, accounts, service requests and other business-critical data.

Siebel InterActive comprises of the following components:

- Siebel Database Server—This server stores information such as organizational structure, responsibilities, product lines, sales personnel, territories and opportunities
- Siebel InterActive Database Connector Server
- Siebel InterActive Web Server—This server is responsible for managing the Web site and requests from Web browsers as well as for authentication of Siebel InterActive users, collecting information, generating ActiveBriefings and caching
- Siebel InterActive News Server is hosted by Siebel Systems and contains a repository with 90 days of news, which is constantly being updated by third-party news providers
- Siebel InterActive Vocabulary Server is hosted by Siebel Systems and holds the repository of the Master IDs
- Siebel InterActive Content Server requests content from an external content provider's server or else is maintained by Siebel itself

With Siebel InterActive, sales, marketing and service professionals can get the information they need immediately, enabling them to spend less time searching for information and more time serving new and exiting customers. Siebel InterActive models the information gathering and using habits of an organization's top performers to significantly reduce the time spent on researching customers and prospects. It empowers users by enabling them to focus on what they can do best—sell, market and provide great customer service.

Siebel provides the following types of InterActive briefings.

(a) Personal ActiveBriefing—Each user of Siebel InterActive receives a personalized ActiveBriefing every morning. This daily electronic newspaper collects and consolidates targeted information from multiple sources. Because it is tailored to the profile of each user, the Personal ActiveBriefings keeps everyone up-to-date on the latest happenings with the company, the customers and the competitors. Personal ActiveBriefings enable the direct launch of Siebel Client to access the records summarized in the ActiveBriefing.

(b) Account ActiveBriefings—When preparing to call on a customer or prospect, sales representatives can review everything they need to know about the customer in a single sheet including recent news, financial performance and externally generated information from sources including Reuters, Business Wire and the SEC EDGAR database as well as opportunity, contact and other related information from the Siebel database.

(c) Competitor ActiveBriefings provides comprehensive reports for use by the sales team in a competitive situation including recent competitor news and product announcements, positioning strategies and the latest recommended resources.

(d) Company ActiveBriefings enables sales, marketing and service professionals to have a wealth of company intelligence that integrates all available third-party information for the more than 100,00 public and private companies in the Siebel InterActive database.

Siebel InterActive includes a one-year subscription to the Company Information Service (CIS). CIS includes targeted business news stories via NewsEDGE, company profiles and financial information on more than 10,000 US and foreign public companies from Market Guide, plus Information Access Company's Ward's Business Directory, which includes profiles on more than 100,000 public and private companies. EDGAR, the Electronic Data Gathering, Analysis and Retrieval system, performs automated collection, validation, indexing, acceptance and forwarding of submissions by companies and others to SEC. Direct links to relevant SEC filings are also integrated into Account, Competitor and Prospect ActiveBriefings. Current stock prices are provided for public companies from Quote.com at www.quote.com. Siebel InterActive also links users to a 52-week price and volume history from StockMaster at www.stockmaster.com.

## 9.3.2 Siebel Personalization

Siebel Personalization provides for creation of personalization rules applied to applets and views that are viewed by the corresponding user. For instance, a personalized message can alert the user to update user profiles or review current open service requests.

## 9.3.3 Siebel eBriefings

Siebel eBriefings are online briefing reports that provide charts, tabular displays and a narrative that explains business trends and drivers. Siebel eBriefings are displayed in Microsoft Word to enable managers and business analysts to further customize briefing documents.

### 9.3.4 Siebel eCollaborations

eCollaboration allows customers browsing the eService site to obtain immediate access to live assistance from customer care representatives. Customer requests are queued and routed to the appropriate agents along with real-time customer profiling information depending on the chosen mode of communication—textual chat, telephone call or voice over Internet.

The agents can take customers:

- On Web tours
- Jointly fill out forms
- Do product demonstrations
- Take control of customer's desktops
- Troubleshoot customer's problems

### 9.3.5 Siebel eSearch

Enterprises can build a flexible knowledge base consisting of data and files inside the Siebel eBusiness Applications or in external systems. The same knowledge base is available across various channels of communications—users can locate this information by using full-text search. Siebel eSearch allows users to search this knowledge base for:

- Solutions to problems
- Resolution documents
- Product news
- External documents

Call center agents use this knowledge base to answer customer queries over the phone or through email.

Siebel Smart Answer uses linguistic analysis techniques and content analysis algorithms to perform natural language searches to retrieve solution data. The system also has self-learning capabilities whereby it learns from successful outcomes across multiple channels—over the Web, through mail or the call center.

Siebel Advanced Search uses fuzzy logic to make searching more intuitive and effective.

### 9.3.6 Siebel eAdvisor

Siebel eAdvisor provides interactive advice and guidance to help customers identify the ideal solution that would satisfy their needs optimally. Siebel eAdvisor emulates the need analysis approach of an enterprise's sales, service or consulting staff through a dialog with the customer that includes 'what if' scenarios, choices and instant feedback.

### 9.3.7 Siebel eConfigurator

Siebel eConfigurator delivers a dynamic online buying experience by guiding customers through product selection and customization to deliver the ideal personalized solution. Siebel eConfigurator quickly identifies the valid purchase options as well as presents cross and upsell purchase options based on the customer's profile and selections on prior occasions.

### 9.3.8 Siebel ePricer

Siebel ePricer enables organizations to provide customers with the relevant price information based on the reference information on contract details, ordered quantity, etc. Siebel ePricer facilitates effecting consistent pricing by enabling enterprises to define and enforce complex pricing rules as well as provide specialized pricing by product, account or other criteria.

### 9.3.9 Siebel eAuction

Siebel eAuction is a comprehensive dynamic commerce solution that helps enterprises to increase return on inventory, test product pricing, create branded marketplaces, develop new sales channels, and create better customer experiences through cross-selling and target promotions.

### 9.3.10 Siebel eSmartScript

Siebel eSmartScript provides agents with a robust, workflow based, dynamically generated user interface to guide an interaction with a customer. SmartScript can be invoked automatically based on business rules or through screen pop-up windows when used in conjunction with Siebel CTI. By providing agents with a complete call script tailored to the customers' needs, businesses ensure the quality of calls, prevent data entry errors and reduce training times. In addition, this option includes the Siebel Script Wizard, an easy-to-use dialog that enables agents to quickly enter data into any view within Siebel Communication.

Siebel eSmartScript is integrated with Siebel SmartScript enabling the sharing of troubleshooting scripts between the Siebel eService site and customer care representatives using Siebel Call Center. Scripts can be created and administered easily using a drag and drop, flowchart-based design interface. This leads to many benefits including increased call quality, fewer data-entry errors and also reduced training time.

### 9.3.11 Siebel eTraining

Siebel eTraining is a comprehensive solution for creating, hosting and managing end-user training. It provides the following services:

- Catalog of training courses
- curriculum information in the case of certification and degree programs
- An automated course registration system
- A library of training materials
- A skills testing system for testing the effectiveness of training and assessing the proficiency level of the trainees

Most of the related administration tasks are performed via the training administration screens:

- Courses
- Classes
- Curriculums
- Enrollments
- Training library
- Training locations
- Test questions
- Tests
- Test results

## 9.4 SUMMARY

This chapter introduced the phenomenon of Internet-enabled eBusinesses in terms of the basic eBusiness business models and pricing models, following which we presented important strategy patterns like targeting the right customers, owning the customers' total experience and fostering customer loyalty. We introduced the basic categories of eBusiness applications, namely, business-to-customer (B2C), business-to-business (B2B) and customer-to-customer (C2C). Following this, we described the main components of the Siebel eBusiness applications like eSales, eService, eChannel and eMarketing. In the last section, the chapter described briefly a host of special eBusiness options.

Chapter 10

# Siebel Applications Environment

In this chapter we look at the Siebel Application Environment consisting of the Siebel Enterprise Server and its components, Siebel Data Warehouse, Siebel eBusiness Applications Integration (eAI), Workflow and Wireless. But first, the chapter introduces the concept of distributed applications and architecture that underlies the architecture of Siebel applications.

The Siebel Applications Architecture is discussed at three layers:

(a) Data Objects Layer
(b) Business Objects Layer
(c) User Interface Objects Layer

## 10.1 DISTRIBUTED APPLICATIONS

Distributed applications consist of a collection of heterogeneous but fully autonomous components that can execute on different computers. Whilst each of these components has full control over its constituent sub-parts, there is no master component that possesses control over all the components of a distributed system. Thus, for the system to appear as a single and integrated whole, the various components need to be able to interact with each other via pre-defined interfaces through a computer network.

The characteristic global features of a successful distributed application are as follows.

- Distributed systems are heterogeneous arising from the need to (say) integrate components on a legacy IBM mainframe, with the components newly created to operate on a UNIX workstation or Windows NT machine.
- Distributed systems are scalable in that when a component becomes overloaded with too many requests or users, another replica of the same component can be instantiated and added to the distributed system to share the load amongst them. Moreover, these instantiated components can be located closer to the local users and other interacting components to improve the performance of the overall distributed system.
- Distributed systems execute components concurrently in a multi-threaded mode via multiply invoked components corresponding to the number of simultaneously invoked processes

- Distributed systems are fault-tolerant in that they duplicate components on different computers so that if one computer fails another can take over without affecting the availability of the overall system.
- Distributed systems are more resilient in that whereas distributed systems have multiple points of failure, the unaffected components are fully operational even though some of the components are not functional or are malfunctioning. Moreover, the distributed system could invoke another instance of the failed components along with the corresponding state of the process (characterized by the program counter, the register variable contents and the state of the virtual memory used by the process) to continue with the process.
- Distributed systems demonstrate invariance or transparency with reference to characteristics like:
  - Accessibility, either locally or across networks to the components
  - Physical location of the components
  - Migration of components from one host to another
  - Replication of components including their states
  - Concurrency of components requesting services from shared components
  - Scalability in terms of the actual number of requests or users at any instance
  - Performance in terms of the number and type of available resources
  - Points of failure be it a failure of the component, network or response

> Performance transparency is achievable through the technique of load balancing that is based on the replication transparency. The middleware layer transparently decides on the balancing decision to select the replica with the least load to provide the requested service. Furthermore, the performance can also be prevented from degrading by continuously monitoring the patterns of access to components and migrating the components appropriately to minimize remote access.

### 10.1.1 n-tier Applications Architecture

In the '80s, the prior monolithic architecture began to be replaced by the client/ server architecture, which split applications into two pieces in an attempt to leverage new inexpensive desktop machines. Distributing the processing loads across many inexpensive clients allowed client/ server applications to scale more linearly than single host/ single process applications could, and the use of off-the-shelf software like Relational Database Management Systems (RDBMS) greatly reduced application development time. While the client could handle the user interface and data display tasks of the application, and the server could handle all the data management tasks, there was no clear solution for storing the logic corresponding to the business processes being automated. Consequently, the business logic tended to be split between the client and the server; typically, rules for displaying data became embedded inside the user interface and the rules for integrating several different data sources became stored procedures inside the database. Whereas this division of logic made it difficult to re-use the user interface code with a different data source, it also made it equally difficult to use the logic stored in the database with a different front-end user interface (like ATM, mobile, etc.) without being required to redevelop the logic implemented in the earlier interface. Thus, a customer service system developed for a particular client system (like a 3270 terminal, a PC or a workstation) would have great difficulty in providing telephony and Internet interfaces with the same business functionality.

The client/ server architecture failed to recognize the importance of managing the business rules applicable to an enterprise independent of both the user interface and, the storage and management of enterprise data. The three-tiered application architecture of the '90s resolved this problem by sub-dividing the application into three distinct layers:

- Data management, which stores and manages data independent of how it is processed and displayed by the other layers
- Business logic, which implements the business logic to process data independent of how it is stored or displayed by the other two layers
- Presentation, which formats and displays the data independent of the way it is interpreted/ processed and stored by the other two layers.

With the advent of Internet in the past few years, the three tiers were split even further to accommodate the heterogeneity in terms of the user interfaces, processing systems or databases existing in various parts of an enterprise.

> The power of the n-tier architecture derives from the fact that instead of treating components as integral parts of applications, components are treated as standalone entities, which can provide services for applications. Applications exist only as cooperating constellation of components and each component in turn can simultaneously be part of many different applications.

### 10.1.1.1 The n-tier Architecture Advantage

The n-tier architecture has many advantages over the more traditional client/ server architecture.

- Agile software—The n-tier architecture is useful in creating more flexible and easily modifiable software. By treating software components as standalone data providers, middleware service providers, business service providers and service consumers, the n-tier architecture creates software infrastructure of re-usable parts.
- Maintainable software—The n-tier architecture is useful in creating more maintainable and easily upgradeable software. Because software components are standalone re-usable parts of business logic, they are used from the same place without need for multiplication or replication and are therefore, easier to change and upgrade rendering the application as a whole more easily maintainable.
- Reliable software—The n-tier architecture is useful in creating more testable, more easily debuggable, and thus more reliable software. Flexible and maintainable software does not automatically imply reliable software, but because software components are standalone packets of business logic, bugs can be localized more easily and their functionality can be calibrated more accurately rendering the application as a whole more reliable.
- Reduced complexity—The n-tier architecture is useful in creating more streamlined, simplified and standardized software because the software components paradigm eliminates the need for custom interconnections between disparate constituents of a composite application (that includes

existing and legacy systems) that increase in complexity rapidly with the increase in the number of disparate constituents. For instance, for a composite application constituted of n applications and m data sources, the problem of corresponding n x m interconnections is barely manageable even for small values of n and m. However, in the n-tier architecture this problem is resolved to a great extent by interfacing all components to (say) a single standardized data bus—this reduces the problem of m x n interconnections to that of only n + m interconnections! All components can connect with each other via connections to this singular data bus without the need for multiple customized single-purpose interconnects between each pair of components.

The interfacing approach of point-to-point interfaces between two applications would be prohibitively expensive for EAIs that may involve tens and hundreds of such interfaces. EAIs also adopt the alternate approach of instituting an information broker whereby all systems communicate with the information broker by uploading data into the same while simultaneously translating it into a single format and protocols native to this central broker. Because information is routed through the information broker, rather than going directly among different systems, this simplifies the problem considerably and it becomes easy to connect disparate systems via their respective adapters for this broker that use the singular format and protocols of this central broker. Any future systems have to devise only one 'adapter' to integrate with the central broker to start communicating transparently with all other systems. The exchange of data between the various systems interconnected by EAI is governed by the business rules determined by the user; and the message broker routes the messages according to these rules. However, the data in the messages is translated enroute into whatever format is required by the concerned application.

- Simplified systems management—The n-tier architecture is useful in reducing the effort of systems management especially of the software on client machines, particularly for large enterprises that may have tens of thousands of client machines or even for enterprises that have multi-located and decentralized IT/ IS operations. For instance, for conventional client/ server systems the plan for deploying a new version of any application would immediately run into a difficulty of choosing between:
    - Changing the entire installed base of clients in a single massive effort during which the normal operations come to a complete standstill
    - Undergoing a long and expensive but more regulated phase-in of the new software, during which IT/ IS is required to support multiple and mutually incompatible versions of the server and client codes, and above all, the new application is available to only a part of the target user base.

n-tier architecture by reason of its software-on-demand paradigm reduces the need for physical updates of the client machines considerably; in many of these cases the updates can be distributed through HTTP and a Web browser or through separately available automatic application distribution systems. But in the case of applications with zero footprint clients like Siebel, this need is completely eliminated. Moreover, as the majority of the code resides in the business logic, middleware and data layers that are typically deployed on centralized, back-end servers supported by professional staff, the updates and enhancements to these layers are relatively painless.

### 10.1.1.2 Limits of the n-tier Architecture

While the n-tier architectures deliver all the advantages associated with distributed systems they also have a down side. The n-tier systems are workable only because of a network-based data bus for communications between the various tiers.

Such a communications layer will have the following adverse effects:

- Add to the latency of the system and degrade overall performance
- Libraries of software components (and classes) required for interfacing with the data bus will typically increase the size of the application

However, the system architects usually take these problems into account at the time of planning and designing the overall enterprise infrastructure and architecture. And, in the event that these problems become noticeable (because of dramatic increase in business and transaction volumes) or foreseeable (because of envisaged M&A activities, etc.), the enterprise architecture is revisited in its entirety.

## 10.1.2 Enterprise Component Architecture

Large corporations that have already invested vast sums of money in existing enterprise applications, infrastructure, hardware and in their employees cannot change overnight. Moreover, the software skills and techniques that are essential for Web-based applications development are different from those prevalent in most of the companies. Consequently, enterprises need to learn new development techniques, new methodologies and new ways of fitting all these solutions together if their transition to e-commerce is to be successful. In this sub-section we will briefly examine why a successful enterprise should be based on enterprise component architecture as embodied in Siebel applications.

Flexible applications need to be constructed by assembling a variety of components (functional modules) to create newer products and services. Although the initial components will have to be developed from scratch, over time and with accumulation of basic components applications will be assembled more and more from increasing re-use of the existing components. However, to accomplish this, the software needs to be designed as component-based applications and there must be an infrastructure to support the component-oriented development of applications. An organizational structure that enables change is based on re-usable elements that are re-configurable in a scalable framework. In the componentized architecture, a system is considered as a group of components sharing a common interaction framework and serving a common purpose. A framework is a set of standards constraining and enabling the interactions of compatible system components; where the component itself is an autonomous system sub-unit with a self-contained identity, purpose and capability, and is capable of interacting with other components.

Component architecture then is a high level description of the major components of a system and the relationship between them. Enterprise component architecture defines the enterprise's infrastructure for components as well as defines:

- How compliant components are built
- How components are stored and cataloged
- How components are located and re-used

## 10.1.3 Enterprise Component Model

A component model can be described as a set of Application Programming Interfaces (APIs) and an architecture, which enables developers to define and create software components, which also have an ability to be connected dynamically together and inter-operate with other components. Most components operate within a possible nested hierarchy of containers, that is, components.

> Typically, an architecture is a more abstract description while a model is a more concrete description—similar to the distinction between classes and instances in object-oriented development environments (see Chapter 5, sub-section "Object-orientation").

Component models provide an array of mechanisms and services for interoperation of components:

- Self-discovery of components enables rendering of information on supported interfaces and methods to other components. This enables components to publish its capabilities as well as interact with other components dynamically.
- Properties of components determine the state, behavior or appearance of the component.
- Customization of components enables the properties of a component to be set or modified from within a component or externally by another component/ container.
- Persistence of components involves the process of saving and restoring a component's current state.
- Event control of components enables a component to create (or generate) an event for another component or to respond to an event. Pre-defining various kinds of events can also differentiate the occurrence of different kinds of events.

## 10.1.4 Distributed Application Requirements

As described earlier, an application is made up of three main constituents, namely, data, servers and clients. A large-scale system is one that is capable of supporting simultaneously hundreds of thousands of components that run in a server, dozens or hundreds of servers, and tens of thousands of clients. The key to building large-scale applications is optimum resource utilization involving two aspects:

- Determining the critical resources in a system
- Devising a mechanism to not only use the resources efficiently but to also enable selective addition of more resources as required.

### 10.1.4.1 Resource Management

Siebel Enterprise Server manages a pool of Siebel servers, mediates the coordination between them and balances the workload among them. The modularity of the enterprise component architecture enhances scalability by adding, as required, more resources to the system configuration (see later section "Siebel Enterprise Server").

The Siebel server itself uses several different resource pools to manage critical resources.

- Data connection links the server to the database; each server has one or more connections to the database. For applications to scale well, a server employs a database connection pool to re-use connections amongst the component/ client rather than using one connection for each component/ client.

- Components' process threads are effectively the flow of control corresponding to the one that the component is using while processing resources on the server. A component has two aspects—behavior as demonstrated via executing threads and the state of the business entity being processed. Each component uses several additional resources such as memory, database connections, locks, etc. The server apparently supports many components concurrently by maintaining a pool of threads that are shared among the many components that need to be executed. When needed, the server creates the instance of (or restores the state of) the component for use in any application; subsequently, the server saves the component's state, flushes the component from the server and re-deploys those resources for other components. This process of saving and restoring a component's state is termed as *state management.*
- Client connection links the client to the application via a server. For each client, there is an associated connection on the server and the corresponding information regarding the client and connection is also stored on the server. For the application to support tens of thousands of clients the number of such client connections in the pool should be minimized.

### 10.1.4.2 Application Management

Application management refers to the tasks necessary to set up the application and to keep the application running successfully and includes the following.

- Configuration—is the ability to set up the system and assign resources, including specifications of the number of servers, the number of clients supported concurrently, assignment of servers to particular machines, assignment of components to servers, and so on. For high availability, the configuration is changeable dynamically while the system is in operation.
- Monitoring—is the ability to get statistics about the system's configuration and operation including the number of connected users, the status of the servers, resources utilization of the servers, throughput and response times, and so on. For high availability, tracing and troubleshooting, systems automatically monitor information such as server status and also respond to detected errors or pre-defined events.
- Controlling—is the ability to effect system configuration and operations including the ability to start and stop servers or components, modify parameters, and so on.

### 10.1.4.3 Application Deployment

Application deployment relates to the issues of initial deployment, securing the application and upgrading it. The ideal deployment scenario involves no special software on the client at all, as is the case with browser-based thin clients.

The application architecture must support application versions and the ability for multiple versions of the same application to operate simultaneously. Security is also a critical requirement for the deployment of an application (see Chapter 17, sub-section "Privacy and Security").

## 10.2 SIEBEL APPLICATIONS ARCHITECTURE

This section describes the Siebel application architecture as a layered structure consisting of the data objects, business objects and the user interface objects. At the end of the section we will discuss the operating architecture of Siebel applications.

Siebel Tools is targeted for application development and maintenance of the functionality at the different layers that correspond broadly to the 3-layer architecture of the Siebel applications, namely:

- The Database-tier for storing data in the Siebel Database Server and Siebel File System
- The Middle-tier enterprise server which deploys BusObjects and includes the Siebel Server, Gateway Server (providing Name Server and connection brokering services), and Server Manager components
- The Presentation-tier clients including the HTML and thin clients, mobile clients and connected clients

The later has been further sub-divided into logical and physical user interface objects.

Figure 10.1 shows the Siebel Applications Architecture Framework.

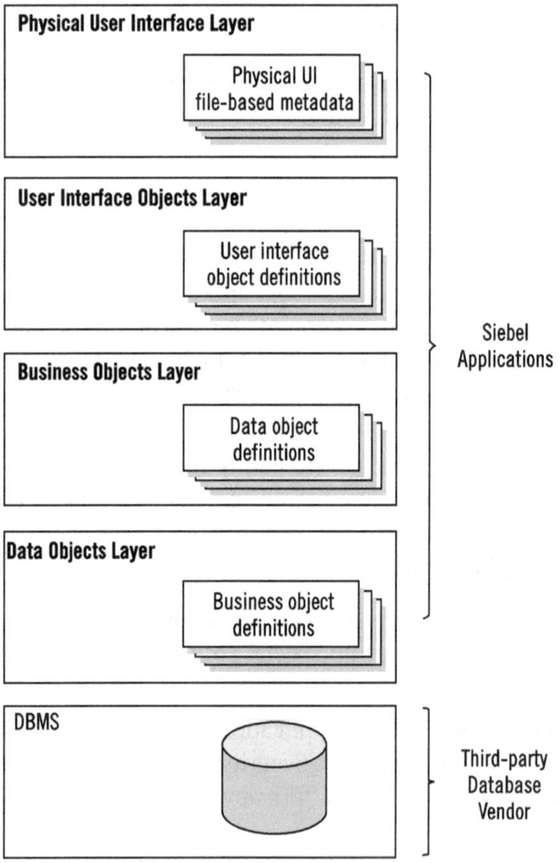


**Fig. 10.1 Siebel Applications Architecture Framework**

## 10.2.1 Business Objects

A business object represents a major functional area of the enterprise—every major business area has a corresponding business object. A business object is a collection of related business components. For instance, the account business object consists of Accounts, Products, Issues, Activities and Contacts.

Each business object has one business component that serves as the master or driving business component. This master business component provides focus for the business object and typically, has the same name as the business object. The Accounts business component has only one parent, which is the Account business object. A link would be required for the other business components (Products, Issues, Activities and Contacts) with the Account business object. A business component can be defined once in terms of a logical collection of columns from one or more tables, and is then usable in many different business object contexts.

## 10.2.2 Data Objects Layer

Data objects layer maintains an object-oriented abstraction of the native data stored in the databases; this abstraction frees developers from knowing and working with the particulars of a specific database. This feature enables migration of a Siebel application from one DBMS to another without having to modify the repository file where the metadata is stored.

Data objects layer creates the SQL objects that automatically generate the most effective and efficient SQL code for the access, manipulation and update of the required data for the underlying database.

### 10.2.2.1 Data Object Types

Data objects are of the following types:

- Table object types
  Column
  Index
  User Key
- Enterprise Integration Manager (EIM) Interface Table object types

Siebel applications store and retrieve data from a relational database management system (DBMS). In Siebel Tools, there exists one Table, Column and Index object definition for each physical database table, column and index.

### 10.2.2.2 Tables

A table object definition is the direct representation of a physical database in a DBMS.

(a) Base Tables

For a business component a base table provides most of its essential fields; for an extension table the base table corresponds to the table that it extends.

The corresponding properties of the Table object type are as follows:

- Name of the table in the DBMS

- Type of the table

  Data (Public) original set of tables implemented in Siebel applications

  Data (Private) are like public data tables but cannot be extended

  Intersection that implements a many-to-many relationship between two data tables

  Extension adds more columns to a data table; and names have _X suffix

  Interface is used by EIM to import initial data for populating one or more Base

  Tables; and names have _IF or _XMIF suffix

  Internal (Database View, Dictionary, Journal, Log, Repository, Virtual Table and Warehouse)

  Base table for the extension table, otherwise is blank

  User name that is a more descriptive table name

  Alias that is a more explanatory name

(b) Data Tables

Data Tables comprise most of the tables in Siebel applications. They serve as the base tables for the business components and provide data for fields. They can be public or private.

(c) Extension Tables

Extension tables provide additional columns to a data table that cannot be added directly into the original table (because of inherent limitations of the underlying DBMS or because of the table being populated with data) without violating DBMS or Siebel application restrictions and have _X suffix. These columns are not physically part of the base table but are available for use in a business component alongside the base table as if they *apparently* were part of the base table.

Extension tables are of the following two types:

1. Standard extension tables are provided by Siebel Systems and have a pre-defined one-to-one relationship with the base tables.
2. Custom extension tables are created via Siebel Database Designer for custom extensions of data (Public) Tables.

Extension table rows exist only for those base table rows that have extension data to store.

One-to-many extension tables have type value of 'Data (Public)' and names have the suffix _XM. Siebel applications come with a standard set of one-to-many applications. They are used to create multi-value groups and master–detail views that are based on custom business components. The Link object creates the one-to-many relationship between the master and detail business components.

(d) Intersection Tables

An intersection table implements a many-to-many relationship between two business components. For instance, one opportunity can be associated with many contact persons and one contact person can be associated with many opportunities, and is implemented as two links and an intersection table designated by means of type having value 'Data (Intersection)'.

### 10.2.2.3 Column Objects

A column object is the direct representation of a database column in a DBMS.

(a) Column Object Type

The corresponding properties of the Column object type are as follows:

- Name of the database column in the database table
- Default value when new rows of this table are added
- Physical Type identifies the data type of the column in the database
  Character for fixed length text
  Long text
  Varchar variable length text for memo type fields, row ids and foreign key values
  Number
  Date
  Date Time
  Time
- Precision specifies the number of digits in a number column (for integer columns it is 10 and for non-integer columns it is 22)
- Scale that specifies the maximum number of digits after the decimal point (for integer columns it is 0 and for non-integers it is 7).
- Primary Key if TRUE that the column is the primary key for the table
- Type of the column

  Data (Public) original set of columns implemented in Siebel applications

  Data (Private) are reserved for Siebel use only for managing the EIM process

  De-normalized duplicates the data in a column in another (base) table for performance reasons

  Extension adds either standard extension or custom extension columns to a base table, or custom extension columns in an extension table

  System columns are read-only and used for various purposes

(b) Data Columns

Data columns comprise most of the columns in Siebel applications. They serve as foreign keys that point to rows in other tables or provide data for fields. They can be public or private. A developer cannot modify the properties of data columns, unlike extension columns.

(c) Extension Columns

Extension columns have 'Extension' as value for Type and are of three kinds:

1. Standard extension columns in a base table
2. Custom extension columns in an extension table; names have _X prefix
3. Custom extension column in a base table

(d) System Columns

System columns have 'System' as value for Type. Some common system columns are described below:

- ROW_ID provides a unique identifier to the rows in the table
- CREATED provides the creation date and time of each record
- CREATED_BY stores the ROW_ID of the S_EMPLOYEE record of the record creator
- LAST_UPD provides the date of last update of each record
- LAST_UPD_BY stores the ROW_ID of the S_EMPLOYEE record of the last record
- updater
- PAR_ROW_ID is a foreign key to the ROW_ID column of the base table

### 10.2.2.4 Indexes

A column object is the direct representation of a database index in a DBMS. Siebel provides a set of standard indexes that have the S_ prefix.

The corresponding properties of the index object type are as follows:

- Name of the database index
- Unique TRUE/ FALSE depending on whether multiple rows with the same value are allowed
- Type of index

  Primary Key index is on ROW_ID column

  User Key index is developer-specified

  Extension index is created by default when developer adds an index

  System index included in the standard Siebel application

### 10.2.2.5 EIM Interface Tables

Interface tables are intermediate database tables between the Siebel application database and other databases.

The object types used in EIM configuration are as follows:

- EIM Interface Table
- EIM Interface Table Column
- Interface Table User Key Usage
- EIM Table Mapping
- Attribute Mapping
- Foreign Key Mapping
- Foreign Key Mapping Column
- User Key
- User Key Column
- User Key Attribute
- User Key Attribute join

#### 10.2.2.6 Field Data Types

Field data types are used to identify the type of data retrieved from and sent to the database server.

Some of the field data types are as follows:

- DTYPE_BPOOL
- DTYPE_CURRENCY
- DTYPE_DATETIME
- DTYPE_ID
- DTYPE_INTEGER
- DTYPE_NOTE
- DTYPE_NUMBER
- DTYPE_PHONE
- DTYPE_TEXT
- DTYPE_TIME

### 10.2.3 Business Objects Layer

Business Objects layer contains the business logic for the business components as well as behavior determining methods for various entities in sales, marketing and service entities. Siebel BusObjects are designed to be configured via Siebel Tools rapidly to meet their business requirements while ensuring a clear and consistent upgrade path for future releases.

#### 10.2.3.1 Business Components

A business component is a logical entity that associates columns from one or more tables into a single structure that provides a layer of wrapping over tables, so that applets reference business components rather than the underlying tables. Consequently, this also separates the role of the developer from the database administrator.

Various kinds of Business Components (BC) are associated with tables as follows.

(a) Base table—provides the most important columns for use as fields in the business component. Every business component has a base table assigned to it. A business component can also have a default sort specification and/or search specification, providing records to applets in a predetermined sort order and according to a selection criterion.

(b) Joined table—provides rows on a one-to-one basis to the business component as a result of a foreign key relationship between the joined table and the business component's base table. The data obtained by a business component through a join is read-only in that business component. Every record in the business component may or may not have a corresponding row in the joined table.

(c) Extension table—is a special kind of joined table where the data obtained by a business component is updatable in that business component. Extension tables allow columns to be virtually added to a base table rather than be added physically to it. This enables the base table to be expanded without violating the DBMS or design constraints as well as avoids complicated database restructuring operations.

(d) Intersection table—provides the means to display all combinations of data in a many-to-many relationship instead of only one of the constituting one-to-many relationships (which is provided by joined tables). Intersection data is data that resides in columns other than the two required foreign key columns in the intersection table and is specific to the intersection of the two master business components.

(e) Virtual table—provides a means to represent external data as a virtual business component within a Siebel application.

Virtual business component supports:

- Insert, delete, query and update operations
- Applets
- Access via object interfaces
- Scripting of business component events

### 10.2.3.2 Fields

A field associates a column with a business component obviating the need to know the tables or join of their origin. They are the source of data for controls and list columns in Applets. A field represents information from a database column obtained through the corresponding column object definition in the base table, extension tables and joined tables of the business component, or it could be a *calculated field* whose values are derived from the values in the other field.

### 10.2.3.3 Joins

A join object definition creates a relationship between a business component and a table other than the base table and allows the business component to use columns from that table. For instance, the master–details relationship joined table is implemented with a foreign key column in the business component detail table. The join uses the foreign key in the business component to obtain rows on a one-to-one basis from the joined table, even though the two do not have a one-to-one relationship.

### 10.2.3.4 Links

A link implements a one-to-many or master–detail relationship between business components based on their base tables. The Link object type makes possible master–detail views, in which one record of the master business component displays with many detail business component records that correspond to the master. For instance, one Opportunity record can have many Product records.

The corresponding object definitions are as follows:

- Link defines the master–detail relationship between two business components
    - Master Business Component (BC)
    - Detail Business Component (BC)
- Source (primary key) field is a field in the master BC that uniquely identifies records in the BC
- Destination (foreign key) field is a field in the detail BC that points back to the master record in the BC

Links are also used in the implementation of multi-value group (MVG) applets. The relationship between the business component of the originating applet and the business component of the MVG applet is one-to-many. For instance, a MVG applet may be used to list the addresses, industries or sales team members associated with an Account.

### 10.2.3.5 Multi-value Links

A multi-value link implements a special use of the Link object type, which is the maintenance of a list of records attached to a control or list column in an Applet. The Multi-Value Link object type is a child (or sub-class) of the BC object type. Multi-value fields are populated with data from a record in the detail BC because of the multi-value link.

The corresponding object definitions are as follows:

- Master BC fields are displayed in the applet from which the MVG applet is initiated
- Multi-value fields are the fields in the master BC that are populated by the current record in the detail BC through the multi-value link
- Key field is the primary key for that BC
- Multi-Value Link defines the relationship between the link and fields in the master BC

  Destination Link

  Destination BC

  Primary Id Field
- Link specifies a master–detail relationship between the two BCs
- Detail BC
- Foreign Key Field
- Primary Id Field

### 10.2.3.6 Business Objects

The benefit of business objects is re-usability. The same business component can be used in various different sets of relationships by including it in multiple business objects. A business object implements a business model tying together a set of interrelated business components using links that provide a foundation for views or screens.

The corresponding object definitions are as follows:

Business Object

Business Object Component

Link

Business Component

Link Object

Master BC

Detail BC

## 10.2.4 User Interface Objects Layer

The user interface objects layer predominantly consists of an applet layer, which manages the user interaction for Siebel and customer-developed applications and components.

### 10.2.4.1 Logical User Interface Objects Layer

This section describes objects in the Logical User Interface Objects layer in the Siebel architecture.

#### *10.2.4.1.1 Applications*

Siebel applications are collections of screens that are appropriate to a select class of users and can be invoked from the desktop by double clicking an icon.

#### *10.2.4.1.2 Screens*

A screen is a logical collection of views. Since a screen typically contains views only of one business object. A screen is implemented as a Screen object definition with Screen View child object definitions.

#### *10.2.4.1.3 View*

A view is a collection of applets that appear at the same time on the same screen. A Siebel application window displays one view at any one time; the current active view is changed by selecting a different view from the View bar or from a menu sub-option in the Screens menu.

The various types of views are as follows:

- List-form View displays data from the same business component—the list applet appears above the form applet that displays the same information (with additional fields) as the currently selected record in the list applet. The form applet also has buttons that provide Add, Delete and Copy functionality.
- Master–detail View displays a form applet and a list applet with data from two business components related by a link. The form applet appears above the list applet—the form applet displays one record from the master business component and the list applet displays all records from the detail business component that have as their master record the record currently displayed in the form applet.

#### *10.2.4.1.4 Applets*

An Applet is a data entry form composed of control that occupies some portion of the Siebel application window and provides capabilities for viewing, entry, modification and navigation of a business component's data. An applet is associated with only one business component (though one business component can be associated with multiple applets).

An applet can be configured to:

- Allow Data entry
- Provide a scrolling table of data rows
- Display business graphics

- Display a navigation tree
- Display a Web browser

etc.

The various types of applets are as follows.

- List Applet displays data in a scrolling list table format akin to a spreadsheet or word processor table. Applet list rows correspond to the records in the business component and Applet list columns correspond to fields in the business component.
- Form Applet displays data in a data entry form.
- Pick Applet provides a list or table of selection values from which the user selects a value or record.
- Multi-value Group (MVG) Applet is used for entry, maintenance and viewing of a list of detail records associated with one or more fields in the currently displayed master record.
- Chart Applet graphically displays data from a business component in a bar chart, line graph, pie chart, scatter diagram, etc.
- Association Applet provides the ability to associate records of two business components that have a many-to-many relationship.
- Web Applet entails a Web browser that displays Web pages or briefings documents.
- Tree Applet is used to create a view like Windows Explorer that allows the user to navigate hierarchically through a structured list of objects.
- File Attachment Applet entails access to external documents including spreadsheets, word processing, documents and presentations.

Applets are created and modified in the Applet Designer in Siebel Tools. We will discuss issues related to definition and configuration of Applets in Chapter 11 "Siebel Tools".

### 10.2.4.2 Physical User Interface Objects Layer

This section describes objects in the Physical User Interface Objects layer in the Siebel architecture.

#### *10.2.4.2.1 Templates*

A Siebel template SWT file defines the layout and formatting of elements of the user interface such as views, applets and controls; it consists of markup language (HTML, WML, XML, etc.) statements interspersed with Siebel Web Engine (SWE) specific tags (whose names have prefix 'swe'). Web browsers require HTML to define the layout and formatting of the page; this information is furnished to the Siebel Web Engine when rendering Siebel objects in the repository definition of the application.

Siebel templates are re-usable by objects in the repository because they only have placeholders—templates are filled with data and user interface elements by mapping the corresponding views, applets controls, etc., from Siebel Tools to a particular placeholder in the template. Siebel also provides for nesting of template files whereby a particular template file can include another one.

Various types of templates are as follows.

(a) Web Page Templates specify the layout of the display as a whole including the location of screen bar, view bar(s) and view(s).

(b) View Templates are used for displaying a view; they specify the location of applets and other page level controls on the view as well as the formatting of the elements within the view.

(c) Applet Templates specify the location of the fields and controls for an applet as well as formatting of the elements within the applet. The various types of Applet Templates correspond to the following:

- Form Applets
- List Applets
- Multi-value Group and Pick Applets
- Toggle Applets
- Tree Applets
- Catlog Style List Applets and Pick Lists

#### *10.2.4.2.2 Tags*

The process of configuring a Web application separates the layout and formatting from the application definition and binding to data. You can use Siebel tags to determine the layout and formatting of controls in your applications. Siebel tags are special tags inserted into the template files that specify the manner in which the objects defined in the repository are laid out and formatted in the final HTML page in the user's Web browser.

## 10.3 SIEBEL ENTERPRISE SERVER

The Siebel Enterprise Server is configured, managed and accessed as a single logical entity regardless of the number or configuration of the underlying Siebel Servers. It does not have any processes of its own and thus, does not have any distinct 'state' of its own. The Siebel Enterprise Server is a logical grouping of Siebel Servers that support groups of users accessing the same database server. This enables the Siebel Server parameters to be defined at the enterprise level, which are then applicable to every Siebel Server and Server Component within the enterprise. The Enterprise Server can be configured, managed and monitored as a single, allowing the Siebel administrator to start, stop, monitor, or set/reset parameters for Siebel Servers within an enterprise. For example, starting and shutting down operations at the enterprise level is automatically affected on every Siebel Server defined within the enterprise.

Siebel Enterprise Applications are built on an advanced, Web-based enterprise server architecture that provides a wide variety of features for deploying and supporting heterogeneous Siebel users enterprise-wide. It corresponds broadly to the common 3-tier architecture with the following layers:

- The Presentation-tier clients including the HTML and thin clients, mobile clients and connected clients
- The Middle-tier enterprise server which deploys BusObjects and includes the Siebel Server, Gateway Server (providing Name Server and connection brokering services), and Server Manager components
- The Database-tier for storing data in the Siebel Database Server and Siebel File System

Figure 10.2 shows the Siebel Server Architecture Framework.

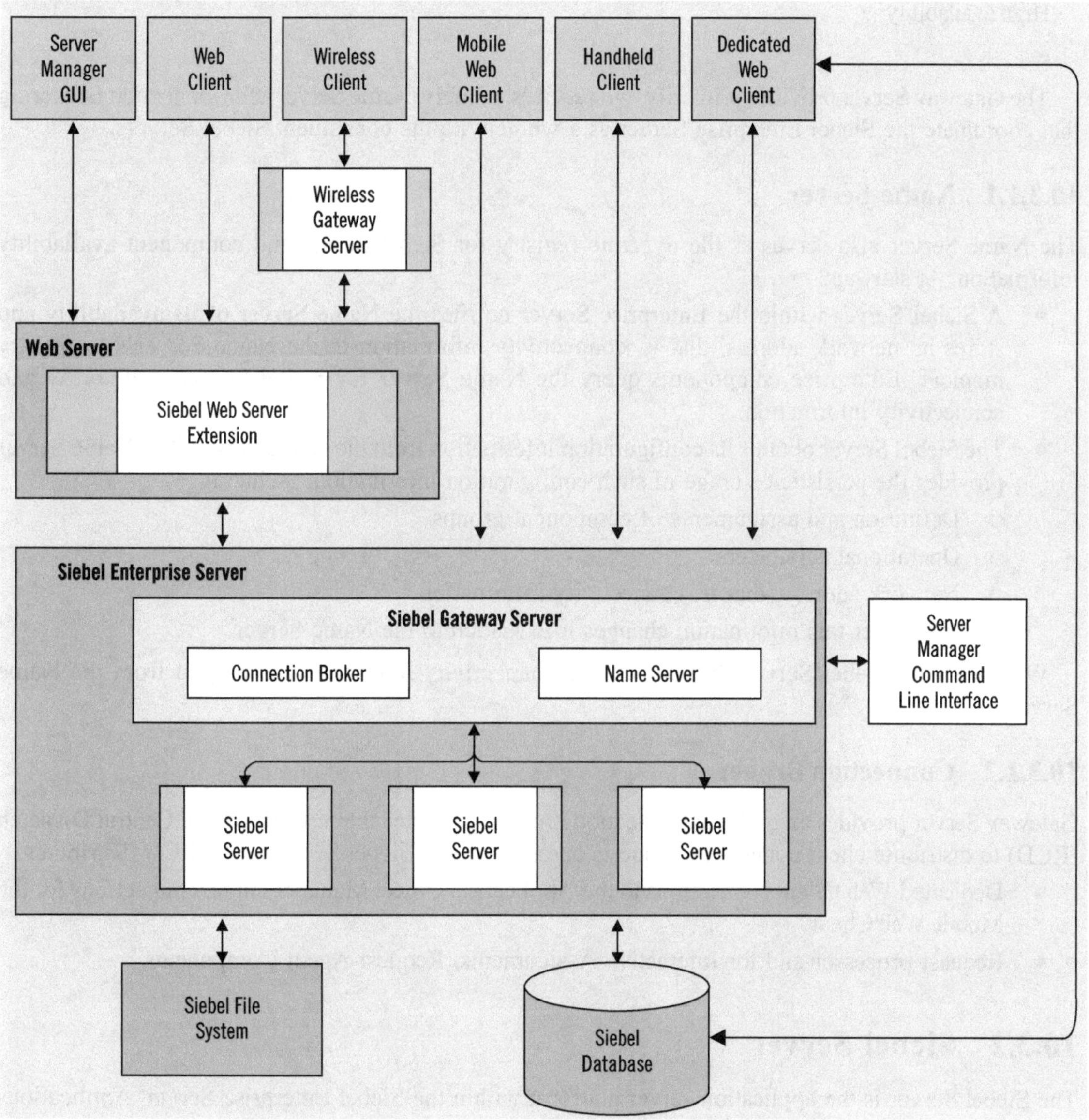


**Fig. 10.2 Siebel Server Architecture Framework**

## 10.3.1 Siebel Gateway Server

The Siebel Gateway Server serves as the singular access point for Siebel Servers and also provides, across the whole of the Siebel Enterprise Server, enhanced facilities like:

Scalability

Load balancing

High availability

etc.

The Gateway Server provides primarily two services, namely, Name Server and Connection Brokering that coordinate the Siebel Enterprise Server as a whole with the constituent Siebel Servers.

#### 10.3.1.1 Name Server

The Name Server also serves as the dynamic registry for Siebel Server and component availability information. At start-up:

- A Siebel Server within the Enterprise Server notifies the Name Server of its availability and stores its network address, that is, connectivity information in the Name Server's temporary memory. Enterprise components query the Name Server for Siebel Server availability and connectivity information.
- The Siebel Server obtains its configuration information from the Name Server. The Name Server provides the persistent storage of such configuration information, including:
  - Definition and assignments of component groups
  - Operational parameters
  - Network address, that is, connectivity information
  - Whenever this information changes it is written to the Name Server

Whenever the Siebel Server shuts down the connectivity information is purged from the Name Server.

#### 10.3.1.2 Connection Broker

Gateway Server provides an optional connection brokering service that uses Resource Central Dispatch (RCD) to distribute client connection requests across multiple Siebel Servers. The RCD distributes:

- Dedicated Web Client connections to the Application Object Manager but no connections for the Mobile Web Client
- Request processor and for Interactive Assignments, Request Agent Components

### 10.3.2 Siebel Server

The Siebel Server is the application server platform within the Siebel Enterprise Server. Applications that execute on the Siebel Server are implemented via components that share common control, administration and monitoring functionality regardless of the different processes they execute. Siebel Server supports both multi-process and multi-threaded components, and can operate components in background, batch and interactive modes.

The Siebel Server supports a wide variety of components, executing in both multi-process and multi-threaded models, as follows:

- Siebel Workflow

- Siebel Assignment Manager
- Siebel Enterprise Integration Manger
- Siebel Applications Object Manager
- Siebel Remote
- Siebel Replication Manager

These components support various functions such as:

- Automatic assignments of new accounts, opportunities, service requests and other records.
- Operation of business logic for Siebel Web Clients
- Connectivity and access to the database server and file system
- Integration with legacy or third-party solutions
- Workflow management

The Siebel Server runs a system service that monitors and controls the state of every server component operating on that Siebel Server. Many of these Siebel Server components can operate on multiple Siebel Servers to support an increased numbers of users or larger batch workloads.

## 10.3.3 Siebel Server Components

The Siebel Server components are designed to scale effectively across multiple processors in a single Siebel Server or across multiple Siebel Servers. The Siebel Administrator has complete flexibility regarding the distribution of the server components across multiple servers within an enterprise.

Siebel supports multiple component types. Each component is configured with a set of parameters and performs a specific function or job. Components defined at the enterprise level are called component groups. Component Groups are logical groupings of server components that are parts of a process, such as Siebel Remote or Workflow Management. For example, defining Component Groups enables starting or stopping of all components that are required for any given process. Siebel also enables user-defined component groups. Component Groups are then assigned to one or more Siebel Servers within the enterprise on which they can execute tasks.

At the time of installation of Siebel Enterprise Server, predefined components for each component type are automatically configured and assigned to each Siebel Server within the enterprise. One can either run an entire suite of Siebel application deployment using these predefined components or customize them to suit specific requirements.

## 10.3.4 Siebel ISS Transaction Server

Transact provides the integration points for the exchange of data between the Siebel Application and third-party Order Management System (OMS) enabling:

- Using of third-party shopping cart system(s)
- Simplification of order submissions from Siebel applications to the desired OMS
- Saving and restoration of configurations
- Sharing of configurations

**Table 10.1 Pre-defined Siebel Server Component Groups**

| Component Group Name | Component Name |
|---|---|
| Assignment Management | Batch Assignment<br>Assignment Manager |
| Siebel Call Center | Service Object Manager<br>Call Center Object Manager<br>email Response Object Manager<br>eService Object Manager |
| Communications Management | Communications Inbound Manager<br>Communications Session Manager<br>Communications Configuration Manager<br>Smart Response Manager<br>eMail Manger<br>Page Manager |
| Content Center | Content Project Publish<br>Content Project Start |
| Dun and Bradstreet | Update Manager |
| Data Quality | Data Quality Manager |
| eCommerce | Dynamic |
| Enterprise Application Integration | Business Integration Batch Manager<br>Business Integration Manager<br>Enterprise Integration Manager<br>MQSeries Server Receiver<br>MQSeries AMI Receiver<br>EAI Object Manager<br>MSMQ Receiver<br>MSMQ Receiver (threadpool)<br>WCS MQSeries Receiver |
| Siebel eChannel | Partner Manager Object Manager |
| | eChannel Object Manager |
| | eChannel (threadpool) |
| Siebel eDocuments | Document Server |
| Siebel Employee Relationship Management | Employee Relationship Management Object Manager |
| Forecast Service Management | Forecast Service Manager |
| Field Service | Field Service Cycle Counting Engine |
| | Service Order Fulfillment Engine |
| | Field Service Mobile Inventory Transaction Engine |
| | Service Order Locator Engine |
| | Preventive Maintenance Engine |

*(Contd.)*

| Component Group Name | Component Name |
|---|---|
| | Field Service Replenishment Engine |
| | Appointment Booking Engine |
| | Optimization Engine |
| | Invoice Engine |
| | Field Service Object Manager |
| Handheld Synchronization | Handheld Field Service CE |
| | Handheld Sales Palm |
| | Handheld Sales CE |
| Incentive Compensation | ICM Calc Engine |
| | ICM Calc Workbook Import |
| | ICM Order Import |
| | ICM Quota Import |
| | Incentive Compensation Manager |
| Siebel ISS | Siebel Product Configuration Object Manager |
| | eSales Object Manager |
| | eAuction XML Interface to SWE Object Manager |
| | eCustomer Object Manager |
| Marketing | Data Dictionary Manager |
| | List Manager |
| | Marketing Server |
| | Marketing Object Manager |
| | eEvents Object Manager |
| Oracle Connector | Oracle Receiver |
| Siebel Remote | Database Extract |
| | Generate New Database |
| | Replication Agent |
| | Synchronization Manager |
| | Transaction Manager |
| | Transaction Processor |
| | Transaction Router |
| | Parallel Database Extract |
| Siebel to Siebel Connector | HA Upgrade MQSeries Server Receiver |
| | Siebel to Siebel MQSeries Receiver |
| | Siebel to Siebel MSMQ Receiver |
| Siebel Sales | Sales Object Manager |
| | Sales Object Manager (threadpool) |
| | eTraining Object Manager |

*(Contd.)*

| Component Group Name | Component Name |
|---|---|
| | eBriefings Object Manager |
| SAP Connector | SAP IDoc Receiver for MQSeries |
| | SAP IDoc Receiver |
| | SAP IDoc AMI Receiver for MQ Series |
| | SAP Send Transaction |
| | SAP Process Transaction |
| | SAP BAPI TRFC Receiver |
| Siebel Anywhere | Upgrade Kit Builder |
| System Management | Server Request Processor |
| | Server Manager |
| | Siebel Server |
| | Server Request Broker |
| | Siebel Server Scheduler |
| | File System Manager |
| Siebel Wireless | Siebel Sales Webphone |
| | Siebel Service Webphone |
| | Siebel eChannel Web Phone |
| | Siebel eService Web Phone |
| Workflow Management | Generate Triggers |
| | Workflow Process Batch Manager |
| | Workflow Process Manager |
| | Workflow Action Agent |

The three-layered Transact architecture is described as follows.

(a) The Client—The Transact Client-side Engine residing within the Siebel application, manages the communication between your Siebel application and the Transact Server-side components via the Transact API. While working in a Siebel application, clicking on 'Save Configuration' saves a record of selected items of a particular page set into the Transact Server RDBMS. On Clicking 'Add to Cart' the configuration is added to the shopping cart. A number of such configurations can also be saved to the Configuration List, which can be viewed from the Siebel application by clicking 'View Configuration List' and can be drilled-down to view the individual configurations.

(b) The Application Server—The Transact Java Engine runs on an application server that manages communications to the remote systems. It uses Enterprise Java Beans (EJBs) to store, retrieve and pass on data from your Siebel application to Transact as configurations.

The Transact Java Engine consists of the following three layers:

- Communication Layer—This is made-up of Java Servlets that accept requests from the browser and direct them to the correct EJB for processing and later send the output back to the browser or the Order Management System (OMS).

- Business Logic Layer—This is made-up of session EJBs that create, manipulate, modify and remove data objects from the Data Object Layer.
- Data Object Layer—This is made-up of entity EJBs that map onto the corresponding relational database tables and contain methods for the access and modification of data objects.

(c) The Remote System—This layer contains two components, namely, the RDBMS that contain the relational SQL tables corresponding to the entity beans in the Data Object Layer and the Object Management System (OMS) that is responsible for the shopping cart User Interface (UI). OMS receives the XML passed from the Transact Server. It also responds to browser requests from the Siebel application with HTML.

When a configuration is added to the shopping cart, Transact connects to the corresponding OMS. This entails the following:

- Connecting 'Add to Cart' button in Siebel application to your shopping cart using the eAdvisor Javascript API.
- Write a style sheet to customize the layout/ format of the corresponding configuration
- Optionally add a URL in OMS to link back to the Siebel application configuration

There may be more than one OMS accepting submissions from a single Siebel application.

## 10.3.5 Siebel Application Object Manager

Siebel Application Object Manager corresponds to the Business Objects Layer and Data Objects Layer of the Siebel architecture (see Figure 5.6). The Siebel Application Object Manager is used primarily to support Siebel Web Client connections.

Siebel Application Object Managers are hosted as components in the Siebel Server that enables it to service multiple Siebel Web Client users; they can be configured to run as multi-threaded processes in the Siebel Server.

The behavior of Siebel Application Object Manager components is controlled by a number of parameters that are accepted at the time of start-up.

## 10.3.6 Siebel Clients

All Siebel eBusiness Applications include one or a mixture of the various Siebel Clients that connect to various servers to request and analyze data.

### 10.3.6.1 Siebel Client Types

The various types of clients supported by Siebel eBusiness Applications are as follows:

- Siebel Web Client—This runs in a standard browser that connects through a Web server to the Siebel Server, which executes business logic and accesses data from Siebel Database.
- Siebel Dedicated Web Client—This connects directly to a database server for access to all data without storing any data locally; except for the data, all other applications are on the client machine.

- Siebel Mobile Web Client—This is designed for accessing database locally obviating the need to be connected to a server; the data is stored locally on the client machine.
- Siebel Handheld Client—This is designed for PalmOS-enabled mobile devices with a Web browser and Internet service.
- Siebel Wireless Client—This is designed for wireless-enabled mobile devices with a Web browser and Internet service.

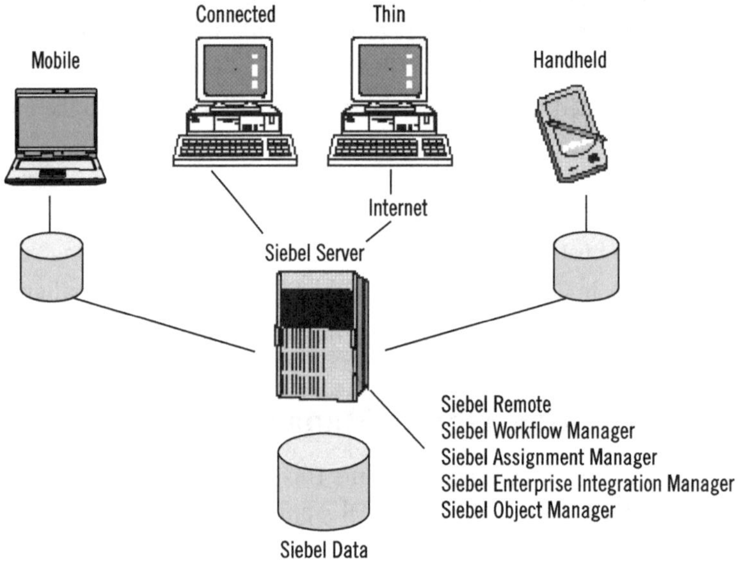


**Fig. 10.3 Clients Supported by Siebel eBusiness Applications Environment**

Figure 10.3 shows the various clients supported by the Siebel eBusiness Applications environment.

## 10.3.7 Siebel File System

The Siebel File System consists primarily of a shared directory that can be accessed via networks by the Siebel Server that stores the physical files that are used by the Siebel clients. Siebel clients can also access the appropriate Siebel Server directly via the File System Manager (FSM) server component that processes these requests through interaction with the Siebel File System directory.

In certain cases like that of Siebel Mobile Web Client in a connected mode, one can connect directly to the Siebel File System bypassing the File System Manager.

## 10.3.8 Siebel Report Server

Siebel Reports provides robust report generation and report viewing capabilities. Siebel Reports include a built in report writer and more than 200 pre-built reports. These standard reports can be modified or news ones can be added either in Siebel Tools or Actuate eReport Designer Professional; though report re-design work frequently requires making changes and additions in both places.

Reports can be created or modified in:

- Siebel Tools by creating and modifying Report or other object definitions (which are executed at run time) and setting properties within them. Siebel Tools modifications use the Report, Report Field, Report Locale, Sub-Report, Sub-Report Field, View Report, and View Report Locale object types, affecting the:
- Specific views of the reports attached to Reports menu
- Data structures exported from the Siebel Applications to the datastreams of the corresponding Actuate report
- In Actuate eReport Designer Professional, by creating and modifying Report Object Design (ROD) files, which are then compiled and executed. ROD file modifications alter various classes and sub-classes that define report behavior, appearance, data acquisition, and so on.

Users have access to the power of Query by Example (QBE) to generate ad hoc reports online or view reports in graphical format. Siebel Smart Reports go far beyond traditional tabular lists of information to provide at a glance, summary dashboards, graphical analysis tools and all the rich detail necessary to make rapid, informed decisions. The summary dashboards provide an overview of the topic covered in the report, and, enable sales and service professionals to know immediately where to focus their efforts. Siebel Smart Reports cover key areas of sales, marketing, customer service and call center performance. This base application is required for all customers that use the Siebel Report Designer included with Siebel Tools (see Chapter 11, sub-section "Siebel Report Designer").

## 10.3.9 Siebel Executive Information System (EIS)

Siebel Executive Information System (EIS) enables sales and service professionals to dynamically display information in a variety of online graphical formats. Siebel EIS comes with more than 90 pre-defined sales and service graphical charts, and the ability to configure new graphics that are tailored uniquely to your requirements.

## 10.3.10 Siebel Remote

Siebel Remote enables true mobile computing by providing a complete exchange of information between your mobile computer and the corporate server. Mobile users can access the power of Siebel Communications, and later synchronize to upload local changes to the server, initiate requests for information and download any new information from the corporate server. Synchronization occurs as a background process, enabling users to continue to work while synchronizing in parallel.

The Siebel Remote Server runs the Siebel Remote components and manages synchronization sessions with a pre-identified group of mobile Web clients. This server acts as the interim storage area for data required to synchronize mobile databases with the Siebel database server. The Siebel Remote Server components are as follows:

- Synchronization Manager
- Database Extract
- Transaction Processor

- Transaction Router
- Transaction Merger

Mobile Web clients use a local database containing Siebel applications tables to store data for user access. The local database also maintains a local transaction log to store transactions created by the mobile user. Mobile Web clients can also use a local Siebel File System to store files from the Siebel File System. Siebel Mobile Web Client normally operates as a standalone unit with a portion of the server database downloaded to the local database on the laptop. Mobile Web Clients connect and communicate periodically with the Siebel Server using a modem across public telephone lines, LAN or WAN. Siebel Remote client software is installed on the Siebel Mobile Web Client laptop, which communicates directly with the Synchronization Manager component on the Siebel Server to synchronize the mobile node with its parent.

Siebel Remote mobile users synchronizing against a local regional node decrease the network costs and improve the performance and reliability of the synchronization process.

## 10.3.11 Siebel Replication Manager

Siebel Replication Manager distributes copies of data in order to support subordinate Siebel installations called Regional Nodes. Each Regional Node is either, a child of the parent node termed, the Headquarters Node or another Regional Node. Typically, a Regional Node is separated geographically from Headquarters Node, though that is not essential technologically.

Each Regional Node is a separate Enterprise Server with a Siebel Database, Siebel Servers and Siebel File System for an identified sub-set of the connected and mobile users. A Regional Node contains either full or a partial set of the parent data including database records and file attachments. Each Regional Database is associated with a routing group that determines how much of the data from the parent node will be replicated to the regional database. When the Regional Database is assigned to a routing group, the data replicated to the Regional Database is the sum total of all the data visible to both connected and mobile users assigned to that Regional Node. Siebel Replication Manager applies standard Routing Rules to determine the data at the parent node that is synchronized with the Regional Node. Siebel Replication Agent synchronizes each Regional Node with its parent to make sure the data is kept updated.

The list of components of Siebel Replication Manager is as follows:

- On Headquarters Siebel Server
  - Transaction Processor
  - Transaction Router
  - Transaction Merger
  - Synchronization Manager
  - Database Extract
  - Parallel Database Extract
  - Generate New Database
- On Regional Siebel Server
  - Regional Database Initialization

- Replication Agent
- Transaction Processor
- Transaction Router
- Transaction Merger
- Synchronization Manager
- Database Extract
- Parallel Database Extract
- Generate New Database

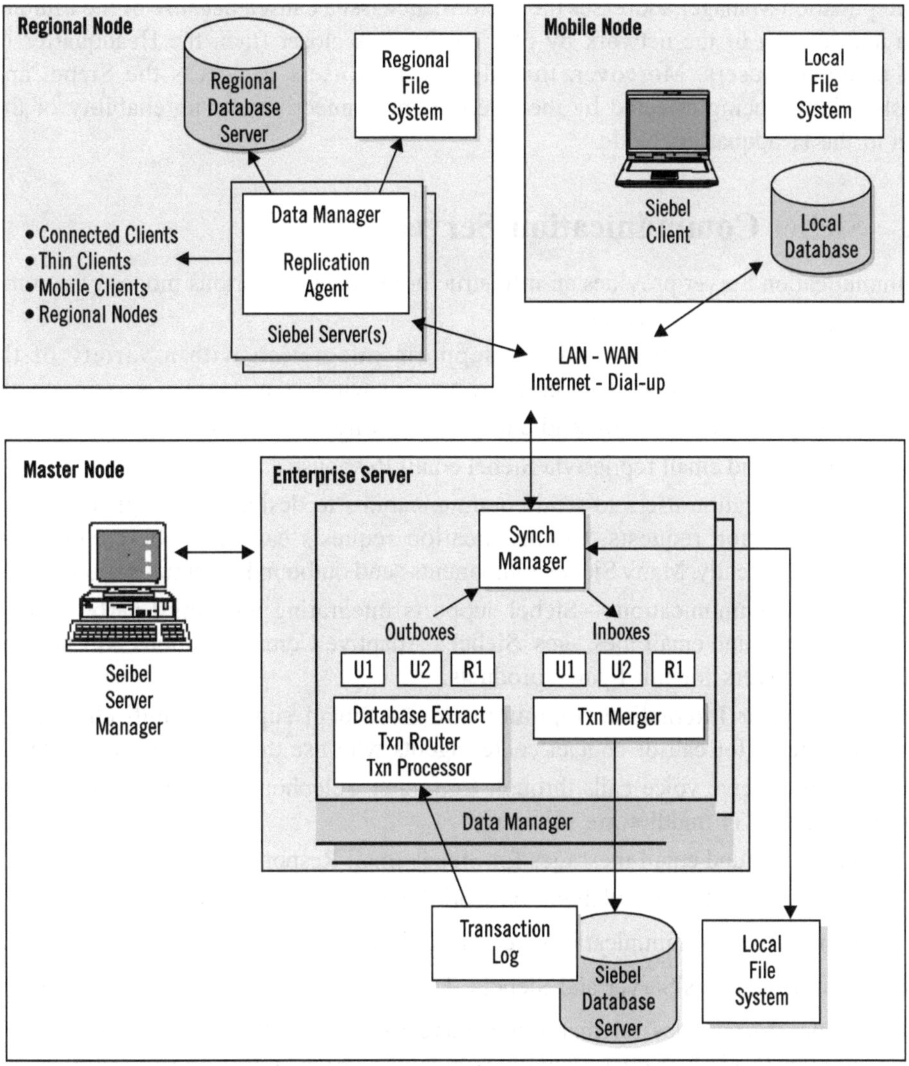


**Fig. 10.4 Siebel Remote and Replication Manager Architecture**

Thus, Siebel Replication Manager supports multiple users and also provides extensions to the master database and file system. Replication Manager synchronizes the master data with its parent server-based Siebel Database and File System rather than with a laptop-based local system.

> As against this, Siebel Remote supports only one user. Remote provides each mobile user with a laptop-based extension of the Siebel Database and File System. Mobile users can access local data while they are disconnected from the parent Siebel Database and File System and must periodically synchronize their local data with the parent database.

Figure 10.4 shows the schematic of the Siebel Remote and Replication Manager.

Siebel Replication Manager addresses the performance issue caused because of the limitations of the bandwidth and latency of the network by placing the data closer (than the Headquarter Node) to a cluster of connected users. Moreover, this also enables users to access the Siebel applications continuously without being affected by the intermittent connectivity or unreliability of the network connection to the Headquarters Node.

## 10.3.12 Siebel Communication Server

Siebel Communication Server provides an infrastructure to support various modes of communications for the Siebel applications users including:

- Outbound communications—Siebel supports integration with a variety of third-party communications systems such as email servers or wireless messaging systems to allow:
  - Siebel application users to send email, fax or wireless messages
  - Agents to send email replies via Siebel email Response
  - Siebel application users to send communications to designated recipients using outbound communication requests. Communication requests can either be created manually or programmatically. Many Siebel components send outbound communications via workflows.
  - Inbound communications—Siebel supports integrating with third-party email servers to process inbound email messages. Siebel's Adaptive Communications API helps in creating custom drivers for third-party products.
- Session-based or Interactive communications—Siebel supports multi-channel interactive communications for call or contact center agents who use the communications toolbar to:
  - Make or receive voice calls through Computer Telephony Integration (CTI) supported by third-party CTI middleware solutions
  - Receive inbound email messages for Siebel email Response
  - Receive inbound Web collaboration work items for Siebel eCollaboration

Figure 10.5 shows the Communications Server Architecture.

(a) Siebel Communications Server and Siebel CTI

Siebel CTI empowers telesales, telemarketing and tele-service professionals with powerful Computer Telephone Integration (CTI), to decrease call times and improve customer intimacy. The Communications Session Manager handles CTI communications. Agents are notified of incoming calls through the communications toolbar for performing a range of call-handling activities using the toolbar and related menu commands. Siebel Reception uses Siebel CTI functionality to provide a user interface for the telephone receptionist to manipulate multiple calls as well as view caller-related detailed information.

Call routing can be handled by:

- Siebel Universal Queuing
- Automatic Call Distributor (ACD)
- CTI middleware
- Third-party vendor's queuing engine (that has been integrated with Siebel Communication Server)

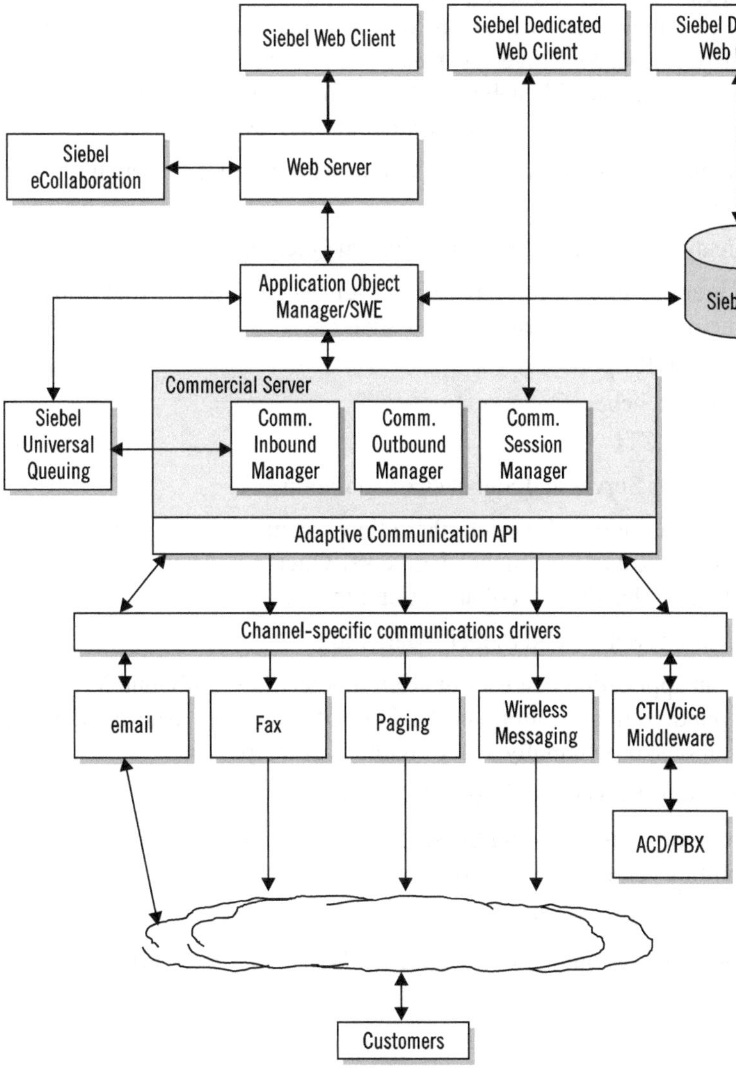


**Fig. 10.5 Communications Server Architecture**

Siebel CTI supports off-the-shelf integration with popular CTI middleware vendors, including Siebel CTI Connect based on Dialogic CT Connect, to provide integrated call handling, call tracking and automated pop-up window capabilities with a broad variety of Automated Call Distributors (ACDs). Siebel CTI includes Siebel Adaptive CTI, a framework that enables middleware vendors, systems integrators, consultants and customers to integrate additional third-party CTI middleware applications and leverage the features of Siebel CTI.

(b) Siebel Communications Server and Siebel eMail Response

Siebel eMail Response, which can be used either as a standalone or as an optional component allows agents to receive or reply to inbound email messages. The Communications Inbound Manager handles inbound email communications while the Communications Outbound Manager handles outbound email for agent replies. The Communications Session Manager also uses Siebel Universal Queuing and communication configurations. Siebel Universal Queuing or even Siebel Assignment Manager can handle inbound email routing in conjunction with Siebel Workflow. Communications administrators can configure response groups to determine the way to process inbound messages.

Siebel provides communications drivers that integrate with a variety of email servers that support SMTP and POP3 protocols.

(c) Siebel Communications Server and Siebel Universal Queuing

Siebel Universal Queuing is an optional infrastructure component that routes to the agents communication work items of pre-defined channels such as:

- email for Siebel email Response
- Web Collaboration for Siebel eCollaboration
- Voice Calls for Siebel CTI

(d) Siebel Communications Server and Siebel eCollaboration

Siebel eCollaboration is an optional module that allows agents to receive and respond to inbound Web collaboration requests, Routed by Siebel Universal Queuing. Agents use the communications toolbar and related features to handle the collaboration requests.

(e) Siebel Communications Server and Siebel eMarketing

Siebel eMarketing is an application that uses the Communications Outbound Manager and workflow processes to send outbound communications in the form of offers and e-newsletters, optionally with Siebel data field substitutions to potentially a large number of recipients.

(f) Siebel Communications Server and Siebel Workflow

Many of the Siebel components including Siebel eMarketing, eSales and eAuction access outbound communications capabilities via Siebel Workflow.

(g) Siebel Communications Server and Siebel Wireless Messaging

Siebel Communications Server outbound messages in Wireless Access Protocol (WAP) compatible format.

## 10.4 SIEBEL DATA WAREHOUSE

As we have seen in Chapter 1, "Customer Capital—Customer Knowledge as the New Capital", real-time information that is collated and analyzed in the proper context is the most important asset of organizations in this century; it is also a tremendous competitive advantage to a company. A company can enhance its effectiveness and the efficiency of its management processes by gaining the ability to quickly extract mission-critical information from a flood of data made available by its operational systems. To achieve this, on one hand companies need solutions that can provide immediate access to information that is relevant for decision-making as well as the ability to analyze it flexibly, and on the other hand, these solutions also need to be integrated with the existing operational systems for easy and fast access to this essential information.

The traditional solution for meeting such divergent goals is known as *data warehousing*. A data warehouse is a separate application environment with a dedicated database that draws on diverse data sources and is designed to support sophisticated query and analysis. The Siebel Data Warehouse (DW) is a state-of-the-art data warehouse solution that gives company members rapid access to data in any desired combination, aggregation or level of detail from Siebel systems, non-Siebel systems and even from external applications.

Siebel uses third-party products from Informatica—Informatica applications extract, transform and load legacy, relational and ERP data into the Siebel Data Warehouse. The Siebel Data Warehouse is a unified data repository of all customer, sales, service, product and marketing data. The Siebel Data Warehouse includes:

- A data integration engine that combines data from the Siebel Transactions Database, other operational products and enterprise data warehouses
- An open architecture to allow organizations to use third-party analytical tools in conjunction with Siebel Data Warehouse using Siebel Analytical Server
- Operational pre-built data extractors to incorporate data from external applications into the Siebel Data Warehouse

Table 10.2 indicates the components of the Siebel DW environment.

**Table 10.2 Components of the Siebel DW Environment**

| Machine | Server Components |
|---|---|
| Siebel Server Machine | Siebel Server<br>Siebel Web Engine |
| Web Server Machine | Web Server Software<br>Siebel Web Server Extension |
| Data Warehouse Server Machine | Informatica Server |
| Administrator Workstation | Informatica Client |

Compared to the traditional data warehousing solutions, the Siebel DW has a tremendous advantage because it can benefit from the simple fact that Siebel itself is a repository-based application environment.

Usual data warehouse solutions are designed to extract and map at the level of the individual database fields because they do not recognize the context of the data. This information on the context and meaning of data has to be established as a separate exercise. Making use of Siebel's metadata and integration concepts, DW extracts, loads and aggregates data in accordance with the enterprise-wide business processes and presents them in a flexible and user-friendly manner customized to the needs of the user.

Also, because of the fundamental integration of DW with Siebel, the results of the DW analysis can also be immediately integrated into the Siebel system, which is the powerful 'second loop' learning that we spoke about in Chapter 1, "The Learning Enterprise". It represents the capability of institutional learning that gives a tremendous advantage to companies in these times of rapidly changing markets. Additionally, Siebel being a highly secure and auditable environment is also a source of correct, clean and reliable data, all of which are major concerns for normal data warehousing projects.

Siebel DW projects can be implemented easily, quickly and cost-effectively. Many time-consuming and painstaking stages of the traditional data warehousing projects are either eliminated completely or are taken care of automatically by the Siebel DW. Some of these stages are as follows:

- Building departmental level data marts leading to the enterprise-wide data warehouse
- Providing complete, correct and reliable data
- Compiling an integrated enterprise-wide, business-driven view of data
- Discovering, defining and building metadata models
- Mapping from Siebel's data stores to the metadata of the data warehouse
- Populating the data warehouse from the Siebel data stores

Siebel DW is also able to take advantage of:

- Integrating an enterprise-wide business processes view of data
- Extensive reporting functions within Siebel
- Siebel's numerous open system solutions for interfacing to differing external systems
- Siebel's leading-edge Basis technology with its n-tier architecture and concomitant benefits like security, integrity, scalability, high availability and inter-operability with a uniform environment

Siebel DW is a comprehensive solution that takes advantage of the capabilities of Siebel but is not limited to Siebel alone.

## 10.4.1 Siebel Analytics

Siebel Analytics Server acts as a portal to structured data residing in one or more data sources—multiple data marts, the Siebel Data Warehouse, an enterprise data warehouse, an operational data store, transaction system databases, personal databases or more. Siebel Analytics Server functions as the integrating component of a complex Decision Support System (DSS) by acting as a layer of abstraction and unification above the underlying databases. When the Siebel Analytics Server accesses heterogeneous databases, any required transformation is handled automatically such as datatype casting or applying multiple complex functions. Siebel Analytics Server can also access XML and legacy data sources.

The Siebel Analytics Server is designed to complement Decision Support Systems to enable business users to analyze large amounts of historic information in various forms:

- Detailed data that provides insights into the specifics of the business is useful in maximizing product strategies or controlling marketing costs
- Snapshot data that shows a view of data in an instant is useful to understand trends and monitor business performance
- Summary data is useful to generate reports at a high level of aggregation to monitor macro level performance of enterprises

Siebel Analytics Server controls the security directly enabling access to be granted based on the dictates of the security policy. Security can be enforced at the level of each user or the user group and privileges can be set to restrict access to even the most fine-grained information.

## 10.5 eBUSINESS APPLICATION INTEGRATION (eAI)

In these times of market change and turbulence, enterprises are confronted with the increasing need to interconnect disparate systems to satisfy the need of the business. It is estimated that 35 to 60 percent of an organization's IT resources are spent on integration (see Chapter 2, sub-section "Extended Collaborative Enterprise"). eBusiness application integration is the creation, maintenance and enhancement of leading-edge competitive functionality of the enterprises' business solutions by combining the functionality of the existing legacy applications, Commercial Off-The-Shelf (COTS) software packages and newly developed custom applications via a common middleware.

Siebel eBusiness Application Integration (eAI) provides components for integrating Siebel eBusiness Applications with external applications and technologies within the enterprise and is designed to work with third-party products.

By employing eAI effectively, an enterprise can leverage its existing enterprise-wide information assets, that is, customer relationships:

- To provide new products and services easily and quickly
- To streamline its internal process and operations
- To strengthen supply relationships
- To enhance customer relationships

Figure 10.6 shows the n-tiered architecture of current applications like Siebel.

As eAI enables enterprise-wide integration of diverse applications across various products and divisions, it provides the enterprise with a 360-degree view of its customer relationships across multiple channels of interaction. Every customer perceives the enterprise as a whole and also expects to be recognized and valued by the enterprise as a whole. As we have seen in Chapter 1, familiarity with customer's earlier interactions and purchases helps frontline members of the enterprise to create opportunities for selling other products or additional add-ons and services to the earlier purchases.

> One of the important objectives of application integration is to achieve the integration between applications with as reduced a level of coupling or inter-dependency as is possible so that the impact of changes in one application do not affect the other application(s).

## 10.5.1 Basic Concepts

The basic concepts related with eAI are described here. A robust and flexible eAI provides a combination of the methods of integration and modes of communication that are embodied into the various models of integration that are deployed within the eAI architecture as discussed later.

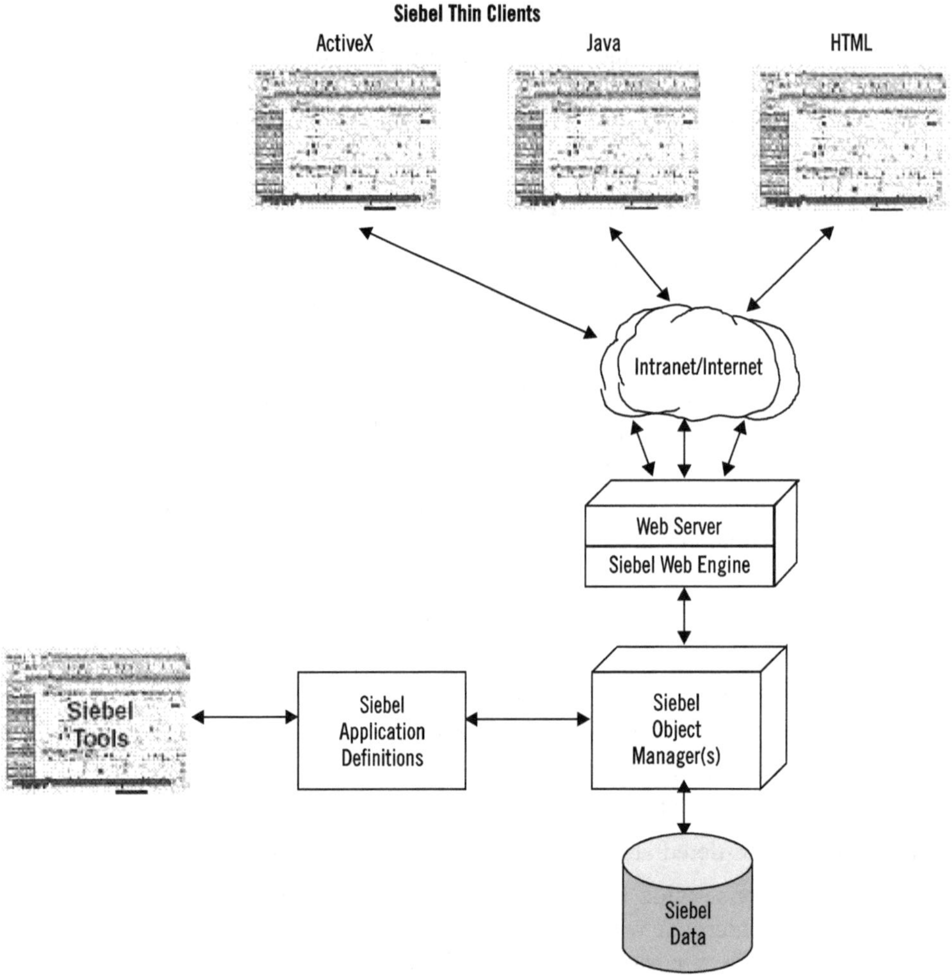


**Fig. 10.6 Siebel n-tier Architecture**

#### 10.5.1.1 Methods of Integration

Methods of integration are the approaches used to guide a request from a sender to a receiver. The two primary methods of integration are as follows.

(a) Messaging—In this approach the sender constructs a message that contains the information on the actions desired as well as the data required to perform these actions—the message contains both the control information and data. Messages provide a lot of flexibility because the control information can be easily changed and extended; they are independent of any of the applications. However, to function correctly the integration messages must be pre-defined precisely so that the messages can be coded and decoded in exactly the same way by all senders and receivers.

(b) Interface—In this approach the sender communicates through an interface, which defines explicitly the actions that can be invoked by an application—the interface is self-describing in terms of the actions that can be taken. Interfaces make the application look like a procedure, or a method or an object. Interfaces are difficult to change and extend; they are associated with a particular application.

### 10.5.1.2 Modes of Communication

The flexibility of systems is critically dependent on the modes of communications that are utilized by the systems. Assuming that a request refers to a communication from a sender to a receiver, the two basic options for communications are as follows.

(a) Synchronous communication—requires the sender of a request to wait until a reply, which is the result of the request, is received before continuing the processing. Synchronous communication between systems implies a high degree of coupling and requires the sender and receiver to coordinate the communications with their internal processing. A reliable network infrastructure is essential for this kind of communication. It is used when the sender requires a notification of the receipt or needs the result of the processing from the receiver. For instance, interactive systems need a synchronous type of communication.

There are three popular types of synchronous communications:

- Request/response
- Transmit
- Polling

(b) Asynchronous communication—allows the sender to continue processing after sending the request without waiting for a reply to this request. The sender does not concern itself with whether or when the request has been received, how it is processed or the results returned from the receiver. Asynchronous communications does not demand a high degree of coupling and also does not require the sender to coordinate the communications with its internal processing. It is used when the communication of information is required without the need to coordinate activities or responses.

There are three popular types of asynchronous communications:

- Message passing—This is used in situations where information needs to be transmitted but a reply is not required. This needs a reliable network for guaranteed delivery.
- Publish/ subscribe—This is used in situations where a reply is not required but unlike all other cases, the recipient is determined based on content of the request and the pre-declared interest of the receiver application. This type of communication is useful for STP type of functional integration (see later sub-section "Straight-Through Processing (STP)" ).
- Broadcast—This is used in situations where again a reply is not needed but the request is sent to all the applications and each receiver decides if it is interested in the request/ message, and accordingly processes that request/ message in accordance with the business and functional logic programmed into each of the receiver systems.

#### 10.5.1.3 Middleware Options

Middleware is software, which enables disparate applications to interact with each other—it facilitates the communication of requests between software components through the use of pre-defined interfaces or messages. The five basic types of middleware are as follows:

- Remote Procedure Calls (RPCs)—is based on the notion of developing distributed applications that integrate at the procedure level but across a network
- Database Access Middleware—is based on the notion of developing distributed applications that integrate at the distributed data level whether in files or databases, but across the network
- Message-Oriented Middleware (MOM)—is based on the notion of developing distributed applications that integrate at the message level, but across the network
- Distributed Object Technology (DOT)—is based on the notion of developing distributed applications that integrate at the interface level but those that make the application look like an object
- Transaction Processing Monitors (TPM)—is based on the notion of developing distributed applications that integrate at the distributed transaction level but across the network.

### 10.5.2 Models of Integration

An integration model defines the approach and configurations used to integrate software applications depending on the nature and methods of the envisaged integration. There are three possible types of integration, namely, presentation, functional and data integration.

#### 10.5.2.1 Presentation Integration

In this model the integration is accomplished by deploying a new and uniform application user interface—the new application appears to be a single application although it may be accessing several legacy and other applications at the back-end. The integration logic, the instructions on where to direct the user interactions, communicates the interaction of the user to the corresponding application using their existing presentations as a point of integration. It then integrates back any results generated from the various constituent applications. Thus, a single presentation could replace a set of terminal-based interfaces and might incorporate additional features, functions and workflow for the user. For instance, a mainframe application can be integrated into a new Microsoft Windows application at the front-end using the screen-scraping technology that effectively copies, maps and imports data from specific locations on character-based screens of the mainframe application onto the new schemas and data structures of the new system.

Presentation integration is the easiest to achieve and can be automated almost 100 percent; however, it is also the most limiting of the three models.

#### 10.5.2.2 Functional Integration

In this model, the integration is accomplished by invoking from other applications functionality or from the business logic of the existing applications by using code level interfaces to the existing applications. This might be achieved at the level of an object or a procedure or via Application Programming Interface (API) if it exists for each of the corresponding applications. The business logic includes the processes and workflow as well as the data manipulation and rules of interpretation. For instance, to change the customer's address in an enterprise application, the functionality of the existing customer order and billing application can be accessed if it is functionally integrated with these later applications. Rather than re-create the logic in the new application it is more efficient and less error-prone to re-use the existing logic. The related concept of Siebel Connectors is discussed later.

Traditionally, Remote Procedure Calls (RPCs), which have been employed for this kind of integration have provided the definitions for access and basic communications facilities. However lately, distributed processing middleware has become the preferred method of integration as it not only provides a more robust approach to the interface definitions and communications but also enables run-time support for inter-component requests. The three categories of distributed processing are as follows:

- Message Oriented Middleware (MOM)—achieves integration by providing for the communication of messages between applications by means of the messages placed in MOM, which itself is implemented in a variety of configurations, including message queuing and message passing. The MOM is then responsible for delivering to the target system. Microsoft's MSMQ, Biztalk, IBM's MQSeries and Talarian's Smart Sockets are examples of MOM.
- Distributed Object Technology (DOT)—achieves integration by providing object interfaces that make applications look like objects. The application can then be accessed by other applications across a network through the object interfaces. OMG's CORBA, Microsoft's COM+ and Sun's Java 2 Enterprise Edition (J2EE are examples of DOT.
- Transaction Processing Monitors (TPMs)—achieve integration by providing critical support for integrity of distributed resources such as databases, files and message queues across distributed architectures by allowing various types of transactions to be managed using a variety of concepts including two-phase commit. BEA's Tuxedo is an example of TPM.

Functional integration that is more flexible than the other two integration models can be applied in three different forms as described below.

#### *10.5.2.2.1 Synchronization*

This corresponds to the coordination of data updates from multiple sources across integrated applications that may have been developed and enhanced over a long period of time. It provides integration that is loosely coupled and predominantly asynchronous. These applications may represent various relationships that a customer may have had with the enterprise, or manage employee or product related information. When an update is made into any of the systems, the update needs to be propagated across all of these systems. Typically, synchronization is implemented by propagating a request that describes the intended action and the corresponding data to each of the relevant systems.

#### *10.5.2.2.2 Component Integration*

Component integration is the integration of applications where a well-defined interface exists that allows a component to be accessed via requests from other components without modifications. The interfaces for each component must identify the specific functions that the component supports. It provides integration that is tightly coupled and predominantly synchronous.

#### *10.5.2.2.3 Straight-Through Processing (STP)*

This corresponds to a coordinated set of automated actions executed across all relevant applications in the correct order of precedence automatically, that is, without human intervention. It provides integration that is tightly coupled and can be both synchronous and asynchronous. This kind of process is commonly associated with workflow though it does not involve decision-making or complicated scheduling. For instance, an order for a product is placed on a Web site; the Order Processing System (OPS) creates the order and notifies the logistics and shipping system to ship the product. When the order is completed, the OPS is notified of the change of status and the billing system triggers a bill for payment. Once the payment is received the OPS is notified to close the order.

### 10.5.2.3 Data Integration

In this model, integration is accomplished by bypassing the existing application business logic, and directly accessing the data created, processed and stored by each of the corresponding applications. For instance, an Oracle-based billing system can be integrated with an IBM-based customer order system using the database gateway technology that integrates the DB2 database with the Oracle database.

This has been one of the earliest models applied for accessing information from databases including:

- Batch file transfer
- Open Database Connectivity (ODBC)
- Database access middleware
- Data transformation

The data integration model provides greater flexibility than the presentation integration model; it simplifies access to data from multiple sources and also allows the data to be re-used across other applications. However, integrating at the data level necessitates rewriting of any functionality required by each of the applications, which implies greater effort for avoiding inconsistencies, standardizing, testing and debugging for each of the applications on an ongoing basis. Since this model is highly sensitive to changes in the data models for each of the applications, this integration model is not very amenable for change and maintenance.

## 10.5.3 Siebel Enterprise Integration Manager (EIM)

Siebel Enterprise Integration Manager (EIM) provides for *batch* interface for highly efficient data integration with external applications. EIM supports bi-directional exchange of large volumes of transaction and event data through pre-built and extensible interfaces.

There are two types of interface tables:

- S-type interface tables that are used in release prior to 6.x
- EIM-type interface tables that are available in 6.x and later releases

Siebel interface tables are intermediate tables that act as a staging area between the Siebel application database and other databases. These tables must be populated with the relevant data before processing it with EIM. EIM uses interface table mappings to map columns from interface tables to Siebel base tables. Siebel Tools can be used to view:

- Interface table mappings to Siebel base tables
- Interface column mappings to Siebel base table columns
- Siebel base table mappings to interface tables

### 10.5.3.1 Pre-defined Interface Tables

Siebel Data Model includes a complete set of pre-defined interface tables. The interface tables are an abstraction layer above the base tables and are used by the EIM to import, update, merge and delete records to and from the base tables.

The Data Model Extension Designer supports the complete customization of EIM tables and allows for:

- Creation of new interface tables
- Addition of columns to existing tables
- Modifications of the mappings between base and interface tables used by EIM to manipulate and modify data records

Table 10.3 gives a list of important Siebel entities that have pre-defined extension tables. Many of these entities have multiple interface tables that provide EIM support for interfacing all of their attributes as well as their relationships to other entities.

**Table 10.3 Important Entities with Pre-defined Interface Tables**

| Account | List of Values (LOV) |
|---|---|
| Account Address | List of Values Relation |
| Account Detail | Market Development Fund (MDF) |
| Account Forecast | Market Segment |
| Account Periods | Note |
| Activities | Opportunity |
| Activity Details | Opportunity 1:M Extension |
| Agreement | Opportunity Detail |
| Agreement Entitlement | Opportunity Forecast |
| Appointment | Opportunity Product Forecast |
| Assessment | Order Item |
| Asset Details | Order Shipments |
| Assets | Order Type |
| Assignment Groups | Orders |
| Assignment Workload | Person Address |
| Broadcast | Personal Account |
| Message | Personal Account 1:M Extension |
| Call List | Personal Account Detail |

*(Contd.)*

| Account | List of Values (LOV) |
|---|---|
| Call Scripts | Positions |
| Campaign Contact | Postal (ZIP) Codes |
| Communication | Price Lists |
| Competitive Metrics | Product |
| Contact | Product Baseline |
| Contact 1:M Extension | Product Comparison |
| Contact Address | Product Consumption |
| Contact Detail | Product Consumption Details |
| Credit | Product Defects |
| Credit Type | Product Forecast |
| Customer Surveys | Product Inventory Location |
| Decision Issues | Product Line |
| Defect Details | Product Shipment |
| Demand Creation Program | Product Targets |
| Employee | Promotion Account |
| Employee Details | Proposal |
| Exception Calendar | Prospect Contact |
| Exchange Rate | Quote Details |
| Expense Reporting | Quote Term |
| External Product | Quotes |
| File Attachment | Returned Merchandise Authorization |
| Financial Asset Liabilities | Sales Methods |
| Financial Income Expense | Sales Quota |
| Financial Instrument Recommendation | Sales Tool |
| Financial Need | Scheduled Calendars |
| Forecast Position | Service Request Details |
| Fulfillment Center | Service Requests |
| Fulfillment Item | Siebel Interactive Search Profiles |
| Fulfillment Recipient | Solutions |
| Group | Source Details |
| Industry | Source Payments |
| Internal Division | Sources |
| Internal Product | State Model |
| Inventory Location | Store Conditions |
| Inventory Transaction | Volume Discounts |
| Item Journal for Quote | |

## 10.5.4 Siebel Object Interfaces

Siebel Object Interfaces are the technology foundation for *online* real-time integration with legacy desktop, Web-based, server-based and mainframe-based legacy applications. They are well-defined, open, customizable and upgradable online interfaces to the Siebel Objects both at the client and application server levels. Object interfaces are also defined through the Siebel Repository and can be customized by changing attributes in the repository and scripting with Siebel VB to adopt them to the existing external models.

Siebel supports object interfaces to communicate with external applications using Siebel Object Manager. Siebel Object Manager communicates using:

- ActiveX Data Controls (ADC) with COM-enabled clients using MTS and Active Server Pages (ASP)
- Java Class Libraries through Java Server Pages, Servlets and Siebel Java Data Beans for Java-enabled clients
- Standard interfaces for COM (Component Object Model) and CORBA (Common Object Request Broker Architecture).

Siebel Virtual Business Components (VBCs) are mechanisms in Siebel eAI by which data from an external system can be viewed in Siebel applications without having to replicate the data within the Siebel database.

## 10.5.5 Siebel eAI and XML

Any data in Siebel applications can be represented as XML and sent over standard Internet protocol like HTTP. Siebel integration objects, which correspond to the data to be loaded into or read from a Siebel Business Object, can be represented as Document Type Definitions (DTDs). Siebel eAI provides components that allow bi-directional exchange of XML documents over a standard protocol such as HTTP. Siebel eAI can be configured to use externally specified DTDs for defining external integration objects.

## 10.5.6 Siebel Connectors

A connector is the access point; it is an interface into the application that defines the requests/ messages that the receiver application will accept while hiding the underlying complexity of accomplishing the integration. Connectors provide access into the application and its presentation, data and functionality while hiding the complexity of creating the actual connections. This makes the software apparently easy to access and integrate. This corresponds to the creation of re-usable components across applications that are more than just APIs because they must be able to handle:

- Requests from other components
- Mapping of requests into the applications
- Maintaining statefulness of the requests
- Providing operational support such as application management, security and error handling

Siebel Pre-built Interfaces provide for out-of-box enterprise scalability of the Siebel applications with major ERP vendors like SAP and PeopleSoft. Siebel also provides pre-built adapters for use by organization standardizing on middleware platforms such as Microsoft BizTalk, webMethods, SeeBeyond, Vitria and TIBCO.

SAP, Oracle and PeopleSoft connectors are built, sold and supported by Siebel. The Connectors for eCommerce such as Broadvision, Ariba and CommerceOne are built, sold and supported by third-party EAI vendors or system integrators.

### 10.5.6.1 Siebel eBusiness Applications Connector

The Siebel-to-Siebel Connector is designed to replicate data between two or more Siebel applications in a master/ slave relationship. Siebel-to-Siebel Connector provides the ability to publish and receive changes that are published by the master nodes and are sent to all subscribing nodes. This connector is intended for situations where a small amount of data such as global customer accounts, needs to be shared in real-time among a number of Siebel instances running the same or different Siebel applications at the same or different locations.

### 10.5.6.2 SAP R/3 Connector

Siebel Connector for SAP R/3 provides an infrastructure that allows Siebel eBusiness Applications to interact with SAP R/3 through standard SAP R/3 technologies. It eliminates the need to code components for transforming and routing data between Siebel applications and SAP R/3. The connector supports both SAP's Business APIs (BAPIs) for real-time interaction and Application Link Enabling (ALE/ IDoc) for asynchronous integration.

### 10.5.6.3 PeopleSoft Connector

Siebel Connector for PeopleSoft provides integration between Siebel applications and PeopleSoft and the connector is configurable and upgradable using Siebel Tools and Siebel eBusiness Applications including Siebel Remote, the built-in technologies for data synchronization. This ensures consistent back office information across all Siebel clients including mobile and wireless Web clients.

### 10.5.6.4 Oracle Applications Connector

Siebel Connector for Oracle applications provides for integration between Siebel applications and Oracle applications including interaction through native Oracle applications interfaces. The connector supports both the older Oracle open interface as well as the newer APIs in Oracle Applications R 11i.

### 10.5.6.5 BizTalk Server Adapter

The Siebel eBusiness platform includes a Siebel adapter for BizTalk to allow the exchange of documents between Siebel Applications and other BizTalk-enabled applications. Siebel eAI provides a standard business service to publish messages to BizTalk and supports integration with BizTalk using MSMQ and COM-based mechanisms. Microsoft BizTalk Server 2000 onwards provides the infrastructure for business-to-business commerce between trading partners through the exchange of XML documents.

MS BizTalk maintains a directory of partner-published documents, enforces a protocol for the publication of XML document schema by partners in the directory and provides for the real-time mapping of exchanged documents.

## 10.6 SIEBEL WORKFLOW

Siebel Workflow enables mapping business processes in the Siebel system and processes them under the control of the workflow system. Like any other workflow management system, Siebel Workflow can process and monitor well structured processes, that contain a sequence of activities involving co-ordination between several people, and which recur regularly.

Office and administrative systems have often been plagued by many problems, including:

- Large in-transit times
- Inwarding or receipt processing
- The tedious recording of information at various stages
- Error-prone duplicate transcriptions of information at various places
- Backward queries
- The tracking of documents
- Locating misplaced documents
- Slowing down of the decision process because of serialization
- The effort to maintain the work task progress through the various stages of the business process

Workflow management systems support the various business processes within a company. They permit close coordination, cooperation and collaboration between the various members of an organization, meeting the essential needs of enterprises of the '90s. They are the best illustration of how technology can be an enabler for corporate-wide process re-engineering (see Chapter 1, sub-section "Enterprise Change Management"). Workflow management systems automate a pre-defined set of related work steps and provide a tool for processing a sequence of steps in an organized manner, with user interaction for obtaining any decisions at various steps.

Workflow management systems help to increase the visibility of processes within enterprises and make it easier to monitor and manage them. Thus, workflow management systems have many advantages like:

- They closely mirror the business processes and its various steps
- Directly support business processes
- Provide quick access to relevant information
- Enforce rules of authorization
- Monitor the completion of individual work steps
- In the case of a bottleneck they initiate escalation procedures
- Automate escalation of events and notifications to concerned parties
- Dramatically reduce throughput times
- Minimize in-transit and wait times

Workflow is the timely management of events to ensure consistent and proper handling of such events. Siebel Workflow enables automation of the organization's workflow processes in sales, marketing and service departments; without automation the policies may not get enforced consistently and hence the consequent benefits may not be realized. Enterprises use Siebel Workflow to enforce consistency as well as adherence to standardized processes through the automatic enforcement of business policies and procedures that enable efficiency, quality service, adherence to contractual agreements and profitability.

Examples of policies are:

- Defining, monitoring and attaining response time objectives for customer callbacks and open service requests
- Specifying and enforcing review policies for important processes like contracts, quotes or product shipments

Siebel Workflow consists of the following three modules.

(a) Workflow processes define a process that consists of one or more process steps such as start steps, decisions points, business services, sub-processcs or tasks. Thc task can be a pre-defined task like update to the Siebel database, email or pager notification, integration message to external systems and call to invoke server tasks; or, it could be a custom task defined by using VB or Siebel eScript. Workflow processes can vary from a simple process such as entering a product order to a complex process such as managing a call center workflow that can comprise multiple smaller processes. Workflow processes can be invoked from:

- Within the Siebel application from a workflow policy, a run-time event or a server component
- From an external system, using COM or CORBA

(b) Workflow policies define policies constituting the conditions and policies that trigger execution of processes. When policy conditions are met, it triggers the policy action to execute the relevant processes.

The basic underlying construct of Workflow Policies is the 'rule'. The structure of a rule is: if all conditions are true, then an action occurs. The rule contains a policy condition and a policy action. This means that when the conditions of the workflow policy are met, an action occurs. A Workflow Policy represents the rules the database monitors; based on the workflow policies rule structure, a workflow policy is composed of conditions and actions. A Workflow Policy condition is a trigger—a circumstance or situation that causes something to happen. A Workflow Policy action is an action invoked by a policy condition being fulfilled.

The workflow policy action contains two parts—the type of action and the corresponding action parameters. Workflow policy programs can be one of the following:

- Send Message
- Send Page
- Send Message Broadcast
- DB Operation
- External Program

- Assignment Request
- Generic Request Server

(c) State models define business object states and state transitions. The state models provide a data-driven method for extending workflow control based on the status of an object (such as a service request or a product defect), namely, Open, Pending or Closed.

State Model is the blueprint of acceptable states and state transition that the state machine enforces during the lifetime of an object. At any instance of time, the state represents where the object is in its lifetime and also controls whether or not data of that object can be modified. A state transition defines the allowable transition of an object from one state to the next. For instance, if required, instead of transitioning directly from a Closed to a Pending state, a service request that has been closed but must be re-opened must go from the Closed state to an Open state, and only then transition onto a Pending state.

State models are used primarily to enforce authorization and transition rules. A state model restricts who can change a given attribute on an object, such as the status on a service request and the conditions that must be met to make the change.

## 10.7 SIEBEL WIRELESS

Siebel Wireless provides real-time access to critical eBusiness information through a wireless device. Using a wireless browser on a mobile phone or handheld device, a user reads, edits and writes new data to the Siebel database.

Siebel uses Siebel's Web-based architecture to deliver wireless access to Siebel content and data. During the wireless connection, the following components are involved:

- A browser-enabled mobile device enabled for accessing the Internet wirelessly and displaying Web pages on a wireless browser
- A wireless gateway server, which translates data from the Internet's HTTP protocol to WAP and vice versa
- A Web server and the Siebel Web Engine serves the Siebel Wireless templates and views that are eventually rendered as Web pages on the user's wireless browser
- A Siebel Server including the necessary Siebel Wireless Object Manager that executes the business logic for the Siebel Wireless Application.
- A Siebel database, which resides on a third-party database server

Figure 10.7 shows a schematic of the Siebel Wireless Architecture.

Siebel Wireless uses the same set of Business Objects, the same development environment of Siebel Tools and the same logical data model as all other Siebel eBusiness Applications. Siebel Wireless takes advantage of pre-built wireless thin client templates and views.

Also, alerts and notifications can be pushed to employees and customers using the Siebel Wireless Messaging and the WAP Push Communications Driver available with Siebel eBusiness Applications.

## 10.7.1 Wireless Messaging

This allows Siebel customers to push one-way (outbound) wireless messages to employees, partners and customers that are defined in the Siebel database. This can also be used to send outbound TAP pages, SMTP wireless email messages and SMS messages through wireless network operators to compatible wireless devices.

Wireless messages can be generated from the Siebel Applications using anyone of these methods:

- Manually from Siebel Web Client
- Manually from the Communications Toolbar
- Automatically through Siebel Workflow Manager based on business rules defined by Siebel customers.

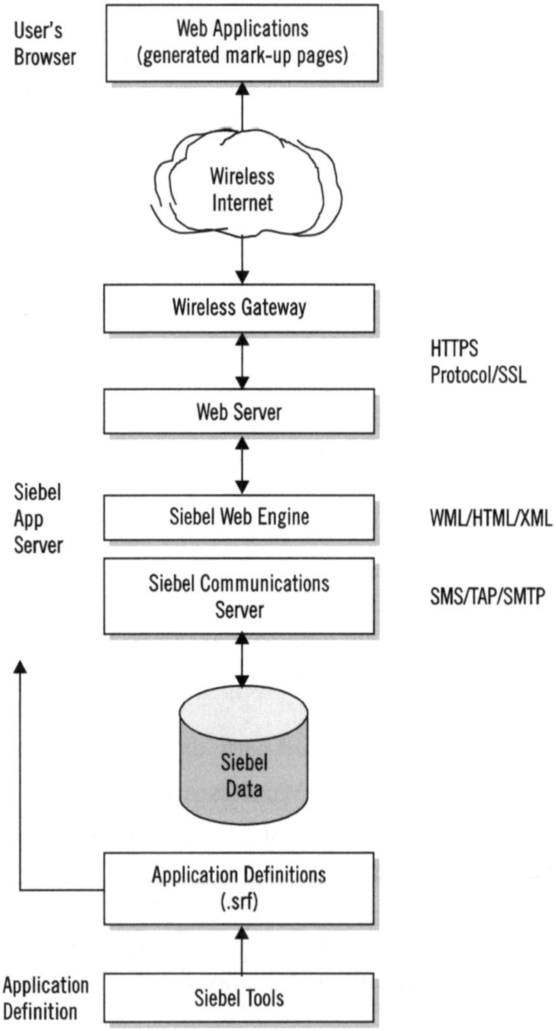


**Fig. 10.7 Siebel Wireless Architecture**

## 10.8 OTHER OPTIONS

Some of the additional options available in the Siebel environment are as follows.

### 10.8.1 Siebel Calendar

Sales, marketing and service professionals can better manage their schedules with a shared calendar that is integrated seamlessly with the activity management system. With Siebel Calendar, users can manage appointments (in an intuitive daily, weekly or monthly format), record repeat appointments, set alarms and receive reminders. All members of your organization can view and schedule appointments for other members. Siebel Calendar also provides support for calendar sharing across mobile and connected users. Siebel offers an Open Scheduling Architecture in Siebel Calendar to enable broad access to contact, calendar and activity information, independent of entry method and synchronization with Microsoft Outlook and Novell Groupwise.

### 10.8.2 Siebel Office

Siebel Office automates the process of sending correspondence, letters, customer satisfaction surveys and literature to your customers. The correspondence system includes complete integration with Microsoft Word, pre-built correspondence templates, personal correspondence templates and automatic mail merge capabilities. The fulfillment system provides support for internal and third-party fulfillment centers to ensure timely completion of fulfillment requests.

### 10.8.3 Siebel Sync

Siebel Sync allows end-users to synchronize information between Siebel eBusiness Applications and a Personal Information Manager (PIM) such as Microsoft Outlook, Lotus Notes or a PalmOS handheld device.

This information could be of various kinds:

- Employee Information
- Personal and Business Contacts
- Appointments
- Calendars
- Activities

All the above information captured via a Siebel application or a PIM can be exported from the Siebel application, imported to the Siebel application or synchronized between the Siebel application and the PIM.

## 10.9 SUMMARY

In this chapter we looked at the Siebel Application environment consisting of the Siebel Enterprise Server and its components, Data Warehouse, Siebel eBusiness Applications Integration (eAI), Workflow and Wireless. The chapter started with an overview of distributed applications, their component architecture, characteristic requirements and models of implementation. We then described the Siebel Applications Architecture comprising of three layers namely, Data Objects, Business Objects and User-interface Objects (along with the constituent elements at the respective layer). Following this, we described the Siebel Enterprise Server and its components like the Gateway Server, Server and Server components, ISS Transaction Server, Application Object Manager, Clients, File System, Report Server, EIS, Remote Server, Replication Manager and finally, the communications Server. Siebel Business applications also provide a standard-based Web architecture for data, functional and presentation integration so that the enterprise can integrate information and processes across marketing, commerce and service. We presented basic principles and models of integration, following which we discussed Siebel Enterprise Integration Manager (EIM) and related components like Siebel XML and Siebel Connectors. eBusiness Application Integration (eAI) empowers enterprises by aligning their partners, employees and customer touch points, processes and channels around the goal of maximizing the value of customer relationships.

In the next chapter we will look at the Siebel Tools that make possible the modification and maintenance of the various components of the Siebel environment discussed in this and earlier chapters.

# Chapter 11

# Siebel Tools

Siebel Tools is an example of interactive enterprise application builders that enable definition, creation and modification via visual manipulation of all of its application components and their services. An application builder environment like Siebel Tools presents all the properties, interfaces, methods and events supported by a component in an easy-to-use GUI format. Siebel Tools is an integrated environment for configuring all aspects of a Siebel application so that a single configuration can be easily maintained, deployed across Windows, Java, HTML and wireless clients, and automatically upgraded to future Siebel product releases.

## 11.1 ENTERPRISE APPLICATION BUILDERS

With the advent of Internet, leading-edge companies used the advances in communication technologies, HTML authoring tools and a range of programming languages like Java, Perl and CGI to custom build eBusiness and eCommerce solutions. These custom built solutions had weaknesses in terms of scalability, reliability, configurability, upgradability and integration with other enterprise applications. A few years ago Sales Force Automation (SFA) and service management solutions were sold as separate packaged applications. However, they are increasingly being delivered as part of an integrated suite of front office solutions at a much lower cost. Integrated sales, marketing, service and eBusiness is quickly becoming the multi-channel architecture of this century. The era of custom built business applications are changing fast with the emergence of professionally built, scalable and customizable off-the-shelf packaged applications.

Never before has it been so easy for a customer to find a desired product or service along with contextual data necessary to make an informed purchase decision. Customers are no more than a click away from a world of comparative information about products, prices and alternatives that are resulting in heightened competition among the suppliers. Companies need to respond rapidly and profitably to this generation of net-savvy and opportunistic customers who are perpetually on the verge of switching or clicking to alternate suppliers. And this implies that the organization's processes and infrastructure must support rapid application development. Business applications will need to operate in an environment of constant change, precipitated by

- External pressures to compete and gain competitive advantage
- Internal pressures to increase efficiency and accountability, and cut costs.

A standard Siebel application comes with a core set of object definitions, which are used as the basis for a solution that has been customized to the specific needs of an enterprise. Siebel Tools provides the facilities and features to customize Siebel applications by modifying and creating object definitions.

### 11.1.1 Programmatic Components of Siebel Application

The key components of a Siebel application are as follows.

- A configuration .cfg file specifies the repository and database files via the names of the data sources and parameters. Every application needs a separate .cfg file as it refers to the name of this application within this file.
- A repository .srf file contains the definition of the configured application or multiple applications. Siebel Tools extracts this information from the database and compiles it to store it in a compressed, binary and read-only file for faster access by the Siebel executable.
- Siebel.exe executable is the installation engine that instantiates and runs objects whose definitions are stored in the repository.

> We are referring to a *.cfg file as cfg file for convenience. We will follow the same convention for other similar type of files like srf.

## 11.2 OVERVIEW OF SIEBEL TOOLS

Siebel Tools is the integrated and full-featured development environment for custom development or enhancement of Siebel standard functionality. It is not a programming language *per se,* but is predominantly a declarative software development tool. It is a powerful object-oriented, client/server application development designed to meet the customization needs of Siebel deployments. Siebel customers can use Siebel Tools to rapidly configure the various aspects of Siebel Applications like the look and feel, behavior and workflow; without modifying the application source code or SQL.

Siebel Tools enables developers to become productive quickly by enabling them to work:

- Top down that starts with the development of the user interface, followed by business component definition and then finally, down to the data structure design
- Bottom up that starts with the database design and then works its way up to the user interface

This flexibility of Siebel Tools enables developers, for instance, to accommodate businesses where visual prototyping is required in the early stages of the project in order to validate the approach with the users.

### 11.2.1 Components of Siebel Tools

The various components of Siebel Tools are discussed as follows.

#### 11.2.1.1 Siebel Business Object (BusObject) Designer

The BusObject Designer gives developers the ability to customize Siebel products quickly and easily. It includes:

- Siebel BusObject Explorer, which is used to modify and manage object definitions and comprises of
    - Hierarchical Object Explorer

- Object List Editor
- Properties Windows Editor

- Siebel Object Visualization Views provides graphical representations of the relationships between the various object definitions in the Siebel BusObject Repository, which in turn helps developers in the configuration process.
- Siebel Applet Designer is an intuitive drag-and-drop visual programming interface that is used to modify and extend applets (which are user interface objects) like list, form, dialog and chart. These objects can be populated with standard windows controls, including buttons, combo boxes, check boxes, labels/text labels and ActiveX controls. These controls can be configured with the Properties Window and written using the integrated Siebel VB Editor.
- Siebel View Designer enables developers to visually modify existing views and construct new ones by simply dragging-and-dropping the desired applets on the View canvas.
- Siebel Menu Designer is a visual programming tool for customizing and extending Siebel menu structures.
- New Object Wizard assists developers to create new objects in the Siebel Repository only by clicking on the type of new object that needs to be created; this Wizard guides one through the entry of properties essential for that type of object. New Object Wizard includes:
  - List Applet
  - Multi-Value Group (MVG) Applet
  - Pick Applet
  - Form Applet
  - Chart Applet
  - BusComp
  - Report
  - View
  - Pick List
  - LOEDB Rowset
  - Integration Object
- BusObject Repository Manager is an efficient multi-user development environment that also provides check-in/ check-out functionality and version control. Typically, a server repository contains the master application definition; each developer can check-out locked projects from the server repository and check-in into their local repositories for making the required changes in the object definitions.
- Siebel BusObject Compiler enables full or incremental compilation of the repository to generate a repository file that is used to run the Siebel Application.

### 11.2.1.2 Programming Environment

As stated earlier Siebel Tools is a predominantly declarative software development tool; however, it also provides facilities for undertaking custom programming as described below.

#### *11.2.1.2.1 Siebel VB and Siebel eScript Scripts*

Siebel Tools provide Siebel Script Editor, Debugger and Compiler for the creation and testing of Siebel VB or eScripts scripts. Siebel VB is a complete Visual Basic (VB) complaint environment for integrating Siebel Enterprise Applications with third-party cooperative applications and extending the base functionality of the Siebel application screens and Business Components. Similarly, Siebel e-Script is a JavaScript-compatible language for Windows as well as UNIX environments that enables developers to write event-specific procedures, known as 'scripts' that operate under the framework of the Siebel Event Model and are associated with objects of specific types such as application, applet, control and business component.

These scripts can be used to program the following:

- Data validation routines that enforce pre and post rules while performing record manipulation operations
- Data manipulation and computational routines that deal with modification of data
- Application launching routines that launch external applications in response to the click of a button or a Siebel event along with the requisite parameters.

#### *11.2.1.2.2 Siebel Object Interfaces*

Siebel Object Interfaces are the technology foundation for online real-time integration of Siebel applications with legacy desktop, Web-based, server-based and mainframe-based legacy applications. They are well-defined, open, customizable and upgradable online interfaces to selected Siebel Objects (that expose their data and functions to custom routines in Siebel VB or Siebel e-Script or external languages) both at the client and application server levels, and are available as COM, ActiveX and CORBA components. These are used to access Siebel Business Objects (with defined methods, events and data) from third-party applications to provide integration with legacy systems and automate Siebel applications from external applications.

Thus, Siebel Object Interfaces provides facilities for:

- Scripting and event handling in Siebel VB and Siebel e-Script
- Accessing data and the user interface using automation interfaces
- Accessing data using COM, CORBA, ActiveX and Java

Object interfaces are also defined through the Siebel Repository via Siebel Tools and can be customized by changing attributes in the repository and scripting with Siebel VB to adopt them to the existing external models. Thus, they can be configured and automatically upgraded to successive releases using Siebel Tools, providing ease of configuration and maintenance.

### 11.2.1.3 Siebel Interactive Designer

Interactive Designer is the environment to author and maintain interactive selling browser-based applications. Interactive Designer is used to create projects that are high level containers from which all aspects of the browser-based applications are referenced.

Interactive Designer is included with any of the following applications:

- eAdvisor

- eCatalog
- eConfigurator

### 11.2.1.4 Siebel Report Designer

Siebel Report Designer enables developers to design reports based on Siebel BusObject. The basic design of the data access is accomplished within Siebel Tools. Layout and format design is done within the Actuate Developer Workbench. Siebel Report is a prerequisite for using Siebel Report Designer.

### 11.2.1.5 Siebel SmartScript

This optional module allows business analysts and customer service managers to define workflow for an interactive situation, which includes both inbound communications such as gathering information to record an adverse event and outbound communications such as informing customers of a new product launch.

Siebel SmartScript provides agents with a robust, workflow-based, dynamically generated user interface to guide the interaction with the customer. Using SmartScript, the desktop dynamically configures itself based on the customer value, skills of the agent and the interest of the customer. By providing agents with a complete script tailored to the customers' needs, businesses ensure the quality of calls, prevent data entry errors, reduce training times and ensure effective integration with the overall marketing campaign. Workflow rules such as address verification or service contract renewal can also be enforced automatically via the script.

Siebel SmartScript guides agents through each customer interaction, suggesting products and services based on the customer's profile, environment, current requirements and buying patterns. Siebel SmartScript helps agents to overcome customer objections, address competitive issues and ask the right questions to resolve problems. Escalations and fulfillments are routed automatically. Administrators can create business process flows and scripts, and change them in real-term to improve productivity without interrupting call center operations.

> Siebel SmartScript can be used to create eSmartScripts that are accessed by customers over the Internet, allowing the same troubleshooting scripts to be shared between customers using the Siebel eService site and call center agents using Siebel Call Center.

### 11.2.1.6 Siebel Database Extension Designer

Customers whose needs exceed the pre-defined extension tables and columns can use the Database Extension Designer option of Siebel Tools to further extend the data model by adding extension tables and columns to contain additional entities and attributes. The Siebel Database Extension Designer renders extensions to the standard Siebel application database. It provides the following extension capabilities.

- Capture additional attributes on entities by adding columns to database tables to store additional information for use by business object definitions (the corresponding user interface objects definition would also have to be changed).

- Carry custom attributes forward with new releases by registering the columns in the Siebel Repository, which helps in carrying the custom columns through the future releases.
- Create custom extension tables to extend the Siebel Data Model by creating new 1:1 extension tables to the Siebel base tables.
- Integrate with Siebel Remote by providing a standard methodology for propagating changes to mobile clients.

This provides a point-and-click interface for extending Siebel application tables when developers need extension even beyond the built-in database extensions. These extensions can be used to capture data from new fields in application screens or from external sources using Siebel Enterprise Integration Manager (EIM). New columns are reflected automatically in the Siebel BusObject Repository and named appropriately to ensure easy migration to future releases of the Enterprise Applications.

The Database Extension Designer also supports extending the Interface Tables used by the Siebel Enterprise Integration Manager (EIM) and adding mappings between the base and the interface tables. This enables enterprises to create bi-directional EIM interfaces to new extension tables and columns, seamlessly integrating them with other applications.

Siebel Anywhere is fully integrated with the Database Extension Designer. It can automatically route and apply logical database changes made in the Siebel Repository to local and replicated databases supported by Siebel Remote and Siebel Replication Manager. This allows the Siebel Administrator to perform seamless application upgrades, including database schema changes, for even the largest communities of remote and mobile users.

#### 11.2.1.7 Siebel Application Upgrader

This radically reduces the time, effort and hence, cost of version upgrades by enabling customers to better determine and compare the changes available in a new release with the customizations from an earlier release. It notifies system administrators about any such conflicts and after merging differences between object definitions it allows administrators to manually override and apply any of the changes.

#### 11.2.1.8 Siebel Object Comparison and Synchronization

It is easy to upgrade Siebel applications because copied objects inherit the behavior of their ancestors. The Upgrade Target property allows copied objects to be upgraded in the same manner as the ancestor objects.

### 11.2.2 Installing Siebel Tools

Pre-installation involves the following tasks:

(a) Verifying the hardware and software platforms

(b) Verifying the chosen DBMS and the connectivity platform

Installation involves the following tasks:

(a) Installing a database server

(b) Installing Siebel Tools including the identification of the database

Post-installation tasks involves:

(a) Verifying successful installation of Siebel
Starting Siebel Tools
Logging on to Siebel Database Server
Entering license key number

(b) Verifying the structure of the Siebel Tools directory as detailed in Table 11.1

**Table 11.1 Siebel Tools Directory Structure**

| SIEBDEV | |
|---|---|
| actuate | Actuate files for generating and running reports |
| afc | Actuate Foundation Class files |
| bin | Actuate binary files |
| cache | Actuate cache files |
| bin | All binary files .exe, .dll, .cfg, .dsn, .enu, .bat<br>All configuration files<br>All user preference files |
| dll | Siebel Tools program files |
| bin | Siebel Tools binary files |
| exe | Siebel Tools executable files |
| classes | Java code files |
| help | Siebel Tools help files |
| enu | American-English language help files |
| local | Local and extracted database |
| files | Local files attachments |
| inbox | Unused by Siebel Tools |
| outbox | Unused by Siebel Tools |
| locale | Language-specific files |
| log | Log files for Siebel Tools operations |
| msgtempl | Message files |
| objects | Siebel .srf files which are the compiled definition files used by Siebel Tools |
| public | HTML and graphics files for uploading; cascading style sheets (CSS) files |
| reports | All report files |
| enu | American-English version of reports |
| rptsrc | Actuate source files for all reports |
| enu | American-English version |
| lib | Report object library .rol files |
| standard | Report object design .rod files |

*(Contd.)*

| SIEBDEV | |
|---|---|
| sample | Sample database sse_samp.dbf |
| files | Sample file attachments |
| inbox | Unused by Siebel Tools |
| outbox | Unused by Siebel Tools |
| scripts | Java scripts |
| search | Saved searches in language-independent and in target-language format |
| sqltempt | SQL statement fragments utilized by Siebel Tools operations |
| temp | Unused by Siebel Tools |
| upgrade | Siebel Web Template .swt files |

(c) Verifying the Siebel Tools Icons that initiate or start the following:
  - Local Database
  - Siebel Tools
  - Siebel Tools Demo
  - Siebel Tools Help

(d) Setting up Siebel Tools ODBC Data Sources for users
  - SQL Anywhere
  - Microsoft SQL Server database
  - DB2 database
  - Oracle database

(e) Setting up for running multiple local databases at the same time (typically Siebel Tools and the Siebel Client simultaneously) by changing the local database configuration

(f) Setting up the Repository names consistently is essential for seamless configuration and testing, performing upgrades, and so on. The conventional repositories recommended are as follows.
  - Production environment is typically termed as Siebel Repository; Siebel eBusiness Applications use this as the default name for the production environment.
  - Test environment typically has the same name as the production environment that simplifies the process of migrating repositories from the test to production environment and also obviates the corresponding need to change the server or client configurations. This environment includes both a Siebel Server and a Database Server of its own.
  - Development environment typically contains a number of repositories especially for different versions of custom configurations corresponding to the various Siebel upgrades. This environment also includes both a Siebel Server and a Database Server of its own.

(g) Setting up the Development Environment

## 11.2.3 Configuring Siebel Tools

The objective of configuring the Siebel applications is to create a target application that satisfies the specific requirements of the enterprise but is also maintainable and upgradable easily. This can be achieved by abiding by the following principles (discussed earlier in Chapter 6, section "Implementation Strategy").

- Leveraging Siebel's standard functionality as far as possible
- Standardizing the approach and strategy of configuration
- Adhering to a standardized, consistent and intuitive user interface
- Maintaining acceptable system performance

The Configuration Development Life Cycle (CDLC) consists of the following steps:

1. Requirements analysis
2. Feasibility analysis in terms of the required time, resources, schedule and activity plan
3. Get management endorsement for proceeding with the project
4. Configuration design
5. Get management endorsement for configuration design document
6. Establish the application development environment
7. Develop the application
8. Use Siebel Tools to create Business components and business objects
9. User Interface Objects
10. Perform Unit Testing
11. Use Siebel Tools Assignment Manager and Workflow Manager to implement the required appropriate assignment and workflow rules
12. Extend the functionality of the application using Siebel VB or Siebel eScript
13. Internationalize/ localize your application
14. Perform System Testing
15. Perform User/Acceptance Testing
16. Conduct User Training

For a Siebel application, all configuration is done at the repository level. The standard Siebel application can be configured in the following way:

- Use Siebel extension tables to modify the standard tables, which would allow (say) the sales team to enter additional information about potential sales leads
- Modify the definitions of some of the business entities for customization
- Create a customized form applet, which would allow (say) call center employees to enter Additional/new/alternate contact information
- Modify the presentation of data in the HTML thin client application

#### 11.2.3.1 Application Enhancement through Scripting and Object Interfaces

Object interfaces are also defined through the Siebel Repository via Siebel Tools and can be customized by changing attributes in the repository and scripting with Siebel VB to adopt them to the existing external models.

#### 11.2.3.2 Internationalization and Localization

Siebel Tools enables global organizations to implement Siebel applications in multiple languages while maintaining a single, unified repository of customer data across the different languages. Features such as a multilingual list of values enable users of different languages to work within the same system while using their native language. Siebel provides multilingual, multi-currency support, as well as support for multiple time zones.

#### 11.2.3.3 Controlling Visibility

Siebel Tools provide the access control mechanisms that enable control of access and visibility of data to the individual user. Siebel provides flexible, efficient and easily maintainable access control depending upon the type of data, the type of parties and the access control mechanisms employed. Data types include master data, customer data and other data like price lists, rate lists, cost lists, etc. Parties are usually of six types, namely, person, organization, position, household, user list, and access group.

Access control is basically of two types:

- View level access control that allows eligible users to see only approved views
- Record level access control that allows the eligible users to see only approved data record(s)

#### 11.2.3.4 Customizing Application Behavior

Siebel applications are highly configurable, that is, achievable by configuring or modifying properties of business objects using Siebel Tools rather than traditional programming.

## 11.3 USING SIEBEL TOOLS

In this section we discuss how Siebel Tools can be used for development, modifications and upgrades at the data objects, business objects and user interface objects layer.

### 11.3.1 Defining Database Extension

Siebel Tools and Siebel applications provide several tools to automate a large part of effort for implementing database extensions.

The planning and design of database extensions involve the following steps:

(1) Perform the requirement analysis for a new column
(2) Establish the approach for introducing the new column: base table, a standard extension table or a custom extension table
(3) Design the extension column—data type, length and default values

(4) Determine the Applet(s), View(s) and Screen(s) where the column will be used
(5) Determine the location of the custom column: base table, a standard extension table or a custom extension table
(6) Determine the method for uploading data into the extension column
(7) Document the database extension design
(8) Determine the plan and schedule for executing the database extension design

The database extension implementation effort involves the following:

- Checking out and Locking the Projects
- Updating the Logical Schema Definition in the Local Environment
  - Creating a Custom Extension Table
  - Adding Extension Columns to Tables
  - Modifying Extension Tables or Columns
  - Deleting Extension Tables or Columns
  - Using Extension with Enterprise Integration Manager (EIM)
  - Adding Custom Indexes
- Applying the Physical Schema Extensions to the Local Database
- Displaying the Schema Extension Data
- Preparing the Server Database Prior to Applying Schema Extensions
- Applying the Changes to the Server Database
- Populating the Extension Tables and Columns

## 11.3.2 Defining Business Objects

The business logic and semantics of the Siebel data are embodied in the Business Objects. The Business Objects need to be defined prior to defining the User Interface Objects layer object types like Applets, Views and Screens. The Business Objects Layer object types like Business Components and Business Objects are the foundations of all Siebel applications.

The sequence to be followed for developing or defining Business Objects in the Siebel Repository is as follows:

- Check out the corresponding project
- Create a Business Component and add it to the corresponding project (or modify an existing one)
- Add fields to the Business Component
- Link the corresponding Business Components
- Associate the Business Component with the corresponding Business Object
- Validate the definitions of Business Objects

### 11.3.2.1 Defining Business Components

Following are the key properties for defining the Business Component object type:

- Class that identifies similar objects types in terms of functionality of navigation, getting or setting field values in records, creating/committing changes/deleting records, undoing/re-doing, bookmarking, searching and sorting
- Name for referencing business components uniquely within the repository
- No Delete, No Insert, No Update (Default is FALSE) for allowing data manipulation operations
- Search specifications for restricting the retrieval of records
- Sort Specifications for ordering records
- Table (Required) from which the records populate the majority of fields in the business components

The corresponding properties of the Field object type are as follows:

- Column (Required unless it is a derived/calculated field) that identifies the column in the default table
- Name user-defined for referencing uniquely within the Business Component
- No Copy if TRUE copies the field's value into the new record during a Copy Record operation
- Read Only if TRUE cannot be changed by the user
- Required if TRUE must be entered before the record can be committed
- Text Length obtained from the database depending on the type
- Type of the field data type

### 11.3.2.2 Defining a Business Object

Following are the key properties for defining the Business Object type:

- Name for referencing business objects uniquely within the repository
- Query List Business Component (Default is Query List) for identifying the business component used to store corresponding pre-defined queries

### 11.3.2.3 Mapping Business Components to Business Objects

The Business Objects are mapped to Business Components, which are in turn mapped onto the corresponding Data Objects.

Figure 11.1 shows an example of such a mapping. Figure 11.2 presents a full set of Business Objects types and their relationships.

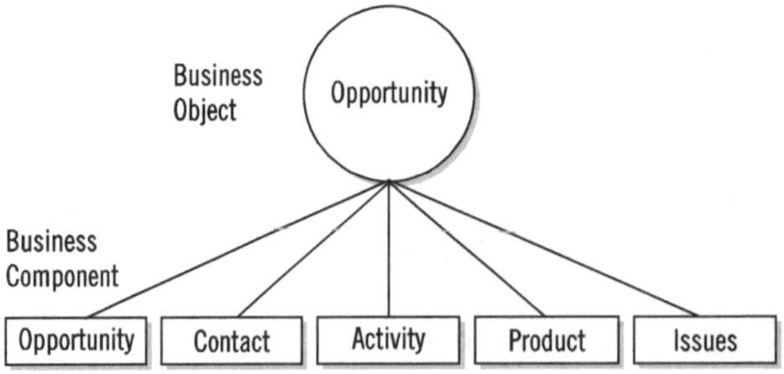


**Fig. 11.1 Mapping Business Components to Business Objects**

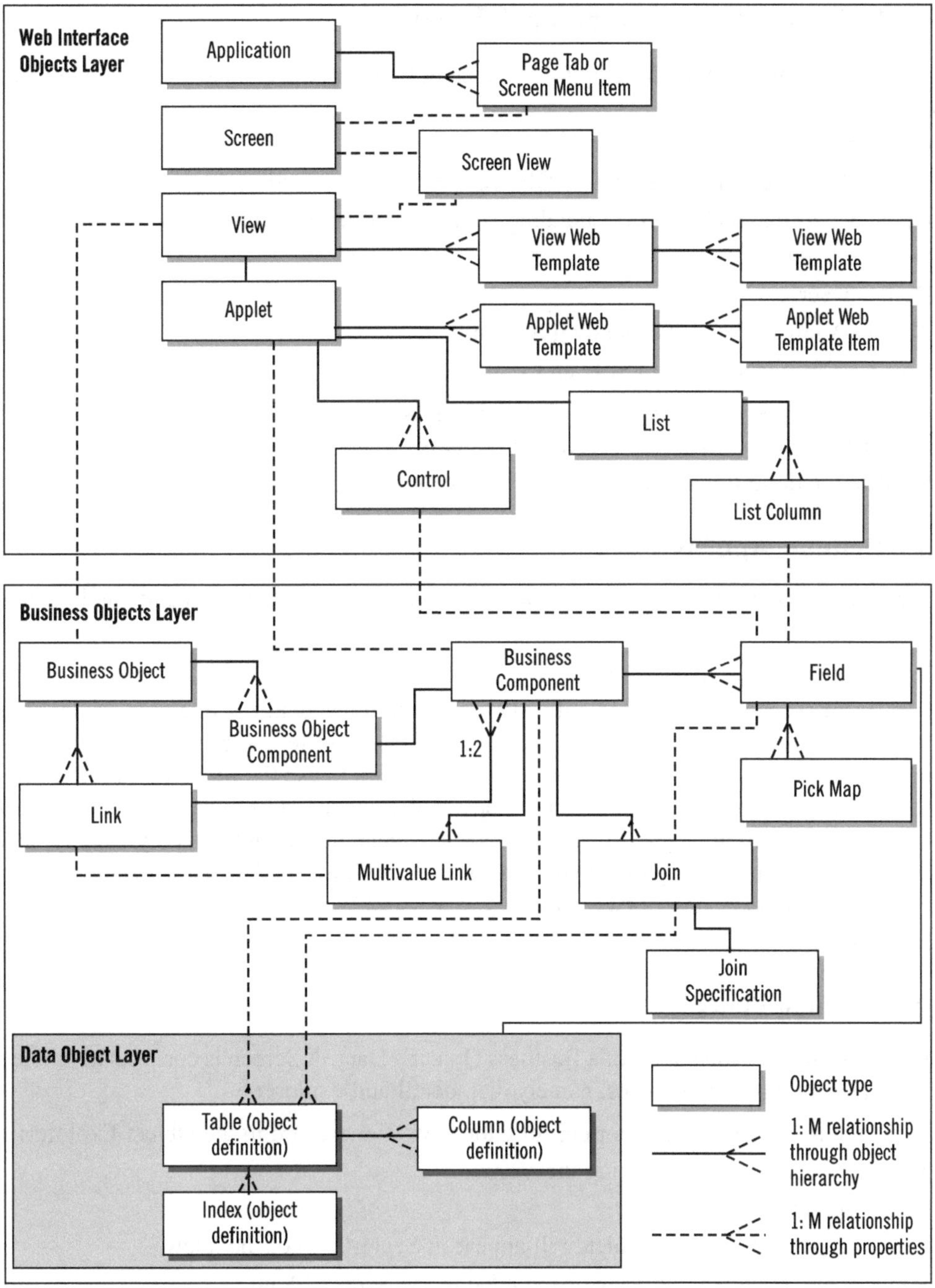


**Fig. 11.2 Full Set of Business Object Types and Their Relationships**

## 11.3.3 Defining User Interface Objects

The sequence to be followed for developing or defining User Interface objects in the Siebel Repository is as follows:

- Check out the corresponding project
- Define the corresponding Business Objects (as described earlier)
- Define an Applet and the corresponding columns and list columns
- Define a View
- Define a Screen
- Add the View to the Corresponding Screen
- Create an Application (or modify an existing one)
- Associate the Screen(s) to the corresponding page tabs
- Associate the Screens to the screen menu items
- Validate the definitions of User Interface Objects

### 11.3.3.1 Defining Applets

Applets are part of Views and provide capabilities for viewing, entry, modification and navigation for data in a business component.

Applet are typically implemented as:

- Form Applets can be populated with Microsoft Windows controls like buttons, text boxes and check boxes or ActiveX controls that can interact with the applet through property settings, methods and events. An entry applet that enables users to use the form for record manipulation, has the button controls New, Delete, Copy and Cancel, and typically appears in list views occupying the bottom horizontal sectors. Form applets that are not entry style are typically used in detail views and occupy the top horizontal sectors. Some applets perform specialized roles as charts, trees and are described later.
- List Applets

### 11.3.3.2 Defining Views

Views define a visual representation of a Business Object's Data. A Screen is constituted of one or more views that appear in three basic styles, namely, list, detail and explorer.

Following are the key properties for defining the new View record in the Object Explorer:

- Name (Required) for referencing the View
- Drop Sectors
- Sector0 Applet (Required) which will appear in Sector0(-7) of the View
- Screen menu if TRUE, the View is included in the Screen Menu
- Title text string used as the window title

### 11.3.3.3 Defining Screens

A screen is a collection or group of related views pertaining to one business function.

Following are the key properties for defining the new Screen record in the Object Explorer:

- Name (Required) for referencing the Screen
- Default View that will be used when the user clicks on a page tab for a Screen
- Bitmap Category containing the logo bitmap that is shown in the View Bar
- View Bar Text that appears below the optional logo bitmap in the View Bar

Screen View is the child object view of a screen. The corresponding properties are as follows:

- 6 Sectors if TRUE the View will be available when the application is running in 6-sector mode
- 8 Sectors if TRUE the View will be available when the application is running in 8-sector mode
- Menu Text displayed in the sub-menu of the Screen menu bar selection
- Sequence specifies the order in which the Views will appear in the cascading menu for the Screen menu item
- Category is a set of Views that appear hierarchically in the View Bar

### 11.3.3.4 Defining Applications

An application is a collection of Screens that are accessible through menus and tabs. The Siebel application object definitions are maintained in a separate project to minimize the locking of the application object definition itself.

The configuration file incorporates the application's name that is read at the time of execution.

### 11.3.3.5 Configuring Pick Applets

Pick applet is a dialog box that appears when the user clicks the drop-down button in certain text boxes or list column cells. When the user selects a row in the list table and clicks the 'Pick' button to accept the selection (or double clicks on the selected row), the pick applet is closed and the user's selected record not only populates the initiating text box/ list column cell but also other related controls/ list column cells in the initiating applet. Typically, the data in the pick applet is from a different business component than the data in the initiating applet.

For instance, in the Opportunity applet, upon clicking the drop-down button in the Account text box and selecting an account, not only does the selected account appear in the Account text box, but even the corresponding site appears in the Site text box in the initiating applet. When the user selects a record in the pick applet, the values of certain list columns in the selected record are copied to the corresponding list column of the initiating (or originating) applet. There is a foreign key in the Opportunity business component identifying the account for each opportunity; when the user selects an account in the Pick Applet, it populates this foreign key field.

A Pick Applet incorporates details on

- Originating applet
- Originating business component

- Originating control or originating list column cell
- Originating Field
- Pick List object definition, which identifies the Pick Applet business component and is referenced by the field of the originating control
- Pick Applet
- Pick Applet Business Component
- Pick maps map a field in the pick Business Component and the corresponding one in the Originating Business Component. The later gets updated with the current value of the pick list field as soon as a record has been picked in the pick applet, unless the user enters a new value manually.
- Join and join specification

The following are the properties for configuring the originating applet:

- Business Component
- Originating control
- Control populated by the Pick Applet
- Controls unrelated to the Pick Applet

The corresponding properties for configuring the pick applet are as follows:

- Business Component
- Class
- Type
- Title

A Pick List can be constrained to display only records that have field values matching corresponding fields in the originating business component's records. Pick applet constraints are defined using the Constrain property in the Pick Map object type.

### 11.3.3.6 Configuring Static Pick Lists

A Static Pick List Applet is a single-column dialog box that appears when the user clicks the drop-down button in certain text boxes or list column cells. On the user selecting a value in the list and clicking the 'Pick' button to accept the selection (or double clicking on the selected value), the static Pick List Applet.

A Static Pick List applet incorporates details on:

- Originating Applet
- Originating Business Component
- Originating control or originating list column cell
- Originating Field
- Static Pick List object definition, which identifies the Pick List applet business component and is referenced by the field of the originating control
- Pick List object
- Pick List Generic Business Component

**Table 11.2 Comparison of Dynamic Pick Applets with Static Pick Lists**

| Pick Applet | Static Pick List |
|---|---|
| Enables the user to select a value to populate a text box with data | Also, enables the user to select a value to populate a text box with data |
| Pick Applet draws values dynamically from a pick applet business component | Static Pick List draws only a pre-defined static list of available selection values that are already configured separately via List of Values Administration View in a Siebel application |
| Pick Applets typically invokes a dialog box with multiple list columns and buttons | Static Pick List invokes only a single-column dialog box |
| Pick Applet populates multiple controls in the originating applet and the corresponding fields in the business component | Static Pick List populates only a single control in the originating applet and the corresponding field in the business component |

- Pick map maps a field in the Pick List business component and the corresponding one in the originating business component. The later gets updated with the current value of the pick list field as soon as a value has been picked in the pick list applet

The Pick List object definition has the following important properties:

- Business component
- Type Field
- Type Value
- Sort Specification

### 11.3.3.7 Configuring Multi-Value Group (MVG) Applets

A multi-value group (MVG) Applet is a dialog box that appears when a user clicks the ellipsis (...) button to the right of certain text boxes or list column cells. It provides a facility to display and maintain a set of records from a business component that is associated with the currently displayed business component in the originating applet. The record with a check mark in the Primary check box is the one whose data appears in the corresponding controls in the originating applet. When the MVG Applet is open, the user can view the entire list of records for this account, not just the primary one. The user can also add, edit and delete address records in this window.

The MVG Applet incorporates details on the following:

- Originating Applet
- Originating Business Component
- Multi-value fields that are populated by multi-value links
- Multi-value Links
- Links

- Multi-value group applet
- Multi-value group business component

### 11.3.3.8 Configuring Association Applets

A many-to-many relationship in Siebel applications is implemented by means of an intersection table and a pair of links. An Association Applet is a dialog box that provides users with the ability to associate a parent record with one or more child records through an intersection table. For instance, Association Applets are provided for assigning Team Members to an Account, Contacts to an Opportunity and Products to a price list.

In the Association Applet, clicking the:

- Add button performs an 'association' entailing newly associating an existing detail record to an existing master record
- New button performs an 'addition' entailing creation of a new detail record followed by an 'association'

An Association Applet invoked from a master–detail view incorporates details on:

  - View whose Business Object establishes the master–detail relationship between the business components whose data is displayed
  - Master Applet
  - Detail Applet
  - Business Components for both master and detail
  - Association Applet
  - List columns that are displayed in the association applet
  - Controls appearing in the Association Applet, namely, Add, New, Close and Find

An Association Applet can also be invoked from multi-value group (MVG) applets.

### 11.3.3.9 Configuring Special Purpose Applets

We described some of the special purpose applets available in Siebel applications.

#### *11.3.3.9.1 Chart Applets*

A Chart Applet graphically presents select and current data from a business component in various formats for analysis of trends, category comparisons and other correlations within the various data.

> Siebel Tools and Siebel Applications use the following convention:
> The horizontal X-axis displays the categories of things like product names
>
> The vertical Y-axis displays the corresponding quantitative data values for (say) the number of service requests
>
> The third Z-axis displays the series of similar qualities/properties that could be numeric/date/text (say) the level or degree of the service request severity

The user can select different chart types through the various chart layout types options also available with a series axis in either 2 or 3-dimensional (2-D or 3-D) options:

- Horizontal Bar
- Stacked Bar
- Pie—displays the relative difference across categories by segmenting a circle based pro rata on the percentage of the various categories; pie charts do not specify a series axis
- Line—displays trends across categories or over time
- Scatter—displays distribution of data like probability distributions; the category axis has to be of numeric rather than date or text type
- Spline—displays one (or more for a series) line curve(s) plotted against an X-Y grid.
- Combo—displays a single bar chart superimposed with a single line chart sharing the same category axis

A Chart Applet contains one or more chart objects that have the following important properties:

- Category Field—name of the text or date field in the business component whose different values are mapped into different categories
- Data Point Field—contains the name of the numeric field that needs to be totaled
- Series Field—contains the name of the text field in the business component whose vales are mapped into different curves
- Data Function Like Sum, Count, Average, etc.

The following chart elements, which are child objects of Chart, are supported—AxisLabel, AxisLineGrid, AxisTitle, Graphic, Legend, Plot, Title, Font, Color, Size and Fill Color. Like all other applets, the business component identified in the Chart Applet provides the data for the category, data point and series axes subject to the current view, the current query and visibility considerations.

A Chart Applet typically provides a choice of Pick Lists for the user to re-configure the presentation or use of data:

- Chart Type Pick list allows a selection of different types of charts for the same data
- Show Pick list allows a selection list of field/ function combinations that determines the values that are displayed on the Y-axis
- By Pick list allows a selection of roles depending on the configuration of certain Chart object properties:

In period Charts the selection is from a list of possible X-axis calendar periods data like day/week/ month/quarter/year, and so on

In source Charts the selection is from a list of possible sources that will populate the X axis

Inversion of the X and Z axes

- Second 'By' Pick List allows a selection of source fields that populates the Z-axis

### *11.3.3.9.2 Tree Applets*

A Tree Applet is used to create an Explorer View that allows the user to navigate hierarchically through a tree of folders in the left hand sectors of the screen and the corresponding structured list of records of related business components through a pre-defined set of list applets in the right hand sectors. This is similar in operation to the Object Explorer and Object List Editor in Siebel Tools; the particular list applet that appears on the right depends on which node is selected in the tree on the left. A tree applet utilizes the set of master–detail relationships (corresponding to a business data model or entity-relationship diagram) implemented in the business object assigned to the View, which is embodied in the hierarchy of folders displayed in the tree applet. The user expands and collapses these folders to view the records in the corresponding list applet.

For instance, on expanding a Service Request (SR) by double clicking on the document icon, a set of folders (Activities, Attachments, Product Defects, and so on) appears beneath it. On expanding one of these child folders (say) activities, a list of the corresponding Activity detail records appear on the right. The tree applet/explorer view can also be re-configured to (say) include additional folders like Contacts, Customer Surveys and Service Agreements (corresponding to other business components of the same business object) as child folders of Service Request.

Figure 11.3 shows a portion of the master–detail relationships in the Service Request (SR) business object.

The tree node object definition has the following important properties:

- Display Name of the node as appears on the tree applet
- Applet corresponding to a folder
- Position of the tree node's hierarchical position relative to the other nodes and its sequence on its level
- Business Component
- Label Field, which is the key field that is used to populate the names in the record list that appears when the node is expanded by the user
- Selected bitmap index set to value 5 corresponding to the folder symbol

Tree Applets are created and modified in the Applet Designer. Siebel also allows creation of recursive trees wherein all nodes in the hierarchy are of the same object type. Siebel applications provide recursive trees for accounts, activities, campaigns, opportunities, positions and many others. Siebel also enables nested trees and almost any number of nesting is permitted.

#### *11.3.3.9.3 File Attachment Applets*

A file attachment applet provides access to external documents such as spreadsheets, word processing documents, slide presentations, etc., from within the Siebel applications.

In addition to facilities for listing, viewing, editing, adding or removing attachments, the file attachment applet also provides for synchronization and shared access support for the attached documents. Attachment applets utilize functionality built into the Siebel File System.

### 11.3.3.10 Special Purpose Controls

This section briefly discusses the ActiveX and HTML controls whose roles and configurations are more complex than those of text boxes, check boxes, buttons, and so on.

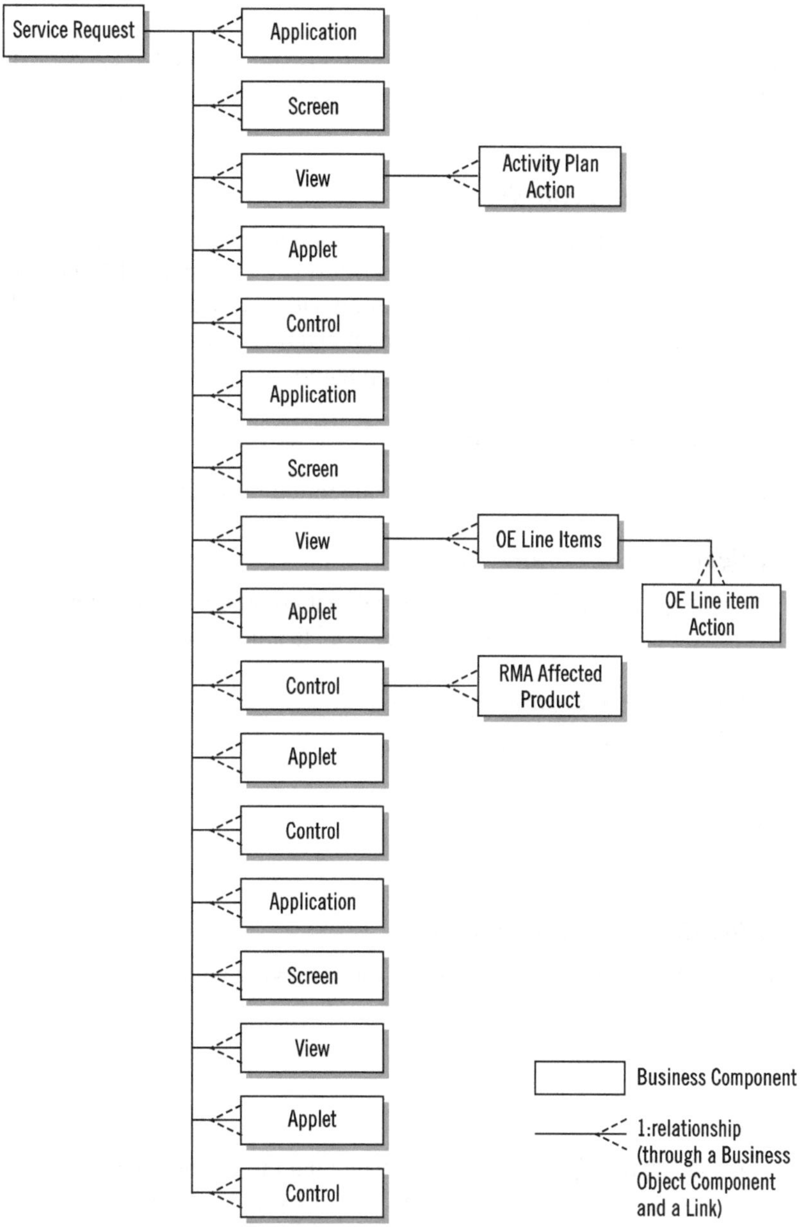


**Fig. 11.3 Service Request (SR) Business Object**

### *11.3.3.10.1 ActiveX Controls*

In Siebel applications, any registered ActiveX control can be incorporated in an applet using the Applet Web Editor. The properties of an ActiveX control can be viewed and modified in the following ways:

- Using the Properties Window

- Using the control's native property sheet

An ActiveX control in an applet exposes a set of methods and events that can be called from scripts written in browser script attached to the control or other objects and events the control generates respectively.

#### *11.3.3.10.2 HTML Content Controls*

Siebel enables configuration of fields to display HTML content by setting the properties of the control in Siebel Tools and defining any necessary supporting information such as URL, host name, syntax and authentication parameters using a set of administration views through the Siebel Web Client. The HTML content can be static HTML or obtained from an external source. For instance, display of static HTML messages to the end-users in the eChannel applications.

### 11.3.3.11 Configuring Templates and Tags

This section describes some of the special behavior supported by templates.

#### *11.3.3.11.1 Configuring Search and Find*

The Siebel Web client supports a unified search model that combines the functions of query, find and search in order to provide users with multiple methods of locating records.

#### *11.3.3.11.2 Configuring Pre-defined Queries*

Configuration of the pre-defined query, also called favorites, involves the following three aspects:

(1) Configuration file
(2) Siebel Web Engine (SWE) tag
(3) Menu/ toolbar command

#### *11.3.3.11.3 Configuring Conditional Tags*

The Siebel Web Engine (SWE) framework supports the following conditional HTML tags:

- <swe:if>
- <swe:switch>
- <swe:case>
- <swe:default>
- <swe:if-var name ="[value]"> is used within an applet to conditionally display parts of the applet; is based on a variable set in a parent view template.

The SWE conditional tags in the Web template can also be checked to display different sections of the template depending on the browser used to access the application.

#### *11.3.3.11.4 Configuring Conditional Mappings for Applets*

Conditional mappings are settings in the repository that modify the appearance of an applet depending on the current target browser group, application, language and 'more/ less' mode. These are implemented with properties in the Applet Web Template object type using the Applet Web Editor and are interpreted by SWE at the runtime.

The areas of conditional mappings are as follows:

- Application specific to that being run by the user
- Browser specific to that being used by the user
- More/Less Mode Specific whereby the user can display more or fewer controls or list columns
- Language specific to the running application

#### *11.3.3.11.5 Configuring Image Support*

This involves configuration for the following:

- Configure images as bitmap objects
- Use image formats
- Use icons for field values
- Use images as links in controls and list columns
- Use images in template files
- Use image catching file manager
- Use icons for hierarchical list applets

#### *11.3.3.11.6 Configuring Templates*

Template configuration features include the following:

- Adding Graphics
- Displaying Server Side Errors
- Adding Sorting Capabilities to applications

## 11.3.4 Defining Access to Information

Access control deals with the access control mechanisms that enable control of access and visibility of information to the individual user. Access control is basically of two types:

- View level access control that allows eligible users to see only approved views
- Record level access control that allows eligible users to see only approved data record(s)

Access control in Siebel applications is implemented through any of these methods:

- Responsibilities control user access to Views through the Screens Menu and View Bar
- Visibility controls user access to records within specific Views based on the ownership of records by individuals or teams
- Routing further restricts the record access of remote users in order to prevent excessive transfer of data over dial-up lines

User access control is based on the user's responsibilities and positions, which are obtained using the user's logon ID as follows:

- First, establish connection with the database system underlying the Siebel application(s)
- Then, Siebel Application Object Manager(s) locates the corresponding database Logon ID value from the Logon Name field in the Employee business component records to retrieve the user's employee record(s).

Typically, users have at least one or more each, of responsibilities and positions. A *responsibility* is a set of users requiring access to the same set of Siebel Views. The set of responsibilities in the Responsibility multi-valued field determines the *view access visibility* to identified View(s) that are available to the logged-on employee.

Similarly, a *position* is a job title within the organization (with a reporting relationship to another supervisory position) that provides the primary basis for the control of record-level access. Based on the user's position being on one or more account, opportunity, campaign sales teams or contact access lists, a user's record access visibility in a particular view may be any of the following visibility types:

- Sales Team visibility conferred via Views such as My Accounts, My Contacts, My Quotes and My Opportunities
- Personal visibility conferred via Views such as My Activities, My Personal Contacts, My Product Defects, My Service Requests and My Proposals
- Manager visibility
- Organizational visibility
- All visibility

As the position in the organization is more stable than the assignment of a particular employee to that position, the records are assigned to positions (or a team position) rather than to individual logon ID's. Also, the set of positions in the Position multi-valued field determines the *record access visibility* to parts of data that are available to the logged-on employee. Thus, access to records like accounts, opportunities, campaigns and contact lists can be limited to individuals within a single organization that have been placed on virtual sales teams for each record.

Siebel also provides, via Siebel Tools and Siebel applications, multiple organizational (multi-org) visibility for customers with large or complex deployments spanning multiple user groups both internal and external to the enterprise. Multi-org visibility can be applied to user data within Siebel eBusiness Applications, including transactional data (such as accounts, contacts and opportunities), reference data (such as price lists) and run-time configuration data (such as Assignment Manager Rules and Product Configurator Models).

Multi-org visibility supports the following kinds of tasks:

- Sharing of data such as sales opportunities across the extended enterprise including channel partners or re-sellers
- Limiting visibility of data such as product prices to each user's context of specific areas of business
- Applying different business logic relevant to disparate internal organizations

Multi-org visibility provides a logical layer at the enterprise, limited and personal levels to restrict further visibility to all data based on the organization or organizations to which user positions have been assigned. While multi-org visibility can be a powerful tool for aggregating business operations and performance related analytics of global and diverse organizations, it is not advisable to use it for intra-enterprise analysis.

Following are the key properties for defining the most significant visibility characteristics of Business Components:

- Visibility Emp MVField—muli-valued field used for maintenance of the list of sales team positions in sales team visibility
- Visibility MVLink—muli-valued link (typically to the Position business component) used for maintenance of the list of sales team positions in Sales Team visibility
- Owner Visibility Field to identify the field used to establish employee-based Personal visibility
- Position Visibility Field to identify the field used to establish position-based Personal visibility
- Organization Visibility Field that identifies objects related to only one organization
- Organization Visibility MVField identifies objects related to multiple organizations
- Organization Visibility MVLink identifies the multi-value link used in organizational visibility
- Contact Visibility Field

Following are the key properties for configuring visibility characteristics of views via the properties of a Visibility Applet:

- Visibility Applet Type containing the value All, Contact, Manager, Organizations, Personal or Sales rep
- Visibility Applet specifies the Applet where the visibility is controlled
- Admin Mode Flag if TRUE, identifies the View that operates in the Admin mode disabling all visibility rules

Siebel applications provide pre-configured user routing rules that cover a combination of implicit security rules (based on responsibility) and assignment rules that determine the mobile user's access to information. The visibility rules described earlier are applicable to both connected and remote users. Remote users, that download a sub-set of database records from the server to their laptops through the synchronization process, have an additional level of restrictions called *Routing* that prevent excessive transfer of data over dial-up lines.

Dock objects are groupings of tables in the database that logically form Siebel Business Components. Each dock object is classified according to a visibility level that could either be at any of the following levels:

- Limited level that specifies a set of records that correspond to a combination of Personal, Sales Team and Manager visibility depending on the dock object and the user logon ID. Limited level routing is specified as default for the Organization (Account), Opportunity, Contact, Service Request, Product Defect, DocQuote, Calendar Item, Forecast and Campaign dock objects.
- Enterprise level that corresponds to All visibility
- Private level used exclusively for routing of non-configurable data.

The docking visibility rules determine which records from the server database are propagated to each mobile user. The information about routing appears in the properties of the Dock Object objects type and it's child object types.

## 11.3.5 Configuring Assignment Objects

Siebel Tools render the custom configuration of the following features of the Assignment Manager (that has been discussed in Chapter 13, sub-section "Siebel Assignment Manager"):

- List of assignment objects that can be assigned to assignment rules
- List of attributes that can constitute assignment criteria
- Behavior of each available assignment object including activation of auto-assignment and creator retention on teams for the assignment object
- Table and column mappings of assignment objects and attributes
- Workflow policy component and the corresponding column mappings of attributes used in the assignment criteria

Siebel Tools allows configuration of the following object types:

- Assignment Object
- Assignment Attribute
- Assignment Attribute Column
- Assignment Criteria
- Assignment Criteria Attribute

Assignment Objects represent assignment entities to which candidates are matched based on assignment rules. Assignment Object is a child object type of the Workflow Policy Object. The parent object provides a set of available column mappings through its child Workflow Policy Component and grandchild Workflow Policy Component column object types that are specified in Assignment Attribute column object definitions as columns to test for value matches, and to monitor for value changes in dynamic assignment.

The major categories of Assignment Object properties are as follows:

- General-purpose and Run-time Properties
  - Name
  - Primary Table
  - Set Primary Employee
  - Set Primary Position
  - Set Primary Rule
  - Calendar Duration Column
  - Calendar Start Time Column
  - Ignore Extra Attributes
  - Auto Re-assign
  - Keep Creator
  - Keep Manual Assigned
  - Keep Manual Assignment Primary Employee
  - Keep Manual Assignment Primary Position
  - Keep Manual Assignment Primary Rule

    - Lock assignment column
    - Replace team members
- Rule Intersection Table Setup Properties—(this is required when an assignment object can be assigned to multiple rules)
    - Rule Table
    - Rule Column
    - Rule Primary Column
    - Rule Primary De-norm Column
    - Rule Primary Manual Column
    - Rule Primary System Column
    - Rule Team Copy Columns
    - Rule Team De-norm Column
    - Rule Team Manual Column
    - Rule Team System Column
- Employee Assignment Properties—This is required when potential assignees candidates are employees rather than positions
- Position Assignment Properties—This is required when potential assignees candidates are positions rather than employees
- Skill Table Setup Properties—This is used to specify the skill table and skill item table for the assignment object. A skill table is used to enable the administrator to add custom attributes for rule evaluation without creating object definitions in the Siebel Tools.

An assignment criterion consists of one or more of the assignment criteria attributes that are implemented as child objects. Assignment criteria attributes make it possible for an assignment criterion to be composed of multiple attributes. For instance, the City-State-Country assignment criteria would have three assignment criteria attributes with values of City, State and Country respectively.

### 11.3.6 Configuring email and Fax

Siebel renders a facility to send email and fax information directly from any View in a Siebel application by invoking the Send Mail or Send Fax command, respectively. The information could be business component information, attachments, product literature and correspondence. Siebel applications integrate with third-party Messaging Application Programming Interface (MAPI) compliant email and fax software.

On invoking the Send Mail or Send Fax command, the opened Message Properties Dialog box enables selection of

- Recipients (from the business component record in the active Applet or from the messaging software's address book)
- Message text (from the fields of the business component record in the active Applet coupled with some pre-defined text or the configured template file)

email and faxes generated from applets can be automatically logged as public or internal Activity records, which is useful for recording sales activities or service request follow-ups. The text of the message is either stored in the comment field or as an attachment if it is beyond a pre-defined length.

Template files are created with a text editor and are located in the sub-directory of the Siebel directory, namely, c:\siebel\msgtempl. The first line of the template file is employed as the subject line of the message and the remaining lines are used along with values populated from the current business records, to form the body of the message text.

## 11.4 MANAGING SIEBEL TOOLS ENVIRONMENT

Managing the Siebel Tools environment involves managing the repositories, cleansing of data and improvement of performance.

### 11.4.1 Managing Repositories

In a multiple repository development environment, archiving is used to share object definitions among various repositories. Archive .sif files that contain object definitions exported from a repository are available for importing into other repositories; in such cases, child object definitions are exported and imported automatically with their parents.

Siebel allows specifying conflict resolution at the object definition level through either of these strategies:

- Ignore the imported object definition
- Ignore the existing definition and override with the imported definition
- Merge the existing with the imported definition on a property-by-property basis

Export of an entire repository is not advisable because of the extended duration required for such a process. Siebel provides various batch .ksh and executable exe programs that are available outside of Siebel Tools for working with the entire repository as a unit in scenarios such as:

- For renaming a repository, all developers need to check in their projects prior to renaming the repository by using Object List Editor of the object explorer. Following the rename, the developers need to do a get on all projects
- For copying a repository, exprep.ksh is used to create an export file that is then imported using imprep.ksh with a new repository name specified in the REPOS_NAME parameter (refer Table 11.3).
- For backing up and restoring a repository, the same batch utility program exprep.ksh is used to generate an export file (typically named customer.dat) in text format containing all object definitions in a repository; this file is imported to re-create the repository using the imprep.ksh program.

*exprep.ksh* is used regularly to make backups of the development repositories on a regular basis to preserve the progressive effort expended in the configuration work. The export file is checked in to the source code control system along with other application components like client cfg and srf files, batch scripts, EIM ifb files and so on.

**Table 11.3 exprep.ksh Parameters**

| Parameter | Description |
| --- | --- |
| SRC_USR | Siebel user name |
| SRC_PSWD | Siebel user password |
| SRC_TBLO | Siebel database table owner<br>For Oracle and Informix, use 'Siebel'<br>For Sybase and Microsoft SQL Server use dbo |
| SRC_ODBC | ODBC data source name |
| SRC_REPOS_NAME | Repository name that should be same as EXP_REPOS_NAME |
| EXP_USR | Export repository user name |
| EXP_PSWD | Export repository password |
| EXP_TBLO | Export repository table owner<br>For Oracle and Informix, use 'Siebel'<br>For Sybase and Microsoft SQL Server use dbo |
| EXP_ODBC | Export repository ODBC data source |
| SRC_REPOS_NAME | Export repository name that should be same as SRC_REPOS_NAME |

The repository and user data need to be migrated in parallel between the development, test and production database environments for the user data, the business objects and the user interface to remain synchronized. The program dev2prod.ksh that is used for schema upgrades performs the following tasks:

- Exports the designated repository from the source database
- Imports the designated repository into the target database
- Exports the logical schema definition from the specified repository to a ddl file
- Synchronizes the physical schema of the target database with this logical schema definition

Patches are applied when there is a need to upgrade a few select objects rather than a majority of objects in the repository. A *patch* spf file unlike an archive file contains two versions of each exported object definitions, one from the pre-upgrade source repository and one from the post-upgrade.

Siebel Tools enables the repository check in/ check out mechanism to interface with third-party source control system such as Microsoft Visual SourceSafe. When source control integration is enabled, each time a project is checked in to the server repository, an archive file containing all the object definitions in the project is also checked in to the source control system. This results in the source control system maintaining a series of successive version of the projects.

## 11.4.2 Data Cleansing

In standard Siebel applications, five business components have data cleansing and are de-duplication enabled, namely, Account, Sub-Account, Business Address and Contact, List Management Prospective Contact. Both of these processes either operate in real-term or in batch mode.

Data cleansing changes names, job titles, addresses and cities to put them in the proper mixed capitalization format, and addresses in the standard US Postal format. In a standard Siebel application, data cleansing operates on the following data:

- Name and location for Accounts and Sub-accounts
- First Name, Middle Name, Last Name and Job Title for contacts and prospects
- Street Address, City, State, Postal Code and Country for business address records

De-duplication detects possible duplications in newly created or modified records of business component types Account, Sub-Account, Contact and Prospect, and prompts for commitment of the new or changed record or use of one of the possible matches.

If a business component is configured for de-duplication, it must also be configured for data cleansing. Both features are disabled by default but can be enabled by setting it in the relevant cfg file. While data cleansing can be turned off for specific records by checking the column labeled Disable Data Cleansing in various lists and multi-value group applets, it is not possible to disable de-duplication for individual records. De-duplication can be disabled for a specific business component by de-activating all of the child user properties by setting the inactive property to TRUE.

## 11.4.3 Improving Performance

Poor application performance and scalability can be addressed to a certain extent by upgrading the basic infrastructure resources at additional costs. However, the basic performance and scalability characteristics of an application are really determined by the application architecture. The Siebel applications are carefully designed to meet all demanding performance and scalability requirements, in all deployment scenarios, at all layers of the Siebel Enterprise Architecture (that correspond broadly to the conventional 3-tier architecture).

(1) Siebel Database Server uses the relational database purely as a data store; the business logic is not implemented in the database in the form of triggers or stored procedures (the database-centric model), but rather on the scalable, middle tier Siebel Enterprise Server and on the Siebel Client. The data-centric model is not only difficult to scale, customize, maintain and upgrade, but it can be scaled only by augmenting the single database server. As against this Siebel provides the ability to scale the deployment across multiple Siebel servers (see following point).

The Siebel Data Model implemented on the Siebel Database Server is carefully designed to provide efficient access paths and rapid execution of the operations prevalent in front office applications by using techniques such as selective de-normalization, primary relationships in 1:M relationships, clustered indexes, and the like. The Siebel Database Server access is performed through a common Data Manager layer that dynamically generates the SQL statements that are tuned to ensure maximum efficiency and performance for the specific database, as well as to reduce network traffic and round trips.

The features of the Data Manager include:

- Use of database optimizer guidelines
- Use of bind variables
- Combining SQL operations
- Database cursors

(2) Siebel Enterprise Server components are designed to scale across multiple Siebel servers in the Enterprise Server, providing a high degree of scalability in the middle tier of Siebel applications. The Enterprise Server provides full support for multi-threaded components that use a single process to handle multiple operations simultaneously, such as multiple user sessions or synchronization requests. The Siebel Gateway Server (see Chapter 10, section "Siebel Enterprise Server") provides dynamic load balancing across multiple parallel instances of server component on multiple Siebel servers. Load balancing is based on real-term monitoring of CPU usage and the number of open network connections on each Siebel server for optimal utilization of Enterprise Server resources. Clients using load-balanced components are configured to connect to the Gateway Server ensuring high availability and continued operation, rather than to a specific Siebel server that may become temporarily unavailable.

(3) Siebel Client—The Object Manager executes Siebel Business Objects and Components on the native Siebel Client and on the middle tier Object Manager that supports the Siebel Thin Client. The Object Manager supports configurable data caching at the business component level, eliminating the need to re-query data from the database server with each use of the business component. Data caching improves performance as data can be retrieved from the cache much faster than from the Database Server and increased by reducing the number of operations executed by the Database Server. Data caching typically is applied to the business components that support pick lists.

Siebel Tools help to detect, diagnose and rectify the sources of performance problems in Siebel applications. In standard Siebel applications the Siebel architecture has been designed and tuned for optimal performance by resorting to strategies such as:

- Database indexes
- Data caching
- RDBMS cursors
- Efficient SQL generation
- Native database APIs

etc.

However, for customized Siebel configurations there are many potential pitfalls that result in unacceptable levels of performance, and these effects can be further aggravated in environments with large databases and wide data distribution across servers. The performance for customized configurations can be benchmarked against that for the standard application. Performance diagnosis is an iterative process spread across the project life cycle:

- During the design stage, performance implications need to be considered.
- During the development phase, changes to potentially troublesome areas (especially multi-valued groups and sort and search specifications in the new and changed business components) and addition of joins, extension tables and indexes need to be considered; accessing unnecessary fields, occurrence of unnecessary joins, multiple joins on the same table or accessing of multi-value group without a primary join especially in a list applet etc. are indications of potential problems.
- During the testing phase, performance bottlenecks using realistic data volumes and distribution needs to be considered; moreover the focus should be on testing the most important but slowest views.

Upon identifying a performance problem, it can be scrutinized further by analyzing the SQL statements by generating an SQL trace file using the */s trace_file* expression as follows:

C:\Siebel\bin\siebel.exe /c config_file /s trace_file

The trace file records the SQL queries (including housekeeping queries) issued by the Siebel application along with the corresponding duration of processing. This can then be analyzed for:

- The number and complexity of SQL statements
- The execution times
- The sort specifications indicated by the sorting criteria in the 'Order by' clauses
- The search specifications indicated by the selection criteria in the 'Where' clauses
- The use of indexes
- The use of temporary tables
- The use of sequential table scans

The basic anti-patterns for poor performance of Siebel applications have been found to be as follows:

- Severe performance impact
  - Multi-Value Group (that entails association of multiple records within a single parent record) performance

    List Applet with Non-Primary Multi-Value Groups
  - Database indexes (are data structures associated with a table that provide references to the records in that table in a particular order and are the basis for the support of sort and search specifications) in sorting and searching

    Sort specification containing one or more joined fields

    Non-indexed search specification on a large table

    Non-indexed sort specification on a large result set
  - Displaying totals in a list applet

    Displaying totals (at the bottom of list columns) in a list applet with a large number of records
  - Other performance bottlenecks

    Search specification on a non-RDBMS supported calculated field

    Setting the cascade delete property to TRUE in a link used in a many-to-many relationship
- Significant performance impact
  - Non-primary multi-value groups appearing in a form applet
  - Several business components used by applets in a view
  - Too many joins, extension tables or primary multi-value groups used in a business component
- Moderate performance impact
  - A business component using a large number of fields
  - Use of outer joins when standard joins are sufficient

## 11.5 MANAGING APPLICATION DEVELOPMENT PROJECTS

The server database stores the master copy of the Siebel Repository. Multiple developers can access them by locking and checking out groups of server repository object definitions to local repository databases for changes and additions, and then checking them back into the server after completing the modifications and testing.

Managing application development projects involves:

- Locking Projects
- Checking-Out Projects
- Creating New Projects
- Checking-In Projects
- Determining Project Differences at Check-In Time
- Compiling Projects

### 11.5.1 Siebel Projects

A Siebel application is delivered with a large number of pre-existing projects. Projects are named sets of related Siebel Objects definitions that reside in the Siebel Repository that can be worked on by teams of application developers.

Project names without any suffix correspond to business object layer definitions that span multiple applications, whereas projects with a suffix indicate business object or user interface definitions that are associated with specific functional areas. For instance, the suffix CC implies a field that contains Call Center user interface data for the Siebel Call Center application.

## 11.6 SUMMARY

This chapter described the Siebel Tools environment including issues related to its installation and configuration. We introduced Business Object Designer, Programming Environment, Interactive Designer, Report Designer, SmartScript, Database Extension Designer and Application Upgrader. In the latter half of the chapter, we also saw details on the use of Siebel Tools for defining the Database, Business and User Interface Objects. The latter includes defining Applets, Views, Screens and applications, and configuring of Pick Applets, Static Pick Lists, MVG Applets, Association Applets, special purpose Applets, special purpose Controls, Templates and Tags, Assignment Objects, and so on. The chapter ended by describing aspects of managing the Siebel Tools environment.

# PART III: THE PRE-IMPLEMENTATION STAGE

This part presents the various activities which are pre-requisite to a Siebel project. Chapter 12 discusses various activities and tasks related to the Siebel project that needs to be there for the Siebel implementation effort. Chapter 13 briefly discusses the installation and administrative aspects of a Siebel installation.z



**The traditional concept of change management is understood generally as a one-time event, but if an organization is looking for the ability to not only handle change management, but the management of changes on a continual basis, then Siebel is a must. Siebel provides a platform for such ongoing changes in the processes critical to the success of a company's business.**

# Chapter 12

# Initiating the Siebel Project

This chapter introduces the various issues that are pre-requisites for initiating a Siebel project. We will discuss the organizational structure recommended for managing a Siebel implementation project. This chapter also details the constitution of the various committees and explains the various supporting issues of training and resource management. The later part of the chapter addresses the various kinds of risks that are associated with a Siebel project and presents measures recommended by Siebel to contain and even minimize their impact. The ground covered here is from the point of view of Siebel's eRoadmap methodology in Chapter 14 as well. The objective of dealing with the same issues from two different views is to illustrate the importance of adapting an integrated methodology like eRoadmap.

## 12.1 SIEBEL EXECUTIVE SPONSOR

The executive sponsor should be the executive with the power to make decisions with respect to processes, finances and the project timeline. He should be a senior member of the organization and represent the business groups of the company. The executive sponsor should also provide resources/ infrastructure support and report project-related issues to the Managing Director (MD) on a regular basis.

## 12.2 SIEBEL PROJECT EXECUTIVE COMMITTEE

Top management commitment is one of the key factors in successful implementation of an Enterprise Resource Planning (ERP) system. Hence, it is important that the top management of the company devote adequate time for planning and review of all the activities from the beginning of the project until it is completed. For the success of the project, it is also important that the commitment is visible to all the employees of the company and is exhibited through the direct involvement and actions of the top management.

An executive committee should consist of

- A CMD or CEO (Chief Executive Officer)
- An Executive Sponsor

- A Project General Manager
- A COO (Chief Operating Officer) or VP of Business Operations
- A CIO (Chief Information Officer) or VP of Systems
- A consultant or any person nominated by the Chairman and Managing Director (CMD)

Executive committee meetings should be held approximately once every four weeks to review the overall progress.

## 12.3 SIEBEL PROJECT STEERING COMMITTEE

The Steering Committee is made up of executives from the client and Siebel. The Steering Committee is an oversight organization charged with providing both project vision and direction. The Steering Committee has the ultimate responsibility for conflict, issue and problem resolution and has the final decision on change and scope management.

The steering committee should consist of:

- An Executive Sponsor
- A Chief Project Officer
- A Technical Team Leader
- Siebel Executive Sponsor
- All key user representatives
- All key consultants
- A technical support project leader
- Senior management representatives
- CMD's nominated consultant

Steering committee meetings should be held every two weeks to take stock of the event-based milestones and other project-related issues.

## 12.4 ROLES OF THE EXECUTIVE AND STEERING COMMITTEE MEMBERS

The roles and responsibilities of the executive and steering committee members should be to:

- Provide direction for the entire project
- Approve and control the project scope and implementation strategy
- Approve identified risks and authorize measures to contain them
- Be responsible for milestone deliverables and project delays
- Authorize the staffing plan for the Siebel project
- Authorize the training plan and budget for the Siebel project
- Help resolve issues, if any, with the implementation partner, coordinate commercial matters and approve payments on completed milestones

- Authorize and ensure infrastructural support (such as Hardware, Software, network, external software, office space, communication lines, OSS, and so on)
- Resolve the issues raised in business process finalization and standardization
- Resolve administrative issues faced by consultants from time-to-time

## 12.5 MISSION AND OBJECTIVES OF THE SIEBEL PROJECT

The mission of the Siebel project should dovetail into the mission and objectives set forth by the company for the next three to five years.

## 12.6 DECIDING THE SCOPE OF THE SIEBEL PROJECT

One of the most important responsibilities to be handled by the executive and Steering Committee is to decide on the scope of the Siebel project. It is recommended that the big bang approach should be adopted here, whereby the company implements most of the standard Siebel modules and also any Siebel industry-specific solutions if available for its areas of business.

Only in the big-bang approach does the company start utilizing the information captured by the Siebel system as a resource like manpower, materials and money, rather than merely as a recording and reporting system. The traditional systems have been hobbled into playing the latter role and have never been able to deliver the productivity gains expected of them.

The company must also decide the phases of implementation following the implementation at the pilot site. The true benefits of an integrated system can be reaped only when all sites and offices of the company are brought on board the Siebel platform. Towards this objective, the pilot site team must be staffed by personnel from all future sites of implementations and the functionality, as implemented at the pilot site, should be as comprehensive as possible, based on the available timeframe and business knowhow with the members of the team.

## 12.7 STARTING THE SIEBEL PROJECT

Initiating the Siebel project primarily involves instituting the project management structure and appointing the Chief Project Officer (CPO). The CPO has to formulate and initiate the mechanism for the selection or nomination process for the members of the team.

The CPO also has to formulate and get approval from the project's steering and executive committees on the project policies, guidelines, strategies to be adopted for minimizing the identified risks, and the methods for reporting on the project's progress, budget and resources.

## 12.8 SIEBEL PROJECT MANAGEMENT STRUCTURE

In this section we look at the organizational structure of a Siebel project.

## 12.8.1 Chief Project Officer (CPO)

The Chief Project Officer (CPO) is also a member of the project's Steering Committee and has enough responsibility and authority to manage day-to-day operational project-related issues and meet all project-related resource requirements.

The company should appoint a senior manager as the full-time CPO. He or she should be familiar with the business environment and the functional and Information Technology (IT) to lead a team of key users and technical consultants who will also participate in the activities of the implementation process and be responsible for the successful implementation of the Siebel system.

The CPO performs the following functions:

- Supervises the entire project
- Is responsible for milestone deliverables and project delays
- Approves and controls the project scope and implementation strategy
- Prepares and gets approval for the staffing plan, including the pilot site and the rollout sites
- Prepares and gets approval for the training plan of the project from the lead super users and end-users at various stages of the project
- Is responsible for getting the relevant business users' time and attention at all relevant stages of the project
- Accepts deliverables and gives signoffs
- Resolves the issues raised in business process finalization and standardization
- Helps resolve issues, if any, with the implementation partner, coordinates on commercial matters, and approves payments on completed milestones
- Resolves administrative issues faced by consultants from time-to-time
- Provides infrastructural support such as hardware, software, network, external software, office space, communication lines, and so on
- Arranges steering and executive committee meetings and the decisions/clearances required from the committees
- Provides guidance to Siebel and its implementation partner on the company's specific business requirements
- Provides all data for loading from the relevant business departments

## 12.8.2 Site Project Managers

The Site Project Managers (SPM) are responsible for the Siebel implementation at various sites and work under the direct guidance of the CPO. They should be part of the Siebel project team for the pilot site from the beginning. This will give them enough exposure and experience on how to handle the implementation at their own respective sites later.

The responsibilities of a SPM include the following:

- Supervision of the entire project onsite
- Responsibility for milestone deliverables and project delays

- Assembling the manpower and resources according to the staffing plan for the Siebel project
- Executing the training plan for the site, including training for the functional and technical team members, super users and end-users at various stages of the project
- Responsibility for getting the relevant site business users' attention at all relevant stages of the project
- Accepting deliverables and giving signoffs
- Resolving administrative issues faced by consultants from time-to-time
- Ensuring infrastructural support (such as H/W, S/W, external software, office space, communication lines, and so on) for the Siebel project
- Providing all data for loading from the relevant business departments

The SPM is also responsible for maintaining the site project's IMG for their respective sites.

## 12.8.3 Module Leaders

The project team should include module leaders who are responsible for each of the major Siebel modules to be implemented for the company. Module leaders should preferably have requisite prior experience in the concerned functional area and also have undergone adequate functional training in Siebel, particularly in his/her module of responsibility.

Module leaders should be identified at the beginning of a project and should be part of the Discover, Design, Configure and Validation stages. They should participate in identifying the processes and documenting them, their gap issues and their resolutions not only for their modules, but for other modules as well. This would enable them to make a more effective contribution later, during the module-level and integration-level testing.

## 12.8.4 Resource Manager

The success of any Siebel project is critically dependent on marshalling the right resources at the scheduled time and place. For an IT project with similar scope and investments, Siebel implementation projects are usually of a much shorter duration. This requires a resource manager who has previously handled the purchasing and resourcing responsibilities in an IT project. He or she should be conversant with the purchase policies and procedures of the organization as well as those for reporting on budgets in a Siebel project.

At the beginning of the project and at appropriate stages later, the resource manager could also be a member of the project Steering Committee. This would enable him to escalate issues quickly on delays in resource approvals, mobilization delays, deliveries, incomplete installations, pending training and support issues, and so on.

## 12.8.5 Training Manager

Unlike the traditional implementations, Siebel implementations involve a much larger number of operational personnel who will be using Siebel on a regular basis. The training manager should be able to execute training for the various groups of personnel as per the training plan at appointed sites.

A major responsibility of the training manager is to ensure the availability not only of instructors, but also to release the various personnel from their normal functions at appropriate times so that they can participate in the scheduled training sessions. He or she must also work with the resource manager to complete the installation of the proper software licenses and authorize the training.

In the training of the functional and technical teams, licenses can be obtained and installed with adequate infrastructural support of the PCs, networking, and so on. Similarly, before commencing training for the end-users the latest company-specific user documents for all requisite modules need to be complete and approved specifically for use in the training sessions.

## 12.9 PROJECT MANAGEMENT POLICIES AND GUIDELINES

The project management policies and guidelines should be finalized and communicated to all concerned at the earliest possible.

### 12.9.1 Project Strategy

As has been mentioned in Chapter 1, section "Information is Relationship", implementing Siebel will benefit the company only when it starts using the information made available by a productive Siebel system as the very essence of relationships. For this, it is essential that all the base modules are implemented and go into production. Otherwise, the system will function merely as a system for recording and reporting on the past performance.

### 12.9.2 Project Planning and Monitoring

The issues of reporting the progress of the project can lead to contention among project members. Considering that Siebel implementation projects are driven by the business managers, even decisions like whether to employ packaged software for management of the Siebel project itself can become a major political issue.

### 12.9.3 Project Resources Requirements

For a successful Siebel implementation, especially for the big-bang approach recommended for millennium enterprises, an adequate measure of resources available at the right time, are essential. These would be in terms of

- The allocation and disbursement of budget finances at appropriate stages.
- The acquisition and on-schedule installation of the server and PC hardware, the networking and communications hardware, the communications monitoring and network management software, O/S and office automation software at the servers and nodes, and finally the Siebel software.
- Staffing by recruitment and subcontracting or deputation from the various departments for Siebel functional teams, technical teams, resource administration, training and logistics teams, super users, and lastly the end-users, for their orientation training and refresher training just before the go-live phase.

- Data from the legacy system or other systems that are operational within the company or its key business partners. This loading of data could be a one-time exercise before the cut-over to the productive Siebel system or on a regular basis at predetermined periods during the business cycle every month. The loading process could itself be in the batch mode or be a real-time interface that transfers data and updates between Siebel and other systems on an ongoing basis.

### 12.9.4 Project Training Requirements

Siebel implementation projects engender large training requirements. Traditional implementations however, are closely administered by a centralized computer facility and are confined to a smaller number of end-users. Moreover, these end-users are also not actually involved with the operations of the business; on the contrary, they are often usually personnel only responsible for transcribing transactions and other information into the system.

CRM, in the true sense of the word, brings computerization to the desktops of the operational people. Thus, the training requirements for a Siebel project implementation would be huge and may easily involve 10 to 20 percent of the manpower of a company.

A company may have to undertake Siebel-related training for three different groups of personnel:

(1) The select group of managerial personnel who are key members of their departments and have been nominated as the members of the functional team.

(2) The group of key users who form the core of the super users to be entrusted with the task of live-scale testing of the system and also training the end-users.

(3) All other end-users who will be using the system as part of their routine operational duties. As an important part of the strategy for post-implementation support, the third group is trained primarily by the members of the second group, the super-users.

The managerial personnel group will be trained with an overview of Siebel and their module(s) of interest. The key user group will be trained with an overview of their module and all of the critical processes of interest. The end-users group will be trained only in the processes that are routinely used by them on a daily basis.

## 12.10 RISK MANAGEMENT IN A SIEBEL PROJECT

Because the Siebel project is an implementation of a standard package, the risks associated with it are different from those traditionally associated with software implementations. The major risks of traditional software projects are as follows:

- Lack of resources
- Lack of appropriate resources
- Lack of clarity, completeness and certainty on the scope and functionality
- Requirements capture and analysis
- System design that is effective, efficient and at the same time flexible for changes in the future
- Development of the system based on this design and testing using this design as a reference
- Training various group of users on the new system

- Interfacing real-time with other application systems
- Loading all relevant and up-to-date data into the new system
- Parallel runs with the new system
- Switching to the new system
- Missing deadlines
- Disputes regarding roles, responsibilities and performance criteria
- User disagreements or non-participation
- Software or infrastructure failures

In addition to the above risks, Siebel projects have other risks, which include:

- Requirements capture and analysis
- Understanding what the Siebel system can provide
- Evaluating and focusing on the gaps in functionality
- Configuring and customizing the Siebel system correctly
- Integration testing of the Siebel system
- Training all groups of users almost in tandem
- Loading all relevant and up-to-date data into the new system
- Switching directly to the new system without full parallel runs phase

The risks associated with the requirements capture and requirements analysis, are no different than those with the traditional projects. Especially for future enterprises of the millennium, it is important to have shorter timelines for the project implementations.

A company implementing Siebel can adopt several strategies for minimizing the risks inherent in the project. The most important one is to do away with the requirement analysis phase, but at the same time implement functionality that represents the optimal practices for the processes that are critical to business. This is effectively achieved by adopting Siebel's recommended best of business practices that come bundled along with the system.

## 12.10.1 Selecting the Most Critical Processes

A company should evaluate and select the processes that are critical to its business and focus on implementing them effectively to add maximum value for optimal effort.

## 12.10.2 Implementing Best-of-Business Processes

Siebel embodies the best-of-business processes derived from its experiences with companies throughout the world. The success of Siebel in providing comprehensive functionality within a shorter timeframe compared with traditional implementations is based on the strategy of leveraging the commonality that is found in similar processes prevalent in companies within an industry.

Re-usability has been a powerful concept in enhancing productivity and the quality of delivered software in the areas of traditional software development. Siebel, in particular, extends this concept of re-usability to the design of mission-critical systems. It packages such universal commonalties of functionality for rapid and successful implementations.

Before adding re-usability to the library of the best-of-business processes however, the company should document, rationalize and standardize the company's select group of processes that are to be implemented using Siebel.

### 12.10.2.1 Documentation of Processes

Documenting the various business processes permits the true comprehension of the characteristic structure and dynamics of the business environment within a company. This involves recording various details on the business processes like name, purpose, responsible function, process description, including inputs and outputs, and sub-processes. This also includes interfaces with other functions and systems, exceptional conditions, areas for improvement, impact analysis of suggested scenarios, and so on.

### 12.10.2.2 Rationalization of Processes

Many of the systems and procedures adopted by traditional systems were influenced by the architecture of the systems themselves. For instance, these earlier systems were designed to be used by IT-literate personnel managed and supported by a centralized IT function. In contrast, because of the end-user orientation of CRM packages like Siebel as well as the online availability of data on all aspects of company operations, Siebel permits the rationalizing of many processes. This could be in terms of eliminating sequential wait periods for approvals, acknowledgements prior to further processing, collating status updates from various departments before compiling the latest positions on inventory, and so on.

In enterprise-wide integrated packages like Siebel, many of these facilities and features become available automatically as a part of the architecture of the system. Thus, such process steps could be eliminated entirely from the business processes.

### 12.10.2.3 Standardization of Processes

Every plant or office site of a company develops its own character and culture, which is a result of the company's recommended corporate environment blending with the local situations. Such local practices have strong adherents and generate loyalty and pride. These factors often harm the progress of implementing a fairly uniform system, even if it is a computerized system like Siebel, across the organization at all of its sites and offices.

The CPO must take ample measures to ensure the broad acceptance within the organization of standardized implementation. This can be ensured by:

- Rapid implementation at the pilot site
- Rapid rollout of Siebel at other company sites and offices
- Deputation of key personnel from all sites for the teams at the pilot sites, even at the risk of overstaffing these teams
- Judicious selection and documentation of functionalities for implementation at the pilot sites
- A democratic and transparent process of standardization based on the pre-defined criteria of value addition in terms of customer friendliness, quality, timeliness, costs, and so on

- Configuration and customization of the maximum possible functionality at the pilot site keeping in view the businesses and practices prevalent at all other sites and offices.

## 12.10.3 Centralized Base Reference Configuration

A company can experience the real payoff of implementing a CRM like Siebel only when it has implemented Siebel at all of its plants, facilities and offices. Traditional computerized systems have a much more difficult time implementing standardized processes across all locations of their organizations. Since a Siebel project entails implementing both best of business and standardized processes, it leads to fairly standard implementation solutions across all of its sites.

A company should plan to implement a fairly comprehensive functionality at its pilot site. This is termed as the Centralized Base Reference Configuration (CBRC). This can simply be transplanted at each of the rollout sites in the subsequent stages of the project. Such an approach engenders faster customization, training, integration testing and finally, go-live stages.

## 12.10.4 Siebel eRoadmap Methodology

The eRoadmap implementation methodology is the latest tool introduced by Siebel for rapid implementation of the Siebel system within an organization. eRoadmap is a structured implementation approach and can help you achieve a faster implementation with quicker user acceptance, well-defined roadmaps and efficient documentation at various stages. Siebel eRoadmap focuses on the key strategic and tactical areas that must be addressed to maximize the customer's return on investment while minimizing their business risk to ensure the successful completion of a Siebel project. The Siebel implementation is comprised of activities logically grouped into eight distinct stages to ensure proper project management and control throughout the life cycle of the project. However, the stages are iterative in nature enabling customers to realize 'quick hit' benefits of implementing CRM in the short-term, while also making possible revisiting earlier stages and fine-tuning for better results.

The eight stages of eRoadmap methodology are:

1. Plan
2. Define
3. Discover
4. Design
5. Configure
6. Validate
7. Deploy
8. Sustain

By promoting the best-of-business practices for implementation, Siebel does away with the time-consuming and tedious steps of requirements capture and analysis mentioned earlier.

The popularity, effectiveness and reliability of such an approach was established by the great success achieved by a similar methodology adopted for the traditional software application development in the 1980s. The Structured Systems Analysis and Design (SSAD) methodology introduced by Gane and

Sarson essentially skipped the then popular practice of first analyzing the existing system and went directly into analysis of the proposed system. The design of the proposed system was therefore a radically different interpretation of the future requirements of a company without being encumbered by the constraints, practices and prejudices of the past systems and procedures prevalent within the organization.

As explained, with Siebel this process is taken a step further by optimizing the traditional design and development stages of the project life cycle by utilizing a library of best of business, pre-implemented processes for any industry. We will discuss all phases of eRoadmap in detail in Part IV of this book.

## 12.11 CHANGE MANAGEMENT IN A SIEBEL PROJECT

Initiating and confronting change are the two most important issues facing companies today. The ability to change business processes contributes directly to your 'innovation' bottom line. The traditional concept of change management is understood generally as a one-time event, but if an organization is looking for the ability to not only handle change management, but the management of changes on a continual basis, then Siebel is a must. Siebel provides a platform for such ongoing changes in the processes that are so critical to the success of a company's business.

As we have stated earlier, business processes that reside or are internalized within the minds of an organizations' employees are difficult to change simply because we naturally find change difficult. However, processes that reside in or are internalized within computerized systems are easy to change. Thus, Siebel-supported processes are much easier to change and execute than the conventional computerized system because Siebel implements a model of the enterprise that is comprehensive and consistent.

Change management is essential but employees are apprehensive because of:

- Fear of job reductions
- Fear of losing responsibility and control
- Anxiety arising out of a perceived inadequacy of their background
- Fear of failure
- Loss in the sense of ownership
- Sheer inertia for changing and learning new systems

The issues become further aggravated because of lack of clarity in terms of:

- Why changes are needed?
- What changes are needed?
- Who is accountable for what?
- How will the performance and progress be measured?

The issues arising because of changes resulting from the implementation of Siebel can be resolved by:

- Demonstrated support from senior management
- Wide and rapid information dissemination on the Siebel project
- Adequate training and refresher programs

- Accelerated progress and effectiveness with the Siebel system
- Rotation of job responsibilities or replacement

## 12.12 SIEBEL PROJECT SUB-TEAMS

We now discuss the roles and responsibilities for the members of the Siebel team at a high level.

(a) Siebel Project Team

The Siebel project team has responsibilities for:

- Studying and streamlining the business processes
- Standardizing the business processes across all offices
- Studying the system and configuring it to suit the business processes with the help of the module consultant
- Generating necessary documentation
- Preparing a training manual
- Training users
- Completing tasks according to the implementation plan
- Working on data collection and the purification of uploads to the system
- Supporting the users after going live
- Implementation at rollout sites

(b) Business Analysis Team

The business analysis team is responsible for defining the business requirements and turning those requirements into a business design. It is also responsible for providing feedback during the user labs and ultimately for signoff of the end-user acceptance criteria. A Siebel business analyst helps to provide an understanding of the built-in Siebel business processes.

The business analysis team of consultants is responsible for:

- Training the Siebel team members in respective modules
- Helping the team map processes in the system
- Finding solutions for the gaps observed after mapping
- Guiding the team during the integration test
- Meeting the milestone deadlines of the module
- Providing necessary inputs for programming
- Helping the team during discussions with users in case of any problems

The business analysis team tends to be staffed with IT business analysts but should also include dedicated time from end-users defined in the extended project team.

(c) Siebel Technical Team

The technical team members are responsible for:

- Identifying the list of customizations using user exits, new reports using, and so on
- Preparing the project Siebel programming and documentation standards

- Writing programs, and reports using tools such as Reports
- Identifying interfaces and data to be uploaded into the Siebel system from legacy and non-Siebel systems
- Specifying the interfaces and data uploads
- Programming the interfaces and data upload programs
- Unit testing and integration testing

The Technical Architecture team provides technical architecture design recommendations, including network, capacity and performance planning. They are responsible for the acquisition, installation and implementation of architecture infrastructure (servers, clients and connectivity) to support development, test and production efforts.

The Systems and Data Integration team's primary focus is on creation of interfaces, data conversion programs and cleansing of legacy data. They are responsible for the design as well as development of programs.

The Configuration team is responsible for assisting in the technical design as well as building and testing the screen configurations and applications extensions. They will also be responsible for the technical documentation.

The Deployment team is responsible for developing the deployment strategy including the identification of the pilot group, schedule and approach to deploying the new system to the entire organization. They are also responsible for the initial administrative data, establishing the help desk facilities and procedures, and the long-term production support strategy.

The End-user Training team is responsible for creating the training curriculum, developing the instructor and end-user training materials, as well as delivering the training.

The members of the Siebel Administration team will have to be skilled in three different areas—basic system administration, database administration and operating system administration.

The various tasks involved with the Siebel administration area are as follows:

- Starting and stopping the system
- Daily administration
- Performing daily checks
- Monitoring system logs
- Monitoring system/database alerts
- Process monitoring
- Update monitoring
- Batch input monitoring
- Managing user and system background jobs
- Print administration
- Spool administration and tuning
- Managing user information, authorization and profiles
- Error analysis and troubleshooting using logs, traces and program dumps

- Planning and managing the disaster recovery site

The database related tasks are as follows:

- Performing regular database backups per the backup strategy
- Performing Siebel database administration activities using utilities for backup and for archiving logs
- Performing regular archive log backups
- Monitoring and managing table spaces, indices, index extent sizes, and so on
- Other operating system and network-related tasks are as follows:
    - Installing upgrades
    - Coordinating with the H/W and other vendors for follow-ups on reported problems
    - Monitoring network loads and identifying bottlenecks

## 12.13 SUMMARY

In this chapter we looked at various aspects preparatory to launching the Siebel project. We covered issues dealing with the planning, organization and managing of Siebel projects. We discussed the organizational structure recommended for managing a Siebel implementation project. We also described the constitution of the various committees and explained details on several related aspects like planning, monitoring, resource management and training. In the last part of the chapter, we focused on the various elements of risks that may jeopardize the success of a Siebel project as well as measures to mitigate them.

In the next chapter we will look into infrastructure planning and pre-requisites for the Siebel implementation project.

# Chapter 13

# Siebel Administration and Set up

In this chapter we look into the infrastructure planning and prerequisites for the Siebel implementation project and describe the initial set up and ongoing administration tasks that are essential for implementing Siebel. The chapter gives an overview of the administrative and initial set up tasks related with the Siebel applications environment that we had discussed in Chapter 10.

## 13.1 SIEBEL SERVER ADMINISTRATION

The Siebel Server is the middleware tier platform that supports both the back-end and interactive processes for every Siebel Client. These processes are components within the Siebel Server architecture executing in both multi-process and multi-threaded models:

- Siebel Server Manager
- Siebel Server Components
- Siebel ISS Transaction Server
- Siebel Application Object Manager
- Siebel Clients
- Siebel File System
- Siebel Report Server
- Siebel Remote
- Siebel Replication Manager
- Siebel Communications Etc.

In the following, we look at the administering environment and some aspects of the setting and configuration of these components.

### 13.1.1 Siebel Server Manager

The Siebel Server Manager is the management console for the Siebel Enterprise Server and Siebel Server. It provides the facility to configure the parameters determining the operations of each of the components as also the Siebel Servers that it can run on.

Siebel Manager can be used to:

- Manage the configuration of the Siebel Enterprise Server, Siebel Servers, components and tasks
- Operate the Siebel Servers, components and tasks including start, stop, pause and resume
- Monitor the status and collect statistics across the Siebel Enterprise Server, Siebel Servers, components and tasks

The Siebel Server runs as a system service that monitors and controls the state of every server component operating on that Siebel Server. It runs as a Windows service in a Windows environment and as a daemon process in a UNIX environment.

Siebel Server Manager can be operated using the following two interfaces:

Graphical User Interface (GUI) by employing the Server Administration views in the Siebel application client

- Enterprise Server Administration
  - Starting the Enterprise Server
  - Shutting Down the Enterprise Server
- Siebel Server administration
  - Monitoring the Siebel Server
  - Starting the Siebel Server
  - Shutting Down the Siebel Server
- Component Group and Server Component Administration
- Component Job Administration
- Component Request Administration
- Server Task Administration
  - Monitoring Server Tasks
  - Administering Server Tasks
- Parameter administration
  - Administering Task Parameters
  - Administering Server Parameters
  - Administering Component Parameters
  - Administering Task Parameters
- State Value Administration
  - Sub-system state values
  - Component-specific state values
- Statistic Administration
  - Sub-system state statistics
  - Component-specific state values statistics
- Event Logging Administration
  - Configuring Events

    Configuring Server Events

Configuring Component Events

- Viewing Event Logs

  Server Event Logs

  Component Event Logs

Command-line interface for regular batch processing: The command-line interface of the Server Manager is the **srvrmgr** program. The Server Manager commands are grouped in several categories as listed below:

- Help
- Environment
- List
- Server Management
- Component Group Definition
- Component Definition
- Component Management
- Task Management
- Parameter Management
- Named Sub-system Management
- List Definition
- Event Logging
- Preferences

## 13.1.2 Siebel Server Components

The Siebel Server components are designed to scale effectively across multiple processors in a single Siebel Server or across multiple Siebel Servers. The Siebel Administrator has the complete flexibility regarding the distribution of the server components across multiple servers within an enterprise. When the Siebel Enterprise Server is installed, pre-defined components are automatically configured for each component type and assigned to each Siebel Server within the enterprise. One can either run the entire suite of Siebel application deployment using these pre-defined components or customize them to suit specific requirements. Please refer to Table 10.1 for a select list of the pre-defined Siebel Server Component groups.

The setting up and administration of Siebel Server Components involves:

- Component group and server component administration
  - Configuring Component Groups and Server Components

    Creating Component Groups

    Creating Defined Components

    Assigning Components Groups to Siebel Services

    Enabling Assigned Component Groups at the Enterprise Level

    Synchronizing Server Components

Re-configuring server components
- Administering component groups and server components
  Administering Server Components
  Administering Component Groups
  Configuring Automatic Restart
  Configuring Database Reconnect
  Monitoring component group status
- Component Job Administration
- Component Request Administration
  - Running Component Requests
  - Deleting Component Requests
  - Monitoring Component Requests
  - Running Repeating Component Requests
  - Deleting Repeating Component Requests
  - Monitoring Repeating Component Request Status

### 13.1.3 Siebel ISS Transaction Server

After installing Siebel ISS Transaction (Transact) Server, the following properties need to be set in the **app_config.js** file that is located in the Custom directory where the Siebel browser-based application has been installed.

**Table 13.1 Transact Properties that are Required to be Set in App_config**

| Property | Description |
|---|---|
| Transact Active | Turns on/off Transact |
| Transact Not Active Msg. | Sets the message that appears if a user tries to access Transact functionality when TRANSACT_ACTIVE is set to 'false' |
| Transact URL | Sets the URL of Siebel Transact |
| Transact Third-party Cart | Determines if a third-party cart is to be used |
| Transact Show Cart URL | Sets the URL for using the third-party cart |
| Transact Cart Winargs | Sets the Windows properties for the shopping cart that is used for opening a window for the third-party cart |
| Transact Cart Target | Determines if the Transact cart will appear in a window ('_new') or in a frame ('framename') |

**Table 13.2 Transact Properties that are Required to be Set in the Property Editor**

| Property | Description |
|---|---|
| Transact Log Debug | Sets the Transact log to debug on or off. When 'off', only errors are logged, but when it is 'on' all activities are recorded in detail |
| Transact Log Filename | The filename of the Transact log file. This property requires an absolute path |
| Transact URL | The URL of Transact relative to that of the Application Server |
| eAdvisor URL | The URL of the Siebel eAdvisor application |
| Use Third-Party Cart | Determines whether or not Transact is using a third-party shopping cart |
| OMS URL | Sets the URL of the Order Management System (OMS) that will accept XML from Transact |
| Transact Cart XSLT | The URL or absolute file path of the XSLT style sheet that Transact will use to convert data to the desired XML format |
| Form Post JSP Page | While using a third-party cart, for using a form post. Enter the name of the JSP page that is used for dynamically creating this form |
| SMTP Server | Sets the name of the e-mail server via which configuration e-mails will be sent |
| Configuration Time-Out Period | Sets the number of days after which the configuration files are removed from the configuration list |
| Use Multiple OMS | Determines whether or not using multiple OMS |
| Multi-OMS Redirect | If using multiple OMS, sets the URL that will be displayed after the user clicks 'add to cart' |
| email Flag | Determines whether or not using the e-mail function |
| Display shopping cart flag | Determines whether or not the shopping cart will be displayed after the user clicks 'Add to Cart' |
| Shopping cart opener | If using customized shopping cart, modifies this parameter to refer to the previous frame context |
| Login required action | Specifies login required actions from **mar_guest_ok** parameter |
| List quote database table name | Specifies the database table name for list quote action |
| List package database table name | Specifies the database table name for list package action |
| List quote/package database user id | Specifies the database user ID for list quote/package action |
| List quote/package database user password | Specifies the database user password for list quote/package action |
| List package/quote database source name | Specifies the data source name for list package/quote action |

For instance, when a user clicks 'Add to Cart', the selected products are sent to the Order Management System (OMS). Using different OMSs for different page sets will need:

- Setting the Use Multiple OMS property in the Properties Editor to 'true'
- Implement the InitAltOMSUrl function to specify the OMS URL that will be accessed by each page set

## 13.1.4 Siebel Application Object Manager

Siebel Application Object Managers are hosted as components in the Siebel Server that enables it to service multiple Siebel Web Client users; they can be configured to run as multi-threaded processes in the Siebel Server.

The behavior of Siebel Application Object Manager components is controlled by a number of Application Object Manager-specific and generic parameters that are accepted at the time of start-up. By adjusting the value of generic and component-specific parameters the performance of the Siebel Application Object Manager can be enhanced. While setting up the eBusiness applications various parameters affecting the performance such as the type of application, language code, compression setting, encryption setting, number of processes for each component, number of threads/ tasks per process, envisaged number of users, and so on need to be considered.

A list of such parameters is given below:

- Compression Type
- Encryption Type
- Error Flags
- Flush Frequency
- Language Code
- Log print Timestamp
- Maximum Number of Archived Trace Files
- Maximum Trace File Size
- Password
- Static Port Number
- Trace Flags
- User Name
- Load Balanced
- Maximum MT Servers
- Minimum MT Servers
- Maximum Tasks
- Multi-Threaded
- Session Manager

The Siebel Application Object Managers can be monitored at the following three levels:

- Server level using the Siebel Server

- Component level using the Application Manager components
- Task level using the Application Object Manager tasks

  Each of these levels allow:

  - Use of the Server Administration views to monitor

    State values

    Statistics

    Log file
  - Use of the Server Components Parameters views to set the Application Object Manager-specific parameters. At the component event level, SQL Tracing can also be enabled to view the SQL select Application Object Managers.
  - Start, stop, pause or resume any Siebel Application Object Manager tasks

Application Object Manager-specific statistics that can be viewed at the component level or the task level are listed in Table 13.3.

**Table 13.3 Application Object Manager-specific Statistics**

| Property | Description |
|---|---|
| Average Connect Time | Average connect time for an Application Object Manager session |
| Average Reply Size | Average size of reply message generated by the Application Object Manager |
| Reply Messages | Total number of reply messages sent by the Application Object Manager |
| Total Reply Size | Total size (in bytes) of reply messages received by the Application Object Manager |
| Average Request Size | Average size of request messages received by the Application Object Manager |
| Average Request Per Session | Average number of requests received by the Applications Object Manager per Application Object Manager session |
| Request Messages | Total number of request messages received by the server |
| Total Request Size | Total size in bytes of request messages received by the Application Object Manager |
| Average Response Time | Average Application Object Manager response time to a request |
| Total Response Time | Total Application Object Manager response time in seconds |
| Average Think Time | Average time between requests from the client |
| Total Think Time | Total client think time in seconds or the total amount of elapsed time between client requests |

## 13.1.5 Siebel Clients

Siebel Mobile and Dedicated Web clients use configuration files to hold the information that determines, at startup, the behavior of the clients.

**Table 13.4 A Select List of Configuration Files and Associated Siebel Applications**

| Configuration File | Application |
|---|---|
| emailresp.cfg | Siebel email Response |
| erm.cfg | Siebel Employee Relationship Management |
| market.cfg | Siebel Marketing |
| pmanager.cfg | Siebel Partner Manager |
| service.cfg | Siebel Service |
| sfs.cfg | Siebel Field Service |
| siebel.cfg | Siebel Sales |
| uagent.cfg | Siebel Call Center |

Setting up of Mobile Web Clients involves activities like:

- Establishing Autodial Preferences
- Setting up Synchronization Parameters
- Registering the Mobile Web Client
- Using Routing Models
- Running Database Extract for a Mobile Web Client
- Initializing a Mobile Web Client database
- Creating Mobile Web Client User Accounts and Privileges

## 13.1.6 Siebel File System

Siebel Clients can also access the appropriate Siebel Server directly via the File System Manager (FSM) server component that processes these requests through interaction with the Siebel File System directory.

Sfscleanup.exe is the Siebel File System Cleanup command-line utility located within the bin sub-directory within the Siebel Server root directory. This utility will perform one of the several operations to each file in the file attachment directory depending on the type of the file and the set of parameters given for execution.

## 13.1.7 Siebel Remote

Siebel Remote enables true mobile computing by providing a complete exchange of information between your mobile computer and the corporate server. Mobile users can also synchronize to upload local changes to the server, initiate requests for information and download any new information from the corporate server.

Siebel Remote administration involves activities like:

- Starting and Stopping Siebel Remote Server Components
  - Generate New Database
  - Database Extract
  - Synchronization Manager
  - Transaction Processor
  - Transaction Router
  - Transaction Merger
- Monitoring of the Siebel Remote operations involve:
  - Monitoring Mobile Client Status
  - Monitoring Transaction Logs
  - Monitoring Siebel Remote Server Operations Status
  - Siebel Remote Transmission Failure
  - Siebel Remote Server Failure
  - Siebel Remote Server Media Failure
  - File Server Media Failure
  - Database Server Failure
  - Database Server Media Failure
  - Client Database Failure

Data synchronization

- Managing synchronization frequency
- Managing Mobile Web client
- Changing Routing Models
- Adding New Mobile Users

#### 13.1.7.1 Dock Objects and Routing

Siebel applications provide pre-configured user routing rules that cover a combination of implicit security rules (based on responsibility) and assignment rules that determine the mobile user's access to information.

Each mobile user is associated with one Routing model including a set of routing rules that collectively determine whether a record will be routed to a mobile client. These models define what data and what follow-up transactions will be routed to mobile Web clients belonging to that model. The local database sizes are reduced by a careful application of the docking rules; the docking visibility rules determine which records from the server database are propagated to each mobile user. This helps in minimizing the size of the local databases and the connect time to download a database extract and to synchronize; this results in enhancing the scalability and performance of the synchronization process.

Some of the routing models available out-of-the-box are as follows:

- Sales Representative Standard
- Sales Manager Standard
- Field Technician
- Senior Field Engineer
- Field Engineer
- Consultant
- Analyst

## 13.1.8 Siebel Replication Manager

Siebel Replication Manager distributes copies of data in order to support subordinate Siebel installations called Regional Nodes. As we have seen in Chapter 10, each Regional Node is a separate Enterprise Server with a Siebel Database, Siebel Servers and Siebel File System for an identified sub-set of the connected and mobile users.

Setting up of the Siebel Replication Manager involves activities like:

- Defining the Regional Node
  Registering a Regional Node
  Adding Mobile Users to the Regional Node
- Extracting the Regional Database
- Initializing the Regional Database
- Configuring Replication Manager for Mobile Web clients
- Starting a Replication Agent

Administration of Siebel Replication involves:

- Activating, De-activating and Re-activating a Regional Node
- Managing Components supported on a Regional Node
- Managing Mobile Databases on a Regional Node
- Managing Synchronization
- Managing Security and Authentication
- Performing Backup and Recovery of Data

## 13.1.9 Siebel Communications

Siebel provides a sample configuration data in the Siebel database; the Communications Administration screen allows this pre-configured data to be modified to customize the Siebel Communications Server and Siebel eBusiness Applications to provide support for the envisaged business processes and communications channel. Communication configurations are primarily used by components like Siebel CTI, Siebel Reception, Siebel CTI Connect, Siebel e-Collaboration and even Siebel eMail Response in cases where the in-bound messages are routed using universal queuing or a similar queuing/routing package. Table 13.5 lists major communications configuration elements that are frequently created in the process of configuring the Siebel Communications Server.

**Table 13.5 Major Communications Configuration Elements**

| Configuration Element | Description |
|---|---|
| Communication configuration | Set of related data, including parameters, for communications used for agents working with channels like voice, email, and, Web collaboration |
| Universal Queuing (UQ) | Set of related data applicable to Siebel Universal Queuing |
| Communications driver | Commonly a library file, including parameters, that the Communications Server uses to interface to a communications system like voice or email or fax |
| Profile | Provides access to communications driver for specific contexts |
| Agent | Contact center agent, manager or other user in communications configuration |
| Automated Call Distributor (ACD) queue (agent queue) | A queue on the ACD that agents can log into; Agents can also log into multiple queues |
| Tele-set | Physical phone device used in a call center |
| Extension | Extension for tele-set |
| Mobile device | A device that can receive a wireless message |
| Event handler | Means for evaluating information received from the communications driver |
| Event response | Determines the response invoked by the event handler |
| Event log | Specifies logging behavior for event response |
| Command | Means for performing a communications action |
| Command data | Data applicable for a command |
| Response Group | Determines processing of out-bound communications such as email, fax or voice calls |
| Communications template | Provides structure or format for out-bound message using email, fax or wireless message; allows Siebel field data substitutions |
| Outbound communication request | A request to send content from communications template (optionally with field substitution) to recipients associated with an account using email, fax, wireless message or other channels |

The communications configuration data also includes communication drivers and profiles, through which Siebel Communications Server can interface with external systems such as CTI middleware, e-mail servers or wireless messaging systems.

Common types of drivers provided by Siebel are:

- Communications driver that supports interactive voice communications, that is, computer telephony integration (CTI), Dialogic CT Connect

- Communication drivers that support interactive communications capabilities for email and Web collaboration channels using the communication toolbar
- Communications driver that supports in-bound and out-bound communications for email server using SMTP/ POP3 protocols
- Communications drivers that support outbound communications for wireless messaging systems compatible with WAP, SMS, etc.
- Communications drivers that support other out-bound communications protocols like FTP

Communications drivers are commonly based on library files, such as DLL (Dynamic Link Libraries) files on Microsoft Windows or shared object files on UNIX. Each driver file must be written to support the Siebel Adaptive Communications API. Using this API, third-party vendors can write communications drivers to support a variety of third-party communications systems like CTI middleware, e-mail servers and wireless messaging systems.

Most of the communications drivers provided by Siebel Systems support single channel types, such as voice, wireless messaging, and so on. For instance, the driver Internet SMTP/ POP3 Server supports the email channel. Each communication driver record includes a *channel string* that is used by the driver to identify the channel type. For communication drivers that support multiple communications channel types, driver records corresponding to specific channels reference different sub-sets of channel-specific functionality depending on different channel strings within the same driver file.

### 13.1.9.1 Communications Configuration Process

The communications configuration process involves the following:
(a) Determining the Communications Deployment needs including:

- Determining the Siebel applications and other products that are envisaged in the implementation including Siebel Call Center, Siebel Service, Siebel Field Service, Siebel Sales, Siebel email Response, Siebel Wireless and related components like Siebel CTI, Siebel CTI Connect, Siebel eCollaboration, Siebel eMarketing, Siebel Universal Queuing, Siebel Wireless Messaging, and so on
- Determining whether the third-party products support the Siebel Adaptive Communications API
- Determining the communications channels and external communication systems that are envisage to be supported by the implemented system including voice, email, fax, Web messaging, etc.
- Determining the number of agents for each supported channel
- Determining which Siebel applications features, technologies or advanced technologies are envisaged in the implementation like global or distributed deployments, applications integration, work-item routing, multi-tenancy, send email, Send Fax, Send Wireless Message, workflow-based communications, the customer Dashboard, and so on
- Determining data and applications visibility issues related to the communications activities
- Determining available relevant infrastructure and resources for the envisaged implementation including tele-sets, extensions, workstations, ACD queues, and so on
- Determining the logic of customer interaction or dialog for in-bound or out-bound communications via the call center or the contact center

- Determining the requirements for performance, scalability, architecture, and

(b) Set up the Siebel Server software including:

- Application Object Managers for the various Siebel Applications including Siebel Call Center, Siebel email Response, and so on
- Server Request Broker which coordinates between the Application Object Managers and the Siebel Server components
- Siebel Server Components including:
  Communications Session Manager
  Communications Configuration Manager
  Communications In-bound Manager
  Communications Out-bound Manager

(c) Configure the Siebel Communications Server including the configuration elements, configuration drivers and profiles, etc. discussed earlier. Communications functionality for the Siebel applications is primarily configured using the Communications Administration screen via any one of the following views:

- Views for defining Communications Configurations, Drivers, Profiles, Agents and Tele-sets
- Views for Generating Reports or Reviewing Run Time Status Data
- Views for defining Templates and for Out-bound communications
- View for defining In-bound communications
- View for defining Web Collaboration communications
- View for Specifying message broadcast settings

Events can also be specified for the communications configuration. Siebel supports three types of events namely:

- Event handlers
- Event responses
- Event logs

Generally, event logs are created first followed by the event responses that are then associated with the event logs; the event handlers are then created and associated with the corresponding event responses.

(d) Configure the external communications system

This includes configuring PBX or ACD (Automatic Call Distributor) switches, CTI middleware, and so on.

(e) Put the Communications Server in Production

### 13.1.9.2 Communications Administration

This includes administration of the following server components:

(a) Communications Configuration Manager—loads and caches communications configuration data for agents using functions supported by the communications Session Manager

(b) Communications Session Manager—supports multi-channel interactive sessions for agents using the communications toolbar for work items like voice, email and Web collaboration

(c) Communications In-bound Manager—processes in-bound work items, such as for email integration required for Siebel email Response

(d) Communications Out-bound Manager—processes outbound communications for email, fax or wireless message channels. Provides out-bound capabilities for Siebel email Response, send email, Send Fax and Send Wireless Message Commands. It also supports communication requests directly or indirectly through Siebel Workflow.

## 13.1.10 Authentication and Access

This section addresses the issues for providing employees, partner users and customers, access to Siebel applications.

### 13.1.10.1 User Registration

A user is registered for some or all of the Siebel applications with varying levels of access to the Siebel's database and features. Registering users entails creating a user record in the Siebel database that enables a user to be authenticated at login.

A user can be registered in the following ways:

- Self-registration by the prospective user at the Web site
- Internal registration by an administrator at the company
- External registration by a designated administrator at a customer or a partner company; this is typically implemented in business-to-business relationships

Several Siebel applications, especially Siebel customer-facing and partner applications, can be configured to allow or disallow users to self-register.

Siebel applications can also be configured to allow or disallow anonymous browsing that typically applies to Siebel customer-facing or partner applications. The anonymous user is a record in the Siebel database that also performs functions during user authentication and user self-registration. In case of an external authentication system, the anonymous user also has the corresponding record in the user directory. Unregistered users gain access to application views and the database via the anonymous user.

### 13.1.10.2 User Authentication

Authentication is the process of verifying the identity of a user. User authentication can be handled separately by each application; however, there are benefits in terms of lessening of the complexity of deployment in using a consistent approach to authentication across all the applications in a system.

Siebel supports three approaches and architectures for authenticating users:

- Database authentication relies on the underlying application database for implementing user authentication
- Security adapter authentication provides authentication to external systems
- Web single sign on (Web SSO) uses an external authentication service to authenticate users

Siebel Authentication Manager running within the Siebel Object Manager receives user credentials from a source determined by one of the authentication strategies described above, namely:

(a) If no security adapter is identified, the authentication manager concludes that database authentication has been implemented and proceeds with interpreting the user credentials as a database account and passes them to the application's Object Manager. The later opens a database connection using the account and identifies the user by the account. When the user logs in to a Siebel application, the user effectively enters the database username and password.

(b) If a security adapter has been identified without specifying a Web single sign on (Web SSO), the authentication manager concludes that external authentication by a security adapter has been implemented and proceeds to invoke the security adapter to authenticate the user credentials through the directory. A directory stores information that allows users to connect to a database, such as a Siebel User ID and database account, external to the Siebel database. The directory could be any one of the Siebel-supported Lightweight Directory Access Protocol (LDAP) server or Microsoft's Active Directory Server (ADS); the Siebel LDAP adapter or ADSI adapter is used to communicate between the authentication manager and the directory. The security adapter retrieves information on the database account, a Siebel User ID and possibly roles from the directory. The application's Object Manager opens a database connection using the account and identifies the user by the Siebel User ID.

(c) If a security adapter has been identified along with the specification of a Web single sign on (Web SSO) the authentication manager concludes that Web SSO has been implemented and that the user has been pre-authenticated by an external authentication service, and proceeds to invoke the security adapter to verify that the user credentials come from a trusted source. The authentication manager returns information on the database account, a Siebel User ID and possibly roles from the directory. The application's Object Manager opens a database connection using the account and identifies the user by the Siebel User ID.

### 13.1.10.3 Access Control

Access control deals with the access control mechanisms that enable control of access and visibility of data to the individual user. A Siebel screen, which represents a broad area of functionality, is a collection of views or applets.

Siebel provides flexible, efficient and easily maintainable access control depending upon the type of data, the type of parties and the access control mechanisms employed. Data types include master data, customer data and other data like price lists, rate lists, cost lists, etc. Parties are usually of six types, namely, person, organization, position, household, user list and access group.

The basic access control mechanisms include:

- Personal access control which restricts access to the personal data only to that particular person.
- Position-based access control typically reflects the reporting relationships among positions; for employees or partner users holding multiple positions, the access is determined by the active position. Position-based access control could be of three types, namely, single, sales team or manager.
- Organization-based access control can be deployed in three ways, namely, single, multiple or sub-organization; at any time, a user can be associated only with one organization to which the user's active position belongs.

- 'All' access control provides access to all records with a valid owner that could be a person, a position, a sales team or even an organization depending on the view modes that are available for the business component.
- Access group access control access is a means to control access by various types of access groups to various categories of data: groups are groups of parties, such as organizations, divisions, positions, or user list, except for a person, and categories are groups of data that are in turn organized into catalogs. Access groups do not allow access to individual master data but only to catalogs and categories of master data. Siebel allows creation of a hierarchy of access groups: if an access group is associated with a category, its descendent groups are also associated with the category.

## 13.1.11 Siebel Assignment Manager

Siebel Assignment Manager enables specific tasks to be assigned to the most qualified people by using the pre-defined assignment rules and strategies. Siebel Assignment Manager provides an extensive set of pre-built objects, rules, criteria and attributes to meet the automatic personnel assignment requirements of any enterprise.

The various components of Assignment Manager are as follows.

(a) Assignment Objects—represent assignment entities to which candidates are matched based on assignment rules. The Assignment Manager provides pre-defined objects:

- Sales objects like opportunity and campaign that represent an entity to which a team of people or positions work collectively until the entity is deemed to be complete or expired.
- Service objects like service request and product defects that represent an entity that typically, has a finite life cycle and the owner has the final responsibility for the successful completion of the assigned task.
- Sales and Service objects like account, contact, activity and projects that have hybrid characteristics of both the sales and service objects.

(b) Candidates—represent the people that are to be evaluated as potential assignees for the assignment objects. Depending on the type of assignment rules employed, candidates can be of many types, namely, positions, employees, teams or organizations.

- Positions are typically used as candidates in sales organizations, which enables for example, a sales representative to inherit the opportunities, accounts and contacts from another representative via re-assignment for that particular position.
- Employees are typically used as candidates in service organizations that enable, for example, to assign to a service request or activity only those employees that have the related specific skills and are also available for such an assignment.
- Teams are typically used as candidates in sales organizations that enable, for example, assignment of a group of individuals including a sales representative and a sales consultant who possess various skills or job functions.
- Organizations are typically used as candidates to enable a group of positions that has limited visibility to particular application data. For example, the distributors can be given access to the

product information but their visibility for access to price lists for these products may be restricted.

(c) Assignment Rules—are used to match assignment objects to candidates. For any assignment object, multiple assignment rules can be active at the same time, just as the assignment rule (which supports multiple selections) can also be applicable to multiple objects. Assignment rules use scores to rate candidates and its pre-determined assignment logic to select potential assignees.

(d) Assignment Criteria—are sets of conditions describing the attributes of objects or candidates, or both, that are evaluated to determine optimal assignment. Each criterion uses many types of comparison methods to determine if the candidates meet the criteria and candidates who satisfy the criteria will have the criteria score added to their total score. Siebel Assignment Manager provides pre-defined criteria related to sales and service organizations but customized criteria can also be created using Siebel Tools. Criteria values are details consisting of one or more attributes associated with criteria that are compared to an object or a candidate.

(e) Workload Criteria—is a special criteria type used to balance the load between candidates especially with service assignments. This criterion prevents employees from being overloaded in that candidates who have workloads in excess of the maximum workload will be eliminated from the assignment rule.

The workload criteria applies a workload score calculated as follows:

$$\text{Workload score} = \text{Score} * (1 - (\text{current workload}/\text{maximum workload}))$$

(f) Availability-based Assignment—entails confirming the availability of an employee for an assignment along with the following factors:

- Skills
- Expertise codes to eliminate under-qualified candidates
- Weighting factors to find the most qualified candidate by eliminating the over-qualified candidates

(g) Modes of Operations—available for running the Assignment Manager are as follows:

- Interactive
- Dynamic
- Batch
- Mobile
- Contact De-normalization
- Product De-normalization

Interactive assignment allows users to invoke the Assignment Manager to view the generated list of assignees and then override or confirm them on an immediate basis. It is invoked with the assign button in an applet displaying records from a business component that is configured and administered for automatic assignment through the Assignment Manager. Administration of Assignment Manager for interactive assignment entails setting the corresponding parameters in the cfg file. Siebel Tools can also be configured to add interactive assignment functionality to a workflow policy object.

> We are referring to a *.cfg file as cfg file for convenience. We will follow the same convention for other similar types of files like srf.

## 13.2 SIEBEL ENTERPRISE INTEGRATION MANAGER (EIM)

Siebel Enterprise Integration Manger (EIM) provides for *batch* interface for highly efficient data integration with external applications.

EIM uses a configuration file that specifies the EIM process to be performed, namely, import, merge, delete or export, and the corresponding parameters. Either multiple processes can be defined within the EIM configuration file and then a specific process can be invoked by using the appropriate process parameter, or multiple EIM configuration files can be created and then EIM can be specified to use the appropriate file.

As regards the parameters, these are of four types:

(1) General Process parameters
(2) Import Process parameters
(3) Export Process parameters
(4) Delete Process parameters

## 13.3 SIEBEL SYNC

By modifying the files listed in Table 13.6 certain features of Siebel Sync can be customized.

**Table 13.6 Siebel Sync Translation and Configuration Files**

| File Name | Description |
|---|---|
| Translation.txt | Contains information on mapping for transfer of information mutually between PIM and Siebel |
| Siebelsettings.cfg | Controls the synchronization process enabling or disabling the import and export options |
| Pimsunc.cfg | Determines the queries that expose Siebel applications data to Siebel Sync, enabling or disabling modifications by the user |
| Siebel.ini | Launches the Lotus Notes and Palm OS hand-held installers |

Siebel Sync administration involves tasks like:

- Installing Siebel Sync that comes separate from the Siebel Applications
- Defining queries in Siebel Applications to limit the number of records that are exported from a Siebel Application ensuring the synchronization process
- Selecting advanced synchronization options to customize it for specific requirements
- Creating filters for PIM data to prevent private data from being written to the Siebel applications
- Establishing field mappings in the Translation.txt file
- Setting up synchronization with a localized PIM
- Changing Siebel Sync configurations

# 13.4 SIEBEL APPLICATIONS SET UP

In this second half of this chapter, we discuss the various set up tasks related to the Siebel applications.

Figure 13.1 shows the Organization Model.

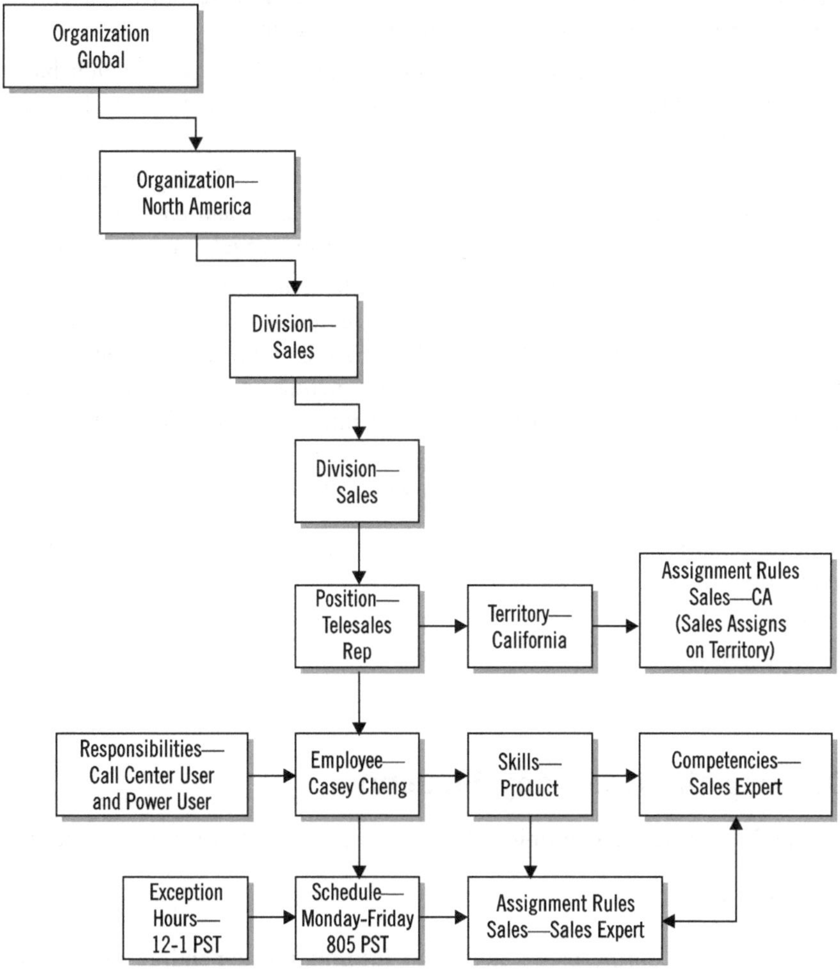


**Fig. 13.1 Organization Model**

## 13.4.1 Initial Set up

A successful installation of a Siebel system will have the following software:

- Siebel Gateway Server
- Siebel Server
- Siebel Database Server

- Siebel eBusiness Applications
- Siebel Tools or Siebel Dedicated Web Client

1. A Siebel system comes with the initial default administrative user ID of 'SADMIN' and password of 'SADMIN'. The Siebel database server installation script creates the corresponding Siebel administrator account automatically.
2. The Siebel license key is a series of numbers (up to 45 digits), which has associated information regarding license status (valid/expired), maximum number of concurrent users and date of expiry.
3. The Siebel application license contains some seed data, including organization, division, position, responsibility and employee records. This seed data can be used for testing or training or as a template while creating real data during a Siebel implementation.
4. Siebel eBusiness Applications include a complete sample database for a reference demo organization for undertaking demonstrations, evaluations and exploration of Siebel's functionality along with Siebel Client and Siebel Tools. The sample database that ships with the Siebel system has a built-in license key that includes access to all views and modules for a period of a year from the original license's initial shipment date. The sample database includes a number of demo user accounts that have pre-defined roles/responsibilities that reflect the particular demo user's position within the reference demo organization.

At the time of starting of the Siebel application from a Siebel Dedicated Web Client, the application can enable connection to any one of these data sources:

- Local Database
- Sample Database
- Enterprise Server Database

## 13.4.2 Defining the Company Structure

The enterprise's defined structure determines the access or visibility of the data within the enterprise.

### 13.4.2.1 Defining Views

As described earlier, views define user's access to information depending on their responsibilities within the enterprise. An enterprise has several kinds of relationships amongst its organizations, responsibilities, positions and people. The relationship between a person and the corresponding position is many-to-many; just as a person can have one or more positions, each user can also be assigned one or more responsibilities. While the responsibility determines which views the user has access to, the position determines the sub-set of data the user has access to.

### 13.4.2.2 Defining Organizations

Organizations are the major entities that constitute the enterprise. Siebel allows defining a multi-level hierarchy of organizations, divisions and positions. Siebel also enables defining skills for assigning employees to certain projects, service requests, and so on; skills have associated competencies that vary according to the type of the skill. Skills assigned to an organization are applicable to all employees assigned to that organization, whereas skills assigned to a position only apply to the employees assigned to that position. Siebel application's deployment allows organizations to be expanded to include external organizations such as channel partners and resellers. Siebel BusObjects can be enabled for a single or multiple organizations or none.

The definition of organizations entails the following benefits:

- Enables the enterprise to be partitioned into logical groups
- Enables limitation of access or visibility based on the organizational structure to which the positions are assigned
- Enables determination of access to both the master data (products, services, price lists, and so on) and customer data (accounts, opportunities, service requests, and so on)
- Enables assignment of skills to organizations that allows the Assignment Manager to route transactions based on the organizational structure
- Enables the setting up of multi-tenancy for call centers

#### 13.4.2.3 Divisions

Divisions are constituents of organizations and are helpful in grouping positions, reporting and for maintaining default currencies.

#### 13.4.2.4 Setting Up Position and Position Skills

A 'Position' represents a job slot within an organization. For an organization, each position is typically associated only with one employee; but in the case of job-sharing situations a position may be associated with more than one employee. However, in the later case, only one of the employees is the primary one. For instance, only the primary employee appears in the Account Team, Opportunity Sales Team, and Contact Access lists, even though all the employees in these teams can access the My Accounts, My Opportunities and My Contact Views. Positions can also be set up in a multi-level hierarchy. Positions and position skills are relevant in Siebel Assignment and Siebel Workflow modules.

If an employee needs to have access or visibility across multiple organizations, a position must be created in each of these organizations and that employee must be assigned to each of these corresponding positions.

#### 13.4.2.5 Setting Up Responsibilities

The views of Siebel application's information and functions that the users have access to are determined by responsibilities and correspond to the job functions within the organization. All users must have responsibilities assigned to them because without any responsibility a user cannot access any views and hence, cannot use the Siebel applications. Generally, the assignment of responsibilities to an employee is performed in the Employee Administration View rather than the Responsibility Administration View, although it can be done in either place. However, the later place is more efficient when responsibilities have to be defined for a larger number of employees. Definition of a responsibility entails specifying the views that are available to that responsibility and for this the seed responsibilities that come with the Siebel license are used as a base and then customized for specific requirements.

For instance, the System Administrator responsibility allows access to all views and should not be associated with end-users. System Preferences view should be accessible only to a select group of administrators because this view controls many system-wide functions like server logic and processing for Siebel Remote and Territory Assignment.

**Table 13.7 Responsibilities Seed Data**

| Name | Description |
|---|---|
| Web Anonymous User | Views provided for anonymous browsing |
| Web Registered User | Views provided for a typical registered user |
| Web Delegated Customer Administrator | Includes views of the Web registered user plus views for administering users |
| Web Corporate User | Views for eSales corporate user |
| Web Purchasing Manager | Views for eSales purchasing manager |
| eAuction Registered Bidder | Views for eAuction registered bidder |
| eAuction Registered Lister | Views for eAuction registered lister |
| eAuction Auction Administration | Views for administering auctions, catalogs and categories, but not administering users |
| Unregistered Partner Agent | Views provided for anonymous browsing |
| Self-registered Partner Agent | Limited set of views provided for a user who self-registers |
| Partner Relationship Manager | Views for eChannel partner portal partner relationship manager |
| Partner Operations Manager | Views for eChannel partner portal partner operations manager, including views for administering users |
| Partner Sales Manager | Views for eChannel partner portal partner sales manager |
| Partner Service Manager | Views for eChannel partner portal partner service manager |
| Partner Service Rep | Views for eChannel partner portal partner service rep |
| Registered Customer Wireless | Views provided for a registered eService user on a wireless device |
| Web Training Manager | Views that allow an administrator to see his or her direct reports' course and curriculum enrolment information |
| Training Administrator | Views that allow complete administrator of courses and enrollees |

### 13.4.2.6 Setting Up Employees and Employee Skills

The database administrator first defines a database user (with an user id and password) who can then be set up as a Siebel application user by adding a user record in each Siebel application. Then the user's personal information is added and he is assigned at least one responsibility to enable him to have access to any view. Additionally, positions, responsibilities, organizations and territories can be associated with an employee. Additional information including assignment rules, availability, utilization, requisite field engineer tools and so on, can also be recorded.

Siebel applications recognize the following types of users:

- Employees—individual internal users who have login privileges
- Partners—individual users in partner companies who maybe granted access to some of the data via a position in order to access any view
- Customers—individual external users who have login privileges to access some data without any position
- Persons—includes employees, partners and contacts with or without login privileges

In the case of a large number of employees, a large number of records can be added automatically by employing processes such as EIM import, database scripts or custom code.

### 13.4.2.7 Setting Up Access Groups and Categories

As described earlier, access groups are groups of parties such as organizations, divisions, positions or user lists. To assign (say) an individual partner to an access group, the individual partner needs to be first added to one of the user lists and that list needs to be associated with the access group. On the other hand, categories are groups of data that are in turn organized into catalogs. For instance, a category could contain all product literature and FAQs about a specific product. For example, the appropriate categories and access groups can be created to provide access to master data on a particular line of products to employees and partners who are involved with the selling of that product line.

### 13.4.2.8 Setting Up Preferences

Preferences control how Siebel applications operate in a particular enterprise's environment.

### 13.4.2.9 Setting Up Pre-defined Queries

Pre-defined queries automate some of the standard queries that are required routinely by the enterprise's users. The user does not have to create and run the query but merely select the query from the queries drop-down list. Pre-defined queries can be of the following types:

- Public queries that are available to all users of the application
- Private queries that are available only to the person who created them

### 13.4.2.10 Setting Up Lists of Values (LOVs)

LOVs correspond to the parameter tables of the traditional systems. A LOV is a set of values that populate a pick list, which is accessed when a user clicks a drop-down list in the user interface. Drop-down pick list can be of two types:

- A static pick list has a selection list that is a static list of values
- A dynamic pick list has a selection list that is a dynamic list of values populated in real-term, usually from the latest transactional data

The List of Values (LOV) record has fields shown in Table 13.8.

**Table 13.8 Some List of Value (LOV) Fields**

| Field | Description |
|---|---|
| Type | The type of list of values (the field name) |
| Display Value | Value is displayed in the drop-down list |
| Translate | When checked, indicates that internationalization is needed |
| Multilingual | When checked, indicates that the list of values is part of a Multilingual List of Values (MLOV) |
| Language Independent Code | This (along with the Display Value for MLOVs) identifies uniquely a list of values item for a particular LOV type. MLOVs enable a single generic list item to support multiple display values for users who access Siebel applications in different languages |
| Parent Language Independent Code (LIC) | Is used in hierarchical lists of values where the values displayed are constrained by the values selected in the parent drop-down LOV |
| High | Extra field for use by pick maps or for customization |
| Low | Extra field for use by pick maps or for customization |
| Active | When checked, indicates that the value is displayed to the end-user; else it is not displayed and hence, not available |

Siebel applications come with a standard LOV as part of the seed data that support the static pick on screens across the whole of Siebel applications. These are used as a base and then customized for specific requirements. Siebel provides facilities to set up new LOVs, add or modify values to the existing LOVs, inactivate values or constrain values depending on selections in other lists.

### 3.4.2.11 Setting Up Communications Related Standard Codes or Parameters

Communications related parameters required by the Siebel applications include:

- Default Country
- Languages
- Case Sensitivity
- Zip Codes
- Date Formats
- Global Time Zone Support
- Telephone Formats
- Pager Companies
- email, Fax and Mail accounts
- Industry

### 13.4.2.12 Setting Up Finance and Accounts Related Information

Finance and accounts related information required by Siebel applications include:

- Defining and activating Currencies
- Currency Conversions including Exchange Rates, Euro and Triangulation along with features like price lists, quotes, rate lists, and impacted reports like expense, forecasting and opportunity pipeline report
- Expense types like Food, Car Rental, Airfare, etc.
- Payment terms including names like Net 30, Net 60, number of days, discount type, discount days, due date of payments, etc.
- Accounting periods used in accounting, time sheets, expense reports, incentive compensation, forecasting, etc.
- Setting up Web browsers and capabilities including adding new Web browsers, configuring Parent and child Web browsers, etc.

## 13.5 SUMMARY

In this chapter we looked at the infrastructure planning and pre-requisites for the Siebel implementation project. The chapter described the initial setup and ongoing administration tasks that are essential for the Siebel implementation. We described administrative details related to the server manager and components, ISS transaction server, application object manager, clients, file system, remote, replication manager, communications, and user authentication and access. We also described an overview of administering Enterprise Integration Manager (EIM) and Siebel applications.

# PART IV: THE IMPLEMENTATION STAGE

This part presents in detail Siebel's eRoadmap implementation methodology through all its phases. Chapter 14 introduces the concept and context of eRoadmap and gives details on the eight stages of eRoadmap viz. Plan, Define, Discover, Design, Configure, Validate, Deploy, and Sustain.



**Siebel is very flexible. But in order to configure it correctly, not only is one required to know the business process requirements of the company, but one must be well acquainted with the Siebel functionality even before starting on the configuration. In typical Siebel projects, this is right at the initial stages of the project. This is the root cause for the large amount of effort and time required for completing the mapping and configuration of the base Siebel system in all Siebel projects. Although all the required functionalities are already available in Siebel all along, it takes some time to discover and use it correctly.**

Chapter 14

# Siebel eRoadmap Methdology

We discussed various aspects of initiating the Siebel project in Chapter 12 "Initiating the Siebel Project." In this chapter we will discuss the various stages of the eRoadmap methodology, which covers similar ground. The objective of dealing with the same issues from two different views is to illustrate the importance of adapting an integrated methodology such as eRoadmap. In this chapter, we see Siebel's view on executing a rapid implementation project. Siebel eRoadmap focuses on the key strategic and tactical areas that must be addressed to maximize the customer's return on investment while minimizing their business risk to ensure a successful completion of a Siebel project. The Siebel implementation is comprised activities logically grouped into eight distinct stages to ensure proper project management and control throughout the life cycle of the project. However, the stages are iterative in nature enabling customers to realize the 'quick hit' benefits of implementing CRM in the short-term, while also making possible re-visiting earlier stages and fine-tuning for better results.

This chapter is based on eRoadmap documentation published by Siebel. Users of this methodology must tailor it suitably to fit the needs of particular projects.

Only an overview of the Siebel eRoadmap methodology is given here. The importance of referring to the original Siebel eRoadmap documentation cannot be overemphasized. What we have presented in this chapter are the essential details of the various stages of the eRoadmap methodology. However, this chapter is not intended as a replacement for the colossal amount of instructive documentation, guidelines, checklists, templates, samples, questionnaires, and so forth provided and recommended for use by Siebel. Those are well-proven instruments and for an actual project it is highly recommended that you procure the version of eRoadmap corresponding to the version of your installation and use it in conjunction with the implementation project.

Some of the material in the following sections may seem repetitive. However, on closer scrutiny you will note that activities like project management, infrastructure support management, project reviews, etc., are common throughout all the stages of the project, and are referred to appropriately in the beginning and end of each stage. Similarly, since many activities go through the stages of planning and execution, we will refer to all such activities through their different stages during the various stages of the project. They are not being repeated; they are only part of the eRoadmap process checklist recommended by Siebel.

## 14.1 WHY DO SIEBEL IMPLEMENTATIONS SEEM SO COMPLEX?

The prime reason for the apparently longer duration of Siebel implementation projects is due to the peculiar complexity of the product. The contradictory demands of comprehensibility and flexibility are satisfactorily addressable in Siebel by reason of its repository-oriented architecture (in this chapter, we have mainly focused on the functionality aspects of this repository rather than the technical ones, which are also substantial). Fundamentally, this is not much different from the trend of parameterized packages that have been gaining ground among application software packages since the '80s. The main difference is the extent or degree of parameterization; Siebel is parameterized to a much larger extent. It is this property that enables it to be flexible enough to be configurable to the requirements of several industries.

The difficulty in implementing Siebel arises from the fact that the success of the implementation project depends on correctly mapping all of the company's customer-facing business process into the Siebel system. This entails the correct configuration of all the required process right at the beginning or at the initial stages of the project. As we have seen earlier, Siebel addresses the problem of providing usable application software systems by effectively short-circuiting the problematic requirements analysis phase, which is the bane of the traditional Software Development Life Cycle (SDLC) (see Chapter 2, sub-section "CRM System Represents the New Department Store Model of Implementing Computerized Systems"). Because of the demand for correct configuration right at the beginning, however, we are back to confronting essentially the same problem.

The majority of the risks for the ultimate success of the project are also dependent on this initial mapping being completed correctly, consistently and completely. Unlike the SDLC, where the end-users are expected to know only their requirements thoroughly, in the new dispensation they have the additional burden of having to become quite familiar with the functionality provided by Siebel. Thus, Siebel is very flexible but in order to configure it correctly, not only is one required to know the business process requirements of the company but one must also be well acquainted with the Siebel functionality even before starting on the configuration. In typical Siebel projects, this is right at the initial stages of the project. This is the root cause for the large amount of effort and time required for completing the mapping and configuration of the base Siebel system in all Siebel projects. Although all the required functionality is already available in Siebel, it takes some time to discover and use it correctly.

## 14.2 SIEBEL IMPLEMENTATION BEST PRACTICES

As stated in Chapter 2, Siebel elevates IT strategy as a part of the business strategy in which people, processes and technology are all organized around delivering value to their customers.

Based on experience with more than 3,500 Siebel initiatives, Siebel identifies the following best practices:

(a) Establish measurable business objectives
(b) Align your organization
(c) Develop an implementation strategic plan
(d) Establish program management
(e) Develop a user adoption strategy

(f) Phase the implementation
(g) Train users
(h) Monitor progress

These best practices have been developed over more than 10 years of product market experience and projects implementation experience.

> It must be noted that processes like change management, risk management or program management are not one-time but ongoing exercises. Periodic assessments will need to be performed during and after the implementation for effective (say) risk mitigation.

### 14.2.1 Enterprise Change Management

Apart from the tasks related directly to the deliverables of the Siebel project, eRoadmap puts a major focus on the change management issue related to the implementation of Siebel. Siebel implementation has a fundamental and far-reaching effect on the organizational and human resources aspects of the company, although not in the conventional sense of a corporate-wide Business Process Re-engineering (BPR) effort (please refer to Chapter 7 "Siebel and Business Process Management").

This organizational change management task deals with a series of change processes that facilitates diagnosing and managing change issues in order to optimize the organizational processes for sustaining the momentum required by the eRoadmap methodology. To contain the attendant risks, eRoadmap has devised a full array of processes like impact analysis, the assessment of baseline risks, program management, user-adoption strategy, organizational alignment, user training and knowledge transfer. We have dealt with some of these aspects of the change management process earlier (see Chapter 6, section "The People Factor").

## 14.3 INTRODUCING THE SIEBEL eROADMAP METHODOLOGY

The eRoadmap implementation methodology is the latest tool introduced by Siebel for an accelerated implementation of the Siebel system within an organization. eRoadmap provides a process-oriented, clear and concise implementation roadmap for individual implementation projects. This roadmap acts as a project guide that specifies stages, identifies milestones and generally sets the pace for the entire project to deliver a live system at top speed and quality utilizing the optimal budget and resources. eRoadmap is a structured implementation approach and can help you achieve a faster implementation with quicker user acceptance, well-defined roadmaps and efficient documentation at various stages.

The eight stages of the eRoadmap methodology are as follows.

(1) Plan stage—The team develops comprehensive strategies that serve as the baseline for the various subsequent stages of the implementation. This ensures that measurable objectives have been established, alignment of the enterprise has occurred and a vision has been articulated.
(2) Define stage—Siebel consultants work with client personnel to organize the project team, set the project approach and scope, and establish project management controls. The project sponsor then officially launches the project by presenting its objectives and timetable to the extended project team.

(3) Discover stage—The project team refines and documents the functional and technical requirements of the company's business goals. This consists of creation of detailed business process flows, documentation of detailed system requirements, and completion of a gap analysis of stated requirements against Siebel functionality.

(4) Design stage—The project team designs the solution using application screen flows and design layouts to map the requirements developed in the discover stage.

(5) Configure stage—The project team configures the application, creates any required extensions and integrates any external interfaces needed to support the system.

(6) Validate stage—The project team completes this in two parts. First, it conducts a full-function system test of the application with production data. Key users then perform an acceptance test to validate user requirements. The test environment evaluates the functionality, usability, scalability, reliability and performance.

(7) Deploy stage—The team conducts a production pilot that provides all the system's features to users in a segment of the organization's business environment, such as a region or district. Feedback from the production pilot guides the full rollout. Activities in this stage include final configuration revisions, production environment tuning, user training and data conversion.

(8) Sustain stage—The team measures the results, including user adoption and customer satisfaction. These are used as the inputs for the next phase of the implementation.

The eRoadmap consists of a wealth of checklists, spreadsheets, questionnaires, answers, document templates, recommendations, and so on. It also provides guidelines on important issues and includes guidebooks, learning tools and accelerators on more technical issues related to the Siebel infrastructure, installation and operations. The various reviews and checklists available from eRoadmap verify not only the implementation project itself, but also the stability and integrity of the system along each stage of the project.

The eRoadmap also includes change management tasks and accelerators that will be necessary for handling the changes in the organization resulting from the deployment of Siebel. The roadmap suggests measures that will raise the awareness of the impact of Siebel implementation and provide insight and guidance on how to manage this change. eRoadmap represents a totality of all the experience and wisdom gained by Siebel, its implementation partners and its customers.

Figure 14.1 illustrates the stages of eRoadmap methodology. We will discuss each of these stages. Figure 14.2 describes the major deliverables for each of these stages.

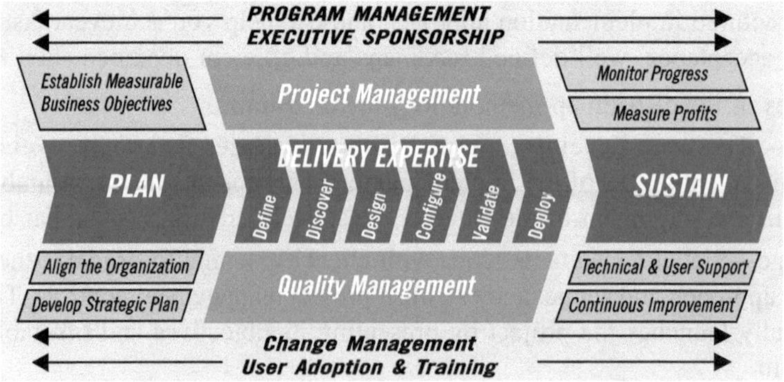


Fig. 14.1 eRoadmap Methodology Stages

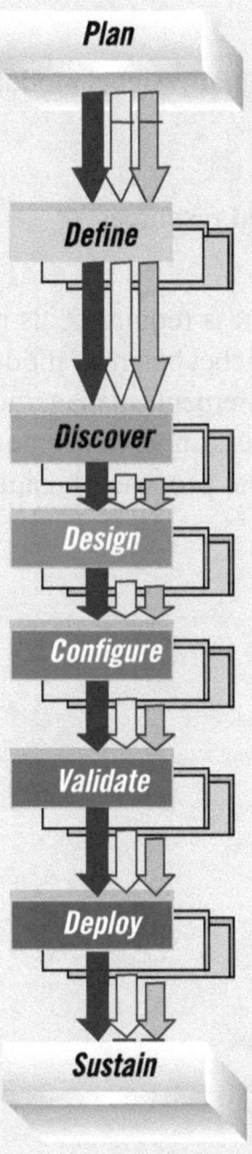


| | | |
|---|---|---|
| Plan | Strategies are developed that will serve as the baseline for single or multiple implementation phases. High level business requirements. Integration strategy, and technical architecture developed. | • Plan solution Blueprint<br>• Plan Strategy eRoadmap<br>Optional Implementation Readiness Review |
| Define | The project team is organized and then sets the project approach and scope. Establishes project management controls | Solution Scope<br>Product & Quality Management Controls<br>Product Quality Review Schedule<br>Optional Baseline Siebel eSurvey<br>Individual Capabilities Assessment<br>Getting Started Workshop |
| Discover | The team documents and refines the functional and technical requirements of the client's business goals | Detailed Business Requirements<br>Detailed Gap Analysis<br>Options Serves Process making sales Effectiveness Assessment |
| Design | The team designs prototypes using application screen flows and design layouts to map the requirements | Solution Design Document<br>Test Plans<br>Options Executive Alignment Workshop |
| Configure | The team configures the application, any required extensions, and external interfaces to support the system | Unit-Tested Solution<br>Optional MCS Software Integration |
| Validate | The team conducts a full function test of the application with production data, then key users perform an acceptance test | System Test Results<br>User Acceptance Test Results Detailed Gap Analysis<br>Optional Management Alignment Workshops |
| Deploy | The team conducts a full-functional production pilot to a segment of users | Production Pilot<br>Feedback from Production Pilot, which guides the full deployment<br>Optional MCS Process Implementation Workshops |
| Sustain | The project team conducts assessments and completes transition and support activities to contribute to the optimization of the Siebel product implementation and generation of high customer satisfaction | Implementation effectiveness Review<br>Ownershop Transfer<br>Measurement<br>Optional Siebel eSurvey |

**Fig. 14.2 Major Deliverables for Each Stage of eRoadmap Methodology**

## 14.4 PLAN STAGE

In this section, comprehensive strategies are developed that will serve as the baseline for single or multiple implementation phases. Siebel ePlan provides the essential blueprint for turning an organization's eBusiness vision and strategy into reality. The purpose of the ePlan is to execute the first pass at requirements analysis and application design for a Siebel implementation and to gain a high level understanding of customer functional and technical requirements of the customer. ePlan helps to optimize the Return on Investment (ROI) on the Siebel software and implementation project by leveraging the core functionality of Siebel; it also optimizes the project timeline, effort and costs by enhancing the use of Siebel's 'standard' that is, 'out-of-the-box' functionality.

Thus, ePlan

- Determines the business scope of the Siebel implementation, including how many Siebel modules will be required and what should be implemented
- Determines the complexity of the Siebel solution
- Proposes an initial project plan including estimated time, cost and required resources
- Proposes a customer-specific implementation strategy

The first step of ePlan involves conducting business workshops wherein business requirements are gathered for all business processes and their constituting activities. ePlan utilizes Siebel business models that have been pre-mapped to the corresponding Siebel functionality as well as requirements management toolkit (RMT) to create a solution blueprint document. The use of Siebel business models promotes greater use of 'standard' Siebel functionality. The solution blueprint identifies the proposed business solution and Siebel solution as well as the integration strategy.

The contents of the solution blueprint are:

(a) Proposed Business Solution

Organization Structure

Organization roles

Business Process Models including all Business Processes

Business Requirements

(b) Proposed Siebel Solution

Siebel Modules

Siebel views mapped to Business Processes

Gap Analysis

Data Management Strategy

(c) Integration Strategy

Integration requirements

Middleware strategy

(d) Technical Architecture

Topology

Network strategy

Client/server deployment

In the second stage of the ePlan, the relationship between business requirements, Siebel functionality and Siebel processes are analyzed and transformed by the RMT (along with other data, such as the organizational structure, channels, products and business objectives) to create an optimal implementation strategy. The resulting strategy eRoadmap includes a phased implementation plan, associated costs, timeframes and the level of effort necessary to complete the implementation. The strategic baseline thus created is used as reference for the analysis and implementation during the subsequent eRoadmap stages.

The strategy eRoadmap consists of:

- Phased implementation plan including timeline by stage
- Envisaged effort by stage
- Envisaged cost by stage

The ePlan strategic view can be validated and supported by a detailed Implementation Readiness Review (IRR) to provide specific guidance to mitigate implementation risks and address areas that could dramatically increase implementation success. The IRR can either be conducted preferably in parallel to the ePlan (before key implementation decisions have been taken) or following the ePlan to assess implementation risks, technical development and deployment strategy, potential sponsorship issues, education concerns, sources of resistance and project vision.

## 14.5 DEFINITION STAGE

In this section, we discuss setting up the right context for the Siebel project. The discussion addresses the issues of goals, objectives, scope, strategies and plans for the Siebel project. This establishes a framework for all subsequent stages, activities and tasks performed as a part of the implementation project. This stage deals with instituting the project organization, including the teams, roles and responsibilities. The project infrastructure including hardware and networking issues is determined and finalized. Sizing and benchmarking of the envisaged installation are performed and the acquisition of the Siebel system is initiated. At the end of the preparatory stage, the project starts officially with a kick-off meeting attended by the members of the executive and steering committees, project team members and Siebel consultants.

The Business Analysis team is responsible for defining the high level business parameters such as:

- Refining Business Objectives to ensure that the project stays focused on achieving the business goals
- Refining high level project scope to act as a reference for scope extensions at various subsequent stages.

This stage deals with the preparation and finalization of the project charter, implementation strategy and establishment of the project organization, as well as plans for various activities of the project, such as the budget, schedule, resources, and so forth.

### 14.5.1 Mission and Objectives of the Siebel Project

The project mission helps in orienting company-wide effort towards the success of the implementation as well as ensuring focus on the most significant aspects of the project.

The project charter establishes the success-defining criteria for the project. In view of the major investments of time, money and resources to be expended in the envisaged project, the first step is to seek the business drivers that the Siebel implementation aims to assist, after it goes in production. These aims could be knowledgeable responses to customer queries, quick turnaround times, minimization of errors in registering requirements for products and services, making the best pricing available to a valued customer, up-to-the-minute tabs on delivery schedules, error-free dispatches of goods and invoices, proper follow-up on payables, and so forth. Consequently, there is a need to define how the performances will be measured and to define a threshold of performances. It is important to realize that Siebel implementation is not an end in itself but a means toward the achievement of the business objectives of the company, which is not unlike any other similar major effort undertaken within the company.

Project benchmarks lay down the thresholds of performance that the Siebel implementation project must deliver in the envisaged timeframe. These include benchmarks for the implementation project itself, including milestones for achieving the various stages, and so on, but they also include business benchmarks on the post-implementation business processes in terms of pre-defined measures in tune with the goals and the objectives of the project.

## 14.5.2 Siebel Project Management Structure

These aspects have been dealt in Chapter 12 "Initiating the Siebel Project".

The following teams comprising the overall project team have been defined in that chapter at a high level:

- Siebel Technical Account Managers
- Siebel Expert Service Consultants
- Siebel Project Quality Reviewers
- Business Analysis Team
- Technical Architecture Team
- Configuration and Design Team
- Change Management and Training Team
- Deployment Team
- Systems and Data Integration Team
- End-user Training Team

Detailed descriptions of the roles and responsibilities of each team are defined later.

## 14.5.3 Project Management Policies

This addresses the task of establishing various standards to be adapted for the Siebel project, which includes project communications, recording project activities and milestones, system documentation, application-related quality standards, and issues on change management, team building, and so on.

### *(a) Prepare and Update Project Plan*

The aim of this task is to prepare a project plan in view of the goals, objectives, strategies, resources and budgets allocated for the project. This includes a resource utilization plan and a budget plan, as well as a schedule for achieving the project milestones. Obviously, this is not a static, but a dynamic plan that is fine-tuned as the project progresses through the various pre-defined milestones.

- Project Work Plan—It is vital to create a detailed plan of schedules, tasks and activities that aids in keeping control of the project effort. A clearly defined and disseminated plan also helps in orienting and focusing everyone concerned toward the achievement of the agreed objectives. The work plan addresses key variables such as activities and related tasks, milestones and deliverables, periods and deadlines, and dependencies of tasks, as well as the responsibility centers for these tasks.
- Project Budget Plan—A proper plan delineating all envisaged expenses can help in arrangement of proper funding and also for management of the project. The expenses budgeted cover consultancy fees, hardware, software, training, traveling, and so on.
- Project Resource Plan—The project resource plan deals with the allocation of manpower in required numbers and with the requisite background at the various stages of the project. Although Siebel implementation is very critical to the future strategy of the company, all necessary personnel cannot be allocated to the project on a full-time basis. The reason is simply because the company must run its business in the meantime! The size of the core team with its contingent of full-time members is rather small. Therefore, it has to be supplemented with members from the concerned departments and functions during the project. The Siebel resource plan enables proper planning and resourcing at the level of the company as a whole. The Siebel project resource plan dovetails into the human resources plan for the company.

### *(b) Organize the Team*

This task involves identifying, interviewing and allocating people to the various roles identified later. This also includes arranging for the requisite project infrastructure and administrative support personnel.

### *(c) Prepare Training Plan*

This task ensures that all members of the core and extended teams undergo proper training that might have been identified as an essential prerequisite for their roles on the team. It is also essential to ensure that members are trained in their areas of responsibility and in keeping with the role at right junctures; otherwise, too wide a gap between training and the actual delivery of learned skills might deteriorate the performance. In case of the latter occurrence, the plan must have provisions for refresher courses to ensure meaningful participation of all members in the project effort.

The training programs could be conducted in-house, at Siebel training centers or at a partner's training facilities. The courses will vary depending on the scope and the background of the various members of the team.

### *(d) Team-building Plan*

This task relates to all measures and plans undertaken for building a cohesive team, which is critical for the success of the project. It helps in arranging team events and programs for recognizing outstanding performance and contributions to successful completion of project tasks and also celebrations on achievement of major milestones. It helps in making the arrangements, scheduling these events, keeping a tab on the expenses, and so on.

### *(e) Project Communications*

This sub-task deals with scheduling of planned and ad hoc meetings, norms for agendas and recording of minutes, conducting meetings, and reporting on the issues, actions and status, as well as communicating with concerned people outside the project team.

### *(f) Project Monitoring*

This relates to the method of recording the effort expended by various consultants, project reporting, task start and end dates, quality reviews and feedback, maintenance of schedules, planning or rescheduling, approval procedures for new schedules, and so forth. This helps in maintaining the project schedule as per the project work, budget and the resource plan.

### *(g) Project Documentation Standards*

This task relates not only to the project work documentation but also to business processes, configuration and customization settings, company-specific enhancements, end-user documentation, and Siebel Services reports and inputs.

### *(h) Scope Management Plan*

These tasks relate to maintenance of the scope of the Siebel implementation project, request for changes, justification for requested changes, assessment of the impact of changes, pending requests and records of implemented changes. The scope management plan also helps to manage the approval processes for the numerous requests received during the course of the project. This is a very important activity because it is customary to get numerous requests for increases in scope of the functionality, which has a direct effect on the resource requirements, overall schedule, and budgets.

### *(i) Issues Management Plan*

This task relates to recording and follow-up on ongoing issues. It is very useful for reviewing and checking the status on suggested actions and resolutions, as well as following-up on open issues.

### *(j) Organizational Change Management Plan*

Organizational change is a very critical issue for the Siebel project plan. This task seeks to account for the various risks that influence the successful outcome of the Siebel project at the levels of the organization, team and individual members of the company. This plan acts as the framework for the various initiatives that are launched during the design stage. The plan identifies the activities, methods, deliverables, deadlines and reporting processes for status on the change management effort within the company.

### *(k) Strategy of Using Siebel Services*

Siebel provides many services at different stages of the project that provide specialized expertise for accomplishing the related tasks and activities in the optimal way. The various services available from Siebel are:

- Technical Services
  Siebel Support Web
  Siebel Support Offerings
- SiebelNet Business Services
  SiebelNet Hosting
  SiebelNet Managed Services
  SiebelNet Deployment Services
  SiebelNet Helpdesk Services
  SiebelNet Hardware Services
- Professional Services
  Scoping Analysis
  Project Management Services
  Design and Implementation Services
  Project Quality Reviews
  Upgrade and Migration Services
  Technical Experts
  Subject Matter Experts

***(l) Quality Plan***

This task deals with planned or on-demand reviews of the level of quality of various project tasks and activities and therefore, assessment of the risk and corrective measures or recommendations. This includes design reviews, configuration reviews, team walkthroughs, scheduled project quality reviews and periodic project audits. It also deals with third-party audits and follow-up on their feedback and recommendations.

## 14.5.4 Project Management Standards and Guidelines

The purpose of this stage is to establish standards and procedures for both the functional and technical aspects of the Siebel project. It relates to the standards applicable in areas of system configuration, testing, authorizations, enhancements and productive operations.

***(a) Implementation of Project Review Standards***

This deals with the issue of presenting a review of the project status at various stages. It includes updates on the milestones crossed, the status of various planned tasks, influencing or impacting factors, position of resource availability and utilization, infrastructure issues, performance issues, identified delays and corrective measures, and so forth. A standardized approach to review presentation makes it easier for comparison and assessment of progress across a period, as well as background references to the decisions made and supporting data for them.

### *(b) System Configuration Standards*

This task establishes the norms for undertaking and managing customization-related activity using Siebel Tools and Siebel Repository. This task defines standards for the authorizations for access to Siebel Tools, documentation on the customization and changes, and release and transportation of the customizations to the testing and eventually, to the production environment.

### *(c) End-user Documentation Standards*

This relates to the standards for the documentation and training programs and materials for the training of end-users. The documentation should be designed so that it is easy for a person to follow and perform his or her job.

### *(d) Testing Standards*

eRoadmap primarily follows an iterative approach to testing in which the same areas and functionality may be visited at more and more focused levels. The testing starts at the level of the configuration, proceeds to the business process level, and goes further to the user-acceptance level.

This task defines the overall strategy throughout the life cycle of the implementation project. The testing is done at the following levels of granularity:

- Unit Testing
- System Testing
- Integration Testing
- User acceptance Testing
- Stress and volume Testing

  and later,
- Upgrade Testing

### *(e) Post-implementation Services and Support Standards*

This task deals with planning the strategy for handling the post-implementation phase in terms of:

- Siebel Support
- Siebel Help Desk

This task dovetails into the general strategy of Siebel support of the post-implementation phase (see Chapter 15, section "Supporting Siebel").

### *(f) System Authorizations Standards*

This task deals with defining the policies, standards and procedures for maintaining the user's access to information, which is implemented through control of responsibilities, visibility and routing (see Chapter 11, sub-section "Configuring Access to Information").

### *(g) System Problems Reporting and Error Handling Standards*

This task primarily aims to set a project-wide system for addressing reported problems and their resolutions. This task addresses the issue of establishing a system that can transition smoothly to the help desk system envisaged in the post-implementation phase.

### (h) Change Control Management Standards

In a Siebel implementation there will be many occasions for admitting changes in the system that are in the nature of extensions or modifications of the Siebel software. This task deals with laying down the rules for requesting and justifying changes, specifying the changes, changing system documentation, testing and QA of the changes, and so on.

### (i) Siebel Tools Programming Standards

This relates to the specification, development, testing and implementation of programs including reports, and so on. It is advisable to maintain Siebel-recommended standards for programming, naming conventions, company-specific tables, screen layout style guides, repository objects, and so on.

## 14.5.5 Siebel Project Team Roles

The project sub-teams roles are detailed as follows.

### (a) Steering Committee Team

- Client Executive Sponsor is typically at the vice president level and has overall responsibility for project success. He takes the lead role in communicating a clear project vision, staffing and especially change management and has the final word on issue resolution, project budget and project direction.
- Client Business Sponsor ensures that the project implementation meets business requirements, develops project strategy, assists the project management team with project scope management, leads change management, communications strategy, resolves escalation issues, commits required resources, conducts project business reviews, and accepts and signs-off on project deliverables.
- Siebel Executive Sponsor is typically at the vice president level and has overall responsibility within the Siebel organization for communication, issue escalation, quality assurance and customer satisfaction.

### (b) Project Management Team

- Client Business Project Manager ensures that the project meets the organization's business objectives, develops project strategy, leads change management, resolves escalation issues, commits resources, and accepts and signs-off on deliverables.
- Client IT Project Manager manages the design and implementation of the Siebel application configurations and other related application development to ensure that the implementation meets the technical requirements, including those for the budget, performance, disaster recovery and so on.
- Siebel Project Manager serves as the primary interface with the client organization, creates detailed project plan, manages the Siebel project team, forecasts resources, costs and schedules, reports project status, manages the customer acceptance of deliverables, directs the change process, ensures adherence to the Siebel implementation methodology, quality reviews, and assists in managing project risks, issue resolution, change management, training, and so on.

### *(c) Business Analysis Team*

- IT Business Analyst interviews business users to determine and document business process flows and functional requirements. These are used subsequently to develop the test plans and criteria to determine client acceptance of the Siebel applications.
- Siebel Business Analyst compares the enterprise requirements against standard Siebel functionality in order to begin defining the changes that must be implemented to meet the target functional requirements.

### *(d) Technical Architecture Team*

- System Architect is responsible for monitoring, maintaining and planning for all application server, hardware and software systems.
- Database Administrator designs and implements data mapping from external sources and integrated applications. The DBA also performs data modeling, optimizes the database, performs database maintenance and administration, and develops backup and disaster recovery strategies.
- Siebel System Administrator is responsible for ongoing maintenance of Siebel processes and supporting data including:

Enterprise Integration Manager (EIM)

Workflow Manager

Mobile User Synchronization

### *(e) Configuration Team*

- Configurators analyze, design, build and test screen configurations and application extensions. They also contribute to the technical documentation and the knowledge transfer needed to enable the enterprise to support the system in the post-implementation phase. The lead configurator is usually a Siebel team member.
- Web Developers meld Siebel's Web capability to fit the enterprises's requirements. They design, build and test the functionality to ensure interaction with their customers seamlessly via the Web.

### *(f) Deployment Team*

- Deployment Team Leader develops and administers the plans, policies and procedures that determine the migration from development to test and finally, to the final production environment.
- Application Administrators maintain the supporting data by making timely updates to List of Values (LOVs), application setup data and other parameters that contribute to customization.
- Help Desk supports end-users of the application and troubleshoots system errors.

### *(g) Systems and Data Integration Team*

- Data Architects design and develop the interfaces to legacy applications, prepare data maps and data extracts, scrub legacy data, and design, build and test data exchange processes and programs.
- EIM Developer focuses on the creation of interfaces developed using EIM.

***(h) End-user Training Team***

- End-user Training Manager is responsible for developing the end-user training plans and curriculums.
- Curriculum Developers create the training materials including labs for both end-users and instructor guides. The material guides the end-users through realistic scenarios and ways to handle the situation in the Siebel system.

***(i) Extended End-user Team***

- Key End-users also termed as super or power users are knowledgeable users of the prior systems and give input on the requirements and also participate in user acceptance testing to ensure that the implemented system supports the envisaged functionality.
- Marketing Administrator is responsible for setting up and maintaining marketing information used in the Siebel applications to support the Sales and Marketing teams of the enterprise.

## 14.5.6 Checklist for Definition Stage

- Project Planning and Start-up
    - Supporting Materials
    - Project Startup Checklist
    - Set up Project in Project Tracking System
    - Prepare/Revise Initial Project Plan
    - Supporting Materials
    - Project Plan
    - Develop Client Communication Plan
    - Develop Baseline Risk Analysis
    - Supporting Materials
    - Project Risk Analysis Workbook
    - Assess Contingency Plan
    - Conduct Initial Customer Planning Meeting
    - Prepare Project Control Document
    - Supporting Materials
    - Project Control Document Template (see Table 14.2 for an outline of the project control document (PCD))
    - Project control document example
    - Conduct Follow-up Planning Meeting
    - Prepare Work Environment
    - Supporting Materials
    - Project Binder Template

- Project Closeout Requirements
    - Project Archive Requirements (a list of project files is given in Table 14.1)
    - Project Profile Report
      Customer Information
      Project Information
      Project Metrics
      Project Challenges and Lessons Learned
      Technical Implementation Profile
      Post-implementation Support
    - Staff Appraisals
    - End-user Satisfaction Surveys
- Project Control/ Reporting Processes
    - Establish Change Control Process
    - Supporting Materials
    - Change Control Agreement
    - Establish Issue Tracking Process
    - Supporting Materials
    - Issue Resolution Procedure
    - Issue Log Template
    - Establish Risk Tracking Process
    - Establish Status Tracking and Reporting Processes
    - Supporting Materials
    - Project Status Reporting Guidelines
    - Project Status Report Template
- Project Kick-off
    - Prepare for Kick-off Meeting
    - Conduct Kick-off Meeting
- Business Definition
    - Supporting Materials
    - Functional Requirements Definition Process
    - Document Business Strategy
    - Review Business Drivers
    - Review and Refine Project Objectives, Scope, Process Supporting Requirements
    - Supporting Materials
    - High Level Process Overview
    - Scope Definition Worksheet
    - Identify ROI Measurements to be used
    - Document Current Benchmarks

- Identify Critical Success Factors
- Project Team Training
  - Define Training Plans for Project Team
  - Register and Schedule Team Training
- Project Quality Review
  - Conduct Project Quality Review
  - Sign-off Definition Stage
  - Supporting Materials
  - Deliverables Acceptance Form

**Table 14.1 Archival Project Files**

| Topic | List of Files |
|---|---|
| Ongoing Project Management | Status Reports |
| | Project Meeting Minutes |
| | Steering Committee Minutes |
| | Change Request Log |
| | Change Requests |
| | Issue Tracking Log |
| | Risk Log |
| | Purchase Orders |
| | Customer Correspondence |
| | Deliverable/Stage Acceptance Records |
| | Project Quality Reports |
| | Timesheets and Expenses Reports |
| Plan Stage | Solution Blueprint |
| | Strategy eRoadmap Document |
| Define Stage | Proposal |
| | Project Control Document (PCD) |
| | Contract |
| | Project Kick-off Meeting |
| Discover Stage | Business Flow Diagram |
| | User Interview Documentation |
| | Functional Requirements Matrix |
| | Entity Activity Diagram |
| | Interface Diagram |
| | Data Mapping Matrix |
| | Logical ERD |
| | Gap Resolution Document |

*(Contd.)*

| Topic | List of Files |
|---|---|
| | Visibility Requirements Matrix<br>Technical Architecture Requirements Document<br>Support Architecture Requirements Document<br>Capacity Planning Questionnaire and Recommendations |
| Design Stage | System Architecture Design Document<br>UI Design Document<br>Feedback Tracking Documentation<br>Design Workshop Minutes<br>Workflow Manager Design Document<br>Assignment Manager Design Document<br>State Machine Design Document<br>Siebel VB/COM Design Document<br>Report Design Document<br>Application Data Administration Document<br>Data Conversion Plan<br>EIM Mapping Design Document<br>Functional Test Plan Scenarios<br>User Test Scenarios<br>Integration Test Plans<br>System Test Plans<br>Test Environment Specifications<br>Configuration Design Review Document<br>Siebel VB/COM Design Review Document |
| Configure Stage | Territory Grouping Matrix<br>Assignment Testing Matrix<br>Workflow Testing Matrix<br>Remote Synchronization Matrix<br>Configuration Review Report |
| Validate Stage | Functional Test Results<br>User Acceptance Test Results<br>Integration Test Results<br>System Tests Results<br>Defect Log<br>Defect Reports |
| Deploy Stage | Data Conversion Results<br>User Training Plans<br>Support Training Plans<br>Project Debrief Document |

**Table 14.2 Outline of a Project Control Document (PCD)**

| Item | Details |
|---|---|
| Project Definition | Summary of Project Objectives |
| | Project Deliverables and Milestones<br>Project Scope<br>Critical Success Factors<br>Success Metrics<br>External Dependencies<br>Project Completion and Acceptance Strategy |
| Project Organization | Project Reporting Structure<br>Project Roles and Responsibilities<br>Third-party Responsibilities |
| Quality Assurance | Quality Control of Project Objectives<br>Expert Services Reviews<br>Project Quality Reviews<br>Test Strategies<br>Configuration Management<br>Data Integrity Strategy |
| Project Controls | Progress Meetings and Reporting<br>Escalation Process<br>Change Requests<br>Risk Tracking<br>Issue Tracking<br>Project Filing<br>Deliverable Acceptance |
| Assumptions | |
| Initial Project Plan | |
| | Work Breakdown Structure<br>Project Timetable |

## 14.6 DISCOVER STAGE

During this stage, the project team refines and documents the functional and technical requirements of the company's business goals. This includes:

- Refining and documenting the functional, technical, architecture, data, capacity, performance and training requirements
- Completing a Gap Analysis to highlight the difference between the client's requirements and standard features of the relevant Siebel applications, and how to handle these differences

- Setting up the development environment, which includes all server, client and network hardware and software, and building the required databases
- Identifying the custom functionality and interfaces to the external systems
- Developing the deployment and end-user training strategies

Many of these and related issues have been dealt with in Chapter 7 “Siebel and Business Process Management”.

### 14.6.1 Define the AS-IS Processes

This stage establishes the starting point by defining the enterprises’ current business processes. During the ‘AS-IS’ process modeling, the enterprise highlights the business processes and sub-processes that require change.

### 14.6.2 Establish the TO-BE Processes

This documents the characteristics of the modified, or re-engineered or new processes envisaged in the Siebel implementation. The processes may be altered to achieve the stated objectives in terms of improved efficiency, productivity, turnaround time, quality, and so on.

### 14.6.3 Fit/Gap Analysis

This assesses the functionality that can be made available by Siebel applications vis-à-vis the functionality that has been identified as essential in the ’TO-BE’ processes. In order to decide on the strategy that can be adopted to bridge this gap the differential between these needs to be ascertained.

### 14.6.4 Checklist for Discover Stage

- Ongoing Project Management Activities
    - Manage Project Plan and Actuals
    - Write Status Reports
    - Supporting Materials
    - Project Status Report Template and Guidelines
    - Manage Financial Information
    - Supporting Materials
    - Budget Template
    - Manage Change Control
    - Supporting Materials
    - Change Order Request and Authorization Forms
    - Maintain Issue Log

- Maintain Risk Log
- Conduct Project Status Meetings
- Conduct Client Briefings
- Conduct User Communications
- Perform day-to-day Meetings and Issue Management

- Identify Ongoing Project Infrastructure Support Requirements
  - Identify Database Admin Requirements
  - Identify Server Management Requirements
  - Identify Network Administration Requirements
  - Identify Desktop Environment Requirements
  - Identify Siebel Application Administration Requirements
  - Supporting Materials
  - Environment Management Strategy
- Functional Requirements
  - Define/Customize Customer Interview Questionnaires
  - Supporting Materials
  - Scope Questionnaire Example
  - Prepare for Functional Requirements Kick-off Meeting
  - Conduct Functional Requirements Kick-off Meeting
  - Prepare for Business Process/Function Sessions
  - Supporting Materials
  - Business Process Scenario Example
- Develop Business Process/Function Requirement
  - Supporting Materials
  - Business Requirements Matrix
  - Create Business Process Flow Diagrams
  - Prepare for Reporting Requirements Session
  - Facilitate Reporting Requirements Session
  - Develop Reporting Requirements
  - Prepare for Workflow Requirements Session
  - Facilitate Workflow Requirements Session
  - Develop Workflow Requirements
  - Prepare for Organization Requirements Session
  - Facilitate Organization Requirements Session
  - Develop Organization Requirements
  - Prepare for Localization Requirements Session
  - Facilitate Localization Requirements Session

  - Develop Localization Requirements
- Operational Requirements
  - Prepare for Operational Requirements Sessions
  - Facilitate Ongoing Support Requirements Session
  - Supporting Materials
  - Help desk Planning Guidelines
  - Facilitate end-user Training Requirements Session
  - Supporting Materials
  - End-user Training Strategy
  - Facilitate Rollout Requirements Session
  - Develop Operational Requirements
  - Supporting Materials
  - Deployment Strategy
- Conversion/Interface Requirements
  - Identify External Interfaces
  - Identify Data Conversions
  - Determine Interface Performance/Timing Requirements
- Data Requirements
  - Document Functional Data Requirements
  - Supporting Materials
  - Data Requirement Matrix
  - Overlay Interface Data Requirements
  - Develop Integrated Data Requirements
  - Supporting Materials
  - ER Diagram Example
- Identify System Capacity and Architecture Requirements
  - Schedule Sizing Review (three weeks prior)
  - Gather Data for Sizing Review
  - Conduct Sizing Review with Siebel Expert Services
  - Identify System Architecture Requirements
- Identify Acceptance Criteria
  - Identify Key User Roles and Decision-makers
  - Gather/Review Current Systems Response Times
  - Gather/Review Application Performance Expectations
  - Identify/Document Key Functional Areas for Phase I
- Develop Gap Analysis
  - Write Gap Analysis Document

- Integrate and Approve Requirements
  - Review Requirements and Reconcile Conflicts
  - Integrate Requirements
  - Supporting Materials
  - Requirement Matrix
  - Obtain Sign-off on Integrated Requirements
  - Supporting Materials
  - Deliverable Acceptance Form
- Setup Development Environment
  - Create Development Environment
  - Build Development Database
- Project Quality Review
  - Conduct Project Quality Review
  - Sign-off Discovery Stage
  - Supporting Materials
  - Deliverable Acceptance Form

## 14.7 DESIGN STAGE

This stage addresses converting gaps from the analysis of enterprise requirements and Siebel applications into solutions.

This stage involves the following activities:

- System Design Specification that includes data models, screen definitions, business rules, reports, external interfaces and custom software development
- Unit and Integrated Test Plans describe the approach for the implemented solutions to be unit-tested in a standalone mode and again after it is integrated with other systems or applications
- Acceptance test plan identifies the tests that must be run and test criteria that must be successfully met for the system to have successfully implemented the agreed upon specifications.
- Data Conversion Design documents the plan for migrating legacy data into the Siebel environment

### 14.7.1 Use Cases and Process flows

Ivor Jacobson's Objectory method was one of the first (object-oriented analysis and design) methods to treat typical work interactions or scenarios termed as use cases, in a formal manner. A use case is a set of scenarios towards achievement of a single purpose. A simple format for capturing a use case involves describing its primary scenario as a sequence of numbered steps and alternative scenarios as variations on that sequence.

Use cases are of two types:

- Business use cases that are helpful in highlighting the flow of control in business processes
- System use cases that are useful in highlighting the procedural details of taking decisions

## 14.7.2 Solution Design

These solutions include setup or specific configurations, customizations or extensions of Siebel applications during the implementation. This also addresses the documentation of the envisaged solution along with the supporting setup documents:

- Technical and application architecture
- Performance testing approach and programs
- Create data conversion scripts and programs
- Initial testing and training documents

The technical architecture is designed to support standard Siebel applications, custom solutions, ancillary applications and third-party solutions.

## 14.7.3 Checklist for Design Stage

- Ongoing Project Management Activities
  - Manage Project Plan and Actuals
  - Write Status Reports
  - Supporting Materials
  - Project Status Report Template and Guidelines
  - Manage Financial Information
  - Supporting Materials
  - Budget Template
  - Manage Change Control
  - Supporting Materials
  - Change Order Request and Authorization Forms
  - Maintain Issue Log
  - Maintain Risk Log
  - Conduct Project Status Meetings
  - Conduct Client Briefings
  - Conduct User Communications
  - Perform Day-to-day Meetings and Issue Management
- Ongoing Project Infrastructure Support
  - Provide Database Administration Support
  - Provide Server Management Support
  - Provide Network Administration Support
  - Provide Desktop Environment Support
  - Provide Siebel Application Administration Support
- Define System Architecture
  - Prepare for Architecture Kick-off

  - Conduct Architecture Kick-off with Siebel Expert Services
  - Define Technical Architecture
  - Define Support Architecture
  - Refine Technical Architecture to Reflect Interfaces Design
  - Integrate Support Architecture with Technical Architecture
  - Design/Plan for Migrating Changes from Development to Test to Production Environments
  - Perform Application and System Infrastructure Strategy Review
- Application Design
  - Prepare Questions and Issues for Configuration Kick-off
  - Conduct Configuration Kick-off with Siebel Expert Services (three weeks lead time)
  - Map Physical Data Model
  - Supporting Materials
  - Business Object Design Template
  - Business Component Design Template
  - Business Component Design Example
  - Design User Interface
  - Supporting Materials
  - Screen, View and Applet Design Template
  - Applet Layout Example
  - Design VB/COM Business Rules
  - Design Report Definitions
  - Conduct Configuration Design Review with Siebel Expert Services
  - Conduct VB/COM Design Review with Siebel Expert Services
- Workflow/Business Rule Design
  - Design Workflow Manager Policies/Rules
  - Supporting Materials
  - Workflow Policy Template and Example
  - Design State Models
  - Design Assignment Objects, Rules
  - Supporting Materials
  - Assignment Manager Template and Example
- Application Data Administration
  - Supporting Materials
  - Application Data Administration Definition Process
  - Example Organization and Position Charts
  - Application Data Administration Worksheet
  - Siebel Reporting Hierarchy (position and divisions)
  - Define Application Users

- Identify Literature Items
- Define and Document Reference Data (list of values)
- Document Multinational Formats and Localization Plan
- Review Siebel Administration Screens to Identify Appropriate Reference Data

- Conversion Design
  - Create Data Conversion Plan
  - Define Data Cleaning Plan
  - Design Initial Data Load
  - Document EIM Mappings
  - Supporting Materials
  - EIM Mapping Template and Example
  - Review Mappings with Application Design Team
  - Document EIM Processing Design
  - Conduct EIM Mapping and Design Processing Review
- Interface Design
  - Review Interface Requirements
  - Design Recurring Data Interfaces
  - Document EIM Mappings
  - Supporting Materials
  - EIM Mapping Template and Example
  - Review Mappings with Application Design Team
  - Document EIM Processing Design
  - Design Archival Strategy and Interfaces
- Data Mapping
  - Document User Interface/Business Object Data Mapping
  - Supporting Materials
  - EIM Mapping Template and Example
  - Conduct Data Mapping Review
- Application Support Design
  - Define Help Desk Process
  - Design End-user Documentation
  - Design Run Book for Operations Staff
  - Design End-user Training Programs
- System and Integration Test Planning
  - Identify Key User Roles and Data Flows
  - Design User Test Scenarios

  - Review End-to-end Interfaces and Data Volumes
  - Review Data Visibility Hierarchies and Volumes
  - Identify Key System Infrastructure Risk Areas
  - Identify Type of Sample Data and Volumes Required for Testing Purposes
  - Design Integration Test Scenarios
  - Design Performance Test Scenarios
  - Define Test Environment (Hardware and Software Requirements)
  - Design Process to Build Test Data
  - Create Integrated System Test Document
  - Supporting Materials
  - System Testing Process and Description
  - System Test Plan
- Expert Services Reviews
  - Review Feedback from Design Reviews
  - Refine Design Based on Review Feedback
- Project Quality Review
  - Schedule Project Quality Review (three weeks lead time)
  - Conduct Project Quality Review
  - Sign-off Design Stage
  - Supporting Materials
  - Deliverable Acceptance Form

## 14.8 CONFIGURATION STAGE

This stage includes the following activities:

- Configure fully the Siebel applications to satisfy the envisaged specifications
- Develop a support plan for satisfying the identified requirements for supporting databases, networks, servers and applications as well as help desk procedures, problem resolution procedures and escalation procedures
- Prepare an end-user training program that is targeted to users attaining a desired level of proficiency
- Assemble a comprehensive test environment including installation of the hardware, software and databases
- Formulate a deployment plan to facilitate the migration from the test environment to production pilot implementation and eventually to a full production environment
- Review to ensure the veracity of the configuration effort

Many of these and related issues have been dealt with in Chapter 11 "Siebel Tools" and Chapter 13 "Siebel Administration and Set up".

## 14.8.1 Application Configuration

This corresponds to configuring the Siebel applications in terms of the:

- Various Siebel modules
- Configuration files
- Defining configuration parameters in the installed system
- Configuring List of Values (LOVs)
- Configuring Multi-Value Group (MVG)
- etc.

## 14.8.2 Application Extensions

This deals with two different types of extensions:

1. Programmatic extensions for altering the business logic by using environments like Siebel VB and Siebel e-Script
2. Database extensions which in turn can be achieved by using either the Siebel provided extension tables or custom extension tables when developers need extension even beyond the built-in database extensions

## 14.8.3 Application Interfaces

All of the enterprises' processes must integrate seamlessly to achieve optimum results. The combination of the in-scope business processes and existing systems or manual processes help in identifying the required points of integration. The issues related to application interfaces need to be considered carefully because they have far-ranging upstream and downstream impacts.

## 14.8.4 Checklist for Configuration Stage

- Ongoing Project Management Activities
  - Manage Project Plan and Actuals
  - Write Status Reports
  - Supporting Materials
  - <u>Project Status Report Template and Guidelines</u>
  - Manage Financial Information
  - Supporting Materials
  - <u>Budget Templates</u>
  - Manage Change Control
  - Supporting Materials
  - <u>Change Order Request and Authorization Forms</u>
  - Maintain Issue Log

- Maintain Risk Log
- Conduct Project Status Meetings
- Conduct Client Briefings
- Conduct User Communications
- Perform Day-to-day Meetings and Issue Management

- Ongoing Project Infrastructure Support
  - Provide Database Administration Support
  - Provide Server Management Support
  - Provide Network Administration Support
  - Provide Desktop Environment Support
  - Provide Siebel Administration Support
- Customize Physical Database
  - Implement Database Extensions to User Tables
  - Create EIM IF Table Extensions and Related Mappings
- Application Development
  - Configure/Unit Test Application and Reports for User Review Session 1 (URS)
  - Supporting Materials
  - Application Unit Testing Guidelines
  - Conduct URS 1
  - Obtain and Document User Feedback
  - Conduct Configuration Review with Siebel Expert Services
  - Conduct VB code Review with Siebel Export Services
  - Conduct Data Mapping Audit with Siebel Export Services
  - Refine Application and Reports—Unit Test for Final URS
  - Supporting Materials
  - Application Unit Testing Guidelines
  - Obtain User Sign-off on Application and Reports for Final URS
  - Supporting Materials
  - Deliverables Acceptance form
- Build Assignment Manager Rules
  - Build Assignment Manager Rules
  - Review and Set Object Parameters
  - Setup/Review Organization/Position Hierarchies
  - Create Assignment Rules/Criteria
  - Unit Test Assignment Rules
  - Conduct Data Mapping Review with ES
  - Conduct Assignment Manager Review

- Build Workflow Manager Rules
  - Review/Configure Workflow Objects in Tools
  - Modify/Create Programs in Tools (if needed)
  - Create Workflow Manager Policies
  - Unit test Workflow Rules Policies
  - Conduct Workflow Manager Implementation Review
- Remote Synchronization
  - Set Remote Synchronization System Preferences
  - Customize Remote Synchronization Rules if necessary
  - Unit Test Remote Synchronization Rule Changes
- Interface Development (Recurring Interfaces)
  - Obtain Sample Data Set from Source Locations
  - Create Program to Load Interface Tables
  - Create IFB Control Files for Import/Update Interfaces
  - Unit Test Import/Update Interfaces
  - Create IFB Control Files for Export Interfaces
  - Unit Test Export Interfaces, Including Load to External Systems
  - Review/Adjust Data Cleansing Plan Based on Interface Unit Test Results
  - Conduct EIM configuration and Performance Review
- Conversion Development
  - Create Extract Program(s)
  - Consolidate Data from Disparate Systems, if desired
  - Perform Pre-processing of Data as required
  - Create IFB Control Files for Conversions
  - Unit Test Source to Siebel Interfaces with Small Data Set
  - Adjust Conversion Programs Based on Unit Test Results
- Data Administration
  - Create Reference Data from Design
  - Create Required Marketing Admin Data
  - Create Required Mobile Client Admin Data
  - Create and set up Literature Files and Correspondence Templates on File Server
  - Create Application Metadata for in-Scope Siebel Modules
- Test and Product Environment
  - Set up Test Environment (hardware and software)
  - Build Test Database
  - Install Siebel Software in Test Environment
  - Set up Production Environment (hardware and software)

    - Build Production Database
    - Install Siebel Software In Production Environment
- Deployment Plans
    - Develop Deployment Plan
    - Supporting Materials
    - Rollout Planning Matrix
    - Training Curriculum Plan
    - Identify Resources required for Deployment
    - Sign-off Deployment Plan
    - Supporting Materials
    - Deliverables Acceptance Form
- System Test Plan
    - Document Testing Objectives
    - Document Scenarios to be used in User Interface Functional Training
    - Create User Interface Performance Test Plan
    - Create EIM Test Plan for Conversions and Integrations
    - Create Assignment Manager Test Plan
    - Create Workflow Test Plan
    - Create Mobile User Test Plan
    - Define Application Integration Tests that demonstrate End-to-end Data Flows
    - Define Multi-user and System Performance Tests
    - Approve Test Plan
- Project Quality Review
    - Conduct Project Quality Review
    - Sign-off Configuration Stage
    - Supporting Materials
    - Deliverable Acceptance Form

## 14.9 VALIDATION STAGE

This stage includes the following activities:

- Test the implemented Siebel applications in compliance with the Unit and Integrated Test Plans formulated during the design stage
- Implement the Training Plan developed during the configuration stage for especially the pilot end-users
- Establish the Production environment including installation of the hardware, software and databases

### 14.9.1 Production Pilot

This is undertaken for gaining experience of a productive Siebel module under normal operating conditions within the enterprise.

### 14.9.2 Feedback from Production Pilot

The running of a production pilot becomes the best input for full-scale implementation of a complete suite of Siebel applications or its rollout at various facilities of the company spread throughout the country or even elsewhere.

The production pilot could give valuable feedback in terms of:

- Functional Requirements
- Technical Infrastructure Requirements
- Data Management Requirements
- Security and Access Requirements
- Interface Requirements
- Performance Requirements
- Reporting Requirements
- Audit and Control Requirements
- Training Requirements
- Documentation Requirements
- Support and Help Desk Requirements

### 14.9.3 Checklist for Validation Stage

- Ongoing Project Management Activities
  - Manage Project Plan and Actuals
  - Write Status Reports
  - Supporting Materials
  - <u>Project Status Report Template and Guidelines</u>
  - Manage Financial Information
  - Supporting Materials
  - <u>Budget Template</u>
  - Manage Change Control
  - Supporting Materials
  - <u>Change Order Request and Authorization Forms</u>
  - Maintain Issue Log
  - Maintain Risk Log

- Conduct Project Status Meetings
- Conduct Client Briefings
- Conduct User Communications
- Perform day-to-day Meetings and Issue Management

- Ongoing Project Infrastructure Support
  - Provide Database Admin Support
  - Provide Server Management Support
  - Provide Network Admin Support
  - Provide Desktop Environment Support
  - Provide Siebel Admin Support
- Prepare Test Environment for Integrated System Testing
  - Migrate Development Repository into System Test Environment
  - Customize Physical Database
  - Build/Import Test Data in Test Environment
  - Create SRF from Test Environment Repository
  - Configure Client Machines to Mirror Production Environment
  - Configure Web Servers
  - Generate Triggers in Test Environment
- Execute Integrated Test Plan Testing
  - Run User Interface Test Scenarios Using all Client Types
  - Run All Reports and Verify Results
  - Run User Interface Performance Tests Using All Client Types
  - Run EIM Tests for Conversions and Integrations
  - Run Assignment Manager Tests
  - Run Workflow Tests (Workflow Manager, State Model)
  - Run Mobile User Tests
  - Run Application Test Scenarios Demonstrating End-to-end Data Flows
  - Run Multi-user and System Performance Tests
  - Review and Tune SQL Optimization and Index Usage
  - Review and Tune Database and Operating System
  - Compare Test Results with Expected Results and Document Findings
  - Analyze and Document Potential System Bottlenecks
  - Implement Changes Based on Test Results and Iterate Tests
  - Establish System Upgrade Plans as required based on System and Capacity Test Results
  - Obtain Customer Sign-off
  - Supporting Materials
  - Deliverable Acceptance Form

- End-user Training Development
  - Develop Training Modules
  - Supporting Materials
  - Training Curriculum Plan
  - Develop Training Exercises
  - Insert Screen Shots
  - Review Training Materials
  - Supporting Materials
  - Training Documentation Sample
  - Walk through Training Materials
  - Adjust Training Materials (All and Screen Shot Refreshes)
  - Insert Training Notes
  - Create Training Database
  - Create Training Installation Kit
  - Walk through Finalized Training Materials
  - Sign-off Training Course and Materials
  - Supporting Materials
  - Deliverable Acceptance Form
- Prepare for Production Pilot
  - Migrate Repository into Production Environment
  - Customize Physical Database
  - Convert Data for Production Pilot
  - Configure Servers and Client Machines
  - Create Setup Data in Production Environment
  - Generate Triggers in Production Environment
  - Run Assignment Manager for Initial Assignments
  - Perform Production Readiness Review with Siebel Expert Services
  - Schedule Batch Files for System Integrations
  - Train Operations Support Team
  - Obtain Customer Sign-off to Begin Pilot
  - Supporting Materials
  - Deployment Readiness Checklist
  - Production Environment Monitoring Worksheet
  - Deliverable Acceptance Form
- Project Quality Review
  - Conduct Project Quality Review
  - Obtain Customer Sign-off

- Supporting Materials
- Deliverable Acceptance Form

# 14.10 DEPLOYMENT STAGE

This stage focuses on bringing all elements of the implementation together to successfully transition from the production pilot to full deployment.

The activities during this stage include:

- Conducting the user training
- Implementing help desk

## 14.10.1 User Training

This task ensures that all end-users undergo the requisite Siebel training prior to the go-live phase. It should be in line with the plan and schedule data prepared during the realization stage. The training plan should ensure adequate coverage of all types of end-users but at the same time avoid redundant training. The latter is not only a drain on the resources but can also lead to losing precious time on a project, which may be under a tight schedule at this stage of the project.

The end-users can be broadly classified into

- Transaction users
- Query and analysis users
- Information users

The various sub-tasks involved in completing this task are as follows.

### *(a) Prepare for End-user Training*

This task deals with arranging the general logistics and also the Siebel environment for training including loading the company-specific training data into the training environment.

### *(b) Conduct End-user Training*

The purpose of this sub-task is to conduct end-user training. After completing this training the end-users should be able to handle their routine tasks on the Siebel system confidently.

### *(c) Review and Assess Post-training Skills*

The purpose of this task is to assess the effectiveness of the training in making the end-users comfortable with Siebel for their operational requirements. The feedback and suggestions should be used to suitably modify the future cycle of training courses. This assessment can also lead to identifying the requirement of all users to go through additional courses to enhance their use of the Siebel system. These courses could focus on specific areas of interest like reporting or querying information.

## 14.10.2 Data Conversion

This involves first reviewing the checklist of all processes and procedures that are essential for the successful conversion of data into the Siebel system including:

- Data to be converted
- Specifications of the data conversion
- Conversion programs
- Conversion program test data
- Conversion program test results both in terms of performance and converted data
- Manual conversion processes and procedures

Following this the conversion of all master and transaction data is performed.

## 14.10.3 Implement Help Desk

The deployment plan prepared during the configuration stage in terms of the processes and procedures as well as the roles and responsibilities of the personnel that man the help desk are refined here.

### *(a) Refine Help Desk Procedures*

This sub-task deals essentially with refining the various kinds of communication processes that are essential for the functioning of a help desk:

- Reporting and recording problems
- Handling, solving and tracking problem messages
- Escalating unsolved problem messages
- Escalating pending problem messages to Siebel
- Delivering information on solutions
- Demonstrating the solution

### *(b) Establish the Help Desk Facility*

This task involves organizing and installing the help desk facility, including:

- Installing the office infrastructure
- Installing the technical infrastructure
- Allocating personnel and resources to the help desk
- Training workshops for the help desk personnel
- Creating Help Desk users for the corresponding help desk personnel

### *(c) Organize Help Desk Resources and Staff*

This sub-task deals with the allocation and training of help desk personnel. The roles and responsibilities of the help desk personnel are defined and circulated to all end-users throughout the organization.

***(d) Long-term Production Support Strategy***

Here you define a long-term strategy for supporting the Siebel system to address the issues of:

- The post-implementation system changes
- Subsequent release upgrades
- The increase in scope resulting from the growth of business
- Training new employees resulting from the employee turnover

## 14.10.4 Checklist for Deployment Stage

- Begin Production Pilot
  - Update Converted Production Data if necessary
  - Train Pilot Users
  - Install/Update Software on Pilot User Machines
- Support Production Pilot
  - Monitor System
  - Support End-users
  - Review System Usage and Problem Reports
  - Conduct Pilot Review Sessions with End-users
  - Document End-user Feedback and Prioritize Change Requests
  - Make System Changes as Required
- System Rollout
  - Train End-users
  - Implement Help Desk
  - Train Operations Staff and Hand-off System
- Project Closeout
  - Complete Project Closeout Checklist
  - Supporting Materials
  - Project Closeout Checklist
  - Archive Project Files
  - Write De-briefing Report
  - Supporting Materials
  - Project Profile Worksheet
  - Write Staff Appraisals
  - Supporting Materials
  - Team Member Review Form
  - Survey End-user Satisfaction

## 14.11 SUSTAIN STAGE

The sustain stage deals with activities that contribute to the optimization of the Siebel product implementation and generation of high customer satisfaction. During this stage, the project team conducts Ownership Transfer activities such as End-User Education, Management Coaching Workshops and Field Reviews, as well as measurement activities such as Sales Effectiveness eSurveys, Executive Reviews and Implementation Effectiveness Reviews (IER).

The technical implementation challenges and risks rather than the technical issues are predominantly due to human factors related to the change. IER specifically addresses these issues by focusing on the end-user's experience with the implemented Siebel application. IER is usually conducted 2-3 months after the deployment.

The purpose of IER is to:

- Identify the end-user effectiveness of the implemented Siebel applications
- Identify the gaps that adversely affect the end-user effectiveness and hence, the user adoption
- Establish a baseline to benchmark the success of improvement programs and releases in future

For issues directly related to the end-users the IER involves analyzing the Help Desk logs, system usage statistics, assessing the effectiveness of training materials and user guides, and so on.

## 14.12 eROADMAP, BPM AND CHANGE MANAGEMENT

When a company adopts eRoadmap methodology for implementing Siebel, its success depends on how quickly it can implement changes in its Business Processes that are in line with the best-of-business processes in Siebel. While using Siebel, it is advisable that the company should avoid undertaking a Business Process Management (BPM) effort in conjunction with the Siebel implementation. It is recommended that the company should implement a vanilla Siebel functionality initially. Once the implementation stabilizes, then custom functionalities could be judiciously introduced later. The vanilla approach cuts down on maintenance as well as speeds up the time to production and benefits of the new system.

## 14.13 SUCCESS PATTERNS FOR SIEBEL IMPLEMENTATION PROJECTS

It is logical at this stage to summarize the lessons learned from the past Siebel implementation projects in the form of a checklist that can be referred to easily.

The following is a checklist of patterns of successful Siebel implementation projects.

***Success Pattern 1:*** Direct Involvement of the top management throughout the project

***Success Pattern 2:*** Clear project organization structure and strong project management

***Success Pattern 3***: Proper visibility and communication throughout the project

***Success Pattern 4:*** A company-wide Change Management Plan

***Success Pattern 5:*** Allocation of appropriate budget and resources

***Success Pattern 6:*** Deputation of experienced achievers and key managers on the project and not by people who can be spared from the department

***Success Pattern 7:*** Project must be driven by the user departments rather than the IT-department and implement only user-driven functionality

***Success Pattern 8:*** Implementation of the pilot site followed by the rollout sites

***Success Pattern 9:*** Big Bang implementation of at least the base components

***Success Pattern 10:*** Clear scope and control on functional creep during the project

***Success Pattern 11:*** Comprehensive Training of Siebel team members

***Success Pattern 12:*** Standardizing business processes and preferably implementing Siebel standard functionality

***Success Pattern 13:*** External consultants used mainly to train the core team and not for executing the project

***Success Pattern 14:*** Plan, monitor and manage the project schedule throughout the project.

***Success Pattern 15:*** Interface with existing or legacy systems for specialized or low-priority functionality

***Success Pattern 16:*** Ready support infrastructure and systems as per project schedule

***Success Pattern 17:*** Support and manage infrastructure throughout the project for high availability

***Success Pattern 18:*** Train all concerned end-users close to deployment

## 14.14 SUMMARY

We started the chapter with an understanding of why Siebel projects seem to be so complex. Following this we discussed the background and context of Siebel's rapid implementation methodology for Siebel implementation,namely, eRoadmap. We also presented details of all the stages of the eRoadmap implementation cycle—plan, define, discover, design, configure, validate, deploy and sustain. We have also presented a checklist for each stage. We wrap the chapter by presenting a reference list of success patterns for Siebel implementation projects.

# PART V: THE POST-IMPLEMENTATION STAGE

Chapter 15 provides a brief overview of the post-implementation issues associated with the support of a Siebel system in production.



**All front office deployments have performance and scalability requirements that must be met to support efficient business operations and commitments on completing the required workloads on schedule. Good performance is not only important to ensure user satisfaction and the ongoing use of the application but is also critical to the efficiencies and operating costs of the supported business processes. All front office deployments also have application scalability requirements not only in terms of the total number of users, processes and data volumes that can be supported but also in terms of the deployed network, server and other resources to control deployment costs.**

# Chapter 15 Supporting Siebel

In this chapter we will look at post-implementation support of Siebel within an organization. In traditional application software systems, ongoing maintenance is known to account for more than 50 percent of the total cost of any system.

Siebel simplifies ongoing changes in the delivered functionality of a system because of:

- Comprehensive functionality
- Inherent flexibility
- A comprehensive and efficient upgrade strategy

In this short chapter we will highlight some of these aspects that are related to supporting the Siebel implementation and hence its Return on Investment (ROI). We will end the chapter by looking at the issue of building up consultants and teams for sustaining the momentum and effectiveness of the Siebel implementation and then retaining them to maximize the advantages to the company.

## 15.1 SIEBEL ROLLOUT

One of the major issues after completing the base site of Siebel is the its rollout to the company's other plant sites and office locations. As mentioned in Chapter 6 "The Siebel Implementation Project Cycle" and Chapter 12 "Initiating the Siebel Project", Siebel deployment at other sites is simplified by adopting the following measures during the pilot site implementation:

- Rationalizing the processes
- Standardizing the processes
- Compiling a comprehensive set of processes relevant to all businesses and locations
- Including members from the other sites and offices in the implementation process

The deployment effort involves the following steps.

(1) Siebel installation—this involves the installation of the infrastructure and Siebel licenses based on the experience gained from the first site implementation.

(2) Uploading base configuration—this involves importing the base configuration prepared, implemented and stabilized to all other sites.

(3) Uploading data—this corresponds to the loading of basic data that is common to the operations of the company at all locations. This basic customization data may differ at each site to the extent that the facility addresses different industries, market segments, and so on. This may be

reflected in the fact that the supplier community may be different at each of these facilities. There may also be differences because of differing rules and regulations at different sites.

(4) Integrated training—this involves conducting an integrated and tightly scheduled training session conducted for Siebel support personnel, power users and end-users at the respective sites. Unlike the case of the pilot site, the training for the rollout sites can be done on the company-specific implementation, an opportunity that is unavailable for the pilot sites.

(5) Integration testing—this involves conducting integrated and tightly scheduled integration testing using the test scripts that were prepared for the pilot site as the base. This approach makes this exercise highly focused and efficient.

The above applies to cases where every plant or pilot site has exactly the same configuration. In reality this may not be the case. Correspondingly, you may have another step for customizing Siebel for the specific requirements of the rollout sites. This may involve the configuration of new organization structures such as sales offices or purchasing departments, or of new business processes specific to the new sites. New authorizations may need to be set up to accommodate differing roles or requirements of the rollout sites and may involve setting up new reports, new forms and additional interfaces to the legacy systems of the plant or pilot site. If the pilot site or plant is in a different country (for example Canada), there will be significant changes due to different tax regulations, reporting requirements and other country-specific requirements.

## 15.2 CONTINUOUS CHANGE

This activity deals with ongoing changes that may be adopted in order to enhance the efficiency and effectiveness of the Siebel system. This may consist of

- Ongoing training
- Performance monitoring and fine-tuning
- Siebel Releases/ upgrades management

This change activity also provides the opportunity to address some of the aspects that were decided to be out of the project's scope for the base implementation. It must be noted that we are not referring to any extensions or enhancements to the functionality provided by Siebel per se, but to the functional modules and processes that may not have been implemented during the first wave. Thus, ancillary modules like eCollaboration, eEvents, eAuction, Siebel Data Warehouse and even important functionality like Siebel Incentive Compensation may get implemented in the second wave of implementation.

This activity may also deal with the implementation of functionalities or systems that add value by overlaying on the base modules:

- Enterprise Integration Applications (EAIs)
- Enterprise Resources Planning (ERP) Systems
- Siebel Workflow
- Document Management Systems
- Siebel Data Warehouse
- Business Intelligence (BI)

- Siebel eBusiness Options like eAuction
- Automatic Data Collection (ADC) Systems
- Mobile Data Capture Systems
- Wireless Applications Systems
- Supply-chain Management (SCM) Systems

We have dealt with some of these systems in the other chapters of the book.

## 15.3 SIEBEL GLOBAL ENTERPRISE SUPPORT

Siebel Technical Support works towards the Siebel applications becoming a mission critical tool in the sales, service and marketing activities of the enterprise.

### 15.3.1 Siebel Technical Support

Siebel Technical Support assists all supported customers and partners to resolve problems encountered in running Siebel applications. Its prime objective is to deal with all reported issues promptly.

Siebel Technical Support utilizes the Web as its primary support delivery vehicle to provide fast, up-to-date technical support and the most comprehensive access to information needed by any enterprise.

#### 15.3.1.1 Designated Contacts

Siebel Technical Support provides assistance to an enterprise through its employees nominated as Designated Contacts, who undergo the Siebel eBusiness essentials course or the Core Consultants course as specified in the enterprises Software License and Services Agreement (SLSA). These contacts work with Siebel Technical Support through Siebel SupportWeb for finding solutions and submitting new questions. Designated Contacts have the responsibility of supporting other Siebel users at your site.

#### 15.3.1.2 Second Line Support

Siebel Systems uses its own implementation of Siebel eBusiness Applications, specifically Siebel Service and Siebel eService, to provide second line support to your Designated Contacts. The designated contacts provide support to reference users within the enterprise like employees manning the Help Desk, who in turn can provide support to the end-users.

#### 15.3.1.3 Siebel SupportWeb

Siebel Technical Support maintains Siebel SupportWeb to provide users with a comprehensive resource for product information and solutions, including issues previously encountered by other companies. Designated Support Contacts are provided with full access accounts.

Through Siebel SupportWeb, Siebel Technical Support provides round-the-clock access to product information and answers to common support issues raised by Siebel customers. Siebel SupportWeb is the primary means for Designated Contacts to log Service Requests (SRs) to Siebel Technical Support. The SRs should contain the following requisite information:

- Siebel Product and Version
- Database and Version
- Client Operating System
- Application Server Operating System
- Siebel Product Area
- Severity Level
- Environment where the problems is occurring (Development/Production/Test)
- Relevant error numbers and error messages as they appear on the screen
- Steps to reproduce the problem against the standard Siebel product

Table 15.1 lists the areas that are covered by the SupportWeb.

**Table 15.1 Siebel SupportWeb Areas**

| Area | Description |
|---|---|
| Using Technical Support | This contains detailed information on working with Technical Support, such as how to report a problem, determine severity level and escalation procedures. This information is also available in French, German, Spanish, Brazilian Portuguese and Japanese |
| Support Search | This allows quick and easy search by querying on keywords across Service Requests, Technical Notes, FAQs and Siebel Alerts |
| Frequently Asked Questions (FAQs) | These are a comprehensive collection of questions and answers from previous support interactions |
| Siebel Notes | These document current information on specific topics related to the implementation, configuration and use of Siebel applications |
| Siebel Alerts | These highlight key points or product behavior that maybe useful in a Siebel implementation or upgrade. It typically includes information on a workaround or application of a maintenance release |
| Statement of Direction | This presents new and enhanced features planned by Siebel Systems for upcoming releases of Siebel applications. This is helpful to customers to decide/plan for deploying future releases |
| Maintenance Release Notes | These contain information on the fixes included in the maintenance release that help enterprises to decided on the benefit of a particular release for their company |
| Installation/Upgrade Document | This contains the relevant documentation including Installation Guides, Release Notes, Addenda and Upgrade Guides for Siebel Products |
| Documentation Updates | These contain the changes that have been effected between revisions of the Siebel Bookshelf |

*(Contd.)*

| Area | Description |
|---|---|
| My Service Requests | This gives individual customer employees access to their own Service Requests created by them and also update them if Required |
| My Company's Service Request | This enables customer employees access to all Service Requests within the enterprise and also update them if required |
| Submit a Service Request (SR) | This enables creation of an SR, if Siebel SupportWeb knowledge base does not reveal an answer to a specific question |
| Find SR | This enables easy querying on current SRs |
| Help | This provides answers to questions on the use of the Siebel SupportWeb service itself |
| Update Profile | This maintains the contact information to enable Siebel Technical Support to inform on any updates to the concerned SRs |
| Enhancements | This enables access to all enhancement requests within the enterprise and the corresponding SRs |
| Maintenance Release Requests | This enables tracking the status of an individual's maintenance release requests from within the SupportWeb account |
| File Update/Download | This renders a secure FTP site for transferring files to Siebel Technical Support or downloading files from Siebel Systems like Technical Notes or maintenance releases |

**Table 15.2 Severity Level Definitions**

| Severity Level | Description | Response Time |
|---|---|---|
| Level-1 | Critical Business Impact | One hour |
| Level-2 | Significant Business Impact | Two hours |
| Level-3 | Some Business Impact | One day |
| | Standard Severity | |
| Level-4 | Minimal Business Impact | Two days |

### 15.3.1.4 Siebel Support Offerings

Siebel Systems offers a range of support programs to suit the needs of companies with varied business requirements. The programs and features within various support offerings are described.

(a) Standard Support is the base level of technical support provided by Siebel Systems for customers that only have basic service needs. Siebel SupportWeb is Siebel Systems' basic channel for supporting customers via Designated Contacts who can create and update Service Requests (SRs), view answers to questions or issues encountered by end-users, check the status of Enhancement Requests and Maintenance Release Requests. They can also use SupportWeb to query the technical support knowledge base for alerts, technical notes, FAQs and upload/download files.

Standard Support includes the following:

- Second tier technical support, wherein Siebel technical support engineers provide support (during business hours) to up to two Designated Contacts who are Siebel trained contacts at your company and are responsible for providing support to other users at your company
- Software maintenance releases are provided on a regular basis for product defects/bugs that impact business significantly
- Software updates for currently licensed and supported products (example: v6.0 to v6.3)
- Siebel Systems provides one copy of software updates to be shipped to one designated shipping site
- Major software version upgrades are provided for the products (example: v6.0 to v7.0)
- Each customer is entitled to two designated support contacts who receive direct support from Siebel's technical support engineers
- Each customer also receives one read-only account to SupportWeb for the entire project team. The read-only account provides access to the extensive knowledge base in Siebel SupportWeb but not to the Service Request (SR) or Enhancement Request areas.

(b) Gold Support is available for those customers who have the need for more comprehensive support. Gold Support incorporates all features within the standard support plus the following additional features:

- 24 × 7 support for production related Severity Level 1 and Severity Level 2 issues
- A total of six Designated Contacts who receive direct support from Siebel technical support engineers
- Siebel Systems provides one-off software updates for up to three designated shipping sites
- Onsite Technical Services are provided for production-related issues and critical implementation or upgrade issues that cannot be resolved remotely and that may have significant impact on the business
- Multiple region support for a company that has multi-located facilities across the globe

(c) Additional Support Options enables customizing the support program including features like:

- Additional designated support contacts
- Additional software shipping sites
- Support for an additional database server platform
- The Rollout Support Option provides Standard Support customers with 24 × 7 support in weekly increments during implementation or upgrade phase. This enables an enterprise to extend the support coverage to 24 × 7 for Severity 1 and 2 issues during those critical periods for minimizing risks, and resolve issues quickly and accurately to complete the installation/ upgrade without incident.

## 15.3.2 SiebelNet Business Services

SiebelNet Business Services allows companies to outsource the hosting, management and support of their Siebel eBusiness Applications enabling customers to focus on their core competencies. By using SiebelNet Business Services customers avail of the following benefits:

- Fastest speed to market with Siebel eBusiness functionality
- End-to-end solution from a single vendor
- Highest possible service levels to customers and to end-users with guaranteed Service Level Agreements (SLAs)
- Planned investment and, clear control and visibility of project costs

### 15.3.2.1 SiebelNet Hosting

SiebelNet Hosting is a family of applications outsourcing services designed to help customers deploy and manage their Siebel eSales, eMarketing and eService systems. Siebel Hosting provides Internet or network-based access to customers' configured Siebel eBusiness Applications through a flexible, cost-effective and support infrastructure.

SiebelNet Hosting service includes the underlying database software, operating systems, server hardware, data storage, support staff, network connectivity and all the expertise to proactively manage and host your Siebel implementation.

### 15.3.2.2 SiebelNet Managed Services

SiebelNet Managed Services provide customers with a remote management solution for in-house Siebel eBusiness developments. It is designed specifically for enterprises that have implemented Siebel but do not have the IT resources to manage and optimize their Siebel implementations.

Siebel Managed Services include:

- Remote DBA services
- Network and system administration
- Performance planning and tuning
- Application upgrade support
- Report creation
- Complete second-level help desk support

### 15.3.2.3 SiebelNet Deployment Services

SiebelNet Deployment Services enable customers to use SiebelNet's expertise for in-house deployments. SiebelNet Deployment Services offers IT-challenged enterprises an alternative implementation solution. It is designed for enterprises that are averse to outsourcing but require development support in rolling out hardware and software implementations. SiebelNet Development Services include software, hardware and bandwidth provisioning, configuration, installation, performance tuning and application management best practice.

### 15.3.2.4 SiebelNet HelpDesk

SiebelNet provides customers with a first level end-user support without staffing an internal help desk for application support. SiebelNet HelpDesk is designed to increase an end user's productivity while simultaneously reducing the costs of supporting a Siebel eBusiness Applications implementation. SiebelNet

HelpDesk offers quick answers to end-user questions so that the enterprise may reap the full benefit of Siebel eBusiness Applications.

### 15.3.2.5 SiebelNet Hardware Services

SiebelNet Hardware Services enables companies to outsource the setup and maintenance of their computer hardware and inventory. SiebelNet Hardware Services' objective is to minimize the amount of time that representatives are devoid of laptops and thus, maximize the productive time of sales representatives calling on their prospects.

## 15.4 SUPPORT HELP DESK

The success of a Siebel implementation is dependent to a great extent on the deployment of an enterprise-wide and properly resourced help desk. This is especially critical during and immediately after the deployment stage because this is when the system is used by a large number of users for whom the system is new, unfamiliar and even disorienting. For companies that do not have a history of computerization this may be a very trying period.

The majority of the problems reported during this period may be due to a lack of knowledge, human errors, system bugs or technical problems with printers, network connections, and so on.

Some of the issues involved with instituting a help desk include:

- Defining the standards for identifying problems
- Defining and establishing the method for registering problems
- Defining the standards and procedures for problem diagnosis and resolutions
- Defining and establishing the service levels and response times for problem resolution
- Defining the standards and procedures for communicating the solution
- Defining the standards and procedures for tracking unresolved and pending problems
- Defining the procedure for escalating overdue, unresolved problems
- Establishing help desk logistics
- Implementing a help desk application system
- Defining the help desk team organization and the corresponding requisite skills and resources
- Appointing and training the help desk team

All unresolved problems are finally referred to Siebel Support Services described earlier.

## 15.5 SIEBEL APPLICATION'S PERFORMANCE AND SCALABILITY

This section provides an overview of key performance and scalability factors that also act as the input for capacity planning and sizing efforts. All front office deployments have performance and scalability requirements that must be met to support efficient business operations and commitments on completing the required workloads on schedule. *Performance* is typically referred to as the speed of the application in performing a given task such as synchronizing a database, importing a number of records or completing a series of operations through the client user interface. Performance is commonly measured in operations completed per unit time. *Scalability* typically refers to the application's ability to support multiple operations simultaneously, such as the number of concurrent connected users performing business operations or mobile users synchronizing their databases.

Good performance is not only important to ensure user satisfaction and the ongoing use of the application but is also critical to the efficiencies and operating costs of the supported business processes. Poor performance, even in a small call center, leads to increased staffing and operational costs, longer hold times and lower customer satisfaction. All front office deployments also have application scalability requirements not only in terms of the total number of users, processes and data volumes that can be supported but also in terms of the deployed network, server and other resources to control deployment costs

Poor application performance and scalability can be addressed to a certain extent, by upgrading the basic infrastructure resources at additional costs. However, the basic performance and scalability characteristics of an application are really determined by the application architecture. Siebel applications are carefully designed to meet all demanding performance and scalability requirements, in all deployment scenarios, at all layers of the Siebel Enterprise Architecture (that correspond broadly to the conventional 3-tier architecture):

- Siebel Database Server uses the relational database purely as a data store; the business logic is not implemented in the database in the form of triggers or stored procedures (the database-centric model) but rather on the scalable, middle-tier Siebel Enterprise Server and on the Siebel Client. The data-centric model is not only difficult to scale, customize, maintain and upgrade, but it can be scaled only by augmenting the single database server.
- Siebel Enterprise Server components are designed to scale across multiple Siebel Servers in the Enterprise Server, providing a high degree of scalability in the middle-tier of Siebel applications.
- Siebel Client—The Object Manager executes Siebel Business Objects and Components on the native Siebel Client and on the middle-tier Object Manager that supports the Siebel Thin Client. The Object Manager supports configurable data caching at the Business Component level, eliminating the need to re-query data from the database server with each use of the Business Component. Data caching typically is applied to the Business Components that support Pick Lists.

## 15.6 UPGRADING SIEBEL APPLICATIONS

Siebel applications provides a comprehensive suite of customization and upgrade tools that allow Siebel application users to benefit quickly and easily from new releases of Siebel software. This approach allows customers to tailor the software to their unique requirements while ensuring a clear and consistent upgrade path for future releases.

Siebel applications have the following characteristics:

- The ability to easily upgrade all levels of a multi-tiered application
- Flexible application installation programs that can be customized to install only the applicable components for major or minor releases of uniquely configured application software

- Database extensibility that enables developers to extend the application's database schema without compromising vendor support or consistency of the application upgrade path
- Application configuration capabilities that take advantage of new object-oriented programming capabilities and allow developers to customize the way the software works without modifying or altering source code

> Siebel Systems has pioneered the use of configurable business object that allow enterprises to configure an application to fit their unique needs by simply configuring and modifying the properties and attributes of an object while eliminating the need to change 4GL application source code or SQL code. Using Siebel Tools, Siebel customers can customize the look and feel, content and workflow of Siebel applications by simply modifying Siebel object definitions.

## 15.6.1 Siebel Anywhere

Siebel Anywhere is designed specifically to address the software upgrade problem of large and geographically distributed Siebel applications. Siebel Anywhere solves the problem of managing software applications on remote and mobile systems. Siebel Anywhere provides integrated database schema distribution, Siebel applications software distribution and third-party software distribution capabilities to all remote users.

Siebel Anywhere allows the Siebel System Administrator to apply upgrades to dedicated Web clients, mobile Web clients and Siebel Servers. The Siebel Administrator has full control over the upgrades distributed and applied by Siebel Anywhere.

Upgrades can include:

- Custom configurations
- New versions of Siebel eBusiness Applications
- Custom extensions to the database schema
- Custom files
- Third-party files or applications

Siebel Anywhere uses pull-based technology for retrieving upgrade kits, which include:

- Siebel Upgrade Kit Wizard for collecting relevant information
- Siebel Upgrade Kit Builder for creating the kit
- Siebel Upgrade Wizard for installing the kit on the clients

Once the upgrade kit is created, it is stored on the Siebel File System for retrieval and application by Siebel Anywhere subscribers.

An upgrade configuration is a collection of upgrade components that define how to version check different software modules. A Siebel Anywhere subscriber belongs to one upgrade configuration and can include the following:

- Mobile Web clients of eBusiness Applications such as Siebel Sales/ Field Service/ Call Center.
- Dedicated Web client which is the standard mobile Web client in server connected mode
- Siebel Tools clients requiring version checks of tools software

- Siebel Servers operating against the Siebel Server Database
- Siebel Servers operating against Replication Manager regional databases

## 15.7 SIEBEL ONLINE HELP DEVELOPMENT

Siebel provides facilities for developing and providing customized online help for Siebel applications. These are primarily sub-divided into the following.

(1) Employee applications like Siebel Call Center and Siebel Sales that are primarily used internally by the employees of the enterprise. The help system is context sensitive and is delivered in the HTML format. When a user accesses the help, the application calls the Siebel Web Engine (SWE) GotoPage method to display the correct help topic in a separately invoked browser window. If accessed directly, the starting page of the employee applications help is named as siebstarthelp.htm

(2) Customer Applications like Siebel eSales and Siebel eService that are primarily used by external partners, customers and prospects of the enterprise. The help system is also delivered in the HTML format but is not context sensitive. When a user accesses the help, the application calls the Siebel Web Engine (SWE) GotoURL method to display the start of the help system in a separately invoked browser window. The starting page of the customer applications help system is named as siebcomgeneric.htm

### 15.7.1 Location of Help Files

The location of the Siebel applications help files depends on the following:

- Location of your Siebel applications
- Type of the Siebel client, which could be Siebel Web Client, Siebel Dedicated Web Client or Siebel Mobile Web Client.
    - Siebel Web Client runs in a standard browser from the client PC and does not require any software or database on the client PC. The browser connects through a Web server to the Siebel eBusiness Application server, which executes business logic and accesses data from the database server.
    - Siebel Dedicated Web Client is a Microsoft Windows client delivered through a Web browser and also provides direct connectivity to a database server. It requires software to be installed on the client machine, but does not require a local database/ Web server/ Siebel eBusiness Application server (though Siebel Server may still be needed for the functioning of Assignment Manager and Replication Manager.
    - Siebel Mobile Web Client is a Microsoft Windows client delivered through a Web browser that accesses a small footprint local database. It requires the same software as that installed on the client machine but periodically, the client must access the Siebel Remote Server through a dial-up, WAN or LAN connection to synchronize mutually data changes with the Siebel Database on the database server and the Siebel File System.

In the case of customer applications, it only depends on the location where the enterprise installs the Siebel eBusiness Applications.

## 15.7.2 Online Help and Siebel Tools

For employee applications, a screen or a view is linked to a help topic (identified by a Help Id object) by using the Help Identifier property of the corresponding Screen/ View objects within Siebel Tools. Each Help Id object has a HTML help URL property that is used to identify the HTML file that contains the help topics for the relevant Screen or View.

In the case of customer applications, a container Web Page object is used to establish the link between the application and corresponding help start page.

## 15.7.3 Customizing and Adding Help

For employee applications, on adding a custom Screen/ View to the Siebel eBusiness Applications, the corresponding help screen can be created by using Siebel Tools to define the Screen/ View object with a Help Identifier property and then adding a Help Id object with a HTML Help URL property for the screen.

| The standard Siebel eBusiness Applications do not include help files for views. |
|---|

An enterprise can also customize the contents of a Screen to suit their specific Siebel implementation requirements.

For customer applications, the enterprise can add or change the help links to establish a link with a different application.

## 15.7.4 Migrating Help

In case the enterprise has created task-specific customized online help for earlier versions of Siebel applications, rather than migration of the prior content to the latest versions, it is best to re-create it in the latest version. This is primarily because of the major changes in the screen navigation that have been brought about by Siebel Systems.

# 15.8 RETAINING AND RETRAINING SIEBEL CONSULTANTS

Until recently Siebel implementations were essentially considered complete after implementing the modules of interest to the organization. However, with the growing importance of virtual corporations or extended enterprises enabled by the Internet, companies are undertaking numerous development efforts. These involve various enhancements and interfacing Siebel with supply-chain management systems and other customer-facing applications, including sales force automation, call center applications, and so on. Thus, retaining the Siebel implementation team may be critical for the organization to maintain the momentum of implementing satellite systems that interface with Siebel or overlay the operational systems of Siebel.

## 15.8.1 The Retention Horizon

If one recalls that companies are advised to nominate their key performers to work as part of the Siebel implementation in order to ensure its success, the effect of Siebel-trained employees quitting the organization in search of better opportunities is doubly damaging. In such cases, the company not only loses Siebel experts who are familiar with the specifics of their implementation, but it may also be deprived of some of its best performers. It is critical for a company to retain its implementation team members at least for twice the period of implementation.

Even if the retention of the core team is achieved at a cost that may double the budgeted figures, it will enable a company to extend its competitiveness further by rapidly implementing additional systems that overlay or interface with Siebel. These systems include:

- EAI systems
- Other Web-enabled Applications
- Workflow systems
- Data Warehouse (DW) systems
- Business Intelligence (BI) systems
- SCM systems
- ERP systems
- Performance enhancement programs like BPR, Activity-Based Management (ABM), Balance Scorecard, and so on

## 15.8.2 Extending the Boundaries of Expertise

Apart from an increase in remuneration and compensations, training in advanced features and functionalities of Siebel and other enterprise applications can be a powerful method of retaining Siebel talent within your organization.

A Siebel Tools developer's skills could be upgraded by:

- Training and participation in EAI systems like computerized telephone integration, barcodes, security and access systems, data capture systems and computer recognition systems
- Training in data warehousing projects using the Siebel Data Warehouse solution or other third-party solutions that use data from the Siebel system
- Training in Siebel Workflow for participating in workflow, document management and wireless projects to be undertaken by the company
- Training in electronic data interchange (EDI) using systems like MSMQ, IBM MQSeries, etc.
- Training in Web-based application development projects in HTML, XML, VB/ ASP, JSP/ Servlets, EJB, Java, JavaScript, Visual Basic VBScript, and so on
- Training in related functional modules depending on background and aptitude

A Siebel applications administration consultant's skills could be upgraded by:

- Training in Siebel Tools development and further opportunities available in that activity
- Training and participation in enterprise infrastructure upgrade projects

- Training and participation in Web infrastructure projects
- Training and participation in enterprise infrastructure management projects including Web-enabled systems management, network management and performance monitoring systems

A business/ functional consultant's skills could be upgraded by:

- Cross-training in different modules. Sales, Service, Call Center and Field Service consultants could be cross-trained in either module as well as other related modules like Product Configurator, Campaigns, Incentive Compensation, and Time & Expense Reporting. Similarly, eSales, eService, eMarketing, eChannel consultants could be cross-trained in either module as well as other related modules like ePricer, eCollaboration, InterActive, eAuction, eEvents and eTraining.
- SCM systems
- ERP systems
- Performance enhancement programs like BPR, activity-based management and Balance Scorecard

## 15.9 SUMMARY

In this chapter we looked at the post-implementation period of a Siebel implementation. We visited aspects of Siebel deployment and rollouts, ongoing configuration changes and enhancements, Siebel support services, Siebel Release and Upgrades, and Help Desk. In the last section we looked at measures for ensuring the longevity of the Siebel team member's association with the company.

# PART VI: SIEBEL IMPLEMENTATION AND BEYOND

Chapter 16 presents various aspects related to valuing the ROI of a Siebel implementation using the method of Balance Scorecard. In the last chapter of the book, Chapter 17, we visit several aspects of the intelligent customer-centric enterprise and how Siebel is gearing up for enabling relationship-based enterprises to address these emerging challenges in the 21st Century.



**An enterprise-wide solution like Siebel, which embodies the process-oriented view of the organization, must provide the means for evaluating and maximizing the value delivered by the enterprise to all of its stakeholders. From the perspective of the collaborative enterprise, it is evident that a single stakeholder cannot sustain an appreciable ROI for itself at the cost of the other stakeholders. An ROI for different stakeholders is not in opposition to each other; it is not a "zero-sum game."**

Chapter 16

# Valuing the Relationship-based Enterprise

Chapter 1 of this book "The Relationship Based Enterprise" dealt at length on the collaborative nature of today's enterprises. In the subsequent chapters we have seen various aspects of Siebel that enable an enterprise to operate as an integrated, enterprise-wide, process-oriented, information-driven, real-time enterprise. We have also seen that as organizational and environmental conditions have become more complex, global and therefore more competitive, processes provide a framework for dealing effectively with the issues of performance improvement, capability development and adaptation to the changing environment.

In turn, continued value addition along every business process has become an essential prerequisite for viability not only of a particular process but also of the organization as a whole. Here is the fundamental rationale for measuring and valuing an enterprise in terms of the value determinants that are relevant to all stakeholders of an organization. These include not only the traditionally known stakeholders of a company, like the company's investors and customers but the suppliers, managers and employees of the company as well.

An enterprise-wide solution like Siebel, which embodies the process-oriented view of the organization, must provide the means for evaluating and maximizing the value delivered by the enterprise to all of its stakeholders. The first half of this chapter provides a fairly detailed introduction to such a perspective on the value created by an enterprise. It also discusses the now popular Balance Scorecard (BSC) approach for valuation of an enterprise. It suggests an interpretation of the scorecard in terms of the value to the five primary stakeholders of an enterprise namely, customers, vendors, investors, and managers and employees.

## 16.1 ENTERPRISE STAKEHOLDERS

An organization is defined by a constellation of collaborations. All collaborative relationships are truly stakeholder relationships; thus, a company is truly a continuum of collaborative stakeholder relationships. A corporation is embedded in a network of interdependent stakeholder relationships that are defined mutually and dynamically. The competitive response of an organization is the result of all such stakeholder relationships or collaborations. One of the earliest proponents of what is known as stakeholder theory is R. E. Freeman, author of "Strategic Management: A Stakeholder Approach". The stakeholders are investors, owners, management, political groups, customers, community, employees, trade associations, suppliers, alliance partners, government, competitors, and so forth.

There are two kinds of stakeholders—primary and secondary. Primary stakeholders are those entities that are affected directly by the success or decline of a company such as investors, financial institutions, customers, suppliers/ vendors, employees, and so on. Secondary stakeholders like the media, government and regulatory agencies that are affected only indirectly by the varying fortunes of the company, but they definitely exercise influence on the functioning of the company. Sometimes this influence may not only exceed the influence of the primary stakeholders but may also prove to be decisive for the enterprise.

The five stakeholders of primary importance who create value for an enterprise are:

(1) Customers
(2) Investors
(3) Vendors
(4) Managers
(5) Employees

Collaborations are characterized by contracts that can range from explicit to the implicit. These contracts specify or allude to what the company can expect from each stakeholder in order to achieve its objectives and what each stakeholder can expect in return from the organization. For instance, explicit contracts are contracts whereby a customer pays a predetermined amount of money to avail of the company's products or services. Similarly, implicit contracts are contracts whereby an employee gets a promotion depending upon his performance with reference to the expectations set at the beginning of the concerned period.

It is with reference to these contracts, whether implicit or explicit, that every stakeholder invests capital in the continued and envisaged future success of the company. This capital could be financial, managerial, intellectual, environmental, social, and so forth. The continued involvement, interest and commitment of the stakeholders are dependent on the stakeholders getting a reasonable Return on Investment (ROI). This ROI could be different for different stakeholders. For customers it could be in terms of assured competitive products, services, support and upgrades in the future. For vendors it could be in terms of assured supply of contracts on favorable terms. For investors it could be in terms of an assured dividend in the future. For the managers it could be in terms of an assured rise up the corporate ladder and for the employees of the company it could be in terms of assured security, professional development and career growth.

### 16.1.1 From 'Built to Last' to 'Built to Perform' Organizations

In the early 1980s Peters and Waterman published a study of forty-three major American corporations. The sample included such household names like Disney, Boeing, IBM, Mars, McDonalds, Dupont, Levi-Strauss, Procter and Gamble, 3M, Caterpillar, Hewlett Packard, Kodak, Wang and Atari. All forty-three companies were selected because they had been innovative and adaptable over reasonably long periods, that is, they were 'built to last' organizations. The study reached the conclusion that the cause of the excellence displayed by these companies lay in eight prominent attributes that they shared in common.

The eight attributes were:

(1) Stick to the knitting
(2) Close to the customer
(3) Productivity through people
(4) Autonomy and entrepreneurship
(5) Hands-on and value-driven
(6) Bias for action
(7) Simple form and lean staff
(8) Simultaneous loose-tight properties

Each of them had a characteristics pattern of actions, position, posture and process associated with them. The conclusion drawn was that if others imitate these eight attributes they too would become excellent.

The eight attributes plan proved to be a disappointment because within five years, two-thirds of the companies in the sample had slipped from the pinnacle. Since then, a number of other studies have followed but none appears to have found the best away for all companies to excel in business. For instance, except for General Electric, none of the top 12 companies that made up the Dow Jones index in 1900 survive today. Almost 40% of the names which made up the Fortune 500 ten years ago have disappeared, whilst of the 1970 list, 60% have been acquired or have folded-up. Clearly, the best run and most widely admired companies are unable to sustain their market beating levels of performance for an extended period of time. The very processes that enable them to survive over the long-term, thwart them from renewal and reinvention, and finally fossilize them.

This seems to suggest that one of the fundamental tenets of business that a company should be 'built to last' is seriously flawed. Rather than aim for continuity, enterprises should aim for changes or variations to ensure 'built to perform' organizations (see section "The Performance Prism"). Analogous to Michael Porter's concept of the value chain that essentially reflects costs at various stages, one can conceive of a casual 'performance chain' running from activities to costs to revenues to the valuation of the enterprise in the capital markets. Enterprises should innovate, renew and reinvent themselves and their businesses in order to survive in the turbulent market environment. Please also refer to Appendix F "Enterprise Evolution by Market Selection" for an alternate view on the success and survival of companies that is inspired by Darwin's 'Theory of Evolution by Natural Selection' in biosciences.

## 16.2 ASPECTS OF ENTERPRISE VALUE

From the perspective of the collaborative enterprise, it is evident that a single stakeholder cannot sustain an appreciable ROI for itself at the cost of the other stakeholders. For instance, shareholder value cannot be maximized indefinitely by reducing product quality or customer service, negotiating arbitrarily lower rates from suppliers/ vendors or by cutting down remuneration of the employees. An ROI for different stakeholders is not in opposition to each other; it is not a "zero-sum game." We have already seen concrete proof of this in the last century when manufacturing quality and cost were mistakenly believed to be in opposition to each other. As has been shown in the '90s, an enterprise can achieve excellent quality *at reduced costs.*

Although companies focus on creating value for all constituencies, these efforts do not or are not able to address all the constituencies simultaneously. An enterprise does not usually have the capabilities to track the information that is essential for maintaining a cross-functional view of the impact of efforts for

- Improving value addition activities at local activity centers.
- Minimizing the non-value addition activities at local activity centers.

The apparent improvement in value addition or non-addition activities needs to be tracked enterprise-wide across all functions and constituencies. This is because value addition or non-value addition at a local level may not be so for the company as whole. It has been well accepted by now that maximizing only the output of each constituting organizational unit or activity cannot maximize the output of the organization as a whole. A unit may often have to undertake activities that are essentially non-value added at the operational level of the unit for overall efficiency and effectiveness of the organization. Siebel provides such a system that generates, retains, analyzes and reports on parameters that can track activity level measures of performance, revenues and expenditures. More importantly, Siebel highlights cross-functional dependencies of activities across the enterprise.

## 16.2.1 Value to Customers

Value to customers is one of the most important values that are created by the company. Customers value the product and services not only in terms of its innate use but also in terms of its price relative to the competition. This in turn leads to other satellite criteria that ultimately lead to customers' continued patronage of the company's products. Customers look for:

- Responsiveness
- Price
- Quality
- Flexibility
- Utility
- Variability or the range of options
- Reliability
- Standardized interfaces and auxiliary systems
- Durability
- Maintainability
- Upgradability
- Support
- Service
- Innovation

Some of these properties characterizing a product/ service may be in opposition to each other; the constellation of values that become applicable may vary from one product to another. Moreover, over the course of time, even the values for one particular product or closely related products may undergo changes. As we have seen in Chapter 7, sub-section, "Value-Added View of Business Processes", the value shifts may happen because of competitive products, changes in technology or changes in the regulatory conditions. In fact, in the absence of other causes value shifts may also occur merely because of the customer's illusive urge for innovation and the need for more than ordinary experiences. Added to this is the complication arising from the fact that the customer base itself is not static and keeps on changing dynamically, depending on the shift in Critical Value Determinants (CVDs).

The customary way to determine the relative importance of value determinants is through customer satisfaction surveys and subsequent customer value analysis to generate normalized customer satisfaction indices. These indices may differ depending on the objectives of the customer value analysis.

## 16.2.2 Value to Shareholders

Shareholders expect a reasonable ROI in the long-term. It must be mentioned that whereas none can deny that higher returns are the basic motives for any investment, shareholders also value their contribution in the creation of wealth and job opportunities for their community. They derive immense satisfaction by sharing the created wealth with the community through the employees of the company. If a company demonstrates that it is utilizing its capital competitively and has a viable strategy that will sustain this rate of return or better it in the future, they will continue to maintain their financial interests in the company.

From the traditional earnings point of view, for industrial enterprises geared to mass production strategies the investors look for Return on Capital Employed (ROCE), Earnings per Share (E/S), Return on Assets (ROA), etc., in terms of integrity and quality of accounting information like:

- Relevance
- Reliability
- Neutrality
- Fidelity
- Verifiability
- Comparability
- Consistency

However, the earnings point of view has not proven to be a reliable indicator of the value of a company. It is primarily oriented towards existing and past values and is not geared to address its arc in the future. Earnings, is a static concept that uses linear projections based on the figures of the last accounting year. The underlying assumption in the traditional approach is that a company's value can be forecast based on its reported earnings. That this is erroneous has been established beyond doubt by the fact that market values of successful companies have always been greater than twice its book value.

On the other hand, the cash flow perspective sees value as a function of the expected future cash flows, which reflects the company's value in the long-term and makes due allowance for the attendant risks. Unlike the accounting approach, in the cash flow approach, a strong correlation has been found to exist between the market price per share and predicted value per share based on cash flow forecasts.

According to the cash flow perspective, the investors look for:

- Increased future surplus cash flows
- Assured future cash dividends
- Share price appreciation

For a company with relatively small capital the earnings and cash flow perspective may not produce appreciably different results, but even in such cases when we factor in accounts payable and inventories the two approaches may provide highly divergent views.

## 16.2.3 Value to Managers

By convention, in the discussions on stakeholders, senior managers are usually grouped with owner/investors, which is incorrect. Managers with their responsibilities for driving the growth and profitability of the company, have a different perspective of the values that are important to them vis-à-vis the owner/investors.

Senior managers look for the following:

- The freedom to articulate the vision of the organization and translate the same into objectives for the organization
- The latitude to focus on a select set of strategies and tactics
- The latitude to form the management team that believes in this vision and gels with this approach
- The facility to define the measures of performances for the organization as a whole as well as the individual business and operational managers
- The authority to allocate and deploy systems and resources for executing the plans
- The authority to institute and implement systems for measuring and reporting on the measures of performance for different functions and levels of the organization at predefined time periods or on an ad hoc basis
- The latitude to mold the policies and procedures in line with the company's vision
- The latitude to commit Research and Development (R&D) efforts on technological and managerial issues that they perceive to be of importance for the future
- Remuneration that is commensurate with risks and targeted tasks

With the increase in the pace and pulse of businesses, the leeway available for CEOs and other senior executives has been diminishing continuously. The window of tolerance for failing revenues or periods of executing corrective strategies is progressively becoming smaller. In such circumstances, the hard-driving managers become conscious of the value that is catalyzed by them for the enterprise and the returns that they accrue to themselves. It is a supreme irony of our times that with their increasing power and prestige the CEOs and members of a management team are also most vulnerable to being summarily replaced due to perceived non-performance.

## 16.2.4 Value to Employees

As described in Chapter 1, section "Management by Collaboration", the dynamic changes in the market and global competition being confronted by companies have resulted in more flexible organizations. These organizations are populated with empowered workers who are multi-skilled with enhanced responsibilities. No organization can sustain the generation of value at high levels for extended periods without a corresponding value-add to the employees of the company.

Employees value factors such as the following:

- Opportunities for participating and contributing significantly to the activities of the enterprise
- Reasonable compensation
- Opportunities to learn, develop skills and handle challenging roles
- Access to all relevant information and resources for making decisions and discharging their responsibilities creditably
- Opportunities for recognition and rewards
- Opportunities for advancement
- Opportunities for training

The integrated, real-time and transparent access to relevant data provided by Siebel empowers the traditionally deprived members of the organization to make timely decisions and derive the satisfaction of being involved meaningfully in ensuring the well being of the company.

In many ways, the value for the employees is analogous to the value for the external customers. Like the customers of the company, the effectiveness of employee value is gauged through employee satisfaction surveys that are administered on a periodic basis.

## 16.2.5 Value to Vendors

Recently, vendors have been getting increased recognition for the value that they add not only to the final output of an enterprise but also to its profitability. Vendors play a major role in enhancing the overall performance of the organization be it in terms of quality, input costs, overheads, responsiveness to the changes in the market, and so forth. Increasingly, they are perceived more as enterprise partners rather than as the traditional adversaries to be browbeaten to lower prices.

Vendors in turn look for the following values in the value-creating enterprise of a company:

- Steady order commitments
- Optimal lead-times
- Immediate information on deliveries, rejects, returns, and so on in terms of the quantity and control information (such as delivery note numbers and batch numbers)
- Systematic invoice verification
- Prompt payments for verified and accepted invoices
- Interfaces with an enterprise-wide, implemented system like Siebel
- Sharing changes in production schedules
- Sharing changes in the positions of inventories vis-à-vis the production orders, and so on
- Sharing results and analysis of quality tests on supplied materials
- Participation in plans of new products, models, technologies and production processes

As mentioned in Chapter 1, section "The Virtual Organization", only mature a Customer Relationship Management (CRM) system like Siebel can provide the backbone for holding together the virtual value chain across such collaborative relationships with vendors.

# 16.3 ECONOMIC VALUE ADD (EVA)

Economic Value Add (EVA) is a new type of managerial accounting criterion that recognizes that capital, whether equity or borrowed, is simply another resource used in the enterprise.

Traditional accounting methods that are transaction based take into account sales (i.e., revenue) and expenses (i.e., purchase and interest payments) for computing profitability that is determined by the measure of the Return on Investment (ROI) defined by:

Return = (Revenue – Expense)

EVA treats both stockholder capital (i.e., equity capital with zero dividends and its average return of about 6% higher than long-term governmental bonds as its cost) and borrowed capital (with its interest payment as its cost) as expense items. Consequently, if the enterprise uses a combination of the borrowed and shareholder capital, the cost of capital is a weighted average of the two costs. Since EVA is computed as revenue less expenses (including all expenses such as purchases, capital and taxes), it is a genuine measure of the value created from the enterprise operations at various levels.

Once the capital is seen as a resource, the focus shifts from a simplified Return on Investment (ROI) to the Yield on Investment (YOI) that primarily measures revenue generated for the capacity scheduled. The emphasis shifts to minimizing the amount of resources used to generate the revenue, that is, to increase the efficiency with which the stockholder equity is used. Accordingly the managers are prompted to aim for the following at the operational level:

- Use less capital
- Earn more profit without using more capital
- Invest capital in as high-return projects as possible

Because of the critical role played by employees in the operations of the enterprise, most EVAs incorporate a method for distributing bonuses and dividends to the employees. EVA effectively expands the definition of ownership beyond that of shareholders (who share the risk of the venture) to include the employees whose participation and commitment also contributes to the success of the enterprise.

# 16.4 VALUE-BASED MANAGEMENT

In order to deliver superior stakeholder value, especially shareholder value, a company's management must not only be able to formulate strategies but should also be able to execute them. Value-based Management (VBM) ensures the implementation of a corporate strategy by directly linking the strategy, finance and operations within a company. By linking strategic objectives to resource allocation and performance management, the operational decision-making is focused fully on delivering the strategic objectives.

To be effective VBM entails combining the internal, external, historic and predicted views with the financial and non-financial drivers of the business. Leveraging VBM essentially involves the following four steps:

(1) Understanding what factors drive value

(2) Finding out where value is created or destroyed
(3) Establishing value as the criterion for decision-making
(4) Embedding value into the corporate culture

The financial-oriented VBMs currently in vogue are primarily aimed at operationalizing the VBM so that individual members of a company can perceive and identify with the shareholder value that is contributed by the various functions and activities within the organization. But it must be noted that it is already recognized that a financial-oriented view needs to be supplemented with a value-add view of manufacturing directly. ERP systems basically perpetuate the philosophy of a top-down, build-to-stock and supply-driven mass-producing manufacturing strategy. The value-add view of manufacturing is in line with the increasing emphasis on:

- Demand pull reflected in order changes
- Flow manufacturing entailing fast changeovers

Like the Corporate Performance Monitor (CPM) discussed later, it is possible to envisage a Manufacturing Performance Monitor (MPM) that monitors in real-time, manufacturing processes in terms of the various technical and economic value drivers.

## 16.4.1 Time Value of Customers and Shareholder Value

As suggested in Chapter 1, a company's market valuation or shareholder value is the sum total of the envisaged Lifetime Values (LTVs) of its current and future customers, that is, its customer capital. Customer capital is like a miner's canary—the bird whose death signals dangerous conditions in mines. It is the most accurate (if grisly) leading indicator of the enterprise's competitive advantage as well as that of its partners and competitors.

In this framework, the total value of the company, its market capitalization, is equal to the present value of the sum total of the predictable Lifetime Value (LTV) of its current and future customers, discounted for risk. Figure 16.1 shows the CLTV curve—a graph of Customers Projected Lifetime Value against Time. The earlier quarters are more accurate as they are based on information on the sales pipelines, work-in-process and backlog orders that contribute to make these earlier numbers more reliable. But further out on the curve, the envisaged numbers are based more on extrapolations of investments and trends. With the increasing risks associated with the progressive forecasts into the future, the present value placed on them progressively decreases to zero. *The area under the curve represents a particular customer's contribution to the organization's market capitalization.* The objective of any management team to increase the shareholder value then translates to increasing the area under this curve.

As is evident from the CLTV curve in Figure 16.2, this is achievable in the following two ways:

(1) Increasing the Customer Value Differential (CUG) that reflects the gap between the measure of customer's Lifetime Value (LTV) for your company vis-a-vis for your closest competitors. The CUG can be enhanced by:
   - Migrating the customers to higher value alternatives of the current offerings
   - Increasing the range/type of offerings
   - Increasing the total quantum of consumption of current offerings

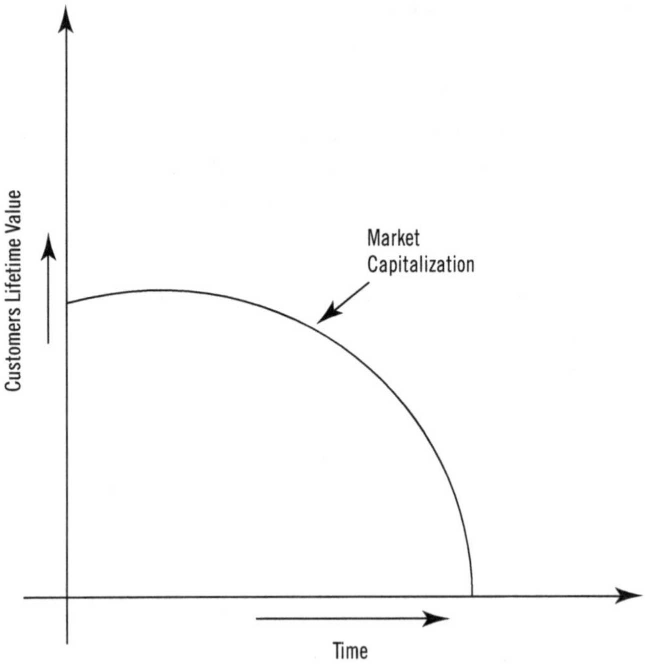


**Fig. 16.1 Market Capitalization in Terms of Customer Lifetime Value (CLTV)**

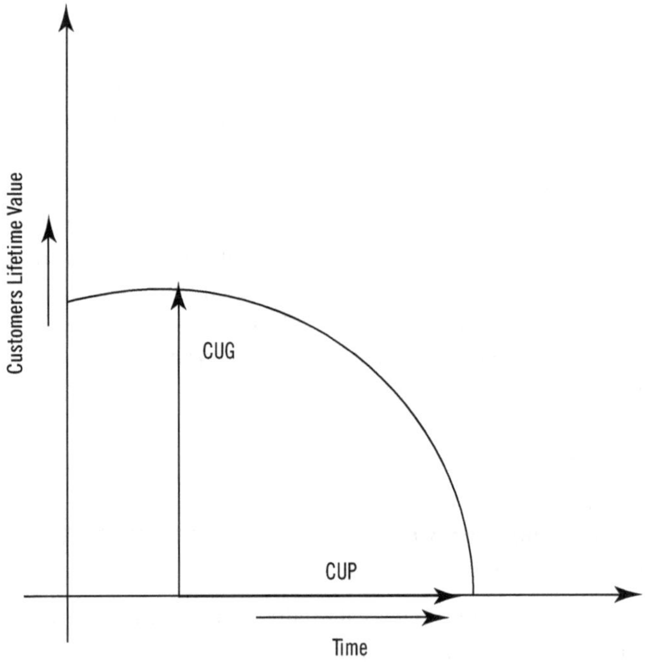


**Fig. 16.2 Higher Market Capitalization in terms of Higher CUGs and Longer CUPs**

- Reducing dramatically the cost of serving the existing customers
- Acquiring new customers

The increase in CUG affects the height of the curve because, assuming the cost structure is unaltered CUG directly impacts both sales and gross margins positively to show up as increased earnings.

(2) Increasing the length of the Customer Value Differential Period (CUP) for which the enterprise can sustain the CUG once the superior returns generated by the enterprise start attracting additional competition.

A long CUP is typically a function of high barriers to entry for competitors who are intent on a portion of the same market, or high switching costs for customers and partners contemplating defecting to the enterprise's competitors. Long CUPs contribute to higher stock price by increasing the duration of the period of such customer differential. Long CUPs effectively represents a reduction in the long-term risks, resulting in much lower discount rates applied to such risks, which in turn results in extending the curve even further towards the right side.

Thus, the management of shareholder value effectively transforms into sustaining increasingly higher customer Lifetime Values (LTVs) for longer durations of time, that is, higher CUGs and longer CUPs. Although CUGs and CUPs are interdependent, CUPs primarily represent the sustainability of CUGs; and the enterprise must focus first on CUPs and then on CUGs. This is because while the effects on CUGs are short-lived and can be corrected easily, the effects on CUPs are more far-reaching and have a bigger impact on stock price than CUGs. Generally, traditional enterprises with P&L focus already have the tool for managing the CUGs, but they do not have a tool to manage the CUPs.

All line functions need to re-evaluate their old metrics to ensure that they are current with the customer-centric and customer responsive stance of the 21st century enterprises. These issues are discussed next.

## 16.5 BALANCE SCORECARD (BSC)

The BSC is a VBM system based on four distinct perspectives for evaluating the performance of a company—financial, customer, internal and learning. The BSC aims to provide a balance between the external and internal measures of performance, between short and long-term objectives, between financial and non-financial measures, and between lagging and leading indicators. It is not limited to being merely a measurement and control system, but has actually developed over the course of time into a full-featured management system for the successful implementation of a company's strategy.

As discussed in Chapter 1, section, "Customer Capital—Customer Knowledge as the New Capital", in this post-industrial and post-modern era of information, the focus of capital and investments has changed dramatically. In the industrial era, all measures and managerial assessments were geared towards the efficiency with which financial capital could be allocated for capturing as quickly as possible the economies of scale to maximize the Return on Capital Employed (ROCE). In this post-modern computerized era however, a company's competitiveness resides primarily in the collaborative systems, processes and people that enable it to be flexible and reconfigure rapidly in response to the changes in the marketplace.

It should be noted that a company's emphasis is not on the capability to ingest the latest technology per se, because that would continue to change in future too. The emphasis is related more to the capability to confront any changes in the market with a strategy that will not only make the customers continue to value the company's products and services, but also differentiate them effectively from those provided by the competitors. This is the subtle reason why a few years ago General Motor's much known foray into highly automated manufacturing facilities to beat the Japanese on productivity and quality was not very successful.

Thus, a company needs a management system to assess and evaluate its strategy in terms of competitiveness and performance in the future. There is also the important need for the company to be able to dynamically monitor the progress and performance of the execution of these strategies, which will then enable the company to administer any corrections or adjustments based on the real-time operational feedback received from such a system. The BSC is precisely such a strategic management system that enables an enterprise to monitor and manage the execution of its value adding and value creating strategies effectively. Enterprises also need an information system that would empower them to implement the BSC.

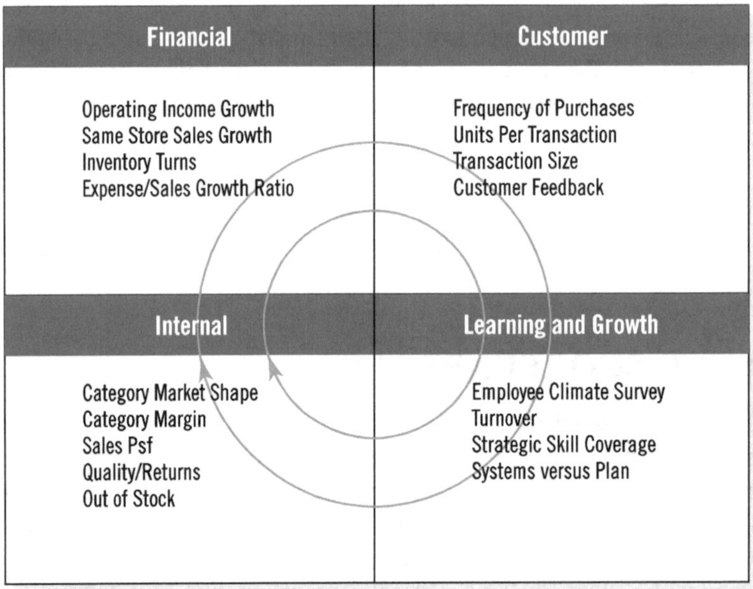


**Fig. 16.3 The Balance Scorecard (BSC) Framework**

BSC provides companies with a framework for translating its vision and strategy into a coherent set of performance measures. BSC derives the objectives and measures of the value determinants or the corresponding performance drivers based on the vision and strategy of the company. As shown in Figure 16.3, the BSC framework is constituted of the following four perspectives:

- Financial
- Customer

- Internal business processes
- Learning and growth

BSC retains the financial perspective of the company's performance that is essentially based on past performance and is valid for short-term performance in the immediate future. However, it supplements this traditional perspective with that of the customer and the internal system, process and people, which determines the company's value-generating potential and hence long-term financial performance in the future.

The customer's perspective ensures the continual relevance of the products and services provided by the company. The internal perspective of business processes and the people ensures that the company surpasses the customer's expectations on critical value determinants like quality, timeliness, innovation and service. It is in this sense that the BSC represents a balance between the external value determinants of the customers and shareholders, and the corresponding internal value drivers of the critical systems, business processes and people.

There are two kinds of value drivers—outcome and performance. Outcome drivers are lagging indicators like financial measures that are objective, quantifiable, and are past facing. On the other hand, performance drivers are leading indicators that link with the company's strategy and provide the rationale for achievements of the outcome drivers. Although performance drivers are future facing, the impact and effectiveness of performance drivers on the outcome drivers is highly subjective. This is compensated by the dynamic nature of the BSC system that treats evaluation and feedback as an important element of the framework. The value drivers are constantly under tests for continued relevance in the market and any deviations observed in the customer's value determinants are immediately cascaded in terms of the changes in the value drivers' measures or the value drivers themselves. This corresponds to the learning and growth perspective of the BSC framework. It represents the capability of institutional learning, which is the powerful concept of "double loop" learning that we spoke about in Chapter 1, sub-section "The Learning Enterprise" that gives tremendous advantages to companies in these times of rapidly changing markets.

In fact, the whole BSC framework is based on a perceived cause-and-effect relationship between the various strategies, organizational elements and processes of the enterprise. It is in the context of these assumptions that the BSC also incorporates the cause-and-effect relationships in terms of the relationships between the various outcome and performance drivers. For instance, the ROCE driver (in the financial perspective) is dependent on customer loyalty (in the customer perspective). Customer loyalty is dependent on the organization's product quality and responsiveness (in the internal business processes perspective), which in turn is dependent on the minimization of product defects, knowledge of the customer's prior transaction history, recorded preferences, and so on (learning and growth perspective). It is because of this that the multiple objectives and measures of BSC do not entail complex tradeoffs but can easily be integrated into a consistent framework of 20 to 25 value drivers that can help navigate the strategy of the company successfully through the turbulent market space.

The strategic management of enterprises using BSC involves the following stages.

- Mapping the company strategy into the BSC framework in terms of the strategic objectives and drivers for BSC. This may also involve reconciling or prioritizing among various objectives or defining differing objectives and drivers for different divisions. This stage identifies all processes that are critical to the strategic performance of the enterprise. It must be noted that the BSC is a methodology for implementing a company strategy and not for formulating one.

- Communicating the link between the strategic objectives and measures throughout the organization at all levels. This may also involve operationalizing the defined set of measures to the specifics of the local circumstances for the various departmental and functional units of the company. BSCs are usually defined at the level of Strategic Business Units (SBUs), but for a multi-divisional company the defined BSC may incline more towards the financial perspective.
- Setting targets, devising aligned strategic initiatives and planning/scheduling initiatives to achieve a breakthrough performance. This may also include financial planning and budgeting as an integrated part of the BSC. From the customer's perspective this step should include requirements of both existing and potential customers.
- Enhancing performance through feedback and learning based on operational data and reviews. This may entail re-prioritizing or changing the performance thresholds or even the value drivers themselves. The latter may become necessary either because of the changes in the marketplace or because the selected set of value drivers may be ineffectual.

Figure 16.4 shows the BSC approach to create a strategy-focused organization.

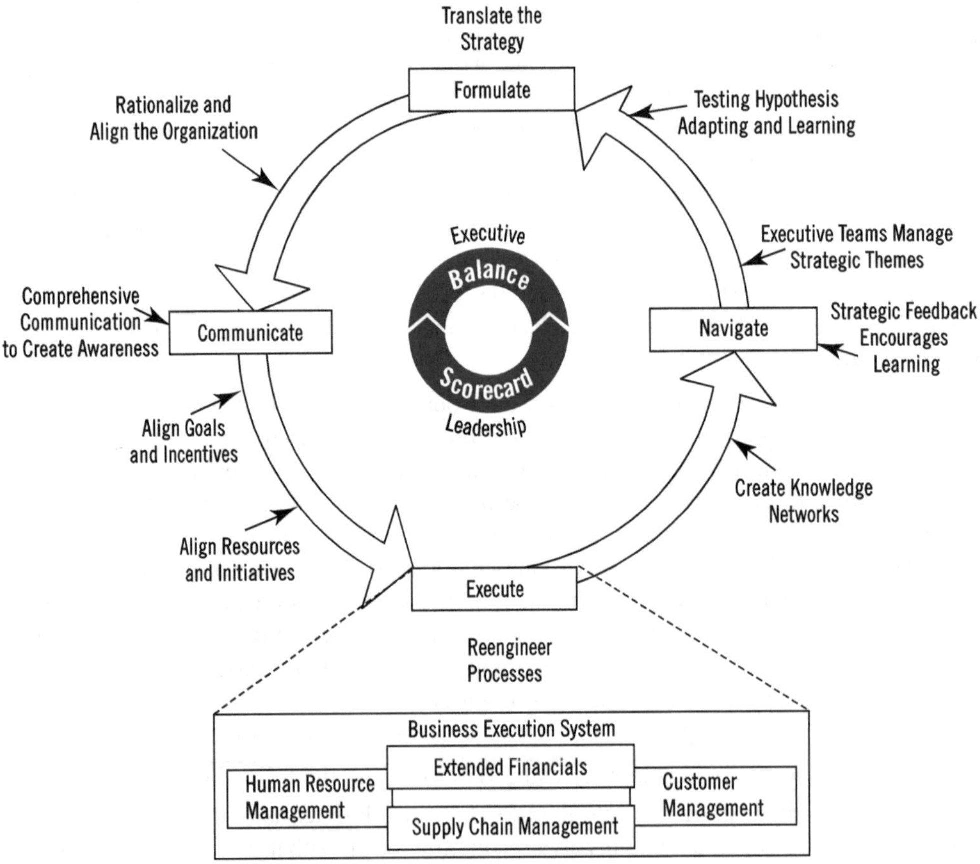


**Fig. 16.4 The BSC Approach to Create a Strategy-focused Company**

In the BSC framework the financial perspective enables a reality check of the strategic management activity of the enterprise. This is because all strategic initiatives meant for improving the quality, flexibility and customer satisfaction may not necessarily translate into improved financial results. If the improved operational outcome as seen from the other three perspectives defined by the company does not end in improved financial results, it may be a powerful indicator of the need for reformulation of the strategy itself. All cause-and-effect relationships that knit a BSC program must eventually link to financial objectives. Therefore, the financial perspective is pre-eminent among all perspectives of the BSC framework.

The standard BSC framework talks of only four perspectives, but if required, the framework can be supplemented with additional perspectives of stakeholders as discussed in "Enterprise Stakeholders." In view of the increased importance of Supply-Chain Management (SCM) for the extended collaborative enterprises of today, a prime candidate for addition would be the suppliers/ vendors of the company. As we will discuss in the final chapter, the suppliers will play as critical a role in the success of the enterprise as any of its constituent SBUs for the extended collaborative enterprises. In the remaining part of this section, we will briefly look at the various perspectives of the standard BSC framework.

## 16.5.1 Financial Perspective

As mentioned earlier, the financial performance measures indicate whether a company's strategy, implementation and execution are translating into bottom-line financial results. Depending on the business strategy, the financial objectives could be in terms of:

- ROCE, Economic Value Add (EVA) or operating income, and maintaining the market share
- Rapid sales growth and increased market share
- Maximize the generation of cash flow

## 16.5.2 Customer Perspective

The customer perspective mainly addresses the customer and market-oriented strategies that will deliver improved financial results. This involves the identification of the market segments of interest, the value propositions for each of these segments and the measures that will help in ascertaining the performance of the company in the selected segments.

The basic outcome measures for this perspective may be:

- Customer Acquisition
- Customer Satisfaction
- Customer Retention
- Customer Profitability

## 16.5.3 Internal Business Processes Perspective

The internal business processes perspective provides focus on the business processes that are critical to the success of the enterprise. The processes selected for improvement could be the existing processes (as discussed in Chapter 7, section "Selecting Business Processes for BPM") or they could also be entirely new processes conceived as a consequence of the strategy of the company. For instance, an excellent example of such a process could be the provision for a Web-based procurement of a company's goods and services.

Siebel contributes directly to a company's performance in this perspective through its now familiar library of best-of-business scenarios and processes as well as its ability to incorporate innovative processes or variations on the existing processes by means of rapid reconfiguration of the IMG.

## 16.5.4 Learning and Growth Perspective

The learning and growth perspective addresses the need to build and maintain an appropriate infrastructure for the long-term growth and success of the company. Contributions from the other perspectives, especially regarding envisaged shifts in customer value, may identify the technologies and products essential to the continued relevance of the company's offerings in the marketplace. These contributions may encompass the following:

(1) People's skills
(2) Information and support systems
(3) Organizational processes and procedures

This perspective comprehensively covers employee-related issues like employee satisfaction, employee training, advancement and promotion policies, employee-friendly policies and procedures, productivity multiplying application environments, and so forth. Siebel is an enabling environment for supporting the management of all these perspectives, an aspect that is considered in the next section.

***Balance Scorecard (BSC) and Activity-based Costing (ABC)***

The Balance Scorecard (BSC) describes how enterprises create value for customers and shareholders by measuring the customer value proposition and linking critical enterprise processes and intangible assets to customer value creation. In a sense, it generalizes the economists' classic 'demand curve' by representing how price, costs and other attributes of the product or service contribute to creating customer value. On the other hand, ABC (or more specifically TDABC) provides enterprises with an accurate model of the cost, capacity utilization of their processes and hence, profitability of servicing their customers (i.e., producing and delivering their products and services) and managing customer relationships. In this sense, it generalizes the economists' classic 'supply curve' to capture the economics of the multi-product and multi-customer enterprises.

ABC provides a model of cost while the BSC describes a model of value creation. They both provide complementary levers for implementing and measuring an enterprise strategy. For instance, enterprises whose BSC describes a low-cost strategy critically need ABC to ensure that the cost of creating value does not exceed the cost of executing this low-cost strategy; similarly, enterprises whose BSC describes a differentiation strategy critically need ABC to ensure that the cost of creating differentiated value does not exceed the cost of achieving this differentiation. On the other hand, truly accurate customer profitability metrics enabled by

TDABC, such as percentage of unprofitable customers and quantum of losses incurred in unprofitable customer relationships, provide the link between customer satisfaction and loyalty, and improved financial performance (see Chapter 7, sub-section "Time-Driven Activity-Based Costing (TDABC)").

# 16.6 THE PERFORMANCE PRISM

Though the balance scorecard takes a far broader view than shareholder value, no mention is made of end-users, employees, suppliers, regulators or local communities. The best way for organizations to survive and prosper in the long-term is to address the wants and needs of all their stakeholders, and deliver value to each of them. Most long-term investors already realize that for companies to be successful over time they must address multiple constituencies. The only sustainable way of delivering shareholder value in the 21$^{st}$ Century is to deliver stakeholder value. The performance prism provides a framework for ensuring better stakeholder relationships (A. Neely et al.).

## 16.6.1 The Performance Prism Framework

The performance prism framework is based fundamentally on the notion of stakeholder value rather than that of shareholder value. It does not assume that the only stakeholders that matter are the shareholders and customers. It results in the organization being best positioned to deliver best value to all of its stakeholders by ensuring that the organization's strategies, processes and capabilities are aligned and integrated with each other.

On the other hand, the Performance Prism also recognizes the fact that organizations are becoming increasingly demanding of their stakeholders too. For instance:

- Investors—capital for growth, greater risk-taking, long-term support
- Customers—profitability, retention, loyalty, advocacy, feedback
- Employees—flexibility, multi-skilling, cross-training
- Suppliers—more outsourcing, fewer vendors, integration
- Alliance partners—cross-selling, co-development, cost sharing
- Regulators—cross-border consistency, early involvement

The Performance Prism consists of five interrelated perspectives on performance that pose specific vital questions:

- Stakeholder satisfaction—which are the key stakeholders and what do they want or need?
- Stakeholder contribution—what does the enterprise want and need from the stakeholders on a reciprocal basis?
- Strategies—what strategies are needed to satisfy the wants and needs of the stakeholders while also satisfying the requirements of the enterprise?
- Processes—what processes need to be in place to enable the enterprise to execute its strategies?
- Capabilities—what capabilities need to put in place to allow the enterprise to operate its processes?

## 16.7 CUSTOMER-CENTRIC ACTIVITY-BASED REVENUE ACCOUNTING (ABRA)

As indicated in Chapter 7, note on "Theory of Constraints (TOC)", a singular drive to minimize costs to the exclusion of all other factors underlies many a disastrous managerial decision. In analogy with ABC, one can conceive of ABRA, which involves assigning revenues and costs explicitly to *both* individual customers, as well as processes or activities. Like ABC, ABRA also envisages the enterprise as a collective whole of activities. ABRA engenders the firm to be designed around customer-facing units where activities, costs and revenues converge on the customer. ABRA enables the fundamental shift from the enterprise to the customer by shifting the focus from the performance of the *enterprise* as a whole to that of the *activities* performed by the enterprise (along with their associated costs and revenues).

ABRA is based on the following:

- Activities of the enterprise
- Activity costs
- Revenues resulting from activities
- Measure of performances as the revenues resulting from activities less the cost of performing them

Like ABC, ABRA also identifies activities, activity revenues, revenue drivers and revenue objects. Because value addition for the customer cannot be observed directly, the contribution of activities to customer revenues is estimated by analyzing the relevant data. After assessing the activity costs by using ABC, the profitability of each activity is assessed by comparing activity revenues with activity costs. Ultimately, ABRA separates the offerings that contribute to customer profitability from those incurring costs.

ABC is useful wherever the enterprise offerings are clearly separable from the underlying specifications and can also be made to particular specifications known to add value for the customer; the corresponding activities and costs can be identified, optimized (including elimination), and performance can be improved without varying these specifications. In contrast, ABRA maybe useful in improving performance in cases like delivery of services (which are innately time-dependent and perishable) where the specifications adding value are not fully known and moreover, are inseparable from the corresponding activity or activities.

1. By allocating costs to customers and revenue to activities and hence, by enabling comparison of revenues to costs customer by customer and activity by activity, ABRA also provides the rationale for evaluating and compensating individual performance.
2. An ABRA-like approach can also be used for focusing on transactions driving customer loyalty or retention; the costs and revenues will change suitably to aspects that are relevant to the changed context

## 16.8 ENHANCEMENT OF MEASURES OF PERFORMANCES (MOPS) BY SIEBEL

It is important to define the right measures for assessing a company's performance and its progress towards its declared goals and objectives. Siebel assists in monitoring and managing the Measures of Performances (MOPs) to enhance the company's operational performance. With its integrated and real-time availability of operational data, Siebel has the enabling environment to create, monitor and manage enterprise value. Siebel provides the empowered platform for SMEs to address the competitive demands of the rapidly changing marketplace and be successful in terms of:

- Improved customer relations and management
- Reduced cycle time
- Improved quality
- Increased sales volumes
- Improved margins
- Reduced product development time
- Reduced manpower for routine operations
- Improved market share

The process of monitoring the MOPs can be guided by the value determinants that have been identified for the company. The value determinants can then be prioritized as well as customized suitable for the different activities within the company. Additions and deletions to the selected measures will be likely, depending on the market situations or alterations in the emphasis and focus of the measures already implemented.

The following lists show some of the performance factors that could be considered for measuring the excellence of the processes in Siebel.

The sales and distribution performance factors are as follows:

- The number of new customers
- The number of one-time customers
- The number of customers retained
- The number of repeat orders and type
- The customer order-to-delivery time
- The number of non-standard or customized orders
- The number of errors per order shipped
- The percentage of back orders as a percentage of total orders
- The percentage of on-time first delivery to customers
- The percentage of on-time complete deliveries to customers

The quality performance factors are as follows:

- The number of defects and their type
- The elapsed time for rework and its type
- The number of customer complaints and their type

- The elapsed time for the first response
- The elapsed time for the delivered resolution
- The average number of customer interactions between problem reporting and resolution, and the type of interactions

Given the multiplicity of dependencies and influencing factors, the selection of the right measures is a complex task. There is a need for a framework under which multiple measures are integrated and related to each other so that a set of measurements should not be perceived to be in opposition to others. Moreover, there is also a need to have the right balance between the financial and non-financial measures, which is the focus of the section, "The Performance Prism".

## 16.9 SUMMARY

This chapter introduced the perspectives on the value created by an enterprise from the point of view of its five major stakeholders, namely, customers, investors, vendors, managers and employees. In the first part of the chapter, we presented the value determinants relevant to all these stakeholders of an enterprise. We then described the concept of Value-based Management (VBM) that ensures the implementation of a corporate strategy by directly linking the strategy, finance and operations within a company. Following this, we proposed *a direct connection between the sum total of time value of all customers of an enterprise with its market capitalization* and therefore, shareholder value. We introduced BSC as a VBM system based on four distinct perspectives for evaluating the performance of a company: financial, customer, internal and learning. The generated value can be monitored and managed by CRM systems like Siebel in terms of the Measures of Performances (MOPs) characterizing the operations of the company. With an eye on extension or customization of VBM systems for specific requirements of an enterprise, we introduced the generic framework of the Performance Prism. At the end of the chapter we looked at a sample list of improvements in MOPs that have been achieved in various companies by the implementation of Siebel CRM.

# Chapter 17 Beyond the Relationship-based Enterprise

In this last chapter of the book, we will look at the long-term implications and prospects of the, '*Information is Relationship*' vision. We will look at the significance of using customer intelligence to enable highly proactive and customer-responsive *decision on desktops*. Following this we will examine application outsourcing and a more refined variation of the Application Service Providers (ASPs) model, namely, Private ASP. Web services are another leading-edge technological solution for creating and delivering cooperative applications over the Internet.

Although gathering a certain amount of information is necessary for companies to personalize and serve their customers better, consumers are rightly concerned about the abuse of their privacy. We will discuss various aspects of customer privacy and security.

Finally, we will identify that, '*Information is Relationship*' leads to the possibility of '*Relationships on Demand*', which in turn, makes possible '*Instant Relationships*'.

## 17.1 INTELLIGENT CUSTOMER-CENTRIC ENTERPRISE

Business Intelligence (BI) systems must provide business users, trading partners and corporate clients of an enterprise, rapid and easy access to the eBusiness applications, services and information that they need in order to compete effectively.

BI systems must provide the following capabilities:

- Channel and cross-channel analysis and campaign applications that measure and analyze the success of the Internet as a sales and marketing channel
- One-to-one marketing analysis applications that customize and personalize applications, products, services and information offered to consumers and clients, especially via the Internet
- Analysis of content, customer and merchandize selling applications to track how users navigate the enterprises' Web sites and use them to buy products
- Supply chain analysis applications that enable the enterprise to work with trading partners to optimize the product supply chain to match the demand for products sold especially through the Internet

- A singular and integrated Web interface to give internal and external users and applications a secure and managed access to enterprise application, services and information.

## 17.1.1 How Intelligent is Your Enterprise?

Each piece of information in the enterprise, including that which resides in the company's information systems, has a value. This value is primarily associated with the manner in which this piece of information is utilized by the enterprise to remain competitive, provide good customer service and optimize eBusiness operations.

In analogy with the Metcalfe's Law for networks (see Chapter 7's note on "*Metcalfe's Law and Network Effects*"), the value of customer information can be assessed to be proportional to:

$$n^m \times d$$

Where,

$n$ is the average number of active users

$m$ is the average number of employees involved in any business process from different departments

$d$ is the number of interacting departments involved in the primary business processes of the enterprise.

## 17.1.2 Decisions on Desktops (DoD)

*'Decisions on desktops' (DoD),* is the 21st century analog of Bill Gates' vision of 'PCs on every desktop' in the 80's. The DoD vision in turn is dependent on attaining *Business Intelligence (BI) on desktops*.

Amid the hyper-competitive environment of the Internet, the systems must enable users to tap the intelligence latent in their data by integrating and analyzing raw data for insights into key business metrics. Desktop-based BI tools should enable real-term, interactive access, analysis and manipulation of mission-critical corporate information to provide users with valuable insight into key indicators to identify business problems and opportunities.

From their desktops, end-users especially those involved with customer-facing functions, should be able to probe, slice, skewer and dice data to assess trends and anomalies in various departments.

- The finance department needs information on profitability in order to adapt cost structures for maximizing value addition.
- The product planning department needs information on sales rates in order to optimally plan for production and to negotiate the most advantageous contracts with vendors.
- The sales department needs information on which products are selling, to which demographic population, in which market spaces, by which channel.
- The marketing department needs information on who is buying what products in order to create intelligent marketing and advertising programs.
- The customer relationship department needs information on its customers to retain them, to adapt its customer-facing practices and mechanisms, to drive repeat business and to win new business.

Enterprise Information Portals (EIP) like Siebel InterActive give users a single Web-based interface to business information and to the applications that generate business information regardless of where they reside. The enterprise can personalize and customize the information and applications accessed through an EIP to match:

- Authorization level of each user
- Role of the user

EIPs enable complete access to the information flow right from back to front-office operational applications to business intelligence and collaborative systems, and back to operational systems as a closed-loop information supply chain.

## 17.2 APPLICATIONS OUTSOURCING (AO)

Applications are evolving from those that facilitated a single business function (e.g., accounting, payroll) to integrated application environments that facilitate business processes spanning entire enterprises or the extended enterprises. This evolution entails more people, planning and ongoing management, especially for mission-critical applications that must maintain a high level of availability. With such increasing complexity and the increased amount of time and skill needed to keep up with the rapidly changing technology cycles, organizations are increasingly seeking outside assistance to deploy, manage and enhance their applications.

Application Outsourcing (AO) is a service wherein responsibility for the deployment, management and enhancement of a packaged or customized software application is handed out contractually to an external service provider. AO entails specific activities and expertise aimed at managing the software application or set of applications. Contractual Service Level Agreements (SLAs) are set at the application level and include responsibilities for:

- Application availability
- Application performance
- Application enhancement

Figure 17.1 presents the positioning of the various types of application outsourcers based on the type of application being outsourced (proprietary vs. packaged) and the configuration/location of the service provision (one-to-one or one-to-many).

The salient characteristics of the various categories are as follows:

(1) Top left quadrant—represents *data center service providers* that provide application hosting services and support to other divisions and are typically managed internally by the enterprises

(2) Bottom left quadrant—represents the *application maintenance service providers* that provide hosting, maintenance and support of custom developed application at the enterprises' site(s)

(3) Top right quadrant—represents the *application service providers* that provide operations and maintenance of both packaged and custom developed application to disparate enterprises using the same outsourcing infrastructure (hardware, software, networks, operational staff, etc.). We will describe this category in the sub-section "CRM Application Service Providers (ASPs)" later.

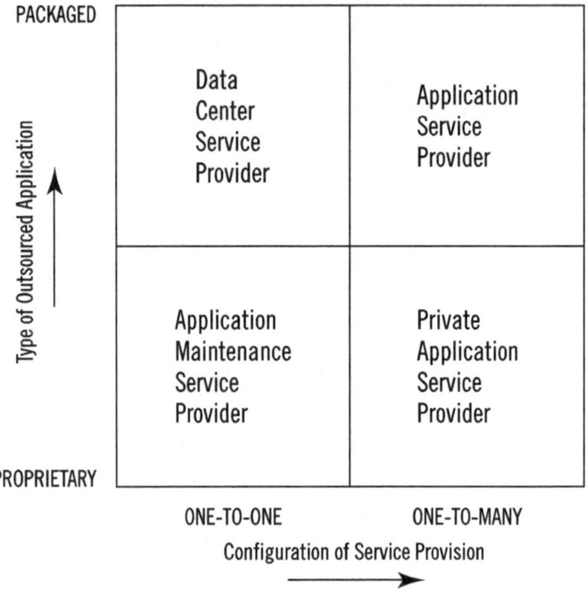


**Fig. 17.1 Types of Applications Outsourcers**

(4) Bottom right quadrant—represents the *private application service providers* that provide operations and maintenance especially of custom applications to an ecosystem of enterprises involved in a particular area of business. We will describe this category in the sub-section "Private ASPs" later.

The top reasons cited by enterprises for resorting to outsourcing are as follows:

- Free internal resources for more strategic projects
- Offload functions that are difficult to manage
- Receive cash infusion from transfer of assets to outsourcers
- Replace capital expenditure with pay-as-you-use operational expenses
- Gain access to world class IT expertise
- Reduce costs for research, development and successful deployment
- Reduce investment risk in a rapidly changing environment
- Obtain additional manpower on an as and when needed basis

In the simplest case, the application is merely hosted for the customer. AO typically does not include responsibility for the underlying business processes or functions; a more comprehensive engagement like Business Processing Outsourcing (BPO) may include operations assessment, process improvement and change management services. When standard applications are being outsourced, the level of staff and asset transfer to this facility maybe minimal and the application itself maybe provided via a license or lease agreement included in the overall service agreement. On the other hand, for more customized applications the contract may include the transfer of people and assets associated with the outsourced application.

### 17.2.1 CRM Application Service Providers (ASPs)

The basic idea behind the Application Service Provider (ASP) computing model is that a provider hosts and manages applications that users can access over networks like Internet. This is the final step towards software manifesting as a service. The market is evolving towards a state where companies will pay for the software as services on a usage basis, as they do traditionally with utility services like electricity and gas. This market was pioneered in 1998 by startups such as Breakaway Solutions, USinternetworking, Corio, etc. The ASP model typically involves lease-to-own options on software. It entails renting access at a low rate to the functionality of ERPs, CRMs, SCMs, etc. over the Internet. In contrast, traditional outsourcing requires upfront purchase of software licenses and often charges large fees for contracted services. Recently however, many ASPs are also experimenting with other pricing models that involve charges for initial customization, migration and integration, plus a flat monthly fee depending on the use of functionality and services, or even a percentage of the customer's revenue. The ASP services could range from infrastructure, co-location, co-hosting, dedicated hosting right through to even hosted businesses such as hosted buying services or hosted customer relationship management services.

The level of the packaged application could vary from discrete applications (like Web-based transaction application for conducting a commerce-based transaction) to environment applications (like CRM). The level of service provided by an ASP can range from simple hosting of application(s) to managing the application environment. Hosting is a standardized service that is based on a high volume and low-cost business model in which applications are hosted at a site and accessed remotely. Managing an application environment goes beyond simple hosting and may include upfront consulting, customization and extensions of the application, and ongoing application technical support.

Factors driving the ASP solutions are as follows:

(a) Enabling Technologies

- Pervasiveness of the Internet
- Access and declining cost of bandwidth capacity
- Shared applications in a client/server environment
- Browsers as an accepted GUI application
- Potential of eCommerce and eBusiness solutions

(b) Technical Drivers

- Utilization of emerging technologies and best-of-breed applications
- Accelerated application development
- Rapidly changing and increasing complexity of technology
- Obtain business domain, functional and vertical industry expertise
- Shortage skilled IT labor
- Transfer of risk regarding application ownership by the super users

(c) Business Drivers

- Minimize Total Cost of Ownership (TCO) by at least 30% to 50%
- Predictability of cash flows by eliminating the uncertainties of post-implementation software-related expenditures

- Focus on core competencies and strategic objectives
- Improve efficiency of internal IT staff by freeing them to focus on processes and systems to leverage core competencies
- Improve coordination efforts on a global basis

However, merely hosting and managing an application is not adequate and needs to be augmented for the creation of proprietary and sustainable customer relationships with value added variations like:

- Domain Expertise Emphasis
- Vertical Industry Emphasis
- Vertical Exchange Emphasis
- Infrastructure Emphasis
- Security Infrastructure Emphasis
- Full Service Provider Emphasis
- Aggregator Emphasis

Some of the challenges faced by the ASP concept are:

- Security of Information
- Scope and Flexibility of Services
- Overall Quality of Service and Support
- Adaptability of Software

Application Service Providers (ASP) present a real opportunity to replace the in-house IT department. Smaller companies also need the full functionality of high-end applications such as ERP, SCM or CRM that cannot be afforded by them. ASPs meet the needs of MME companies that cannot afford the substantial upfront investments in establishing the infrastructure, knowledgeable and experienced staff, ongoing administration and monitoring services, better backup and recovery methods, and so forth. The top reasons that are cited by companies for renting applications are guaranteed performance levels, high availability, responsive service and support. The cost of ownership of hosted applications can be 25% cheaper than managing the applications internally. Other criteria for companies to contract ASPs are lower upfront costs, faster implementations, higher redundancy, larger scalability of hardware and bandwidth, automatic upgrades, quicker distribution and deployment, and data storage, backup and recovery capabilities.

The SiebelNet Business Services that include application-hosting services enable customers to evaluate, implement and operate Siebel eBusiness Applications online (see Chapter 15, sub-section "SiebelNet Business Services"). This enables companies to perform detailed evaluations and prototype company-specific solutions via the Internet prior to deciding to purchase or actually purchasing the CRM product. Customers also have the facility to implement and continue using CRM functionality via the Web browser.

Using Application Service Providers (ASPs) has many advantages, such as:

- Enabling a company to concentrate on enhancing the competitiveness of its core functions
- Enabling a company to outsource the enhancing competitiveness of its non-core but still-critical functions like implementing Call Center operations

- Re-engineering critical but non-core functions and processes quickly
- Comprehensive industry-specific and company-specific evaluations
- Rapid prototyping of company-specific implementations
- Lower upfront investments in hardware and software, technical manpower resources and training
- Reduced risks of initial erroneous decisions in pricing, reliability, scalability, bandwidth and security
- Flexibility of options like hosting, co-hosting and co-location
- Time-to-implement at a lower cost
- Time-to-go-live at a lower cost
- Time-to-benefit at a lower cost
- Time-to-full ownership at a lower cost
- Time-to-deploy at other sites at a lower cost
- Higher service-level guarantees
- Better customer service
- Reduced administration, management, maintenance and support costs

## 17.2.2 Siebel on Demand

Siebel On Demand provides organizations with all the comprehensive Siebel CRM capabilities along with the power of Siebel's software development, infrastructure management and operational services to maximize the business value of their software investment. Delivered to users over the Internet, Siebel On Demand frees IT organizations from day-to-day maintenance, upgrades and software management while providing unparalleled levels of availability, reliability and security. This results in a far more efficient and Cost-effective Approach to Managing CRM and Siebel technology over the long-term.

Siebel On Demand achieves operational excellence and low Total Cost of Ownership (TCO) using standardization and automation as key enablers to improve customers' experience across the entire software ownership life cycle, including in the core service areas like:

- Infrastructure management
- Service level management
- Security management
- Software management
- IT governance

## 17.2.3 Private ASPs

It has been well-established that the largest cost component in an applications life cycle is the effort expended on maintenance and upgrades and this is valid even in cases of packaged software implementations by reason of the customizations that are indispensable. The key idea underlying the Private ASP is that, *the high cost of maintenance and upgrades* (*and operations*) *is spread across the boundary of the enterprise to include the associated ecosystem of at least the exclusive suppliers*. The viability of this business model can be illustrated from the fact that the customization requirements for implementing enterprise systems (ERP, SCM, CRM, etc.) at General Motors's partner/ subsidiary Delphi Electronics are going to be similar to or will be heavily influenced by the customization requirements of General Motors itself. From there it is not very difficult to see that there will be major advantage in combining the implementation projects and teams, training programs, testing centers, rollout projects, IT centers, disaster recovery centers, and so on.

We will describe this concept by taking Ford as the hypothetical example. A Private ASP is an extended ASP service, managed and operated by a major player like Ford for itself and its partners—both customers and vendors. All customization and upgrade issues are dictated mainly by Ford, unlike in the case of a traditional ASP where they may have to customize for each customer independently, *which basically makes the traditional ASP model unviable.*

Private ASP = (SCM + CRM like Siebel + Net Markets) on ASP basis for Ford and its participating partners

> None of the partners need to be compelled to join the Private ASP. Ford however, must mandate that such partners need to integrate and be compatible with its Private ASP at their own cost. Licensing issues are simplified in that all software licenses are owned via the Private ASP instituted jointly by Ford and/ or its partners.

The composite value proposition for Ford and its partners involves the following:

(1) Easy to add/ integrate new vendor partner
(2) Value proposition of a NetMarket—Ford can service an enlarged base of vendors for more competitive bidding but within the class of these preferred partners/ vendors
(3) Value proposition of an ASP for reduced application management, operations and maintenance costs
(4) Value proposition of implementation, management and maintenance of a CRM for individual partners who do not have a CRM which is also the same CRM as used by Ford (at much reduced cost than outside of the private ASP)
(5) Value proposition of an EAI provider, especially for integrating internal and proprietary applications of Ford and its individual partners (at much reduced cost than outside of the private ASP)
(6) Value proposition of profitable IT services via the private ASP for Ford and/ or its partners
(7) Value proposition of an outsourcing service in terms of assets, manpower, support, training, etc.
(8) Value proposition of SCM implementation, operations and management for itself and its partners—this would be of great benefit in the long-term

### 17.2.3.1 What Does a Private ASP Offer?

A Private ASP offers the following.

- Provides applications services to a restricted business ecosystem of Ford and its participating partners.

- Provides individual enterprise-oriented services for Ford and each of the partners through separate instances of each of these applications.
- It also provides individual company-specific services for internal applications like HRMS, CRM, email, etc., to Ford and its partners separately. Thus, if there are 100 partners who have joined Ford's Private ASP program, there maybe 100 different implementations of HRMS, CRM, etc., (from different vendors) systems for the specific requirements for each of these partners but handled by the same entity—the Private ASP.

Ford can own the Private ASP facility fully and run it as a profit center. It can charge its partners on subscription (and/or even on transaction basis) along with a possible lump sum enrollment fee. Or, Ford can float a separate company along with its participating partners to establish and run this Private ASP; the Private ASP can then charge via a uniform model for all its delivered services, to all members of the Private ASP.

## 17.3 APPLICATION FUNCTIONALITY AS WEB SERVICES

Web services are new standards for creating and delivering co-operative applications over the Internet. Web services allow applications to communicate irrespective of the platform or the operating system. By using Web Services, developers can eliminate major porting and quality testing efforts, potentially saving millions of dollars. They will radically change the way that applications are built and deployed in future.

As explained in Chapter 10, sub-section "Enterprise Component Architecture", a developer can create an application out of re-usable components. But what good is it to have a large library of re-usable components if nobody knows that they exist, where they are located, and how to link to and communicate with such programmatic components? Web services are standards for finding and integrating object components over the Internet. They enable a development environment where it is no longer necessary to build complete and monolithic applications for every project. Instead, the core components can be combined from other standard components available on the Web to build the complete applications that run as services to the core applications.

Some of the past approaches for enabling program-to-program communications included combinations of program-to-program protocols such as Remote Procedure Call (RPC) and Application Program Interfaces (APIs) coupled with architectures such as Component Object Model (COM), the Distributed Component Object Model (DCOM) and the Common Object Request Broker Architecture (CORBA). But, without a common underlying network, common protocols for program-to-program communication and a common architecture to help applications to declare their availability and services, it has proven difficult to implement cross-platform program-to-program communication between application modules. These previous attempts to set up standards for accomplishing these objectives were not very successful because:

- They were not functionally rich enough and are difficult to maintain as best-of-breed
- They were vendor-specific as opposed to using open and cross-vendor standards
- They were too complex to deploy and use

The use of Web Services standards holds the potential for correcting each of these deficiencies. This new approach presents applications as services to each other and enables applications to be rapidly assembled by linking application objects together.

With the advent of Internet and its protocols, most vendors and enterprises have graduated to a common communication and network protocol—the Internet's TCP/ IP protocol. And with the availability of Web standards such as eXtended Markup Language (XML), Simple Object Access Protocol (SOAP), Universal Description, Discovery and Integration (UDDI) and Web Services Definition Language (WSDL), vendors enable customers to:

(1) Publish specifications about application modules via WSDL
(2) Find those modules (either on the internal Intranet or on the Internet) via the UDDI
(3) Bind the applications together to work seamlessly and cooperatively and deliver the holistic functionality of composite application via SOAP and XML.

Major hardware vendors and certain key software vendors are looking at these new Web standards for providing solutions for program-to-program communication. IBM's WebSphere Server environment, Sun Microsystems's Open Network Environment (ONE) constituting of various Sun technologies and third-party products, and Microsoft's .NET initiatives deliver Web Services based solutions.

The significance of Web Services for the future is by reason of the following.

- Web Services will enable enterprises to reduce development costs and expand application functionality at a fraction of the cost per traditional application development and deployment method.
- Web Services will enable Independent Software Vendors (ISVs) to bring products to market more quickly and respond to competitive threats with more flexibility.
- Web Services will enable enterprises to re-use existing legacy application functionality with the latest applications and technologies.
- Web Services will obviate the need of porting applications to different hardware platforms and operating systems at great expense.
- Web Services enable applications to communicate irrespective of platform or operating system.
- Web Services will have the effect of leveling the playing field because it will enable even specialized boutique application firms to compete easily with well-established and resourceful Original Equipment Manufacturers (OEMs).
- Web Services will enable only those OEMs to flourish that focus on providing comprehensive implementations and highly productive application development environments for Web Services.
- Web Services will enable applications to be packaged not only as licenses but also as services; this will give a big fillip to ASP services (as discussed in the earlier section) and will consequently expand the overall market size tremendously.
- Web Services will enable Value Added Resellers (VARs) to rapidly add new functionality to current product offerings or to customize the existing applications of customers.
- Web Services will enable enterprises to adapt better to the changing market conditions or competitive threats

## 17.4 PRIVACY AND SECURITY

The advent of Internet has transformed the familiar issues of security and privacy beyond recognition. This is primarily because of the following:

- Every computer can be accessed and influenced by any other computer anywhere on the Internet; this effectively eliminates the concept of locality
- Businesses that are supported on such an extended and open IT-substrata are vulnerable to scrutiny and monitoring by interested parties
- Browsing and visitations of Web sites to gather information in turn also exposes the visitor's behavior itself to interpretation and analyses

Consumer privacy issues and concerns have a drastic effect on the enterprise's ability to market to, connect with and create an ongoing relationship with, your customers (see Chapter 1, sub-section "Permission Marketing", and especially Naomi Klein). Consumers are gravely concerned regarding the abuse of their privacy, but gathering a certain amount of information is necessary for companies to personalize and serve their customers better. Thus, there is a need for a balance between protecting a consumer's privacy and the need for enterprises to target and personalize their offerings to the customers. In 2000, US Federal Trade Commission recommended fair information practices of *notice*, *choice*, *access* and *security*. Enterprises need to adhere to these practices when creating and implementing their privacy policies. Third-party privacy seals are a good way to gain the trust of consumers because these third-party consumer privacy protection organizations certify the enterprise's privacy policy.

There are two types of privacy seal programs. One has strict guidelines that prohibit sites from sharing consumer information that they collect with other business partners, or from using it for direct marketing programs. Secure Assure, which has 200 member companies, offers an audit program but requires members to adhere to a stringent privacy guideline stating that the eBusiness will never share a consumer's private information with a third-party. Other privacy seal programs award stamps-of-approval to sites that simply stick to whatever privacy policy promises they have made. The oldest and most well known privacy seal program is Electronic Frontier Foundation's TRUSTe (www.truste.org), which was started in 1997 and has more than 1300 companies as members including AOL and eToys.

The threat to information privacy and security can never be eliminated but controls and technologies can be applied to reduce the risks to acceptable levels. The challenges faced by the various enterprises in this regard are described here.

### 17.4.1 Privacy

There are a number of aspects to privacy.

(a) The captured user behavior representing the navigation and interaction of the user with the system(s). To identify a particular user the Web server writes/ updates a small *cookie* file that is stored on the user system to record predetermined pieces of information, such as identity of every page visited by the user and every search performed by the user. While this enables enterprises to provide customer-focused services, the compilation of the historic log of searches and Web site visits have major implications for privacy-related issues.

(b) The transmitted user data as it travels across public networks is vulnerable to being tapped much like telephone calls or being scrutinized at the Web servers as is done for calls passing through telephone exchanges. This is resolved through encrypting, by employing a special *algorithm* (i.e., a process) to convert a normal *plaintext* message into an apparently unintelligible *ciphertext* message that can be converted back into plain text by using a deciphering key, which is usually a 40 bits (i.e., a large) number.

The two basic types of encryption algorithms are as follows.

- Symmetric key algorithms/schemes rely on a single key to both encrypt and decrypt a message. It is vulnerable to the key being revealed publicly rendering the system unusable, or the original message can be tampered with without being detected playing havoc with the integrity of the system.
- Pubic key algorithms/schemes work on the principle that the keys can only work in pairs—one private key (that is maintained private) matches with exactly one public key (that is made public); the key used to encrypt a message cannot be used to decrypt it, and vice-a-versa. When the user wants to send a message, it is encrypted with the publicly available public key of the target recipient and on receipt, only the recipient can decrypt the message using the corresponding private key available solely with the recipient.

> A common compromise solution is to use symmetric keys to encrypt the messages but to use public keys to manage the symmetric keys; consequently, the symmetric key can be used for a set of transactions, also termed as the 'session key'.

However, the largest vulnerability is attributable to the use of the public network, which is also the reason for its ubiquity. This is resolved by establishing a *Virtual Private Network* (VPN) between the various nodes of the network. A VPN effectively functions as an extremely secure link via the Internet (termed as a 'tunnel') between these nodes, without the need to lay physical wires between these nodes to create a private network at great cost. Thus, the VPN between an enterprise and its partners is set up via the Internet with hardware devices at each node on the VPN network; adding another trading partner merely entails adding another security device at their end and configuring the VPN network to include it.

(c) The stored user data is discussed in the sub-section "Integrity". The protection of access to stored information is dealt with in the next sub-section.

## 17.4.2 Intrusion

Intrusion is similar to intruders breaking into a building and is countered by the analog concept of an electronic firewall. The firewall generally sits between the enterprise and the Internet, and monitors all traffic coming in (or going out) from your business, primarily at two levels namely,

(a) Network level where it does the following:

- Restricts access for all, some or specific users, to all, some or specific applications
- Scans e-mails for deleting suspect attachments
- Strips ActiveX controls and Java applets from Web pages

- Screens access to URLs to prevent non-business and illegal Internet surfing
- Scans network activity for irregular activities

(b) Application level

Evidently, a faulty firewall may not achieve its objective, but is also more damaging in that it engenders a false sense of security.

## 17.4.3 Integrity

This relates to the reliability of the transactions not having been altered without being detected unfailingly.

The common approaches adopted to ensure integrity are as follows.

(a) Secure Socket Layer (SSL) is the most commonly used security scheme on the Internet for the exchange of information between the browser/client and the remote server.

(b) VPN is suitable for a community or ecosystem of partners.

(c) Secure Electronic Transactions (SET) is a specialized security protocol for dealing with credit card transactions primarily as a part of the financial transactions.

(d) Electronic signatures are akin to the total at the end of a column of numbers that is unrelated to the individual numbers but can be used to ascertain the authenticity of the full message. If this number signature is encrypted with a private key, anyone can read the message using the public key for decryption; but if the message has been modified in any way, the signature would no longer match the text. Thus electronic signatures are direct indicators of the authenticity of the messages.

(e) For any encryption, the requisite public key is reliably obtained from a trusted third-party called the Certification Authority (CA) that provides this information in the form of a certificate consisting of:

  - The public key and verification of who the key belongs to
  - An expiry date indicating period of validity
  - Level of trust indicating the degree of verification that has been undertaken to ascertain the genuineness of the ownership of the key by a particular individual or party

(f) Secure email commonly uses S/MIME (Secure Multi-purpose Internet Mail Extensions) that utilizes encryption and certification to provide the needed security to messages.

The totality of infrastructure and system for managing public keys is referred to as a Public Key Infrastructure (PKI), which includes:

- An hierarchy of CAs starting with a root Certification Authority (rootCA) that focuses only on verifying the veracity of all these layers of CAs
- Resolution for a number of issues like Government regulation of CAs, legal admissibility of the certificates, liabilities in the case of a failure or fraud, etc.

### 17.4.4 Business Disruption

The common ways in which an electronic attack can disrupt the enterprise's business are as follows.

- Viruses which are the most common form of attack can result in incidental damages like wiping of hard disks, overwriting or deletion of files, program crashes, computers or networks slowing down or even grinding to a halt. Even relatively harmless e-mails/ messages in large volumes can also clog the networks and disk spaces to render the system unusable for prolonged periods. E-mail, which is the 'killer app' of the Internet, is also the most frequent conduit for entry and spreading of viruses within enterprises.
- Denial of Service attacks (DOS) though not fatal can be equally damaging. This is similar to a telephone exchange or a call center being swamped by a barrage of spurious calls during a critically timed tele-service event.

> Consider a user receiving a message "URGENT: A new virus 'Happy Valentine' has been detected that, if opened, would wipe your hard disk. Please e-mail this message urgently to everyone you know". If this message itself has an infected attachment, it will lead to an endemic! Even if this message is uninfected, the volume of the resulting messages itself may slow down or even paralyze the network pipes.

## 17.5 MOBILIZING THE ENTERPRISE AND RELATIONSHIPS

Mobilization is fundamentally about extending your enterprise's capacity to do business. The ability to handle and process both personal and public information while mobile is very compelling. Mobilization enables enterprises to extend their networks to mobile enterprises effectively while protecting the investments in legacy systems and current technologies. Mobilizations achieve the following.

- Enable enterprises to distribute enterprise intelligence to wherever, whenever and whichever device it is needed, enabling accelerated decisions.
- Support the broadest range of enterprise touch points possible. The distinction between PDAs, wireless phones and handheld PCs (such as Microsoft's Tablet PC) is becoming blurred; PDAs are receiving mobile phone functionality and in turn, mobile phones are receiving the functionality of PDAs with calendaring and contact database utilities. And all of them are converging further to access e-mail, Web pages, Internet, and wired and wireless infrastructure from anywhere and anytime.
- Leverage the use of legacy information assets while continuing to maintain their local autonomy, integrity and relevance.
- Isolate current and future intellectual property and mobile applications from infrastructure and technology innovation and improvements.

Two outstanding benefits of mobilization are increased productivity, and real-term gathering and dissemination of information. The mobilized enterprise becomes more productive via the gathering and dissemination of real-term information enabling the enterprise to respond quickly and appropriately to new problems and opportunities. For instance, a mobile Sales Force Automation (SFA) application that enables a company to respond to opportunity quickly. If a salesperson has access to inventory information while he is with a customer, the order processing can be handled immediately. Thus, the mobile solutions designed to take into account the needs of the mobile worker enables the enterprise to be more customer-focused, more productive, more responsive, more flexible and more profitable.

The mobile solutions transform the organization from a command-and-control hierarchy into a responsive and adaptive enterprise wherein:

- Technology adapts pervasively to the business processes
- Enterprise resources are extended securely to any environment
- Collaboration is supported at all touch points within the workflow
- Distance and time cease to be impediments to productivity
- Enterprise responds in real-term

Mobile technology transforms organizations and has the potential to significantly increase overall productivity, adaptability and responsiveness of the enterprise.

## 17.6 PROSPECTS FOR THE FUTURE—RELATIONSHIPS ON DEMAND!

If it is true that '*Information is Relationship*', then it readily admits the possibility of '*Relationships on Demand*', with far-reaching implications. Customer and customer interaction related information available on demand makes it possible for the front end employees to substitute this information for a possibly intrusive interaction with the customer for ascertaining their routine needs every time.

As we have stated in Chapter 1, companies have a wealth of knowledge in the files and records that customer-facing employees have on customer interactions. Freeing this knowledge from the shackles of experience, institutionalizing it and transferring it in real-time to all employees, so that they are empowered to leverage or build further on the relationships with particular customers is the best way to leverage this knowledge.

More significantly, this customer information does not have to be disseminated to everyone on a routine basis, but only whenever required. This finally would be the realization of any marketer's dream—*instant relationships*!

## 17.7 SUMMARY

In this last chapter of the book, we looked at the long-term implications and prospects of the vision of, *Information is Relationship* proposed in this book. We also looked at the significance of using customer intelligence to enable a highly proactive and customer-responsive vision of '*decision on desktops*'. Following this we looked at Application Outsourcing and a more refined variation of the Application Service Providers (ASPs) model, namely, Private ASP. We also introduced the concept of Web services as another leading-edge technological solution for creating and delivering cooperative applications over the Internet. As consumers are rightly concerned regarding the abuse of their privacy, we discussed various aspects of the customer privacy and security. Finally, we identified that *Information is Relationship* leads to the possibility of '*instant relationships*'.

# Appendix A

# Selecting Siebel Implementation Partners

Selecting the right kind of implementation partner is very critical.

For successful implementation of Siebel, it is critical for the company to define the objectives and the role of the Siebel consulting firm. The prime objective for the firm should be:

- To help and guide the Siebel implementation
- Train the core implementation team of the company
- Transfer knowledge of Siebel product and functionality to members of the company on the implementation team

This will ensure that the company can continue the momentum of the Siebel implementation into its subsequent phases even after the exit of the consultants.

Siebel implementation partners should be selected on the basis of:

(a) Siebel implementation projects portfolio

(b) Siebel consultants and their experience

(c) Industry-specific expertise

(d) Project consulting experience

(e) Implementation methodology

(f) Location of additional office sites

It should be noted that unlike in the case of the earlier projects that were predominantly for Fortune 500 companies, projects for the Small and Medium Business (SMB) enterprises with revenues ranging from $25 million to $500 million, would require smaller teams with multi-skilled consultants. SMB enterprise would not require or be able to afford individual consultants for different functional areas of CRM.

Appendix B

# Traditional Siebel Consulting Partners–USA**

## NATIONAL LOGO PARTNERS

1 Andersen Consulting .
2 Cap Gemini America
3 CSC Consulting America (CSC)
4 Deloitte & Touche (D&T)
5 Dynamic Data Solutions
6 Electronic Data Systems Corp. (EDS)
7 Ernst & Young (E&Y)
8 Hewlett-Packard Company (HP)
9 IBM Corporation (IBM)
10 Intelligroup, Inc.
11 KPMG Peat Marwick
12 Modis Solutions
13 Origin Technology in Business
14 PriceWaterhouseCoopers
15 Resource Support Associate Inc.
16 Siemens Nixdorf Info Systems, Inc.

## IMPLEMENTATION PARTNERS

1 Abacus Software
2 ACSYS IT
3 AG Consulting (Div. of ADP)
4 Akili Systems Group
5 Application Partners LLC
6 Applied Integration Services
7 Argus Integrated Sokutions, Inc.
8 Arthur Andersen LLP
9 Atlantic Duncans International
10 Atlas Software
11 Braun Technology Group
12 BrightStar Information Technology Group
13 Bristlecone, Inc.
14 Bureau Van Dijk Computer Services, Inc.
15 CAI/ Advanced Solutions
16 Cap Gemini America, Inc.
17 CaRD America, Inc.
18 cdg & associates, inc.
19 Ciscorp
20 Clarkson Potomac Group, Inc.
21 Client Server Solutions, Inc.
22 Complete Business Solutions Inc.
23 Computer Task Group, Inc.
24 Conley, Canitano Assoc, Inc.
25 Cybertech International Co.
26 d.d.synergy USA
27 DA Consulting Group
28 Debis Information Services
29 Delphi Consultants, Inc.
30 Delta Consulting, Inc.
31 Deno Morris, Inc.
32 Dynamic Resources, Inc
34 EA Consulting
35 Eisner Consulting
36 EMAX Solution Partners, Inc.
37 Executive Consultants
38 Gamma Computer, Inc.

39 Global Core Strategies
40 Grant Thornton LLP
41 Grom Associates Data Processing Cons.
42 Hewlett-Packard Company
43 Holland Software Solutins LLC
44 Honeywell, Inc.
45 HPC Heck & Partner Consulting
46 HR Link Group, Inc.
47 IBM Corporation
48 IDS Sheer, Inc.
49 IMG America, Inc.
50 IMI Systems
51 Integration Associates
52 Integration Software Consulants
53 Intelligroup, Inc.
54 International Management Group, Inc.
55 IT Services Inc.
56 Kelly-Levey & Associates
57 Knightsbridge Solutions, Inc.
58 Kurt Salmon Associates, Inc.
59 Litton PRC
60 Logical Choice of Technologies, Inc.
61 Magnus Management Consultants USA Inc.
62 Mahindra Consulting
63 Management & Application Support
64 Maganement Resources of VA, Inc.
65 Meatra America, Inc.
66 Metamor Enterprise Solutions
67 Miracle Software Systems, Inc.
68 Modis Solutions, Inc.
69 Multivision International, Inc.
70 Murray & West
71 Nanobyte Software Inc.
72 Nexus Technology, Inc.
73 OAO technology Solutions, Inc.
74 Optimum Consulting America, Inc.
75 Osprey Systems, Inc.
76 Pegasus System+B25s, Inc.
77 Phaedra Software Solutions
78 Plaut Consulting, Inc.
79 POWERhaus Consulting, LLC
80 Preimer HR Solutions, Inc.
81 Prescient Consulting LLC
82 Prism Consulting Group, LLC
83 Prism Consulting Services
84 Radiant Systems Inc.
85 RCG International, Inc
86 realTECH, Inc.
87 Realtime Consulting, Inc.
88 Reed Business Systems Consulting
89 Resource Support Associates
90 RPM Associates
91 RWD Technologies, Inc.
92 Schmidt Vogel & Partner America, Inc.
93 Science Application International Corp. (SAIC)
94 Seal Consulting, Inc.
95 Seltmann, Cobb & Bryant, Inc.
96 Seimens Nixdorf Info Systems, Inc.
97 SLI Consulting, Inc.
98 Soft Guide International, Inc.
99 Solbourne Solutions Consulting, Inc.
100 Spearhead Systems Consultants (US) Ltd.
101 SPO America, Inc.
102 Syskoplan Consulting Group, Inc.
103 Technology Solutions Corp.
104 The Amber Group, Inc.
105 The Hunter Group, Inc.
106 The INC Group, Inc.
107 The Owens Group, Inc.
108 Transaction Information Systems
109 Triple-I
110 TSI International Software
111 VGS, Inc.
112 Walldorf Technology Group
113 Whittman-Hart, LP

## HARDWARE PARTNERS

1 Amdhal Corp.
2 Compaq Computer Corp.
3 Data General Corp.
4 Dell Computer Corp.
5 EMC Corporation
6 Hewlett Packard Corp.
7 Hitachi Data Systems Corporation

8 IBM Corporation
9 NCR World Headquarters
10 Sun Microsystems, Inc.
11 Unisys Corporation

## CONSULTING PARTNERS

1 Informix Software Inc.
2 Intel Corporation
3 Microsoft Corporation
4 Oracle Corporation

## CONSULTING PARTNERS

**Base**

1 2Grow BV
2 Abacus Software Group
3 Acadia University
4 Acando AB
5 Aces International
6 Active CRM Support
7 Adacel Technologies Limited
8 Adjoined
9 ADS Financial Services Solutions
10 Advanced Information Services Inc.
11 Advanced Programming Resources, Inc
12 alabus ag
13 Ambient Consulting
14 AMC Technology L.L.C.
16 Avanzit Tecnologia, S.L.
17 Axias NV
18 b-next AG
19 B2B Workforce
20 BASF IT Services Ltd.
21 Bay Street Solutions
22 BD Consultores S.A.
23 BDR Consulting
24 Beacon Technologies LLC
25 BEKK Consulting AS
26 BFGP Sistemas, C.A.
27 Birlasoft
28 BIT Institute (Mannheim University)
29 Blue Hammock
30 BMC Software
31 Cluster Reply
32 Cognizant Technology Solutions
33 Cohen Brown Management Group, Inc
34 Computer Information Systems
35 Consultores De Sistemas S.a. De C.v.
36 CPM SA
37 CRM Solutions
38 CRM-IT
39 CRMSmart Pty Ltd.
40 CRP Solutions, Inc
41 Customer Systems
42 Cybertech Systems
43 EDGE Services, Inc.
44 ELCA Informatique SA
45 Elcimai Informatique
46 entory AG
47 Envisage Solutions, Inc.
48 ePairs, Inc
49 Equarius, Inc.
50 Erudite Systems Limited
51 eRUNWAY. Com
52 eSMS, Inc
53 Everest Field Technologies
54 Evosoft GmbH
55 GEDAS DE MEXICO, SA DE CV
56 Global Edge Technologies (Pty) Ltd.
57 GNC Consulting, Inc
58 Gold CRM Consulting L.L.C.
59 Green House Group Pte Ltd.
60 Greenbrier & Russel
61 Grupo IT Deusto S.L.
62 GSI - Group ABS
63 GST S.p.A.
64 H & A Consulting, Inc.
65 Haverstick Consulting
66 HCL Technologies America, Inc.
67 HOGART Ltd.
68 I-flex Solutions limited
69 IBERDROLA / IBERINCO
70 Innovatica, S.A.
71 Innovent Solutions
72 Insert Sistemas
73 Integrated Systems Solutions, Inc.

74 Intersoft Technology Partners
75 Intertrade ITS
76 Intesol Corporation
77 iORMYX Inc.
78 iRevolution Consulting Inc.
79 ISYDE S.r.l.
80 IT Frontier
81 IT/net Group Inc.
82 ITApps Limited
83 IT NET UK Limited
84 jambou
85 Kainos Software Ltd.
86 MetricSphere, LLC
87 Mind Information Services SA
88 Miracle Software Systems
89 Mitsubishi Information
90 Mphasis
91 Mummert + Partner
92 National Computer Systems Pte Ltd.
93 Navint (formerly Nextera)
94 Neoris De Mexico, S.A. de C.V.
95 NetComm Solutions, Inc.
96 NETRAGON AG
97 OZSoft Consulting Corpn
98 Pascada Consulting GmbH
99 Patni Computer Systems
100 PBSE, Inc.
101 Pcom (Europe) Limited
102 Plutus Enteprises
103 Polaris Software Lab Limited
104 Pride S.p.A.
105 Princeton Consulting
106 RWD Technologies
107 SAIC
108 Samsung SDS
109 Sapient Corporation
110 Satyam Computer Services Ltd.
111 SchlumbergerSema
112 SevenThree Limited
113 Syntegra (USA) Inc.
114 Syntel, Inc.
115 syskoplan
116 SysTech Integrators, Inc
117 Systor AG
118 T-Nova Deutsche Telekom Innovatinsgesellschaft mbH EZ Darmstadt
119 T-Systems ITS GmbH (Formerly debis Systemhaus)
120 Taldor Computer Systems Ltd.
121 TDS Consulting GmbH
122 TEAM PARTNERS GROUP
123 Team4 GmbH
124 TecniData, BC
125 The Keena Group, Inc.
126 TicaretNet
127 TietoEnator Corp.
128 Watch Hill Partners, Incorporated
129 Watermark Spain
130 Wipro
131 Wola Net S.A.
132 Xform, Inc.

**Strategic**

1 BearingPoint, Inc (formerly KPMG)
2 Siemens Business Services GmbH & Co. OHG

**Premier**

1 Akibia
2 CSK CORPORATION
3 eLoyalty
4 Escador
5 Headstrong, Inc.
6 SKURA Software, Inc.
7 TeleAp
8 Watson Wyatt Worldwide
9 Xansa
SOFTWARE

**Base**

1 360Commerce, Inc.
2 Acapel
3 Actional Corporation
4 Actuate Corporation
5 ADC Software Systems, Inc.
6 Agile Software Corporation
7 Altitude Software

8 Avistar Communications Corporation
9 Axeda Systems Inc.
10 BackWeb Technololgies
11 Baltimore Technologies
12 BAM! Software Inc.
13 Banter
14 ClickSoftware, Inc
15 COGNOS
16 Compuware Corporation
17 Comshare Incorporated
18 Convergent Systems Limited
19 Corechange, Inc
20 Cramer Systems Inc.
21 Crystal Decisions - a Seagate Company
22 CSG Systems
23 edocs
24 EISI
25 Elity Systems, Inc.
26 Eloquent, Inc
27 Embarcadero Technologies, Inc.
28 EMC Corporation
29 Empirix Inc.
30 ePeople, Inc.
31 Epicentric
32 Ericsson
33 Everypath Inc.
34 Global Knowledge, Inc
35 GoAmerica Communications Corp.
36 HERMES SoftLab USA Inc.
37 HighDeal, SA
38 Hummingbird Ltd.
39 HyperSpace Communications, Inc.
40 Ibermatica SA
41 Interactive Intelligence
42 Interwoven, Inc.
43 Intraspect Software, Inc.
44 IPC Information Systems, Inc.
45 Journee Software Corporation
46 Kabira Technologies
47 Kintana
48 MDSI Mobile Data Solutions Inc.
49 Micromuse, Inc.
50 Mobilesys, Inc.
51 Mobius Management Systems Inc.
52 Motive Communications Inc.
53 Narus, Inc.
54 NaviSys Inc.
55 Ncorp Limited
56 Netegrity
57 OTG Software Inc.
58 Outstart, Inc
59 PALMWARE SA
60 PASCO CORPORATION
61 Pegasystems Inc.
62 Peopleclick
63 Pepper Technologies AG
64 Planlinx, Inc.
65 Plumtree Software
66 Precise Software Solutions LTD.
67 Presence Technology
68 Primus
69 RSA Security
70 Salentica Systems Ltd.
71 SAS Institute
72 Scribe Software Corporation
73 SearchSoftware America
74 Segue Software, Inc.
75 ServiceWare
76 Servigistics
77 Shipcom Wireless Inc
78 Sierra Atlantic Inc.
79 Silicon Energy Corp.
80 Siperian, Inc
81 Syntegra UK
82 Syntellect
83 Viafone
84 Visual Mining Inc.
85 Waveset Technologies
86 Wicom Communications Oy Ltd.
87 Witness Systems

**Strategic**

1 Acxiom
2 Alcatel
3 BEA Systems
4 Convergys Corporation
5 Jacada, Inc.

6 Mercury Interactive
7 SeeBeyond
8 TIBCO
9 Vitria Technology
10 webMethods, Inc.

**Premier**

1 Concerto Software (formerly Davox and CELLIT, Inc)
2 Group 1
3 Hyperion
4 Mercator Software Inc
5 Portal Software, Inc.
6 WRQ, Inc.

## MANAGEMENT

**Base**

1 A. T. Kearney
2 Bain & Company, Inc.
3 Peppers & Rogers

## NO CATEGORY

**Global Strategic**

1 Accenture
2 Avaya Inc.
3 Hewlett-Packard Company
4 Microsoft
5 PricewaterhouseCoopers

## CONTENT

**Base**

1 Bank of America
2 Holden International

**Premier**

1 Medical Data Management PORTFOLIO

**Premier**

1 BizProLink Networks
2 ClearCube
3 comScore
4 Everdream
5 Satmetrix Systems
6 SeeCommerce
7 Systemcorp.
8 VitalLink

## ACE

**Base**

1 CSC
2 eVerge Group
3 Seurat Company
4 Tata Consultancy Services
5 TIER1 Innovation LLC

## PLATFORM

**Base**

1 EPICLINK SPA
2 Intermec Technologies Corporation
3 Itronix Corporation
4 NCR Corp.
5 Neoteris, Inc.
6 Sirius Computer Solutions, Inc.

**Strategic**

1 Pitney Bowes, Inc.
2 Precision Response Corporation
3 Xerox Corporation

****Please check for the latest Oracle Siebel CRM Consulting Partners List***

# Appendix C
# Traditional Siebel CRM Third-Party Solutions**

| COMPANY | | CATEGORY | PRODUCT |
|---|---|---|---|
| **Base** | | | |
| 1 | 360Commerce, Inc. | eCRM | 360 Stoe, 360 Enterprise |
| 2 | Acapel | Internet Telephony | KISARA Siebel 2000 JPN version 1.02, 2.2 |
| 3 | Actional Corporation | eCRM | Actional Control Broker version 3.1 SoapSwitch version 3.5 and e-Reporting 3.2, 4.0, 5.0 |
| 4 | Actuate Corporation | eCRM, eProcurement and Net Marketplaces | Actuate Reporting System version 3.2 and eReporting Suite version 4.0, 5.0 |
| 5 | ADC Software Systems, Inc. | | Easy Phone version 5.1 Altitude uCI2000+ Easy Phone version 5.1 |
| 6 | Agile Software Corporation | Product Life Cycle Management | Agile Product Collaboration, Cost Management, etc. |
| 7 | Altitude Software | Contact Center Solutions | Altitude Unified customer interaction 6.2 |
| 8 | Avistar Communications Corporation | | Video Conference Solutions AvistorVOS, |
| 9 | Axeda Systems Inc. | DRM System | eMation DRM version 2.0, 2.5 |
| 10 | BackWeb Technololgies | Offline Infrastructure | Proactive Portal Server, Backweb e-Accelerator,Backweb Foundation |
| 11 | Baltimore Technologies | Security | Baltimore Unicert, OmniRoot,Baltimore SelectAccess |
| 12 | BAM! Software Inc. | File Handling | BamSplitItPro 2.0 |
| 13 | Banter | Customer Care Applications | Banter Server, Banter Workbench,Banter reply |

| | | | |
|---|---|---|---|
| 14 | ClickSoftware, Inc | Web Optimization Solution | Service Optimatization Suite, |
| 15 | COGNOS | Business Intelligence | Cognos BI Series 7,Cognos Analytic Applications |
| 16 | Compuware Corporation | Automated Testing | QACenter, EcoSystems |
| 17 | Comshare Incorporated | Corporate Performance Management | Comshare MPC,Comshare Decision,Comshare FDC |
| 18 | Convergent Systems Limited | Communication and eLearning | |
| 19 | Corechange, Inc | Business-to-Mobile | Coreport |
| 20 | Cramer Systems Inc. | Automated Network Inventory/ Telecom Services | Crammer 4 Datasheet |
| 21 | Crystal Decisions-a Seagate Company | Access, Analysis and Reports Solutions | Crystal Enterprise 9,Crystal Reports, Crystal Analysis |
| 22 | CSG Systems | CRM and Billing | CSG kenan/BP,Kenen Revenue Settlements,Kenan Rating Server,Kenan prepaid, CSG ICMS |
| 23 | edocs | eBilling and Account Management | eaSuite |
| 24 | EISI | Financial Planning | NaviPlan 8.0 |
| 25 | Elity Systems, Inc. | Marketing Automation/ Workflow | |
| 26 | Eloquent, Inc | Sales Automation Solution | LaunchForce |
| 27 | Embarcadero Technologies, Inc. | Database/Application Management | Data Voyager,DBArtisan, Describe, DT/Studio,Embarcadero Change Manager,Embarcadero Job Scheduler,Embarcadero Performance Center,Embarcadero SQL Debugger, Embarcadero SQL Profiler, Embarcadero SQL Tuner, ER/studio, ER/Studio Repository, Rapid SQL |
| 28 | EMC Corporation | Information Storage | |
| 29 | Empirix Inc. | Web Testing and Monitoring Solutions | eTest, eLoad,eLoadexpert,eTester, eManager Enterprise, BeanTest,FirstAct,OneSight, FarSight, |
| 30 | ePeople, Inc. | Web-based Collaborative CRM | Teamwork |
| 31 | Epicentric | Enterprise Portal | Vignette V7 |
| 32 | Ericsson | Telecom | |
| 33 | Everypath Inc. | Mobile Task Automation | Everypath Studio, Everypath Server, Everypath connector, Everypath smart client, Everypath Administration console |

| | | | |
|---|---|---|---|
| 34 | Global Knowledge, Inc | IT Education/ Training | |
| 35 | GoAmerica Communications Corp. | Wireless Data Services | |
| 36 | HERMES SoftLab USA Inc. | Application Management Solution | HERMES SoftLab Siebel eBusiness SMART Plug-in, HERMES SoftLab custom java application |
| 37 | HighDeal, SA | Pricing and Billing | |
| 38 | Hummingbird Ltd. | Document Management, DW/ BI | OpenDocs, CyberDocs, ETL |
| 39 | HyperSpace Communications, Inc. | Accelaration Technology | Hyperspace, Hyperspace SSL,Hyperspace ISAPI |
| 40 | Ibermatica SA | Consulting | |
| 41 | Interactive Intelligence | IP Telephony Software | Communite 2.2, Enterprise Interaction Center 2.2 |
| 42 | Interwoven, Inc. | Enterprise Content Management | Interwoven 5 |
| 43 | Intraspect Software, Inc. | Enterprise Collaboration Software | Intraspect 5 |
| 44 | IPC Information Systems, Inc. | | |
| 45 | Journee Software Corporation | Customer-centric Enterprises with Real-time Data | |
| 46 | Kabira Technologies | eBusiness Infrastructure | |
| 47 | Kintana | Technology Chain Management | Accelerator For Siebel 2.6.1 eBusiness Applications 3.1.0a |
| 48 | MDSI Mobile Data Solutions Inc. | Workforce Management Systems | Advantex Enterprise Gateway |
| 49 | Micromuse, Inc. | Service and Business Assurance Software | Netcool Suite |
| 50 | Mobilesys, Inc. | Content Management, Auctions | eCAT, Bizcafe |
| 51 | Mobius Management Systems Inc. | Web Site/Document Management | |
| 52 | Motive Communications Inc. | Digital Connection | Motive ServiceNet Platform version 4 |
| 53 | Narus, Inc. | Enterprise Resource Planning | ViewDirect for Networks Version 3.2 |
| 54 | NaviSys Inc. | Platform-neutral Software Solutions and Strategic Counsel | NaviSys Front Office ™ Suite |
| 55 | Ncorp Limited | Intelligence Technology | Intelligence Predictive Analytics version 3 |
| 56 | Netegrity | eBusiness/ B2B Security Solutions | |
| 57 | OTG Software Inc. | Taken over by Legata Systems | |
| 58 | Outstart, Inc | Enterprise Learning | Evolution, Trainersoft 8,studio, softsim, Manager |
| 59 | PALMWARE SA | | |

| | | | |
|---|---|---|---|
| 60 | PASCO CORPORATION | Geographic Information System | PasCal |
| 61 | Pegaus Systems Inc. | | |
| 62 | Peopleclick | Workforce Management System | ClickXGrms, ClickXGvms, clickAAP, clickEM |
| 63 | Pepper Technologies AG | | |
| 64 | Planlinx, Inc. | | |
| 65 | Plumtree Software | eMarkets Platforms, Portals | Plumtree Enterprise Web suite |
| 66 | Precise Software Solutions LTD. | Performance Management Solutions | Precise i3 ver. 6.2 |
| 67 | Presence Technology | Call Center Software | |
| 68 | Primus Knowledge Solutions | Knowledge Management Solutions | |
| 69 | RSA Security | Security Solutions | |
| 70 | Salentica Systems Ltd. | eCRM and BI | Salentica Analytic |
| 71 | SAS Institute | Business Intelligence | |
| 72 | Scribe Software Corporation | Demand Chain Management Solutions | |
| 73 | SearchSoftware America | Identity System | SSA-NAME3, SSA-CJK Support |
| 74 | Segue Software, Inc. | Web Testing and Monitoring Solutions | |
| 75 | ServiceWare Technologies | KM Solutions for Service, Support | MindSync |
| 76 | Servigistics | Service Parts Management | Servigistics 7.1 |
| 77 | Shipcom Wireless Inc | Enterprise Application Integeration | Mobile EAI, CATAMARAN |
| 78 | Sierra Atlantic Inc. | eBusiness | |
| 79 | Silicon Energy Corp. | Energy Management Software | |
| 80 | Siperian, Inc | Customer Data Management System | |
| 81 | Syntegra UK | Consulting and Systems Integration | |
| 82 | Syntellect | Speech-enabled Customer Self-service | Vista 4.0 |
| 83 | Viafone | Mobile Enterprise Solutions | |
| 84 | Visual Mining Inc. | Data Mining Solutions | |
| 85 | Waveset Technologies | Secured Identity Management Solutions | Waveset Lighthouse |
| 86 | Wicom Communications Oy Ltd. | Call Center Solutions | Wicom CSS 3, |
| 87 | Witness Systems | Customer Interaction Recording | |

| | | | |
|---|---|---|---|
| | **Strategic** | | |
| 1 | Acxiom | Innovative Database Marketing Services, Advanced Technologies | Customer Data Integration |
| 2 | Alcatel | G-plus Adapter for Siebel 7 | Genesys Framework 5.0 and 5.1, 6.0, 6.3.1 |
| 3 | BEA Systems | Web Application Server | |
| 4 | Convergys Corporation | Billing and Customer Care Solutions | |
| 5 | Jacada, Inc. | Legacy Integration and Web Enablement | |
| 6 | Mercury Interactive | Testing Solution | WinRunner QuickTest for R/3 |

| | | | |
|---|---|---|---|
| 7 | SeeBeyond | eBusiness and Application Integration (eAI) Solutions | e*Way version 3.6, 4.1, 4.5 |
| 8 | TIBCO | Middleware and Enterprise Application Integration Solution | TIB/Adapter For Siebel version 2.0, 1.0.0, 3.2, 4.1 |
| 9 | Vitria Technology | eBusiness Applications Platform | BusinessWare |
| 10 | webMethods, Inc. | Enterprise Web Services | webMethods Enterprise 4.1.1, 5.0, 4.6 |

| | | | |
|---|---|---|---|
| | **Premier** | | |
| 1 | Concerto Software (formerly Davox and CELLIT, Inc) | Customer Interaction Management | EnsemblePro, ContactPro, Ensemble,Unison,LYRICall |
| 2 | Group 1 | Data Quality | Datasight, Code-1Plus, GeoTax, MoveForward |
| 3 | Hyperion | Business Performance Management Solutions | |
| 4 | Mercator Software Inc | Integration Solutions | Mercator |
| 5 | Portal Software, Inc. | End-to-end Solution for the Convergent Services | Infranet 6.1, 6.2 |
| 6 | WRQ, Inc. | Bi-directional Communication | Verastream Integration Broker v8.0, eBusiness Application 9.2 |

**** Please check the latest Oracle Siebel CRM Third-Party Solutions List***

# Appendix D

# CRM Industry Analysis

The CRM industry has many consultants and analysts whose sole responsibility is CRM research and reviews. These consultants can provide detailed reviews of any reputable CRM solution on the market. Suggested CRM experts:

- **ISM-Information Systems Management, Inc.**—Awards the Top 15 CRM Solutions annually. This award is considered the 'Oscar Awards' of the CRM industry.
- **Patricia Seybold Group**—The Patricia Seybold Group is the customer-centric executives' first choice for strategic insight, technology guidance and eBusiness best practices. Founded in 1978 and based in Boston, Massachusetts, the firm offers customized consulting, strategic research and executive coaching.
- **MetaGroup**—META Group helps companies make Technology (IT) decisions by providing research and analyst consultation relevant to their specific business needs. META Group offers advisory services, consulting/ benchmarking and access to various IT publications. META Group addresses the latest technologies, industry trends and business challenges
- **OVUM**—Ovum is an independent research and consulting company offering expert advice on IT, Telecommunications and eCommerce.
- **Giga Information Group**—Giga Information Group provides research, advice and coaching on technology for eBusiness. Giga helps clients make strategic decisions about the technologies, people and processes needed to excel in the new digital economy.

Appendix E

# Oracle Fusion Architecture

Oracle Fusion Architecture is the basis for Oracle's next generation fusion applications that will combine the best ideas and processes of the Oracle eBusiness Suite, PeopleSoft, JD Edwards and Siebel applications.

## E.1 SERVICE ORIENTED ARCHITECTURE

Leading companies are tackling the complexity of their application and IT environments with Service Oriented Architecture (SOA), which facilitates the development of modular business services that can be easily integrated and re-used—creating a truly flexible, adaptable IT infrastructure. With an SOA approach, enterprises' IT organization will focus more resources and budget on innovation and on delivering new business services.

SOA has the following benefits:

- Reduces development time and cost—SOA services are easily re-used and can be rapidly assembled into new, composite applications
- Lowers maintenance costs—Re-usable services reduce the number and internal complexity of IT services
- Higher quality services—Increased service re-use creates higher quality services through multiple testing cycles from different service consumers
- Lower integration costs—Standardized services know how to work together, enabling disparate applications to quickly and easily connect
- Reduces risk—Fewer, re-usable services provide greater control over corporate and IT governance policies and reduce the overall compliance risk

## E.2 ORACLE FUSION MIDDLEWARE FOR SIEBEL

Oracle Fusion Middleware for Siebel is a market-leading suite of middleware products that are precertified with Siebel applications to optimize sales and customer service. This innovative solution delivers real-time intelligence, greater flexibility and a lower total cost of ownership across all business processes and associated systems that touch a customer.

- Increase your capacity for growth and change—Siebel-certified middleware solutions extend CRM functionality to accelerate sales force automation, campaign efficiency and sales execution. Relevant middleware products are Oracle SOA Suite, Oracle BPA Suite.
- Improve business insight—Pervasive business intelligence improves pipeline visibility, increases cross and up sell opportunities, and identifies sales trends. Relevant middleware products are Oracle Business Intelligence Suite, Oracle WebCenter, Oracle Data Integrator.
- Mitigate risk and drive compliance—Best-in-class security and document management protects access to sensitive customer and sales information across sales and distribution channels. Relevant products are Oracle Identity Management Suite, Oracle Enterprise Content Management.
- Empower users for productive interactions—Unified, role-specific customer, sales, and service access to processes, and information for increased customer satisfaction and issue resolution. Relevant middleware products are Oracle WebCenter, Oracle Enterprise Content Management.

## E.3 ORACLE FUSION APPLICATIONS—NEXT GENERATION ENTERPRISE APPLICATIONS

Oracle Corporation is building Oracle Fusion Applications that are being designed to unify best-of-business capabilities from all Oracle applications including Siebel CRM 8.0 in a complete suite delivered on Oracle's open technology.

Applications Unlimited is Oracle's commitment to continue providing enhancements to current Siebel, JD Edwards EnterpriseOne, JD Edwards World, Oracle e-Business Suite and PeopleSoft product lines beyond the delivery of Oracle Fusion Applications. With Oracle's unique Applications Unlimited and Lifetime Support policy enterprises will not be forced to upgrade to Fusion Applications, but can decide when and if they choose to upgrade.

# Appendix F

# Enterprise Evolution by Market Selection

As we saw in Chapter 16, section "From 'Built to Last' to 'Built to Perform' Organizations", the best run and most widely admired companies are unable to sustain their market-beating levels of performance for an extended period of time. The very processes that enable them to survive over the long-term thwart them from renewal and reinvention and finally, fossilize them.

## F.1 THE PARADOX OF ENTERPRISE SUCCESS—SURVIVAL OF THE ALIGNED BUT THE SUCCESS OF THE VARIATOR

The theory of evolution, in particular Darwin's 'Theory of Evolution By Natural Selection' has been deployed as a model for application in diverse fields ranging from 'hard' sciences (like physical sciences) to 'soft' sciences (like ecology, economics, social, political sciences and even in philosophy for the allied problems of growth of knowledge, theory selection, etc.) In this appendix we shall explore the interesting possibility of applying this model to the growth and development of enterprises. Thus, businesses or enterprises are primarily organic systems that struggle for survival in the environment of the 'market'. This is not to suggest that companies are organisms with characteristics of sex, reproduction, etc., but primarily to throw more light on our understanding of the problem of change and sustained competitiveness, and performance, growth and success of companies. It may also be fascinating to see the many common business terms interpreted in a new light.

In this appendix we are proposing that the only true solution for longevity and success of companies is to ***variate***! As we discussed earlier, in a trend identified with the publication of *In Search of Excellence*, comprehensive efforts have been undertaken worldwide to identify the prescriptive characteristics for 'excellent companies'. However, time and again, corrective measures adopted by companies based on such prescriptions, have belied expectations. This is because the companies end up focusing exclusively on a singular or a small set of guiding principles to the exclusion of all others, way beyond the limits of their validity and time. No enterprise can build a competitive advantage that is sustainable indefinitely—every advantage eventually erodes. In fact, fine-tuned systems for today's success may actually *increase* the chances of failure tomorrow! Short-term effectiveness can sow the seeds of failure by hindering long-term adaptability. Most declining companies did not lack the technology to succeed; rather, this resulted from their failure to embrace variations and change effectively.

Using the evolutionary metaphor, the world of business can be understood in terms of individual companies, the market environment and in terms of variations—the generation of novelty, retention and selection. These variations, unlike the more familiar innovations, are not necessarily confined to products alone but can extend to visions, goals, objectives, plans, services, business or production processes, organizational structures, communications, systems, rules and procedures, partnerships, and so on. We are suggesting here that it is the result of such continuous and experimental variations, at varied levels of the enterprise or time-scales wrought by an enterprise in itself and its surrounding environment that may result in its continued competitiveness and therefore, long-term performance, survival and success.

## F.2 THE RIDDLE OF EXCELLENCE

It seems that the very strategies, which contribute to the competitiveness, excellence and success of an enterprise, in time lead to their decline resulting from organizational inertia, complacence and inflexibility because of over emphasis and adherence on these very 'proven' routines.

Large successful firms have greater resources and the forward momentum of established products and customers to carry them through times of distress and mismanagement. However, many of what were once the biggest, best financed and most professionally managed companies have slid from the top ranks while others have dropped from the lists altogether. Still others, who were earlier small or non-existent, have risen to displace them. Many of the new entrants are formed around semiconductors, software, supercomputers and biotechnology—technologies that few had imagined were commercially viable a generation ago. And the few who survived like Motorola and Hewlett-Packard, have so altered their products and technologies that they are scarcely recognizable as the same companies. Texas Instruments had taken the momentous decision to exit out of the traditional chip business to concentrate more on the design and development of Digital Signal Processing (DSP) chips.

> We are proposing that there is nothing fundamentally wrong per se with any of the traditional strategies and techniques. However, it is unlikely that a single approach or principle will permanently resolve all issues faced by enterprises and also remain a valid panacea for all times in future. Adherence to one or a small set of guiding principles way beyond its domain of relevance or time is singularly responsible for the decline or even destruction of enterprises.

Failure to variate is a prime source of business failure. There is an essential tension between variation (or instability) and stability (or inertia) within the companies. Initiating change or confronting change are the two most important issues facing the companies today. To succeed both today and in the future, companies must play two different games simultaneously. First, they must continually get better at competing in the short-term, which requires increasing alignment among strategy, structure, processes, culture and people. Second, they must also simultaneously introduce strategic changes to ensure long-term competitiveness. However, this balancing game alone will not ensure long-term success; short-term effectiveness can sow the seeds of failure by hindering long-term adaptability. As companies grow they develop structures, processes and systems that are inter-linked, making further changes difficult, costly and time-consuming to implement. Structural inertia rooted in size, complexity and such interdependence sets in. In fact, fine-tuned systems for today's success may actually increase the chances of tomorrow's failure. While consistency, reliability and efficiency are crucial, so too are characteristics such as flexibility, responsiveness (i.e., variation), etc.

In a sense, this is the more fundamental version of the universally recognized 'productivity paradox' which results from a tension arising from trying to achieve two mutually contradictory goals. On one hand, companies strive for economies of scale, while on the other hand they are confronted increasingly with the dilemma of the economies of scope. For companies, an unhappy by-product of success in one dimension has been rapid deterioration in the other, which has led to their decline, if not demise, much sooner than anticipated. Rather then work towards competitive responses (possibly entailing even radical changes) with unfailing regularity, companies have chosen to defend from their traditional bastions. They keep building upon, reinforcing and modifying what has made them successful. Time and again they have demonstrated remarkable creativity in defending their entrenched products, technologies and processes, which have often reached unimaginable heights of productivity and performances. The evolutionary metaphor and model based on biological evolution goes a long way to unravel the mystery of the solution to the problem of growth and development of businesses. The evolutionary model readily explains, in analogy with the decline, decay and death of species in the biological world, the trauma associated with the change management within companies and its consequences like down-sizing. Similarly, according to this model, excessive proliferation of companies along with their products is thwarted either because of the competition or because of the limited capacity of the market environment.

Traditionally, the pursuit of sustainable advantage has long been the focus of strategy. But advantages can last only until competitors have duplicated or outmaneuvered them. No enterprise can build a competitive advantage that is sustainable; every advantage erodes. The configuration of markets and competition are constantly threatened by uncertainty, dynamism and heterogeneity because of short product life cycles, short product design cycles, new technologies, frequent entries by new entrants, repositioning by incumbents, and so on. Protecting advantages becomes increasingly difficult; therefore, disruption of the competitor's or even one's own advantages is the approach for long run survival. The traditional goal of strategies has been to find a grand and long-term strategy that sustains itself for years, if not for decades. However, such strategies take too long to create the assets needed to pull off this grand strategy. Such long-term strategy is often outmaneuvered or rendered irrelevant because of the dramatic changes in the circumstances and the environment. Instead of long-range plans and competitive advantages companies aim for a series of small and short-term advantages, which combined together effectively creates a long-term sustainable advantage for the enterprises. It is much easier and less risky to create a home run rather than a series of base hits.

The only true solution for longevity of enterprises is to variate. As indicated earlier, the world of business can be understood in terms of individual companies, the market environment and in terms of variations—the generation of novelty, retention and selection. Competitiveness is not a state that can be reached once and for all and held on to; competitiveness is a process. Thus, the approach suggested here involves a fundamental transition of viewing business from a state of 'being' to a process of 'becoming'.

This approach can help structure the understanding of the opportunities and the challenges that confront us. Variations are the engine of business development and growth. The process variation means the process whereby business agents act to transform new knowledge, inventions and/or scientific techniques, that is, know-how into business value, often through products, production processes and/ or changes to the organization. The variations may be technological, organizational and/ or market environment in orientation. Thus, the variations could be in products, services, business or production process, organization structures, procedures, processes and rules, and so on.

In the evolutionary model discussed in the next section, business variations can be understood to lead to sustenance and growth of companies. It provides a way of conceptualizing variation, not as a final result but as a complex process involving many stages through which the know-how seeking agents respond to environmental conditions and in turn, effect or even create newer states of environmental conditions.

## F.3 EVOLUTION OF ENTERPRISES

In the evolutionary model of businesses, we are primarily dealing with two entities, companies and the market environment; companies exist within the market environment and could be individual or multi-individual companies. Companies are like individual organic systems within the various species of industries akin to the macro-level niches occupied by species in the biological environment. Companies interact with the internal and external environment constantly; they take sustenance in terms of the resources, namely, money, manpower and material (and now, possible information as the fourth resource) and produce outputs that are let out into the market. It is the success of such life-sustaining bi-directional exchanges that ensures not only the survival but also the growth of companies. Indeed, the very process of interaction or exchange between the organic system and the environment defines their existence. Isolated enterprises, for all practical purposes, may not exist at all and indeed, cannot exist!

> We must point out that there is no equilibrium here; on the contrary this happens because of being very much away from the equilibrium. It has also been established that being away from equilibrium only enhances self-organization and complexity—evolution inexorably moves in the direction of increasing complexity of organic systems.

The Cartesian paradigm has dominated the scientific world for the last three centuries. It acknowledges only stability, order, uniformity, linearity, locality and equilibrium in Nature. In truth, it is the stable, orderly, uniform, linear, local and uniform systems that are aberrations in Nature. Physical sciences have themselves revealed the extreme limitations of this traditional mechanistic, reductionist and deterministic view of the world. It is now being understood that under non-equilibrium conditions, entropy may give rise to order, organization and complexity. In the evolutionary model, equilibrium is only a prescription for decline and death for an enterprise. However, the market environment like Nature, is not boundless. It has limited resources as also a limited ability to absorb their produce—the former refers to the sources of investments and the later to the customers. Just like organisms in the natural environment, the companies therefore have to compete both for resources and customers. However, this competition in Nature is not totally destructive but symbiotic in nature.

In our model, in response to the changes in the market environment, not unlike mutations in the biological evolution, it is the variations or differentiations that are wrought by the companies that increase their effectiveness to perform and survive in the changed environment or in other words, their competitiveness. These changes or variations the companies have undergone to increase competitiveness could be in terms of their strategies, structures, functions, resources consumed, and outputs produced. These variations and the resulting differentiations are different for different companies. The variations (or breakthroughs) could manifest in terms of new products, product improvisations, re-launch of products (or services), new strategies, diversifications, mergers, acquisitions, and so on. The variations or differentiations themselves could be enforced by the market environment or originate internally.

> Individuals in the companies bring about the variations. Like genes in the biological evolution, the entrepreneurs are the 'active' agents, that is, agents of change in the corporate evolution. Here we use the term entrepreneurs to mean any person, owner or employee, who initiates changes or confronts changes in the market environment and is responsible for taking proactive or reactive decisions. The entrepreneurs affect actions based upon variations generated by them in terms of introducing new products, positioning, packaging, etc., into the market environment. Since different people in different companies shall come up with different variations, the resulting differentiations shall be different in the case of each company.

The exchange interaction with the market environment is essential for the survival and growth of the companies. It is driven by the difference of the value potential between the company and the market environment. Historically also, money is merely a convenient representation of the magnitude of any business transaction, which is essentially about exchange of value. Companies create or add value to the input resources; and it is this value in the form of products or services provided by the companies, if appreciated by the market, which is accepted by the market environment leading to the sustenance of the companies. The market constituents and therefore, in general terms the market environment, values the produce of the enterprise in terms of low costs (and hence, end-user price), higher quality, faster response times, greater variations and lately, clear, correct and complete information for making decisions. Even small differences in the delivered value may lead to major deviations in the competitiveness and performance of the companies. If we agree that customers are no different from these same sets of companies in the market environment but play only a different role (and at a different scale or level), one could state that all these values are always with reference to the customers; it is truly the customers who define what is low cost or good quality or faster response times and great variations. Many a company has come to grief by ignoring this simple fact. Furthermore, because of the dynamic nature of the mutual interaction between the market environment and the customer companies, these values continuously undergo change. Thus, for survival the companies must not only monitor their competitors' value chains continuously but also the changes in them on a continuous basis.

> Indeed, one can associate value chains not only to companies but also to any association (partnership or alliance or consortium or cartel) of companies and even to industry segments of the market environment. Any major disparities between the value chains of the constituents with the higher-level value chains are indicators of imminent shakeouts in the market environment. The market environment will weed out any entities with value chains deviating appreciably from the minimum standard for being 'fit' with these higher-level value chains. One of the critical criteria for 'fitness' is the ability of the company (or value chain) to variate, that is, learn, institutionalize this learning or knowledge, and adapt over time. Amongst competing companies even small and apparent differences in value streams and value chains can result in tremendous differences in the resulting performance of the companies.

Thus, all segmentation and positioning strategies employed by the companies as also the consequent promotional strategies like advertising, etc., are similar to the differentiation strategies brought to play in the biological environment. The market scanning, competitor intelligence, business forecasting and at the extreme, scenario planning exercises undertaken by companies, are similar to the constant scanning or sensing done by organic systems both for food or for sensing any approaching danger.

The response of the market for such introductions or changes may be negative or affirmative. Since there are many companies in the market environment addressing similar situations, this is the corporate analogue of the process of natural selection—the market response may either encourage or discourage the continuation of these variations. For a company as a whole the total effect of such variations is the sum total of all such variations for the various products and services provided by the company (or group of divisions or companies). In case of the positive market response *as a whole*, companies may reinforce these variations even further and may perform better, and emerge stronger and more successful. Alternatively, if they face rejections of these variations as a whole, the companies' performance may be affected adversely and they may have to identify and work on other variations.

The interactions between the companies and the market are dynamic and constantly undergo changes. The market environment influences and selects the best-fit companies and in turn the variations introduced by the competing companies affect this very market environment. This may happen because of:

(i) Changes brought about in the configuration of the market by all the companies constantly competing against each other

(ii) Changes that occur fundamentally in the market environment

(iii) Changes brought about by customers

Changes of the second category may occur because of several reasons like:

- Natural cataclysms or sudden changes in political situations (like military coups, landslide victories for opposition parties after a prolonged periods as in Britain, or dramatic changes in demographics because of large influx of refugee populations into or from neighboring countries)
- The sudden promulgation or withdrawal of regulatory frameworks (like license policies and export policies) by the governments
- Discovery of radically new resources of energy like atomic energy or sudden depletion of traditional derived energy sources like petroleum

> According to this model, not only suppliers but also customers compete amongst themselves for providing their custom. In other words, there is competition amongst customers!

However, there are some major differences between the biological and business evolution being proposed here.

(i) Unlike biological evolution, business evolution can be very much faster. Entrepreneurs who are the agents of the business evolution and therefore, evolution of companies, can try out a large range of alternatives, which can be subjected much more rapidly to selection.

(ii) Unlike biological evolution where mutations in genes are essentially random in nature, companies can direct variations along certain directions or paths, or directly control the generation of novelties or variations corresponding to their perceptions of the market environment. Thus, companies internalize some selection mechanisms in order to generate variations that they hope will be successful in the market.

(iii) The alternative that is ultimately selected is better than other alternatives only in relation to the localized market environment and not necessarily to any ideal, universally best alternative. This implies that success and progress is not general and permanent but can only be discussed in relation to specific and local conditions—it is context-specific and ephemeral.

The evolutionary perspective inherently consists of a dynamic and co-evolving perspective of the complex interactions between companies, variations and the market environment. Ultimately, all evolution is concerned with the growth and development of the know-how (or company's 'extended phenotype' a la Richard Dawkins) for survival in the market environment. Know-how is increasingly important for variations because it involves the creation of a new resource—information (see Chapter 1, note on "Information as a New Resource"). But, the market co-evolves because of the variations wrought by the competing companies; business variations give opportunities for productivity gains which lead to increased production, competitiveness and market share. Often, the variations are truly associated with the creation of know-how or its applications to specific questions, problems and challenges. Know-how refers not only to technology, techniques, skills, etc., but also to information about learned routines (e.g., the survival rates of different strategies in a dynamically and perpetually changing environment in the context of a particular company).

The business variations are the outcome of a myriad of knowledge-seeking activities whereby the agent's perceptions and actions are translated into practice. The resulting pattern of business change is characteristically *evolutionary* because it involves the development and diffusion of business variations, as well as novelty and selection among alternatives. Biological evolution provides a useful model for the evolution of businesses because it implies, on one hand, that a variety of unique events are important. On the other hand, it also implies that these unique, micro-level events and diversities still add up to an aggregate identifiable pattern of business change—that of survival and growth of business firms or companies. Correspondingly, in the evolution of businesses through variations the unit of variation is the know-how, the unit of selection is the product or service delivered to the customer, and the unit of evolution is the development and growth of the enterprise.

This completes the basic characteristics of the evolutionary model of businesses. Within this general framework it is fascinating to map the standard business issues into the evolutionary model and seek solutions within this, and then re-translate them into the normal business framework for comparison with conventional wisdom. Often, even if this does not result in a solution radically different from the traditional one, it at least unfolds a completely new perspective on the concerned issues, which in itself is extremely fulfilling and satisfying.

## F.4 THE APPLICATIONS

At a finer level, motivated by the use of DNA fingerprinting in the biological world, this model suggests that the competitiveness of companies can be analyzed and interpreted meaningfully by using their corresponding value streams or their aggregates—the value chains. This is what value chains have been used for in the past few decades by the corporates! Value-oriented analysis (even in its ethical dimension) underlies such concepts like competitive advantage, core competencies, competitive leverage,

BPR, and so on. Furthermore, even testable predictions can be made by studying the structure and changes occurring in the value streams and hence the value chains of any business. Since testable and repeatable predictions is the hallmark of any serious scientific theory we would like to emphasize that the evolutionary model, which we are proposing here, is a respectable candidate for becoming the "Theory of Business" (David Harper).

For sustainable success, companies must also understand how and when to initiate variations and or change. Variations are a central determinant of longer-run success and failure for commercial companies. Most of the declining companies did not lack the technology to succeed; rather, the decline resulted from companies failing to embrace variation and change effectively. As we have stated earlier, initiating change or confronting change are the two most important issues facing the companies today, and the ability to manage for today and for the future simultaneously is critical for long-term survival and success.

Although the generation of variations involves adaptive and anticipatory changes in relation to the market environment, they will differ for different companies because each of them differs in their characteristics, experiences and resources, in short, their know-how. The companies' varying know-how will affect their decisions and actions; companies will make differing choices leading to diversity and therefore, competition. Analogously, within the enterprises the selection process for variations is dependent on the complex results of many factors such as scientific, technological, economic and political. Companies will select to respond to markets based not only on their know-how but also on their perceptions of the market as well as their vision about how to change those prevalent conditions in the future. Thus, the innovatory response of an enterprise to or for changes in the market cannot be specified in simple variables; it is essentially dependent on the company's know-how, its context and its business vision. Its success cannot be predicted with certainty and can be tested only by introducing it in the market environment. Whether the resulting variative response of the enterprise is perceived externally as radical or incremental may only be a matter of degree, local context and finally, momentary. Immediately, a new iteration cycle of anticipation, variation and market selection is set in motion. A radical variation may actually be the result of a myriad of incremental variations in the company's products, processes or organizations.

However, enterprises do not truly have free choice between all available technologies; they can only choose close to what they know and do. The survival of the non-optimal Querty typing keyboard is an illustration of how tenacious such dominant designs or preferred paths can become. Many technical changes, which are possible in theory are deemed too costly and are not explored in practice. Enterprises are likely to respond with technologies similar to those that they already possess or have understood in their context, to have strategic significances. Therefore, one implication of the evolutionary perspective for business competition is that existing firms are most likely to continue using their old knowledge, techniques and skills, or at least their old routines for searching or generating novelty and knowledge. Existing companies will only make numerous improvements along with their companies' chosen path to make it competitive rather than searching for radical variations. Only new enterprises unfettered by past experiences and accumulated experience are likely to go in for radically new technologies and variations. A radical variation disrupts the competencies or competitive advantages of existing companies as the market leaders in the existing markets or possibly in the redefined markets.

For instance in the motorcar industry, at the turn of the century bicycles and horse-driven carriages were threatened by the horse-less carriage, soon to be called the automobiles. There were several competing alternative energy sources and different steering mechanisms and arrangement of passenger compartments. In a very short period however, a dominant design emerged epitomized by the Model T Ford. This design consisted of an internal combustion engine, steering wheel on the left, brake pedal on the right and clutch on the left. Once this standard emerged, the focus of competition shifted primarily to optional features, cost or the power of the engine. This lasted until General Motors introduced a radically new concept in cars—the fully enclosed steel automobile. A majority of the companies continue to make gasoline engines whereas some are experimenting with electric engines. They are quite different technologies but competing paths for similar functions.

There is a causal and reciprocal relationship between market environment and variations. Variative success usually leads to faster enterprise growth and hence, to concentration of market power. Although, at the formative stage of any market segment variation may come from the new entrants, often variations by incumbents may act as a barrier to entry. In fact, it is the knowledge from the feedback that provides the strategic incentive for incumbent monopolists to variate. Most product variations tend to occur in the early stages of the product life cycle. Most of the variations occurring towards the end of the product life cycle are process variations. Process variations are more likely to increase rather then reduce economies of scale, thus reinforcing the tendency towards greater concentration. Enterprises, which already have relatively low costs are able to reduce their average cost faster than the others. However, radical and rapid business changes resulting from disruptive variations, which destroy established companies' capabilities and competencies may be de-concentrating. Large enterprises depend in a large measure on tried and trusted variative routines and are poor in improvising coordinated responses to novel situations. This may arise because of the sunken costs, inherent lags in decision process, deployed standards of procedures and task allocations, sheer structural inertia, and so on. Many large enterprises that have multi-divisional structures are also able to show agility in responding to rapid and radical changes especially in technologies that depend for their development on a wide accumulated competence across divisional boundaries. However, such enterprises have to live with tension between the tendencies for corporate centralization to exploit such synergies and de-centralization to enhance the ability to variate effectively.

IBM successfully entered the PC market through a separately dedicated unit set up far from the firm's headquarters, an independent Team Taurus put Ford Motor Company back on the map, and General Motors entered the small car market through the Saturn Motor Company. In each instance, the task of creating the competencies needed to successfully bridge into chosen markets hinged on creating organizational units with a clear mandate and a great deal of independence from the staff, committees and other encumbrances of the parent company. Predictably, spinning-off separate and independent organizational units does not always lead to success. Xerox's attempt to revitalize itself through Xerox Palo Alto Research Center (PARC) facility is a notable example. PARC was the ultimate fount of creative genius, creating technology for the modern PC, the fax machine, Ethernet, the now ubiquitous Windows user interface and the laser printer. However, most have found a way to the marketplace and achieved undoubtedly astounding market success not through Xerox but via other newer companies.

The importance of business vision can be understood in its ability to sometimes overcome the limitations imposed by the core competence of the corporations. For companies facing major opportunities or threat, current competencies may cloud the enterprises' field of vision and hence, limit its ability to perceive the potential. With a strong vision often driven by entrepreneurial individuals with authority to implement it, the enterprise may develop new competencies and thereby move into new technologies. This implies first that while radical change is taken to be disruptive and incremental change less so, the perception of change as being 'radical' or 'incremental' is dependent on a vision of where the business is going. If a vision correctly anticipates a market change in the future path of a business or technology, then radical may become incremental. Second, this also implies that only newer or existing companies with related competencies or those with strong incentives/ disincentives are likely to move quickly into a new technology.

Appendix G

# References


Barabasi, Alberto Laszlo, *Linked: The New Science of Networks,* Perseus, New York, 2002.

Bebczuk, Ricardo, *Asymmetric Information in Financial Markets,* Cambridge University Press, London, 2003.

Cairncross, Francis, *The Death of Distance,* Harvard Business School Press, Boston, 1997.

Compaine, Benjamin M. and William H. Read, *The Information Resources Policy Handbook,* The MIT Press, Cambridge, 1999.

Coveney, Peter and Roger Highfield, *Frontiers of Complexity: The Search for Order in a Chaotic World,* Random House, New York, 1995.

Dawkins, Richard, *The Extended Phenotype: The Long Reach of the Gene*, Oxford University Press, London, 2000.

Delmater, Rhonda and Monte Hancock, *Data Mining Explained: A Manager's Guide to Customer-Centric Business Intelligence,* Butterworth-Heinemann, London, 2001.

Dove, Rick, *Response Ability: The Language, Structure, and Culture of the Agile Enterprise,* John Wiley, New York, 2001.

Dyche, Jill, *The CRM Handbook,* Addison-Wesley, New York, 2002.

Edvinsson, Leif and Michael S. Malone, *Intellectual Capital,* Harper Business, New York, 1997.

Harper, David, *Entrepreneurship and the Market Process,* Routledge, London, 1996.

Kalakota, Ravi and Marcia Robinson, *E-Business 2.0: Roadmap for Success,* Addison-Wesley, Massachusetts, 2000.

Kaplan, Robert S. and Steven R. Anderson, *Time-Driven Activity-Based Costing,* Harvard Business School Press, Boston, 2007.

Davis, Frank W. and Karl B. Manrodt, *Customer-Responsive Management: The Flexible Advantage,* Blackwell, Massachusetts, 1996.

Gupta, Sunil and Donald Lehman, *Managing Customer as Investments: The Strategic Value of the Customers in the Long Run* Wharton Science Publishing, 2005.

Kale, Vivek, *Implementing SAP R/3: The Guide for Business and Technology Managers,* Sams, Indianapolis, 2000.

Keiningham, Timothy, Terry Vavra, Lerzan Aksoy and Henry Willard, *Loyalty Myths: Hyped Strategies that will Put You Out of Business and Proven Tactics that will Really Work,* John Wiley, New York, 2005.

Levinson, Paul, *The Soft Edge,* Routledge, London, 1997.

McGrath, Michael E., *Product Strategy for High Technology Companies,* McGraw-Hill Trade, New York, 2000.

McKenzie, Richard, *Digital Economics: How Information Technology Has Transformed Business Thinking*, Praeger Publishers, Westport, Connecticut, 2003.

Klein, Naomi, *No Logo,* Picador, New York, 1999.

Neely, A., C. Adams and Mike Kennenerley, *The Performance Prism: The Scorecard for Measuring and Managing Business Success,* Prentice-Hall, London, 2002.

Papows, Jeff, *Enterprise.com,* Nicholas Brealey, London, 1999.

Postrel, Virginia, *The Future and Its Enemies: The Growing Conflict Over Creativity, Enterprise and Progress,* Free Press, New York, 1998.

Peppers, Don and Martha Rogers, *The One to One Future,* Doubleday, New York, 1997.

Reichheld, Frederick F., *The Loyalty Effect: The Hidden Force Behind Growth, Profits and Lasting Value,* Harvard Business School Press, Boston, 2001.

Seybold, Patricia B., *Customers.com,* Crown Business, New York, 2001.

Siebel, Thomas M., *Taking Care of eBusiness,* Doubleday, New York, 2001.

Shapiro, Carl and Hal R. Varian, *Information Rules,* Harvard Business School Press, Boston, 1999.

Sheth, Jagdish N. and A. Parvatiyar, *Relationship Marketing,* Sage Publications, 1999.

Slywotzky, Adrian J. and David J. Morrison, *How Digital Is Your Business?* Nicholas Brealey, London, 2000.

Tiwana, Amrit, *Knowledge Management Toolkit,* Prentice-Hall, New York, 2002.

Tapscott, Don, (Ed.), *Creating Value in the Network Economy,* Harvard Business School Press, Boston, 1999.

Vandermerwe, Sandra, *Customer Capitalism,* Nicholas Brealey, London, 1999.

# Subject Index

## C

# Author Index

## Author's Profile

Vivek Kale has more than two decades of professional experience, including ten years managing ERP, CRM and extended-ERP projects in SAP, PeopleSoft, Siebel, and Oracle Applications. His experience includes designing, developing, and consulting on large application software, eBusiness, knowledge management, and data warehousing solutions. He has handled and consulted on various aspects of enterprise-wide information modeling, enterprise architectures, business process re-design, and, eBusiness architectures. He is the author of *Implementing SAP R/3: The Guide for Business and Technology Managers, Sams (2000).* Vivek lives in Mumbai, India with his wife and two daughters.

Made in United States
Troutdale, OR
05/07/2026

49097154R00319